HTML
Black Book

Steven Holzner

President, CEO *Keith Weiskamp*	**HTML Black Book** © 2000 The Coriolis Group. All Rights Reserved.

This book may not be duplicated in any way without the express written consent of the publisher, except in the form of brief excerpts or quotations for the purposes of review. The information contained herein is for the personal use of the reader and may not be incorporated in any commercial programs, other books, databases, or any kind of software without written consent of the publisher. Making copies of this book or any portion for any purpose other than your own is a violation of United States copyright laws.

President, CEO
Keith Weiskamp

Publisher
Steve Sayre

Acquisitions Editor
Charlotte Carpentier

Marketing Specialist
Tracy Schofield

Project Editor
Pat DuMoulin

Technical Reviewer
Scott Duffy

Production Coordinator
Laura Wellander

Cover Designer
Jody Winkler

Layout Designer
April Nielsen

CD-ROM Developer
Michelle McConnell

Limits Of Liability And Disclaimer Of Warranty
The author and publisher of this book have used their best efforts in preparing the book and the programs contained in it. These efforts include the development, research, and testing of the theories and programs to determine their effectiveness. The author and publisher make no warranty of any kind, expressed or implied, with regard to these programs or the documentation contained in this book.

The author and publisher shall not be liable in the event of incidental or consequential damages in connection with, or arising out of, the furnishing, performance, or use of the programs, associated instructions, and/or claims of productivity gains.

Trademarks
Trademarked names appear throughout this book. Rather than list the names and entities that own the trademarks or insert a trademark symbol with each mention of the trademarked name, the publisher states that it is using the names for editorial purposes only and to the benefit of the trademark owner, with no intention of infringing upon that trademark.

The Coriolis Group, LLC
14455 N. Hayden Road, Suite 220
Scottsdale, Arizona 85260

480/483-0192
FAX 480/483-0193
http://www.coriolis.com

Library of Congress Cataloging-in-Publication Data
Holzner, Steven.
    HTML black book / by Steven Holzner.
       p. cm.
    Includes index.
    ISBN 1-57610-617-9
    1. HTML (Document markup language)   I. Title.

QA76.76.H94 H63   2000
005.7'2–dc21   00-022687
CIP

Printed in the United States of America
10 9 8 7 6 5 4 3 2 1

14455 North Hayden Road • Suite 220 • Scottsdale, Arizona 85260

Dear Reader:

Coriolis Technology Press was founded to create a very elite group of books: the ones you keep closest to your machine. Sure, everyone would like to have the Library of Congress at arm's reach, but in the real world, you have to choose the books you rely on every day *very* carefully.

To win a place for our books on that coveted shelf beside your PC, we guarantee several important qualities in every book we publish. These qualities are:

- *Technical accuracy*—It's no good if it doesn't work. Every Coriolis Technology Press book is reviewed by technical experts in the topic field, and is sent through several editing and proofreading passes in order to create the piece of work you now hold in your hands.

- *Innovative editorial design*—We've put years of research and refinement into the ways we present information in our books. Our books' editorial approach is uniquely designed to reflect the way people learn new technologies and search for solutions to technology problems.

- *Practical focus*—We put only pertinent information into our books and avoid any fluff. Every fact included between these two covers must serve the mission of the book as a whole.

- *Accessibility*—The information in a book is worthless unless you can find it quickly when you need it. We put a lot of effort into our indexes, and heavily cross-reference our chapters, to make it easy for you to move right to the information you need.

Here at The Coriolis Group we have been publishing and packaging books, technical journals, and training materials since 1989. We're programmers and authors ourselves, and we take an ongoing active role in defining what we publish and how we publish it. We have put a lot of thought into our books; please write to us at **ctp@coriolis.com** and let us know what you think. We hope that you're happy with the book in your hands, and that in the future, when you reach for software development and networking information, you'll turn to one of our books first.

Keith Weiskamp
President and CEO

Jeff Duntemann
VP and Editorial Director

Look For These Related Books From The Coriolis Group:

Active Server Pages Solutions
by Al Williams, Kim Barber, and Paul Newkirk

Java Black Book
by Steven Holzner

XML Black Book
by Natanya Pitts-Moultis and Cheryl Kirk

Also Recently Published By Coriolis Technology Press:

Windows 2000 Professional Advanced Configuration and Implementation
by Morten Strunge Nielsen

Windows 2000 Systems Programming Black Book
by Al Williams

Windows 2000 Registry Little Black Book
by Nathan Wallace

Windows 2000 Mac Support Little Black Book
by Gene Steinberg and Pieter Paulson

To Nancy, for more reasons than there are numbers to count.

&

About The Author

This is the 60th book written by **Steven Holzner**. His books have sold well over one million copies, and they have been translated into 16 languages. A former *PC Magazine* contributing editor, he is a graduate of MIT and earned his Ph.D. at Cornell University. He has been on the faculty at both universities.

He and Nancy travel extensively and spend time at their homes near Tanglewood, Massachusetts, in the Austrian Alps, and in a small, picturesque New England coastal town.

Acknowledgments

This book was exceptionally fortunate in having an outstanding team working on it. First, I'd like to thank the technical reviewer, Scott Duffy, for his microscopic attention to detail—very much appreciated. You did a great, conscientious job; thanks for your hard work and long hours. And the same to the project editor, Pat DuMoulin, who did an amazing job and caught many issues before they became problems (note to Coriolis: don't forget to give Pat a promotion!). Pat, you were great.

Also, I'd like to thank Charlotte Carpentier, acquisitions editor, for her attentiveness and hard work; Laura Wellander, the production coordinator who kept things on track with good grace; Michelle McConnell, the CD-ROM developer, new on the job, who jumped in with both feet; Anne Marie Walker, the copyeditor who waded through everything and got the manuscript into such good shape; Shelly Crossen, the eagle-eyed proofreader; Edwin Durbin, the accomplished indexer; April Nielsen, who designed the interior; and Jody Winkler who designed the cover. Thanks to all: Great job!

Contents At A Glance

Table Of Contents

Chapter 6
Creating Tables **297**

Chapter 13
Dynamic HTML: Changing Web Pages On The Fly 735

Introduction

Welcome to the big book of Hypertext Markup Language (HTML). This book is designed to be as comprehensive—and as accessible—as is possible for a single book on HTML. In fact, this book is written to be the only Web development resource you'll need. Nearly everything is in here, ready for you to use.

You'll find coverage of every HTML tag with at least one example showing how it works. I'll discuss not only all the official HTML 4 tags, but also all the additional tags supported by Microsoft Internet Explorer and Netscape Navigator (as far as I know, no other book can make that claim).

That's just part of the story, of course—we'll put HTML to work in depth, pushing the envelope as far as it can go. Writing Web pages with HTML is not some ordinary and monotonous task: It inspires artistry, devotion, passion, exaltation, and eccentricity—not to mention exasperation and frustration. I'll try to be true to that spirit and capture as much of the excitement and fun of HTML in this book as I can.

Besides covering every aspect of HTML, this book adds other up-to-date skills you can use to create modern Web pages. You'll get a detailed tour of Dynamic HTML, JavaScript, Java, XML, and writing Perl Common Gateway Interface (CGI) scripts. And we won't just gloss over the surface of those topics like so many other HTML books do—you'll get a real working knowledge of them all. (Of course, we can't cover all those topics in as much detail as a dedicated book on each subject would. For that level of depth, I recommend my *Java Black Book* (The Coriolis Group, ©2000) and my *Perl Black Book* (The Coriolis Group, ©1999).

What's In This Book

This book is designed to give you as much of the whole HTML story as one book can hold. We'll not only see the full HTML syntax—from the most basic to the newest HTML tags—but also dig into every major way in which HTML is used today.

There are hundreds of real-world topics covered in this book, including connecting HTML to databases on Web servers; creating and using HTML tables, lists, images, frames, image maps, and Java applets; and a great deal more. We'll create Web pages that can send email, create and use cookies, redirect browsers, change themselves on the fly, react to the time of day, and so on. And each of these topics will be presented using examples showing how they work. That's one important aspect of this book—there's an example for every important topic, ready to be typed in and used (and you can find them all on the CD-ROM, as well as a huge amount of free and powerful software).

The material you need to create dazzling Web pages is here. In addition to standard HTML, I'll dig into Dynamic HTML as well, so our Web pages can come alive by responding to mouse movements, rewriting themselves as directed by the user, and binding to databases.

You'll also find JavaScript, 'which allows us to add code to Web pages and create cookies, add Web page controls like text fields and checkboxes, and even add animated graphics. You'll learn how to determine what browser the user has, open new browser windows, display dialog boxes, and more.

Besides JavaScript, I'll also take an in-depth look at using Java to create Java applets, showing you how to program in Java, and how to embed the applets we create in Web pages. Using Java applets, we'll display images, radio buttons, and other items.

We'll also take a look at HTML's cousin, Extensible Markup Language (XML), which has been getting a great deal of attention these days. We'll learn how to use XML to format data in XML documents that you can read in and manipulate, create XML data islands, and bind data to record sets in Internet Explorer. Many people consider XML the future of the Web, and we'll be in on the ground floor.

We'll also dig into CGI (Common Gateway Interface) programming—those Internet scripts that make your Web pages come alive by allowing you to write programs that create Web pages dynamically. Using the Perl programming language, we'll learn how to write CGI scripts that reside on Web servers. I'll discuss how to create and use nearly all of the HTML controls in Web pages: text fields, text areas, checkboxes, scrolling lists, radio buttons, password fields, popup menus, hidden data fields, Submit and Reset buttons, and more.

This book is divided into separate, easily accessible topics—nearly 500 of them. Some of the topics we'll cover are as follows:

- Working with the full HTML 4 syntax
- Setting Web page colors
- Formatting text
- Creating Web page headings
- Setting font point size directly

- Displaying special characters—character entities
- Formatting text with tables
- Creating transparent, interlaced, and animated GIF images
- Displaying alternate text in place of images
- Aligning text and images
- Setting Web page background images
- Tiling images—creating image mosaics
- Creating overlapping images
- Creating graphical hyperlinks
- Giving hyperlinks access keys
- Creating navigation bars
- Creating clickable footnotes
- Emailing with hyperlinks
- Downloading files with the HTTP and FTP protocols
- Creating client-side image maps
- Creating server-side image maps
- Creating lists
- Nesting lists
- Creating tables
- Setting table colors
- Using images in tables
- Nesting tables
- Redirecting browsers
- Creating links to external multimedia files
- Adding background sounds
- Embedding multimedia and plug-ins in a Web page
- Creating inline sounds
- Creating inline videos
- Using scrolling marquees
- Using Internet Explorer multimedia controls
- Using external style sheets
- Using embedded style sheets

- Using inline styles
- Creating and using style classes
- Applying styles to text and fonts
- Applying styles to margins, indentations, and alignments
- Positioning elements using styles
- Creating JavaScript code
- Working with data in JavaScript
- Working with JavaScript operators
- Creating JavaScript objects
- Handling events in browsers
- Determining browser type in code
- Creating self-modifying Web pages
- Reloading images at runtime
- Opening a new browser window
- Configuring and writing to a new browser window
- Creating Alert, Confirmation, and Prompt dialog boxes
- Writing to the browser's status bar
- Navigating with the **location** and **history** objects
- Creating cookies with JavaScript
- Creating and using buttons, checkboxes, hidden data, image controls, Submit buttons, password controls, radio buttons, Reset buttons, text fields, text areas, HTML areas, and select controls
- Using dynamic styles
- Toggling style sheets on and off
- Creating dynamic tables
- Using conditional comments to set content on the fly
- Creating amazing **MouseOver** effects
- Creating graphics animation
- Using Vector Markup Language (VML)
- Setting element visibility
- Printing Web pages
- Using dynamic fonts

- Using visual effects—filters and transitions
- Dragging and dropping
- Using data binding
- Creating Internet Explorer behaviors
- Working with Java
- Creating Java applets
- Embedding applets in Web pages
- Reading parameters in applets
- Creating XML documents
- Creating XML document type definitions (DTDs) and schemas
- Accessing XML data by loading XML documents and with XML data islands
- Parsing XML to get element and attribute content
- Handling events while loading XML documents
- Using data binding with the XML applet and XML data islands
- Handling hierarchical data in XML documents
- Controlling XML data access using record sets
- Creating Perl CGI scripts
- Handling Perl input and output
- Creating scalar variables in Perl
- Using Perl variable interpolation
- Using Perl arrays and hashes
- Using Perl operators
- Creating Web pages from CGI scripts
- Using non-object-oriented CGI programming
- Debugging CGI scripts

In addition, a very important resource on the accompanying CD-ROM deserves mention—a complete, searchable HTML tag reference, htmlref.html. This handy reference opens in your browser and allows you to search for any official HTML, Internet Explorer, or Netscape Navigator tag. They're all listed, and all the details are there. You'll find all the details in the text as well, of course, but the HTML tag reference on the CD-ROM is already in HTML format, ready to be viewed in your browser.

As you can see, there's a lot of HTML power coming up—and hopefully what HTML has to offer will prove as irresistible to you as it does to so many others.

Conventions Used In This Book

There are one or two conventions I use in this book that you should be aware of. For example, when a particular line of HTML or code needs to be pointed out, I'll highlight it in this way:

```
<HTML>

    <HEAD>
        <TITLE>
            Using the &lt;TT&gt; Tag
        </TITLE>
    </HEAD>

    <BODY>
        At this point, the program should display:
        <BR>
        <TT>Warning! The CPU is on fire. Do you wish to quit?</TT>
    </BODY>

</HTML>
```

I'll also add tips and notes to the text like this:

TIP: This is a tip. Tips provide added information, such as where to go on the Internet for certain resources or how the unexpected behavior of a particular HTML tag can be used to your advantage.

NOTE: This is a note. Notes add information that you should be aware of, such as why it's not a good idea to use an HTML tag in a certain way or to point out when a certain browser doesn't actually do what you expect it should.

Each HTML tag has its own reference both in the text and in the complete HTML tag reference called htmlref.html on the CD-ROM. For example, here's what such a reference looks like for the **<TT>** tag:

<TT>

Purpose: Displays text in a monospace "teletype" font.

Start Tag/End Tag: Required/Required

Supported: [2, 3, 3.2, 4, IE1, IE2, IE3, IE4, IE5, NS1, NS2, NS3, NS4]

Attributes:

- **CLASS**—Class of the element (used for rendering). [3, 4, IE4, IE5, NS4]

- **DIR**—Gives the direction of directionally neutral text (text that doesn't have inherent direction in which you should read it). Possible values: **LTR**: left-to-right text or table and **RTL**: right-to-left text or table. [4, IE5]

- **ID**—Unique alphanumeric identifier for the tag, which you can use to refer to it. [3, 4, IE4, IE5, NS4]

- **LANG**—Base language used for the tag. [3, 4, IE4, IE5]

- **LANGUAGE**—Scripting language used for the tag. [IE4, IE5]

- **STYLE**—Inline style indicating how to render the element. [4, IE3, IE4, IE5, NS4]

- **TITLE**—Holds additional information (which might be displayed in tool tips) for the element. [3, 4, IE4, IE5]

Note in particular the expressions in square brackets: [3, 4, IE4, IE5, NS4]. This key indicates where a particular item is supported. In this case, the expression indicates that the item is supported in the official HTML specification for HTML 3 and HTML 4, as well as in the Microsoft Internet Explorer browser versions 4 and 5, and in the Netscape Navigator browser, version 4. Using these expressions, you can determine exactly which items are supported in what official HTML specification, and in which versions of the two major browsers, Microsoft Internet Explorer and Netscape Navigator.

What You'll Need

To use this book and display Web pages on the Internet, you'll need a connection to an Internet Service Provider (ISP) and a way of installing your HTML documents on that ISP. I address this in more detail in Chapter 1—see "Installing A Web Page" in the In Depth section—and of course, you can get more details from your ISP.

You'll need a way to create actual HTML documents. Such documents are just plain text files filled with HTML statements and declarations. To create an HTML document, you should have an editor program that can save files in plain text format or a dedicated HTML editor. See "Creating A Web Page" in the In Depth section of Chapter 1 for more information.

You should also have the latest version of a good Web browser, one that supports at least most of HTML 4 as well as JavaScript and Java. In particular, this book was written using Microsoft Internet Explorer 5 and Netscape Communicator 4.7. You can find a list of modern Web browsers and where to get them in "Viewing A Web Page" in the In Depth section of Chapter 1.

Other Resources

Throughout this book, I'll list many online resources in the In Depth sections of the chapters for additional information. The following list contains the primary resources for HTML development, including the official HTML home page at the World Wide Web Consortium (W3C), which is the organization that sets the HTML standards:

- *http://developer.netscape.com/docs/manuals/htmlguid/index.htm*—Netscape's HTML guide.

- *http://msdn.microsoft.com/workshop/c-frame.htm#/workshop/author/default.asp*—Microsoft's HTML reference and help.

- *www.w3.org/MarkUp/*—W3C's HTML home page.

There are quite a few HTML resources listed in the first chapter. If you want to take a look at some online HTML tutorials in addition to this book, there are many on the Web (a casual Web search for "HTML tutorial" turns up 28,048 pages). Here is a starter list:

- *http://echoecho.com/html.htm*—Contains a tutorial that is fairly extensive.

- *http://hotwired.lycos.com/webmonkey/teachingtool/*—Contains a basic tutorial that also points out some advanced material.

- *http://html.digitalsea.net*—Contains the "Learn HTML In Seven Easy Steps" tutorial.

- *http://search.yahoo.com/search?o=1&p=html+tutorial/*—Includes Yahoo's list of HTML tutorials.

- *www.htmlprimer.com*—Includes a number of HTML tutorials.

- *www.xencon.com/Tutorial/toc.htm*—Includes basic and some advanced HTML material.

There are also a number of Usenet groups for HTML authors (note that not all these groups may be available on your Usenet server):

- *alt.html*—The busiest of the HTML groups. A free-form forum, and a good place to go for help.

- *alt.html.critique*—For people who want to have others check their sites and get feedback on HTML programming practices.

- *alt.html.editors.enhanced-html*—Another group that offers mutual help on HTML authoring.

- *alt.html.writers*—This group is a more advanced forum on HTML.

- *microsoft.public.htmlhelp*—Microsoft's public HTML help site.

And that's all the introduction needed. Now it's time to get into HTML, starting with Chapter 1.

Chapter 1

Essential HTML

In Depth

Welcome to the big book of HTML. HTML is the language you write Web pages in, and if you want to create Web pages, you've come to the right place. This book is packed with all that you need (and much more).

Many people think writing Web pages is a difficult process—which is why many people don't do it—but the truth is that it's easy once you get the fundamentals down. The easiest way to see this is through examples, and unlike many other books, this is an example-oriented book. We're not going to wade through chapters of obscure theory as many books do before getting to the heart of the matter—we'll start creating Web pages right away, putting HTML to use. As we'll see, HTML is the language you use to tell Web browsers how to display your Web page, and once you've mastered the basics, you'll soon be creating terrific Web pages.

What's HTML All About?

What's HTML all about? HTML (Hypertext Markup Language) is the language you use to create Web pages. Left to themselves, Web browsers would take the text and images in your Web page and wrap them up into what looks like a single paragraph without any line breaks. With HTML, you act much like an editor does, *marking up* a page to indicate its format, telling the Web browser where you want a new line to begin or how you want text or images aligned, and more. In other words, HTML is all about specifying the structure and format of your Web page.

Here's an example. Unlike some other books, where you have to wait until page 215 (literally) before seeing any Web pages, we're going to get right to the HTML. This Web page is a simple one. It displays the text "Web page number one!" in a Web browser's title bar and the text "Welcome to HTML!" in the Web browser itself:

```
<HTML>
    <HEAD>
        <TITLE>
            Web page number one!
        </TITLE>
    </HEAD>

    <BODY>
        <H1>
            Welcome to HTML!
        </H1>
```

```
    </BODY>
</HTML>
```

The results of this HTML appear in Microsoft Internet Explorer in Figure 1.1.

We're going to dissect the parts of a page like this in this chapter. The first thing to note is that all the HTML terms here, like **<BODY>** are enclosed in angle brackets, **<** and **>**, and such terms are called *tags*. For example, I use the **<HTML>** tag to indicate that this Web page is written in HTML. In this case, I straddle the entire document with the **<HTML>** *starting* or *opening tag* and the corresponding *ending* or *closing tag*, **</HTML>** (the closing tag is always the same as the opening tag, but with a */*):

```
<HTML>
    <HEAD>
        <TITLE>
            Web page number one!
        </TITLE>
    </HEAD>

    <BODY>
        <H1>
            Welcome to HTML!
        </H1>
    </BODY>
</HTML>
```

Figure 1.1   Our first Web page.

NOTE: *Formally speaking, there is a tag that should precede the* **<HTML>** *tag in a Web page—the* **<!DOCTYPE>** *tag, which indicates the exact language and version of that language used to create the Web page. Review the Immediate Solutions section "**<!DOCTYPE>**—Starting An HTML Page." In practice, however, Web browsers currently make no use of this tag in HTML-based Web pages, and following the usage of most other books, I will omit it in most examples. However, you should know that officially, the first tag in a Web page is the* **<!DOCTYPE>** *tag.*

Collectively, a starting tag, an ending tag, and everything between them make up an HTML *element*. In this example, every element I use has both an opening and closing tag. Using those tags, I'm creating the two necessary sections of a Web page—its head and body—with the **<HEAD>** and **<BODY>** tags:

```
<HTML>
    <HEAD>
        <TITLE>
            Web page number one!
        </TITLE>
    </HEAD>

    <BODY>
        <H1>
            Welcome to HTML!
        </H1>
    </BODY>
</HTML>
```

As we'll see, the head section includes information about how your Web page should be displayed, and the body includes the actual material you want to display. In the previous code, I'm using the **<TITLE>** tag in the page's head to indicate that the text the Web browser should display in its title bar is "Web page number one!". And I'm also using the **<H1>** tag in the page's body to indicate that the Web browser should display the text "Welcome to HTML!" in the actual page, using heading style number one (H1). This creates big type in bold. You can see the result in Figure 1.1.

This example helps make the idea of HTML more concrete. As you can see, I've used the HTML tags **<HTML>**, **<HEAD>**, **<TITLE>**, **<BODY>**, and **<H1>** to structure and create our first Web page. HTML is based on tags like **<HEAD>** and **<BODY>**. Tags like **<HEAD>** and **<BODY>** can enclose other tags as you saw in the previous example, allowing you to create complex nested structures in your documents. (This fact is important in XML, Extensible Markup Language, which many people consider the successor to HTML, when creating involved data structures.)

Note that the **<H1>** tag, which displays an H1 (in big, bold type), needs a closing tag **</H1>** to enclose the text you want to set in that heading style as shown here:

```
<H1>
    Welcome to HTML!
</H1>
```

On the other hand, the **<P>** tag, which starts a new paragraph of text (and skips some space between paragraphs), doesn't need a closing tag **</P>**. However, you can use one if you want (if you just start a new paragraph with a new **<P>** tag, the browser will know what to do). For that reason, closing tags are *optional* for the **<P>** element and you can omit them as I do here:

```
<P>
    Here's a paragraph of text.
<P>
    Here's another paragraph!
```

In addition, some elements, like the **<H1>** element, are designed to enclose some text between the opening and closing tag. Others, like the **<META>** element, called *empty elements*, are not. Here's an example in which I set the name of the author of a Web page to "Steve" using a **<META>** element:

```
<HEAD>
    <TITLE>
        Web page number one!
        <META NAME="Author" CONTENT="Steve">
    </TITLE>
</HEAD>
```

Because some HTML elements need closing tags and others don't, and because some can have text between the opening and closing tag and others can't, I'll be sure to specify how every tag works as we cover each one in this book. I'll also give at least one example of each tag at work.

Note the terms **NAME** and **CONTENT** in the previous example, which I set to the values **Author** and **Steve** respectively. These terms are called *attributes*, and they're another important part of working with HTML tags.

Using Tag Attributes

HTML tags tell Web browsers how to format and organize your Web pages, but there's more to tell here—you can actually customize most tags using attributes.

An attribute is a keyword that you use in an opening tag to give more information to the Web browser. It follows this format:

```
<TAGNAME ATTRIBUTE = VALUE>
```

In the following example, I use the **ALIGN** attribute of the **<H1>** tag and set it equal to **CENTER** to indicate that I want the text in this tag to appear centered on the Web page:

```
<HTML>
    <HEAD>
        <TITLE>
            Web page number one!
        </TITLE>
    </HEAD>

    <BODY>
        <H1 ALIGN = "CENTER">
            Welcome to HTML!
        </H1>
    </BODY>
</HTML>
```

The result appears in Figure 1.2, where, as you can see, the text has indeed been centered.

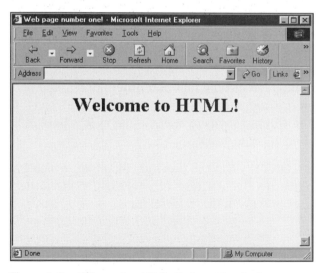

Figure 1.2   Using a tag attribute to center text.

You can have a number of attributes in the same opening tag, like this:

```
<TAGNAME ATTRIBUTE1 = VALUE1 ATTRIBUTE2 = VALUE2>
```

Because tag attributes are so important, I'll list all the attributes for each tag as I introduce that tag in the text. I'll also indicate what browser supports what tag and in what version.

Now that we know what we're talking about and how it looks, it's time to dig deeper into what's going on. You know that HTML stands for Hypertext Markup Language, but what's *hypertext* anyway? The term has become more familiar to people in recent years. I'll take a look at its origins in the next section.

The History Of HTML

Where did HTML—and for that matter, Web pages—come from? It's worth taking a look at HTML's history, and I'll do that in overview here. The first person to actually use the word hypertext was Ted Nelson in the 1960s. Was he a computer expert? No, his specialties were philosophy and sociology. Ted Nelson originally came up with an idea for a system he called Xanadu (**www.xanadu.net**), which allowed nonsequential text access. That is, instead of needing to read text from first to last as you normally would when scrolling through it, you could skip around in it at will, much as you would browse around a magazine.

The idea was a simple one—words or phrases in what Ted Nelson called a *hyperfile* would bring up associations with other words or phrases in the same or other documents. The idea was that hypertext would be a fully interconnected way to skip around as the thought took you. In this way, Nelson created what he called the *hyperworld*.

We all know the result as implemented in modern Web browsers with *hyperlinks*— you can move from location to location just by clicking a link. Although it took a long time to catch on, there's simply no doubting its tremendous success. I can still remember the time I first saw an early version of the National Center for Supercomputing Applications (NCSA) Mosaic browser at work at Cornell University. It was shown to me by a member of the anthropology department who clicked a link, waited for a few minutes, and then saw new text appear. "That," he said with great satisfaction, "came from California." I was completely amazed—and knew I had to get into this stuff.

1. Essential HTML

The idea of hypertext still needed an actual working implementation and that took many more years. Around 1990, Tim Berners-Lee, an English scientist at the European Laboratory for Particle Physics (better known as CERN), was working on a system he called Enquire that let him make associations between text for his own personal use. He got so interested in the process that he perfected it, creating the foundation of the World Wide Web that we know today. It was Tim Berners-Lee who created the first Web server, came up with the term HTML, the term HTTP (Hypertext Transport Protocol, which specifies how hypertext is sent on the Internet), and the term URL (Uniform Resource Locator) to represent a World Wide Web address (more on URLs in a few pages).

To create HTML, Tim Berners-Lee knew that he would need a markup language, so he chose SGML (Standard Generalized Markup Language), which was a general markup language that had been around for a long time and was already in use on computers for specialized applications. Using SGML, you can *define* markup languages, specifying their rules and grammar. You do that by creating a *document type definition* (DTD) of the type. We'll see how to create a DTD when working with XML later in this book. Tim Berners-Lee created a DTD for HTML specifying the early syntax of HTML, and so HTML, and therefore Web pages, were born.

TIP: As we'll see, the **<!DOCTYPE>** tag, which formally begins Web pages, specifies the actual DTD in use for the HTML you utilize in the Web page itself.

In 1992, Dan Connolly started developing HTML 1 (the original version is now called HTML 0), which included the idea of a document's head and body with the **<HEAD>** and **<BODY>** tags as well as the **<TITLE>** tag and others. David Raggett created HTML+, which incorporated images into HTML. By then many people began to see the exciting possibilities, and the World Wide Web Consortium (called W3C at **http://w3c.org**), the people responsible for the official form of HTML itself, was formed. The W3C created HTML 2, which included new tags like **<FORM>**, allowing you to place buttons, drop-down list boxes, text fields, and more (collectively called *controls*) in Web pages.

TIP: Here are some W3C resources that might be of interest: W3C itself is at **http://w3c.org**. You can find the actual HTML standards at **http://w3c.org/MarkUp/**, cascading style sheets at **http://w3c.org/Style/**, the new document object model (DOM) at **http://w3c.org/DOM/**, working with math on the Web at **http://w3c.org/Math/**, working with graphics at **http://w3c.org/Graphics/**, the Web Accessibility Initiative for people with disabilities at **http://w3c.org/WAI/**, and XML information at **http://w3c.org/XML/**.

HTML 3 followed not long after HTML 2, but it was a very ambitious standard that in the end broke into factions—and in fact, HTML 3 was never fully approved. By that time, however, Web browsers had already taken the lead and W3C finally approved HTML 3.2, which in reality just acknowledged the tags that were already in popular use. With HTML 4, W3C has taken the lead again and is once more in charge of the standards (which is not to say that the popular browsers are following in all cases). HTML 4 is the current standard, and I'll take a closer look at it in the next section.

HTML 4

There are many new features in HTML 4, and a number of them will only have meaning if you already know how to work with HTML. So, if the material in this section doesn't make too much sense, don't worry—I'll be covering all of it in more detail throughout the book.

Two big changes in HTML 4 were the addition of IDs and *event capturing* for nearly all tags. You can now specify an ID for just about every tag using the ID attribute like this: **<H1 ID = HEADING1>**. In this case, I've named the **<H1>** heading **HEADING1** and can refer to it that way in code (using languages such as JavaScript or VBScript). Event capturing is closely aligned with dynamic HTML, which we'll discuss later in Chapters 13 and 14, and lets your tags "come alive" in new ways. For example, if I use the **ONCLICK** attribute like this: **<H1 ONCLICK = HANDLE_CLICK>**, when the user clicks this H1 heading, the code in a function I've created and named **HANDLE_CLICK** will be called. Using event capturing in this way, you can create special effects, like highlighting hyperlinks, when the mouse moves over them.

Another big change was the move from using tags to format text to using *style sheets*. For example, you can use the **<B>** tag to display text as bold and **<I>** to display it in italics, but with HTML 4 you're supposed to use style sheets to create these effects. This is a big change for most HTML programmers, and I'll cover style sheets in some detail in Chapter 9. However, because this is such a big change to a cherished part of HTML, it's a safe bet that formatting tags like **<B>** and **<I>** will be around for some time to come, so I'll cover them as they stand today as well.

The **<OBJECT>** tag was expanded to include Java *applets* (which we'll see later in Chapter 16) as well as just about any kind of external file you want to include in a Web page. In fact, **<OBJECT>** now seems intended to supersede the **<APPLET>**, **<EMBED>**, and eventually even the **<IMG>** tag, which you currently use to embed images.

You can find the official HTML 4 specification, version 4.01, as of this writing at **www.w3.org/TR/1999/REC-html40-1-19991224/**. (HTML 4.01 fixes a few minor bugs in the specification for version 4.) Note that this document will probably have been superseded by the time you read this. You can always find the latest HTML 4 specification at **www.w3.org/TR/REC-html40/**.

TIP: *In fact, there are three forms of HTML 4 that are officially recognized—strict, transitional, and frameset. For the differences between these forms, see the Immediate Solutions section "<!DOCTYPE>—Starting An HTML Page." With virtually all modern browsers, however, you don't need to specify the form of HTML 4 you're using; the browser will understand from the tags you're using.*

HTML 4 also introduces a number of new tags. You can see these in Table 1.1.

Deprecated Features

It's difficult for W3C to make universal changes to HTML because there are many HTML authors out there who are accustomed to the old ways. For that reason, W3C marks features it wants to eliminate from HTML as *deprecated*. When something is marked as deprecated, it means that it'll be removed from HTML in a future version. It's usually good practice to avoid deprecated tags, although common ones like **<CENTER>** will be around for a long time, so I'll cover them in this book (in fact, it will be a while before the functionality of the deprecated tags is available using style sheets in many browsers).

HTML 4 with its emphasis on style sheets deprecated quite a lot of tags including the **<CENTER>**, **<BASEFONT>**, **<FONT>**, **<STRIKE>** (also called **<S>**), and **<U>** tags. These tags all format text. W3C decided that such formatting should take place with style sheets instead.

Table 1.1   New tags in HTML 4.

Tag	Does This
<ACRONYM>	Marks a group of letters that stand for something else.
<BUTTON>	Adds functionality to invoke scripts, calculates values, performs formatting, and more. A fully featured button for use in forms. Can be used for far more than just a Submit or Reset button.
<COLGROUP>	Identifies a column in a table for easy formatting.
<FIELDSET>	Groups elements in forms as logical groups.
<INS> and **<DEL>**	**<INS>** marks text as newly inserted with the date of insertion and **<DEL>** marks text as deleted with the date of deletion.
<LEGEND>	Gives the elements in form captions.
<Q>	Used for inline quotes (like an inline version of **<BLOCKQUOTE>**).

Besides deprecating many formatting tags, W3C has deprecated a number of tag attributes that determine appearance, such as the **ALINK**, **VLINK**, **BGCOLOR**, **COLOR**, and **LINK** attributes of the **<BODY>** tag. In addition, these tags are now considered deprecated: **<APPLET>** (replaced by **<OBJECT>**), **<ISINDEX>** (which generates a text field that the user can type into and has been replaced by the **<INPUT>** tag in forms) as well as **<DIR>** and **<MENU>** (which create vertical lists of items and so duplicate the **<UL>** tag).

Removed Features

Some features that were deprecated a long time ago have been removed from HTML 4. These features include the **<XMP>**, **<PLAINTEXT>**, and **<LISTING>** tags, which let you display preformatted text. These have now been taken over by the **<PRE>** tag.

As you can see, HTML is an evolving standard. In fact, it's evolving even more than indicated by the work of the W3C. Keep in mind that W3C only sets the HTML standards; it's the actual browsers that implement it. And the companies that create the browsers have a lot to say about what's going on.

Browser Wars

The browser giants today are Netscape Navigator and Microsoft Internet Explorer. Both of them deviate to some degree from the HTML standard as set by W3C. For example, there are quite a few tag attributes that W3C has defined as standard that neither Netscape Navigator nor Internet Explorer implement. And there are quite a few attributes—and even tags (like the Netscape Navigator **<LAYER>** tag and the Internet Explorer **<MARQUEE>** tag)—that are not part of the HTML standards at all, but are implemented by one or the other of the big browsers. In fact, things differ by browser version—some attributes only appear in Internet Explorer 5, for example.

As you can imagine, it's quite a zoo out there when you come to the actual implementation of HTML in the various browsers, and that's one of the areas this book is designed to clarify. I'll list the attributes that are part of the HTML standard, which ones are supported by what browser, and even which version of what browser.

The actual split between browsers really cracked wide open when Netscape first introduced the idea of dynamic HTML, which Microsoft has elaborated tremendously, and which I'll cover later in Chapter 13. However, the difference is evident even when working with HTML itself. Tags that are supposed to be interpreted the same way end up giving different results (for example, the very common **
**

tag creates a vertical space that ends up being different in both Netscape Navigator and Internet Explorer). For this reason, when you create a Web page, it's best to actually test it out in a variety of browsers before releasing it to the world. And that brings us to the topic of actually creating Web pages for use in browsers. We'll start in the next section.

Creating A Web Page

We've already seen an example Web page:

```
<HTML>
    <HEAD>
        <TITLE>
            Web page number one!
        </TITLE>
    </HEAD>

    <BODY>
        <H1>
            Welcome to HTML!
        </H1>
    </BODY>
</HTML>
```

How do you get this page into a Web browser as shown in Figure 1.1? All you have to do is enter this HTML into a file, and then open that file in your Web browser. To create that file, you can use common editors like Windows WordPad or Notepad if you save the page in text format. You can even use a word processor like Microsoft Word, but note that you cannot save normal Web pages in .doc format (which includes many special formatting characters that Web browsers won't understand)—they must be saved in text format from the Save As dialog box.

TIP: *Here's the test—if you can type the page using the **type** command in a DOS window and see the example code without any funny looking characters, you're doing okay (the real test, of course, is how your browser displays the page).*

The name you give the Web page doesn't matter as long as you give it the extension .html to indicate that it's an HTML document. For example, you might enter the previous text into a file named one.html. Because of the fact that MS-DOS used to only recognize three-letter extensions, you can also use the extension .htm and not have a problem with most browsers.

That's the process. Just enter the previous HTML in a file and save the file in text format, giving it the extension .html, such as one.html. Congratulations—you've just created your first Web page!

In fact, there are many tools called HTML editors to help you with the process—many of which will even write the HTML for you. I'll take a look at some of these in the next section (note that for this book, all you need is a simple text editor like Windows WordPad or Notepad, or vi or emacs in Unix).

What HTML Editors Are Available?

There are a great number of HTML editors available for you to use in creating Web pages. Here's a starter list:

- *Adobe PageMill (**http://adobe.com**)*—An editor that helps automate the whole process of site design and implementation.

- *Allaire's HomeSite (**www.allaire.com**)*—A simple, but powerful, editor.

- *Amaya (**www.w3.org/Amaya/**)*—A WYSIWYG (what you see is what you get) HTML editor from W3 Corporation.

- *American Cybernetics Multi-Edit (**www.amcyber.com**)*—An HTML editor that works well for programmers.

- *BBEdit (**www.barebones.com**)*—An easy-to-use Macintosh HTML editor.

- *Claris Home Page (**www.claris.com**)*—An editor with mostly WYSIWYG for beginners with some additional tools.

- *ExperTelligence's Webber (**www.webbase.com**)*—An editor that includes good support for checking your HTML.

- *Hot Dog Express (**www.sausage.com**)*—An easy-to-use editor for beginners.

- *Hot Dog Pro (**www.sausage.com**)*—A more powerful version of the Hot Dog Express editor including many advanced features, such as site management.

- *HoTMetaL Pro (**www.softquad.com**)*—An extensive, powerful, and venerated HTML editor.

- *MicroEdge's Visual SlickEdit (**www.slickedit.com**)*—An editor that works well for programmers. It lets you work faster than many graphic-based editors.

- *Microsoft FrontPage (**www.microsoft.com**)*—An editor contained in a powerful package that integrates directly with your Web site.

- *Netscape Composer (**www.netscape.com**)*—An editor that comes with the Netscape Communicator, more or less WYSIWYG. It is easy to use, but somewhat limited.

So, after you've created a Web page, how do you install it on your Web site? I'll take a look at that in the next section.

Installing A Web Page

To install a Web page like one.html on the World Wide Web, you use an Internet Service Provider (ISP), such as America Online (AOL), CompuServe, or any one of thousands of local companies (including, increasingly, phone companies that let you connect through fiber optics). You can also use Web sites like GeoCities (**www.geocities.com**) that let you install Web pages free of charge (there are hundreds of such sites now—just use a Web search engine to search for the phrase "free web page" and be prepared for many matches: I got 53,113 matches). The actual installation process depends on your ISP, but I'll go over the process in general here.

What's My URL?

ISPs have their own ways of storing Web pages, and only they will be able to tell you what your page's Web address, its URL, will be. For example, if your ISP is named "starpowder.com" and your account's name is "steve", your Web page's URL when you install it may be **http://www.starpowder.com/steve/one.html**.

Note the parts of this URL: It begins with "http" indicating that we're using HTTP, the Web browser protocol, which is what you use to look at Web pages in browsers. Next is the name of the ISP followed by the name of your account and then the name of the actual page itself, "one.html". What your Web page's actual URL will be depends on the ISP; for example, it's common to place a tilde (~) before the account name like this: **http://www.starpowder.com/~steve/one.html**. You might even end up with something like this: **http://www.starpowder.com/customers/steve/one.html**. This is something only your ISP can tell you, so make sure you ask it.

Uploading A Page

How do you actually send your Web page to your ISP? This also depends on your ISP. Some ISPs (like GeoCities) let you use a Web browser-based interface that asks you for your account name and password, and it lets you indicate what file to upload. All you have to do is click a button and your Web page is uploaded to the ISP.

It's far more common, however, to use a File Transfer Protocol (FTP) program to send your Web page to your ISP. You'll need an FTP program for that, and often your ISP can provide you with one free of charge. FTP programs exist just for the purpose you want here—to send files across the Internet. In this case, you want to upload your Web page to your ISP. To do that, you need to ask your ISP what its FTP address is. Typically, it'll be much the same as its URL except with ftp instead of http, like this: **ftp://ftp.starpowder.com**. You also need to give your username and password to the FTP program so it knows where to place the Web page you're uploading. You might even have to set the uploaded page's security protection so it will be accessible on the Internet (your FTP program should do this by default—you shouldn't have to worry about it). If you get stuck, ask the people at your ISP who will have dealt with similar questions many times before.

There are dozens of FTP programs out there for you to choose from. For example, two good sources of shareware programs for Windows are TUCOWS (The Ultimate Collection Of Winsock Software, **www.tucows.com**) and CWSApps (**http://cws.internet.com/home.html**). Here are the FTP programs available at CWSApps (there are reviews of each at the CWSApps site):

- 3D-FTP
- AbsoluteFTP
- Bullet Proof FTP
- CuteFTP
- FTP Explorer
- FTP Icon Connection
- GetRight
- John Junod's WS-FTP
- LeechFTP
- Rhino Software's FTP Voyager
- TransSoft's FTP Control
- WinTelnet & FTP Pro
- WSN-FTPC

Here's an example using CuteFTP to connect to a site. When you start the program, CuteFTP's Site Manager dialog box appears as shown in Figure 1.3. You click the Add Site button and in the dialog box that opens, you enter the FTP address of your ISP (such as "ftp.starpowder.com"), your username (such as "steve") and your password (such as "open sesame"). Click OK to close the dialog box and add this new site to the Site Manager, then select the site with the mouse and click the Connect button.

This connects to your account on your ISP, shown in Figure 1.4. In the left window, is your local directory. You use the drop-down list boxes at the top to move to the directory with your Web page, one.html. In the right window, there's a listing of your account on your ISP, shown in Figure 1.4. To upload your Web page, all you have to do is to use the mouse to drag the one.html file from the left window to the right window, and the FTP program will do the rest. That's it—now your Web page is uploaded, installed on your ISP, and ready to view.

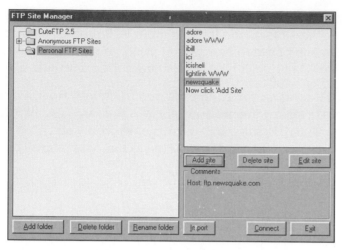

Figure 1.3   CuteFTP's Site Manager dialog box.

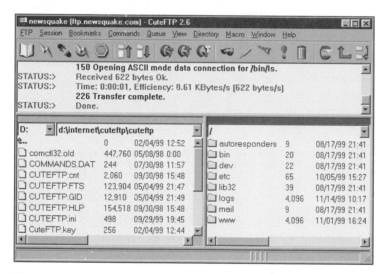

Figure 1.4   CuteFTP at work.

TIP: One last point: The default Web page for your site should be called index.html (or index.htm) because Web browsers will look for a page with that name if no particular Web page is specified. For example, these refer to the same page: **www.starpowder/steve/** and **www.starpowder/steve/index.html**. Note that if your Web server uses Microsoft Internet Information Server (IIS), the default page is named default.htm. I'll discuss more Web site design issues throughout the book.

Viewing A Web Page

You use a Web browser to view your new Web page. There are two ways to view a Web page: locally and from the Internet. Local pages are on your own computer. To open them, you just use the Open item in the Web browser's File menu. For example, say one.html was stored in c:\www. You can open that file directly in your browser with the Open item in the File menu. In addition, both Netscape Navigator and Internet Explorer let you enter the location of a Web page by typing it directly into a box (labeled Address in Internet Explorer, as you can see in Figure 1.1, and Location in Netscape Navigator). You can type c:\www\one.html directly into that box. On the other hand, if you want to open a Web page from the Internet, you just connect to the Internet and enter the URL of that page directly into that box.

TIP: *A great way to "debug" your Web pages is to work on them locally. Open them in your Web browser, and each time you make a new change to them, save that change in your editor and reload the page (use the Reload button in Netscape Navigator and the Refresh button in Internet Explorer). This will save you from having to upload the page to your ISP each time you want to test a change.*

As you might expect, there are quite a few browsers available for you to use. Here's a partial list:

- *Alis Technology's Tango (**www.alis.com**)*—A browser that is good for handling Arabic, Devangari, Chinese, Japanese, and Kanji characters.

- *Amaya (**www.w3.org/Amaya/**)*—A browser used by W3C to test new HTML with, and a good way to keep up on the latest features.

- *HotJava (**http://java.sun.com/products/hotjava/**)*—Sun Microsystem's browsers, which are well integrated with current Java versions.

- *Lynx (**www.lynx.browser.org**)*—A text-based Web browser, popular in Unix shell accounts.

- *Microsoft Internet Explorer (**www.microsoft.com/ie/**)*—Microsoft's browser, now in Release 5. Internet Explorer is trying hard to become the king of browsers. Free and huge, it's become the choice of many. One of the two top browsers.

- *NCSA Mosaic (**www.ncsa.uiuc.edu/SDG/Software/Mosaic/**)*—One of the early and most popular browsers; it stopped development in 1997.

- *Netscape Navigator (**www.netscape.com**, part of the Netscape Communicator suite)*—The original big browser, now in competition with Internet Explorer. Navigator was the first one to come up with dynamic HTML and many other innovations. One of the two top browsers.

- *Opera (**www.operasoftware.com**)*—A small and innovative browser from Norway for Windows.

Now that your Web page is up, how do you know it'll work in all these browsers? Other than testing it in all of them, one way is to use an HTML *validator*.

Checking Your Web Page

HTML validators are programs that will check your Web page for compliance with the HTML 4 standard. Many such programs are free and exist on the Web; all you do is enter the URL of the page you want checked, and you'll get a full report. Here are some validators available on the Web:

- *CAST's Bobby (**www.cast.org/bobby/**)*—A validator that lets you test for accessibility features as well as standard HTML.

- *CSE 3310 HTML Validator (**www.htmlvalidator.com**)*—A commercial validator used by thousands of users.

- *Neil Bower's Weblint (**www.cre.canon.co.uk/~neilb/weblint/**)*—An HTML validator written in Perl that operates online.

- *WebTechs Validation Service (**www.webtechs.com/html-val-svc/**)*—A validator that lets you check an entire page or just sections of HTML.

That's it! We've taken a look at what HTML is, where it comes from, how to use it to create Web pages, how to install and view those Web pages, and even how to check them. It's now time to get some hands-on experience in the Immediate Solutions section, beginning with how to start a Web page. Let's start writing some HTML.

Immediate Solutions

<!DOCTYPE>—Starting An HTML Page

Purpose: Formally starts an HTML document, indicating the version of HTML used.

Start Tag/End Tag: Required/None

Supported: [2, 3, 3.2, 4]

Attributes:

• None

The novice programmer says, "OK, I'm ready to start my Web page! Where do I begin?" "With the **<!DOCTYPE>** tag," you say, in your capacity as Web Wizard. "**<!DOCTYPE>**?" the NP says, "Never heard of it!"

The **<!DOCTYPE>** tag is formally the first tag of HTML documents. Here's a typical **<!DOCTYPE>** tag, which should go at the beginning of a Web page:

```
<!DOCTYPE HTML PUBLIC "-//W3C//DTD HTML 4.0//EN">
<HTML>
    <HEAD>
        <TITLE>
            Web page number one!
        </TITLE>
    </HEAD>

    <BODY>
        <H1>
            Welcome to HTML!
        </H1>
    </BODY>
</HTML>
```

This tag indicates that the "top element" of the document is the **<HTML>** tag (as it must always be for HTML documents), and that the required DTD (the DTD defines the syntax for the language) is public (as opposed to the other alternative, SYSTEM). It also indicates that the sponsoring organization is "W3C", that the "public text class" of the item being referred to is a DTD, and that the "public text definition" is HTML 4. Finally, it indicates that the language used is English (EN = English).

If you use the **<!DOCTYPE>** tag in the previous example, it indicates that you want to use strict HTML 4 in your document. Any non-HTML 4 elements or usage will be considered an error. There are three possible DTDs for HTML 4: strict HTML 4, transitional HTML 4 (which includes support for deprecated items), and frameset HTML 4 (which includes support for transitional HTML 4 plus frames). Here are the corresponding **<!DOCTYPE>** tags:

```
<!DOCTYPE HTML PUBLIC "-//W3C//DTD HTML 4.0//EN">
<!DOCTYPE HTML PUBLIC "-//W3C//DTD HTML 4.0 Transitional//EN">
<!DOCTYPE HTML PUBLIC "-//W3C//DTD HTML 4.0 Frameset//EN">
```

If you're using HTML 3.2, you'd use this **<!DOCTYPE>** tag:

```
<!DOCTYPE HTML PUBLIC "-//W3C//DTD HTML 3.2 Final//EN">
```

The browser is supposed to know how to get the various DTDs for HTML itself, but if not, you can actually specify where to find them like this:

```
<!DOCTYPE HTML PUBLIC "-//W3C//DTD HTML 4.0//EN"
        "http://www.w3.org/TR/REC-html40/strict.dtd">

<!DOCTYPE HTML PUBLIC "-//W3C//DTD HTML 4.0 Transitional//EN"
        "http://www.w3.org/TR/REC-html40/loose.dtd">

<!DOCTYPE HTML PUBLIC "-//W3C//DTD HTML 4.0 Frameset//EN"
        "http://www.w3.org/TR/REC-html40/frameset.dtd">
```

In practice, browsers ignore this tag because they expect the document to be in HTML. I'll omit this tag for the most part as well. On the other hand, you should know this tag exists (if for no other reason than HTML validators will often notice that it's missing and complain about it), and you'll often see it in the Web pages created by large corporations (such as Microsoft) or by professional Web packages (like the CGI.pm package in Perl, which lets you create Web pages in code as we'll see later in Chapter 20).

<HTML>—Starting An HTML Page

Purpose: Starts the HTML document and contains that document surrounding everything else except the **<!DOCTYPE>** tag.

Start Tag/End Tag: Optional/Optional

Supported: [2, 3, 3.2, 4, IE1, IE2, IE3, IE4, IE5, NS1, NS2, NS3, NS4]

Attributes:

- **CLASS**—Class of the element (used for rendering). [IE4, IE5]

- **DIR**—Gives the direction of directionally neutral text (text that doesn't have inherent direction in which you should read it). Possible values: **LTR**: left-to-right text or table and **RTL**: right-to-left text or table. [4]

- **ID**—Unique alphanumeric identifier for the tag, which you can use to refer to it. [IE4, IE5, NS4]

- **LANG**—Base language used for the tag. [4, NS4]

- **VERSION**—Deprecated. Version of the language used. HTML version information is now stored in the **<!DOCTYPE>** tag. [1, 2, 3, 3.2]

- **XMLNS**—Declares a namespace for custom tags in an HTML document. [IE4, IE5]

"Say," asks the novice programmer, "how do I tell the Web browser that my document is written in HTML?" "You use the HTML tag," you say. "Ah," the NP says, "makes sense."

Practically speaking, **<HTML>** is almost always the first tag in an HTML page, and the **</HTML>** tag is the last tag. *Everything* else in the Web page goes between those two tags and is technically part of the **<HTML>** element.

Here's an example that we've already seen:

```
<HTML>
    <HEAD>
        <TITLE>
            Web page number one!
        </TITLE>
    </HEAD>

    <BODY>
```

```
      <H1>
           Welcome to HTML!
      </H1>
   </BODY>
</HTML>
```

TIP: *It's worth noting that the start and end tags for **<HTML>** are typically optional. Most browsers will assume, by default, that the document is HTML. However, it's possible that some browsers will have problems, so it's a good idea to include this tag.*

Creating The Structure Of A Web Page: Head And Body

"Can you take a look at my Web page?" the novice programmer asks; "I think it's a doozy." "Hm," you say, "where's the head section? Where's the body?" "Do I need those?" the NP asks. You smile and say, "Pull up a chair."

There is a certain structure for HTML documents as defined in the HTML DTD created by W3C. Formally speaking, to be legal HTML, a Web page must start with the **<!DOCTYPE>** tag followed by the **<HTML>** tag. The **<HTML>** element must contain both a **<HEAD>** element and a **<BODY>** element. The **<HEAD>** element contains general information about the document, and the **<BODY>** element contains the contents of the document. Another thing to note is that, formally, the **<HEAD>** element must contain a **<TITLE>** element (the **<BODY>** element is not required to contain any other elements):

```
<!DOCTYPE HTML PUBLIC "-//W3C//DTD HTML 4.0 Transitional//EN">
<HTML>
    <HEAD>
        <TITLE>
            Web page number one!
        </TITLE>
    </HEAD>

    <BODY>
        <H1>
            Welcome to HTML!
        </H1>
    </BODY>
</HTML>
```

Because Web pages are divided very specifically into head and body sections, I'll take a look at those sections in overview in the remainder of this chapter.

`<HEAD>`—Creating A Web Page's Head

Purpose: Contains the head of an HTML document, which holds information about the document, such as its title.

Start Tag/End Tag: Optional/Optional

Supported: [2, 3, 3.2, 4, IE1, IE2, IE3, IE4, IE5, NS1, NS2, NS3, NS4]

Attributes:

- **CLASS**—Class of the element (used for rendering). [IE4, IE5]

- **DIR**—Gives the direction of directionally neutral text (text that doesn't have inherent direction in which you should read it). Possible values: **LTR**: left-to-right text or table and **RTL**: right-to-left text or table. [4]

- **ID**—Unique alphanumeric identifier for the tag, which you can use to refer to it. [IE4, IE5, NS4]

- **LANG**—Base language used for the tag. [4, IE4, IE5, NS4]

- **PROFILE**—Gives the location of one or more white-space separated metadata profile URLs for the current document, which can hold a great deal of information about the document. [4]

- **STYLE**—Inline style indicating how to render the element. [NS4]

- **TITLE**—Holds additional information (as might be displayed in tool tips) for the element. [NS4]

The novice programmer wants to know, "What's so important about a Web page's head?" "Well," you say, "among other things, every Web page needs one to be proper HTML. There are certain tags, like **`<TITLE>`**, which can only appear in the page's head, and it's possible to request just a Web page's head, and search engines often do, so it's important to put lots of information in the head." "You've sold me," says the NP.

Each properly defined HTML page should have a head, which you create with the **`<HEAD>`** tag:

```
<HTML>
    <HEAD>
        <TITLE>
            Web page number one!
        </TITLE>
    </HEAD>
```

```
<BODY>
    <H1>
        Welcome to HTML!
    </H1>
</BODY>
</HTML>
```

The head of a Web page holds information about the page, such as its title (in fact, to be proper HTML, each head needs a title), keywords for search engines, a base address for URLs, and more.

You can use the standard attributes in the **<HEAD>** tag, such as **CLASS**, **ID**, **STYLE**, and so on, and one attribute particular to **<HEAD>**: the **PROFILE** attribute. This attribute can hold a list of URLs that contains metadata about the page that would be returned with the **<META>** tag (coming up in a few pages), such as the page's author, copyright, description, and more. Note that although **PROFILE** is part of the HTML 4 specification, neither Netscape Navigator nor Internet Explorer supports it yet.

Here are the HTML elements that can appear in the head:

- **BASE**—Base URL for the document
- **BASEFONT** [IE]—Base font for the document
- **BGSOUND** [IE]—Background sound
- **ISINDEX**—Rudimentary input control
- **LINK**—Indicates a relationship between the document and another object
- **META**—Header information
- **NEXTID** [IE]—Hint for the **NAME** value to use when creating a new hyperlink element
- **NOSCRIPT**—Holds text that only appears if the browser does not support the **SCRIPT** tag (some browsers might not display text from elements in the **<HEAD>** element, so you might want to place **<NOSCRIPT>** outside the **<HEAD>** element)
- **SCRIPT**—Holds programming script statement, such as JavaScript
- **STYLE**—Includes style information for rendering
- **TITLE**—The Web page's title, which appears in the Web browser

I'll cover the following tags throughout the book: working with **<BGSOUND>** in Chapter 8 about multimedia, **<ISINDEX>** in Chapter 12 about working with controls and forms, **<LINK>** and **<BASE>** in Chapter 5 on hyperlinks, **<STYLE>** in Chapter 9 on style sheets, **<SCRIPT>** in Chapters 10 and 11 on JavaScript (the document head is a good place to store scripts you'll use throughout the page), and so on. I'll take a look at the two important tags that can only appear in the head in this chapter: **<TITLE>** and **<META>**. These two topics are discussed in the next two sections.

<TITLE>—Giving A Web Page A Title

Purpose: Contains the title of the HTML document, which will appear in the Web browser's title bar and is used by search engines to refer to the document. Each **<HEAD>** element should include a **<TITLE>** element.

Start Tag/End Tag: Required/Required

Supported: [2, 3, 3.2, 4, IE1, IE2, IE3, IE4, IE5, NS1, NS2, NS3, NS4]

Attributes:

- **CLASS**—Class of the element (used for rendering). [NS4]
- **ID**—Unique alphanumeric identifier for the tag, which you can use to refer to it. [IE5, NS4]
- **LANG**—Base language used for the tag. [4, IE4, IE5, NS4]
- **STYLE**—Inline style indicating how to render the element. [4, NS4]

"Hm," says the novice programmer, "why does the HTML validator say: 'Error 34405: Missing **TITLE** element' when I run it on my Web page?" You smile and say, "Probably because you didn't include a **<TITLE>** element in the page's head. It's required for proper HTML pages, and it must be in the head." "Well that's it," the NP says, "no more HTML validators for me."

The **<TITLE>** element indicates that document's title to the browsers. The text in the **<TITLE>** element is displayed in the browsers' title bars, shown in Figure 1.1.

It's a good idea to keep the text in the title relatively short and to the point. Keep in mind that people may read the title out of context—as when it's displayed by a search engine, so try to establish a little context if you can. For example, rather than call your page "View 5", you might say, "The Austrian Alps At Sunset". You might also keep in mind that besides the list of keywords you embed in your Web page (see the following section), many search engines search a Web page's title first. So, if there are special keywords you want people to use to find your page, the title is one place to put them.

We've already seen an example **<TITLE>** element at the beginning of this chapter:

```
<HTML>
    <HEAD>
        <TITLE>
            Web page number one!
        </TITLE>
    </HEAD>

    <BODY>
        <H1>
            Welcome to HTML!
        </H1>
    </BODY>
</HTML>
```

The result of this HTML appears in Figure 1.1. Note that if you omit the title in a Web page, no browser (none that I know of, anyway) will react badly. In general, browsers are written to be very forgiving; however, I recommend that you do give all but the shortest pages a title because the title bar of the browser is a natural place for the user to check when they're looking at your pages.

TIP: *Some browsers will have problems if you use titles longer than 256 characters. In addition, some browsers may use the title as the name of the file to save the Web page in, if the user requests the browser to save it. Be careful when defining multiple titles; Netscape Navigator will use the first one you've defined, for example, but earlier versions of Internet Explorer will use the last one.*

<META>—Giving More Information About Your Web Page

Purpose: Includes "metadata" about your Web page consisting of keywords for search engines, refresh rates for client pull, and more. Metadata is passed as name/value pairs like this: **NAME="DESCRIPTION", VALUE="Western view of the Alps"**, or **HTTP-EQUIV="REFRESH" CONTENT="5"**.

Start Tag/End Tag: Required/Omitted. This element contains no content.

Supported: [2, 3, 3.2, 4, IE2, IE3, IE4, IE5, NS1, NS2, NS3, NS4]

Attributes:

- **CONTENT**—Required attribute giving the content of a name/value pair. The actual value you use depends if you're using the **NAME** or **HTTP-EQUIV** attribute. [2, 3, 3.2, 4, IE2, IE3, IE4, IE5, NS1, NS2, NS3, NS4]

- **DIR**—Gives the direction of directionally neutral text (text that doesn't have inherent direction in which you should read it). Possible values: **LTR**: left-to-right text or table and **RTL**: right-to-left text or table. [4]

- **ID**—Unique alphanumeric identifier for the tag, which you can use to refer to it. [NS4]

- **HTTP-EQUIV**—Connects the **CONTENT** attribute to an HTTP header field. If a browser asks for the page, the value of the content attribute will be passed to the browser as part of the HTTP header. [2, 3, 3.2, 4, IE2, IE3, IE4, IE5, NS1, NS2, NS3, NS4]

- **LANG**—Base language used for the tag. [4, NS4]

- **NAME**—Connects the **CONTENT** attribute to a name, such as "Keywords". When a Web browser or other agent requests the data connected to the name, the value of the **CONTENT** attribute will be sent. [2, 3, 3.2, 4, IE2, IE3, IE4, IE5, NS1, NS2, NS3, NS4]

- **SCHEME**—Specifies a predetermined format to be used to interpret the **CONTENT** attribute value. [4]

"I've finished my Web page," the novice programmer says, "but how do I get the search engines to notice it?" "Besides submitting the URL to the search engines," you say, "you should use the **<META>** tag to indicate the keywords for your Web page that the search engines use to allow people to find your page."

The **<META>** element lets you provide information about your page in two ways. First, by connecting values to names, such as **Steve** to **Author** so that those who want to find out who the author of the page is can check the value corresponding to the author term. Second, by placing information in HTTP headers, you can determine the page's behavior, for example, when you want the Web browser to refresh the page automatically every few seconds.

One very common use for the **<META>** element is to include keywords that search engines will store to help people find your page. For example, if you want to connect the keywords **vacation**, **sun**, and **Austria**, to your Web page, you would do that with a name/value pair by setting the **NAME** attribute to **keywords** and the **CONTENT** attribute to **vacation, sun, Austria** like this:

```
<META NAME="keywords" CONTENT="vacation, sun, Austria">
```

You can also specify the language for the tag, such as the following U.S. English, British English, and French versions:

```
<META NAME="keywords" LANG="en-us" CONTENT="vacation, sun, Austria">
<META NAME="keywords" LANG="en" CONTENT="holiday, sun, Austria">
<META NAME="keywords" LANG="fr" CONTENT="vacances, soleil, Austria">
```

Here's a popular way to use the HTTP header, called *client pull*. In this case, you can instruct a browser to keep refreshing your page every few seconds by creating an HTTP **REFRESH** header with the **HTTP-EQUIV** attribute. In the following code, I instruct the Web browser to refresh the page every five seconds:

```
<META HTTP-EQUIV="REFRESH" CONTENT="5">
```

Another popular use for **<META>** is to override the browser's caching system by using the **EXPIRES** value to give a time when the page expires (you've probably seen the warning "Page has expired" in your browser). Browsers must not cache the requested page beyond the date given. Here's an example:

```
<META HTTP-EQUIV="EXPIRES" CONTENT="date">
```

You can also use the **<META>** element in Internet Explorer 4 and later versions to allow special effects to occur while the page is loading or unloading. Here's how that works in general:

```
<META HTTP-EQUIV="[event]" CONTENT="Duration=[seconds],
Transition=[transition]">
```

In this case, ***event*** can be Page-Enter, Page-Exit, Site-Enter, or Site-Exit; ***seconds*** is the transition time in seconds; and ***transition*** is an integer from 0 to 23 that represents a transition effect.

You can also use **REPLY-TO** to give an email address that users can reply to if they want to get in touch with you. Here's an example:

```
<META HTTP-EQUIV="REPLY-TO" CONTENT="steve@starpowder.com">
```

Many HTML editors use the **GENERATOR** value for **NAME** when giving the name of the editor that generated the code, like this:

```
<META NAME="GENERATOR" CONTENT="SuperDuperHTMLEditorPro">
```

The **<META>** element should be used to include information about the page's author, a description of the page, and a copyright notice. Here's how that might look:

```
<HTML>
    <HEAD>
        <META NAME="AUTHOR" CONTENT="Steve">
        <META NAME="DESCRIPTION" CONTENT="My Web Page">
        <META NAME="COPYRIGHT" CONTENT="Copyright 2000 by Steve">
        <TITLE>
            Web page number one!
        </TITLE>
    </HEAD>

    <BODY>
        <H1>
            Welcome to HTML!
        </H1>
    </BODY>
</HTML>
```

</HEAD>—Ending A Web Page's Head

"Hey," says the novice programmer, "I've written my entire Web page, but nothing appears in my Web browser. Is it a bug? Here's the HTML." "It's not a bug," you say, "you've just forgotten to end your **<HEAD>** element, and because nothing in that element is displayed in a Web browser except the title, you end up with a blank page." "Oh," says the NP, "darn."

Don't forget to end your page's **<HEAD>** element with the **</HEAD>** tag:

```
<HTML>
    <HEAD>
        <TITLE>
        Web page number one!
        </TITLE>
    </HEAD>

    <BODY>
        <H1>
        Welcome to HTML!
        </H1>
    </BODY>
</HTML>
```

<BODY>—Creating A Web Page's Body

Purpose: Contains the body of the HTML document, which includes the content that will actually appear in the Web browser. The entire content of the Web page is placed in the page's **<BODY>** element.

Start Tag/End Tag: Optional/Optional

Supported: [2, 3, 3.2, 4, IE1, IE2, IE3, IE4, IE5, NS1, NS2, NS3, NS4]

Attributes:

- **ALINK**—Deprecated. Color of hyperlinks as they're being clicked. Set it to a color value or predefined color name. [3.2, 4, IE4, IE5, NS1, NS2, NS3, NS4]

- **BACKGROUND**—Deprecated. The URL of a graphic file to be used in tiling the browser's background. [3, 3.2, 4, IE1, IE2, IE3, IE4, IE5, NS1, NS2, NS3, NS4]

- **BGCOLOR**—Deprecated. The color of the browser's background. Set it to one of the predefined colors or a color value. [3.2, 4, IE1, IE2, IE3, IE4, IE5, NS1, NS2, NS3, NS4]

- **BGPROPERTIES**—Indicates if the background should scroll when the text does. If you set it to **FIXED**, the only allowed value, the background will not scroll when the text does. [IE2, IE3, IE4, IE5]

- **BOTTOMMARGIN**—Specifies the bottom margin, the empty space at the bottom of the document, in pixels. [IE4, IE5]

- **CLASS**—Class of the element (used for rendering). [3, 4, IE4, IE5, NS4]

- **DIR**—Gives the direction of directionally neutral text (text that doesn't have inherent direction in which you should read it). Possible values: **LTR**: left-to-right text or table and **RTL**: right-to-left text or table. [4, IE5]

- **ID**—Unique alphanumeric identifier for the tag, which you can use to refer to it. [3, 4, IE4, IE5, NS4]

- **LANG**—Base language used for the tag. [3, 4, IE4, IE5, NS4]

- **LANGUAGE**—Scripting language used for the tag. [IE4, IE5]

- **LEFTMARGIN**—Specifies the left margin, the empty space at left of the document, in pixels. [IE2, IE3, IE4, IE5]

- **LINK**—Deprecated. Color of hyperlinks that have not yet been visited (identified by the browser). Set it to a color value or predefined color name. [3.2, 4, IE1, IE2, IE3, IE4, IE5, NS1, NS2, NS3, NS4]

- **MARGINHEIGHT**—Gives the height of the margins at top and bottom of the page in pixels. [NS4]

- **MARGINWIDTH**—Gives the width of the left and right margins of the page in pixels. [NS4]

- **RIGHTMARGIN**—Specifies the right margin, the empty space to the right of the document, in pixels. [IE4, IE5]

- **SCROLL**—Specifies whether a vertical scrollbar appears to the right of the document; can be **YES** (the default) or **NO**. [IE4, IE5]

- **STYLE**—Inline style indicating how to render the element. [4, IE3, IE4, IE5, NS4]

- **TEXT**—Deprecated. Color of the text in the document. Set it to a color value or a predefined color. [3.2, 4, IE1, IE2, IE3, IE4, IE5, NS1, NS2, NS3, NS4]

- **TITLE**—Holds additional information (as might be displayed in tool tips) for the element. [3, 4, IE4, IE5]

- **TOPMARGIN**—Specifies the top margin, the empty space at the top of the document, in pixels. [IE2, IE3, IE4, IE5]

- **VLINK**—Deprecated. Color of hyperlinks that have been visited (identified by the browser). Set it to a color value or predefined color name. [3.2, 4, IE1, IE2, IE3, IE4, IE5, NS1, NS2, NS3, NS4]

"What's so important about the **<BODY>** element?" the novice programmer asks; "Do I need to use it?" "Not if you don't want anything to appear in your Web page," you say. "Hey," the NP says, "I do!" "Then you should use the **<BODY>** element," you say.

The **<HEAD>** element is where you place information about your page; the **<BODY>** element is where you place the content of the page. This is an important tag and a big one as you can see by its large number of attributes. What casual users think of as your Web page, all goes into the body element: headings, text, images, multimedia elements, animated graphics, and more.

We've already seen a rudimentary example where the content of a page is just an H1 heading:

```
<HTML>
    <HEAD>
        <TITLE>
            Web page number one!
        </TITLE>
    </HEAD>
```

```
    <BODY>
        <H1>
            Welcome to HTML!
        </H1>
    </BODY>
</HTML>
```

Again, notice the great number of attributes available for this tag. Because it encloses the entire body of the document, this is a natural place to set attributes that affect the entire displayed content. For example, to add a left margin of 200 pixels to a page, you can use the Internet Explorer **LEFTMARGIN** attribute:

```
<HTML>
    <HEAD>
        <TITLE>
            Web page number one!
        </TITLE>
    </HEAD>

    <BODY LEFTMARGIN = 200>
        <H1>
            Welcome to HTML!
        </H1>
    </BODY>
</HTML>
```

The result appears in Figure 1.5.

Figure 1.5   Setting margins in Internet Explorer.

On the other hand, the **LEFTMARGIN** attribute is specific to Internet Explorer. You can set margins in Netscape Navigator using the attribute **MARGINWIDTH**. Here, I'm setting the horizontal margins to 200 pixels:

```
<HTML>
    <HEAD>
        <TITLE>
            Web page number one!
        </TITLE>
    </HEAD>

    <BODY MARGINWIDTH = 200>
        <H1>
            Welcome to HTML!
        </H1>
    </BODY>
</HTML>
```

The results of this HTML appear in Figure 1.6.

If you've written HTML before, you may be startled to see that many cherished attributes (as of HTML 4) are now considered deprecated, like these:

- **ALINK**—The color of links as they're clicked.
- **BACKGROUND**— The URL of a background image to use to tile the browser's background.
- **BGCOLOR**—The color of the browser's background.
- **LINK**—The color of hyperlinks that have not yet been visited.

Figure 1.6   Setting margins in Netscape Navigator.

- **TEXT**—The color to use for the text in the page.
- **VLINK**—The color of hyperlinks that have been visited.

Instead of using these attributes, you're now supposed to use style sheets, which we'll discuss in Chapter 9.

In the following code, I set the background color of a page to white, its text color to black, the color of hyperlinks (which I create with the **<A>** tag as we'll see in Chapter 5 on hyperlinks) to red, the color of activated links (when they're clicked) to blue, and the color of already visited links to green, all using attributes of the **<BODY>** element:

```
<HTML>
    <HEAD>
        <TITLE>
            This is a Web page!
        </TITLE>
    </HEAD>

    <BODY BGCOLOR="white" TEXT="black" LINK="red" ALINK="blue"
        VLINK="green">
        Welcome to my page!
        If you don't like it, you can go to
        <A HREF="http://www.w3c.org">W3C</A>.
    </BODY>
</HTML>
```

This page, including the hyperlink to W3C (which actually appears in green in this case, because I've been to the W3C site before), is shown in Figure 1.7. As you can see, it works, but the fact is, it's not strict HTML 4.

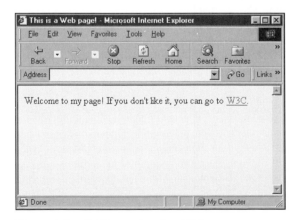

Figure 1.7   Setting colors in a Web page.

To make the same page adhere to the HTML 4 standard, you'd use style sheets as I'll do in Chapter 9. Here's how this page looks using a **<STYLE>** element to set up the same colors:

```
<HTML>
    <HEAD>
        <TITLE>This is a Web page!</TITLE>
        <STYLE type="text/css">
            BODY {background: white; color: black}
            A:link {color: red}
            A:visited {color: green}
            A:active {color: blue}
        </STYLE>
    </HEAD>

    <BODY>
        Welcome to my page!
        If you don't like it, you can go to
        <A HREF="http://www.w3c.org">W3C</A>.
    </BODY>
</HTML>
```

The result of this HTML is shown in Figure 1.7. I've just used a style sheet instead of HTML elements to specify colors. In fact, this brings up the question of just how do you specify colors in Web pages—to find out, take a look at the following section, "Setting Web Page Colors," for the details.

TIP: *One nice effect in Internet Explorer is to turn off background scrolling, which you do by setting the* **SCROLL** *attribute to* **NO**. *Only the content, like text and images of the page, will scroll when the user manipulates the scrollbars. This gives the user the feeling that the content is being displayed on a glass sheet that moves up and down against a stationary background. To make this effect noticeable, of course, you have to provide background graphics using the* **BACKGROUND** *attribute. Also note that if you use the* **BACKGROUND** *attribute and the* **BGCOLOR** *attribute in the same page, the* **BGCOLOR** *attribute is ignored.*

Setting Web Page Colors

"Say," says the novice programmer, "I'm writing a page that shows the company's annual budget—how do you color text red?" "You can use color values or predefined colors," you say, "but what do you want red for?" "To show how far we're in the hole," the NP says. "Uh oh," you say.

Many HTML elements and attributes let you specify colors. For example, you can set the **TEXT** attribute of the **<BODY>** element to a specific color, which changes the color of the text in the document's body. There are two ways to specify colors in Web pages that browsers will recognize: refer to predefined colors by name or by color values (also called RGB [Red, Green, Blue] triplets). I'll take a look at them both here.

NOTE: It's still common for programmers to specify colors using HTML elements and attributes, even though they have actually been deprecated. W3C encourages you to use style sheets instead.

Using Predefined Colors

The W3C has added the names of 16 colors to HTML, which browsers are supposed to recognize. They are listed in Table 1.2.

You can use these names directly when you want to specify a color, as in this example:

```
<HTML>
    <HEAD>
        <TITLE>
            Web page number one!
        </TITLE>
    </HEAD>

    <BODY TEXT="RED">
        <H1>
            Welcome to HTML!
        </H1>
    </BODY>
</HTML>
```

The result of this HTML appears in Figure 1.8, and it works as intended.

As you know, the big browsers have a way of outpacing W3C. Both Internet Explorer and Netscape Navigator have defined additional colors. You'll find the predefined colors for Internet Explorer in Table 1.3 and the predefined colors for Netscape Navigator in Table 1.4.

Table 1.2   Colors recognized by browsers.

aqua	black	blue	fuchsia
gray	green	lime	maroon
navy	olive	purple	red
silver	teal	white	yellow

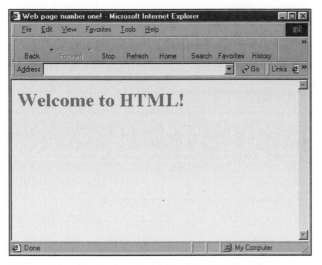

Figure 1.8   Setting a color to red in a Web page.

Table 1.3   Predefined colors in Internet Explorer.

aliceblue	antiquewhite	aqua	aquamarine
azure	beige	bisque	black
blanchedalmond	blue	blueviolet	brown
burlywood	cadetblue	chartreuse	chocolate
coral	cornflowerblue	cornsilk	crimson
cyan	darkblue	darkcyan	darkgoldenrod
darkgray	darkkhaki	darkmagenta	darkolivegreen
darkorange	darkorchid	darkred	darksalmon
darkseagreen	darkslateblue	darkslategray	darkturquoise
darkviolet	deeppink	deepskyblue	dimgray
dodgerblue	firebrick	floralwhite	ghostwhite
gold	goldenrod	gray	green
greenyellow	honeydew	hotpink	indianred
indigo	ivory	khaki	lavender
lavenderblush	lawngreen	lemonchiffon	lightblue
lightcoral	lightcyan	lime	maroon
navy	olive	purple	red
silver	teal	white	yellow

Table 1.4   Predefined colors in Netscape Navigator.

aliceblue	antiquewhite	aqua	aquamarine
azure	beige	black	blanchedalmond
blue	blueviolet	brown	burlywood
cadetblue	chartreuse	chocolate	coral
cornflowerblue	cornsilk	crimson	cyan
darkblue	darkcyan	darkgoldenrod	darkgray
darkgreen	darkkhaki	darkmagenta	darkolivegreen
darkorange	darkorchid	darkred	darksalmon
darkseagreen	darkslateblue	darkslategray	darkturquoise
darkviolet	deeppink	deepskyblue	dimgray
dodgerblue	firebrick	floralwhite	forestgreen
fuchsia	gainsboro	ghostwhite	gold
goldenrod	gray	green	greenyellow
honeydew	hotpink	indianred	indigo
ivory	khaki	lavender	lavenderblush
lawngreen	lemonchiffon	lightblue	lightcoral
lightcyan	lightgoldenrodyellow	lightgreen	lightgrey
lightpink	lightsalmon	lightseagreen	lightskyblue
lightslategray	lightsteelblue	lightyellow	lime
limegreen	linen	magenta	maroon
mediumaquamarine	mediumblue	mediumorchid	mediumpurple
mediumseagreen	mediumslateblue	mediumspringgreen	mediumturquoise
mediumvioletred	midnightblue	mintcream	mistyrose
moccasin	navajowhite	navy	oldlace
olive	olivedrab	orange	orangered
orchid	palegoldenrod	palegreen	paleturquoise
palevioletred	papayawhip	peachpuff	peru
pink	plum	powderblue	purple
red	rosybrown	royalblue	saddlebrown
salmon	sandybrown	seagreen	seashell
sienna	silver	skyblue	slateblue
slategray	snow	springgreen	steelblue

(continued)

Table 1.4   Predefined colors in Netscape Navigator (continued).

tan	teal	thistle	tomato
turquoise	violet	wheat	white
whitesmoke	yellow	yellowgreen	

Creating Color Values

You can also specify colors using color values. Color values are expressed as *rrggbb*, where *rr* is the value you want to use for the red component of the color ranging from 0 through 255 and expressed as a hexadecimal (base 16) two-digit number, *gg* specifies the green component, and *bb* specifies the blue component. The only trick here is getting used to using hexadecimal values ranging from 00 to *ff* (hexadecimal *ff* = 255 because hexadecimal digits range from 0 to 9 and then from a to f).

Here's an example; the color value for pure red is **ff0000** (you can use lowercase or uppercase letters, so this is the same as **FF0000**). Although not required by many browsers, you indicate this number as hexadecimal by placing a sharp symbol (**#**) in front of it like this: **#ff0000**. To be safe, you should also enclose the value of attributes in quotation marks if the value is text. So you would specify pure red to a browser as "**#ff0000**". Here's how the previous Web page would look using a color value instead of the predefined value **RED**:

```
<HIML>
    <HEAD>
        <TITLE>
            Web page number one!
        </TITLE>
    </HEAD>

    <BODY TEXT = "#ff0000">
        <H1>
            Welcome to HTML!
        </H1>
    </BODY>
</HTML>
```

As color value examples, I'll list the actual color values for each of the W3C pre-defined colors (for example, note that back is **#000000**, blue is **#0000ff**, and white is **#ffffff**):

- Aqua = **#00ffff**
- Black = **#000000**

- Blue = **#0000ff**
- Fuchsia = **#ff00ff**
- Gray = **#808080**
- Green = **#008000**
- Lime = **#00ff00**
- Maroon = **#800000**
- Navy = **#000080**
- Olive = **#808000**
- Purple = **#800080**
- Red = **#ff0000**
- Silver = **#c0c0c0**
- Teal = **#008080**
- White = **#ffffff**
- Yellow = **#ffff00**

TIP: *How do you make sure that a color value appears as you want it to? The best way is to check it out in your browser. Another way is to find a color picker or color chooser online (just use a search engine to search for those terms), which often lets you use scrollbars to select the red, green, and blue settings for color values interactively.*

Adding Text To A Web Page

The novice programmer wants to know, "How do I add simple text to a Web page? What tag do I use?" You smile and say, "You don't use any tag at all. You just put the text right into the Web page." The NP asks, "Just like that? No tag?" "Just like that," you say.

I'll cover how to work with text in Chapter 2, but it's worthwhile getting the basics down now. In its simplest form, it's easy to enter plain text into a Web page; you just place that text in the page like this:

```
<HTML>
    <HEAD>
        <TITLE>
            Web page number one!
        </TITLE>
    </HEAD>
```

```
    <BODY>
        <H1>
            Welcome to HTML!
        </H1>
        This is simple text that appears in this page.
    </BODY>
</HTML>
```

The result of this HTML appears in Figure 1.9.

That's all it takes to display simple text in a Web page. You just place that text into the **<BODY>** element.

Figure 1.9   Displaying simple text in a page.

Basic Text Formatting

"Hey," says the novice programmer, "you said I could just enter text into a Web page, but when I try to skip to the next paragraph in the text, my browser just ignores it." "That's because browsers format what you type," you say, "so you have to use the **<P>** tag to start a new paragraph."

We'll see how to format text in Chapter 2, but again it's worth taking a quick look here to get some basic skills down. For example, to center text you can use the **<CENTER>** element, and to start a new paragraph (much as if you had typed "Enter" in a word processor) you can use the **<P>** tag. Here's an example:

```
<HTML>
    <HEAD>
        <TITLE>
            Web page number one!
        </TITLE>
    </HEAD>

    <BODY>
        <H1>
        Welcome to HTML!
        </H1>
        <CENTER>
        This is simple text that appears in this page.
        <P>
            Here's a new paragraph!
        </CENTER>
    </BODY>
</HTML>
```

The results of this HTML appear in Figure 1.10. As you can see, the **<CENTER>** tag has centered the text, and the **<P>** tag skips to a new paragraph leaving some space between paragraphs. We'll discuss both of these elements in more detail later.

Figure 1.10   Displaying simple formatted text in a page.

<!-->—Comments And Server-Side Includes

<!--*comment*-->

Purpose: Annotates a Web page with a comment in the HTML that you can read by looking at the HTML, but will not be displayed in the Web browser.

Start Tag/End Tag: Required/Required. This element contains no content.

Supported: [2, 3, 3.2, 4, IE1, IE2, IE3, IE4, IE5, NS1, NS2, NS3, NS4]

Attributes:

• None

"There's one more basic skill you should have," you tell the novice programmer. "What's that?" the NP asks. "You should know how to comment a Web page using the HTML **COMMENT** tag."

You place HTML comments in a Web page to clarify what's going on at the HTML level. Comments do not appear in the Web browser itself. You use them to annotate a Web page so that you or someone else can tell what's going on in the code at a later time. You enclose an HTML comment in the <!--*comment*--> tag like this: <!--**This is a comment**-->. Here's an example where I've annotated this Web page with comments:

```
<HTML>
    <!-- This is the head of the page-->
    <HEAD>
        <!-- This title will appear in the browser's title bar-->
        <TITLE>
        Web page number one!
        </TITLE>
    </HEAD>

    <!-- This is the body of the page-->
    <BODY>
        <H1>
        <!-- Here's an H1 element that makes up the body-->
        Welcome to HTML!
        </H1>
    </BODY>
</HTML>
```

None of these comments will appear in the browser, but they'll all be in the HTML, so you can take a look at them when you want. Since comments are in the HTML, they'll be downloaded with the rest of the page. So, if you have a lot of comments, bear in mind that they can affect download time.

Another use for the **<!-->** tag is to create *server-side includes*. You can use server-side includes to send commands to or get data from many Web servers. You embed server-side includes in HTML pages, and you give those pages the extension .shtml, not .html. Table 1.5 lists of some of the popular server-side includes.

I'll take a look at some server-side includes here by writing an example named ssi.shtml. In this case, I'll just display the values of various server-side include variables, such as the name of the document (ssi.shtml):

```
Document name: <!--#echo var="DOCUMENT_NAME" -->
```

Since the server I'll use is Unix based, I'll also execute the Unix command **uptime** to find out how long the server has been up:

```
Up time: <!--#exec cmd="uptime" -->
```

Table 1.5   Popular server-side includes.

Server-Side Include	Does This
<!--#config errmsg="Uh oh"-->	Sets the format for error messages
<!--#config sizefmt="%d"-->	Sets the format for displaying file sizes
<!--#config timefmt="%s"-->	Sets the format for displaying dates
<!--#echo var="DATE_GMT" -->	Echoes the Greenwich Mean Time (GMT) and date
<!--#echo var="DATE_LOCAL" -->	Echoes the local date and time
<!--#echo var="DOCUMENT_NAME" -->	Echoes the document's name
<!--#echo var="DOCUMENT_URI" -->	Echoes the document's virtual path and name
<!--#echo var="LAST_MODIFIED" -->	Echoes the date the document was last modified
<!--#exec cgi="cgi/script.cgi"-->	Executes a Common Gateway Interface (CGI) script
<!--#exec cmd="shell command"-->	Executes a shell command
<!--#flastmod file="file.txt"-->	Displays the time a file was last modified
<!--#fsize file="file.txt"-->	Displays the size of a file
<!--#include file="file.txt"-->	Displays a given file

Here's the full Web page, ssi.shtml:

```
<HTML>
    <HEAD>
        <TITLE>
            Server Side Includes
        </TITLE>
    </HEAD>

    <BODY>
        <CENTER>
            <H1>
                Server Side Includes
            </H1>
        </CENTER>
        <H3>
            <P>
                Document name: <!--#echo var="DOCUMENT_NAME" -->
            <P>
                Document path: <!--#echo var="DOCUMENT_URI" -->
            <P>
                Server name: <!--#echo var="SERVER_NAME" -->
            <P>
                Local date: <!--#echo var="DATE_LOCAL" -->
            <P>
                Up time. <! #exec cmd="uptime" -->
        </H3>
    </BODY>
</HTML>
```

The results appear in Figure 1.11. As you can see, the server itself has filled in the values of the variables I want to display and has also executed the **uptime** command displaying how long the server has been up.

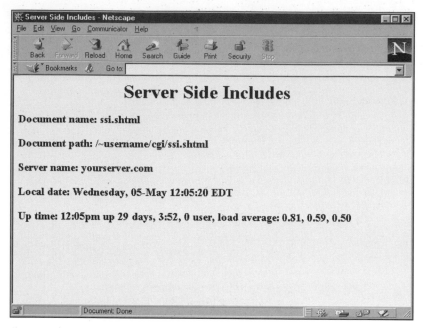

Figure 1.11   Using server-side includes.

</BODY>—Ending A Web Page's Body

To end the Web page's body, use the **</BODY>** tag:

```
<HTML>
    <HEAD>
        <TITLE>
        Web page number one!
        </TITLE>
    </HEAD>

    <BODY>
        <H1>
        Welcome to HTML!
        </H1>
    </BODY>
</HTML>
```

</HTML>—Ending A Web Page

To end a Web page, use the closing **</HTML>** tag, which should always be the last tag in a Web page:

```
<HTML>
    <HEAD>
        <TITLE>
        Web page number one!
        </TITLE>
    </HEAD>

    <BODY>
        <H1>
        Welcome to HTML!
        </H1>
    </BODY>
</HTML>
```

Chapter 2

Working With Text

(continued)

In Depth

HTML specializes in handling text, and we're going to take advantage of that in this chapter. The most basic element of Web pages in general is not animated images, multimedia elements, Java applets, or ActiveX controls—it's text. And this is the chapter where we begin creating real Web pages that show what's possible when working with text in HTML.

Originally, HTML could only handle text, not even simple images. So, throughout its history, HTML has had much opportunity to elaborate on how it works with text. There are literally dozens of HTML tags dedicated to this purpose. In this chapter, I'll take a look at how to set text styles in Web pages. I'll discuss everything from using bold, italics, and alternate fonts to creating headings and more—using the tags available in HTML. In Chapter 3, I'll take a look at how to arrange text in a Web page by indenting it, spacing it vertically, and even overlapping it. Because creating Web pages has so much to do with displaying text, the material in both this chapter and Chapter 3 is essential information.

Working with text, and especially styling text, has changed considerably in HTML 4. I'll start with an overview of these changes.

Formatting With HTML Tags

As we saw in the previous chapter, if you place just plain text in a Web page, Web browsers will simply treat it as a word processor would—by displaying it in the current default font. To set the actual style of text as displayed in a Web page, you can use text style tags, like **<I>** to make text italic and **<B>** to make text bold. The text between the opening **<I>** tag and the closing **</I>** tag will appear in italics in a Web page. You can even nest text style tags. For example, if you place some of the text between **<I>** and **</I>**, in addition to tags, such as **<B>** and **</B>** to make it bold, then that text will actually appear in italic *and* bold.

Here's an example showing how this works:

```
<HTML>
    <HEAD>
        <TITLE>
            Using italics
        </TITLE>
    </HEAD>
```

```
<BODY>
    <P>
        <I>Here is some text displayed in italics and
        <B>bold</B> too.</I>
    </BODY>
</HTML>
```

The result of this HTML appears in Figure 2.1. The displayed text is indeed in italics and the word "bold" appears in bold.

As you see from this example, it was simple enough to set the style of text used in this page. However, this kind of direct formatting is somewhat rudimentary, and HTML 4 has advanced beyond it. Now you use style sheets instead of simple tags. Here's an example that reproduces the previous Web page. I'll set the style of the **<P>** tag to italics and use a **<SPAN>** tag (which we'll see more about soon) to set the style of the word "bold" to bold. You might think that you could use the font-style style to set both italic and bold styles, but in fact you use font-weight to set bold style.

```
<HTML>
    <HEAD>
        <TITLE>
            Using italics
        </TITLE>
    </HEAD>

    <BODY>
```

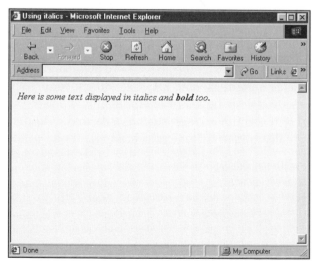

Figure 2.1   Using HTML tags to format text.

```
        <P STYLE="font-style: italic">
            Here is some text displayed in italics and
            <SPAN STYLE="font-weight: bold">bold</SPAN> too.
    </BODY>
</HTML>
```

This code produces the page you see in Figure 2.1. Actually, style sheets were not really introduced to set the styles manually tag by tag as I've done here, but rather to set the styles for whole documents and libraries of documents. The way this typically works is that you set the style for entire tags all at once, as you see in the following example, where I'm making the **<P>** tag display italic text:

```
<HTML>
    <HEAD>
        <TITLE>
            Using italics
        </TITLE>
    </HEAD>

    <STYLE>
        P {font-style: italic}
    </STYLE>

    <BODY>
        <P>
            Here is some text displayed in italics and
            <SPAN STYLE="font-weight: bold">bold</SPAN> too.
    </BODY>
</HTML>
```

There are a number of ways to apply styles to text the new HTML 4 way. Some of them are quite sophisticated, and we'll cover them a little later in the book, in Chapter 9. On the other hand, it's also true that this new way is more complex than the old. Even though the World Wide Web Consortium (W3C) now endorses the use of style sheets, you can be ss/e that the old way of doing things will be around for a long time to come.

Tags like **<I>** and **<B>** are called *physical styles* in HTML; that is, they specify exactly how the browser should display text. In addition to physical styles, there are also *logical styles*, which leave the actual styling up to the browser. For example, one logical style is **<EM>** for emphasized, and the actual interpretation of this tag is up to the browser. In practice, **<EM>** is usually displayed as italics. I'll take a look at the physical styles first in this chapter, then the logical styles.

Physical HTML Styles

Here's a list of the HTML physical style tags:

- **<B>**—Displays bold text.
- **<I>**—Displays italic text.
- **<TT>**—Displays "teletype" text; usually rendered in a monospace font (where each character has the same width).

HTML 3.2 added these physical HTML styles:

- **<BIG>**—Displays text larger than usual.
- **<S>** and **<STRIKE>**—Displays strikethrough, which has been deprecated in HTML 4.
- **<SMALL>**—Displays text smaller than usual.
- **<SUB>**—Displays a subscript.
- **<SUP>**—Displays a superscript.
- **<U>**—Displays underline, which has been deprecated in HTML 4.

TIP: *One reason the **<BIG>** and **<SMALL>** elements were introduced was to allow people with disabilities to access the Web. Browsers can display text in larger font, and if you specify a text size that you think is large, that size may in fact be smaller than what the person is used to reading. In such cases, it's better to use the **<BIG>** tag and leave the details up to the browser.*

Physical styles were defined to let you format your text exactly, but there are also a number of tags—the logical style tags—that let you specify your intention and leave the details up to the browser.

Logical HTML Styles

You use logical styles when you want to leave the formatting up to the browser. For example, when you want to emphasize text strongly, you can use the **<STRONG>** tag. Here's the list of the logical HTML tags:

- **<ADDRESS>**—Address
- **<CITE>**—Citation or reference to another source
- **<CODE>**—Code (program listing) text
- **<DFN>**—Defining instance of the enclosed term
- **<EM>**—Emphasized text
- **<KBD>**—Text the user should enter

- **<SAMP>**—Sample output (as from programs)
- **<STRONG>**—Strongly emphasized text
- **<VAR>**—Variable or programming term from code

HTML 4 adds these logical tags:

- **<ABBR>**—Abbreviation
- **<ACRONYM>**—Acronym

TIP: *In fact, there is one more logical style, **<BLOCKQUOTE>**, that I'll deal with in Chapter 3. This style indents its text rather than just setting its style.*

You can see the beginnings of working with style sheets in the preceding lists. The logical styles are one step up from the physical styles, like **<B>** and **<I>**, in that they leave the formatting up to the user environment. Because formatting is content based, the logical styles include tags for all sorts of situations, such as defining a new term, displaying output from programs, requesting user input, and so on. Of course, using this method was naturally doomed to failure because no one can anticipate all the styles that will be needed in all documents. So, the next step was to incorporate style sheets, which is the way things work today.

In fact, far from the rich formatting that W3C was hoping these logical styles would provide, they have been implemented in virtually all browsers only as simple italics, bold, and monospace font as you see in Table 2.1.

Table 2.1   How logical tags are rendered.

Tag	Rendered As
<ABBR>	Italics or plain text
<ACRONYM>	Italics or plain text
<ADDRESS>	Italics
<CITE>	Italics
<CODE>	Monospace font
<DFN>	Italics or plain text
<EM>	Italics
<KBD>	Bold or standard monospace font
<SAMP>	Monospace
<STRONG>	Bold
<VAR>	Italics

I'll put all these styles to work in one page. In the following example, I'm using the **
** tag, which we'll see in the next chapter, to introduce a line break:

```
<HTML>
    <HEAD>
        <TITLE>
            Using logical styles
        </TITLE>
    </HEAD>

    <BODY>
        <ABBR>This is &lt;ABBR&gt; style.</ABBR>
        <BR>
        <ACRONYM>This is &lt;ACRONYM&gt; style.</ACRONYM>
        <BR>
        <ADDRESS>This is &lt;ADDRESS&gt; style.</ADDRESS>
        <BR>
        <CITE>This is &lt;CITE&gt; style.</CITE>
        <BR>
        <CODE>This is &lt;CODE&gt; style.</CODE>
        <BR>
        <DFN>This is &lt;DFN&gt; style.</DFN>
        <BR>
        <EM>This is &lt;EM&gt; style.</EM>
        <BR>
        <KBD>This is &lt;KBD&gt; style.</KBD>
        <BR>
        <SAMP>This is &lt;SAMP&gt; style.</SAMP>
        <BR>
        <STRONG>This is &lt;STRONG&gt; style.</STRONG>
        <BR>
        <VAR>This is &lt;VAR&gt; style.</VAR>
    </BODY>
</HTML>
```

NOTE: The terms **<** and **>** in the previous code example are called character entities and are used to display the angle bracket characters (**<**) and (**>**) respectively in a Web page. Because **<** and **>** are identified as part of HTML tags by browsers, using character entities solves the problem of utilizing them in a Web page. You can use these codes, which begin with an ampersand (**&**) and end with a semicolon (**;**) to display characters that might have other meanings to the browser. You can also use character entities to display characters that you might not find on your keyboard, such as characters with accents or umlauts. I'll list every character entity (and there are a lot of them) available in HTML 4 in this chapter.

The results of this page appear in Netscape Navigator in Figure 2.2 and in Internet Explorer in Figure 2.3. Note that the **<ADDRESS>** style adds a line after itself.

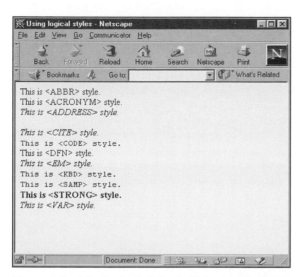

Figure 2.2   The logical styles in Netscape Navigator.

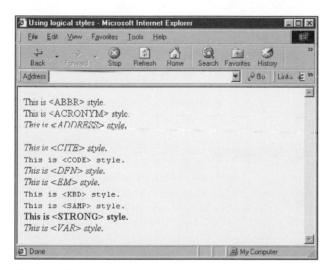

Figure 2.3   The logical styles in Internet Explorer.

And because the **<ABBR>** and **<ACRONYM>** are too new to have been imple-mented in either browser yet, they are implemented in plain text.

TIP: *Note in particular how both the **<ABBR>** and **<ACRONYM>** elements are displayed in Netscape Navigator and Internet Explorer. Because they're not actually implemented in those browsers (except that in Internet Explorer 5 **<ACRONYM>** elements are displayed as plain text, but the value of the **TITLE** attribute is displayed in a tool tip), the browsers just ignore the tags and display the text as plain text. The fact that browsers ignore tags they don't understand will be important when we start working with scripts to manage other browsers that don't handle scripts.*

Setting Fonts

In addition to using the physical and logical tags to style text, you can also use the **<FONT>** tag to set text color, font face (such as Times New Roman, Arial, and so on), and size. With the new emphasis on style sheets, **<FONT>** has been deprecated in HTML 4, but in fact it's still a very popular tag. Here's an example showing how it works. In this case, I'll display text in Arial font in blue like this:

```
<HTML>

    <HEAD>
        <TITLE>
            Using the &lt;FONT&gt; Tag
        </TITLE>
    </HEAD>

    <BODY>
        <FONT SIZE=6 COLOR="#0000ff" FACE="Arial">Here is some text!</FONT>
    </BODY>

</HTML>
```

The results of this code appear in Figure 2.4 in a large, blue Arial font. On the other hand, note that you specify font size in the **<FONT>** tag with simple values from 1 through 7, not with point size directly.

Figure 2.4   Using the **<FONT>** tag.

TIP: *In fact, there is a way you can specify a font's point size; in Netscape Navigator, you can use the **POINT-SIZE** attribute with the **<FONT>** tag. And you can use style sheets to do the same thing in Internet Explorer.*

Headings

The heading element tags are, **<H1>**, **<H2>**, **<H3>**, **<H4>**, **<H5>**, and **<H6>**. These elements create the "headlines" in your Web pages by displaying bold text in a variety of sizes—**<H1>** being the largest. We've already seen **<H1>** at work in the previous chapter, but all six tags, **<H1>** through **<H6>**, exist. Here's an example of how these tags work:

```
<HTML>

    <HEAD>
        <TITLE>
            Using the &lt;H1 - H6&gt; Tags
        </TITLE>
    </HEAD>

    <BODY>
        <CENTER>
            <H1>Here is an &lt;H1&gt; heading</H1>
            <BR>
            <H2>Here is an &lt;H2&gt; heading</H2>
            <BR>
            <H3>Here is an &lt;H3&gt; heading</H3>
            <BR>
            <H4>Here is an &lt;H4&gt; heading</H4>
            <BR>
            <H5>Here is an &lt;H5&gt; heading</H5>
            <BR>
            <H6>Here is an &lt;H6&gt; heading</H6>
        </CENTER>
    </BODY>

</HTML>
```

You can see the results of this HTML in Figure 2.5, which shows the relative sizes of all six heading tags, **<H1>** through **<H6>**.

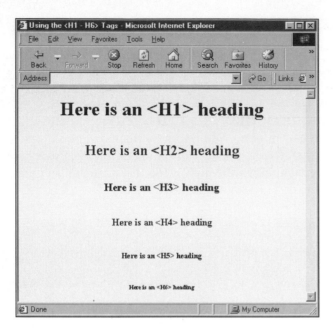

Figure 2.5   The heading tags, **<H1>** through **<H6>**.

Some Removed Tags

Over the years, some text style tags have gone from deprecated to *removed status*, which means that they're no longer supported in HTML 4. They still work in browsers, however. Here are the removed elements designated as obsolete by W3C:

- **<LISTING>**
- **<PLAINTEXT>**
- **<XMP>**

These three tags do essentially the same thing—display text "as is" without being interpreted by the browser. Instead of using these tags, you should now use the **<PRE>** tag (preformatted text), which I'll cover in Chapter 3.

Besides all the tags mentioned already, there are some other tags that I'll take a look at in this chapter, such as Netscape Navigator's **<BLINK>** tag, which makes text blink and the **<Q>** tag for inline quotations.

That's it, then—there's a lot of text handling coming up here, so I'll turn to the Immediate Solutions section now and start by explaining how to display plain text.

TIP: *In this chapter, you'll start seeing significant differences between the HTML used in Internet Explorer and the HTML used in Netscape Navigator. One way to handle these discrepancies is to check what browser the user has and adjust your HTML accordingly. I'll show you how to do this in the Immediate Solutions section, "Determining Browser Type In Code" in Chapter 11.*

Immediate Solutions

Displaying Plain Text

The novice programmer has a problem and says, "All I want to do is to display some plain text in a Web page, no formatting, nothing special. How do I do that?" "Easy," you say, "just put the text directly into the Web page's body."

If you put plain text into a Web page's body, the Web browser will display it in its current default font, color, and font size. On the other hand, Web browsers will not respect the line breaks you've added to the text (unless you use a special tag like **<PRE>** for preformatted text as we'll see in the next chapter) and will wrap everything into a single paragraph. Here's an example:

```
<HTML>
    <HEAD>
        <TITLE>
            Using Plain Text
        </TITLE>
    </HEAD>

    <BODY>
        Hey what gives?
        This text is all supposed to be on different lines!
        But it looks like it's all been put in the same paragraph!
    </BODY>
</HTML>
```

The result appears in Figure 2.6, and as you can see, all the text has been wrapped into the same paragraph.

If you want to separate the text into paragraphs, you can use the tag **<P>** for paragraph, which we saw in Chapter 1. Each sentence will now begin on a new line:

```
<HTML>
    <HEAD>
        <TITLE>
            Using Plain Text
        </TITLE>
    </HEAD>
```

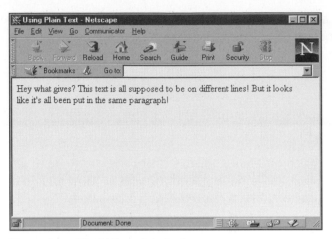

Figure 2.6   Displaying plain text.

```
<BODY>
     Hey what gives?
     <P>
     This text is all supposed to be on different lines!
     <P>
     But it looks like it's all been put in the same paragraph!
</BODY>
</HTML>
```

For more about text formatting, see Chapter 3.

<H1> Through <H6>—Creating Web Page Headings

Purpose: Creates a heading in the Web page, like a headline, using bold font and various sizes. **<H1>** creates the largest text and **<H6>** the smallest.

Start Tag/End Tag: Required/Required

Supported: [2, 3, 3.2, 4, IE1, IE2, IE3, IE4, IE5, NS1, NS2, NS3, NS4]

Attributes:

- **ALIGN**—Specifies the alignment of text in the heading. Set to **LEFT** (the default), **CENTER**, **RIGHT**, or **JUSTIFY**. [3, 3.2, 4, IE4, IE5, NS1, NS2, NS3, NS4]

- **CLASS**—Class of the element (used for rendering). [3, 4, IE4, IE5, NS4]

- **CLEAR**—Stops text from flowing around other elements. [3]

- **DIR**—Gives the direction of directionally neutral text (text that doesn't have inherent direction in which you should read it). Possible values: **LTR**: left-to-right text or table and **RTL**: right-to-left text or table. [4, IE5]

- **ID**—Unique alphanumeric identifier for the tag, which you can use to refer to it. [3, 4, IE4, IE5, NS4]

- **LANG**—Base language used for the tag. [3, 4, IE4, IE5]

- **LANGUAGE**—Scripting language used for the tag. [IE4, IE5]

- **STYLE**—Inline style indicating how to render the element. [4, IE4, IE5, NS4]

- **TITLE**—Holds additional information (as might be displayed in tool tips) for the element. [3, 4, IE4, IE5]

The Web page style czar gives you a call and says, "About your new Web page— where's the style, the zing, the pizazz?" You ask, "*Pizazz*?" "Why doesn't the page reach out and grab me?" the Web page style czar says. "I'll add some headings," you say. The Web page style czar says, "Great!"

Headings act much like headlines in newspapers. They present text in bold and often are larger than the text they appear above. There are six heading tags, all beloved by HTML programmers: **<H1>**, **<H2>**, **<H3>**, **<II4>**, **<H5>**, and **<H6>**. **<H1>** creates the largest text and **<H6>** the smallest with a smooth progression between those levels.

In fact, headings are not just about big bold text—they really act like headings by getting their own line in the Web page (even if you use a heading tag in the middle of other text, it'll get its own line in the page) and starting a new paragraph.

You can add other formatting in a heading using different tags, such as the **<I>** tag to make all or part of the heading italic, or **<S>** to strike out all or part of the heading, and so on.

Here's an example that was presented in the beginning of this chapter:

```
<HTML>

    <HEAD>
        <TITLE>
            Using the &lt;H1 - H6&gt; Tags
        </TITLE>
    </HEAD>
```

```
<BODY>
    <CENTER>
        <H1>Here is an &lt;H1&gt; heading</H1>
        <BR>
        <H2>Here is an &lt;H2&gt; heading</H2>
        <BR>
        <H3>Here is an &lt;H3&gt; heading</H3>
        <BR>
        <H4>Here is an &lt;H4&gt; heading</H4>
        <BR>
        <H5>Here is an &lt;H5&gt; heading</H5>
        <BR>
        <H6>Here is an &lt;H6&gt; heading</H6>
    </CENTER>
</BODY>

</HTML>
```

The results of this HTML appear in Figure 2.5, where you can see every heading HTML 4 supports. Headings are good tags, and I encourage you to use plenty of them. They help break up monotonous text and let the structure of your page stand out immediately.

TIP: Some people consider the skipping of heading levels to be bad practice. For example, you might have an **<H2>** heading followed by an **<H3>** followed by an **<H2>**, but not an **<H1>** heading followed by an **<H3>** followed by an **<H4>** because you'd skip the **<H2>** that way.

<B>—Creating Bold Text

Purpose: Sets the text style to bold.

Start Tag/End Tag: Required/Required

Supported: [2, 3, 3.2, 4, IE1, IE2, IE3, IE4, IE5, NS1, NS2, NS3, NS4]

Attributes:

- **CLASS**—Class of the element (used for rendering). [3, 4, IE4, IE5, NS4]

- **DIR**—Gives the direction of directionally neutral text (text that doesn't have inherent direction in which you should read it). Possible values: **LTR**: left-to-right text or table and **RTL**: right-to-left text or table. [4, IE5]

- **ID**—Unique alphanumeric identifier for the tag, which you can use to refer to it. [3, 4, IE4, IE5, NS4]

- **LANG**—Base language used for the tag. [3, 4, IE4, IE5]

- **LANGUAGE**—Scripting language used for the tag. [IE4, IE5]

- **STYLE**—Inline style indicating how to render the element. [4, IE3, IE4, IE5, NS4]

- **TITLE**—Holds additional information (as might be displayed in tool tips) for the element. [3, 4, IE4, IE5]

"Hey," says the novice programmer, "I want some words to stand out in my page. Is there any way to do that?" "Well," you say, "you can use the **<B>** tag to set those words in bold." "Swell!" says the NP and is gone like a shot.

The **<B>** element encloses text that you want to display in bold. You can use this tag together with other styles, like **<I>**, as we see in this next example, which was also shown at the beginning of this chapter:

```
<HTML>
    <HEAD>
        <TITLE>
            Using italics
        </TITLE>
    </HEAD>

    <BODY>
        <P>
            <I>Here is some text displayed in italics and
            <B>bold</B> too.</I>
    </BODY>
</HTML>
```

The results of this HTML appear in Figure 2.1. The **<B>** tag is a favorite among many HTML programmers, and it's easy to use.

<I>—Creating Italic Text

Purpose: Displays text in italics.

Start Tag/End Tag: Required/Required

Supported: [2, 3, 3.2, 4, IE1, IE2, IE3, IE4, IE5, NS1, NS2, NS3, NS4]

Attributes:

- **CLASS**—Class of the element (used for rendering). [3, 4, IE4, IE5, NS4]

- **DIR**—Gives the direction of directionally neutral text (text that doesn't have inherent direction in which you should read it). Possible values: **LTR**: left-to-right text or table and **RTL**: right-to-left text or table. [4, IE5]

- **ID**—Unique alphanumeric identifier for the tag, which you can use to refer to it. [3, 4, IE4, IE5, NS4]

- **LANG**—Base language used for the tag. [3, 4, IE4, IE5]

- **LANGUAGE**—Scripting language used for the tag. [IE4, IE5]

- **STYLE**—Inline style indicating how to render the element. [4, IE3, IE4, IE5, NS4]

- **TITLE**—Holds additional information (as might be displayed in tool tips) for the element. [3, 4, IE4, IE5]

"That darn Johnson," the novice programmer says, "read my page about mountaineering and skipped over all the warnings. Now that darn Johnson is in the hospital and I'm talking to lawyers!" "Hm," you say, "Next time, why not set the warnings in italics with the **<I>** tag to emphasize them?"

You can use the **<I>** element to display italicized text. You can also combine this style with other styles as we saw in the beginning of this chapter:

```
<HTML>
    <HEAD>
        <TITLE>
            Using italics
        </TITLE>
    </HEAD>

    <BODY>
        <P>
            <I>Here is some text displayed in italics and
            <B>bold</B> too.</I>
    </BODY>
</HTML>
```

The results of this HTML appear in Figure 2.1. The **<I>** tag is another favorite among many HTML programmers, and it's easy to use when you want to italicize text.

<TT>—Creating "Teletype" Text

Purpose: Displays text in a monospace "teletype" font.

Start Tag/End Tag: Required/Required

Supported: [2, 3, 3.2, 4, IE1, IE2, IE3, IE4, IE5, NS1, NS2, NS3, NS4]

Attributes:

- **CLASS**—Class of the element (used for rendering). [3, 4, IE4, IE5, NS4]

- **DIR**—Gives the direction of directionally neutral text (text that doesn't have inherent direction in which you should read it). Possible values: **LTR**: left-to-right text or table and **RTL**: right-to-left text or table. [4, IE5]

- **ID**—Unique alphanumeric identifier for the tag, which you can use to refer to it. [3, 4, IE4, IE5, NS4]

- **LANG**—Base language used for the tag. [3, 4, IE4, IE5]

- **LANGUAGE**—Scripting language used for the tag. [IE4, IE5]

- **STYLE**—Inline style indicating how to render the element. [4, IE3, IE4, IE5, NS4]

- **TITLE**—Holds additional information (as might be displayed in tool tips) for the element. [3, 4, IE4, IE5]

The big boss appears and says, "How's the training manual coming?" "Pretty well," you say, "I'm just getting to the part where I display the program output in a **<TT>** element." "What's that?" the BB asks. "Monospace font," you say.

You can use the **<TT>** tag to create monospace font, which is effective for displaying program output and arranging text and numbers into columns. Here's an example:

```
<HTML>

    <HEAD>
        <TITLE>
            Using the &lt;TT&gt; Tag
        </TITLE>
    </HEAD>
```

```
<BODY>
    At this point, the program should display:
    <BR>
    <TT>Warning! The CPU is on fire. Do you wish to quit?</TT>
</BODY>

</HTML>
```

The result of this HTML appears in Figure 2.7. Another good element to use for displaying program output is **<SAMP>**.

TIP: *Although this tag is similar to the **<PRE>** tag (as we'll see in Chapter 3), it is by no means identical. The **<PRE>** tag displays text completely "as is", whereas the **<TT>** tag ignores line breaks, for example.*

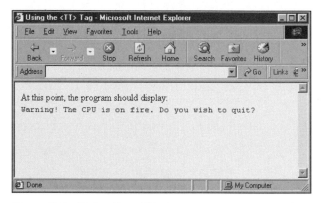

Figure 2.7   Using the **<TT>** tag.

<U>—Underlining Text

Purpose: Underlines text. Deprecated in HTML 4.

Start Tag/End Tag: Required/Required

Supported: [3, 3.2, 4, IE1, IE2, IE3, IE4, IE5, NS3, NS4]

Attributes:

- **CLASS**—Class of the element (used for rendering). [3, 4, IE4, IE5, NS4]

- **DIR**—Gives the direction of directionally neutral text (text that doesn't have inherent direction in which you should read it). Possible values: **LTR**: left-to-right text or table and **RTL**: right-to-left text or table. [4, IE5]

- **ID**—Unique alphanumeric identifier for the tag, which you can use to refer to it. [3, 4, IE4, IE5, NS4]

- **LANG**—Base language used for the tag. [3, 4, IE4, IE5]

- **LANGUAGE**—Scripting language used for the tag. [IE4, IE5]

- **STYLE**—Inline style indicating how to render the element. [4, IE3, IE4, IE5, NS4]

- **TITLE**—Holds additional information (as might be displayed in tool tips) for the element. [3, 4, IE4, IE5]

"I can create bold font and italics in Web pages," the novice programmer says, "but what about underlining?" "Well, you can use the **<U>** tag, but it's deprecated." "The **<U>** tag," the NP says, "thanks!" "Hm," you say.

You can use the **<U>** tag to underline text in HTML, but you should note that this element has been deprecated in HTML 4. Here's an example:

```
<HTML>

    <HEAD>
        <TITLE>
            Using the &lt;U&gt; Tag
        </TITLE>
    </HEAD>

    <BODY>
        You can <U>underline</U> text with the &lt;U&gt; tag.
    </BODY>

</HTML>
```

The result of this HTML appears in Figure 2.8.

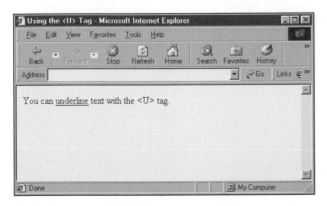

Figure 2.8   Using the **<U>** tag.

`<S>` And `<STRIKE>`—Striking Text Out

Purpose: Displays text in strikethrough style. Deprecated in HTML 4.

Start Tag/End Tag: Required/Required

Supported: [3, 4, IE1, IE2, IE3, IE4, IE5, NS3, NS4]

Attributes:

- **CLASS**—Class of the element (used for rendering). [3, 4, IE4, IE5, NS4]
- **DIR**—Gives the direction of directionally neutral text (text that doesn't have inherent direction in which you should read it). Possible values: **LTR**: left-to-right text or table and **RTL**: right-to-left text or table. [4, IE5]
- **ID**—Unique alphanumeric identifier for the tag, which you can use to refer to it. [3, 4, IE4, IE5, NS4]
- **LANG**—Base language used for the tag. [3, 4, IE4, IE5]
- **LANGUAGE**—Scripting language used for the tag. [IE4, IE5]
- **STYLE**—Inline style indicating how to render the element. [4, IE3, IE4, IE5, NS4]
- **TITLE**—Holds additional information (as might be displayed in tool tips) for the element. [3, 4, IE4, IE5]

The novice programmer appears and says, "I'm ready to write version 2 of my online manual, but I want to indicate what's been revised since version 1. Is there any way to do that?" "Well, you can use the **`<STRIKE>`** tag, but it's deprecated." "The **`<STRIKE>`** tag," the NP says, "thanks!" "Hm," you say.

The **`<S>`** and **`<STRIKE>`** tags are used for the same effect (HTML 2 used **`<STRIKE>`**, HTML 3 called it **`<S>`**, HTML 3.2 called it **`<STRIKE>`** again, and in HTML 4, both are available although deprecated); they let you strike out text. Both tags are deprecated in favor of style sheets in HTML 4.

Here's a quick example of the **`<STRIKE>`** tag at work:

```
<HTML>

    <HEAD>
        <TITLE>
            Using the &lt;STRIKE&gt; Tag
        </TITLE>
    </HEAD>

    <BODY>
        You <STRIKE>ain't allowed to</STRIKE> shouldn't use
```

```
            the &lt;STRIKE&gt; tag, because it's deprecated.
    </BODY>

</HTML>
```

The result of this HTML appears in Figure 2.9.

TIP: *Note that HTML 4 lists both **<S>** and **<STRIKE>** (even though they're deprecated), and HTML 3.2 only lists **<STRIKE>**. So, if you really want to use this tag instead of style sheets, it's best to use **<STRIKE>**.*

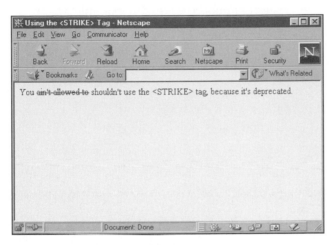

Figure 2.9   Using the **<STRIKE>** tag.

<BIG>—Creating Big Text

Purpose: Renders text in a bigger font than the current default. Often used for emphasis.

Start Tag/End Tag: Required/Required

Supported: [3, 3.2, 4, IE3, IE4, IE5, NS2, NS3, NS4]

Attributes:

- **CLASS**—Class of the element (used for rendering). [3, 4, IE4, IE5, NS4]
- **DIR**—Gives the direction of directionally neutral text (text that doesn't have inherent direction in which you should read it). Possible values: **LTR**: left-to-right text or table and **RTL**: right-to-left text or table. [4, IE5]
- **ID**—Unique alphanumeric identifier for the tag, which you can use to refer to it. [3, 4, IE4, IE5, NS4]

- **LANG**—Base language used for the tag. [3, 4, IE4, IE5]

- **LANGUAGE**—Scripting language used for the tag. [IE4, IE5]

- **STYLE**—Inline style indicating how to render the element. [4, IE3, IE4, IE5, NS4]

- **TITLE**—Holds additional information (as might be displayed in tool tips) for the element. [3, 4, IE4, IE5]

You use the **<BIG>** tag to make text somewhat bigger than the current default (normally by one font size, using the standard HTML 1 to 7 simple values mentioned in the In Depth section "Setting Fonts"). Here's an example:

```
<HTML>

    <HEAD>
        <TITLE>
            Using the &lt;BIG&gt; and &lt;SMALL&gt; Tags
        </TITLE>
    </HEAD>

    <BODY>
        Here's some text that's <BIG>big</BIG>.
        <P>
        And here's some text that's <SMALL>small</SMALL>.
    </BODY>

</HTML>
```

The results of this HTML appear in Figure 2.10.

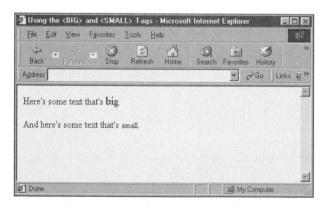

Figure 2.10   Using the **<BIG>** and **<SMALL>** tags.

So why should you use **<BIG>** instead of, say, the **<FONT>** tag, which lets you specify the actual size of text? One reason is that browsers are now displaying text larger for visually disabled users, and if you specify a font size with **<FONT>**, the result may actually be smaller than the rest of the text. **<BIG>** is intended to mean "bigger than the default" text.

TIP: *What does "big" really mean? In terms of the now deprecated* **<FONT>** *tag, the default font size for text is usually size 3, and browsers usually implement* **<BIG>** *as size 4 when compared to default text. You can also nest* **<BIG>**, *which increases the font size by one size for each such element (by using the standard HTML 1 to 7 simple values mentioned in the In Depth section "Setting Fonts").*

<SMALL>—Creating Small Text

Purpose: Renders text in a smaller font than the current default.

Start Tag/End Tag: Required/Required

Supported: [2, 3, 3.2, 4, IE1, IE2, IE3, IE4, IE5, NS2, NS3, NS4]

Attributes:

- **CLASS**—Class of the element (used for rendering). [3, 4, IE4, IE5, NS4]

- **DIR**—Gives the direction of directionally neutral text (text that doesn't have inherent direction in which you should read it). Possible values: **LTR**: left-to-right text or table and **RTL**: right-to-left text or table. [4, IE5]

- **ID**—Unique alphanumeric identifier for the tag, which you can use to refer to it. [3, 4, IE4, IE5, NS4]

- **LANG**—Base language used for the tag. [3, 4, IE4, IE5]

- **LANGUAGE**—Scripting language used for the tag. [IE4, IE5]

- **STYLE**—Inline style indicating how to render the element. [4, IE3, IE4, IE5, NS4]

- **TITLE**—Holds additional information (as might be displayed in tool tips) for the element. [3, 4, IE4, IE5]

You use the **<SMALL>** tag to make text somewhat smaller than the current default (normally by one font size, using the standard HTML 1 to 7 simple values mentioned in the In Depth section "Setting Fonts"). Here's an example:

```
<HTML>

    <HEAD>
        <TITLE>
            Using the &lt;BIG&gt; and &lt;SMALL&gt; Tags
        </TITLE>
    </HEAD>

    <BODY>
        Here's some text that's <BIG>big</BIG>.
        <P>
        And here's some text that's <SMALL>small</SMALL>.
    </BODY>

</HTML>
```

The results of this HTML appear in Figure 2.10.

So why should you use **<SMALL>** instead of the **<FONT>** tag, which lets you specify the actual size of text? One reason is that browsers are now displaying larger text for visually disabled users, and if you specify a font size with **<FONT>**, the result may actually be a great deal smaller than the rest of the text. **<SMALL>** is intended to mean "smaller than the default" text.

TIP: *What does "small" really mean? In terms of the now deprecated **<FONT>** tag, the default font size for text is usually size 3, and browsers usually implement **<SMALL>** as size 2 when compared to default text. You can also nest this element, which normally reduces the font size by one size for each such element (by using the standard HTML 1 to 7 simple values mentioned in the In Depth section "Setting Fonts").*

<SUB>—Creating Subscripts

Purpose: Styles text as a subscript.

Start Tag/End Tag: Required/Required

Supported: [3, 3.2, 4, IE3, IE4, IE5, NS2, NS3, NS4]

Attributes:

- **CLASS**—Class of the element (used for rendering). [3, 4, IE4, IE5, NS4]
- **DIR**—Gives the direction of directionally neutral text (text that doesn't have inherent direction in which you should read it). Possible values: **LTR**: left-to-right text or table and **RTL**: right-to-left text or table. [4, IE5]

- **ID**—Unique alphanumeric identifier for the tag, which you can use to refer to it. [3, 4, IE4, IE5, NS4]

- **LANG**—Base language used for the tag. [3, 4, IE4, IE5]

- **LANGUAGE**—Scripting language used for the tag. [IE4, IE5]

- **STYLE**—Inline style indicating how to render the element. [4, IE3, IE4, IE5, NS4]

- **TITLE**—Holds additional information (as might be displayed in tool tips) for the element. [3, 4, IE4, IE5]

"I'm working on my new online novel," the novice programmer says, "but is there any way to display subscripts as in H_2SO_4?" "Sounds exciting," you say, "and you can indicate subscripts with the **<SUB>** tag."

The **<SUB>** tag lets you create subscripts in a Web page. Here's an example:

```
<HTML>

    <HEAD>
        <TITLE>
            Using the &lt;SUB&gt; and &lt;SUP&gt; Tags
        </TITLE>
    </HEAD>

    <BODY>
        <P>
            "Don't drink that pure H<SUB>2</SUB>SO<SUB>4</SUB>, Jim,"
            I said.
            "It's not very good for you."
        <P>
            "Good point," Jim said,
            "I remember that from our previous adventure<SUP>1</SUP>."
        <BR>
        <BR>
        <BR>
        <HR>
        <SUP>1</SUP><I>The Astounding H<SUB>2</SUB>SO<SUB>4</SUB>
        Adventure</I>, now available in paperback.
    </BODY>

</HTML>
```

The results of this HTML appear in Figure 2.11. As you can see in the figure, the subscripts in the text are displayed appropriately.

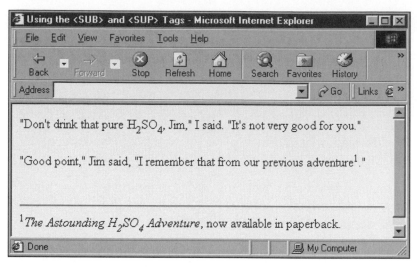

Figure 2.11   Using the **<SUB>** and **<SUP>** tags.

<SUP>—Creating Superscripts

Purpose: Styles text as a superscript.

Start Tag/End Tag: Required/Required

Supported: [2, 3, 3.2, 4, IE1, IE2, IE3, IE4, IE5, NS2, NS3, NS4]

Attributes:

- **CLASS**—Class of the element (used for rendering). [3, 4, IE4, IE5, NS4]
- **DIR**—Gives the direction of directionally neutral text (text that doesn't have inherent direction in which you should read it). Possible values: **LTR**: left-to-right text or table and **RTL**: right-to-left text or table. [4, IE5]
- **ID**—Unique alphanumeric identifier for the tag, which you can use to refer to it. [3, 4, IE4, IE5, NS4]
- **LANG**—Base language used for the tag. [3, 4, IE4, IE5]
- **LANGUAGE**—Scripting language used for the tag. [IE4, IE5]
- **STYLE**—Inline style indicating how to render the element. [4, IE3, IE4, IE5, NS4]
- **TITLE**—Holds additional information (as might be displayed in tool tips) for the element. [3, 4, IE4, IE5]

The big boss appears and says nervously, "About this online annual report for the company—I want to explain the reason we lost so much money last quarter to the stockholders." "Do you really want to explain your trip to Las Vegas?" you say. "Hm," says the BB, "maybe we should bury it a little. Let's add it in a footnote." "OK," you say, "I'll use the **<SUP>** tag."

The **<SUP>** tag lets you create superscripts in a Web page. Here's an example:

```
<HTML>

    <HEAD>
        <TITLE>
            Using the &lt;SUB&gt; and &lt;SUP&gt; Tags
        </TITLE>
    </HEAD>

    <BODY>
        <P>
            "Don't drink that pure H<SUB>2</SUB>SO<SUB>4</SUB>, Jim,"
            I said.
            "It's not very good for you."
        <P>
            "Good point," Jim said,
            "I remember that from our previous adventure<SUP>1</SUP>."
        <BR>
        <BR>
        <BR>
        <HR>
        <SUP>1</SUP><I>The Astounding H<SUB>2</SUB>SO<SUB>4</SUB>
        Adventure</I>, now available in paperback.
    </BODY>

</HTML>
```

The results of this HTML appear in Figure 2.11. As you can see, the superscripts in the text are displayed as they should be.

TIP: *As with other HTML tags, you can nest **<SUP>** tags inside other tags. Nesting is useful if the explanatory text for footnotes is in some other document—in which case, you can make the superscript footnote numbers into hyperlinks to that document.*

<EM>—Emphasizing Text

Purpose: Emphasizes text; usually rendered as italics.

Start Tag/End Tag: Required/Required

Supported: [2, 3, 3.2, 4, IE1, IE2, IE3, IE4, IE5, NS1, NS2, NS3, NS4]

Attributes:

- **CLASS**—Class of the element (used for rendering). [3, 4, IE4, IE5, NS4]
- **DIR**—Gives the direction of directionally neutral text (text that doesn't have inherent direction in which you should read it). Possible values: **LTR**: left-to-right text or table and **RTL**: right-to-left text or table. [4, IE5]
- **ID**—Unique alphanumeric identifier for the tag, which you can use to refer to it. [3, 4, IE4, IE5, NS4]
- **LANG**—Base language used for the tag. [3, 4, IE4, IE5]
- **LANGUAGE**—Scripting language used for the tag. [IE4, IE5]
- **STYLE**—Inline style indicating how to render the element. [4, IE3, IE4, IE5, NS4]
- **TITLE**—Holds additional information (as might be displayed in tool tips) for the element. [3, 4, IE4, IE5]

The **<EM>** logical style emphasizes text. In practice, this element is usually rendered in italics. Here's an example showing how to use this tag:

```
<HTML>
    <HEAD>
        <TITLE>
            Using logical styles
        </TITLE>
    </HEAD>

    <BODY>
        This is the <EM>second</EM> time it's happened.
    </BODY>
</HTML>
```

You can see this style in Netscape Navigator shown in Figure 2.2 and in Internet Explorer shown in Figure 2.3.

`<STRONG>`—Strongly Emphasizing Text

Purpose: Emphasizes text strongly; usually rendered in bold.

Start Tag/End Tag: Required/Required

Supported: [2, 3, 3.2, 4, IE1, IE2, IE3, IE4, IE5, NS1, NS2, NS3, NS4]

Attributes:

- **CLASS**—Class of the element (used for rendering). [3, 4, IE4, IE5, NS4]

- **DIR**—Gives the direction of directionally neutral text (text that doesn't have inherent direction in which you should read it). Possible values: **LTR**: left-to-right text or table and **RTL**: right-to-left text or table. [4, IE5]

- **ID**—Unique alphanumeric identifier for the tag, which you can use to refer to it. [3, 4, IE4, IE5, NS4]

- **LANG**—Base language used for the tag. [3, 4, IE4, IE5]

- **LANGUAGE**—Scripting language used for the tag. [IE4, IE5]

- **STYLE**—Inline style indicating how to render the element. [4, IE3, IE4, IE5, NS4]

- **TITLE**—Holds additional information (as might be displayed in tool tips) for the element. [3, 4, IE4, IE5]

You use **`<STRONG>`** when you want to strongly emphasize text. In practice, **`<STRONG>`** text is usually rendered as bold text. Here's an example showing how to use **`<STRONG>`**:

```
<HTML>
    <HEAD>
        <TITLE>
            Using logical styles
        </TITLE>
    </HEAD>

    <BODY>
        <STRONG>Do not</STRONG> press the ejector seat button!
    </BODY>
</HTML>
```

You can see this style in Netscape Navigator shown in Figure 2.2 and in Internet Explorer shown in Figure 2.3.

<CODE>—Displaying Program Code

Purpose: Styles text as program code in a monospace font.

Start Tag/End Tag: Required/Required

Supported: [2, 3, 3.2, 4, IE1, IE2, IE3, IE4, IE5, NS1, NS2, NS3, NS4]

Attributes:

- **CLASS**—Class of the element (used for rendering). [3, 4, IE4, IE5, NS4]

- **DIR**—Gives the direction of directionally neutral text (text that doesn't have inherent direction in which you should read it). Possible values: **LTR**: left-to-right text or table and **RTL**: right-to-left text or table. [4, IE5]

- **ID**—Unique alphanumeric identifier for the tag, which you can use to refer to it. [3, 4, IE4, IE5, NS4]

- **LANG**—Base language used for the tag. [3, 4, IE4, IE5]

- **LANGUAGE**—Scripting language used for the tag. [IE4, IE5]

- **STYLE**—Inline style indicating how to render the element. [4, IE3, IE4, IE5, NS4]

- **TITLE**—Holds additional information (as might be displayed in tool tips) for the element. [3, 4, IE4, IE5]

The **<CODE>** element styles text as program code. It is usually rendered in a monospace font where each character has equal width. Here's an example showing how to use **<CODE>**:

```
<HTML>
    <HEAD>
        <TITLE>
            Using logical styles
        </TITLE>
    </HEAD>

    <BODY>
        You can try this Web page in your browser:
        <CODE>
            <BR>
                &lt;HTML&gt;
            <BR>
                &lt;HEAD&gt;
            <BR>
                &lt;TITLE&gt;
```

```
        <BR>
              This is my page.
        <BR>
              &lt;/TITLE&gt;
        <BR>
              &lt;/HEAD&gt;
        <BR>
              &lt;/HTML&gt;
      </CODE>
    </BODY>
</HTML>
```

You can see this style in Netscape Navigator shown in Figure 2.2 and in Internet Explorer shown in Figure 2.3.

TIP: The **<CODE>** element is expressly for displaying code samples. If you just want to display monospace text, it's better to use the **<TT>** element, because that's **<TT>**'s job. If the browser displays **<CODE>** elements in a different way from **<TT>** elements, the user can be confused if you use **<CODE>** for monospace text and not for code samples. Note that like **<TT>**, **<CODE>** ignores line breaks.

<SAMP>—Displaying Sample Program Output

Purpose: Styles text as sample program output; usually rendered in a monospace font.

Start Tag/End Tag: Required/Required

Supported: [2, 3, 3.2, 4, IE1, IE2, IE3, IE4, IE5, NS1, NS2, NS3, NS4]

Attributes:

- **CLASS**—Class of the element (used for rendering). [3, 4, IE4, IE5, NS4]

- **DIR**—Gives the direction of directionally neutral text (text that doesn't have inherent direction in which you should read it). Possible values: **LTR**: left-to-right text or table and **RTL**: right-to-left text or table. [4, IE5]

- **ID**—Unique alphanumeric identifier for the tag, which you can use to refer to it. [3, 4, IE4, IE5, NS4]

- **LANG**—Base language used for the tag. [3, 4, IE4, IE5]

- **LANGUAGE**—Scripting language used for the tag. [IE4, IE5]

- **STYLE**—Inline style indicating how to render the element. [4, IE3, IE4, IE5, NS4]

- **TITLE**—Holds additional information (as might be displayed in tool tips) for the element. [3, 4, IE4, IE5]

You use the **<SAMP>** element to display program output or sample text. This element usually renders text in a monospace font; here's an example using **<SAMP>**:

```
<HTML>
    <HEAD>
        <TITLE>
            Using logical styles
        </TITLE>
    </HEAD>

    <BODY>
        At this point, the program displays:
        <SAMP>Sorry, wrong password!</SAMP>
    </BODY>
</HTML>
```

You can see this style in Netscape Navigator shown in Figure 2.2 and in Internet Explorer shown in Figure 2.3.

TIP: *The **<SAMP>** element is expressly for displaying sample text. If you just want to display monospace text, it's better to use the **<TT>** element, because that's **<TT>**'s job. If the browser displays **<SAMP>** elements in a different way from **<TT>** elements, the user can be confused if you use **<SAMP>** for monospace text and not for sample text. Note that like **<TT>**, **<SAMP>** ignores line breaks.*

<KBD>—Displaying Text The User Is To Type

Purpose: Displays text that the user is supposed to enter, usually in a bold or standard monospace font.

Start Tag/End Tag: Required/Required

Supported: [2, 3, 3.2, 4, IE1, IE2, IE3, IE4, IE5, NS1, NS2, NS3, NS4]

Attributes:

- **CLASS**—Class of the element (used for rendering). [3, 4, IE4, IE5, NS4]
- **DIR**—Gives the direction of directionally neutral text (text that doesn't have inherent direction in which you should read it). Possible values: **LTR**: left-to-right text or table and **RTL**: right-to-left text or table. [4, IE5]

- **ID**—Unique alphanumeric identifier for the tag, which you can use to refer to it. [3, 4, IE4, IE5, NS4]

- **LANG**—Base language used for the tag. [3, 4, IE4, IE5]

- **LANGUAGE**—Scripting language used for the tag. [IE4, IE5]

- **STYLE**—Inline style indicating how to render the element. [4, IE3, IE4, IE5, NS4]

- **TITLE**—Holds additional information (as might be displayed in tool tips) for the element. [3, 4, IE4, IE5]

You use the **<KBD>** element to display text that you want the user to type (for example, when writing a training manual and you want to indicate what users should type into their computer). The text in this element is usually displayed in a bold or standard monospace font. Here's an example:

```
<HTML>
    <HEAD>
        <TITLE>
            Using logical styles
        </TITLE>
    </HEAD>

    <BODY>
        Now type this: <KBD>Search all records</KBD>.
    </BODY>
</HTML>
```

You can see this style in Netscape Navigator shown in Figure 2.2 and in Internet Explorer shown in Figure 2.3.

<VAR>—Displaying Program Variables And Arguments

Purpose: Styles text as a program variable or argument; usually rendered in italics.

Start Tag/End Tag: Required/Required

Supported: [2, 3, 3.2, 4, IE1, IE2, IE3, IE4, IE5, NS1, NS2, NS3, NS4]

Attributes:

- **CLASS**—Class of the element (used for rendering). [3, 4, IE4, IE5, NS4]

- **DIR**—Gives the direction of directionally neutral text (text that doesn't have inherent direction in which you should read it). Possible values: **LTR**: left-to-right text or table and **RTL**: right-to-left text or table. [4, IE5]

- **ID**—Unique alphanumeric identifier for the tag, which you can use to refer to it. [3, 4, IE4, IE5, NS4]

- **LANG**—Base language used for the tag. [3, 4, IE4, IE5]

- **LANGUAGE**—Scripting language used for the tag. [IE4, IE5]

- **STYLE**—Inline style indicating how to render the element. [4, IE3, IE4, IE5, NS4]

- **TITLE**—Holds additional information (as might be displayed in tool tips) for the element. [3, 4, IE4, IE5]

Often, when writing technical material that involves programming, the style is to highlight program variables or arguments within text to distinguish them from the standard text font. You can use the **<VAR>** element to do this. This element usually displays its text in italics. Here's an example:

```
<HTML>
    <HEAD>
        <TITLE>
            Using logical styles
        </TITLE>
    </HEAD>

    <BODY>
        The Perl <VAR>$input</VAR> argument will hold 5.
    </BODY>
</HTML>
```

You can see this style in Netscape Navigator shown in Figure 2.2 and in Internet Explorer shown in Figure 2.3.

<DFN>—Defining New Terms

Purpose: Styles text to indicate the first time a term is used—that is, to indicate that you're defining the term; usually rendered as italics.

Start Tag/End Tag: Required/Required

Supported: [3, 3.2, 4, IE1, IE2, IE3, IE4, IE5]

Attributes:

- **CLASS**—Class of the element (used for rendering). [3, 4, IE4, IE5]

- **DIR**—Gives the direction of directionally neutral text (text that doesn't have inherent direction in which you should read it). Possible values: **LTR**: left-to-right text or table and **RTL**: right-to-left text or table. [4, IE5]

- **ID**—Unique alphanumeric identifier for the tag, which you can use to refer to it. [3, 4, IE4, IE5]

- **LANG**—Base language used for the tag. [3, 4, IE4, IE5]

- **LANGUAGE**—Scripting language used for the tag. [IE4, IE5]

- **STYLE**—Inline style indicating how to render the element. [4, IE3, IE4, IE5]

- **TITLE**—Holds additional information (as might be displayed in tool tips) for the element. [3, 4, IE4, IE5]

You can use the **<DFN>** element when introducing a new term. In practice, however, this element is usually just rendered in italics. Here's an example:

```
<HTML>
    <HEAD>
        <TITLE>
            Using logical styles
        </TITLE>
    </HEAD>

    <BODY>
        This is known as a <DFN>SNAFU.</DFN>
    </BODY>
</HTML>
```

You can see this style in Netscape Navigator shown in Figure 2.2 and in Internet Explorer shown in Figure 2.3.

<CITE>—Creating A Citation

Purpose: Styles text as a citation; usually rendered in italics.

Start Tag/End Tag: Required/Required

Supported: [2, 3, 3.2, 4, IE1, IE2, IE3, IE4, IE5, NS1, NS2, NS3, NS4]

Attributes:

- **CLASS**—Class of the element (used for rendering). [3, 4, IE4, IE5, NS4]

- **DIR**—Gives the direction of directionally neutral text (text that doesn't have inherent direction in which you should read it). Possible values: **LTR**: left-to-right text or table and **RTL**: right-to-left text or table. [4, IE5]

- **ID**—Unique alphanumeric identifier for the tag, which you can use to refer to it. [3, 4, IE4, IE5, NS4]

- **LANG**—Base language used for the tag. [3, 4, IE4, IE5]

- **LANGUAGE**—Scripting language used for the tag. [IE4, IE5]

- **STYLE**—Inline style indicating how to render the element. [4, IE3, IE4, IE5, NS4]

- **TITLE**—Holds additional information (as might be displayed in tool tips) for the element. [3, 4, IE4, IE5]

You can use the **<CITE>** element to indicate that certain text is a citation. Usually, this text is rendered in italics. Here's an example:

```
<HTML>
    <HEAD>
        <TITLE>
            Using logical styles
        </TITLE>
    </HEAD>

    <BODY>
        Yogi Berra said, <CITE>I didn't really say everything I said</CITE>.
        Or did he?
    </BODY>
</HTML>
```

You can see this style in Netscape Navigator shown in Figure 2.2 and in Internet Explorer shown in Figure 2.3.

<ABBR>—Displaying Abbreviations

Purpose: Styles text as an abbreviation.

Start Tag/End Tag: Required/Optional

Supported: [4]

Attributes:

- **CLASS**—Class of the element (used for rendering). [4]

- **DIR**—Gives the direction of directionally neutral text (text that doesn't have inherent direction in which you should read it). Possible values: **LTR**: left-to-right text or table and **RTL**: right-to-left text or table. [4]

- **ID**—Unique alphanumeric identifier for the tag, which you can use to refer to it. [4]

- **LANG**—Base language used for the tag. [4]

- **LANGUAGE**—Scripting language used for the tag. [4]

- **STYLE**—Inline style indicating how to render the element. [4]

- **TITLE**—Holds additional information (as might be displayed in tool tips) for the element. [4]

You use the **<ABBR>** element to indicate that a term is an abbreviation. This element is new in HTML 4 and has not been implemented by the major browsers yet, but will probably be implemented as italics or boldface. Here's an example:

```
<HTML>
    <HEAD>
        <TITLE>
            Using logical styles
        </TITLE>
    </HEAD>

    <BODY>
        MIT is on Massachusetts Avenue, which people call
        <ABBR TITLE="Massachusetts Avenue">Mass Ave</ABBR>.
    </BODY>
</HTML>
```

TIP: *W3C suggests using the **TITLE** attribute to hold the expanded version of the abbreviation.*

<ACRONYM>—Displaying Acronyms

Purpose: Used to display acronyms.

Start Tag/End Tag: Required/Required

Supported: [4, IE4, IE5]

Attributes:

- **CLASS**—Class of the element (used for rendering). [4, IE4, IE5]

- **DIR**—Gives the direction of directionally neutral text (text that doesn't have inherent direction in which you should read it). Possible values: **LTR**: left-to-right text or table and **RTL**: right-to-left text or table. [4, IE5]

- **ID**—Unique alphanumeric identifier for the tag, which you can use to refer to it. [4, IE4, IE5]

- **LANG**—Base language used for the tag. [4, IE4, IE5]

- **LANGUAGE**—Scripting language used for the tag. [IE4, IE5]

- **STYLE**—Inline style indicating how to render the element. [4, IE4, IE5]

- **TITLE**—Holds additional information (as might be displayed in tool tips) for the element. [4, IE4, IE5]

You use the **<ACRONYM>** element to indicate that a term is an acronym. This element is new in HTML 4 and has only been implemented by Internet Explorer. Here's an example:

```
<HTML>
    <HEAD>
        <TITLE>
            Using logical styles
        </TITLE>
    </HEAD>

    <BODY>
        HTML is standardized by the
        <ACRONYM TITLE="World Wide Web Consortium">W3C</ACRONYM>.
    </BODY>
</HTML>
```

TIP: *W3C suggests using the **TITLE** attribute to hold the expanded version of the acronym.*

<FONT>—Specifying A Font

Purpose: Lets you select text size, color, and face. Deprecated in HTML 4.

Start Tag/End Tag: Required/Required

Supported: [3.2, 4, IE1, IE2, IE3, IE4, IE5, NS1, NS2, NS3, NS4]

Attributes:

- **CLASS**—Class of the element (used for rendering). [3, 4, IE4, IE5, NS4]

- **COLOR**—Deprecated. Color of the text; set it to a color value or predefined color [3.2, 4, IE1, IE2, IE3, IE4, IE5, NS2, NS3, NS4]

- **DIR**—Gives the direction of directionally neutral text (text that doesn't have inherent direction in which you should read it). Possible values: **LTR**: left-to-right text or table and **RTL**: right-to-left text or table. [4, IE5]

- **FACE**—Deprecated. The font face can be a list of names separated by commas. The browser will select the first font face from the list it can find in the system it's running on. [4, IE1, IE2, IE3, IE4, IE5, NS3, NS4]

- **ID**—Unique alphanumeric identifier for the tag, which you can use to refer to it. [3, 4, IE4, IE5, NS4]

- **LANG**—Base language used for the tag. [3, 4, IE4, IE5]

- **LANGUAGE**—Scripting language used for the tag. [IE4, IE5]

- **POINT-SIZE**—Size of the text in points (1/72 of an inch). [NS4]

- **SIZE**—Deprecated. Size of the text. Possible values range from 1 through 7. You can also specify sizes relative to the current base font (see the **<BASEFONT>** tag) by placing a + or - in front of the **SIZE** attribute's value. Relative values can range from -6 through +6. [3.2, 4, IE1, IE2, IE3, IE4, IE5, NS1, NS2, NS3, NS4]

- **STYLE**—Inline style indicating how to render the element. [4, IE4, IE5, NS4]

- **TITLE**—Holds additional information (as might be displayed in tool tips) for the element. [3, 4, IE4, IE5]

- **WEIGHT**—Sets the font weight from 100 to 900 (possible values are 100 up to 900 in steps of 100). [NS4]

The **<FONT>** tag is cherished by many HTML authors, but was deprecated in HTML 4 in favor of style sheets. You use this tag to select a font face, size, and color. Here's an example shown earlier in this chapter. In this case, I'm displaying text in a large blue Arial font:

```
<HTML>

    <HEAD>
        <TITLE>
            Using the &lt;FONT&gt; Tag
        </TITLE>
    </HEAD>

    <BODY>
        <FONT SIZE=6 COLOR="#0000ff" FACE="Arial">Here is some text!</FONT>
    </BODY>

</HTML>
```

The results appear in Figure 2.4. You specify font sizes by using the values 1 through 7 or as relative values -6 through +6 if you've set the base font size with the **<BASEFONT>** element (see the Immediate Solutions section "**<BASEFONT>**— Setting The Base Font"). If you're using Netscape Navigator, you can set the font size in points with the **POINT-SIZE** attribute. In practice, font size 1 is about 6 points, font size 2 is about 12 points, and so on, but actual sizes vary by system. Here's an example showing the range of possible sizes:

```
<HTML>
    <HEAD>
        <TITLE>
            Using the &lt;FONT&gt; Tag
        </TITLE>
    </HEAD>

    <BODY>
        <CENTER>
            <FONT SIZE=1>This is font size 1.</FONT>
            <BR>
            <FONT SIZE=2>This is font size 2.</FONT>
            <BR>
            <FONT SIZE=3>This is font size 3.</FONT>
            <BR>
            <FONT SIZE=4>This is font size 4.</FONT>
            <BR>
            <FONT SIZE=5>This is font size 5.</FONT>
            <BR>
            <FONT SIZE=6>This is font size 6.</FONT>
            <BR>
            <FONT SIZE=7>This is font size 7.</FONT>
        </CENTER>
    </BODY>
</HTML>
```

The results of this HTML appear in Figure 2.12.

Sometimes, the system the browser is on may not have the font installed that you've specified. To anticipate any problems, you can specify a list of font faces to use, and the browser will select the first one that it can identify and utilize (note that you specify font names containing multiple words by using single quotes):

```
<FONT SIZE=6 COLOR="#0000ff" FACE="Arial, 'Courier New', 'Times New
Roman'">Here is some text!</FONT>
```

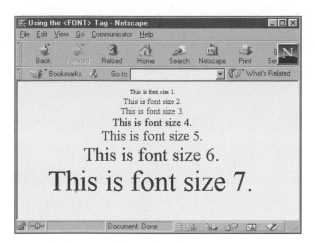

Figure 2.12   Using the **<FONT>** tag.

TIP: *A popular use of **<FONT>** is to color text inline as in this example:* **<EM><FONT COLOR=RED>Warning!</FONT> You're about to delete all your files!</EM>**

Setting Font Point Size Directly

The novice programmer says, "Jeez, what's all this about setting font sizes using values from 1 through 7 with the **<FONT>** tag? I'm used to using the point sizes you see in word processors." "OK," you say, "There is a way to do that." "Tell me all about it!" the NP cries happily.

In Netscape Navigator, you can set font size directly in points (1/72 of an inch) using the **POINT-SIZE** attribute of the **<FONT>** tag. In this example, I'm setting the point size of text to 50 points:

```
<HTML>
    <HEAD>
        <TITLE>
            Using the &lt;FONT&gt; Tag
        </TITLE>
    </HEAD>

    <BODY>
            <FONT POINT-SIZE=50>
                Some big text.
            </FONT>
    </BODY>
</HTML>
```

Internet Explorer, on the other hand, does not support the **POINT-SIZE** attribute, but you can do the same thing with style sheets. In this case, I'm setting the style of the **<P>** paragraph tag to use 50-point text (note that this code works only in Internet Explorer):

```
<HTML>
    <HEAD>
        <TITLE>
            Specific tag styling example
        </TITLE>
    </HEAD>

    <STYLE>
        P {font-size = 50pt}
    </STYLE>

    <BODY>
        <P>
        Some big text.
    </BODY>
</HTML>
```

<BASEFONT>—Setting The Base Font

Purpose: Sets the base font. Relative font changes (created with the **<FONT>** element) are made with respect to the base font. Deprecated in HTML 4.

Start Tag/End Tag: Required/Omitted

Supported: [3.2, 4, IE1, IE2, IE3, IE4, IE5, NS1, NS2, NS3, NS4]

Attributes:

- **CLASS**—Class of the element (used for rendering). [3, 4, IE4, IE5, NS4]

- **COLOR**—Deprecated. Color of the default text; set it to a color value or predefined color. [4, IE1, IE2, IE3, IE4, IE5]

- **DIR**—Gives the direction of directionally neutral text (text that doesn't have inherent direction in which you should read it). Possible values: **LTR**: left-to-right text or table and **RTL**: right-to-left text or table. [4, IE5]

- **FACE**—Deprecated. The font face of default text can be a comma-separated list of font names. The browser will select the first one it can find in the system it's running on. [4, IE1, IE2, IE3, IE4, IE5]

- **ID**—Unique alphanumeric identifier for the tag, which you can use to refer to it. [3, 4, IE4, IE5, NS4]

- **LANG**—Base language used for the tag. [3, 4]

- **SIZE**—Deprecated. Size of default text. Possible values range from 1 through 7. [3.2, 4, IE1, IE2, IE3, IE4, IE5, NS1, NS2, NS3, NS4]

- **STYLE**—Inline style indicating how to render the element. [4, NS4]

- **TITLE**—Holds additional information (as might be displayed in tool tips) for the element. [3, 4, IE4, IE5]

The **<BASEFONT>** element sets the font for default text enclosed in the element, replacing the default font used by the browser. You can specify relative sizes with respect to this default font with the **<FONT>** tag. Note that the **<BASEFONT>** tag is deprecated in HTML 4.

In the following example, I'm setting the base font size to 4 (possible values range from 1 through 7), then temporarily increasing that size to 6 for one word with a **<FONT>** tag by adding 2 to the base font size:

```
<HTML>

    <HEAD>
        <TITLE>
            Using the &lt;BASEFONT&gt; Tag
        </TITLE>
    </HEAD>

    <BODY>
        <BASEFONT SIZE = 4>
        Here's some <FONT SIZE="+2">bigger</FONT> text.
    </BODY>

</HTML>
```

The results appear in Figure 2.13. As you can see, the word I've increased in size is indeed bigger. Keep in mind that **<BASEFONT>** is deprecated, which means it'll disappear from HTML one day. The use of style sheets is a better choice.

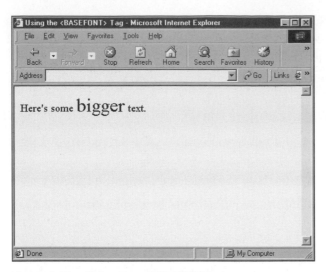

Figure 2.13   Using the **<BASEFONT>** tag.

TIP: *Neither Internet Explorer nor Netscape Navigator apply the **BASEFONT SIZE** attribute value to heading levels. On the other hand, Internet Explorer, but not Netscape Navigator, does apply the **FACE** and **COLOR** values to headings.*

<Q>—Displaying Short Quotations

Purpose: Displays a short, inline quotation.

Start Tag/End Tag: Required/Required

Supported: [4, IE4, IE5]

Attributes:

- **CLASS**—Class of the element (used for rendering). [4, IE4, IE5]
- **DIR**—Gives the direction of directionally neutral text (text that doesn't have inherent direction in which you should read it). Possible values: **LTR**: left-to-right text or table and **RTL**: right-to-left text or table. [4, IE5]
- **ID**—Unique alphanumeric identifier for the tag, which you can use to refer to it. [4, IE4, IE5]
- **LANG**—Base language used for the tag. [4, IE4, IE5]
- **LANGUAGE**—Scripting language used for the tag. [IE4, IE5]
- **STYLE**—Inline style indicating how to render the element. [4, IE4, IE5]
- **TITLE**—Holds additional information (as might be displayed in tool tips) for the element. [4, IE4, IE5]

The **<Q>** tag is for inline quotations that do not include line breaks. It can be used on a word-by-word or character-by-character basis. The **<CITE>** tag is used for longer quotations and **<Q>** for shorter ones. Theoretically, the browser is supposed to add locale-specific quotation marks around the quotation (one of the ideas behind this element is to let the browser select the right kind of locale-specific quotation marks for you), but this element is too new for either Internet Explorer or Netscape Navigator to do anything but render it as plain text. Here's an example:

```
<HTML>

    <HEAD>
        <TITLE>
            Using the &lt;Q&gt; Tag
        </TITLE>
    </HEAD>

    <BODY>
        Yogi Berra said, <Q>I didn't really say everything I said</Q>.
        Or did he?
    </BODY>

</HTML>
```

<BLINK>—Making Text Blink

Purpose: Displays enclosed text as blinking on and off approximately once a second.

Start Tag/End Tag: Required/Required

Supported: [NS1, NS2, NS3, NS4]

Attributes: None

"Hey look," the novice programmer says, "I can make my whole page blink." "Yes," you say, "that's quite an effect." The NP studies the blinking screen for a few moments and says, "Kind of annoying, isn't it?"

The **<BLINK>** tag is a little notorious because the result, text that blinks on and off, can aggravate people (especially when a whole page blinks). Reading such text can be difficult, and if you're looking at other parts of the page, distracting. In fact, many people consider it a little juvenile, so you might want to consider this before using the **<BLINK>** tag. Netscape created this tag early on and still supports it; Internet Explorer now recognizes it, but does not implement this tag. For instance, you can use the tag attributes, like **ID** in Internet Explorer, but the text will not blink. Here's an example:

```
<HTML>

    <HEAD>
        <TITLE>
            Using the &lt;BLINK&gt; Tag
        </TITLE>
    </HEAD>

    <BODY>
        <BLINK>HAPPY NEW YEAR!!</BLINK>
    </BODY>

</HTML>
```

This is not to say **<BLINK>** doesn't have its uses. By blinking the heading "Warning", it can be useful to draw attention.

TIP: *Due, one imagines, to popular request, you can now disable blinking text in Netscape Navigator, but it's not easy and can involve editing the Windows Registry. See the directions at* **www.sightspecific.com/~mosh/WWW_FAQ/ noblink.html** *for examples.*

<INS>—Displaying Inserted Text

Purpose: Styles text as inserted text; used to track document edits and changes. Rendered in Internet Explorer as underlined.

Start Tag/End Tag: Required/Required

Supported: [4, IE4, IE5]

Attributes:

- **CITE**—Text that cites the reason for the insertion. [4]
- **CLASS**—Class of the element (used for rendering). [4, IE4, IE5]
- **DATETIME**—Displays the date and time of the change. [4]

- **DIR**—Gives the direction of directionally neutral text (text that doesn't have inherent direction in which you should read it). Possible values: **LTR**: left-to-right text or table and **RTL**: right-to-left text or table. [4, IE5]

- **ID**—Unique alphanumeric identifier for the tag, which you can use to refer to it. [4, IE4, IE5]

- **LANG**—Base language used for the tag. [4, IE4, IE5]

- **LANGUAGE**—Scripting language used for the tag. [IE4, IE5]

- **STYLE**—Inline style indicating how to render the element. [4, IE3, IE4, IE5]

- **TITLE**—Holds additional information (as might be displayed in tool tips) for the element. [4, IE4, IE5]

The novice programmer says, "It would be great if I could track changes in my online training manual by date and time." "Theoretically," you say, "you can use the **<INS>** tag to indicate what text has been inserted and when." "Great!" says the NP. "Except," you add, "that Internet Explorer is the only browser to implement **<INS>** so far, and it doesn't handle attributes like **DATETIME**, which stores the time of the change." "Great," says the NP.

Together with the **<DEL>** element, the **<INS>** element lets you track changes in the content of HTML documents. **<INS>** indicates insertions and **<DEL>** deletions. Theoretically, you can record the time and date of the change with the **DATETIME** attribute, however browsers do not support this attribute yet. Here's the format to set dates and times: ***YYYY-MM-DDThh:mm:ssTZD*** (following the ISO8601 standard), where:

- ***YYYY***—Four-digit year

- ***MM***—Two-digit month (01 through 12)

- ***DD***—Two-digit day of month (01 through 31)

- ***hh***—Two-digit hour (00 through 23, no A.M./P.M. designation is used)

- ***mm***—Two-digit minute (00 through 59)

- ***ss***—Two-digit second (00 through 59)

- ***TZD***—Time zone designator

The time zone designator is a simple z for Universal Coordinated Time (UTC, formerly Greenwich Mean Time [GMT]) or the number of hours and minutes that your time zone is ahead or behind UTC, like this: ***+hh:mm*** or ***-hh:mm***. For example, because Mountain Standard Time (MST) is seven hours behind UTC, 6:00 P.M. September 2, 2000 is designated as: **2000-09-02T18:00:00-07:00**.

2. Working With Text

Currently only Internet Explorer implements **<INS>** by underlining the enclosed text, but it does not implement the **DATETIME** or **CITE** attributes. Here's an example:

```
<HTML>

    <HEAD>
        <TITLE>
            Using the &lt;INS&gt; Tag
        </TITLE>
    </HEAD>

    <BODY>
        Here is <INS DATETIME="2000-01-01T09:00:00-06:00"
        CITE="Grammar correction">the</INS> page.
    </BODY>

</HTML>
```

<DEL>—Displaying Text As Deleted

Purpose: Marks text as deleted. Rendered as strikethrough text in Internet Explorer.

Start Tag/End Tag: Required/Required

Supported: [4, IE4, IE5]

Attributes:

- **CITE**—Text that cites the reason for the insertion. [4]
- **CLASS**—Class of the element (used for rendering). [4, IE4, IE5]
- **DATETIME**—Displays the date and time of the change (for format, see the **DATETIME** entry in the**<INS>** section). [4]
- **DIR**—Gives the direction of directionally neutral text (text that doesn't have inherent direction in which you should read it). Possible values: **LTR**: left-to-right text or table and **RTL**: right-to-left text or table. [4, IE5]
- **ID**—Unique alphanumeric identifier for the tag, which you can use to refer to it. [4, IE4, IE5]
- **LANG**—Base language used for the tag. [4, IE4, IE5]

- **LANGUAGE**—Scripting language used for the tag. [IE4, IE5]

- **STYLE**—Inline style indicating how to render the element. [4, IE3, IE4, IE5]

- **TITLE**—Holds additional information (as might be displayed in tool tips) for the element. [4, IE4, IE5]

Like the **<INS>** element, **<DEL>** lets you track changes in a document. The **<INS>** tag marks inserted text, and the **<DEL>** tag marks deleted text. Currently, the only browser that implements the **<DEL>** tag is Internet Explorer, and it renders the text in this element as strikethrough (much like the **<STRIKE>** tag would). Note, however, that Internet Explorer does not yet implement the **DATETIME** attribute (which is the date and time of the deletion—for information on the format of this attribute's values, see the previous section "**<INS>**—Displaying Inserted Text")—nor the **CITE** (reason for the deletion) attribute.

Here's an example showing how to use **<DEL>**:

```
<HTML>

    <HEAD>
        <TITLE>
            Using the &lt;DEL&gt; Tag
        </TITLE>
    </HEAD>

    <BODY>
        Here is <DEL DATETIME="2000-01-01T09:00:00-06:00"
        CITE="Grammar correction">the</DEL> the page.
    </BODY>

</HTML>
```

<ADDRESS>—Displaying An Address

Purpose: Displays text styled as an address.

Start Tag/End Tag: Required/Required

Supported: [2, 3, 3.2, 4, IE1, IE2, IE3, IE4, IE5, NS1, NS2, NS3, NS4]

Attributes:

- **CLASS**—Class of the element (used for rendering). [3, 4, IE4, IE5, NS4]

- **DIR**—Gives the direction of directionally neutral text (text that doesn't have inherent direction in which you should read it). Possible values: **LTR**: left-to-right text or table and **RTL**: right-to-left text or table. [4, IE5]

- **ID**—Unique alphanumeric identifier for the tag, which you can use to refer to it. [3, 4, IE4, IE5, NS4]

- **LANG**—Base language used for the tag. [3, 4, IE4, IE5]

- **LANGUAGE**—Scripting language used for the tag. [IE4, IE5]

- **STYLE**—Inline style indicating how to render the element. [4, IE3, IE4, IE5, NS4]

- **TITLE**—Holds additional information (as might be displayed in tool tips) for the element. [3, 4, IE4, IE5]

You use the **<ADDRESS>** tag to indicate an address, authorship, or a signature of some kind. This tag acts much like a **<P>** tag setting its text apart in its own paragraph. It also sets its text in italics in Netscape Navigator and Internet Explorer (I've heard reports that text is also indented in some other browsers). Here's an example where I'm using a **MAILTO** hyperlink (which I'll cover in Chapter 5 on hyperlinks) to let people send email to a page's author:

```
<HTML>

    <HEAD>
        <TITLE>
            Using the &lt;ADDRESS&gt; Tag
        </TITLE>
    </HEAD>

    <BODY>
        I take a firm stand and say: "<I>Maybe</I>"!
        Have comments on my opinion? Write to me!
        <ADDRESS>
            <A HREF="MAILTO:author@starpowder.com">Arthur T. Author</A>
            <BR>
            Negligible, Mass.
        </ADDRESS>
        The opinions expressed are mine.
    </BODY>

</HTML>
```

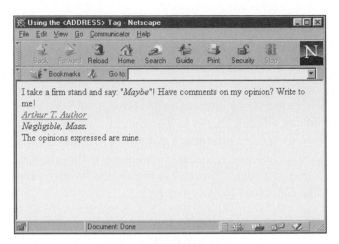

Figure 2.14   Using the **<ADDRESS>** tag.

The results of this code appear in Figure 2.14. As you can see, the address text has been set off in its own paragraph.

<BDO>—Overriding The Bidirectional Character Algorithm

Purpose: Overrides the direction in which text is to be read, so the browser can render text from different languages satisfactorily.

Start Tag/End Tag: Required/Required

Supported: [4, IE5]

Attributes:

- **CLASS**—Class of the element (used for rendering). [3, 4, IE4, IE5]

- **DIR**—Gives the direction of text. Possible values: **LTR**: left-to-right text or table and **RTL**: right-to-left text or table. [4, IE5]

- **ID**—Unique alphanumeric identifier for the tag, which you can use to refer to it. [3, 4, IE4, IE5]

- **LANG**—Base language used for the tag. [3, 4, IE4, IE5]

- **LANGUAGE**—String indicating the language or character set used in the **<BDO>** element. Adheres to Request For Comment (RFC) 1766, which is available on the Internet. [4, IE5]

- **STYLE**—Inline style indicating how to render the element. [4, IE3, IE4, IE5]

- **TITLE**—Holds additional information (as might be displayed in tool tips) for the element. [3, 4, IE4, IE5]

"Hm," says the big boss, "as we open up the Arabic and Hebrew markets, we're running into some trouble because those languages are written and read right to left. The problem is that in documents that mix English and those languages, browsers have no idea how to render character combinations, such as some unicode, correctly." "That's no problem," you say, "I can just use the **<BDO>** element to specify the direction of the text." "Great," says the BB, "you've earned a raise." "Really?" you ask. The BB says, "No, not really."

Languages have an inherent directionality, left to right or right to left, but when you mix languages, it can be difficult to specify directionality. That's a problem when working with some special character combinations, such as those that make up symbol sets like unicode. To fix this problem, you can use the **<BDO>** tag, which is implemented in HTML 4 and in Internet Explorer 5. To specify text direction, you set the **DIR** attribute to **RTL** (right to left) or **LTR** (left to right). You can also specify the language used in the **LANGUAGE** attribute, which is a string from the RFC 1766 standard (you can find this on the Internet at **http://info.internet.isi.edu/in-notes/rfc/files/rfc1766.txt/**).

Here's an example in which I'll reverse the direction of one word:

```
<HTML>

    <HEAD>
        <TITLE>
            Using the &lt;BDO&gt; Tag
        </TITLE>
    </HEAD>

    <BODY>
            There's something <BDO DIR="RTL">funny</bdo> going on here!
    </BODY>

</HTML>
```

The result appears in Figure 2.15 in Internet Explorer. The word "funny" has been reversed. Most people won't have a lot of use for this tag unless their text is in a language like Arabic, or they like reversing text.

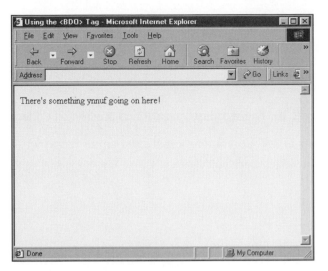

Figure 2.15   Using the **<BDO>** tag.

Displaying Special Characters: Character Entities

"I'm working on my online novel," the novice programmer says, "and I'm having some trouble—the word coöperation keeps coming out as cooperation, no double dots!" "That's an umlaut," you say, "and you can display it using *character entities* in HTML." "Terrific," the NP says, "now I can put the mysterious Monsieur Alphônsé back in the text." "Hm," you say, intrigued.

There are plenty of characters that don't appear on your keyboard you might want to display, such as Greek letters; characters with umlauts, accents, and grave marks; various currency marks; math notation; and more. The W3C has added many of these as *character entities* to HTML. The term character entity comes from SGML (Standard Generalized Markup Language), which calls such codes *entities*; W3C calls them *character encodings*.

A character entity has this format: ***&name;***. Here, ***name*** is the name of the entity. You can also specify a character entity with its number, like this: ***&#number;***. For example, the character entity for ö is ***ö*** so you could place that character in your page like this:

```
<HTML>
    <HEAD>
        <TITLE>
            Using Character Entities
        </TITLE>
    </HEAD>
```

```
<BODY>
    "Thanks for the co&ouml;peration," Jed said grimly to
    the trembling criminal.
</BODY>
</HTML>
```

The result appears in Figure 2.16. The word coöperation is spelled as coded.

The **ö** entity's number is 246, so you can create the same result with this HTML:

```
<HTML>
    <HEAD>
        <TITLE>
            Using Character Entities
        </TITLE>
    </HEAD>

    <BODY>
        "Thanks for the co&#246;peration," Jed said grimly to
        the trembling criminal.
    </BODY>
</HTML>
```

You may have seen Scandinavian, French, or German characters in Web pages, and now you know how it's done. The complete list of character entities in HTML 4 appears in Table 2.2, and although it's long, it's worth taking a look at the list to become familiar with it. When you want to display a special character and don't know how to do it, one of the first things you should consider are character entities.

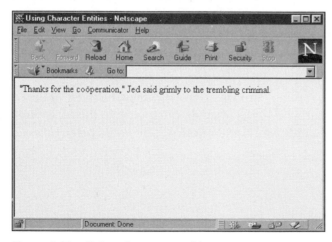

Figure 2.16   Using character entities.

TIP: *In some cases, you can skip the final semicolon in a character entity, but I don't recommend it. The final semicolon is necessary if you want to embed a character entity in the middle of a word, for example, but not when the next character is a space. Because it's so easy to forget the semicolon if you start alternating between using them and not, I recommend that you always use it.*

Table 2.2   Character entities for HTML 4 (note that support varies by browser).

Entity	Numerical	Does This
Aacute	&#193;	Latin capital letter A with acute
aacute	&#225;	Latin small letter a with acute
Acirc	&#194;	Latin capital letter A with circumflex
acirc	&#226;	Latin small letter a with circumflex
acute	&#180;	Acute accent
AElig	&#198;	Latin capital letter AE
aelig	&#230;	Latin small letter ae
Agrave	&#192;	Latin capital letter A with grave
agrave	&#224;	Latin small letter a with grave
alefsym	&#8501;	Alef symbol = first transfinite cardinal
Alpha	&#913;	Greek capital letter alpha
alpha	&#945;	Greek small letter alpha
amp	&#38;	Ampersand
and	&#8743;	Logical and
ang	&#8736;	Angle
Aring	&#197;	Latin capital letter A with ring above
aring	&#229;	Latin small letter a with ring above
asymp	&#8776;	Almost equal to = asymptotic to
Atilde	&#195;	Latin capital letter A with tilde
atilde	&#227;	Latin small letter a with tilde
Auml	&#196;	Latin capital letter A with diaeresis (umlaut)
auml	&#228;	Latin small letter a with diaeresis
bdquo	&#8222;	Double low-9 quotation mark
Beta	&#914;	Greek capital letter beta
beta	&#946;	Greek small letter beta
brvbar	&#166;	Broken bar = broken vertical bar
bull	&#8226;	Bullet = black small circle

(continued)

Table 2.2   Character entities for HTML 4 (note that support varies by browser) (continued).

Entity	Numerical	Does This
cap	&#8745;	Intersection = cap
Ccedil	&#199;	Latin capital letter C with cedilla
ccedil	&#231;	Latin small letter c with cedilla
cedil	&#184;	Cedilla
cent	&#162;	Cent sign
Chi	&#935;	Greek capital letter chi
chi	&#967;	Greek small letter chi
circ	&#710;	Modifier letter circumflex accent
clubs	&#9827;	Black club suit = shamrock
cong	&#8773;	Approximately equal to
copy	&#169;	Copyright sign
crarr	&#8629;	Downwards arrow with corner leftwards
cup	&#8746;	Union = cup
curren	&#164;	Currency sign
Dagger	&#8225;	Double dagger
dagger	&#8224;	Dagger
dArr	&#8659;	Downwards double arrow
darr	&#8595;	Downwards arrow
deg	&#176;	Degree sign
Delta	&#916;	Greek capital letter delta
delta	&#948;	Greek small letter delta
diams	&#9830;	Black diamond suit
divide	&#247;	Division sign
Eacute	&#201;	Latin capital letter E with acute
eacute	&#233;	Latin small letter e with acute
Ecirc	&#202;	Latin capital letter E with circumflex
ecirc	&#234;	Latin small letter e with circumflex
Egrave	&#200;	Latin capital letter E with grave
egrave	&#232;	Latin small letter e with grave
empty	&#8709;	Empty set = null set = diameter
emsp		Em space

(continued)

Table 2.2   Character entities for HTML 4 (note that support varies by browser) (continued).

Entity	Numerical	Does This
ensp		En space
Epsilon	&#917;	Greek capital letter epsilon
epsilon	&#949;	Greek small letter epsilon
equiv	&#8801;	Identical to
Eta	&#919;	Greek capital letter eta
eta	&#951;	Greek small letter eta
ETH	&#208;	Latin capital letter ETH
eth	&#240;	Latin small letter eth
Euml	&#203;	Latin capital letter E with diaeresis (umlaut)
euml	&#235;	Latin small letter e with diaeresis
euro	&#8364;	Euro sign
exist	&#8707;	There exists
fnof	&#402;	Latin small f with hook = function
forall	&#8704;	For all
frac12	&#189;	Vulgar fraction one half
frac14	&#188;	Vulgar fraction one quarter
frac34	&#190;	Vulgar fraction three quarters
frasl	&#8260;	Fraction slash
Gamma	&#915;	Greek capital letter gamma
gamma	&#947;	Greek small letter gamma
ge	&#8805;	Greater-than or equal to
gt	&#62;	Greater-than sign
hArr	&#8660;	Left right double arrow
harr	&#8596;	Left right arrow
hearts	&#9829;	Black heart suit = valentine
hellip	&#8230;	Horizontal ellipsis = three dot leader
Iacute	&#205;	Latin capital letter I with acute
iacute	&#237;	Latin small letter i with acute
Icirc	&#206;	Latin capital letter I with circumflex
icirc	&#238;	Latin small letter i with circumflex
iexcl	&#161;	Inverted exclamation mark

(continued)

Table 2.2   Character entities for HTML 4 (note that support varies by browser) (continued).

Entity	Numerical	Does This
Igrave	Ì	Latin capital letter I with grave
igrave	ì	Latin small letter i with grave
image	ℑ	Blackletter capital I = imaginary part
infin	∞	Infinity
int	∫	Integral
Iota	Ι	Greek capital letter iota
iota	ι	Greek small letter iota
iquest	¿	Inverted question mark
isin	∈	Element of
Iuml	Ï	Latin capital letter I with diaeresis (umlaut)
iuml	ï	Latin small letter i with diaeresis
Kappa	Κ	Greek capital letter kappa
kappa	κ	Greek small letter kappa
Lambda	Λ	Greek capital letter lambda
lambda	λ	Greek small letter lambda
lang	〈	Left-pointing angle bracket = bra
laquo	«	Left-pointing double angle quotation mark
lArr	⇐	Leftwards double arrow
larr	←	Leftwards arrow
lceil	⌈	Left ceiling = apl upstile
ldquo	“	Left double quotation mark
le	≤	Less-than or equal to
lfloor	⌊	Left floor = apl downstile
lowast	∗	Asterisk operator
loz	◊	Lozenge
lrm	‎	Left-to-right mark
lsaquo	‹	Single left-pointing angle quotation mark
lsquo	‘	Left single quotation mark
lt	<	Less-than sign
macr	¯	Macron = spacing macron
mdash	—	Em dash

(continued)

Table 2.2   *Character entities for HTML 4 (note that support varies by browser)* (continued).

Entity	Numerical	Does This
micro	µ	Micro sign
middot	·	Middle dot
minus	−	Minus sign
Mu	Μ	Greek capital letter mu
mu	μ	Greek small letter mu
nabla	∇	Nabla = backward difference
nbsp		No-break space = nonbreaking space
ndash	–	En dash
ne	≠	Not equal to
ni	∋	Contains as member
not	¬	Not sign
notin	∉	Not an element of
nsub	⊄	Not a subset of
Ntilde	Ñ	Latin capital letter N with tilde
ntilde	ñ	Latin small letter n with tilde
Nu	Ν	Greek capital letter nu
nu	ν	Greek small letter nu
Oacute	Ó	Latin capital letter O with acute
oacute	ó	Latin small letter o with acute
Ocirc	Ô	Latin capital letter O with circumflex
ocirc	ô	Latin small letter o with circumflex
OElig	Œ	Latin capital ligature OE
oelig	œ	Latin small ligature oe
Ograve	Ò	Latin capital letter O with grave
ograve	ò	Latin small letter o with grave
oline	‾	Overline = spacing overscore
Omega	Ω	Greek capital letter omega
omega	ω	Greek small letter omega
Omicron	Ο	Greek capital letter omicron
omicron	ο	Greek small letter omicron
oplus	⊕	Circled plus = direct sum

(continued)

Table 2.2   Character entities for HTML 4 (note that support varies by browser) (continued).

Entity	Numerical	Does This
or	∨	Logical or = vee
ordf	ª	Feminine ordinal indicator
ordm	º	Masculine ordinal indicator
Oslash	Ø	Latin capital letter O with stroke
oslash	ø	Latin small letter o with stroke
Otilde	Õ	Latin capital letter O with tilde
otilde	õ	Latin small letter o with tilde
otimes	⊗	Circled times = vector product
Ouml	Ö	Latin capital letter O with diaeresis (umlaut)
ouml	ö	Latin small letter o with diaeresis
para	¶	Pilcrow sign
part	∂	Partial differential
permil	‰	Per mille sign
perp	⊥	Up tack = orthogonal to = perpendicular
Phi	Φ	Greek capital letter phi
phi	φ	Greek small letter phi
Pi	Π	Greek capital letter pi
pi	π	Greek small letter pi
piv	ϖ	Greek pi symbol
plusmn	±	Plus-minus sign
pound	£	Pound sign
Prime	″	Double prime = seconds = inches
prime	′	Prime = minutes = feet
prod	∏	N-ary product = product sign
prop	∝	Proportional to
Psi	Ψ	Greek capital letter psi
psi	ψ	Greek small letter psi
quot	"	Quotation mark = APL quote
radic	√	Square root = radical sign
rang	〉	Right-pointing angle bracket = ket
raquo	»	Right-pointing double angle quotation mark

(continued)

Table 2.2   Character entities for HTML 4 (note that support varies by browser) **(continued).**

Entity	Numerical	Does This
rArr	⇒	Rightwards double arrow
rarr	→	Rightwards arrow
rceil	⌉	Right ceiling
rdquo	”	Right double quotation mark
real	ℜ	Blackletter capital R = real part symbol
reg	®	Registered sign
rfloor	⌋	Right floor
Rho	Ρ	Greek capital letter rho
rho	ρ	Greek small letter rho
rlm	‏	Right-to-left mark
rsaquo	›	Single right-pointing angle quotation mark
rsquo	’	Right single quotation mark
sbquo	‚	Single low-9 quotation mark
Scaron	Š	Latin capital letter S with caron
scaron	š	Latin small letter s with caron
sdot	⋅	Dot operator
sect	§	Section sign
shy	­	Soft hyphen
Sigma	Σ	Greek capital letter sigma
sigma	σ	Greek small letter sigma
sigmaf	ς	Greek small letter final sigma
sim	∼	Tilde operator
spades	♠	Black spade suit
sub	⊂	Subset of
sube	⊆	Subset of or equal to
sum	∑	N-ary sumation
sup	⊃	Superset of
sup1	¹	Superscript one
sup2	²	Superscript two
sup3	³	Superscript three
supe	⊇	Superset of or equal to

(continued)

Table 2.2   Character entities for HTML 4 (note that support varies by browser) (continued).

Entity	Numerical	Does This
szlig	&#223;	Latin small letter sharp s
Tau	&#932;	Greek capital letter tau
tau	&#964;	Greek small letter tau
there4	&#8756;	Therefore
Theta	&#920;	Greek capital letter theta
theta	&#952;	Greek small letter theta
thetasym	&#977;	Greek small letter theta symbol
thinsp		Thin space
THORN	&#222;	Latin capital letter THORN
thorn	&#254;	Latin small letter thorn
tilde	&#732;	Small tilde
times	&#215;	Multiplication sign
trade	&#8482;	Trade mark sign
Uacute	&#218;	Latin capital letter U with acute
uacute	&#250;	Latin small letter u with acute
uArr	&#8657;	Upwards double arrow
uarr	&#8593;	Upwards arrow
Ucirc	&#219;	Latin capital letter U with circumflex
ucirc	&#251;	Latin small letter u with circumflex
Ugrave	&#217;	Latin capital letter U with grave
ugrave	&#249;	Latin small letter u with grave
uml	&#168;	Diaeresis (umlaut)
upsih	&#978;	Greek upsilon with hook symbol
Upsilon	&#933;	Greek capital letter upsilon
upsilon	&#965;	Greek small letter upsilon
Uuml	&#220;	Latin capital letter U with diaeresis (umlaut)
uuml	&#252;	Latin small letter u with diaeresis
weierp	&#8472;	Script capital P = power set
Xi	&#926;	Greek capital letter xi
xi	&#958;	Greek small letter xi
Yacute	&#221;	Latin capital letter Y with acute

(continued)

Table 2.2   Character entities for HTML 4 (note that support varies by browser) (continued).

Entity	Numerical	Does This
yacute	ý	Latin small letter y with acute
yen	¥	Yen sign = yuan sign
Yuml	Ÿ	Latin capital letter Y with diaeresis (umlaut)
yuml	ÿ	Latin small letter y with diaeresis
Zeta	Ζ	Greek capital letter zeta
zeta	ζ	Greek small letter zeta
zwj	‍	Zero width joiner
zwnj	‌	Zero width nonjoiner

Chapter 3

Presenting And Arranging Text

In Depth

The previous chapter was all about using HTML to set text styles, and this chapter is all about the other aspect of working with text—placing and arranging text on the page. In this chapter, we're going to start structuring what goes where in a Web page, which is vitally important to the success of your page. We'll use HTML tags to arrange text into paragraphs and layers, add breaks and margins, set text alignment, create scrolling "marquee" style text, overlap text, and more. This is where we actually start to structure Web pages visually.

Arranging Text

A great deal of designing and creating Web pages is subjective—there's no firm set of rules. Like any visual art, it takes practice and a good feel for aesthetics; some people don't have it and some (like you!) do. I'll talk about some of the subjective elements of Web page design throughout the book, but for now, it's worth noting that the subject matter of this chapter—how and where you place text in a page—has a lot to do with how well your Web page "works."

If we just stopped with the text handling discussed in Chapter 2, we'd be in trouble. That chapter was all about text styles, not presenting text in Web pages. Without adding any structure to the text, Web browsers would take the text and wrap it into a single paragraph ignoring the line breaks you've put in, unless you've also added tags like **<P>** and **
**. There's nothing that makes a Web page more impenetrable than displaying a simple, long block of text.

When it comes to reading Web pages, people have notoriously short attention spans. The back button is in easy reach of the mouse, and with all the multimedia elements flashing at them, people expect something that'll reach out and grab them. For that reason, it can be very important to arrange your text to avoid monolithic blocks. In fact, this is one of the skills that computer book authors are supposed to master, so I'll add a new heading right now to break things up a little.

Breaking Text Up With Headings

A heading does more than just break the text up and avoid monolithic blocks of unremitting words—it also makes the structure of your document evident at a glance. Just by observing the headings in your page, the reader will be able to follow the structure. Headings will periodically remind the reader of what you're doing and where you're directing them.

Using headings is one way to make your document come alive to your readers, allowing them to see the structure and make a decision about reading it. Newspapers use headlines for the same effect. Another popular technique, used primarily in magazines, is to repeat pivotal sentences in blocks of larger type so the readers can view "outtakes" from the text and decide whether the topic interests them.

In general, if you want to catch the audience's attention, it's a good idea to break pages of text into a number of elements. In addition to applying headings, you can also use tips and notes of the kind you see in this book.

TIP: *A hobby of mine is writing and designing advertising for computer book publishers because it's challenging to pack as much as you can into just a few powerful sentences. It's become axiomatic in the advertising world that what attracts a reader's eye to an ad is not the elements of the ad itself, but the white space around the elements in the ad. The idea is that the eye naturally moves to the part of a page that is different—away from big blocks of text. However, this advertising technique has become overrated. One fact is very clear: Overcrowded Web pages do turn readers off.*

Using Paragraphs And Line Breaks

Besides making the structure of your document stand out with headings, you can also separate text with paragraphs and line breaks. It's best to avoid long paragraphs (unless you're a government agency or graduate school instructor and have a captive audience). Because the reader takes a mental breath at the end of each paragraph, similar to finishing a sentence when speaking, shorter paragraphs can help accelerate the reading pace.

The two HTML tags you should use are the **<P>** for paragraph and **
** for break. Some HTML authors think these tags are more or less interchangeable, but they're quite different. The **
** tag allows you to skip to the next line of text and the **<P>** tag starts a new paragraph, which means that the browser will skip some additional vertical space. Here's an example showing both the **<P>** and **
** tags at work:

```
<HTML>
    <HEAD>
        <TITLE>
            Using the &lt;BR&gt; and &lt;P&gt; tags.
        </TITLE>
    </HEAD>

    <BODY>
        Here's a line of text.
        <BR>
        Using the &lt;BR&gt; tag skips to the next line.
        <P>
```

```
            On the other hand, using the &lt;P&gt; tag
            starts a new paragraph.
        </BODY>
</HTML>
```

You can see the result in Figure 3.1. Note that the **
** tag simply made the browser skip to the next line, much like pressing the Enter key in a word processor. The **<P>** tag made the browser skip some additional vertical space to start a new paragraph, much like pressing the Enter key a second time.

There's another big difference between the **<P>** and **
** tags; the **
** element is empty and does not enclose any text (you use **
** by itself), whereas the **<P>** element is a true HTML element that does enclose text. HTML authors often forget the fact that the **<P>** element creates a true paragraph because you can skip the closing **</P>** tag, making this tag seem like the **
** tag. Here's an example that shows the full structure of the **<P>** element complete with closing tag. In this case, I'm emphasizing that the **<P>** tag sets the style of the following paragraph by using the tag's **ALIGN** attribute to center the text in the paragraph:

```
<HTML>
    <HEAD>
        <TITLE>
            Using the &lt;BR&gt; and &lt;P&gt; tags.
        </TITLE>
    </HEAD>

    <BODY>
        Here's a line of text.
        <BR>
        Using the &lt;BR&gt; tag skips to the next line.
        <P ALIGN=CENTER>
        On the other hand, using the &lt;P&gt; tag
        starts a new paragraph.
        </P>
    </BODY>
</HTML>
```

The results appear in Figure 3.2, where you can see that the text I've put into the paragraph is indeed centered. The **<P>** element does set the style for its enclosed text, so it differs substantially from the simple **
** tag.

Aligning text, dividing text into paragraphs, and using other visual elements are a big part of what HTML is all about and what it is designed to do. Here's an

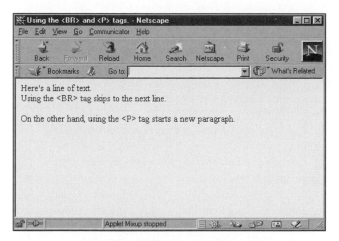

Figure 3.1   Using the **
** and **<P>** tags.

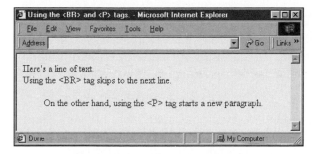

Figure 3.2   Using the **<P>** element to align text.

example showing the difference that arranging text in a Web page can make. The Web page doesn't look too bad here with the text arranged into paragraphs:

```
<HTML>
    <HEAD>
        <TITLE>
            European Train Travel
        </TITLE>
    </HEAD>

    <BODY>
            So, you've decided to take the train in Europe!
        Congratulations, you're in for a great time. There are
        a few things you should know that will make
        things a lot easier.
```

```
            Many train stations are packed with crowds, especially
        in the summer, and you can save yourself a great deal of
        time waiting in lines that can last an hour or more by
        getting a complete train schedule, such as Thomas Cook's
        European Timetable. With a complete train schedule, you'll
        also become the most popular person in the youth hostel.

            In larger stations, you'll find a diagram showing where
        each wagon of the train will stop, so if you have a
        reservation for a specific wagon, you can wait in the right
        place with your luggage.

            Check the destination of the train, the class of the wagon, and
        whether it's a smoking or non-smoking wagon before getting on. This
        information is displayed on a plaque on the wagon.
    </BODY>
</HTML>
```

However, the result in a Web browser is pretty catastrophic, as you see in Figure 3.3. The Web browser has taken the carefully formatted text and lumped it all together. The result is one solid mass of text. Imagine how uninviting 20 pages of the same would be.

Arranging the text and using headings, paragraphs, margins, alignments, and other visual elements as we'll do in this chapter, is what text handling in HTML is all about and exactly what HTML was originally designed to do. Here's an example using HTML formatting tags to present the same text in a better way:

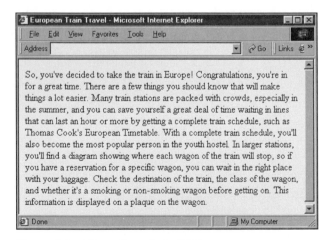

Figure 3.3   First attempt at a Web page.

```
<HTML>
    <HEAD>
        <TITLE>
            European Train Travel
        </TITLE>
    </HEAD>

    <BODY>
        <H1>
            European Train Travel
        </H1>
        So you've decided to take the train in Europe!
        Congratulations, you're in for a great time. There are
        a few things you should know that will make
        things a lot easier. Here's an overview:
        <UL>
            <LI>Getting Train Times
            <LI>Getting On The Train
            <LI>Handling Security
        </UL>

        <H2>
            Getting Train Times
        </H2>
        Many train stations are packed with crowds, especially in
        the summer, and you can save yourself a great deal of time
        waiting in lines that can last an hour or more by getting
        a complete train schedule, such as Thomas Cook's European
        Timetable.
        <P>
        <TABLE BGCOLOR="#d0d0d0">
            <TR>
                <TD>
                    TIP: With a complete train schedule, you'll
                    also become the most popular person in
                    the youth hostel.
                </TD>
            </TR>
        </TABLE>
        <H2>
            Getting On The Train
        </H2>
        In larger stations, you'll find a diagram showing where
        each wagon of the train will stop so if you have a
        reservation for a specific wagon, you can wait in the right
        place with your luggage.
```

```
<P>
Check the destination of the train, the class of the wagon, and
whether it's a smoking or non-smoking wagon before getting on. This
information is displayed on a plaque on the wagon.
    </BODY>
</HTML>
```

In this new page, I've added headings and broken up the text as well as used a bulleted list, which we'll see how to do in Chapter 5, and taken advantage of the fact that you can set the background color of cells in a table to create a plausible style for tips as you see in Figure 3.4. The result is much more accessible than the page shown in Figure 3.3.

Using <DIV> And <SPAN>

Two important formatting elements are the **<DIV>** and **<SPAN>** elements. These elements will become very useful when working with style sheets. Using **<DIV>** (which stands for division) and **<SPAN>**, you can specify a range of text and style it as you want it.

Earlier, we discussed using the **<P>** element to set the style for a paragraph of text, but you may not want to break your text into HTML style paragraphs. For

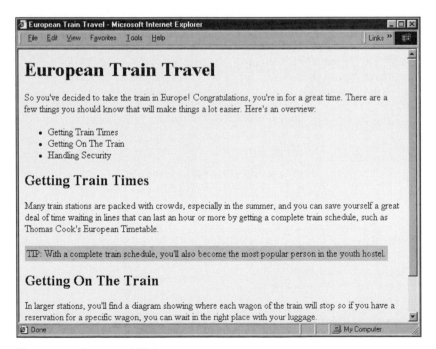

Figure 3.4   Improved Web page.

that reason, HTML includes tags, like **<DIV>** and **<SPAN>**, which let you select the text you want to work with.

You normally use **<DIV>** to select a block of text and **<SPAN>** to select text inline. Here's an example using the **<DIV>** tag with its **ALIGN** parameter to set the alignment of text without using the **<P>** tag:

```
<HTML>
    <HEAD>
        <TITLE>
            Using the &lt;DIV&gt; tag
        </TITLE>
    </HEAD>

    <BODY>

        <DIV ALIGN="LEFT">
            Manager
            <BR>
            SlowPoke Products, Inc.
            <BR>
            Languid, TX
        </DIV>

        <P>
            Dear You:
        <DIV ALIGN="CENTER" STYLE="color: red; font-style: italic">
            When are you going to ship my order?
        </DIV>

        <DIV ALIGN="RIGHT">
            <P>
            President
            <BR>
            NeedItNow, Inc.
            <BR>
            Speedy, CO
        </DIV>

    </BODY>
</HTML>
```

The results appear in Figure 3.5. As you can see in the figure, I've justified whole sections of text as I want them. The **<DIV>** tag really shines when you use styles

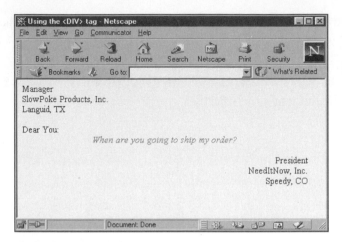

Figure 3.5   Using the **<DIV>** tag.

with it. In the previous HTML, I set the style of the middle **<DIV>** element to display its text in red italics. Using **<DIV>**, you can style whole blocks of text that even contain other HTML elements. This gives you a flexible way of applying styles as we'll see when working with style sheets.

On the other hand, you can use the **<SPAN>** tag to mark sections of text inline or text in the midst of other text. This lets you apply styles in a very precise way, like this:

```
<HTML>
    <HEAD>
        <TITLE>
            Using the &lt;SPAN&gt; tag
        </TITLE>
    </HEAD>

    <BODY>
        This is <SPAN STYLE="font-style: italic">not</SPAN> going to do!
    </BODY>
</HTML>
```

The result of this HTML appears in Figure 3.6. As you can see, working with **<DIV>** and **<SPAN>** is one step up from using a simple **<P>** tag to enclose text. These two tags will become more important as we progress through the book. The possibilities of arranging text using **<DIV>** and **<SPAN>** are endless—in fact, we'll even see how to display overlapping text with these elements.

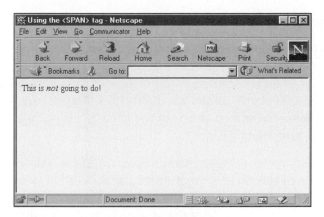

Figure 3.6   Using the **<SPAN>** tag.

Using Layers

One relatively new way of arranging text and other elements in Netscape Navigator (not in Internet Explorer) is to use *layers*. You can divide the display in the browser into successive layers stacked one on top of the other, and you can move these layers.

Because text in a layer is confined to that layer, you can arrange it on top of other layers. In fact, you can specify exactly where each layer is to be placed on the page, so you can create justified text, columns of text, and overlapping text using layers. I'll introduce Netscape Navigator layers in this chapter, giving you a taste of what's to come.

Similar to <**DIV**> and <**SPAN**>, using layers is a powerful technique that we'll explore in a number of places in the book. In particular, layers are accessible to scripting and therefore have become an important part of dynamic HTML.

More Formatting Power

In addition to the aforementioned HTML elements, there is much more coming up in this chapter: visual elements, like *horizontal rules*, which are horizontal lines that you use to break text into sections; Internet Explorer marquees, which let you display text that scrolls across the page; *spacers* that let you set aside some horizontal and vertical space; multiple columns in Netscape Navigator; HTML tables to structure text; and much more. Don't forget—a great deal of HTML is about letting the Web browser know how you want to format a page. I'll give you a guided tour of these elements and structures in the Immediate Solutions section.

Preformatting Text

Before getting to the Immediate Solutions section, however, let me mention one very important consideration—formatting and arranging text can be a frustrating process in HTML, especially when you consider that different users have different screen resolutions (800×600 pixels, 1024×768, 1280×1024, and so on). Web browsers are going to make use of screen space in a variety of ways, possibly reducing your hard work to a hopeless hash.

We'll see various ways of dealing with different screen sizes throughout the book. For instance, you'll learn how to specify how much screen space certain elements should cover as a *percentage* of what's available. In the following code example, I'm creating a table that will cover 95 percent of the available display width in the browser:

```
<TABLE NOBORDER CELLPADDING = "4" WIDTH = "95%">
```

Even so, there are times when you'll be tempted to simply throw up your hands and ask why browsers can't just display your text *the way you've entered it*. In fact, they *can*. To display text exactly as entered in a Web page—line breaks and all—you can use the **<PRE>** tag to tell the browser that the text is preformatted, and it should display the text as is.

In this example, I'm creating and displaying a table that I've entered by hand using the **<PRE>** tag to preserve the formatting exactly as I've entered it:

```
<HTML>
    <HEAD>
        <TITLE>
            Using the &lt;PRE&gt; tag
        </TITLE>
    </HEAD>

    <BODY>
        <PRE>
Name                    Email                   extension
--------------------------------------------------------
David           david@starpowder.com            x4849
Sam             sam@starpowder.com              x4850
Nancy           nancy@starpowder.com            x4851
Jennifer        jennifer@starpowder.com         x4852
Marty           marty@starpowder.com            x4853
Frank           frank@starpowder.com            x4854
        </PRE>
    </BODY>
</HTML>
```

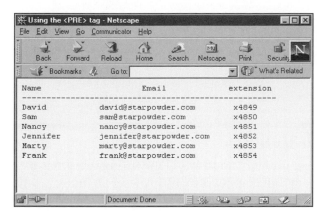

```
Name                 Email                    extension
----------------------------------------------------------------
David                david@starpowder.com       x4849
Sam                  sam@starpowder.com         x4850
Nancy                nancy@starpowder.com       x4851
Jennifer             jennifer@starpowder.com    x4852
Marty                marty@starpowder.com       x4853
Frank                frank@starpowder.com       x4854
```

Figure 3.7   Using preformatted text.

The results of this HTML appear in Figure 3.7. As you can see in the figure, the table in the previous HTML appears in the browser just as I've entered it.

The **<PRE>** tag keeps you from blowing your stack when HTML isn't cooperating, but keep in mind that using it is something of a cop-out. After all, HTML was first invented to help arrange and present text. When you effectively turn browser formatting off, you're turning your back on a lot of power. Still, it's there if you need it, so we'll take a look at it in this chapter.

That's it, then. There's a great deal of text presentation power coming up here, so I'm going to turn to the Immediate Solutions section now and start by taking a look at what happens if you *don't* arrange text the way you want it.

TIP: *In this chapter, you'll start seeing significant differences between the HTML used in Internet Explorer and the HTML used in Netscape Navigator. To handle these discrepancies, you can actually tell what browser the user has and adjust your HTML accordingly. I'll show you how to do this in the Immediate Solutions section "Determining Browser Type In Code" in Chapter 11.*

---

3. Presenting And Arranging Text

Immediate Solutions

Avoiding Plain Text Wrapping

The novice programmer has a problem and says, "I'm writing this great page on train travel and have it all ready, but it appears in my browser all funny." "What do you mean?" you say. "It's all wrapped up into one solid block," the NP says. You smile and say, "Web browsers do that."

The first thing to know about arranging text in a Web page is that Web browsers are going to ignore the line breaks in your page's text (unless you've used a tag, like **<PRE>**, to tell the browser the page is already formatted). We saw this example at the beginning of this chapter:

```
<HTML>
    <HEAD>
        <TITLE>
            European Train Travel
        </TITLE>
    </HEAD>

    <BODY>
            So you've decided to take the train in Europe!
        Congratulations, you're in for a great time. There are
        a few things you should know that will make
        things a lot easier.

            Many train stations are packed with crowds, especially
        in the summer, and you can save yourself a great deal of
        time waiting in lines that can last an hour or more by
        getting a complete train schedule, such as Thomas Cook's
        European Timetable. With a complete train schedule, you'll
        also become the most popular person in the youth hostel.

            In larger stations, you'll find a diagram showing where
        each wagon of the train will stop so if you have a
        reservation for a specific wagon, you can wait in the right
        place with your luggage.
```

```
        Check the destination of the train, the class of the wagon, and
    whether it's a smoking or non-smoking wagon before getting on. This
    information is displayed on a plaque on the wagon.
   </BODY>
</HTML>
```

In the previous code, the text is nicely set in paragraphs, but a Web browser treats line breaks in text as it would any other white space character, such as spaces—it reformats the text. You can see the sad result of this page in Figure 3.3. In fact, the Web browser even changes multiple spaces between words into single spaces, such as those used to indent the text.

So how do you tell a Web browser how to arrange the text the way you want it? That's the job of HTML—just take a look at the following topics.

—Inserting Line Breaks

Purpose: Inserts a line break into a page.

Start Tag/End Tag: Required/Omitted. This element contains no content.

Supported: [2, 3, 3.2, 4, IE1, IE2, IE3, IE4, IE5, NS1, NS2, NS3, NS4]

Attributes:

- **CLASS**—Class of the element (used for rendering). [3, 4, IE4, IE5]
- **CLEAR**—Used to move past aligned images or other elements. Set to **NONE** (the default; just a normal break), **LEFT** (breaks line and moves down until there is a clear left margin past the aligned element), **RIGHT** (breaks line and moves down until there is a clear right margin past the aligned element), or **ALL** (breaks line and moves down until both margins are clear of the aligned element). [3.2, 4, IE1, IE2, IE3, IE4, IE5, NS1, NS2, NS3, NS4]
- **ID**—Unique alphanumeric identifier for the tag, which you can use to refer to it. [3, 4, IE4, IE5]
- **STYLE**—Inline style indicating how to render the element. [4, IE4, IE5]
- **TITLE**—Holds additional information (which might be displayed in tool tips) for the element. [3, 4]

The novice programmer says, "How do I add line breaks to text in a Web page? Browsers seem to treat the line breaks in the actual text as white space, just like space characters." "That's right," you say, "to tell the browser you want to skip to the next line, you use the **
** element."

The **
** element has one use, which is to move to the next line of text. It inserts a line break into your text and is identified by the Web browser much like pressing the Enter key when working with a word processor. Let's review the example from the beginning of the chapter that used the **
** tag:

```
<HTML>
    <HEAD>
        <TITLE>
            Using the &lt;BR&gt; and &lt;P&gt; tags.
        </TITLE>
    </HEAD>

    <BODY>
        Here's a line of text.
        <BR>
        Using the &lt;BR&gt; tag skips to the next line.
        <P>
        On the other hand, using the &lt;P&gt; tag
        starts a new paragraph.
    </BODY>
</HTML>
```

The results of this code appear in Figure 3.1. Using the **
** tag makes the Web browser move to the next line of text.

TIP: *Note that ideally, as with word processors, you're not supposed to insert line breaks directly into your text, but rather break the text up into paragraphs. In HTML, you use the* **P** *tag and let the browser handle breaking the text into lines that match the browser width. That's the reason browsers format text as they do—to work smoothly with the display area available. It's ideal when working with text, but there's no question that* **BR** *comes in handy when working with other elements, like images, to specify that you want each element to be separated vertically.*

This element is an empty element, which means it doesn't take any content. On the other hand, the **
** tag does have attributes, and one attribute in particular is worth mentioning: **CLEAR**. I'll take a closer look at this attribute in Chapter 4 when working with images. **CLEAR** indicates how text should "flow" around images (and around other elements in modern Web pages too).

For example, if I align an image on the left of a page and then type text with line breaks, that text will all appear to the right of the image. However, if I use the line break **<BR CLEAR=LEFT>**, then the next line of text will *appear* after the image, where there's a clear left margin again. Here's an example:

```
<HTML>
    <HEAD>
        <TITLE>
            Using the &lt;BR&gt; tag
        </TITLE>
    </HEAD>

    <BODY>
        <IMG ALIGN=LEFT SRC="image.jpg">
        Here's some text.
        <BR>
        This text is still next to the image.
        <BR>
        <BR>
        <BR>
        <BR>
        <BR>
        <BR>
        <IMG ALIGN=LFFT SRC="image.jpg">
        Here is some new text.
        <BR>
        Now I use the &lt;BR CLEAR=LEFT&gt; tag.
        <BR CLEAR=LEFT>
        This next text starts when there's a clear left margin.
    </BODY>
</HTML>
```

You can see these results in Figure 3.8. Using **<BR CLEAR=LEFT>** makes the next line of text skip past the image to where there's a clear left margin again.

TIP: *In earlier versions of Netscape Navigator, the* **
** *tag skipped some additional vertical space, giving the impression of double spacing. That's been fixed in recent versions.*

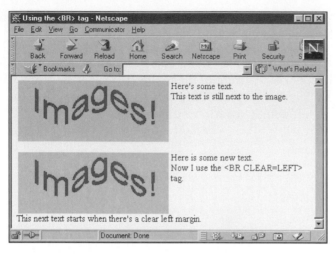

Figure 3.8   Using the **
 CLEAR** attribute.

<NOBR>—Avoiding Line Breaks

Purpose: Tells the browser not to break text into separate lines.

Start Tag/End Tag: Required/Required

Supported: [IE1, IE2, IE3, IE4, IE5, NS1, NS2, NS3, NS4]

Attributes:

- **CLASS**—Class of the element (used for rendering). [IE4, IE5]

- **DIR**—Gives the direction of directionally neutral text (text that doesn't have inherent direction in which you should read it). Possible values: **LTR**: left-to-right text or table and **RTL**: right-to-left text or table. [IE5]

- **ID**—Unique alphanumeric identifier for the tag, which you can use to refer to it. [IE4, IE5]

- **LANG**—Base language used for the tag. [IE4, IE5]

- **LANGUAGE**—Scripting language used for the tag. [IE4, IE5]

Normally, Web browsers take text in a Web page and reformat it to fit the display area they have to work with, including adding line breaks to wrap text as needed. However, there's a way of effectively turning line wrap off. The **<NOBR>** element is not part of the HTML standard, but both Netscape Navigator and Internet Explorer implement it. This tag tells the browser not to introduce line breaks for the text you specify.

Here's an example:

```
<HTML>
    <HEAD>
        <TITLE>
            Using the &lt;NOBR&gt; tag
        </TITLE>
    </HEAD>

    <BODY>
        <NOBR>
            Here's some text in a long line that may
            continue right off the edge of the Web browser's
            available display space.
        </NOBR>
    </BODY>
</HTML>
```

As you can see in Figure 3.9, the result is that the text is displayed in one long line, even though that line extends beyond the browser's display area.

TIP: *It's a good idea to use the **<NOBR>** tag sparingly. Web browsers are designed to format text into the space they have available, and if you change the limits, the results may be unpredictable.*

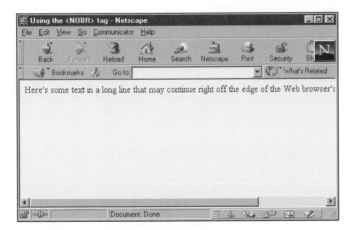

Figure 3.9   Using the **<NOBR>** tag.

\<WBR\>—Allowing Word Breaks

Purpose: Indicates where word breaks are allowed.

Start Tag/End Tag: Required/Omitted. This element contains no content.

Supported: [IE1, IE2, IE3, IE4, IE5, NS1, NS2, NS3, NS4]

Attributes:

- **ID**—Unique alphanumeric identifier for the tag, which you can use to refer to it. [IE4, IE5]

"Hm," says the novice programmer, "I've got a problem—I want to use the **\<NOBR\>** element to avoid letting the browser break my poem into lines, but I also want to specify where breaks should go." "In that case," you say, "you can use the **\<WBR\>** tag to show the browser exactly where line breaks should happen."

The **\<WBR\>** tag tells the browser where a word may be broken at the end of a line, which does not mean it *will* be broken (in fact, most browsers prefer to break lines on word boundaries, preserving whole words, not in the middle of a word). If you use this tag inside an **\<NOBR\>** element, it tells the browser just where line or word breaks should occur.

Here's an example:

```
<HTML>
    <HEAD>
        <TITLE>
            Using the &lt;WBR&gt; tag
        </TITLE>
    </HEAD>

    <BODY>
        <NOBR>
            This is a really, really, really, really long amount of<WBR>
            text, and we only want to let it be broken in one place.
        </NOBR>
    </BODY>
</HTML>
```

<P>—Creating Paragraphs

Purpose: Formats text into a paragraph and adds space before the paragraph.

Start Tag/End Tag: Required/Optional

Supported: [2, 3, 3.2, 4, IE1, IE2, IE3, IE4, IE5, NS1, NS2, NS3, NS4]

Attributes:

- **ALIGN**—Deprecated in HTML 4. Sets the alignment of the text in the paragraph; set to **LEFT** (the default), **RIGHT**, **CENTER**, or **JUSTIFY**. [3, 3.2, 4, IE1, IE2, IE3, IE4, IE5, NS1, NS2, NS3, NS4]

- **CLASS**—Class of the element (used for rendering). [3, 4, IE4, IE5, NS4]

- **DIR**—Gives the direction of directionally neutral text (text that doesn't have inherent direction in which you should read it). Possible values: **LTR**: left-to-right text or table and **RTL**: right-to-left text or table. [4, IE5]

- **ID**—Unique alphanumeric identifier for the tag, which you can use to refer to it. [3, 4, IE4, IE5, NS4]

- **LANG**—Base language used for the tag. [3, 4, IE4, IE5]

- **LANGUAGE**—Scripting language used for the tag. [IE4, IE5]

- **STYLE**—Inline style indicating how to render the element. [4, IE3, IE4, IE5, NS4]

- **TITLE**—Holds additional information (which might be displayed in tool tips) for the element. [3, 4, IE4, IE5]

The **<P>** tag lets you organize your text into *paragraphs*. Paragraphs are relatively rudimentary formatting structures that just refer to blocks of text in which the browser inserts a little vertical space on top to separate them from other elements. Paragraphs in HTML act much like the paragraphs in a word processor. The Web browser formats the text into a paragraph to fit the current page width. You don't have to format your text into paragraphs at all, of course. However, similar to word processors, breaking your documents into paragraphs provides an easy way of formatting your text.

Let's review an HTML example using the **<P>** tag from the beginning of this chapter. Again, note that the end tag **</P>** is optional:

```
<HTML>
    <HEAD>
        <TITLE>
            Using the &lt;BR&gt; and &lt;P&gt; tags.
        </TITLE>
    </HEAD>

    <BODY>
        Here's a line of text.
        <BR>
        Using the &lt;BR&gt; tag skips to the next line.
        <P>
        On the other hand, using the &lt;P&gt; tag
        starts a new paragraph.
    </BODY>
</HTML>
```

You can see the results of this HTML in Figure 3.1 in the In Depth section. Because the **<P>** element is a true HTML element, you can use this tag's attributes to work with the text enclosed in the element. For example, here's how I use the **ALIGN** attribute to center and right justify text:

```
<HTML>
    <HEAD>
        <TITLE>
            Using the &lt;P&gt; tag
        </TITLE>
    </HEAD>

    <BODY>
        <P>
        Here's a standard paragraph. This text is left-aligned.
        <P ALIGN=CENTER>
        Here's a center-aligned paragraph.
        <P ALIGN=RIGHT>
        Here's a right-aligned paragraph.
    </BODY>
</HTML>
```

You can see the result of this HTML in Figure 3.10.

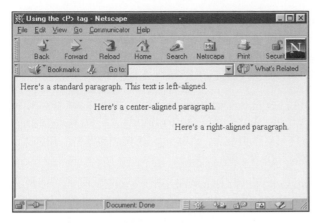

Figure 3.10   Aligning paragraph text.

\<HR\>—Creating Horizontal Rules

Purpose: Draws a horizontal line to separate or group elements vertically.

Start Tag/End Tag: Required/Omitted. This element contains no content.

Supported: [2, 3, 3.2, 4, IE1, IE2, IE3, IE4, IE5, NS1, NS2, NS3, NS4]

Attributes:

- **ALIGN**—Deprecated. Sets alignment of rule, set to **LEFT**, **CENTER** (the default), or **RIGHT**. Note that, if you want to set this attribute, you must also set **WIDTH** attribute. [3.2, 4, IE1, IE2, IE3, IE4, IE5, NS1, NS2, NS3, NS4]

- **CLASS**—Class of the element (used for rendering). [3, 4, IE4, IE5, NS4]

- **COLOR**—Sets the color of the rule. Set to a color value or predefined color. [IE3, IE4, IE5]

- **ID**—Unique alphanumeric identifier for the tag, which you can use to refer to it. [3, 4, IE4, IE5, NS4]

- **NOSHADE**—Deprecated. Renders the rule as two-dimensional, not three-dimensional (the default), in appearance. [3.2, 4, IE1, IE2, IE3, IE4, IE5, NS1, NS2, NS3, NS4]

- **SIZE**—Deprecated. Sets the vertical size of the horizontal rule in pixels. [3.2, 4, IE1, IE2, IE3, IE4, IE5, NS1, NS2, NS3, NS4]

- **STYLE**—Inline style indicating how to render element. [4, IE3, IE4, IE5, NS4]

- **TITLE**—Holds additional information (which might be displayed in tool tips) for the element. [3, 4, IE4, IE5]
- **WIDTH**—Deprecated. Sets horizontal width of rule. Set to actual pixel count or a percentage. [3.2, 4, IE1, IE2, IE3, IE4, IE5, NS1, NS2, NS3, NS4]

Looking over the novice programmer's shoulder, you say, "What are you doing?" "Creating a horizontal line graphic that I can use to divide a Web page's content with," the novice programmer says. "Uh huh," you say, "why don't you just use the **<HR>** element?" The NP says, "The what?"

One easy way to break text vertically is to use horizontal rules by using the **<HR>** element. This is especially useful in longer documents, which Web browsers present as single, monolithic pages that seem to go on forever. A horizontal rule is a horizontal line that serves to break up a page or to group items together.

Here's an example showing a number of ways to display and align horizontal rules. Note that, as with most style attributes, these are officially deprecated in favor of style sheets:

```
<HTML>
    <HEAD>
        <TITLE>
            Using the &lt;HR&gt; tag
        </TITLE>
    </HEAD>

    <BODY>
        Here's what &lt;HR&gt; looks like:
        <HR>
        <BR>
        Here's what &lt;HR ALIGN=LEFT WIDTH=80%&gt; looks like:
        <HR ALIGN=LEFT WIDTH=80%>
        <BR>
        Here's what &lt;HR ALIGN=CENTER WIDTH=80%&gt; looks like:
        <HR ALIGN=CENTER WIDTH=80%>
        <BR>
        Here's what &lt;HR ALIGN=RIGHT WIDTH=80%&gt; looks like:
        <HR ALIGN=RIGHT WIDTH=80%>
        <BR>
        Here's what &lt;HR SIZE=10&gt; looks like:
        <HR ALIGN=CENTER SIZE=10>
        <BR>
        Here's what &lt;HR SIZE=10 NOSHADE&gt; looks like:
        <HR ALIGN=CENTER SIZE=10 NOSHADE>
    </BODY>
</HTML>
```

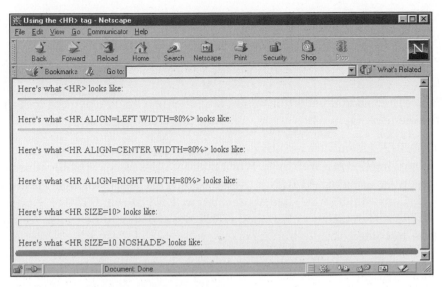

Figure 3.11 Using the **<HR>** element.

You can see the results of this HTML in Figure 3.11, which shows a number of ways to configure horizontal rules. Two more quick notes: To use the **ALIGN** attribute, you must also use the **WIDTH** attribute; and using **<HR>** automatically adds a line break above and below the rule.

<CENTER>—Centering Text

Purpose: Centers its enclosed text in the Web browser. Deprecated in HTML 4.

Start Tag/End Tag: Required/Required

Supported: [3.2, 4, IE1, IE2, IE3, IE4, IE5, NS1, NS2, NS3, NS4]

Attributes:

- **CLASS**—Class of the element (used for rendering). [4, IE4, IE5, NS4]

- **DIR**—Gives the direction of directionally neutral text (text that doesn't have inherent direction in which you should read it). Possible values: **LTR**: left-to-right text or table and **RTL**: right-to-left text or table. [4, IE5]

- **ID**—Unique alphanumeric identifier for the tag, which you can use to refer to it. [4, IE4, IE5, NS4]

- **LANG**—Base language used for the tag. [4, IE4, IE5]

- **LANGUAGE**—Scripting language used for the tag. [IE4, IE5]

- **STYLE**—Inline style indicating how to render the element. [4, IE3, IE4, IE5, NS4]

- **TITLE**—Holds additional information (which might be displayed in tool tips) for the element. [4]

The **<CENTER>** element was introduced by Netscape to fill an early formatting need—centering text in a Web page. Since that time, the same capability has been filled largely by using the **ALIGN** attribute of many HTML elements. The World Wide Web Consortium (W3C) has deprecated **<CENTER>** in HTML 4. Nonetheless, **<CENTER>** remains a cherished HTML tag and should be in use for quite some time to come.

Here's an example of **<CENTER>** at work centering multiline text:

```
<HTML>
    <HEAD>
        <TITLE>
            Using the &lt;CENTER&gt; tag
        </TITLE>
    </HEAD>

    <BODY>
        <CENTER>
            As you can see,
            <BR>
            the &lt;CENTER&gt; tag
            <BR>
            can center multi-line text.
        </CENTER>
    </BODY>
</HTML>
```

You can see the results of this HTML in Figure 3.12.

Because **<CENTER>** was introduced by Netscape and not W3C, the interaction rules for this tag can be different in various browsers. For example, using **<CENTER>** around a table centers the table in some browsers, but centers the text in each table cell in other browsers. It's best to test things out in as many browsers as you can.

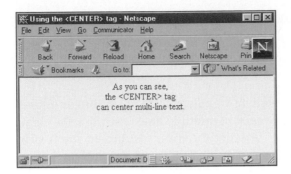

Figure 3.12   Using the <CENTER> tag.

TIP: *Now that the **<CENTER>** tag is deprecated, what should you use to replace it? It turns out that the **<CENTER>** element produces exactly the same effect as using the **<DIV>** element with the **ALIGN** attribute set to **CENTER**. That's what W3C suggests you use.*

<BLOCKQUOTE>—Indenting Quotations

Purpose: Indents and styles text as a quotation. Use for longer, multiline quotations; otherwise use **<Q>**.

Start Tag/End Tag: Required/Required

Supported: [2, 3, 3.2, 4, IE1, IE2, IE3, IE4, IE5, NS1, NS2, NS3, NS4]

Attributes:

- **CITE**—Indicates the source of the quotation. Set to text. [4]
- **CLASS**—Class of the element (used for rendering). [3, 4, IE4, IE5, NS4]
- **DIR**—Gives the direction of directionally neutral text (text that doesn't have inherent direction in which you should read it). Possible values: **LTR**: left-to-right text or table and **RTL**: right-to-left text or table. [4, IE5]
- **ID**—Unique alphanumeric identifier for the tag, which you can use to refer to it. [3, 4, IE4, IE5, NS4]
- **LANG**—Base language used for the tag. [3, 4, IE4, IE5]
- **LANGUAGE**—Scripting language used for the tag. [IE4, IE5]

- **STYLE**—Inline style indicating how to render the element. [4, IE3, IE4, IE5, NS4]

- **TITLE**—Holds additional information (which might be displayed in tool tips) for the element. [3, 4, IE4, IE5]

You use the **<BLOCKQUOTE>** element to indent and set off longer quotations (for shorter quotations that don't consist of multiple lines, use the **<Q>** element). Currently, Netscape Navigator and Internet Explorer just indent the text in the **<BLOCKQUOTE>** element and set it in the default font, but other browsers, like NCSA Mosaic, also set the text in bold.

Here's an example of using the **<BLOCKQUOTE>** element for a longer quotation:

```
<HTML>
    <HEAD>
        <TITLE>
            Using the &lt;BLOCKQUOTE&gt; tag
        </TITLE>
    </HEAD>

    <BODY>
        When it comes to block quotes, W3C says:
        <BLOCKQUOTE>
            We recommend that style sheet implementations provide
            a mechanism for inserting quotation marks before and
            after a quotation delimited by BLOCKQUOTE in a manner
            appropriate to the current language context and the
            degree of nesting of quotations.
            <P>
            However, as some authors have used BLOCKQUOTE merely
            as a mechanism to indent text, in order to preserve
            the intention of the authors, user agents should not
            insert quotation marks in the default style.
        </BLOCKQUOTE>
    </BODY>
</HTML>
```

You can see the results of this HTML in Figure 3.13. Even though the **<BLOCKQUOTE>** tag can be useful, style sheets have become more powerful and allow you to style block quotes to your specification.

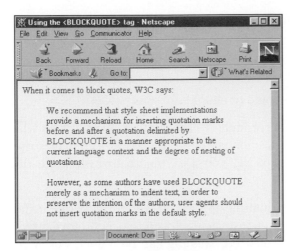

Figure 3.13   Using the <BLOCKQUOTE> tag.

<PRE>—Displaying Preformatted Text

Purpose: Tells the browser that the enclosed text is preformatted and should not be reformatted.

Start Tag/End Tag: Required/Required

Supported: [2, 3, 3.2, 4, IE1, IE2, IE3, IE4, IE5, NS1, NS2, NS3, NS4]

Attributes:

- **CLASS**—Class of the element (used for rendering). [3, 4, IE4, IE5, NS4]

- **COLS**—Indicates the number of columns to use for the text. [NS4]

- **DIR**—Gives the direction of directionally neutral text (text that doesn't have inherent direction in which you should read it). Possible values: **LTR**: left-to-right text or table and **RTL**: right-to-left text or table. [4, IE5]

- **ID**—Unique alphanumeric identifier for the tag, which you can use to refer to it. [3, 4, IE4, IE5, NS4]

- **LANG**—Base language used for the tag. [3, 4, IE4, IE5]

- **LANGUAGE**—Scripting language used for the tag. [IE4, IE5]

- **STYLE**—Inline style indicating how to render the element. [4, IE3, IE4, IE5, NS4]

- **TITLE**—Holds additional information (which might be displayed in tool tips) for the element. [3, 4, IE4, IE5]

- **WIDTH**—Sets the maximum number of characters per line, usually 40, 80, or 132. [2, 3, 3,2, 4]

- **WRAP**—Indicates if the text should or should not wrap. [NS4]

The novice programmer enters screaming, "I can't get it to work!" "Get what to work, NP?" you say. "The company's annual report; there's just no way to do it in HTML, it's too complex!" "Calm down, NP," you say, "you can always use the **<PRE>** tag." "Oh," says the NP.

You can turn off the automatic formatting applied by Web browsers by using the **<PRE>** tag, which tells the browser that the enclosed text is preformatted and should not be interpreted or reformatted. This tag can be a good one if you're stuck in tangles of HTML and want a quick, if somewhat crude, solution because it tells the browser to display the text exactly as is.

Here's an example that we saw in the beginning of this chapter, where I formatted a table for display:

```
<HTML>
    <HEAD>
        <TITLE>
            Using the &lt;PRE&gt; tag
        </TITLE>
    </HEAD>

    <BODY>
        <PRE>
Name                    Email                   extension
- - - - - - - - - - - - - - - - - - - - - - - - - - - - - - - - - - - - - - - - - -
David               david@starpowder.com        x4849
Sam                 sam@starpowder.com          x4850
Nancy               nancy@starpowder.com        x4851
Jennifer            jennifer@starpowder.com     x4852
Marty               marty@starpowder.com        x4853
Frank               frank@starpowder.com        x4854
        </PRE>
    </BODY>
</HTML>
```

The result appears in Figure 3.7. The text is displayed in the Web browser just as I've typed it (note that this includes spaces, so if you don't want your text to appear indented, don't leave leading spaces on the line, remove them as I have done in this code sample).

TIP: *In fact, you can use tags, like **<B>** and **<I>**, to style text inside a **<PRE>** block and the browser will use them. **<PRE>** is usually just used to preserve line breaks and indentation in the original text.*

<MULTICOL>—Creating Columns

Purpose: Breaks text into columns.

Start Tag/End Tag: Required/Required

Supported: [NS3, NS4]

Attributes:

- **COLS**—This required attribute indicates the number of columns you want to break the text into. Set it to a positive integer. [NS3, NS4]

- **GUTTER**—Sets the number of pixels between columns. Set to a positive integer; the default is 10. [NS3, NS4]

- **WIDTH**—Supposed to be the width of each column, actually seems to be the width of all columns plus gutters. The default value is 100 percent of the display width. [NS3, NS4]

The big boss says, "I want you to write the company newspaper. Here's the text." "OK," you say, "I can use the **<MULTICOL>** tag to arrange it in columns, like a newspaper. What's this about how employees are happier if they leave all decisions to upper management?" "Completely true," says the BB, "as studies have shown."

The **<MULTICOL>** tag is a Netscape Navigator-only tag, and as such it's ignored by some HTML resources. However, it exists and can be quite useful. This element arranges its text into columns; you have control over the number of columns, the distance between the columns, and the total width of the result, but not much more. In particular, note that it's up to Netscape Navigator to determine how many lines of text each column will be. It seems to have a proclivity to keep the last column relatively empty and instead adds another line to each column when more text is added.

Here's an example of the **<MULTICOL>** tag at work:

```
<HTML>
    <HEAD>
        <TITLE>
            Using the &lt;MULTICOL&gt; tag
        </TITLE>
    </HEAD>

    <BODY>
        <H1 ALIGN=CENTER>
            Using The &lt;MULTICOL&gt; Tag
        </H1>
        <MULTICOL COLS=3 WIDTH=90% GUTTER=10>
            This text is specifically distributed over
            three columns using the &lt;MULTICOL&gt; tag.
            The &lt;MULTICOL&gt; tag is useful when you
            want to get that "newspaper-like" look, much
            like you see in this case. It's a nice effect
            for some purposes, but not for everybody.
        </MULTICOL>
    </BODY>
</HTML>
```

This HTML is designed to arrange its text into three columns, and as you can see in Figure 3.14, it does just that.

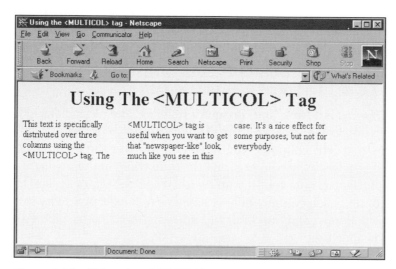

Figure 3.14   Using the **<MULTICOL>** tag.

<SPACER>—Controlling Horizontal And Vertical Spacing

Purpose: Gives you more control over horizontal and vertical spacing.

Start Tag/End Tag: Required/Omitted. This element contains no content.

Supported: [NS3, NS4]

Attributes:

- **ALIGN**—Sets alignment only when the **TYPE** attribute is set to **BLOCK**. Possible values are: **LEFT**, **RIGHT**, **TOP**, **TEXTTOP**, **MIDDLE**, **ABSMIDDLE**, **BASELINE**, **BOTTOM**, and **ABSBOTTOM**. [NS3, NS4]

- **HEIGHT**—Sets the height in pixels of the spacer when the **TYPE** attribute is set to **BLOCK**. [NS3, NS4]

- **SIZE**—Sets the width or height in pixels of the spacer when the **TYPE** attribute is set to **HORIZONTAL** or **VERTICAL**. [NS3, NS4]

- **TYPE**—Sets the type of the spacer. Required attribute. May be **HORIZONTAL**, **VERTICAL**, or **BLOCK**. [NS3, NS4]

- **WIDTH**—Sets the width in pixels of the spacer when the **TYPE** attribute is set to **BLOCK**. [NS3, NS4]

The novice programmer has a problem and says, "Jeez! Isn't there some way to space things the way I want them? I feel like putting in an invisible image of the same color as the background just so I can skip down exactly 100 pixels in my Web page before putting in some text." "There's an easy way to do that," you say, "just use the **<SPACER>** element." The NP says, "Why didn't someone think of this before?"

Web browsers move the elements of your page around to fit the available space. Netscape Navigator actually allows you to create a pseudoelement named a spacer that helps you set the amount of open space around the elements in your page. **<SPACER>** is another of those Netscape Navigator-specific elements that many books omit, but it exists and is useful.

Here's an example. In this case, I'm just creating a spacer 100 pixels high and displaying a line of text right after it:

```
<HTML>
    <HEAD>
        <TITLE>
```

```
            Using the &lt;SPACER&gt; tag
        </TITLE>
    </HEAD>

    <BODY>
        <H1 ALIGN=CENTER>
            Using The &lt;SPACER&gt; Tag
        </H1>
            <SPACER TYPE="VERTICAL" SIZE=100>
            There's an invisible spacer 100 pixels high above this text!
    </BODY>
</HTML>
```

The result of this HTML appears in Figure 3.15. As you can see in the figure, the text has been moved down and starts after the (invisible) spacer.

NOTE: Now that you can use styles to specify text position as well as formatting, it's a better idea to use style sheets instead of spacers.

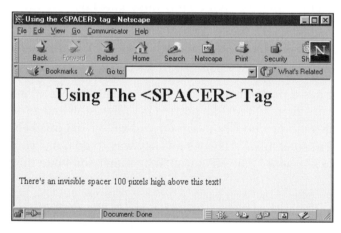

Figure 3.15   Using the **<SPACER>** tag.

<MARQUEE>—Displaying Text In A Scrolling Marquee

Purpose: Displays scrolling text in a "marquee" style.

Start Tag/End Tag: Required/Required

Supported: [IE2, IE3, IE4, IE5]

Attributes:

- **ALIGN**—Sets the alignment of the text relative to the marquee. Set to: **TOP** (the default), **MIDDLE**, or **BOTTOM**. [IE2, IE3, IE4, IE5]

- **BEHAVIOR**—Sets how the text in the marquee should move. Can be: **SCROLL** (the default; text scrolls across the marquee), **SLIDE** (text enters from one side and stops at the other side), or **ALTERNATE** (text seems to bounce from one side to the other). [IE2, IE3, IE4, IE5]

- **BGCOLOR**—Sets the background color for the marquee box. Set to a color value or a predefined color name. [IE2, IE3, IE4, IE5]

- **DIR**—Gives the direction of directionally neutral text (text that doesn't have inherent direction in which you should read it). Possible values: **LTR**: left-to-right text or table and **RTL**: right-to-left text or table. [IE5]

- **DIRECTION**—Sets the direction the text should scroll. Can be: **LEFT** (the default), **RIGHT**, **DOWN**, or **UP**. [IE2, IE3, IE4, IE5]

- **HEIGHT**—Specifies the height of the marquee. The default is the height of the marquee's text. Set to a height in pixels or a percentage of the available display height. [IE2, IE3, IE4, IE5]

- **HSPACE**—Gives the left and right margins outside the marquee. Set to a pixel value (the default is 0). [IE2, IE3, IE4, IE5]

- **LANG**—Base language used for the tag. [IE4, IE5]

- **LANGUAGE**—Scripting language used for the tag. [IE4, IE5]

- **LOOP**—Sets how many times you want the marquee to cycle. Set to a positive integer, or -1 for continuous cycling. [IE2, IE3, IE4, IE5]

- **SCROLLAMOUNT**—Sets the horizontal space between each successive display of the text. Set to pixel values. [IE2, IE3, IE4, IE5]

- **SCROLLDELAY**—Sets the number of milliseconds between each successive display of the text. Set to a positive integer millisecond value. [IE2, IE3, IE4, IE5]

- **STYLE**—Inline style indicating how to render the element. [IE3, IE4, IE5]

- **TITLE**—Holds additional information (which might be displayed in tool tips) for the element. [IE4, IE5]

- **TRUESPEED**—Specifies that exact **SCROLLDELAY** values should be used as given. If you don't use this attribute, values less than 59 are set to 60 milliseconds. Set to **TRUE** or **FALSE** (the default). [IE4, IE5]

- **VSPACE**—Sets the top and bottom spacing margins outside the marquee. Set to a positive pixel value. The default value is 0. [IE2, IE3, IE4, IE5]

3. Presenting And Arranging Text

- **WIDTH**—Sets the width of the marquee; the default value is 100 percent of the available display width. Set to positive integer pixel values or a percentage of the total display width. [IE2, IE3, IE4, IE5]

The novice programmer comes in frowning and says, "I've just got to get their attention." "Whose attention?" you say. "Those mountaineering students that are reading my mountaineering page—I've got to get their attention about the safety warnings, they're dropping off mountains like flies." "Well," you say, "what about the **<MARQUEE>** tag?"

The **<MARQUEE>** element is an Internet Explorer element that displays text in a moving "marquee" (modeled after a moving movie marquee), which can scroll, slide, or bounce in a horizontal strip. It's up to you to set the size of the script in a marquee (similar to **<H1>** or **<H2>** headers). If you don't specify a font, the marquee will use the current default.

Scrolling text (**BEHAVIOR="SCROLL"**) in the marquee does just that—scrolls left to right, top to bottom, or whatever you like by setting the direction with the **DIRECTION** attribute. To make the text keep scrolling, you can set the **LOOP** attribute to a specific value or to **INFINITE** to make it keep scrolling forever. Text that slides (**BEHAVIOR="SLIDE"**) enters from one side, slides to the other, and stays there. It does not repeat, no matter how you use the **LOOP** attribute. Text that bounces (**BEHAVIOR="ALTERNATE"**) moves from one limit and then back to the other, such as left to right and then back. You can make it go on continuously with the **LOOP** attribute.

Here's an example showing various **<MARQUEE>** options at work:

```
<HTML>
   <HEAD>
      <TITLE>
         Using the &lt;MARQUEE&gt; tag
      </TITLE>
   </HEAD>

   <BODY>

      <MARQUEE ALIGN="TOP" LOOP="INFINITE" BEHAVIOR="BOUNCE"
         BGCOLOR="#00FF00" DIRECTION="RIGHT">
         <H2>
            Here's a marquee!
         </H2>
      </MARQUEE>
```

```
<CENTER>
    <H1>
        Using Marquees
    </H1>
</CENTER>

    <MARQUEE ALIGN="LEFT" LOOP="INFINITE" BEHAVIOR="SCROLL"
        BGCOLOR="#FF0000" HEIGHT=40 WIDTH=300 DIRECTION="DOWN">
    <H2>
        Here's another marquee!
    </H2>
    </MARQUEE>

    <MARQUEE ALIGN="TOP" LOOP="INFINITE" BEHAVIOR="SLIDE"
        BGCOLOR="#00FFFF" WIDTH=100% DIRECTION="RIGHT">
    <H2>
        And one more!
    </H2>
    </MARQUEE>

    </BODY>
</HTML>
```

The results of this HTML appear in Figure 3.16.

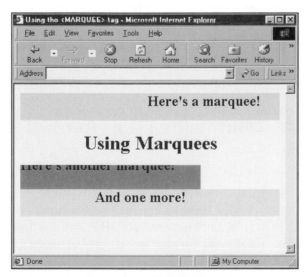

Figure 3.16   Using the **<MARQUEE>** tag.

3. Presenting And Arranging Text

There's no denying the appeal of the **<MARQUEE>** tag for getting attention, but because it's restricted to Internet Explorer, you should be careful before using it. In other browsers, the text in the marquee will simply appear static when displayed.

NOTE: The **<MARQUEE>** tag in Internet Explorer has changed as new versions of the browser have been introduced. For example, versions before Internet Explorer 4 won't understand the **UP** and **DOWN** directions for text.

Note also that there's no easy way to be certain of the speed at which the text in the marquee will travel. You'll have to experiment with the **SCROLLAMOUNT** and **SCROLLDELAY** attributes.

To create a marquee that will work in most browsers, you can use JavaScript instead.

TIP: You can create a multiline marquee with a **<BLOCKQUOTE>** element. You also shouldn't nest **<MARQUEE>** elements. One more tip: If you make the marquee large enough or use multiple marquees next to each other, you can create a striking effect in which the plain text in your Web page appears to be scrolling around by itself.

<DIV>—Formatting Block Text

Purpose: Selects a block of text so you can apply styles.

Start Tag/End Tag: Required/Required

Supported: [3, 3.2, 4, IE3, IE4, IE5, NS2, NS3, NS4]

Attributes:

- **ALIGN**—Deprecated. Sets the horizontal alignment of the element in the page. Set to **LEFT** (the default), **RIGHT**, **CENTER**, or **JUSTIFY**. [3, 3.2, 4, IE3, IE4, IE5, NS2, NS3, NS4]

- **CLASS**—Class of the element (used for rendering). [3, 4, IE4, IE5, NS4]

- **CLEAR**—Used to move past aligned images or other elements. Set to **NONE** (the default; just a normal break), **LEFT** (breaks line and moves down until there is a clear left margin past the aligned element), **RIGHT** (breaks line and moves down until there is a clear right margin past the aligned element), or **ALL** (breaks line and moves down until both margins are clear of the aligned element). [3]

- **DIR**—Gives the direction of directionally neutral text (text that doesn't have inherent direction in which you should read it). Possible values: **LTR**: left-to-right text or table and **RTL**: right-to-left text or table. [4, IE5]

- **ID**—Unique alphanumeric identifier for the tag, which you can use to refer to it. [3, 4, IE4, IE5, NS4]

- **LANG**—Base language used for the tag. [3, 4, IE4, IE5]

- **LANGUAGE**—Scripting language used for the tag. [IE4, IE5]

- **STYLE**—Inline style indicating how to render the element. [4, IE3, IE4, IE5, NS4]

- **TITLE**—Holds additional information (which might be displayed in tool tips) for the element. [3, 4, IE4, IE5]

The **<DIV>** tag provides you with an easy way to refer to a block of text. As discussed at the beginning of this chapter, you can use the **<P>** element to refer to a paragraph of text, but you might not want to divide your document into paragraphs (the type HTML creates, anyway), so you can use the **<DIV>** element instead. Most Web browsers place a line break before and after **<DIV>** elements.

This element is very important when applying styles because you can mark specific blocks of text to apply styles to. We'll discuss more about how this works when we examine styles in Chapter 9. You can also use the attributes of this element to specify attributes of the enclosed text, as you can see in this example from the beginning of the chapter. I use the **<DIV>** element to align text in the page.

NOTE: The **ALIGN** attribute is deprecated in HTML 4, so if you have a style sheet-enabled browser, you might want to switch to style sheets.

```
<HTML>
    <HEAD>
        <TITLE>
            Using the &lt;DIV&gt; tag
        </TITLE>
    </HEAD>

    <BODY>

        <DIV ALIGN="LEFT">
            Manager
            <BR>
            SlowPoke Products, Inc.
            <BR>
            Languid, TX
        </DIV>
```

```
<P>
    Dear You:
<DIV ALIGN="CENTER" STYLE="color: red; font-style: italic">
    When are you going to ship my order?
</DIV>
<DIV ALIGN="RIGHT">
    <P>
    President
    <BR>
    NeedItNow, Inc.
    <BR>
    Speedy, CO
</DIV>
    </BODY>
</HTML>
```

You can see the results of this HTML in Figure 3.5. As you can see, the alignment set in the **<DIV>** element is reflected in the text.

TIP: *In fact, now that the **<CENTER>** tag is deprecated, you're supposed to use a **<DIV>** element with the **ALIGN** attribute set to **CENTER** to replace it.*

You can also position text with the **<DIV>** tag, even overlapping it on the page. See the section "Positioning Text With **<DIV>**" near the end of this chapter. As you'll see in that section, you can use this element to restrict text to a specific rectangular region.

<SPAN>—Formatting Inline Text

Purpose: Selects inline text to let you apply styles.

Start Tag/End Tag: Required/Required

Supported: [4, IE3, IE4, IE5, NS4]

Attributes:

- **CLASS**—Class of the element (used for rendering). [4, IE4, IE5, NS4]
- **DIR**—Gives the direction of directionally neutral text (text that doesn't have inherent direction in which you should read it). Possible values: **LTR**: left-to-right text or table and **RTL**: right-to-left text or table. [4, IE5]

- **ID**—Unique alphanumeric identifier for the tag, which you can use to refer to it. [4, IE4, IE5, NS4]

- **LANG**—Base language used for the tag. [3, 4, IE4, IE5]

- **LANGUAGE**—Scripting language used for the tag. [IE4, IE5]

- **STYLE**—Inline style indicating how to render the element. [4, IE3, IE4, IE5, NS4]

- **TITLE**—Holds additional information (which might be displayed in tool tips) for the element. [4, IE4, IE5]

You can use the **<DIV>** element to select and apply styles to a block of text, but in those cases where you don't have a well-delineated block of text to work with, you can use the **<SPAN>** element to select and apply styles. To clarify—you usually use **<SPAN>** to apply styles inline, for example, in the middle of a sentence. For blocks of text use **<DIV>**, for words or sentences use **<SPAN>**.

In this example, I'm applying a style to a section of text using **<SPAN>**, turning that text red:

```
<HTML>
    <HEAD>
        <TITLE>
            Using the &lt;SPAN&gt; tag
        </TITLE>
    </HEAD>

    <BODY>
        <H2>
            Is my face <SPAN CLASS="redface" STYLE="color: red">red</SPAN>?
        </H2>
    </BODY>
</HTML>
```

You can see the results of this HTML in Figure 3.17. The word "red" appears in red (although in black and white in the figure, of course).

TIP: *Now that the **<FONT>** element is deprecated, the **<SPAN>** element provides a good substitute. Use inline styles to set the font attributes you want, such as we did for Figure 3.17.*

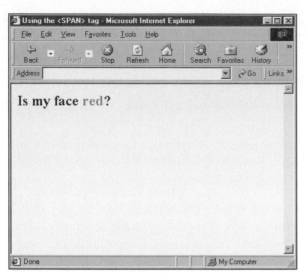

Figure 3.17   Using the **<SPAN>** tag.

Formatting Text With Tables

The novice programmer enters, wailing. "I can't do it! I just can't format this text the way I want it!" "Calm down," you say, "have you tried using tables yet?" "Tables?" the NP says.

One very powerful way to arrange text is with HTML *tables*. Tables were introduced in Netscape Navigator 1.1, implemented in Internet Explorer in version 2, and became standard in HTML 3. Using tables, you can create a grid of cells that displays text and images. Early on, Web page stylists realized that you could turn the border of a table off, making it invisible by using the **NOBORDER** attribute as we'll see in Chapter 6. To their delight, this gave them a way of arranging text into columns and rows on a Web page.

In fact, arranging text using HTML tables is a very common thing to do. And although you can now use the **<DIV>** element to do the same thing (see the section "Positioning Text With **<DIV>**" near the end of this chapter), even the big corporations still use the **<TABLE>** element to arrange text, ensuring that early browsers will know how to handle it. Using **<TABLE>**, you can place text where you want it in a Web page, although it may take some work. For more information on creating tables, see Chapter 6.

As an example, let's say that I want to display a large number of hyperlinks in rows and columns. I can do that using a table and even supply text as a caption, which I can spread over several columns using the **COLSPAN** attribute. Here's how this looks—note how long HTML can get when using tables for even relatively simple tasks:

```
<TABLE NOBORDER CELLPADDING = 4 WIDTH = 95%>
    <TR>
        <TH COLSPAN = 4>
            <H2>
                Travel to these sites around the world
            </H2>
        </TH>
    </TR>
    <TR>
        <TH COLSPAN = 4>
            Ever been to a site in Kenya? Russia? China?
            You can travel to those countries now, because
            each tour below is actually at a site in the
            country it describes! <I>Bon Voyage...</I>
        </TH>
    </TR>
    <TR ALIGN = CENTER>
        <TD>
            <A HREF = "http://www.secyt.gov.ar/arg/introi.html">
                Argentina
            </A>
        </TD>
        <TD>
            <A HREF = "http://www.telstra.com.au/meta/australia.html">
                Australia
            </A>
        </TD>
        <TD>
            <A HREF = "http://croco.atnet.at/tourism">
                Austria
            </A>
        </TD>
        <TD>
            <A HREF = "http://canada.gc.ca/canadiana/cdaind_e.html">
                Canada
            </A>
        </TD>
    </TR>
    <TR ALIGN = CENTER>
        <TD>
```

```
                    <A HREF = "http://sunsite.dcc.uchile.cl/chile/chile.html">
                        Chile
                    </A>
                </TD>
                <TD>
                    <A HREF = "http://www.ihep.ac.cn/tour/china_tour.html">
                        China
                    </A>
                </TD>
                <TD>
                    <A HREF = "http://www.ciesin.ee/ESTCG/">
                        Estonia
                    </A>
                </TD>
                <TD>
                    <A HREF = "http://www.csc.fi/tiko/finland.html">
                        Finland
                    </A>
                </TD>
            </TR>
            <TR ALIGN = CENTER>
                <TD>
                    <A HREF = "http://www.iway.fr/internet-way/fr/france">
                        France
                    </A>
                </TD>
                <TD>
                    <A HREF = "http://www.chemie.fu-berlin.de/adressen/brd.html">
                        Germany
                    </A>
                </TD>
                <TD>
                    <A HREF = "http://www.culture.gr/2/21/maps/hellas.html">
                        Greece
                    </A>
                </TD>
                <TD>
                    <A HREF = "http://www.arctic.is">
                        Iceland
                    </A>
                </TD>
            </TR>
            <TR ALIGN = CENTER>
                <TD>
                    <A HREF = "http://slarti.ucd.ie/maps/ireland.html">
```

```
                Ireland
            </A>
        </TD>
        <TD>
            <A HREF = "http://ece.iisc.ernet.in/india.html">
                India
            </A>
        </TD>
        <TD>
            <A HREF = "http://www.travel.it">
                Italy
            </A>
        </TD>
        <TD>
            <A HREF = "http://www.recruit.co.jp/Jjapan">
                Japan
            </A>
        </TD>
    </TR>
    <TR ALIGN = CENTER>
        <TD>
            <A HREF = "http://www.arcc.or.ke">
                Kenya
            </A>
        </TD>
        <TD>
            <A HREF = "http://www.mty.1tesm.mx/MexWeb/Info2/">
                Mexico
            </A>
        </TD>
        <TD>
            <A HREF = "http://www.govt.nz/nzinfo.html">
                New Zealand
            </A>
        </TD>
        <TD>
            <A HREF = "http://info.fuw.edu.pl/pl/poland.html">
                Poland
            </A>
        </TD>
    </TR>
    <TR ALIGN = CENTER>
        <TD>
            <A HREF = "http://indis.ici.ro/romania/romania.html">
                Romania
```

```
                </A>
            </TD>
            <TD>
                <A HREF = "http://www.kiae.su/www/wtr">
                    Russia
                </A>
            </TD>
            <TD>
                <A HREF = "http://www.technet.sg">
                    Singapore
                </A>
            </TD>
            <TD>
                <A HREF = "http://osprey.unisa.ac.za/south-africa/home.html">
                    South Africa
                </A>
            </TD>
        </TR>
        <TR ALIGN = CENTER>
            <TD>
                <A HREF = "http://www.uji.es/spain_www.html">
                    Spain
                </A>
            </TD>
            <TD>
                <A HREF = "http://www.westnet.se/sweden">
                    Sweden
                </A>
            </TD>
            <TD>
                <A HREF = "http://heiwww.unige.ch/switzerland/">
                    Switzerland
                </A>
            </TD>
            <TD>
                <A HREF = "http://www.chiangmai.ac.th/thmap.html">
                    Thailand
                </A>
            </TD>
        </TR>
        <TR ALIGN = CENTER>
            <TD>
                <A HREF = "http://www.rada.kiev.ua/ukraine.htm">
                    Ukraine
                </A>
```

```
        </TD>
        <TD>
            <A HREF = "http://www.cs.ucl.ac.uk/misc/uk/intro">
                United Kingdom
            </A>
        </TD>
        <TD>
            <A HREF = "http://www.zamnet.zm/zamnet/zntb.html">
                Zambia
            </A>
        </TD>
        <TD>
            <A HREF = "http://cy.co.za/atg/stbroz.html">
                Zimbabwe
            </A>
        </TD>
    </TR>
</TABLE>
```

The result of this HTML appears in Figure 3.18. The hyperlinks appear neatly arranged in rows and columns. In addition, the explanatory text appears centered above it.

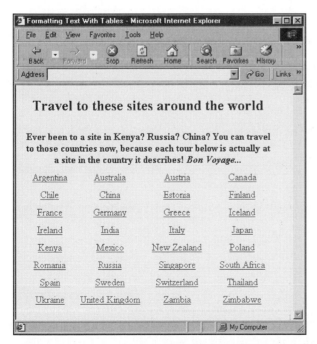

Figure 3.18   Formatting hyperlinks into rows and columns using a table.

You can get more creative, of course, such as flanking an image with two columns of text. Here's a more advanced example that uses the **ROWSPAN** attribute to create a nice effect:

```
<TABLE NOBORDER CELLPADDING = 8 WIDTH = 90%>
    <TR ALIGN = CENTER>
        <TH ROWSPAN = 4>
            <H2>
                High
                <BR>
                culture
                <BR>
                on
                <BR>
                demand!
            </H2>
        </TH>
        <TD>
            Download
            <A HREF="darkness.zip">
                Joseph Conrad's Heart of Darkness
            </A>
        </TD>
    </TR>
    <TR ALIGN = CENTER>
        <TD>
            Listen to some of
            <A HREF = "mozart1.mid">
                Mozart's music
            </A>
        </TD>
    </TR>
    <TR ALIGN = CENTER>
        <TD>
            See a
            <A href="chaplin.html">
                Charlie Chaplin movie
            </A>
        </TD>
    </TR>
</TABLE>
```

The results of this HTML appear in Figure 3.19. As you can see in the figure, you can use tables to format text in a pretty general way.

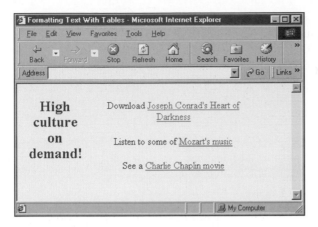

Figure 3.19   Formatting text using a table.

Another popular use of tables is to accentuate Web page elements. Because you can set the background color of the cells in a table, you can surround text in what appear to be colored boxes. I did this earlier in this chapter with this HTML:

```
<HTML>
    <HEAD>
        <TITLE>
            European Train Travel
        </TITLE>
    </HEAD>

    <BODY>
        <H1>
            European Train Travel
        </H1>
        So you've decided to take the train in Europe!
        Congratulations, you're in for a great time. There are
        a few things you should know that will make
        things a lot easier. Here's an overview:
        <UL>
            <LI>Getting Train Times
            <LI>Getting On The Train
            <LI>Handling Security
        </UL>

        <H2>
            Getting Train Times
        </H2>
```

3. Presenting And Arranging Text

```
Many train stations are packed with crowds, especially in
the summer, and you can save yourself a great deal of time
waiting in lines that can last an hour or more by getting
a complete train schedule, such as Thomas Cook's European
Timetable.
<P>
<TABLE BGCOLOR="#d0d0d0">
    <TR>
        <TD>
            TIP: With a complete train schedule, you'll
            also become the most popular person in
            the youth hostel.
        </TD>
    </TR>
</TABLE>
<H2>
    Getting On The Train
</H2>
In larger stations, you'll find a diagram showing where
each wagon of the train will stop so if you have a
reservation for a specific wagon, you can wait in the right
place with your luggage.
<P>
Check the destination of the train, the class of the wagon, and
whether it's a smoking or non-smoking wagon before getting on. This
information is displayed on a plaque on the wagon.
    </BODY>
</HTML>
```

You can see the results of this HTML in Figure 3.4. Tables are good for many text formatting problems—especially when you get creative. However, working with tables can be difficult if you write all the HTML yourself. If you're going to format a great deal of text this way, my advice would be to look into some good HTML editors.

<LAYER>—Arranging Text In Layers

Purpose: Creates a layer with content that can overlap other layers.

Start Tag/End Tag: Required/Required

Supported: [NS4]

Attributes:

- **ABOVE**—Gives the name of the layer that will occur directly above the current layer in the layer z-order (stacking order). Note that only one of these attributes: **Z-INDEX**, **ABOVE**, or **BELOW** can be used for a given layer. Set this attribute to an existing layer **ID** value. [NS4]

- **BACKGROUND**—Indicates a background image to be tiled on the layer (the default for layers is that they are transparent). Set to the image's URL. [NS4]

- **BELOW**—Gives the name of the layer that will occur directly below the current layer in the layer z-order (stacking order). Note that only one of these attributes: **Z-INDEX**, **ABOVE**, or **BELOW** can be used for a given layer. Set this attribute to an existing layer **ID** value. [NS4]

- **BGCOLOR**—Gives the background color of the layer (the default for layers is that they are transparent). Set to a Red, Green, Blue (RGB) color value or a predefined color. [NS4]

- **CLASS**—Class of the element (used for rendering). [NS4]

- **CLIP**—Specifies the viewable area of the layer. Using this attribute, you can set the clipping area to values less than the width and height of the content of the layer. Set this attribute to a comma-separated list of integers specifying the pixel coordinates of the clipping rectangle (**CLIP="100, 100, 400, 400"** or **CLIP="400, 400"**, where the second form relies on the fact that the left and top settings default to 0). Note that the origin is at the top, left corner and pixel values grow moving down and to the right. [NS4]

- **HEIGHT**—Gives the height of the content of the layer and sets up a reference dimension for child layers. Set to positive pixel widths or a percentage of the container. [NS4]

- **ID**—Unique alphanumeric identifier for the tag, which you can use to refer to it. [NS4]

- **LEFT**—Gives the left location of the current layer relative to a parent layer if there is one, or the browser window otherwise. Set to an integer specifying screen position or a scripting expression. [NS4]

- **PAGEX**—Sets the absolute horizontal position of the left boundary of the current layer in relation to the document window. Set to a value giving screen position in pixels or an HTML scripting expression. [NS4]

- **PAGEY**—Sets the absolute vertical position of the top boundary of the current layer in relation to the document window. Set to a value giving screen position in pixels or an HTML scripting expression. [NS4]

- **SRC**—The URL of an HTML document to be inserted in the layer (like using **IFRAME** in Internet Explorer). Set to a URL. [NS4]

- **STYLE**—Inline style indicating how to render the element. [NS4]

- **TOP**—Gives the top location of the current layer relative to a parent layer if there is one, or the browser window otherwise. Set to an integer specifying screen position or a scripting expression. [NS4]

- **VISIBILITY**—Sets whether a layer is visible or not (by default, a layer has the same visibility as its parent layer). Set to: **SHOW** (shows the layer), **HIDE** (hides the layer), or **INHERIT** (giving the layer the same visibility as its parent). For top-level layers without a parent layer, **INHERIT** means the same as **SHOW**. [NS4]

- **WIDTH**—Sets the width of the layer's content, controlling the layer's right margin for wrapping purposes. Set to positive pixel values. [NS4]

- **Z-INDEX**—Lets you specify the stacking order of a layer. Layers that have higher **Z-INDEX** values go above those with lower **Z-INDEX** values. **Z-INDEX** values that are positive stack layers above their parents, while negative ones stack them below their parents. Note that only one of these attributes: **Z-INDEX**, **ABOVE**, or **BELOW** can be used for a given layer. Set this attribute to an existing layer **ID** value. Set this attribute to integer values. [NS4]

The novice programmer has a problem and says, "All I want to do is display some text on top of other text. Why is that so hard?" You smile and say, "It's not so hard—just use the **<LAYER>** element." "Tell me all about it!" the NP says.

The **<LAYER>** element lets you create layers of content in Netscape Navigator. Each layer can hold text, images, and other content and can be stacked on top of other layers.

As you can see by the attribute list, this is an extensive tag. We'll take a closer look at **<LAYER>** when working with dynamic HTML in Chapters 13 and 14 because this element is the main method used by Netscape Navigator to implement dynamic HTML. Layers are accessible from scripting languages, like JavaScript. Using a scripting language, you can move layers around as you like, giving the impression of animation. I'll take a look at this tag now just to get us started. Here's an example showing how to add text to two different layers, stacking one on top of the other using the **LEFT** and **TOP** attributes:

```
<HTML>

<HEAD>
    <TITLE>
        Working with layers
    </TITLE>
```

```
</HEAD>

<BODY>

    <H1 ALIGN="CENTER">
        Working With Layers
    </H1>

    <LAYER NAME="LAYER1">
        <H1>This text is in layer 1.</H1>
    </LAYER>

    <LAYER NAME="LAYER2" LEFT=50 TOP=80>
        <H1>This text is in layer 2.</H1>
    </LAYER>

</BODY>

</HTML>
```

The result of this HTML appears in Figure 3.20. As you can see in the figure, one layer is overlapping another in Netscape Navigator.

There's a lot more to working with layers, and we'll dig into it later in Chapters 13 and 14. Meanwhile, this example shows you some of the possibilities. Unfortunately, this element is not supported by Internet Explorer, so before you use **<LAYER>** to arrange text, take a look at the **<DIV>** element in the section "Positioning Text With **<DIV>**" near the end of this chapter.

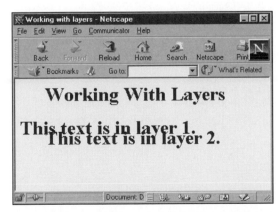

Figure 3.20   Creating overlapping text using layers in Netscape Navigator.

NOTE: *If you place **<LAYER>** tags in an HTML form and draw controls in the layer, they will not be drawn in the browser. You must place the form in the layer as well.*

<NOLAYER>—Handling Browsers That Don't Handle Layers

Purpose: Exposes text and/or HTML in browsers that don't handle layers.

Start Tag/End Tag: Required/Required

Supported: [NS4]

Attributes:

• None

To handle browsers that don't handle layers, you use the **<NOLAYER>** element. The text or HTML in this element appears in browsers that don't support layers, and it is hidden in those that do. In fact, the **<NOLAYER>** element is a great place to put the HTML for a version of your page that doesn't use layers.

Here's an example, displaying a message in browsers that don't support layers:

```
<LAYER SRC=coolstuff.html></LAYER>
<NOLAYER>
    This page looks really great in browsers that support the
    &lt;LAYER&gt; element. Why not get such a browser today?
</NOLAYER>
```

<ILAYER>—Creating Inline Layers

Purpose: Creates a layer with content that can overlap other layers. An inline version of the **<LAYER>** tag.

Start Tag/End Tag: Required/Required

Supported: [NS4]

Attributes:

- **ABOVE**—Gives the name of the layer that will occur directly above the current layer in the layer z-order (stacking order). Note that only one of these attributes: **Z-INDEX**, **ABOVE**, or **BELOW** can be used for a given layer. Set this attribute to an existing layer **ID** value. [NS4]

- **BACKGROUND**—Indicates a background image to be tiled on the layer (the default for layers is that they are transparent). Set to the image's URL. [NS4]

- **BELOW**—Gives the name of the layer that will occur directly below the current layer in the layer z-order (stacking order). Note that only one of these attributes: **Z-INDEX**, **ABOVE**, or **BELOW** can be used for a given layer. Set this attribute to an existing layer **ID** value. [NS4]

- **BGCOLOR**—Gives the background color of the layer (the default for layers is that they are transparent). Set to an RGB color value or a predefined color. [NS4]

- **CLASS**—Class of the element (used for rendering). [NS4]

- **CLIP**—Specifies the viewable area of the layer. Using this attribute, you can set the clipping area to values less than the width and height of the content of the layer. Set this attribute to a comma-separated list of integers specifying the pixel coordinates of the clipping rectangle (**CLIP="100, 100, 400, 400"** or **CLIP="400, 400"**, where the second form relies on the fact that the left and top settings default to 0). Note that the origin is at the top, left corner and pixel values grow moving down and to the right. [NS4]

- **HEIGHT**—Gives the height of the content of the layer and sets up a reference dimension for child layers. Set to positive pixel widths or a percentage of the container. [NS4]

- **ID**—Unique alphanumeric identifier for the tag, which you can use to refer to it. [NS4]

- **LEFT**—Gives the left location of the current layer relative to a parent layer if there is one, or the browser window otherwise. Set to an integer specifying the screen position or a scripting expression. [NS4]

- **PAGEX**—Sets the absolute horizontal position of the left boundary of the current layer in relation to the document window. Set to a value giving the screen position in pixels or an HTML scripting expression. [NS4]

- **PAGEY**—Sets the absolute vertical position of the top boundary of the current layer in relation to the document window. Set to a value giving the screen position in pixels or an HTML scripting expression. [NS4]

- **SRC**—The URL of an HTML document to be inserted in the layer (like using **IFRAME** in Internet Explorer). Set to a URL. [NS4]

- **STYLE**—Inline style indicating how to render the element. [NS4]

- **TOP**—Gives the top location of the current layer relative to a parent layer if there is one, or the browser window otherwise. Set to an integer specifying the screen position or a scripting expression. [NS4]

- **VISIBILITY**—Sets whether a layer is visible or not, by default, a layer has the same visibility as its parent layer. Set to: **SHOW** (shows the layer), **HIDE** (hides the layer), or **INHERIT** (giving the layer the same visibility as its parent). For top-level layers without a parent layer, **INHERIT** means the same as **SHOW**. [NS4]

- **WIDTH**—Sets the width of the layer's content, controlling the layer's right margin for wrapping purposes. Set to positive pixel values. [NS4]

- **Z-INDEX**—Lets you specify the stacking order of a layer. Layers that have higher **Z-INDEX** values go above those with lower **Z-INDEX** values. **Z-INDEX** values that are positive stack layers above their parents, while negative ones stack them below their parents. Note that only one of these attributes: **Z-INDEX**, **ABOVE**, or **BELOW** can be used for a given layer. Set this attribute to an existing layer **ID** value. Set this attribute to integer values. [NS4]

The **<ILAYER>** element is to the **<LAYER>** element as the **<SPAN>** tag is to the **<DIV>** element. It has much the same function, but rather than creating a stand-alone HTML structure, the **<ILAYER>** is supposed to be used inline (in the middle of other text). The **<ILAYER>** element lets you create layers inline, as in this example, where I'm creating a new layer inline to move some text up a little higher on the page:

```
<HTML>

<HEAD>
<TITLE>Working with layers</TITLE>
</HEAD>

<BODY>

    <H1 ALIGN="CENTER">
        Working With Inline Layers
    </H1>

    <BR>
```

```
<H1>
     This text includes some that
     <ILAYER NAME="LAYER1" LEFT=5 TOP=-15>
     <I>pops up</I></ILAYER>
     a little.
</H1>

</BODY>

</HTML>
```

You can see the results of this HTML in Figure 3.21. The **<ILAYER>** element has indeed created a new layer. I positioned this layer using the **TOP** and **LEFT** attributes to push some text up a little.

There's a lot more to working with layers, and we'll dig into it later in Chapters 13 and 14. Meanwhile, the previous example showed you some of the possibilities. Unfortunately, this element is not supported by Internet Explorer, so before you use **<ILAYER>** to arrange text, take a look at the **<DIV>** element in the next section, "Positioning Text With **<DIV>**".

NOTE: *If you place **<ILAYER>** tags in an HTML form and draw controls in the layer, they will not be drawn in the browser. You must place the form in the layer as well.*

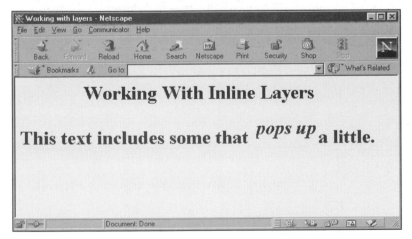

Figure 3.21   Using inline layers in Netscape Navigator.

Positioning Text With **\<DIV>**

"Uh oh," says the novice programmer, "I've got a problem. I want to overlap some text at a specific location in a Web page, so I can't use a table. On the other hand, the **\<LAYER>** tag will do the trick, but it only works in Netscape Navigator!" "Well," you say in your capacity as HTML guru, "you should use the **\<DIV>** tag instead."

You can use the **\<DIV>** tag's **STYLE** attribute to set its position in a Web page as we'll see when we start working with styles and style sheets in Chapter 9. However, because this chapter discusses positioning and arranging text, this tag and its **STYLE** attribute deserve some mention here. Here's an example showing how it works and how it displays overlapping text:

```
<HTML>

    <HEAD>
        <TITLE>
            Using The &lt;DIV&gt; Element To Overlap Text
        </TITLE>
    </HEAD>

    <BODY BGCOLOR=BLACK>

        <DIV STYLE="POSITION:ABSOLUTE; LEFT:100; TOP:30; WIDTH:250;
            HEIGHT:280">
            <FONT SIZE = 4 FACE = "ARIAL" COLOR = WHITE>
                Here's some text that will appear under other text.
                This demonstration shows one way to create overlapping
                text using the &lt;DIV&gt; element.
            </FONT>
        </DIV>


        <DIV STYLE="POSITION:ABSOLUTE; LEFT:100; TOP:0; WIDTH:250;
            HEIGHT:200">
            <FONT SIZE = 7 FACE = "VERDANA" COLOR = RED>
                <CENTER>
                    Overlapping
                    Text!
                </CENTER>
            </FONT>
        </DIV>

    </BODY>
</HTML>
```

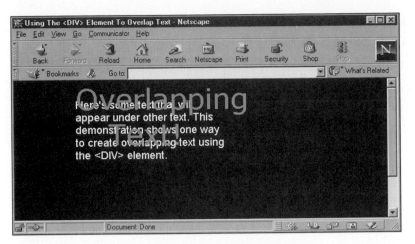

Figure 3.22 Using the <DIV> element to position text.

The result of this HTML appears in Figure 3.22. As you can see in the figure, I've created overlapping text, which will work in both Netscape Navigator and Internet Explorer with the **<DIV>** element. To do so, I've used the **POSITION**, **LEFT**, **TOP**, **WIDTH**, and **HEIGHT** styles. More about these styles when we work with style sheets in Chapter 9.

<RUBY> And <RT>—Creating Ruby (Captioned) Text

<RUBY>

Purpose: Creates a *ruby*, which is a content pair of text and annotation or caption.

Start Tag/End Tag: Required/Required

Supported: [IE5]

Attributes:

- **CLASS**—Class of the element (used for rendering). [IE5]

- **DIR**—Gives the direction of directionally neutral text (text that doesn't have inherent direction in which you should read it). Possible values: **LTR**: left-to-right text or table and **RTL**: right-to-left text or table. [IE5]

- **ID**—Unique alphanumeric identifier for the tag, which you can use to refer to it. [IE5]

- **LANG**—Base language used for the tag. [IE5]

- **LANGUAGE**—Scripting language used for the tag. [IE5]

- **NAME**—Sets the name of the element. Set to alphanumeric text. [IE5]

- **STYLE**—Inline style indicating how to render the element. [IE5]

- **TITLE**—Holds additional information (which might be displayed in tool tips) for the element. [IE5]

<RT>

Purpose: Creates ruby text (the annotation/caption).

Start Tag/End Tag: Required/Optional

Supported: [IE5]

Attributes:

- **CLASS**—Class of the element (used for rendering). [IE5]

- **DIR**—Gives the direction of directionally neutral text (text that doesn't have inherent direction in which you should read it). Possible values: **LTR**: left-to-right text or table and **RTL**: right-to-left text or table. [IE5]

- **ID**—Unique alphanumeric identifier for the tag, which you can use to refer to it. [IE5]

- **LANG**—Base language used for the tag. [IE5]

- **LANGUAGE**—Scripting language used for the tag. [IE5]

- **NAME**—Sets the name of the element. Set to alphanumeric text. [IE5]

- **STYLE**—Inline style indicating how to render the element. [IE5]

- **TITLE**—Holds additional information (which might be displayed in tool tips) for the element. [IE5]

Rubies, new in Internet Explorer 5, are content/caption text pairs. When you want to annotate text or add captions to text explaining that text, you can use rubies. Probably the most common use of rubies is to provide pronunciation guides to foreign language text.

The ruby base element, **<RUBY>**, holds the main content text, and the ruby text itself, **<RT>**, holds the annotation or caption, which is displayed in a smaller font above the ruby base. Here's an example showing how to use these elements:

```
<HTML>
    <HEAD>
        <TITLE>
```

```
        Using the &lt;RUBY&gt; and &lt;RT&gt; tags.
    </TITLE>
</HEAD>

<BODY>

    <FONT SIZE="5">
        <RUBY>
            Here's the text.
            <RT>Here's the annotation.</RT>
        </RUBY>
    </FONT>

</BODY>
</HTML>
```

There's one thing to point out here—by default, the ruby text is very small and nearly unreadable, so I'm using a larger font size for all the text. The result appears in Figure 3.23.

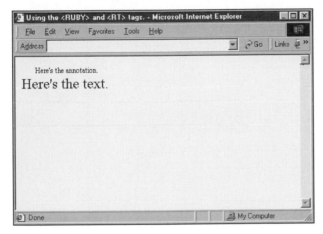

Figure 3.23   Creating ruby text.

Chapter 4

Working With Images

In Depth

This is our chapter on handling images, and as far as I am concerned, we could talk about images on the Web forever. There's so much material here that it would easily fit a book by itself. After all, how can you overestimate the power of graphics in Web pages?

In this chapter, we'll see how to put images in Web pages, how to display alternate text for browsers unable to display images, how to let the text in your page "flow" around images, what kind of images to use and when, how to put borders around images, how to overlap images, and more.

Images In Web Pages

Images are stored in files outside your Web page, which means you upload them to your Internet Service Provider (ISP) as files separate from your Web pages themselves. Using the **<IMG>** element, you can *point* to those images, and the Web browser will read that image from your ISP and place it directly into the page.

Here's an example showing how this works. I'm telling the Web browser that it will find the image I want to use at **www.starpowder.com/steve/image.gif**, that the image is 252 pixels wide and 115 high, and that the text to display while the browser is loading the image or if the browser doesn't display images, is simply, "An image":

```
<HTML>
    <HEAD>
        <TITLE>
            Using the &lt;IMG&gt; tag.
        </TITLE>
    </HEAD>

    <BODY>
        <CENTER>
            <H1>
                Working With Images
            </H1>
        </CENTER>
```

```
        Here's an image:
            <IMG SRC="http://www.starpowder.com/steve/image.gif"
                WIDTH=252 HEIGHT=115 ALT="An image">
    </BODY>
</HTML>
```

The result of this HTML appears in Figure 4.1. As you can see in the figure, the image that I want to load, **www.starpowder.com/steve/image.gif**, appears in the Web page as planned. I've also put some text in the page that appears on the same line as the image, but the result looks a little odd because the image is so much taller than the text. This is one of the issues I'll discuss at some length throughout the Immediate Solutions section—mixing text and graphics in a Web page.

TIP: *Something to bear in mind when working with images is that an URL like **www.starpowder.com/steve/ image.gif** is in fact a perfectly good URL (note that this is just an example, there's no actual image at this URL), one you can enter directly into your browser to see the corresponding image. It's worth keeping that in mind because, if for some reason, your browser can't find an image in your Web page, you can enter its full URL directly to check on the location of the image.*

As we'll see in the Chapter 5, you don't have to specify the full Uniform Resource Locator (URL) of an image to display it in your Web page; you can use a *relative URL*, which gives the location of the image file relative to the current page. If you've placed image.gif in the same directory in your ISP as the Web page itself, you can just refer to the image file by name like this:

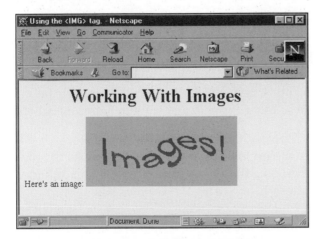

Figure 4.1   Displaying an image in a Web page.

```
<HTML>
    <HEAD>
        <TITLE>
            Using the &lt;IMG&gt; tag.
        </TITLE>
    </HEAD>

    <BODY>
        <CENTER>
            <H1>
                Working With Images
            </H1>
        </CENTER>
        Here's an image:
        <IMG SRC="image.gif" WIDTH=252 HEIGHT=115 ALT="An image">
    </BODY>
</HTML>
```

This HTML works just as the previous page did and has the added advantage that the Web browser can use the same HTTP connection to get the image from a relative URL, saving you some time.

The image in Figure 4.1 is called an *inline image,* one that the browser itself displays as part of your Web page. Inline images must be in a format that the Web browser can handle, such as graphics interchange format (GIF) or Joint Photographic Experts Group (JPEG) format, and for some browsers, Portable Network Graphics (PNG) format (I'll take a look at these formats in the upcoming In Depth section "Graphic Formats").

There are many image formats that exist, such as PICT for the Macintosh, tagged image file format (TIFF), XBM, BMP, and others. You may have applications that can display images in these formats. If your browser can find these programs (for example, if the applications are registered in Windows to handle specific file types), it can download images in these other formats and start the appropriate image-displaying program.

To work with images stored in files or in formats that the browser doesn't handle, or to let users see very large graphic files if they want to, you can link to those image files. Doing so treats those files as *external images* as opposed to inline images. Here's an example in which I treat image.gif as an external image by linking to it with a type of hyperlink that we'll see how to create in Chapter 5:

```
<HTML>
    <HEAD>
        <TITLE>
            Using the &lt;IMG&gt; tag.
        </TITLE>
    </HEAD>

    <BODY>
        <CENTER>
            <H1>
                Working With External Images
            </H1>
        </CENTER>
        Here's an
        <A HREF="image.gif">image</A>.
    </BODY>
</HTML>
```

This page appears in Netscape Navigator in Figure 4.2. When the user clicks the hyperlink to the image, the image itself appears in the browser, as you see in Figure 4.3.

As you start to work with graphics, you'll find it's an area with great depth—there's always something else to know. Broadly speaking, images are divided into two large categories: *photographic images* (also called bitmap or raster graphics) and *vector graphics* (also called line art). As you can gather from its name,

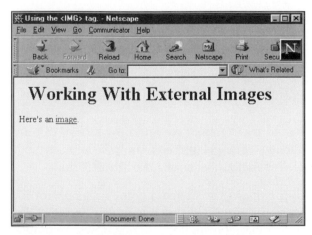

Figure 4.2   Displaying a link to an external image.

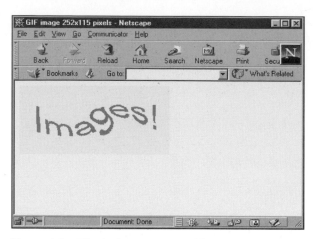

Figure 4.3   Displaying an external image.

line art is drawn art, often containing high-resolution graphics and steep color gradients between elements. Of the two main graphic formats, GIF and JPEG, GIF is better for line art and JPEG is more suitable for photographic images. I'll take a look at these formats in the following section.

Graphic Formats

There are plenty of graphic file formats in existence, some of which I've already mentioned, like PICT, TIFF, XBM, BMP, JPEG, and GIF. You can't count on browsers knowing more than two standard formats, however—GIF and JPEG.

TIP: *Web servers and browsers know what kind of image file format you're using based on its file extension, such as .gif (for GIF files) and .jpg (for JPEG files). It's important to use the file extension for that reason. In fact, if you're working with a nonstandard file format, your ISP may not know how to handle it and try to convert it to text.*

GIF Format

GIF is a format originally created by CompuServe and now stored in a format patented by Unisys. The GIF image format is limited to only 256 colors, so if you want to work with more colors, you should consider the JPEG format.

GIF images use an *indexed color map* (also called a color index, color lookup table [CLUT], or palette) to store the colors used in the image. Each pixel in the image stores a one-byte number ranging from 0 through 255, which points to a location in the palette.

The upshot is that, although you can store high-resolution images with the GIF format, you can only use 256 colors. Which of the 256 colors you use is up to you. If you have a good graphics software program, it will let you set the palette of colors yourself. When a GIF file is actually displayed, the image looks like it contains a lot more than 256 colors. What's really happening is that colors in the palette are *dithered*, which means they are mixed using alternating pixels of various colors. When you convert an image to GIF format, it will be limited to the 256 colors. If you have a smart enough graphics file conversion program (see the In Depth section "Graphics Programs And Resources"), it can create a good palette for you.

TIP: *In fact, if you can use your software to reduce the number of colors in the image or start by drawing an image of only a few colors, the palette can be smaller, and the resulting file can be smaller. In general, it's a good idea to shoot for small palettes and small file sizes to make it easier and quicker to download the image. Using color reduction techniques like this, you can create two-color images of full Web page size that download quicker than a small full-color image would. For example, look at the image in the Web page in Figure 4.1; it has few colors (shown as gray), so even stretched to a huge 1000x460 pixel size (larger than most Web pages), it's only 5K, which downloads in five or so seconds.*

In general, the GIF file format is a good choice for line art graphics, graphics with few colors, and those that have a sharp gradation in color between elements.

There's one significant issue with the GIF format you should know about—it's patented by Unisys Corporation. Actually, Unisys has patented the Lempel Ziv Welch (LZW) data compression and decompression technology used to create and read GIF files. Software that creates or displays LZW-compressed GIF files should have a license from Unisys, or so Unisys says.

Because the GIF compression format is patented, it has had a dampening effect on developing software that uses GIF files. For example, if you write a program that's freeware but displays GIF files and you distribute it, Unisys requires that you license it from them. Their fees start at a rate of several thousand dollars and continue with fees (less than a dollar usually) for each copy of the software you distribute, even if your software is free. There's an ongoing debate about the patent; some people say that only the creation of GIF and other LZW files is patented, not reading and decompressing them. Although Internet Explorer has a license from Unisys, some other major browsers do not.

NOTE: *To see more about the LZW patent and to get licensing information, see* ***www.unisys.com***.

In any case, many people feel that they want to avoid the GIF format. Other formats are being explored including the PNG format, which uses a different compression algorithm. The feeling among some developers is that the GIF format is slowly on the way out, although that remains to be seen.

TIP: *The PNG home page is* **www.cdrom.com/pub/png/png.html**. *To see a list of browsers that support the PNG format, see* **www.cdrom.com/pub/png/pngapbr.html**. *Currently, 48 browsers are listed including Internet Explorer and Netscape Navigator.*

There are two GIF formats, GIF87, which is the standard format and GIF89, which supports *image transparency* and animation (called animated GIFs). Image transparency makes the background color "transparent" so images can appear in a variety of shapes.

In addition, GIF files can be *interlaced*, which means that they appear progressively in the Web browser as they are downloaded. While being downloaded, interlaced GIFs are displayed as full size, but gradually improve in resolution as you've seen in your browser. Many graphics programs let you store GIF images as interlaced. I'll take a look at how the process works in the Immediate Solutions section "Creating Interlaced GIF Images".

JPEG Format

JPEG (often abbreviated to JPG and used as the file extension) takes its name from the group that first created the format. Unlike GIF with its restricted format, you can create JPEG images using a virtually unlimited number of colors. The three popular formats use 256 colors (one byte per pixel, holding a color value from 0 through 255), 65,536 colors (two bytes stored per pixel), or 16,777,216 colors (three bytes stored per pixel).

Like GIF, JPEG files are stored as compressed. JPEG is a compression technology that can store images with various levels of perfection. Conversion software, like LView Pro (**www.lview.com**), will let you set how perfectly an image is stored. Although there's less dithering with JPEG images than with GIF images, the JPEG compression format loses some precision in the image and has a tougher time dealing with sharp gradients in the image. On the other hand, JPEG image files are usually smaller for photographic images, which is what makes them so popular on Usenet where they've just about replaced GIF files entirely.

In general, the JPEG format is a good choice for photographs that don't have sharp gradients and for images that have many colors, but not for line art or high-resolution graphics.

So which is the best format for a particular image, GIF or JPEG? It depends on your image and what you're shooting for. If you have a large image that you want to store in a small file, try JPEG, but you should also try using software that helps you convert the image to a small palette for use in GIF files. You can't tell which format will give you the smallest—and therefore the quickest—downloaded image file until you actually create the file. By putting in some hard work, I've been able to use such small palettes that huge images are packed into small files and downloaded in a snap. When using GIF files, use as few colors as you can get away with. The rule of thumb for 14.4K modems (although most are faster than that now) is that 1K of an image file downloads in one second, so it's best to keep your images smaller than 20K. It's also important to look at the resulting image. JPEG images that have lots of sharp gradients may have considerable distortion when uncompressed.

Wonder what graphics programs are out there to help you create images and convert them to various formats so you can find out which one is right for you? There are thousands of such programs, and I'll take a look at a few of them next.

Graphics Programs And Resources

There are so many graphics programs available that it's just about impossible to list them all. Some are free, some are shareware, some are expensive (and some are *very* expensive). Here's a starter list, beginning with what many people and Web designers consider the cream of the crop—Adobe Photoshop.

- *Adobe Photoshop/Illustrator (**www.adobe.com/prodindex/**)*—Use Photoshop for photographs and Illustrator for line art. These are top of the line applications with seemingly endless resources.

- *Alchemy Mindworks' GIF Construction Set (**www.mindworkshop.com/ alchemy/alchemy.html**)*—Lets you create animated GIFs as well as convert graphics formats and transparent GIFs.

- *Andreas Ley's GIFTrans (**ftp://ftp.rz.uni-karlsruhe.de/pub/net/www/ tools/**)*—Makes transparent GIFs.

- *CorelDRAW!/PHOTO-PAINT (**www.corel.com**)*—Less expensive than Adobe and very powerful. Corel has been around a long time and is the choice of many Web designers.

- *DeBabelizer (**www.equil.com**)*—Lets you perform batch manipulations on many files at the same time, including finding the best palette automatically.

- *GIMP (**www.gimp.org**)*—Gnu Image Manipulation Program (GIMP) graphic editor and photo retouching, works under Unix X Windows.

- *John Bradley's XV Image Viewer (**www.trilon.com/xv/**)*—Unix X Windows package. Multiple file conversions performed.

- *LView Pro (**www.lview.com**)*—Use for interchanging formats, creating transparent GIFs, and displaying files with multiple file formats.

- *Macromedia Freehand Graphics Studio (**www.macromedia.com**)*—Use for creating animated line art.

- *Paint Shop Pro (**www.jasc.com**)*—Use for hobby Web design.

- *SPG's ColorWorks: Web 3 (**www.spg-net.com**)*—GIF animation optimization that can shrink animated GIFs by 50 percent, image library browser, Web graphics spider that downloads all the images from a site, and more.

Of course, you can also use software that comes with your operating system to create images, such as Windows Paint (select Start|Programs|Accessories|Paint). Paint can only create images in .bmp (Windows bitmap) format, however, so you'll need a file format conversion program, like LView Pro, to convert to GIF or JPEG formats.

There are also online graphics programs that let you create graphics online, such as CoolText.Com (**www.cooltext.com**). This service uses GIMP technology to let you create flashy text with a variety of special effects, such as starbursts and special textures.

In addition to these resources, you can also find free art—*clip art*—on the Internet.

Using Clip Art

Many Web developers prefer not to have to create their own graphics—they get it ready-made from the Internet. Such art is called clip art, and although it was originally popular to get snappy images for buttons and navigational aids in Web pages, clip art images are getting more and more involved all the time.

NOTE: *Here's the requisite note on being careful about copyrights when downloading art from the Internet. If you download something from someone else's Web page and use it in your own page, that's a very public act and can be copyright infringement—you're just asking for trouble. People can embed copyright notices inside graphics—it's very easy to do with animated GIFs, for example—so be careful about "borrowing" any art that may be copyrighted. Often a simple email to the Web page's creator can result in getting permission to use some graphics from the site; I've used this method a few times when I saw an outstanding piece of art I wanted to use. Of course, on Web sites that advertise free, noncopyrighted clip art, you're all set.*

There's a great deal of free clip art available. A Web search engine turns up a mere 11,433 matches for the string "free clip art", far too many to mention here. A short starter list will be helpful:

• *Barry's Clip Art Server (**www.barrysclipart.com/index.html**)*—A huge collection of art, and the place I go to first. Also has animated GIFs.

• *iBAND Clip Art Mega Site (**www.iband.com/clip/clipart.html**)*—This site has many categories of art and is worth a look.

• *Wagon Train Animated GIFs (**http://dreamartists.com**)*—A collection of animated GIFs.

• *XOOM's Free Clip Art Library (**http://xoom.com/clips/website/**)*—A pretty good selection of art.

When you go to a site advertising free clip art, you'll see pages and pages of clip art. For instance, see Figure 4.4 to view a page from Barry's Clip Art Server.

TIP: *So how do you copy an image from a clip art page to your own computer? If you're using Netscape Navigator or Internet Explorer on a PC, right-click the image and select Save Picture As in Internet Explorer or Save Image As in Netscape Navigator to store the image on disk. If you're using a Macintosh, press the mouse button on the image you want to copy, and then select Save As to store the image on disk.*

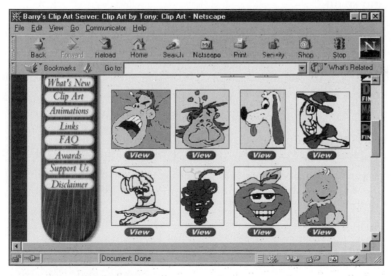

Figure 4.4   Finding clip art.

4. Working With Images

Graphics Color

Now that you're working with graphics programs, it's worthwhile knowing how to handle color in these programs. In Chapter 1, we saw the most common way of specifying colors directly—as color values, also called Red, Green, Blue (RGB) triplets.

Using RGB triplets, colors are expressed as **rrggbb**, where **rr** specifies the red component of the color with values ranging from 0 through 255 expressed as a hexadecimal (base 16) two-digit number, **gg** specifies the green component, and **bb** specifies the blue component. The only trick to utilizing RGB triplets is getting used to hexadecimal values, which range from 00 to *ff* (hexadecimal *ff* = 255 because hex digits range from 0 to 9 and then from a to f).

Here are some examples; the color value for pure red is **ff0000**, bright white is **ffffff**, black is **000000**, gray is **080808**, and yellow is **ffff00**. For more about RGB triplets, see Chapter 1.

The second way of specifying color is by using the Hue, Saturation, Brightness (HSB) method. This technique is modeled after the way you see color. *Hue* is the actual color itself, such as red or blue. Hue is specified with a color wheel that displays colors from 0 to 360 degrees. Red is at 0 and 360 degrees, yellow is at 120, blue is at 240, and so on.

Brightness indicates the intensity of the color. For example, even red can appear very dark without a lot of light shining on it. Brightness varies from 0 to 100.

Finally, *saturation* is the amount of color. The more the saturation, the more intense the color. Saturation values range from 0 to 100; lower values give you pastel-like colors, and higher values give you very intense colors.

Working with RGB values is far more common than using the HSB model, but you should know about both if you are going to work with graphics programs. In fact, most graphics programs that work with color let you specify color either way, so the final choice is up to you. It's a good idea to find out which one you feel more comfortable with.

Creating Images

There are thousands of programs available to create images, and some are very, very costly. However, if you're just starting out, it's a good idea to get at least a file format converter, like LView Pro (**www.lview.com**), which is a program that also lets you create transparent and interlaced GIFs. You can use this kind of utility in conjunction with an application you may already have, such as the Windows Paint program shown in Figure 4.5.

In Figure 4.5, the image I'm working with will be saved in the only format available, Windows BMP format. I can use a file converter to convert the file to GIF or JPEG format. Using LView Pro, open the BMP file, select Save As from the File menu, and save the file in the desired format. You can also customize the palette used for the image with the Retouch menu's Color Depth option. The image appears in LView Pro in Figure 4.6. Note that while the image is being converted to a GIF format, the dimensions of the image, 252×115 pixels, appear in LView Pro's title bar. This is handy information because you'll need these dimensions to use the image in a Web page.

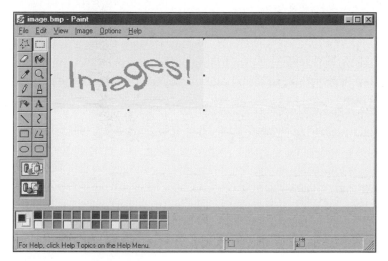

Figure 4.5   Creating images.

Figure 4.6   Opening an image in a file converter.

There are other ways of getting images, of course. You can also scan them in yourself. Scanners are becoming cheaper and cheaper and are supporting higher resolutions. The scanner resolution you use, 72 dots per inch (DPI) or a higher resolution, like 300 DPI, is your decision. It's a good idea to use a high-resolution scan in a small image file to reduce download time, and then expand that image in your Web page (see the Immediate Solutions section "Scaling Images To Different Sizes").

After you've scanned the image, the scanner software might save the image in an unappealing format. For example, some scanners create multimegabyte BMP files. To convert the file, you can use a shareware program, such as LView Pro (**www.lview.com**). The program also allows you to save the file in another format, resize it, and change the shading to lighten or darken it as you like. You can even adjust the contrast. There's no end to the ways in which images can be manipulated.

And there's no end to the ways in which you can work with images in Web pages. There's a lot coming up in this chapter including using images in Web pages, which is an extremely important topic in Web page creation, so I'll start the Immediate Solutions section now.

Immediate Solutions

Creating Transparent GIF Images

"Hey," says the novice programmer, "I've created some terrific icons I want to use as bullets in a bulleted list, but there's a problem—each bullet is supposed to be round, but my graphics program can only store rectangular images." "Ah," you say, "it's time for a transparent GIF." The NP says, "It's time for *what*?"

One powerful aspect of the GIF format files is that they can be *transparent*. What this actually means is that you select a background color to make the background transparent. When the image is displayed, the transparent background allows the underlying image to become visible.

I'll take a look at an example here. Let's start by looking at the image in Figure 4.1. As you can see, it has a very definite rectangular shape. However, by making the background of the image transparent, I can make it appear as though the swirling text is alone on the page.

I start by loading the image into LView Pro, shown in Figure 4.6. Then I select Options|Background Color to open the Select Color Palette Entry dialog box you see Figure 4.7.

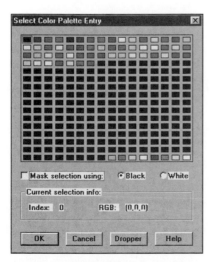

Figure 4.7   Selecting a color to make transparent.

Using this dialog box, I can select the color that I want to make transparent—the image background color. To do that, I click the button labeled Dropper in Figure 4.7, and then move to the image itself. The mouse cursor changes to a medicine dropper shape, and I just click anywhere on the background of the image. LView Pro makes that transparent. Finally, I save the new image using the File menu's Save As option. Be sure to select GIF89, the format that supports transparent GIFs, in the Save File As Type option in the Save Image As dialog box.

The results appear in Figure 4.8. As you can see in the figure, the background of the image is invisible, and the swirling text appears directly in the page.

TIP: *As you can imagine, using transparent GIFs is great when you want to use images that don't look rectangular, such as bullets in front of list items.*

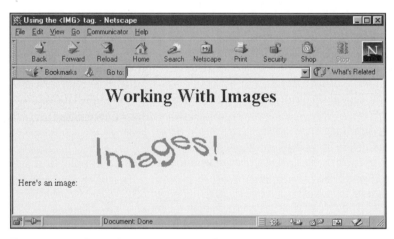

Figure 4.8   Displaying a transparent GIF file.

Creating Interlaced GIF Images

"Jeez," says the novice programmer, "images are great, but they take so long to download! I'm just sitting here watching a blank page in my browser." "Well," you say, "apart from using alternate text for images with the **ALT** attribute, you can use interlaced GIFs to let the browser build the image progressively as it downloads more data." "Swell!" says the NP, " How does it work?"

As mentioned in the introduction to this chapter, interlaced GIFs are written in such a way that the browser can display the whole image almost immediately in very low resolution, adding resolution as time goes on. For example, in Figure 4.9,

Figure 4.9   Downloading an interlaced GIF file.

I'm downloading the image as an interlaced GIF. We'll use this figure as an image map in Chapter 5. You can see that the text in the image is still rather crude at this early stage of the download, but as time goes on, it will get sharper. The idea here is that the user has something to look at instead of staring at a blank space.

How do you create an interlaced GIF? These days, most file format conversion programs store GIF images as interlaced by default. In Figure 4.10, you can see that it's the default setting in LView Pro by opening the Options menu.

TIP: *You can't interlace JPEG images. However, there is a new format being developed called progressive JPEGs. Programs, such as Adobe Photoshop, let you create progressive JPEG files.*

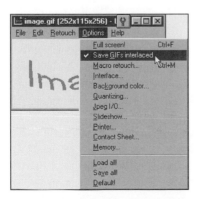

Figure 4.10   The LView Pro Options menu.

Creating Animated GIF Images

"Say," wonders the novice programmer, "what about creating animated images? Can I do that?" "Sure you can," you say, "provided you have the right software."

Animated GIF's have become very popular in Web pages. They're those images that display animation including those annoying banner ads. There are a number of popular applications for creating animated GIF images, such as Alchemy Mindworks' GIF Construction Set (**www.mindworkshop.com/alchemy/alchemy.html**).

You can see the GIF Construction Set at work in Figure 4.11. I'm creating a type of banner ad image using the standard size for each image in the animation (468×60 pixels). As you can see in the figure, the animated GIF starts with a header announcing the format and size of the image. This header is automatically created when you create a new animated GIF, and the default size of the animated GIF is 640×480 pixels. Click the Edit button to edit the header settings and change it to the same size as the GIF files you're going to use in the animation (each of which must be exactly the same size, or some browsers will have problems). If you don't enter the image's correct size, the browser is going to allocate the wrong size for the image in the Web page.

After the header comes a **LOOP** command, which you can add by clicking the Insert button. By selecting the **LOOP** command and clicking the Edit button, you can set the number of times the animation will execute. After the **LOOP** command, I've inserted a **CONTROL** command before each image, which I edited to set the delay for each image to 1/100 of a second. Following each delay is an **IMAGE** command added by clicking the Insert button, which you use to load an image.

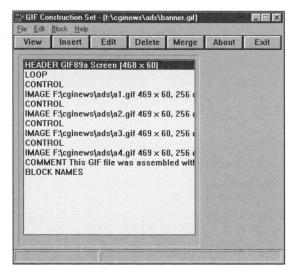

Figure 4.11   Using the GIF Construction Set to make an animated GIF.

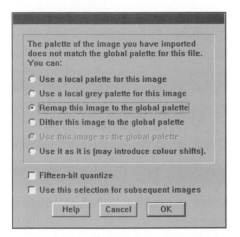

Figure 4.12   Setting a palette in the GIF Construction Set.

When you insert a new image, the GIF Construction Set asks you what palette to use, as you see in Figure 4.12. Although the default selection is Dither This Image To The Global Palette, I recommend you use the Remap This Image To The Global Palette option because it produces the best results.

After you're done creating your **LOOP** and **CONTROL** statements, select File|Save As to save your new animated GIF image.

Testing Your Images

"Hey," says the novice programmer, "my new image looks all funny in my browser." "Kind of wide, isn't it?" you ask. "About 12,000 pixels," the NP says proudly. "Hm," you say.

One thing to bear in mind as you develop your graphics for the Web is that they'll be viewed in a variety of environments and resolutions. A good rule of thumb for image width is that it should be less than 600 pixels wide.

Ideally, you should test your images in a variety of browsers and in a variety of graphical environments. For example, not everyone is going to have their screen resolution set to 1582×1582 pixels, so this is something to consider. In addition, some people are still using screens that can only display 256 colors (or have set their screens to 256 colors in order to use programs that require it), so it's a good idea to take a look at your images after setting your screen to 256 colors.

Another consideration is download time—the general rule here is that 1K of image takes one second to download. A file that's 50K can take 50 seconds to download, which is something to keep in mind because people who browse the Web can have very short attention spans. If your images are more than 20K, you might consider using *thumbnail images* instead. Thumbnails are smaller versions of an image—when clicked, they take the user to the actual image on another page. You can use graphics programs, like LView Pro, to shrink an image, and in fact, there are dedicated applications that produce thumbnail images en masse.

Another way to reduce file size is to use palette reduction as discussed in the introduction to this chapter. If you can reduce the number of colors in an image, you can save a great deal of space. For example, because the image in the Web page in Figure 4.1 uses so few colors, I was able to enlarge it to a huge 1000×460 pixels, but its image file was only 5K. Other images that size, using many colors, would be 100K or more. Smart software, like Adobe Photoshop, is able to help you with a number of palette reduction techniques.

<IMG>—Adding An Image To A Web Page

Purpose: Inserts an image into a Web page.

Start Tag/End Tag: Required/Omitted

Supported: [2, 3, 3.2, 4, IE1, IE2, IE3, IE4, IE5, NS1, NS2, NS3, NS4]

Attributes:

- **ALIGN**—Sets the alignment of text, which follows the **IMG** reference relative to the image on the screen. You use **LEFT** and **RIGHT** to indicate horizontal alignment of the image in the browser window, and the text that follows will wrap around the image. You use the other options to indicate vertical alignment of text relative to the image when the text is on the same line. Possible settings are: **LEFT**, **RIGHT**, **TOP**, **TEXTTOP**, **MIDDLE** (you can also call this setting **CENTER** in Internet Explorer and Netscape Navigator), **ABSMIDDLE**, **BASELINE**, **BOTTOM**, and **ABSBOTTOM**. [2, 3, 3.2, 4, IE1, IE2, IE3, IE4, IE5, NS1, NS2, NS3, NS4]

- **ALT**—According to the World Wide Web Consortium (W3C), this attribute is required. You use this attribute to specify text to be displayed in place of an image for browsers that cannot handle graphics or have graphics disabled. Set this attribute to a string of valid alphanumeric characters. [2, 3, 3.2, 4, IE1, IE2, IE3, IE4, IE5, NS1, NS2, NS3, NS4]

- **BORDER**—Sets whether or not the image has a border, and if so, how thick the border is. If the image is not also a hyperlink, the border color is usually the color of the surrounding text. If the image is a hyperlink, the border color will be the default hyperlink color. Set to 0 for no border, or a positive integer pixel value. [3.2, 4, IE1, IE2, IE3, IE4, IE5, NS1, NS2, NS3, NS4]

- **CLASS**—Class of the element (used for rendering). [3, 4, IE4, IE5]

- **DIR**—Gives the direction of directionally neutral text (text that doesn't have inherent direction in which you should read it). Possible values: **LTR**: left-to-right text or table and **RTL**: right-to-left text or table. [IE5]

- **DYNSRC**—Specifies the URL of an inline video. Set this attribute to a URL. [IE2, IE3, IE4, IE5]

- **HEIGHT**—Indicates the height of the image. Can be omitted, but specifying a value here for the **HEIGHT** and for the **WIDTH** attribute can speed up the downloading of the image. Because the browser can draw a blank space for the image while it's being downloaded, the page elements will not move around. Set to pixel measurements. [3, 3.2, 4, IE1, IE2, IE3, IE4, IE5, NS1, NS2, NS3, NS4]

- **HSPACE**—Sets the horizontal spacing (both left and right sides) around the image. Set to pixel measurements. [3.2, 4, IE1, IE2, IE3, IE4, IE5, NS1, NS2, NS3, NS4]

- **ID**—A unique alphanumeric identifier for the tag, which you can use to refer to it. [3, 4, IE4, IE5]

- **ISMAP**—Indicates that this image is to be used as an image map together with a map file. This attribute is a stand-alone attribute. The map file holds shape names and matching coordinate values that list corresponding URLs to navigate to. [2, 3, 3.2, 4, IE1, IE2, IE3, IE4, IE5, NS1, NS2, NS3, NS4]

- **LANG**—Base language used for the tag. [3, 4, IE4, IE5]

- **LANGUAGE**—Scripting language used for the tag. [IE4, IE5]

- **LONGDESC**—Set to a longer description of the image. This attribute allows descriptive narrative with markup to be used for image descriptions. Set to a URL. [4]

- **LOOP**—Sets the number of times a video will play. You use this attribute together with the **DYNSRC** attribute. Set it to a positive integer, or -1 for a value of **INFINITE** (which makes the video loop forever). [IE2, IE3, IE4, IE5]

- **LOWSRC**—Gives the URL of a low-resolution image, which should be downloaded before the higher resolution image given by the **SRC** attribute. The idea is to present some kind of the image to the user while the higher

4. Working With Images

resolution image is downloading. The low-resolution image is displayed until the high-resolution image is fully downloaded. Set this attribute to a URL. [IE4, IE5, NS1, NS2, NS3, NS4]

- **NAME**—Gives a unique name to the image so you can reference it with scripting code. Set to valid alphanumeric characters. [4, IE4, IE5, NS3, NS4]

- **SRC**—This attribute is required. Specifies the URL of the actual image to display. Set to a URL. [2, 3, 3.2, 4, IE1, IE2, IE3, IE4, IE5, NS1, NS2, NS3, NS4]

- **START**—Sets when a video will start playing. You use this attribute together with the **DYNSRC** attribute. Possible values are: **FILEOPEN** (the video will start as soon as it is downloaded) and **MOUSEOVER** (the video starts playing when the mouse moves over the video). [IE2, IE3, IE4, IE5]

- **STYLE**—Inline style indicating how to render the element. [4, IE4, IE5]

- **TITLE**—Holds additional information (which might be displayed in tool tips) for the element. [3, 4, IE4, IE5]

- **USEMAP**—Gives the URL—usually inside the current document—of a client-side image map, and indicates that the image is to be used as an image map. Note that using **USEMAP** overrides any **<A>** element surrounding the **<IMG>** element. Set to a URL, or an anchor name internal to the file. [3.2, 4, IE1, IE2, IE3, IE4, IE5, NS2, NS3, NS4]

- **VRML**—Gives the URL of an inline Virtual Reality Modelling Language (VRML) world, letting the browser launch a VRML viewer (if there is one on the computer). Set to a URL. [IE2, IE3, IE4, IE5]

- **VSPACE**—Sets the vertical spacing (both top and bottom sides) around the image. Set to pixel measurements. [3.2, 4, IE1, IE2, IE3, IE4, IE5, NS1, NS2, NS3, NS4]

- **WIDTH**—Indicates the width of the image. Can be omitted, but specifying a value for **WIDTH** here and for the image's **HEIGHT** can speed up the downloading of the image. Because the browser can draw a blank space for the image while it's being downloaded, the page elements will not move around. Set to pixel measurements. [3, 3.2, 4, IE1, IE2, IE3, IE4, IE5, NS1, NS2, NS3, NS4]

"I've got my super duper image ready to go! Now how do I actually display an image in a Web page?" the novice programmer says. "It's easy," you say, "just use the **<IMG>** element."

You use the **<IMG>** element to insert images into a Web page as well as image maps and some video clips. To use this element, you supply the URL of the image you want to display in the **SRC** attribute, and specify alternate text if the browser can't find the image or doesn't display images in the **ALT** attribute. W3C considers both of these attributes as required for the **<IMG>** element; interestingly, the **ALIGN** attribute is not deprecated in the **<IMG>** element as it is for virtually every other HTML element that uses it. (The other element that still has an **ALIGN** attribute is the **<OBJECT>** element, see "**<OBJECT>** And **<PARAM>**—Placing An Object Into A Web Page" in Chapter 8; the **ALIGN** attribute is also not listed as deprecated in the **<APPLET>** element, but the **<APPLET>** element itself is deprecated, see "**<APPLET>**—Embedding Applets In Web Pages" in Chapter 16.)

TIP: *Most browsers also let you refer to the **<IMG>** element as **<IMAGE>**.*

NOTE: *As of version 4, the Netscape Navigator **<IMG>** element is supposed to take another attribute: **SUPPRESS**, which you set to values of **TRUE** or **FALSE**. When set to **TRUE** (the default is **FALSE**), the image-loading icon that appears when the image is loading is not supposed to appear, and the tool tip that displays the image's alternate text when the mouse rests on the image is also not supposed to appear. In practice, this attribute doesn't do anything.*

Here's an example using the **<IMG>** element, which we saw in the introduction to this chapter:

```
<HTML>
    <HEAD>
        <TITLE>
            Using the &lt;IMG&gt; tag.
        </TITLE>
    </HEAD>

    <BODY>
        <CENTER>
            <H1>
                Working With Images
            </H1>
        </CENTER>
        Here's an image:
        <IMG SRC="http://www.starpowder.com/steve/image.gif"
            WIDTH=252 HEIGHT=115 ALT="An image">
    </BODY>
</HTML>
```

You can see the result in Figure 4.1. In the Web page, the image appears next to the text in the page. As you can see by the enormous number of attributes you can use with the **<IMG>** tag, there's a lot of depth to this element. I'll work through other uses of this element in the following sections.

TIP: *One thing to remember when working with images—browsers cache images. If you make a change to an image and reload its page, you may see the old version of the image. However, you can see the updated image by clearing the browser's cache. To work with the cache in Netscape Navigator 4, select Edit|Preferences, then in the Preferences dialog box, select the Advanced item, then the Cache item (in Netscape Navigator 3, the Cache setting is in the Options menu); in Internet Explorer, select Tools|Internet Options|General. If you're still having trouble, you should also know that some ISPs cache whole Web pages for quicker access, so if you make a change to a page including the images in it, you may still see the old page and images. One option in this case is to rename the page and the images. Ask your ISP for more details.*

NOTE: *Adobe corporation has two HTML editing products: SiteMill and PageMill. If you use these products, you will find an additional attribute in your **<IMG>** elements used only by SiteMill and PageMill named **NATURALSIZEFLAG**. This attribute indicates the size of the image in these editors.*

Displaying Alternate Text In Place Of Images

"Huh," says the novice programmer, "I just ran my Web page through an HTML validator, and it said something about all my **<IMG>** elements needing a value for the **ALT** attribute—surely that's some kind of bug?" "Nope," you say, "W3C lists the **ALT** attribute as required for the **<IMG>** element." "That's interesting," the NP says, "what does **ALT** do?"

The **ALT** attribute lets you set text that the browser can display before an image is displayed, or text the browser displays if the browser doesn't support graphics. As with the **SRC** attribute, W3C lists **ALT** as a required attribute for the **<IMG>** element for proper HTML 4. It's worth providing text to the **ALT** attribute in an **<IMG>** element because there are still text-only browsers in use by many people, such as Lynx in Unix.

Here's an example using the **ALT** attribute:

```
<HTML>
    <HEAD>
        <TITLE>
            Using the &lt;IMG&gt; tag.
        </TITLE>
    </HEAD>

    <BODY>
        <CENTER>
            <H1>
                Working With Images
            </H1>
```

```
        </CENTER>
        Here's an image:
        <IMG SRC="http://www.starpowder.com/steve/image.gif"
            WIDTH=252 HEIGHT=115 ALT="A sunset view of the Alps.">
    </BODY>
</HTML>
```

The result of this HTML appears in Figure 4.13. In this case, Netscape Navigator can't find the file specified, which it indicates by displaying a broken image icon and the alternate text. The alternate text also appears before the image starts downloading.

The alternate text also appears in a tool tip (those small yellow windows that hold explanatory text), which is displayed when the user lets the mouse rest over the image. See Figure 4.14 for an example. As you can imagine, tool tips are useful for supplying captions for images.

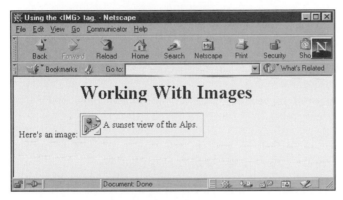

Figure 4.13   Using the **ALT** attribute.

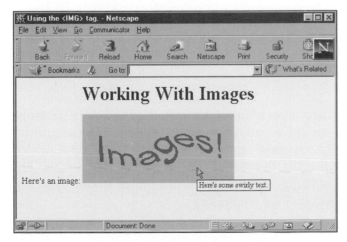

Figure 4.14   Using the **ALT** attribute as a tool tip.

Allocating Space For An Image

The novice programmer has a question. "What about the **WIDTH** and **HEIGHT** attributes in the **<IMG>** element; do I need those?" "Actually," you say, "you don't need them, but there are several good reasons to use them."

The **WIDTH** and **HEIGHT** attributes of the **<IMG>** element provide the width and height of the image in pixels. It's not necessary to supply values for these attributes, but it can be helpful. The following is an example from the beginning of this chapter where I used these attributes:

```
<HTML>
    <HEAD>
        <TITLE>
            Using the &lt;IMG&gt; tag.
        </TITLE>
    </HEAD>

    <BODY>
        <CENTER>
            <H1>
                Working With Images
            </H1>
        </CENTER>
        Here's an image:
        <IMG SRC="http://www.starpowder.com/steve/image.gif"
            WIDTH=252 HEIGHT=115 ALT="A sunset view of the Alps.">
    </BODY>
</HTML>
```

If you don't supply values for these attributes, your browser will still be able to load and display your images. However, if you do supply values for these attributes (be sure to provide a value for *each* attribute), the browser will display a box that is the same size as the image in the page while the image loads, giving the impression that the image is loading faster than it actually does.

In addition, when the Web browser is able to allocate the correct size of the image as the image loads, it doesn't have to rearrange the other elements in the page when the image is finally downloaded. It can determine the correct size of the image from the image file itself. In other words, specifying a size for the image means that all the elements in your page won't have to move around to accommodate that image when its download is complete.

So how do you find the dimensions of an image? You can use a graphics program, like LView Pro, which displays the dimensions of the image in its title bar, or you can simply use your browser. In Netscape Navigator, select View|Document Info; in Internet Explorer, right-click the image and select the Properties item in the menu that appears.

TIP: *As of Netscape Navigator 1 and Internet Explorer 3, you can specify the **HEIGHT** and **WIDTH** values using percentages of the display area like this: **WIDTH="95%"**.*

NOTE: *If you set **HEIGHT** and **WIDTH** to zero, strange things happen. In Netscape Navigator, the image appears with its normal, nonzero size. In Internet Explorer, the image becomes invisible.*

Adding Borders To Images

You can use the **<IMG>** element's **BORDER** attribute to add borders to images. These borders are simple lines of various thicknesses, which you set by giving the **BORDER** attribute a value in pixels. Normally, the color of the border is the same as the current default text color, but if you are using the image as a hyperlink, the border will be the same color as the current default hyperlink color (see Chapter 5 for more details).

Here's an example in which I set the border of an image to eight pixels:

```
<HTML>
    <HEAD>
        <TITLE>
            Using the &lt;IMG&gt; tag.
        </TITLE>
    </HEAD>

    <BODY>
        <CENTER>
            <H1>
                Working With Images
            </H1>
        </CENTER>
        Here's an image with a border:
        <IMG SRC="flower1.jpg"
            WIDTH=85 HEIGHT=129 ALT="An image" BORDER=8>
    </BODY>
</HTML>
```

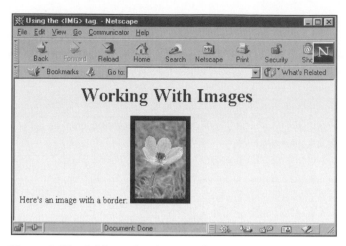

Figure 4.15   Adding a border to an image.

You can see the results of this HTML in Figure 4.15, where a thick border appears around the image. Borders are useful for making images stand out from their surroundings—particularly when the image's background color is the same as the page's background color.

NOTE: *You can remove the border around an image used as a hyperlink by using the setting* **BORDER=0**, *but that's not a great idea because users rely on the border as a visual clue that the image is being treated as a hyperlink.*

Adding Space Around Images

The novice programmer wants to know, "How can I set the spacing between images? There's usually a thin line of blank space between images, but that's not enough." "No problem at all," you say, "just use the **HSPACE** and **VSPACE** attributes."

You can set the horizontal spacing between images with the **HSPACE** attribute, and the vertical spacing between images with the **VSPACE** attribute. You set these attributes to pixel values. Here's an example in which I'm setting the horizontal and vertical spacing between images to eight pixels:

```
<HTML>
    <HEAD>
        <TITLE>
            Using the &lt;IMG&gt; tag.
```

```
            </TITLE>
        </HEAD>

        <BODY>
            <CENTER>
                <H1>
                    Setting Image Spacing
                </H1>
                <IMG SRC="flower1.jpg"
                    WIDTH=85 HEIGHT=129 HSPACE=8 VSPACE=8>
                <IMG SRC="flower1.jpg"
                    WIDTH=85 HEIGHT=129 HSPACE=8 VSPACE=8>
                <IMG SRC="flower1.jpg"
                    WIDTH=85 HEIGHT=129 HSPACE=8 VSPACE=8>
                <IMG SRC="flower1.jpg"
                    WIDTH=85 HEIGHT=129 HSPACE=8 VSPACE=8>
            </CENTER>
        </BODY>
    </HTML>
```

You can see the results of this HTML in Figure 4.16. As you can see in the figure, the images are indeed spaced as they should be.

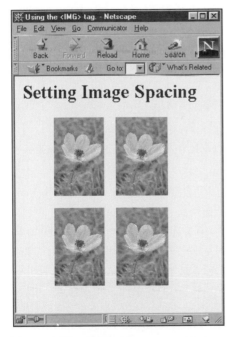

Figure 4.16   Setting image spacing.

TIP: *Want to get rid of all the space between images, even the space that appears there by default? Take a look at the Immediate Solutions section "Tiling Images—Creating Image Mosaics".*

Aligning Text And Images

"OK," says the big boss, "I want you to write the company newsletter. It's supposed to have both images and text, just like a newspaper." "Fine," you say, "I can use the **<IMG>** element's **ALIGN** attribute."

You can use the **<IMG>** element's **ALIGN** attribute (which, unlike other elements' **ALIGN** attributes, is not deprecated in HTML 4) to align text and images. Here are the possible values for this attribute:

- **ABSBOTTOM**—Aligns the bottom of the image with the lowest item in the line of text, even if it's below the baseline of the text. (Netscape Navigator and Internet Explorer only.)

- **ABSMIDDLE**—Aligns the middle of the image with the middle of the largest item in the line of text. (Netscape Navigator and Internet Explorer only.)

- **BASELINE**—Aligns the bottom of the image with the baseline of the text (same as **BOTTOM**, but a somewhat more descriptive term). (Netscape Navigator and Internet Explorer only.)

- **BOTTOM**—Aligns the bottom of the image with the text baseline. This is the default.

- **LEFT**—Positions the image to the current left margin; any text that follows flows around the image's right margin.

- **MIDDLE**—Aligns the vertical midline of the image with the baseline of the text. (You can also call this setting **CENTER** in Internet Explorer and Netscape Navigator.)

- **RIGHT**—Positions the image to the current right margin; any text that follows flows around the image's left margin.

- **TEXTOP**—Aligns the top of the image with the top of the tallest text in the line of text. (Netscape Navigator and Internet Explorer only.)

- **TOP**—Positions the text next to the top of the image.

Vertically Aligning Text

To align text vertically, you can set the **ALIGN** attribute to settings like **TOP**, **MIDDLE**, and **BOTTOM**. Here's an example:

```
<HTML>
    <HEAD>
        <TITLE>
            Using the &lt;IMG&gt; tag.
        </TITLE>
    </HEAD>

    <BODY>
        <CENTER>
            <H1>
                Aligning Text And Images
            </H1>
        </CENTER>
        <IMG SRC="flower1.jpg"
            WIDTH=85 HEIGHT=129 ALIGN=TOP>
        &lt;IMG SRC="flower1.jpg"
            WIDTH=85 HEIGHT=129 ALIGN=TOP&gt;
        <IMG SRC="flower1.jpg"
            WIDTH=85 HEIGHT=129 ALIGN=MIDDLE>
        &lt;IMG SRC="flower1.jpg"
            WIDTH=85 HEIGHT=129 ALIGN=MIDDLE&gt;
        <IMG SRC="flower1.jpg"
            WIDTH=85 HEIGHT=129 ALIGN=BOTTOM>
        &lt;IMG SRC="flower1.jpg"
            WIDTH=85 HEIGHT=129 ALIGN=BOTTOM&gt;
    </BODY>
</HTML>
```

The results of this HTML appear in Figure 4.17, where you can see the three different alignments at work.

Horizontally Aligning Text

You can also use the **ALIGN** attribute to set horizontal alignment. When you do, the text "flows" around the image. For example, if you align the image on the left, the text flows around to the right. Here's an example showing how this works:

```
<HTML>
    <HEAD>
        <TITLE>
            Using the &lt;IMG&gt; tag.
        </TITLE>
    </HEAD>

    <BODY>
```

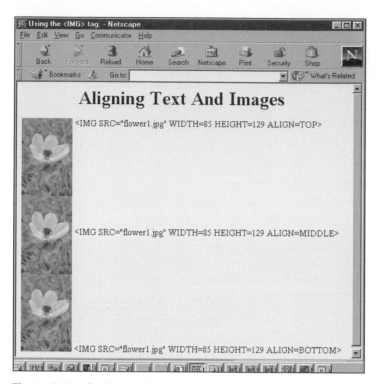

Figure 4.17   Setting vertical alignment.

```
<CENTER>
    <H1>
        Aligning Text And Images
    </H1>
</CENTER>
This example is all about letting text flow around images.
```

```
<IMG SRC="flower1.jpg"
    WIDTH=85 HEIGHT=129 ALIGN=RIGHT>
```

Here's a case where the image is on the right and the text
is on the left. Notice how the text seems to flow around
the image. The image is aligned to the right with this HTML:
<IMG SRC="flower1.jpg" WIDTH=85 HEIGHT=129 ALIGN=RIGHT>.
The result looks quite impressive and professional, giving
your page a stylish boost. On the other hand, notice what
happens if you align the image to the left instead of to the
right, as you see here in the image immediately below. In
this case, the text is flowing around to the right of the image.
Here, the HTML used to align the image is:

```
<IMG SRC="flower1.jpg"
        WIDTH=85 HEIGHT=129 ALIGN=LEFT>
```

<IMG SRC="flower1.jpg" WIDTH=85 HEIGHT=129 ALIGN=LEFT>
With this alignment, text continues on the right side of the
image, wrapping around the image as needed. Using alignments
like this makes it easy to present images and text together,
much as you'd see in a newspaper. It's a nice effect that
gives your pages some impact. Note that if the spacing is
too tight for you, you can increase the <IMG> element's
HSPACE and VSPACE settings.
    </BODY>
</HTML>

The results appear in Figure 4.18. As you can see in the figure, once you align an image, the text flows around it respecting that alignment.

On the other hand, what if you want to stop text from wrapping around images? No problem—take a look at the next section for the details.

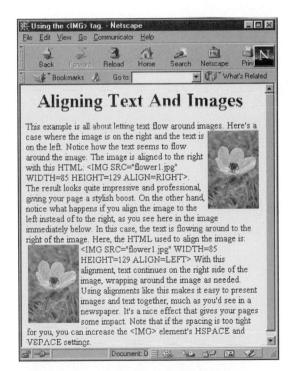

Figure 4.18   Setting horizontal alignment.

Avoiding Text Wrapping

"I need more control," the novice programmer says, "I want to stop text from wrapping around images after a certain point. Can I do that?" "Actually," you say, "you can. Just use the **CLEAR** attribute of the **
** element."

At times, you might want to stop filling in the text next to an aligned image and skip to a point beyond the image. You can't do that with a standard **
** or **<P>** element, but you can do it if you use the **CLEAR** attribute for these tags. Here are the possible settings for this attribute:

- **ALL**—Move to a point past the image where both margins are clear.

- **LEFT**—Move to a point past the image where the left margin is clear.

- **RIGHT**—Move to a point past the image where the right margin is clear.

The idea is that you use the **CLEAR** attribute to indicate when text should start again—when the left margin is clear, the right margin, or both.

Here's an example. In this case, I stop text from wrapping around two images using the **CLEAR** attribute of the **
** element:

```
<HTML>
    <HEAD>
        <TITLE>
            Using the &lt;IMG&gt; tag.
        </TITLE>
    </HEAD>

    <BODY>
        <CENTER>
            <H1>
                Aligning Text And Images
            </H1>
        </CENTER>

        This example is all about letting text flow around images.

        <IMG SRC="flower1.jpg"
            WIDTH=85 HEIGHT=129 ALIGN=RIGHT>

        Here's a case where the image is on the right and the text
        is on the left. Notice how the text seems to flow around
        the image. Now I use &lt;BR CLEAR=RIGHT&gt;,
```

```
    <BR CLEAR=RIGHT>

    <IMG SRC="flower1.jpg"
        WIDTH=85 HEIGHT=129 ALIGN=LEFT>

    which skips to a point where the right margin is free
    again. Now the right margin is clear, but there's an
    image to the left. I can skip to a point where the left
    margin is clear again with &lt;BR CLEAR=RIGHT&gt;,

    <BR CLEAR=LEFT>

    which means that this text will continue after the image
    when the left margin is clear again.

    </BODY>
</HTML>
```

You can see the results of this HTML in Figure 4.19. Using the **CLEAR** attribute lets you move past images and stops text from flowing around them.

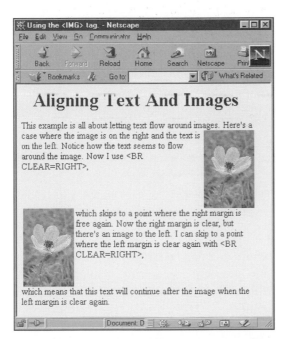

Figure 4.19   Using the **
** element's **CLEAR** attribute.

Scaling Images To Different Sizes

Browsers will respect the size you set for an image using the **<IMG>** element's **WIDTH** and **HEIGHT** attributes by using the size specified in preference to the image's actual size. For this reason, you can use these attributes to *scale* images, changing their size. In this example, I'm doubling the horizontal and vertical dimensions of an image with the **WIDTH** and **HEIGHT** attributes:

```
<HTML>
    <HEAD>
        <TITLE>
            Using the &lt;IMG&gt; tag.
        </TITLE>
    </HEAD>

    <BODY>
        <CENTER>
            <H1>
                Scaling Images
            </H1>
        </CENTER>
        Here's an image (&lt;IMG SRC="image.gif"
            WIDTH=252 HEIGHT=115&gt;):
        <BR>
        <IMG SRC="image.gif"
            WIDTH=252 HEIGHT=115 ALT="An image">
        <BR>
        Doubled in both dimensions (&lt;IMG SRC="image.gif"
            WIDTH=504 HEIGHT=230&gt;):
        <BR>
        <IMG SRC="image.gif"
            WIDTH=504 HEIGHT=230 ALT="An image">
    </BODY>
</HTML>
```

The results appear in Figure 4.20, where you can see the image in its normal and doubled sizes. This technique has one practical application: You can install high-resolution small images on your ISP so they'll download quickly, and then increase their size in the browser using the **WIDTH** and **HEIGHT** attributes. If your images are long on download time, you might want to consider using this method.

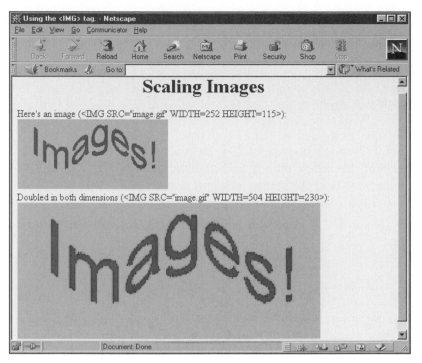

Figure 4.20   Scaling an image by doubling both dimensions.

Using The **LOWSRC** Attribute For Image Previews

"Darn," says the novice programmer, "the high-resolution images in my page are still loading too slowly for users who are moving on to other pages." "Well," you say, "what about using a low-resolution version of the image, which you can display with the **LOWSRC** attribute while the larger image is downloading? By the way, how big is the high-resolution image?" "It's 12000×8000 pixels," the NP says. You say, "Uh oh."

You can use **LOWSRC** in browsers, like Netscape Navigator and Internet Explorer, to give the URL a fast-loading low-resolution version of an image. This attribute is not standard HTML. When you use **LOWSRC**, you specify a URL for both this attribute and the **SRC** attribute, which holds the URL for the larger, high-resolution image. Here's an example:

```
<IMG SRC="maximage.gif"
    LOWSRC="minimage.gif"
    ALT="A view of the Alps."
    WIDTH=12000
    HEIGHT=8000
>
```

Setting Page Background Images

"Help!" the novice programmer cries. "What's wrong, NP?" you say. "I want to use a cool background image that I found on the Internet for my Web page," the NP says, "but I have no clue how to do it!" "It's easy," you say, "just use the **BACKGROUND** attribute of the **<BODY>** element. By the way, NP, is that image copyrighted?" "Uh oh," says the NP.

You've undoubtedly seen Web pages with graphical backgrounds. Using such backgrounds is one of the most common and dazzling of Web page effects. To add a background image to your Web page, you simply assign the URL of the image you want to use to the **BACKGROUND** attribute of the **<BODY>** element, like this:

```
<HTML>
    <HEAD>
        <TITLE>
            Using background images.
        </TITLE>
    </HEAD>

    <BODY BACKGROUND="flower.jpg">
        <CENTER>
            <H1>
                Horticulture!
            </H1>
        </CENTER>
        <BR>
        <BR>
        <BR>
        <H2>
            Don't you just love horticulture? I know I do!
        </H2>
    </BODY>
</HTML>
```

TIP: There are thousands of free background images available for you to use on the Internet. For example, I just located 13,729 Web pages matching the search text "free backgrounds" in a Web search engine (and I've spent many hours among those pages in the past). Some of these backgrounds are very cool and contain textures and impressive designs—take a look! Just make sure they're really available for use in terms of copyright before using them.

The results of this HTML appear in Figure 4.21, where as you can see, the browser has used the image I indicated to tile the background of the page.

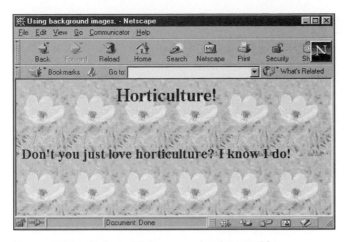

Figure 4.21   Giving a Web page a background image.

4. Working With Images

TIP: *In recent versions of Netscape Navigator and Internet Explorer, you can use animated GIFs as backgrounds. But be careful—the results can be very distracting, not to mention annoying.*

TIP: *Is your background image overwhelming your foreground text in your Web page? That's a common problem, but one that's easy to fix. You can use a graphics program, like LView Pro (**http://lview.com**), to lighten the image to pastel colors that won't interfere with the foreground. To do that in LView Pro, select Retouch/Gamma Corrections and slide the scrollbars to the right. You can also create stunning backgrounds including effects, such as making images appear to be engraved or etched, with graphics packages, like PhotoStudio 2000 (**www.arcsoft.com**).*

Using The **<OBJECT>** Tag To Insert Images

W3C has great plans for the **<OBJECT>** element, originally introduced by Microsoft and now meant to replace the Netscape **<APPLET>** element, among others. In fact, according to W3C, you're supposed to be able to use the **<OBJECT>** element in place of the **<IMG>** element (we'll discuss the **<OBJECT>** element, which is a big one, in Chapter 8).

Here's an example. Note that I'm specifying the image type as **IMAGE/GIF** so the browser knows what kind of data it will be dealing with. **IMAGE/GIF** is the GIF format's Multipurpose Internet Mail Extensions (MIME) type (for more on MIME types see Chapter 8):

```
<HTML>
    <HEAD>
        <TITLE>
            Using the &lt;OBJECT&gt; tag.
        </TITLE>
    </HEAD>

    <BODY>
        <CENTER>
            <OBJECT SRC="flower1.gif" TYPE="IMAGE/GIF" STANDBY="A flower">
            </OBJECT>
        </CENTER>
    </BODY>
</HTML>
```

I'd like to show you how this would look in a browser, but unfortunately neither Netscape Navigator nor Internet Explorer implement this use of the **<OBJECT>** element. When they do, however, it'll be worth knowing about because you'll be able to handle PNG format images (see the "Images In Web Pages" section at the beginning of this chapter for more details) smoothly even in browsers that don't handle that format. For instance, in this example, I'm giving the browser an alternate GIF image if it doesn't support PNG:

```
<HTML>
    <HEAD>
        <TITLE>
            Using the &lt;OBJECT&gt; tag.
        </TITLE>
    </HEAD>

    <BODY>
        <CENTER>
            <OBJECT SRC="flower1.png" TYPE="IMAGE/PNG" STANDBY="A flower">
                <OBJECT SRC="flower1.gif" TYPE="IMAGE/GIF"
                    STANDBY="A flower">
                </OBJECT>
            </OBJECT>
        </CENTER>
    </BODY>
</HTML>
```

Using Images To Replace Missing Content

Sometimes, when you do something fancy, some browsers won't understand how to display your code. For example, say you have a fancy image that you created with a Java applet where the graphical letters in the message dance around. Now say that the Web page is loaded into a Web browser that doesn't understand Java— nothing will show up. On the other hand, using the **<IMG>** element, you can present at least a static version of the message. Here's how: Just use the **<IMG>** inside the **<APPLET>** or **<OBJECT>** element:

```
<HTML>
    <HEAD>
        <TITLE>
            Using the &lt;OBJECT&gt; tag.
        </TITLE>
    </HEAD>

    <BODY>

        <APPLET CODE="myterrificapplet.class"
            CODEBASE="http://www.starpowder.com/steve" WIDTH=450
                HEIGHT=150>
            <PARAM NAME="PARAM1" VALUE="READY">
            <PARAM NAME="PARAM1" VALUE="SET">
            <PARAM NAME="PARAM1" VALUE="GO">
            <IMG SRC="staticappletimage.gif">
        </APPLET>

    </BODY>
</HTML>
```

The browser that doesn't understand Java will ignore the **<APPLET>** and **<PARAM>** elements (see "**<APPLET>**—Embedding Applets In Web Pages" in Chapter 16 and "**<OBJECT>** And **<PARAM>**—Placing An Object Into A Web Page" in Chapter 8 for more on these elements) and only see the **<IMG>** element, which will display the static image you specified to replace the moving one.

Tiling Images—Creating Image Mosaics

You may have seen larger images broken up into pieces in Web pages. The individual pieces are downloaded separately and when they're all downloaded, the whole image is complete. One reason this is done is to increase download time. If you break a large image into four pieces, a browser can open four HTTP connections to the server instead of just one. When server connections are slow, using the tiling technique allows the browser to create multiple connections to the server, resulting in accelerated download time.

So how do you break an image into several pieces in a Web page and then put them together again? One way to do this is to simply put **<IMG>** elements right next to each other without any white space (including line breaks) between them. This prevents the browser from adding spaces between the images. Here's an example:

```
<HTML>
    <HEAD>
        <TITLE>
            Tiling images.
        </TITLE>
    </HEAD>

    <BODY>
        <CENTER>
            <H1>
                Tiling Images
            </H1>
            <IMG SRC="FLOWER1.JPG" WIDTH=85 HEIGHT=129
            BORDER=0><IMG SRC="FLOWER1.JPG" WIDTH=85
            HEIGHT=129 BORDER=0><IMG SRC="FLOWER1.JPG"
            WIDTH=85 HEIGHT=129 BORDER=0><IMG
            SRC="FLOWER1.JPG" WIDTH=85 HEIGHT=129 BORDER=0>
        </CENTER>
    </BODY>
</HTML>
```

The results of this HTML appear in Figure 4.22. All four copies of the same image are lined up right next to each other without any spacing between them.

What if you wanted to arrange the images in some other way? That's commonly done with tables, which we'll discuss in depth in Chapter 6. Here's an example where I stack images on top of each other in a 2×2 pattern. Note that I turn off all the default table spacing by setting the **CELLPADDING**, **CELLSPACING**, and **BORDER** attributes to 0:

Figure 4.22   Tiling images in a row.

```
<HTML>
    <HEAD>
        <TITLE>
            Tiling images.
        </TITLE>
    </HEAD>

    <BODY>
        <CENTER>
            <H1>
                Tiling Images
            </H1>
            <TABLE CELLPADDING=0 CELLSPACING=0 BORDER=0>
                <TR>
                    <TD>
                        <IMG SRC="FLOWER1.JPG" WIDTH=85 HEIGHT=129
                        BORDER=0><IMG SRC="FLOWER1.JPG" WIDTH=85
                        HEIGHT=129 BORDER=0></TD></TR><TR><TD>
                        <IMG SRC="FLOWER1.JPG" WIDTH=85 HEIGHT=129
                        BORDER=0><IMG SRC="FLOWER1.JPG" WIDTH=85
                        HEIGHT=129 BORDER=0>
                    </TD>
                </TR>
            </TABLE>
        </CENTER>
    </BODY>
</HTML>
```

4. Working With Images

219

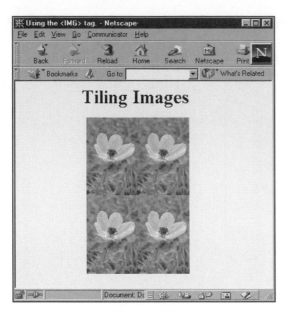

Figure 4.23   Tiling images in two dimensions.

The results of this HTML appear in Figure 4.23.

Creating Overlapping Images

One interesting effect using images is to overlap them in a Web page. You can do this with layers in Netscape Navigator. Here's an example:

```
<HTML>

    <HEAD>
        <TITLE>
            Creating Overlapping Images With Layers
        </TITLE>
    </HEAD>

    <BODY>

        <H1 ALIGN="CENTER">
            Creating Overlapping Images With Layers
        </H1>

        <LAYER NAME="LAYER1">
            <IMG SRC="FLOWER1.JPG" WIDTH=85 HEIGHT=129>
        </LAYER>
```

```
<LAYER NAME="LAYER2" LEFT=50 TOP=80>
    <IMG SRC="FLOWER1.JPG" WIDTH=85 HEIGHT=129>
</LAYER>

<LAYER NAME="LAYER3" LEFT=100 TOP=100>
    <IMG SRC="FLOWER1.JPG" WIDTH=85 HEIGHT=129>
</LAYER>

    </BODY>

</HTML>
```

The results of this HTML appear in Figure 4.24. This technique works, but it's restricted to the only browser that supports layers—Netscape Navigator.

To overlap images with more general HTML, use the **<DIV>** element. Here's a Web page that overlaps images using **<DIV>**, which will work in both Netscape Navigator and Internet Explorer:

```
<HTML>

    <HEAD>
        <TITLE>
            Using The &lt;DIV&gt; Element To Overlap Images
        </TITLE>
    </HEAD>
```

Figure 4.24   Overlapping images with layers.

221

```
<BODY>

    <H1 ALIGN="CENTER">
        Creating Overlapping Images With &lt;DIV&gt;
    </H1>

    <DIV STYLE="POSITION:ABSOLUTE; LEFT:100; TOP:60;">
        <IMG SRC="FLOWER1.JPG" WIDTH=85 HEIGHT=129>
    </DIV>

    <DIV STYLE="POSITION:ABSOLUTE; LEFT:120; TOP:90;">
        <IMG SRC="FLOWER1.JPG" WIDTH=85 HEIGHT=129>
    </DIV>

    <DIV STYLE="POSITION:ABSOLUTE; LEFT:150; TOP:120;">
        <IMG SRC="FLOWER1.JPG" WIDTH=85 HEIGHT=129>
    </DIV>

</BODY>

</HTML>
```

The results of this HTML appear in Internet Explorer in Figure 4.25. As you can see, the copies of the same image appear in a cascade in the figure. Using the **<DIV>** element, you can arrange images as you like. I'll cover this element in greater depth when discussing styles later in Chapter 9.

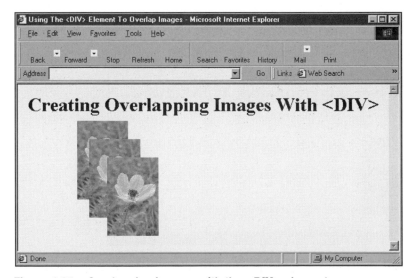

Figure 4.25   Overlapping images with the **<DIV>** element.

Chapter 5

Links and Lists

(continued)

In Depth

This chapter is all about creating links and creating lists in HTML. Both elements are integral to writing Web pages, but of the two, hyperlinks are by far the most popular. The World Wide Web thrives on hyperlinks. Imagine a Web without links, without browsers, without search engines that give you lists of hyperlinks of pages that match your search. What makes the Web a web? Hyperlinks.

Links connect the pages of the Web, letting the user navigate to a new page just by clicking the link. Without them, the Web wouldn't work. Breaking long documents into multiple pages is made possible through hyperlinks, allowing you to navigate from section to section easily without waiting for everything to download at once. And without a mechanism like hyperlinks, it would be impossible to organize Web sites. Hyperlinks are what make the World Wide Web go round.

Hyperlinks and hypertext were created by Ted Nelson in the 1960s, from the design of his famous Xanadu system. The idea was to create a new model of text to let users skip from place to place, and of course, the results are well known to anyone who has even casually browsed the Web. Tired of where you are and want to take a look at something else? Just click the link—usually set off from the surrounding text in color and underlined—and you're there.

There are a number of ways to work with hyperlinks, and I'll cover them in depth in this chapter. Standard hyperlinks are text based; the hyperlink is displayed as simple text. Graphical hyperlinks use images instead of text—click the image and you navigate to the hyperlink's target. I'll also take a look at specialized uses of these two types of hyperlinks, like making footnotes in hyperlinks for easy lookup, and using graphical images, like arrows, specifically for navigation.

I'll also discuss how to create *image maps* in Web pages in this chapter. Image maps are those images that you can click in various different places to make your browser navigate to a new location. Image maps provide an easy graphical way to navigate around a site and to other sites. They are becoming more and more popular, especially in larger sites.

The other types of HTML elements I'll take a look at in this chapter are lists. You use these elements to display lists in a Web page, like this:

- Here's
- a
- list!

You can create all types of lists in HTML, and in fact, lists let you save considerable space in Web pages. Because space is always at a premium, lists present material in a compact format. I'll take a look at list possibilities in this chapter, such as creating bulleted lists, numbered lists, nested lists, even lists that use Roman numerals.

The main topic of this chapter, however, is hyperlinks, so I'll start with those.

Creating Hyperlinks

You use the **<A>** element (A stands for anchor, and we'll see why in this chapter) to create hyperlinks in HTML. The most common form of hyperlink is undoubtedly the text hyperlink, where the hyperlink itself usually appears underlined and in a different color from the surrounding text to set it off from that text. I'll take a look at creating text hyperlinks first.

TIP: *According to the official HTML 4 specification, nested links are illegal, so never use **<A>** tags inside **<A>** elements.*

Creating Text Hyperlinks

The standard form of a hyperlink element looks like this:

```
Find the answers at <A HREF="http://W3C.org">W3C</A>.
```

I'm using the **<A>** tag to set up a hyperlink and using the **HREF** attribute to set the target of the hyperlink to **http://W3C.org** (which is the home page for the World Wide Web Consortium). This is the URL that the browser will navigate to when the user clicks the link. The text inside the **<A>** element will appear in the hyperlink style for the page, which is underlined and usually in a different color from the surrounding text like this:

```
Find the answers at W3C.
```

All the user has to do is to click the W3C hyperlink to be transported to the W3C Web site. Here's a full example, also linking to W3C:

```
<HTML>
    <HEAD>
        <TITLE>
            Creating A Hyperlink
        </TITLE>
    </HEAD>

    <BODY>

        <CENTER>

            <H1>
                Creating A Hyperlink
            </H1>

            Here's a Web site to check out:
            <A HREF="http://W3C.ORG">W3C</A>!
        </CENTER>

    </BODY>
</HTML>
```

The results of this HTML appear in Figure 5.1, where you can see the text hyperlink, ready to be clicked.

NOTE: *You might notice that I made the text of the hyperlink "W3C", not just "Click here" or "Here" or something like that. Web designers consider it better practice to make the hyperlink itself as descriptive as possible.*

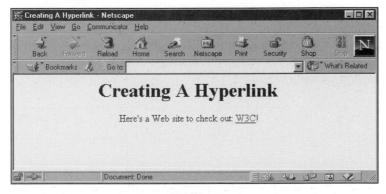

Figure 5.1   Creating a text hyperlink.

Creating Graphical Hyperlinks

In addition to text, you can also use images as hyperlinks, adding a little "pizazz" to your pages. Doing so is easy to do—just put an **<IMG>** element in the **<A>** element instead of text. Here's an example showing how this works:

```
<HTML>
    <HEAD>
        <TITLE>
            Creating A Graphical Hyperlink
        </TITLE>
    </HEAD>

    <BODY>

        <CENTER>

            <H1>
                Creating A Graphical Hyperlink
            </H1>

            <A HREF="http://W3C.ORG">
                <IMG WIDTH=277 HEIGHT=114 SRC="clickme.gif"
                    ALT="Click me to go to W3C!">
            </A>
        </CENTER>

    </BODY>
</HTML>
```

The results of this HTML appear in Figure 5.2. When the user clicks the image in the figure, the browser navigates to the hyperlink's target, **http://W3C.org**. Note also that you can use the **<IMG>** element's **ALT** attribute to add a tool tip to the hyperlink, which appears when the mouse rests over the hyperlink image showing the hyperlink's target, as in Figure 5.2.

TIP: *Want to turn the border of a graphical hyperlink off or make it wider? Use the **<IMG>** element's **BORDER** attribute. **BORDER=0** turns off the border. This is probably not advisable for hyperlinks because the border is how the user knows it's a hyperlink.*

Linking To A Section Of A Document

It's also possible to link to a section of a document instead of linking to the document as a whole. When you navigate to a document using the document's URL, the browser opens the document and positions the top of the document at the top

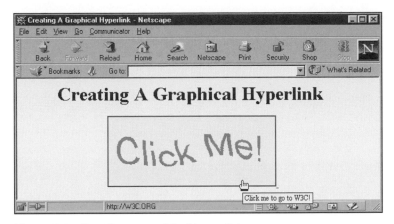

Figure 5.2   Creating a graphical hyperlink.

of the browser window. Say, however, that you've written a training manual with a hundred individual topics in one page—how can you navigate to one of the topics, not just to the top of the page?

You can use *anchors*. Creating anchors is another valuable use of the **<A>** element. Anchors supply a name to a section of a page, so you can use the anchor's name to navigate to that section. Here's how you use the **<A>** element to create a named anchor—note that I'm using the **NAME** attribute of the **<A>** element here, not the **HREF** attribute:

```
<A NAME="SEASHORE">A guide to marine biology.</A>
```

Now that I've named the text in the anchor using the name **SEASHORE**, I can refer to that anchor as **#SEASHORE** (the **#** is essential). For example, here's a hyperlink to that section from another place in the same document:

```
Want to learn more about the <A HREF="#SEASHORE">Sea shore</A>?
```

When the user clicks this hyperlink, the browser will reposition itself in the same page, placing the **SEASHORE** anchor section at the top of the page.

Here's another example. In this case, the user can click a hyperlink to move to the bottom of the page, like this:

```
<HTML>
    <HEAD>
        <TITLE>
            Linking To A Section In A Page
```

```
            </TITLE>
        </HEAD>

        <BODY>

            <CENTER>

                <H1>
                    Linking To A Section In A Page
                </H1>

                Click here to go to the
                <A HREF="#BOTTOM">bottom</A>
                of the page.

                <BR>
                <BR>
                <BR>
                <BR>
                <BR>
                <BR>
                <BR>
                <BR>
                <BR>
                <BR>
                <BR>
                <BR>
                <BR>

                <HR>

                    <A NAME="BOTTOM">This is the bottom of the page.</A>
            </CENTER>

        </BODY>
    </HTML>
```

When the user clicks the hyperlink, shown in Figure 5.3, the browser looks for the hyperlink's target, which is the anchor named **BOTTOM** and navigates to that anchor. You can see the results in Figure 5.4. The browser has moved to the anchor at the bottom of the same page.

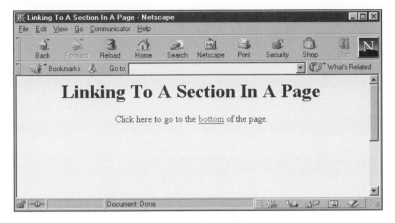

Figure 5.3   Creating an anchored hyperlink.

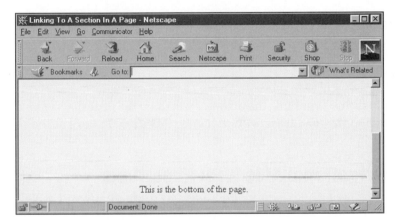

Figure 5.4   Navigating to an anchor.

TIP: *What if you're anchoring text that's in another element, such as a header? For instance, **<H1>What About Oil Painting?</H1>**. Should the **<A>** element be inside or outside of the header? Many browsers will function either way, but some will have problems unless you put the **<A>** tags inside the outer tags to make a well-defined anchor like this: **<H1><A NAME="OILPAINTING">What About Oil Painting?</A></H1>**.*

The anchored section you link to doesn't need to be in the same document at all. You can link to a section inside another Web page as long as you add **#** and the anchor name to the end of the URL, like this: **www.starpowder.com/steve/ fishing.html#BAIT**. Here's an example where I link to the anchored section named **BOTTOM** in the page discussion.html:

```
<HTML>
    <HEAD>
        <TITLE>
```

```
                    Linking To A Section In Another Page
                </TITLE>
            </HEAD>

            <BODY>

                <CENTER>

                    <H1>
                        Linking To A Section In Another Page
                    </H1>

                    Click here to go to the
                    <A HREF="discussion.html#BOTTOM">bottom</A>
                    of the <I>other</I> page.

                </CENTER>

            </BODY>
        </HTML>
```

When the user clicks this hyperlink, the browser will open the page discussion.html and position itself so the anchored section named **BOTTOM** starts at the top of the page.

Creating Navigational Aids With Hyperlinks

One popular use of hyperlinks is to make it easy to navigate around a Web site using image buttons, like arrows. Here's an example that displays arrows to let the user navigate to the next or previous page in a series of pages, or to navigate to the home page just by clicking the appropriate image:

```
<HTML>
    <HEAD>
        <TITLE>
            Creating Graphical Navigational Aids
        </TITLE>
    </HEAD>

    <BODY>

        <CENTER>

            <H1>
                Creating Graphical Navigational Aids
```

```
            </H1>

            Want to get somewhere fast? Click a button below...

            <BR>

            <A HREF="prev.html">
                <IMG WIDTH=172 HEIGHT=117 SRC="left.gif"
                    ALT="Previous"  BORDER=0>
            </A>

            <A HREF="index.html">
                <IMG WIDTH=161 HEIGHT=105 SRC="home.gif"
                    ALT="Home"  BORDER=0>
            </A>

            <A HREF="next.html">
                <IMG WIDTH=172 HEIGHT=117 SRC="right.gif"
                    ALT="Next"  BORDER=0>
            </A>

        </CENTER>

    </BODY>
</HTML>
```

The results of this HTML appear in Figure 5.5. As you can see in the figure, the user can click any of the handy (if slightly oversized in this example) images to make navigation easier.

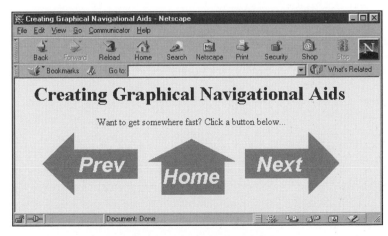

Figure 5.5   Using hyperlinks as navigational aids.

As you know, the target of a hyperlink is a URL, but it turns out that there are many different types of URLs that browsers understand. Knowing what URLs are is essential to the work we'll be doing here, so I'll discuss creating URLs next.

All About URLs

URL stands for Uniform Resource Locator (not, as many people think, Universal Resource Locator). A URL is a Web address. Most people think of URLs as something like this: **http://www.starpowder.com/steve/superduperpage.html**, but in fact there are many forms of URLs, including relative and absolute URLs. I'll take a look at these first.

TIP: *Besides URLs, there are some other acronyms you might encounter when working with hyperlinks: URC (Uniform Resource Citation); URI (Uniform Resource Identifier); and URN (Uniform Resource Name).*

NOTE: *The case sensitivity of file names in URLs can be important. HTML itself is not case sensitive, but some Web servers that run under Unix are and may have trouble finding the right file if you don't use the right case.*

Relative And Absolute URLs

If I wrote something like this, **http://www.W3C.org**, you'd realize that I was referring to a specific URL:

```
<A HREF="http://W3C.org">
```

But what if I wrote this?

```
<A HREF="mountaineering.html">
```

In this example, I'm just giving a file name, mountaineering.html, as the URL—but it's a perfectly valid URL. It's valid because it's a *relative* URL, relative to the current page. If the current page visible in the browser is **http://www.starpowder.com/steve/vacations.html**, then the Web browser will know that the hyperlink in the this HTML points to **http://www.starpowder.com/steve/mountaineering.html** because it keeps the current page's URL, substituting **mountaineering.html** for **vacations.html**.

Using relative URLs can save you a lot of time when writing Web pages because they are shorter and often easier to specify. What's a relative URL relative to? It's relative to the current page or to the URL you've specified with the **<BASE>** element (see "**<BASE>**—Setting The Base For Hyperlinks" in the Immediate Solutions section).

Here are some examples of relative URLs:

- *bigtime.html*—Points to the page bigtime.html in the same directory on the Internet Service Provider (ISP) as the currently open page.

- *archives/bigtime.html*—Points to the page bigtime.html in the directory named archives, which is a subdirectory of the directory the current page is in.

- *archives/old/bigtime.html*—Points to the page bigtime.html in the directory named old, which is a subdirectory of the directory named archives, which is itself a subdirectory of the directory the current page is in.

- *../bigtime.html*—Points to bigtime.html in the directory *above* the directory the current page is in (".." refers to the directory above the current one).

- *../archives/bigtime.html*—Points to bigtime.html in the directory named archives, which is in the directory above the current directory.

Absolute URLs, on the other hand, do not rely on being relative to anything. They specify a page's full Web address, like **http://www.starpowder.com/steve/mountaineering.html**. All the information the browser needs to know is in the URL—the protocol to use to get the page (Hyptertext Transfer Protocol [HTTP]), the name of the ISP to contact, the directory to search on the ISP, and the name of the file to fetch. Here arc somc cxamples of absolute URLs:

- *http://www.starpowder.com/steve/bigtime.html*—Refers to the page bigtime.html in the steve directory of the **www.starpowder.com** server.

- *http://www.w3.org/MarkUp/*—Refers to the page index.html (default.html under the Mircrosoft Internet Information Server) in the MarkUp directory on the **www.w3.org** server.

TIP: *There's one good reason to use relative URLs instead of absolute URLs: If you move all your files en masse to a new directory in your Web server, all absolute links will become invalid (called broken links), but relative URLs will remain valid.*

Besides the standard characters you see in URLs, you might also see something like this from time to time:

```
http://www.starpowder.com/cgi/script.cgi?text=Now+is+the+time&color=blue
```

This kind of URL is used when your Web page sends data to the Web server after the user clicks a Submit button. This data is tacked on to the end of the URL following a question mark (**?**) and consists of parameter pairs. In this example, the text parameter is being set to "Now is the time" (spaces are replaced with plus signs [+] by the browser), and the parameter named "color" is being set to blue. We'll discuss more about this type of URL when working with CGI scripts in Chapter 20.

TIP: *What if your Web page is stored in a directory whose name has a space in it? Can you use a URL like* **http://www.starpowder.com/my cool pages/index.html** *in an* **<A>** *element? You can, but at the very least, you should enclose it in quotation marks—even then some browsers will have problems (such as Netscape 3 and earlier). It's best to use the URL escape code for a space, which is 20. The hexadecimal number 20 is 32 in decimal, which is the ASCII (American Standard Code for Information Interchange) code for a space. For example,* **http://www.starpowder.com/my%20cool%20pages/index.html***.*

You can open the file c:\html\bigtime.html on Windows systems by typing that path and file name directly into the browser, but there's another way of doing the same thing using the file URL type, like this: **file://c:/html/bigtime.htm**. This tells the browser specifically that the data you want to read is stored in a local file (so you don't need a forward slash at the very beginning of the URL). In fact, there are a number of URL types.

Types Of URLs

Here is a list of the different types of protocols you can use to create URLs with:

- *file*—File URLs; the address in the URL refers to a local file.

- *ftp*—File Transfer Protocol, the protocol for transporting files on the Internet. You can also specify an FTP username and password as part of the URL: **ftp://*username*:*password*@ftp.starpowder.com/steve/*filename***.

- *gopher*—This URL uses the Gopher protocol on the Internet; uses a Gopher server to find and get files.

- *http*—Hypertext Transfer Protocol, the protocol you use with Web pages.

- *https*—Secure Hypertext Transfer Protocol, the protocol you use with secure Web pages.

- *mailto*—An email URL; clicking this URL will open the user's email program so he or she can send email to the email address given in the URL.

- *news*—A Usenet URL pointing to a message on Usenet. You can use this kind of URL in two ways: **news:*groupname*** or **news:*messageID***. If your browser supports newsgroups, the first way will display all the posts in a Usenet group. The second way will display an individual message, which you must refer to using a Usenet message ID.

Creating Image Maps

Image maps are another powerful hyperlink technique that makes pages come alive. Image maps provide users with a graphical aid for navigation to a new location. For example, you might want to display an actual map of your site and let the user navigate to each location just by clicking the map in the right place.

There are two kinds of image maps: server-side and client-side image maps. They differ in implementation details: server-side maps are processed on the Web server, and client-side image maps are processed in the Web browser.

Server-Side Image Maps

In the following example, I'll create a server-side image map by surrounding an **<IMG>** element with **<A>** tags, which is how you create hyperlinks. In this case, I'll point to a .map file that holds the image map locations, so when the user clicks in a particular location, the server knows what to do. Here's the HTML:

```
<HTML>
    <HEAD>
        <TITLE>
            Using A Server Side Image Map
        </TITLE>
    </HEAD>

    <BODY BGCOLOR="BLACK">

        <CENTER>
            <A HREF="MAIN.MAP">
                <IMG WIDTH=528 HEIGHT=137 SRC="mainmenu.jpg"
                    BORDER=0 ALT="Image Map" ISMAP>
            </A>
        </CENTER>

    </BODY>
</HTML>
```

Note that I'm referring to a file named main.map on the server; that file connects clickable regions in the image with URLs that the browser will navigate to when those regions are clicked. Here's what's in main.map (we'll see how to create map files like this one in Immediate Solutions sections like "Creating Client-Side Image Maps"):

```
DEFAULT http://www.starpowder.com/steve/index.html#mainmenu
RECT http://www.reuters.com 16,39 127,61
RECT http://www.starpowder.com/steve/search.html 62,71 173,93
RECT http://www.nnic.noaa.gov 98,104 209,126
RECT http://www.starpowder.com/steve/gbook.htm 411,35 522,57
RECT http://www.yahoo.com/Guides_and_Tutorials/ 360,67 471,89
RECT http://www.web21.com/services/hot100/index.html 328,98 439,120
```

You can see the result in Figure 5.6. As you see in the figure, the image map is ready to be clicked, and when the user clicks one of the labels, the browser will navigate to the appropriate URL. Presenting a graphical navigation device like this is a terrific help for users and makes your site more attractive and accessible.

Client-Side Image Maps

In client-side image maps, all the work is done in the browser. You include the map information using **<MAP>** and **<AREA>** elements. Here's an example that performs the same function as the example in the previous section:

```
<HTML>
    <HEAD>
        <TITLE>
            Using A Client Side Image Map
        </TITLE>
    </HEAD>

    <BODY BGCOLOR="BLACK">
```

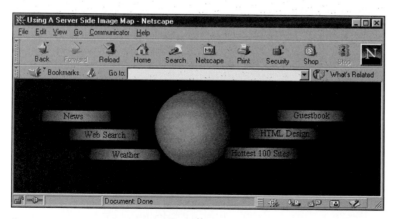

Figure 5.6   A server-side image map.

```
<CENTER>
    <IMG WIDTH=528 HEIGHT=137 SRC="mainmenu.jpg"
        BORDER=0 ALT="Image Map" USEMAP="#IMAP">
    <MAP NAME="IMAP">
        <AREA NAME="LINK1" SHAPE=RECT COORDS="16,39 127,61"
            HREF="http://www.reuters.com">
        <AREA NAME="LINK2" SHAPE=RECT COORDS="62,71 173,93"
            HREF="http://www.starpowder.com/steve/search.html">
        <AREA NAME="LINK3" SHAPE=RECT COORDS="98,104 209,126"
            HREF="http://www.nnic.noaa.gov">
        <AREA NAME="LINK4" SHAPE=RECT COORDS="411,35 522,57"
            HREF="http://www.starpowder.com/steve/gbook.htm">
        <AREA NAME="LINK5" SHAPE=RECT COORDS="360,67 471,89"
            HREF="http://www.yahoo.com/Guides_and_Tutorials/">
        <AREA NAME="LINK6" SHAPE=RECT COORDS="328,98 439,120"
            HREF="http://www.web21.com/services/hot100/index.html">
        <AREA NAME="DEFAULT" SHAPE=DEFAULT
            HREF=
            "http://www.starpowder.com/steve/index.html#mainmenu">
    </MAP>
</CENTER>

</BODY>
</HTML>
```

5. Links And Lists

TIP: *So what kind of image map should you use, server-side or client-side? The older server-side image maps are on their way out. Because they are processed on the server, information has to be sent back to the server and worked on there—which takes time. For a faster response, I recommend client-side image maps (if the user's browser supports them), which are also easier to create.*

Creating image maps and getting the right coordinates for your link regions in the map can be a little difficult. A graphics tool like LView Pro (**www.lview.com**) makes things easier by displaying the location of the mouse in its title bar in pixel coordinates when you click an image. Here are some dedicated image map tools that can make the creation of these maps easier:

• *Imaptol*—A Unix tool, **www.sci.fi/~uucee/ownprojects/**.

• *LiveImage*—A Windows tool, **www.mediatec.com**.

• *Mapedit*—A Windows and Unix tool, **www.boutell.com/mapedit/**.

• *Web HotSpots*—A Windows tool, **www.concentric.net/~automata/ hotspots.shtml**.

Creating Lists

Another popular HTML topic is the creation of *lists*. Lists let you display information in a compact, tight format and are a useful asset to know about. There are three kinds of lists—unordered lists, ordered lists, and definition lists.

Unordered Lists

You can create *unordered lists* with elements like **<UL>**. Each item in the list gets its own element using the **<LI>** list item tag. Here's an example showing how to create a bulleted list:

```
<HTML>

    <HEAD>
        <TITLE>
            An Unordered List
        </TITLE>
    </HEAD>

    <BODY>

        <H1 ALIGN=CENTER>
            Creating An Unordered List
        </H1>

        Here are some items to consider when buying a computer:
        <UL>
            <LI> Speed
            <LI> Cost
            <LI> RAM
            <LI> Disk space
            <LI> CD ROM speed
        </UL>

    </BODY>

</HTML>
```

The results appear in Figure 5.7, where you can see the bulleted vertical list made from all the list items.

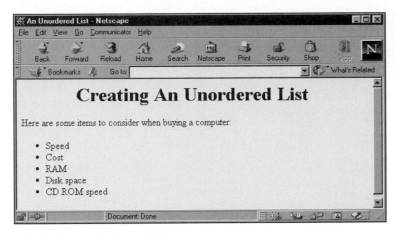

Figure 5.7   An unordered list.

Ordered Lists

While unordered lists display a simple bullet before each list item, *ordered lists* use a number (or lettering) system of some kind to indicate that the items are ordered in some way. Here's an example that creates a simple numbered list using the **<OL>** element:

```
<HTML>

    <HEAD>
        <TITLE>
            An Ordered List
        </TITLE>
    </HEAD>

    <BODY>

        <H1 ALIGN=CENTER>
            Creating An Ordered List
        </H1>

        Here are some items to consider when buying a computer:
        <OL>
            <LI> Speed
            <LI> Cost
            <LI> RAM
            <LI> Disk space
            <LI> CD ROM speed
        </OL>
```

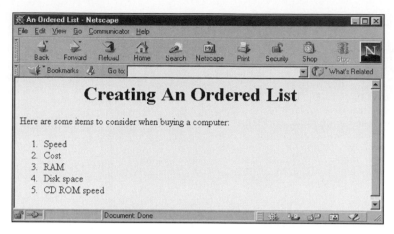

Figure 5.8   An ordered list.

```
    </BODY>

</HTML>
```

The results of this HTML appear in Figure 5.8. You can see that the list in the figure is numbered from one through five. There are other numbering systems possible as we'll see throughout this chapter—everything from letters to roman numerals.

Definition Lists

There's a third type of list—*definition lists*. These lists include both terms and their definitions. You use the **<DL>** element to create these lists, **<DT>** for terms, and **<DD>** for the definition of each term. Here's an example:

```
<HTML>

    <HEAD>
        <TITLE>
            A Definition List
        </TITLE>
    </HEAD>

    <BODY>

        <H1 ALIGN=CENTER>
            Creating A Definition List
        </H1>
```

```
Here are some items to consider when buying a computer:
<DL>
        <DT>Speed<DD>CPU speed in megahertz.
        <DT>Cost<DD>Make sure to keep this down!
        <DT>RAM<DD>Amount of memory in the computer.
        <DT>Disk space<DD>Get plenty of gigabytes.
        <DT>CD ROM speed<DD>Get at least 24X.
</DL>

</BODY>

</HTML>
```

We'll take a look at definition lists in the Immediate Solutions section "**<DL>**, **<DT>**, And **<DD>**—Creating Definition Lists." There's a lot more coming up in this chapter, and we have a lot of ground to cover. I'll turn to the Immediate Solutions section now and start with the **<A>** element.

5. Links And Lists

Immediate Solutions

<A>—Creating A Hyperlink Or An Anchor

Purpose: Creates a hyperlink (use the **HREF** attribute) or an anchor (use the **NAME** attribute).

Start Tag/End Tag: Required/Required

Supported: [2, 3, 3.2, 4, IE1, IE2, IE3, IE4, IE5, NS1, NS2, NS3, NS4]

Attributes:

- **ACCESSKEY**—Assigns a keyboard shortcut to the hyperlink; you usually use a platform-dependent key, like the Alt key in Windows, along with the shortcut to give the hyperlink the focus (when it has the focus, it receives keystrokes). Set to a single (case-insensitive) alphanumeric value. [4, IE4, IE5]

- **CHARSET**—Specifies the character encoding of the target of the hyperlink. Set to a Request For Comments (RFC) 2045 language character set string (the default value is ISO-8859-1). [4]

- **CLASS**—Class of the element (used for rendering). [3, 4, IE4, IE5, NS4]

- **COORDS**—Sets the coordinate values (in pixels) appropriate to the accompanying **SHAPE** attribute to define a region of an image for image maps. Set up **SHAPE** types and **COORDS** definitions as: **SHAPE=RECT COORDS=*"left, top, right, bottom"*; SHAPE=CIRC COORDS=*"centerX, centerY, radius"*; SHAPE=POLY COORDS=*"x1, y1, x2, y2, ... , xn, yn"*.** [4]

- **DIR**—Gives the direction of directionally neutral text (text that doesn't have inherent direction in which you should read it). Possible values: **LTR**: left-to-right text or table and **RTL**: right-to-left text or table. [4, IE5]

- **HREF**—Holds the target URL of the hyperlink. Either this attribute or the **NAME** attribute must be used. Set to a URL. [2, 3, 3.2, 4, IE1, IE2, IE3, IE4, IE5, NS1, NS2, NS3, NS4]

- **HREFLANG**—Specifies the base language of the target indicated in the **HREF** attribute. Set to RFC 1766 values. [4]

- **ID**—A unique alphanumeric identifier for the tag, which you can use to refer to it. [3, 4, IE4, IE5, NS4]

- **LANG**—Base language used for the tag. [3, 4, IE4, IE5]

- **LANGUAGE**—Scripting language used for the tag. [IE4, IE5]

- **METHODS**—Can specify methods to be used in accessing the target. This attribute has disappeared from the HTML 3.2 recommendation. Set to names matching the protocol scheme of the URL in the **HREF** attribute. [2, 3, IE4, IE5]

- **NAME**—Specifies an anchor name, the name you want to use when referring to the enclosed items (such as text, images, and so on) as the target of a hyperlink. Either this attribute or the **HREF** attribute must be used. Set to a string of alphanumeric characters. [2, 3, 3.2, 4, IE1, IE2, IE3, IE4, IE5, NS1, NS2, NS3, NS4]

- **REL**—Specifies the relationship described by the hyperlink. Set to a white space separated list of relationship names. See "**<LINK>**—Setting Link Information" in the Immediate Solutions section for more on the **REL** attribute. [2, 3, 3.2, 4, IE3, IE4, IE5]

- **REV**—Essentially the same as the **REL** attribute, but the syntax works in the reverse direction. A link from A to B with **REL="X"** is the same relationship as a link from B to A with **REV="X"**. Set to a white space separated list of relationship names. [2, 3, 3.2, 4, IE3, IE4, IE5]

- **SHAPE**—Defines the type of region to be defined for mapping in the current **AREA** tag. Used with the **COORDS** attribute. Set to **RECT** (the default), **CIRC**, **CIRCLE**, **POLY**, or **POLYGON**. [3, 4]

- **STYLE**—Inline style indicating how to render the element. [4, IE3, IE4, IE5, NS4]

- **TABINDEX**—Sets the tab sequence of hyperlinks in the page (pressing the Tab key moves from one to the next hyperlink). Set to a positive or negative integer. [4, IE4, IE5]

- **TARGET**—Indicates the named frame for the **HREF** hyperlink to jump to. Set to the name of a frame. [4, IE3, IE4, IE5, NS2, NS3, NS4]

- **TITLE**—An advisory-only title for the target resource. The **TITLE** attribute holds text that will be displayed in tool tips when the mouse rests over the hyperlink. Set to an alphanumeric string. [2, 3, 3.2, 4, IE4, IE5]

- **TYPE**—Specifies the Multipurpose Internet Mail Extensions (MIME) type of the target given in the **HREF** attribute. Set to an alphanumeric MIME type, like image/gif. [4]

- **URN**—Designed to give a more persistent identifier for the **NAME** value of the hyperlink (but never implemented in the main browsers); has been removed from the HTML specification as of HTML 3.2. [2, 3, IE4, IE5]

The big boss appears and says, "We need a hyperlink added to each of the company's Web pages." "OK," you say, "I'll use the **<A>** element. What's the hyperlink to?" "My own Web page," the BB says, "the one with the huge picture of me in it."

The **<A>** element is a big part of what makes HTML work. This is the element you use to create hyperlinks and anchors as discussed in the In Depth section of this chapter. Here's an example that creates a hyperlink to the W3C Web site:

```
<HTML>
    <HEAD>
        <TITLE>
            Creating A Hyperlink
        </TITLE>
    </HEAD>

    <BODY>

        <CENTER>

            <H1>
                Creating A Hyperlink
            </H1>

            Here's a Web site to check out:
                <A HREF="http://W3C.ORG">W3C</A>!
        </CENTER>

    </BODY>
</HTML>
```

You can see the results of this HTML in Figure 5.1. Note that I'm creating a hyperlink by assigning the target URL to the **HREF** attribute. The actual text in the **<A>** element is what will appear as the hyperlink in the Web page. The hyperlink is usually underlined and in a different color than the surrounding text to set it off from that text.

Another popular use of the **<A>** element is to create anchors, which is what the A represents. As discussed in the In Depth section of this chapter, you use anchors to label a section of a Web page as a hyperlink target—see "Creating Anchors And Linking To Sections In A Page" in the Immediate Solutions section for more information and examples.

As you can see by its number of attributes, the **<A>** element is an extensive one in HTML. I'll take a more in depth look at it throughout the following sections.

Setting Hyperlink Colors

"Hey," says the novice programmer, "how do I set the color of a hyperlink? The default value seems to be blue—the same blue as the background of my page!" "There are two ways to do it," you say, "using attributes, like **ALINK**, **VLINK**, and **LINK**, and using styles. Better get some coffee." "OK," says the NP and trots off.

The default color for hyperlinks in a page is blue. Hyperlinks that you've already visited are displayed in violet by default, and when you click a hyperlink, it turns red when the mouse button is down, again by default. You can set these colors with the **<BODY>** element's **LINK**, **VLINK** (visited link), and **ALINK** (active link) attributes.

Here's an example where I set the color of hyperlinks to green, the color of hyperlinks you've already visited to blue, and the color of links as they're clicked to red like this:

```
<HTML>
    <HEAD>
        <TITLE>
            Setting Hyperlink Colors
        </TITLE>
    </HEAD>

    <BODY LINK="GREEN" VLINK="BLUE" ALINK="RED">

    <CENTER>

        <H1>
            Setting Hyperlink Colors
        </H1>

        Here's a Web site to check out:
        <A HREF="http://W3C.ORG">W3C</A>!
    </CENTER>

    </BODY>
</HTML>
```

This works, but as with other style attributes, **ALINK**, **VLINK**, and **LINK** have all been deprecated in HTML 4 in favor of style sheets. So how do you set those colors using style sheets? We'll see more about style sheets in Chapter 9, but here's an example. I'll use the **<STYLE>** element to reproduce the colors in the previous example and also add something new (supported in Internet Explorer only so far): a hover color set to yellow here, which is used when the mouse is over the hyperlink:

```
<HTML>
    <HEAD>
        <TITLE>
            Setting Hyperlink Colors
        </TITLE>
    </HEAD>

    <STYLE TYPE="text/css">

        A:link {color:GREEN}
        A:visited {color:BLUE}
        A:hover {color:YELLOW}
        A:active {color:RED}

    </STYLE>

    <BODY>

        <CENTER>

            <H1>
                Setting Hyperlink Colors
            </H1>

            Click this hyperlink to go to
            <A HREF="http://W3C.ORG">W3C</A>!
        </CENTER>

    </BODY>
</HTML>
```

Creating Graphical Hyperlinks

The Web page design czar is on the phone and says, "The hyperlinks in your page lack oomph." You ask, "*Oomph?*" "That's right," says the WPDC, "can't you spice them up?" "Well," you say, "I can use images instead of text." "Great, do it *now*," says the WPDC and hangs up.

You can make images into hyperlinks using an **<IMG>** element inside an **<A>** element, which can spice up your Web pages considerably—especially if you have some powerful graphics. We saw an example of this in the In Depth section at the beginning of this chapter:

```
<HTML>
    <HEAD>
        <TITLE>
            Creating A Graphical Hyperlink
        </TITLE>
    </HEAD>

    <BODY>

        <CENTER>

            <H1>
                Creating A Graphical Hyperlink
            </H1>

            <A HREF="http://W3C.ORG">
                <IMG WIDTH=277 HEIGHT=114 SRC="clickme.gif"
                    ALT="Click me to go to W3C!">
            </A>
        </CENTER>

    </BODY>
</HTML>
```

You can see the results of this HTML in Figure 5.2. When the users click this image, their browser will navigate to the hyperlink's target, **http://W3C.org**. Note, in particular, that the text you use for the **ALT** attribute of the **<IMG>** element appears as a tool tip when the mouse rests over the image, also shown in Figure 5.2.

TIP: *As noted in the In Depth section of this chapter, the border that appears around the image will use the same colors as the current text hyperlinks. You can regulate the thickness of the border with the **<IMG>** element's **BORDER** attribute.*

The fact that you can use images as hyperlinks is significant because it allows you to use images for navigation. See "Using Graphical Hyperlinks For Navigation" in the Immediate Solutions section of this chapter for more information.

<BASE>—Setting The Base For Hyperlinks

Purpose: Sets the base URL for the hyperlinks in a page.

Start Tag/End Tag: Required/Omitted. This element contains no content. Can only be used in the **<HEAD>** section.

Supported: [2, 3, 3.2, 4, IE1, IE2, IE3, IE4, IE5, NS1, NS2, NS3, NS4]

Attributes:

- **HREF**—Holds the URL you want to use as the base URL of hyperlinks in the page. **HREF** is a required attribute. [2, 3, 3.2, 4, IE1, IE2, IE3, IE4, IE5, NS1, NS2, NS3, NS4]

- **TARGET**—Gives the target frame for hyperlink targets to load to. [4, IE3, IE4, IE5, NS2, NS3, NS4]

"Jeez," says the novice programmer, "you try to do something just a little different, and nothing works." "What do you mean, NP?" you ask. "I have a page I want to use as an index to pages in another directory," the NP says, "and I keep getting fouled up when I have to put in the full URL of each of those pages." "Why didn't you just set the base URL with the **<BASE>** element?" you ask. "Because I never heard of it," the NP says, chagrined.

Relative hyperlinks (see the In Depth section of this chapter) are defined relative to the current page, unless you specify a different base to use for hyperlinks with the **<BASE>** element.

In the following example, I'm setting the base URL for a Web page to **http://www.starpowder.com/images/**. Now when I refer to a file with a relative URL—just the name of the file, in fact, clickme.gif—the browser will look for that file using the full URL **http://www.starpowder.com/images/clickme.gif**:

```
<HTML>
    <HEAD>
        <TITLE>
            Creating A Graphical Hyperlink
        </TITLE>

        <BASE HREF="http://www.starpowder.com/images">

    </HEAD>

    <BODY>
```

```
<CENTER>

    <H1>
        Creating A Graphical Hyperlink
    </H1>

    <A HREF="http://W3C.ORG">
        <IMG WIDTH=277 HEIGHT=114 SRC="clickme.gif"
            ALT="Click me to go to W3C!">
    </A>
</CENTER>

</BODY>
</HTML>
```

Using the **<BASE>** element is a great idea if you have a lot of relative URLs in your pages, and the organization of your Web site has become complex.

<LINK>—Setting Link Information

Purpose: Specifies the relationship of other documents to the current one (such as specifying an external style sheet). **<LINK>** is an element for the **<HEAD>** section of a page.

Start Tag/End Tag: Required/Omitted. This element contains no content.

Supported: [2, 3, 3.2, 4, IE3, IE4, IE5, NS4]

Attributes:

- **CHARSET**—Specifies the character encoding of the target of the hyperlink. Set to an RFC 2045 language character set string (the default value is ISO-8859-1). [4]

- **CLASS**—Class of the element (used for rendering). [2, 3, 4]

- **DIR**—Gives the direction of directionally neutral text (text that doesn't have inherent direction in which you should read it). Possible values: **LTR**: left-to-right text or table and **RTL**: right-to-left text or table. [4]

- **DISABLED**—Indicates that the relationship to other documents is initially disabled. [IE4]

- **HREF**—Holds the target URL of the resource. Either this attribute or the **NAME** attribute must be used. Set to a URL. [2, 3, 3.2, 4, IE3, IE4, IE5]

- **HREFLANG**—Specifies the base language of the target indicated in the **HREF** attribute. Set to RFC 1766 values. [4]

- **ID**—A unique alphanumeric identifier for the tag, which you can use to refer to it. [2, 3, 4, IE4, IE5]

- **LANG**—Base language used for the tag. [4]

- **MEDIA**—Indicates on what device the document will be rendered; possible values: **SCREEN** (the default), **PRINT**, **PROJECTION** (transparent projection devices), **BRAILLE**, **SPEECH**, or **ALL** (style information should be used for all devices). [4, IE4, IE5]

- **REL**—Specifies the relationship described by the hyperlink. Set to a white space separated list of relationship names. [2, 3, 3.2, 4, IE4, IE5, NS4]

- **REV**—Essentially the same as the **REL** attribute, but the syntax works in the reverse direction. A link from A to B with **REL="X"** is the same relationship as a link from B to A with **REV="X"**. Set to a white space separated list of relationship names. [2, 3, 3.2, 4, IE4, IE5]

- **SRC**—Gives the link's source. [NS4]

- **STYLE**—Inline style indicating how to render the element. [4, NS4]

- **TARGET**—Indicates the named frame for the **HREF** hyperlink to jump to. Set to the name of a frame. [4]

- **TITLE**—Holds additional information (as might be displayed in tool tips) for the element. [2, 3, 4, IE4, IE5]

- **TYPE**—Specifies the MIME type of the target given in the **HREF** attribute. Set to an alphanumeric MIME type, like image/gif. [4, NS4]

You use the **<LINK>** element to specify the relationship of the current page to other documents. The actual relationship is specified with the **REL** attribute, which can take these values:

- **REL=ALTERNATE** (Internet Explorer and HTML 4 only)—Specifies an alternate resource.

- **REL=APPENDIX** (Internet Explorer and HTML 4 only)—Specifies an appendix.

- **REL=Bookmark**—Provides links to entry points into a document (the **TITLE** attribute may be used to label the bookmark).

- **REL=CHAPTER** (Internet Explorer and HTML 4 only)—Specifies a chapter.

- **REL=CONTENTS** (Internet Explorer and HTML 4 only)—Specifies the contents section.

- **REL=Copyright**—Specifies a copyright document for the current document.

- **REL=Glossary**—Specifies a document providing a glossary of terms.
- **REL=Help**—Specifies a document providing help.
- **REL=Home**—Specifies a home page.
- **REL=Index**—Specifies a document providing an index.
- **REL=Next**—Specifies the next document.
- **REL=OFFLINE** (Internet Explorer only)—Specifies an offline resource.
- **REL=Previous**—Specifies the previous document.
- **REL=SECTION** (Internet Explorer and HTML 4 only)—Specifies a section.
- **REL=SHORTCUT ICON** (Internet Explorer only)—Specifies a shortcut icon to be used in the Internet Explorer Favorites folder for the page.
- **REL=START** (Internet Explorer and HTML 4 only)—Specifies the start of a resource.
- **REL=StyleSheet**—Specifies an external style sheet.
- **REL=SUBSECTION** (Internet Explorer and HTML 4 only)—Specifies a subsection.
- **REL=ToC**—Specifies a document that holds a table of contents.
- **REL=Up**—Specifies the parent of the current document.

Here's an example showing how to use an external style sheet (which we'll see more about in Chapter 9; note that in the Netscape Navigator, you use **SRC**, not **HREF** here):

```
<HTML>
    <HEAD>
        <TITLE>
            Using An External Style Sheet
        </TITLE>

        <LINK REL="stylesheet" HREF="style.css">

    </HEAD>

    <BODY>

        <CENTER>

            <H1>
                Using An External Style Sheet
            </H1>
```

5. Links And Lists

```
            <P>
                This page uses an external style sheet.
        </CENTER>

    </BODY>
</HTML>
```

Giving Hyperlinks Access Keys

In Internet Explorer, you can use the **<A>** element's **ACCESSKEY** attribute to assign an access key to the hyperlink to make it accessible from the keyboard. Here's an example where I assign the access key "I" to the Internet Explorer link and "N" to the Netscape Navigator link:

```
<HTML>
    <HEAD>
        <TITLE>
            Using Hyperlink Access Keys
        </TITLE>
    </HEAD>

    <BODY>

        <CENTER>

            <H1>
                Using Hyperlink Access Keys
            </H1>
            You might be interested in these two browsers:
            <P>
                <A HREF="http://www.microsoft.com/ie" ACCESSKEY="I">
                    Internet Explorer
                </A>
                <BR>
                <A HREF="http://www.netscape.com" ACCESSKEY="N">
                    Netscape Navigator
                </A>
        </CENTER>

    </BODY>
</HTML>
```

To activate the access key, the user presses a system-specific key and the access key at the same time. For example, in Windows, when the user presses Alt+I, the Internet Explorer hyperlink gets the focus (that is, it appears with a dotted box around it and receives keystrokes); pressing Enter at that point activates the hyperlink.

Using Graphical Hyperlinks For Navigation

The novice programmer wants to know, "Why can't I use the cute arrow buttons for navigation that other Web pages have?" "No reason at all," you say, "give it a whirl."

It's very common to use graphical symbols, like arrows and buttons for navigation, and you can use them by making their images into hyperlinks. Here's an example showing how that works. I use arrow images to let the user navigate to other pages and use the image of a house to let them navigate to the site's home page:

```
<HTML>
    <HEAD>
        <TITLE>
            Creating Graphical Navigational Aids
        </TITLE>
    </HEAD>

    <BODY>

        <CENTER>

            <H1>
                Creating Graphical Navigational Aids
            </H1>

            Want to get somewhere fast? Click a button below...

            <BR>

            <A HREF="prev.html">
                <IMG WIDTH=172 HEIGHT=117 SRC="left.gif"
                    ALT="Previous"  BORDER=0>
            </A>
```

```
                    <A HREF="index.html">
                        <IMG WIDTH=161 HEIGHT=105 SRC="home.gif"
                            ALT="Home"   BORDER=0>
                    </A>


                    <A HREF="next.html">
                        <IMG WIDTH=172 HEIGHT=117 SRC="right.gif"
                            ALT="Next"   BORDER=0>
                    </A>

            </CENTER>

        </BODY>
    </HTML>
```

We first saw the previous example in the In Depth section of this chapter, and you can see the result of this HTML in Figure 5.5. The user has only to click an arrow image or the house image to be transported (I was going to say "instantly transported," but the Web is particularly slow today) to a new page.

Creating Navigation Bars

A popular use of hyperlinks is to create a *navigation bar*. Such bars display a number of small text or graphical hyperlinks that point to the other pages on the site and let users navigate around the site as they desire. Navigation bars are extremely useful if you include them in all the pages in your site because they really open up your Web site to users, who can navigate anywhere from anywhere else. And these bars are unobtrusive, appearing at the bottom or top—or both—of your pages. You'll find that larger commercial Web sites almost invariably use navigation bars.

Navigation bars are usually created using tables to avoid letting the browser reposition the hyperlinks in them. Here's an example:

```
<HTML>
    <HEAD>
        <TITLE>
            Creating Navigation Bars
        </TITLE>
    </HEAD>

    <BODY>
```

```
<CENTER>

    <H1>
        Creating Navigation Bars
    </H1>

    Welcome to my page!

    <BR>
    <BR>
    <BR>
    <BR>
    <BR>
    <BR>
    <BR>
    <BR>

    <TABLE>
        <TR>
            <TD>
                <A HREF="http://www.starpowder.com">
                    <IMG SRC="nav1.gif" VSPACE=1 HSPACE=1
                        BORDER="0">
                </A>
            </TD>
            <TD>
                <A HREF="http://www.starpowder.com/tutorial.htm">
                    <IMG SRC="nav2.gif" VSPACE=1 HSPACE=1
                        BORDER="0">
                </A>
            </TD>
            <TD>
                <A HREF="http://www.starpowder.com/help.htm">
                    <IMG SRC="nav3.gif" VSPACE=1 HSPACE=1
                        BORDER="0">
                </A>
            </TD>
            <TD>
                <A HREF="http://www.starpowder.com/email.htm">
                    <IMG SRC="nav4.gif" VSPACE=1 HSPACE=1
                        BORDER="0">
                </A>
            </TD>
        </TR>
    </TABLE>
```

```
        </CENTER>

      </BODY>
    </HTML>
```

The results of this HTML appear in Figure 5.9. As you can see in the figure, the navigation bar appears at the bottom of the page. Using that bar, the user can navigate to other locations on the site easily. Navigation bars are very useful and I highly recommend them for real Web sites.

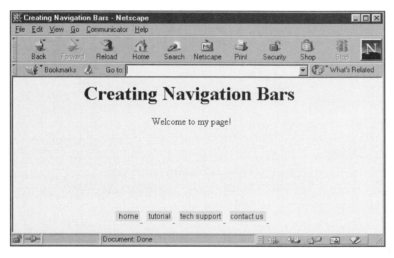

Figure 5.9   Using a navigation bar.

Creating Anchors And Linking To Sections In A Page

"Darn," says the novice programmer, "this hyperlink stuff is no good." "Why?" you ask. "Well," the NP says, "my Web page is about 12,000 lines long, and when I send users there, they get impatient." "Why not send them to the exact section of the Web page instead of to the top of it?" The NP asks, "You can do that?"

You can use the **<A>** element with the **NAME** attribute to enclose a section of a Web page and create an *anchor*. When you create an anchor, you can make it the target of hyperlinks, which allows you to jump to a particular section of a Web page.

TIP: *Although you use the **HREF** attribute in **<A>** elements to create hyperlinks and the **NAME** attribute to create anchors, you can actually use both of these attributes in the same **<A>** element.*

After naming an anchor, you can refer to it by adding a **#** symbol in front of the name and using it in the **HREF** attribute of a hyperlink. When the user clicks that hyperlink, the browser will navigate to the anchor.

Here's an example that we saw in the In Depth section of this chapter, where I set up an anchor named **BOTTOM** at the bottom of a page. This lets the user move there by clicking its hyperlink:

```
<HTML>
    <HEAD>
        <TITLE>
            Linking To A Section In A Page
        </TITLE>
    </HEAD>

    <BODY>

        <CENTER>

            <H1>
                Linking To A Section In A Page
            </H1>

            Click here to go to the
            <A HREF="#BOTTOM">bottom</A>
            of the page.

            <BR>
            <BR>
            <BR>
            <BR>
            <BR>
            <BR>
            <BR>
            <BR>
            <BR>
            <BR>
            <BR>
            <BR>
            <BR>

            <HR>

            <A NAME="BOTTOM">This is the bottom of the page.</A>
        </CENTER>
```

5. Links And Lists

```
        </BODY>
</HTML>
```

You can see the results of this HTML in Figures 5.3 and 5.4.

The target anchor of a hyperlink doesn't have to be in the same document—you can link to an anchored section in another document as well. To do so, you include the URL of that page before the # and the anchor name in the hyperlink like this: **HREF="http://www.starpowder.com/steve/mountains.html#ALPS"**.

Here's another example from the In Depth section of this chapter in which I'm linking to the **BOTTOM** anchor in the previous page, but from another document:

```
<HTML>
    <HEAD>
        <TITLE>
            Linking To A Section In Another Page
        </TITLE>
    </HEAD>

    <BODY>

        <CENTER>

            <H1>
                Linking To A Section In Another Page
            </H1>

            Click here to go to the
            <A HREF="discussion.html#BOTTOM">bottom</A>
            of the <I>other</I> page.

        </CENTER>

    </BODY>
</HTML>
```

NOTE: *Browsers are supposed to be able to navigate to anchors, even if they do not enclose anything (that is, even if the* **<A>** *element is empty). However, some browsers have problems recognizing empty anchor elements.*

Creating Clickable Footnotes

If you use footnotes in your documents, then in the interest of making your pages more accessible, it's a good idea to make those footnotes into hyperlinks—taking full advantage of what hypertext has to offer.

In this example, when the user clicks the reference for footnote 1 (marking the University of Vienna), the browser navigates to the bottom of the page where the footnote is expanded (into "Founded in 1365."):

```
<HTML>
    <HEAD>
        <TITLE>
            Creating Hyperlink Footnotes
        </TITLE>
    </HEAD>

    <BODY>

        <CENTER>

            <H1>
                Creating Hyperlink Footnotes
            </H1>

            Today, we visited the University of Vienna.
            <A HREF="#FOOTNOTE"><SUP>1</SUP></A>.

            <BR>
            <BR>
            <BR>
            <BR>
            <BR>
            <BR>
            <BR>
            <BR>
            <BR>
            <BR>
            <BR>
            <BR>
            <BR>

            <HR>
```

```
            <A NAME="FOOTNOTE">Founded in 1365.</A>
      </CENTER>

   </BODY>
</HTML>
```

You can see the result of this HTML in Figure 5.10, where you see the clickable footnote.

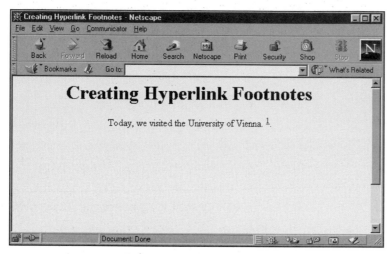

Figure 5.10   Using a hyperlink footnote.

Emailing With Hyperlinks

The novice programmer wants to know, "How can I get feedback from people who admire my Web page?" You smile and say, "You can include an email hyperlink, and when users click it, their email program will open with an empty email already addressed to you." "At last I can hear the applause!" the NP says.

You can use an email hyperlink to let users email you. When they click the hyperlink, it opens their email program and creates an empty message addressed to you. You create an email hyperlink by using the hyperlink protocol mailto: (see "Types of URLs" in the In Depth section of this chapter) followed by your email address. Here's an example showing how this works:

```
<HTML>
   <HEAD>
      <TITLE>
```

```
            Creating A MAILTO Hyperlink
        </TITLE>
    </HEAD>

    <BODY>

        <CENTER>

            <H1>
                Creating A MAILTO Hyperlink
            </H1>

            Want to contact me? Just
            <A HREF="mailto:steve@starpowder.com">email me
            </A>!
        </CENTER>

    </BODY>
</HTML>
```

You can see the result of this HTML in Figure 5.11. When the users click the hyperlink, their email program opens and they can send email to you. As you can see, mailto: hyperlinks provide an easy way to get feedback from people who are viewing your Web page (easier than setting up CGI scripts, for example).

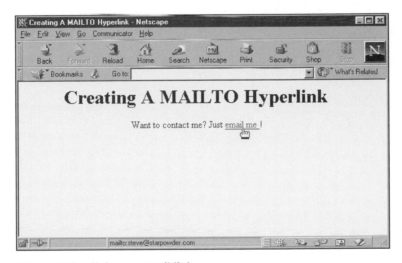

Figure 5.11   Using an email link.

Downloading Files With The HTTP And FTP Protocols

"I've got a Microsoft Word .doc file that I want to let people download," says the novice programmer. "Is there any way I can do it?" "Sure," you say, "just use a hyperlink to the file or use an FTP hyperlink." "How's that?" the NP asks.

Web browsers are capable of downloading files other than HTML pages. If you specify a URL that corresponds to a text file, for example, the Web browser will download it using the standard HTTP protocol (which means that such files are valid hyperlink targets). If the browser thinks it can display the type of file you are downloading, it will; otherwise, it'll ask you if you want to run it, or where you want to save it on disk.

Although the HTTP protocol works for transferring files, it's often faster to use FTP. If you have access to an FTP server, you can upload your files there and provide FTP hyperlinks to them. An FTP hyperlink tells the Web browser to use the FTP protocol instead of HTTP. You can create an FTP hyperlink simply by starting it with FTP instead of HTTP, like this: **ftp://ftp.starpowder.com** (note that the FTP server name usually begins with ftp). You can also provide a username and password for the FTP server, if needed, like this where I'm referring to a specific file: **ftp://*username:password*@ftp.starpowder.com/steve/ *filename***.

Here's an example putting FTP hyperlinks to work:

```
<HTML>
    <HEAD>
        <TITLE>
            Creating An FTP Hyperlink
        </TITLE>
    </HEAD>

    <BODY>

        <CENTER>

            <H1>
                Creating An FTP Hyperlink
            </H1>

            You can get the
            <A HREF =
                "ftp://username:password@ftp.starpowder.com/steve/list.txt">
            list of heroes</A> here!
```

```
        </CENTER>

      </BODY>
    </HTML>
```

<MAP>—Creating Client-Side Image Maps

Purpose: Creates an image map specification; encloses **<AREA>** elements that define the shapes in the image map. Pass the name of this map to the **<IMG>** element's **USEMAP** attribute.

Start Tag/End Tag: Required/Required

Supported: [3.2, 4, IE1, IE2, IE3, IE4, IE5, NS2, NS3, NS4]

Attributes:

- **CLASS**—Class of the element (used for rendering). [4, IE4, IE5]

- **DIR**—Gives the direction of directionally neutral text (text that doesn't have inherent direction in which you should read it). Possible values: **LTR**: left-to-right text or table and **RTL**: right-to-left text or table. [4, IE5]

- **ID**—A unique alphanumeric identifier for the tag, which you can use to refer to it. [4, IE4, IE5]

- **LANG**—Base language used for the tag. [4, IE4, IE5]

- **LANGUAGE**—Scripting language used for the tag. [IE4, IE5]

- **NAME**—Holds the name of the map for reference by other parts of the page. [3.2, 4, IE1, IE2, IE3, IE4, IE5, NS2, NS3, NS4]

- **STYLE**—Inline style indicating how to render the element. [4, IE4, IE5]

- **TITLE**—Holds additional information (which might be displayed in tool tips) for the element. [4, IE4, IE5]

The big boss appears in a cloud of cigar smoke and says, "All our competitors have image maps on their Web sites for easier navigation. We need one like theirs, but better." "What do you mean by better?" you ask. "Bigger," says the BB and disappears.

I first discussed image maps and what they do in the In Depth section of this chapter; image maps present the user with an easy graphical way to use hyperlinks to navigate. All you have to do is click a region in an image map—called a *hotspot*—and the browser navigates to the corresponding URL.

There are two types of image maps—client-side and server-side. Client-side image maps run in the browser, and server-side image maps run in the server. You use the **<MAP>** element to create a client-side image map, which is defined in the Web page itself. To do that, you name the map with the **<MAP>** element's **NAME** attribute and enclose **<AREA>** elements, which define the clickable regions in the image map in the **<MAP>** element, like this:

```
<MAP NAME="IMAP">
    <AREA NAME="LINK1" SHAPE=RECT COORDS="16,39 127,61"
        HREF="http://www.reuters.com">
    <AREA NAME="LINK2" SHAPE=RECT COORDS="62,71 173,93"
        HREF="http://www.starpowder.com/steve/search.html">
</MAP>
```

So how do you set up the **<AREA>** elements and tie the resulting map to an image? Take a look at the following two sections.

<AREA>—Creating Clickable Regions In Image Maps

Purpose: Specifies a clickable region in a client-side image map. Use this element in **<MAP>** elements.

Start Tag/End Tag: Required/Omitted. This element contains no content.

Supported: [3.2, 4, IE1, IE2, IE3, IE4, IE5, NS2, NS3, NS4]

Attributes:

- **ACCESSKEY**—Assigns a keyboard shortcut to the hyperlink; you usually use a platform-dependent key, like the Alt key in Windows, along with the shortcut to give the hyperlink the focus. Set to a single (case-insensitive) alphanumeric value. [4, IE4, IE5]

- **ALT**—This required attribute holds alternate text for the region defined by the **<AREA>** element. [3.2, 4, IE4, IE5]

- **CLASS**—Class of the element (used for rendering). [3, 4, IE4, IE5, NS4]

- **COORDS**—Specifies the actual coordinates for the clickable area. The coordinate system starts at the top-left corner of the image and coordinates get larger as you move down and to the right. Here are the **SHAPE** types and **COORDS** definitions you can use: **SHAPE=RECT, COORDS=**"*left*, *top*, *right*, *bottom*"; **SHAPE=CIRCLE, COORDS=**"*centerX, centerY, radius*"; **SHAPE=POLY, COORDS=**"*x1, y1, x2, y2, ... , xn, yn*". [3.2, 4, IE2, IE3, IE4, IE5, NS2, NS3, NS4]

- **DIR**—Gives the direction of directionally neutral text (text that doesn't have inherent direction in which you should read it). Possible values: **LTR**: left-to-right text or table and **RTL**: right-to-left text or table. [4, IE5]

- **HREF**—Holds the hyperlink target that the browser should navigate to when this clickable area is clicked. Set to a URL. [3.2, 4, IE2, IE3, IE4, IE5, NS2, NS3, NS4]

- **ID**—A unique alphanumeric identifier for the tag, which you can use to refer to it. [3, 4, IE4, IE5, NS4]

- **LANG**—Base language used for the tag. [3, 4, IE4, IE5]

- **LANGUAGE**—Scripting language used for the tag. [IE4, IE5]

- **NAME**—Name used for the element. [NS4]

- **NOHREF**—Specifies that there is no hyperlink target for this **<AREA>** element. This is the default if you don't specify a hyperlink with the **HREF** attribute. This is a stand-alone attribute. [3.2, 4, IE1, IE2, IE3, IE4, IE5, NS2, NS3, NS4]

- **SHAPE**—Specifies the shape of the area. Use this attribute together with the **COORDS** attribute. Possible values: **RECT** (the default, also **RECTANGLE**), **CIRC** (also **CIRCLE**), **POLY** (also **POLYGON**). [3.2, 4, IE1, IE2, IE3, IE4, IE5, NS2, NS3, NS4]

- **STYLE**—Inline style indicating how to render the element. [4, IE4, IE5, NS4]

- **TABINDEX**—Sets the tab sequence of hyperlinks in the map (pressing the Tab key moves from one to the next hyperlink). Set to a positive or negative integer. [4, IE4, IE5]

- **TARGET**—Gives the name of a frame for the **HREF** hyperlink to jump to when clicked. [4, IE3, IE4, IE5, NS2, NS3, NS4]

- **TITLE**—Holds additional information (which might be displayed in tool tips) for the element. [3, 4, IE4, IE5]

You use the **<AREA>** element to define clickable regions in image maps; **<AREA>** elements are enclosed in a **<MAP>** element. You can define three types of shapes in **<AREA>** elements—rectangles, circles, and polygons. You use the **SHAPE** attribute to indicate the shape you want, the **COORDS** attribute to set its actual coordinates, and the **HREF** attribute to set the hyperlink target for the region. Note that the coordinates for image maps start at (0, 0) at the upper left and increase to the right and down—measured in pixels.

Here's how you define the three shapes you can use in client-side areas:

```
<AREA SHAPE=RECT COORDS="left, top, right, bottom" HREF=URL1>
<AREA SHAPE=CIRCLE COORDS="centerX, centerY, radius" HREF=URL2>
<AREA SHAPE=POLY COORDS="x1, y1, x2, y2, ... , xn, yn" HREF=URL3>
```

And here's an example. Note that after defining a client-side image map with the **<MAP>** element, you pass its name to the **USEMAP** attribute of an **<IMG>** element:

```
<MAP NAME="IMAP">
    <AREA SHAPE=RECT COORDS="0, 0, 100, 100" HREF="http://www.w3c.org">
    <AREA SHAPE=CIRCLE COORDS="200, 200, 50" HREF="http://microsoft.com">
    <AREA SHAPE=POLY COORDS="300, 300, 310, 320, 450, 473, 300, 300"
        HREF="http://www.netscape.com">
</MAP>
```

An important point—there's a fourth "shape" you can use in image maps, **DEFAULT**, which is the area not covered by any other **<AREA>** elements. When you set up a URL for **DEFAULT**, that URL is used when the user clicks outside any clickable region.

Want to see a full client-side image map example at work? Take a look at the next section.

NOTE: The number of successive coordinates of polygons has no specific limits or number of points, but HTML limits the values of attribute settings to 1,024 characters. Also, note that if the first and last coordinates of a polygon are not the same, then HTML adds a final segment to close it.

TIP: You can specify an unlimited number of **<AREA>** regions in a client-side image map, and if two regions overlap, the one that was listed first should take precedence.

Creating Client-Side Image Maps

The novice programmer asks, "So exactly how do I create a client-side image map? I know you use **<MAP>** and **<AREA>** elements." "Better pull up a chair," you say, "and we'll go through it."

You create client-side image maps by creating a **<MAP>** element to define the clickable regions in the map and then place **<AREA>** elements, one per clickable region, in the **<MAP>** element (see the Immediate Solutions sections "**<MAP>**—Creating Client-Side Image Maps" and "**<AREA>**—Creating Clickable Regions In

Image Maps" in this chapter). You then assign the name of the **<MAP>** element to the **USEMAP** attribute of the **<IMG>** element, which inserts the actual image map into the Web page.

NOTE: *Netscape Navigator does not allow you to specify an external URL in the **USEMAP** attribute of the **<IMG>** element—you can only use internal anchors.*

In this example, I insert the image into the Web page with an **<IMG>** element, create a map named IMAP with the **<MAP>** element, define the regions in the map with **<AREA>** elements, and assign the name of the map—prefaced with a #—to the image with the **<IMG>** element's **USEMAP** attribute. Here's what it looks like:

```
<HTML>
    <HEAD>
        <TITLE>
            Using A Client Side Image Map
        </TITLE>
    </HEAD>

<BODY BGCOLOR="BLACK">

    <CENTER>
        <IMG WIDTH=528 HEIGHT=137 SRC="mainmenu.jpg"
            BORDER=0 ALT="Image Map" USEMAP="#IMAP">
        <MAP NAME="IMAP">
            <AREA NAME="LINK1" SHAPE=RECT COORDS="16,39 127,61"
                HREF="http://www.reuters.com" ALT="News">
            <AREA NAME="LINK2" SHAPE=RECT COORDS="62,71 173,93"
                HREF="http://www.starpowder.com/steve/search.html"
                ALT="Web search">
            <AREA NAME="LINK3" SHAPE=RECT COORDS="98,104 209,126"
                HREF="http://www.nnic.noaa.gov" ALT="Weather">
            <AREA NAME="LINK4" SHAPE=RECT COORDS="411,35 522,57"
                HREF="http://www.starpowder.com/steve/gbook.htm"
                ALT="Guest book">
            <AREA NAME="LINK5" SHAPE=RECT COORDS="360,67 471,89"
                HREF="http://www.yahoo.com/Guides_and_Tutorials/"
                ALT="Create a Web page">
            <AREA NAME="LINK6" SHAPE=RECT COORDS="328,98 439,120"
                HREF="http://www.web21.com/services/hot100/index.html"
                "Hottest 100 sites">
            <AREA NAME="DEFAULT" SHAPE=DEFAULT
                HREF=
```

```
                    "http://www.starpowder.com/steve/index.html#mainmenu"
                    ALT="Image map">
            </MAP>
        </CENTER>

    </BODY>
</HTML>
```

The results of this HTML appear in Figure 5.12. As you can see in the figure, the image map appears in the page. When the mouse rests over a clickable region in the map, the URL of that region appears in the browser's status bar, and the ALT text for the region appears as a tool tip next to the mouse cursor. When the user clicks a region, the browser navigates to the target URL.

Congratulations, you've just created an image map!

There's one thing to note, however, some older browsers don't support client-side image maps, so take a look at the next section on creating server-side image maps.

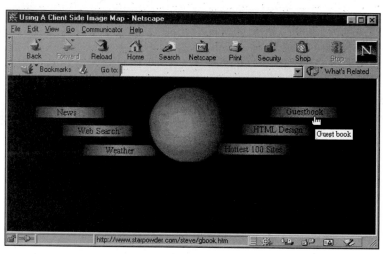

Figure 5.12   A client-side image map.

Creating Server-Side Image Maps

"Uh oh," says the novice programmer, "my favorite Web browser doesn't seem to support client-side image maps. Of course, my browser may be nonstandard." "What's it called?" you ask. "*SuperDuperWebProKing* 5.3, patch level 97," the NP says. "That does sound like a nonstandard browser," you say. "Maybe you should stick with server-side image maps."

Some older browsers don't support client-side image maps. In those cases, you should use server-side image maps, where the work is done on the server. These maps work slowly, but they do work.

To create a server-side image map, you use the **ISMAP** stand-alone attribute of the **<IMG>** element (see the Immediate Solutions section "**<IMG>**—Adding An Image To A Web Page" in Chapter 4). Surround the whole **<IMG>** element that displays the map in a hyperlink **<A>** element. The **<A>** element's **HREF** attribute gives the URL of the *map file* you want to use. The map file specifies the clickable regions in the image map, much as the **<MAP>** element does for client-side image maps. And it's stored on your Web server.

As an example, I'll modify the client-side image map example from the previous section into a server-side image map example here. To do that, I'll create a map file, main.map, and store that on the server. I use the **ISMAP** attribute to connect the image to that map file. Note the use of the relative URL to the main.map file, which I'll store in the same directory as the main Web page:

```
<HTML>
    <HEAD>
        <TITLE>
            Using A Server Side Image Map
        </TITLE>
    </HEAD>

    <BODY BGCOLOR="BLACK">

        <CENTER>
            <A HREF="main.map">
                <IMG WIDTH=528 HEIGHT=137 SRC="mainmenu.jpg"
                    BORDER=0 ALT="Image Map" ISMAP>
            </A>
        </CENTER>

    </BODY>
</HTML>
```

There are two ways to create .map files—using the NCSA (National Center For Supercomputing Applications) format and the CERN (Conseil Européen pour la Recherche Nucléaire) format. Although the NCSA format is more widely used, the format your server uses is something you should determine.

5. Links And Lists

Here's what the image map file from the previous section looks like in NCSA format as stored in the main.map file (note that this follows the format of the **<AREA>** element):

```
DEFAULT http://www.starpowder.com/steve/index.html#mainmenu
RECT http://www.reuters.com 16,39 127,61
RECT http://www.starpowder.com/steve/search.html 62,71 173,93
RECT http://www.nnic.noaa.gov 98,104 209,126
RECT http://www.starpowder.com/steve/gbook.htm 411,35 522,57
RECT http://www.yahoo.com/Guides_and_Tutorials/ 360,67 471,89
RECT http://www.web21.com/services/hot100/index.html 328,98 439,120
```

And here is the same map using the CERN format. Note that unlike the **<AREA>** element, you surround coordinate pairs in parentheses in this format—the URL comes first, and you use **RECTANGLE** instead of **RECT**:

```
DEFAULT http://www.starpowder.com/steve/index.html#mainmenu
RECTANGLE (16,39) (127,61) http://www.reuters.com
RECTANGLE (62,71) (173,93) http://www.starpowder.com/steve/search.html
RECTANGLE (98,104) (209,126) http://www.nnic.noaa.gov
RECTANGLE (411,35) (522,57) http://www.starpowder.com/steve/gbook.htm
RECTANGLE (360,67) (471,89) http://www.yahoo.com/Guides_and_Tutorials/
RECTANGLE (328,98) (439,120)
    http://www.web21.com/services/hot100/index.html
```

Here's the general format for NCSA image map files:

```
DEFAULT URL
RECT URL x1, y1 x2, y2
CIRCLE URL centerX, centerY radius
POLY URL x1, y1 x2, y2 x3, y3 ... xn, yn
```

And here's the general format for CERN image map files. Note that in this format, you use a different spelling for each shape (**CIRC**, **RECTANGLE**, and **POLYGON**), and as previously stated, you surround coordinate pairs with parentheses:

```
DEFAULT URL
RECTANGLE (x1, y1) (x2, y2) URL
CIRC (centerX, centerY) radius URL
POLYGON (x1, y1) (x2, y2) (x3, y3) ... (xn, yn) URL
```

Many servers allow you to place the .map file where you want them (refer to the example at the beginning of this section, where I stored the .map file in the same directory as the Web page that displays the map). But sometimes you'll have to place the .map files in a special, reserved directory on your server (something you'll have to ask your ISP).

For example, the NCSA script that handles image maps is called imagemap, and you might have to store your map files in a directory called /cgi-bin/imagemap/ or /cgi-bin/imagemap/maps like this:

```
<HTML>
    <HEAD>
        <TITLE>
            Using A Server Side Image Map
        </TITLE>
    </HEAD>

    <BODY BGCOLOR="BLACK">

        <CENTER>
            <A HREF="/cgi-bin/imagemap/main.map">
                <IMG WIDTH=528 HEIGHT=137 SRC="mainmenu.jpg"
                    BORDER=0 ALT="Image Map" ISMAP>
            </A>
        </CENTER>

    </BODY>
</HTML>
```

The script that handles CERN format scripts is called htimage, and if you have to place your map files in a special directory, it's typically called /cgi-bin/htimage:

```
<HTML>
    <HEAD>
        <TITLE>
            Using A Server Side Image Map
        </TITLE>
    </HEAD>

    <BODY BGCOLOR="BLACK">

        <CENTER>
            <A HREF="/cgi-bin/htimage/main.map">
                <IMG WIDTH=528 HEIGHT=137 SRC="mainmenu.jpg"
                    BORDER=0 ALT="Image Map" ISMAP>
            </A>
        </CENTER>
```

5. Links And Lists

```
    </BODY>
</HTML>
```

The result of this server-side example looks just like the client-side image map you saw in Figure 5.12, except that all processing goes on in the server. For that reason, the browser will not display the URL of each clickable region as the mouse passes over it, nor will it display tool tips for each region.

So, when do you use client-side image maps and when do you use server-side image maps? It depends on the browser users have; to be safe, you can use *both*. See the Immediate Solutions section "Creating Combined Client-Side And Server-Side Image Maps" for the details.

Creating Image Maps With The <OBJECT> Element

The W3C has indicated that the **<OBJECT>** element should be able to support image maps—however, no browser does this yet. Here's an example showing how such an image map should be set up—note the **<AREA>** elements enclosed in the **<OBJECT>** element:

```
<OBJECT DATA="map.jpg">
    <AREA SHAPE=RECT COORDS="0, 0, 100, 100" HREF="http://www.w3c.org">
    <AREA SHAPE=CIRCLE COORDS="200, 200, 50" HREF="http://microsoft.com">
    <AREA SHAPE=POLY COORDS="300, 300, 310, 320, 450, 473, 300, 300"
        HREF="http://www.netscape.com">
</OBJECT>
```

Creating Combined Client-Side And Server-Side Image Maps

Client-side image maps are faster and more efficient than server-side maps (and can also display tool tips and target URLs), but some older browsers don't support client-side image maps. To provide for older types of browsers, you can create Web pages that support both client-side and server-side image maps. In browsers that support client-side image maps, the client-side map will be used; otherwise the server-side map will be used.

You do this by combining the client-side and image-side techniques. That means you surround the **<IMG>** element that displays the image map in an **<A>** element that points to the server-side image .map file and use the **ISMAP** attribute in the **<IMG>** element. You also use the **USEMAP** attribute and supply a **<MAP>** element with **<AREA>** elements like this:

```
<HTML>
    <HEAD>
        <TITLE>
            Using A Client Side And Server Side Image Map
        </TITLE>
    </HEAD>

    <BODY BGCOLOR="BLACK">

        <CENTER>
            <A HREF="main.map">
                <IMG WIDTH=528 HEIGHT=137 SRC="mainmenu.jpg"
                    BORDER=0 ALT="Image Map" ISMAP USEMAP="#IMAP">
            </A>
            <MAP NAME="IMAP">
                <AREA NAME="LINK1" SHAPE=RECT COORDS="16,39 127,61"
                    HREF="http://www.reuters.com" ALT="News">
                <AREA NAME="LINK2" SHAPE=RECT COORDS="62,71 173,93"
                    HREF="http://www.starpowder.com/steve/search.html"
                    ALT="Web search">
                <AREA NAME="LINK3" SHAPE=RECT COORDS="98,104 209,126"
                    HREF="http://www.nnic.noaa.gov" ALT="Weather">
                <AREA NAME="LINK4" SHAPE=RECT COORDS="411,35 522,57"
                    HREF="http://www.starpowder.com/steve/gbook.htm"
                    ALT="Guest book">
                <AREA NAME="LINK5" SHAPE=RECT COORDS="360,67 471,89"
                    HREF="http://www.yahoo.com/Guides_and_Tutorials/"
                    ALT="Create a Web page">
                <AREA NAME="LINK6" SHAPE=RECT COORDS="328,98 439,120"
                    HREF="http://www.web21.com/services/hot100/index.html"
                    ALT="Hottest 100 sites">
                <AREA NAME="DEFAULT" SHAPE=DEFAULT
                    HREF=
                    "http://www.starpowder.com/steve/index.html#mainmenu"
                    ALT="Image map">
            </MAP>
        </CENTER>

    </BODY>
</HTML>
```

Here's the main.map file (in NCSA format) as stored on the Web server:

```
DEFAULT http://www.starpowder.com/steve/index.html#mainmenu
RECT http://www.reuters.com 16,39 127,61
RECT http://www.starpowder.com/steve/search.html 62,71 173,93
RECT http://www.nnic.noaa.gov 98,104 209,126
RECT http://www.starpowder.com/steve/gbook.htm 411,35 522,57
RECT http://www.yahoo.com/Guides_and_Tutorials/ 360,67 471,89
RECT http://www.web21.com/services/hot100/index.html 328,98 439,120
```

That's all it takes—now you're equipped to handle client-side and server-side image maps.

Creating Lists

The novice programmer appears and says, "How do I display a list in a Web page?" "There are plenty of ways," you say, "using ordered lists, unordered lists, customized lists, the old way, the new way...." "Hold it," the NP says, "I better get some coffee."

You use HTML list elements to display lists in Web pages as discussed in the In Depth section of this chapter. The two broad categories for lists are unordered lists and ordered lists. Unordered lists display a bullet or other graphic in front of each list item, and ordered lists present the items in some progression, numerical or alphabetical.

Here's an example shown at the beginning of the chapter that creates an unordered list:

```
<HTML>

    <HEAD>
        <TITLE>
            An Unordered List
        </TITLE>
    </HEAD>

    <BODY>

        <H1 ALIGN=CENTER>
            Creating An Unordered List
        </H1>
```

```
        Here are some items to consider when buying a computer:
        <UL>
            <LI> Speed
            <LI> Cost
            <LI> RAM
            <LI> Disk space
            <LI> CD ROM speed
        </UL>

    </BODY>

</HTML>
```

The results appear in Figure 5.7, where you can see the bulleted vertical list made from all the list items. Note that lists are indented.

Unordered lists display a simple bullet before each list item; ordered lists use a numbering (or lettering) system to indicate that the items are sequenced in some way. Here's an example that creates a simple numbered list:

```
<HTML>

    <HEAD>
        <TITLE>
            An Ordered List
        </TITLE>
    </HEAD>

    <BODY>

        <H1 ALIGN=CENTER>
            Creating An Ordered List
        </H1>

        Here are some items to consider when buying a computer:
        <OL>
            <LI> Speed
            <LI> Cost
            <LI> RAM
            <LI> Disk space
            <LI> CD ROM speed
        </OL>

    </BODY>

</HTML>
```

The results of this HTML appear in Figure 5.8. You can see that the list in the figure is numbered from one through five. There are other ordering systems possible as we'll see in the following sections—everything from letters to roman numerals.

To create ordered lists, you use the **<OL>** element, and to create unordered lists, you use the **<UL>** element. However, there's one element you use in common with these two tags—the **<LI>** element, which creates a list item. I'll take a look at the **<LI>** element in the next section.

<LI>—Creating List Items

Purpose: Creates a list item to use in ordered or unordered lists.

Start Tag/End Tag: Required/Optional

Supported: [2, 3, 3.2, 4, IE1, IE2, IE3, IE4, IE5, NS1, NS2, NS3, NS4]

Attributes:

- **CLASS**—Class of the element (used for rendering). [3, 4, IE4, IE5, NS4]

- **CLEAR**—Used to move past aligned images or other elements. Set to **NONE** (the default; just a normal break), **LEFT** (breaks line and moves down until there is a clear left margin past the aligned element), **RIGHT** (breaks line and moves down until there is a clear right margin past the aligned element), or **ALL** (breaks line and moves down until both margins are clear of the aligned element). [3]

- **DIR**—Gives the direction of directionally neutral text (text that doesn't have inherent direction in which you should read it). Possible values: **LTR**: left-to-right text or table and **RTL**: right-to-left text or table. [4, IE5]

- **ID**—A unique alphanumeric identifier for the tag, which you can use to refer to it. [3, 4, IE4, IE5, NS4]

- **LANG**—Base language used for the tag. [3, 4, IE4, IE5]

- **LANGUAGE**—Scripting language used for the tag. [IE4, IE5]

- **STYLE**—Inline style indicating how to render the element. [4, IE3, IE4, IE5, NS4]

- **TITLE**—Holds additional information (which might be displayed in tool tips) for the element. [3, 4, IE4, IE5]

- **TYPE**—Deprecated. Specifies the type of list item; for ordered lists, set to **A** (uppercase letters), **a** (lowercase letters), **I** (large roman numerals), **i** (small roman numerals), or **1** (default numbering scheme); for unordered lists set to: **DISC** (default solid bullet), **SQUARE** (solid square), or **CIRCLE** (hollow bullet). [2, 3, 3.2, 4, IE1, IE2, IE3, IE4, IE5, NS1, NS2, NS3, NS4]

- **VALUE**—Deprecated. Specifies the number of the current list item, making it possible to create nonsequential lists. [3.2, 4, IE1, IE2, IE3, IE4, IE5, NS1, NS2, NS3, NS4]

You use the **<LI>** element to create a list item for use in ordered and unordered lists. Here's an example:

```
<HTML>

    <HEAD>
        <TITLE>
            An Unordered List
        </TITLE>
    </HEAD>

    <BODY>

        <H1 ALIGN=CENTER>
            Creating An Unordered List
        </H1>

        Here are some items to consider when buying a computer:
        <UL>
            <LI> Speed
            <LI> Cost
            <LI> RAM
            <LI> Disk space
            <LI> CD ROM speed
        </UL>

    </BODY>

</HTML>
```

The results of this HTML appear in Figure 5.7. To see how to create unordered and ordered lists in detail, take a look at the next few sections.

5. Links And Lists

<UL>—Creating Unordered Lists

Purpose: Creates an unordered list. Surrounds **<LI>** list items.

Start Tag/End Tag: Required/Required

Supported: [2, 3, 4, IE1, IE2, IE3, IE4, IE5, NS1, NS2, NS3, NS4]

Attributes:

- **CLASS**—Class of the element (used for rendering). [3, 4, IE4, IE5, NS4]

- **CLEAR**—Used to move past aligned images or other elements. Set to **NONE** (the default; just a normal break), **LEFT** (breaks line and moves down until there is a clear left margin past the aligned element), **RIGHT** (breaks line and moves down until there is a clear right margin past the aligned element), or **ALL** (breaks line and moves down until both margins are clear of the aligned element). [3]

- **COMPACT**—Deprecated. Stand-alone attribute specifying that compact rendering be used. [2, 3, 3.2, 4]

- **DIR**—Gives the direction of directionally neutral text (text that doesn't have inherent direction in which you should read it). Possible values: **LTR**: left-to-right text or table and **RTL**: right-to-left text or table. [4, IE5]

- **ID**—A unique alphanumeric identifier for the tag, which you can use to refer to it. [3, 4, IE4, IE5, NS4]

- **LANG**—Base language used for the tag. [3, 4, IE4, IE5]

- **LANGUAGE**—Scripting language used for the tag. [IE4, IE5]

- **STYLE**—Inline style indicating how to render the element. [4, IE3, IE4, IE5, NS4]

- **TITLE**—Holds additional information (which might be displayed in tool tips) for the element. [3, 4, IE4, IE5]

- **TYPE**—Deprecated. Specifies the type of list item; for unordered lists set to: **DISC** (default solid bullet), **SQUARE** (solid square), or **CIRCLE** (hollow bullet). Note that in Internet Explorer, you must set these values to lowercase (**disc**, **square**, or **circle**). [2, 3, 3.2, 4, IE1, IE2, IE3, IE4, IE5, NS1, NS2, NS3, NS4]

To create an unordered list, surround the list items, which are defined with the **<LI>** element, using the **<UL>** element. Here's an example, shown at the beginning of the chapter:

```
<HTML>

    <HEAD>
        <TITLE>
            An Unordered List
        </TITLE>
    </HEAD>

    <BODY>

        <H1 ALIGN=CENTER>
            Creating An Unordered List
        </H1>

        Here are some items to consider when buying a computer:
        <UL>
            <LI> Speed
            <LI> Cost
            <LI> RAM
            <LI> Disk space
            <LI> CD ROM speed
        </UL>

    </BODY>

</HTML>
```

You can see the results of this HTML in Figure 5.7. Note that you can also customize unordered lists—see the Immediate Solutions section "Creating Customized Unordered Lists."

\<OL\>—Creating Ordered Lists

Purpose: Creates an ordered list. You use this element to surround **\<LI\>** list items.

Start Tag/End Tag: Required/Required

Supported: [2, 3, 3.2, 4, IE1, IE2, IE3, IE4, IE5, NS1, NS2, NS3, NS4]

Attributes:

- **CLASS**—Class of the element (used for rendering). [3, 4, IE4, IE5, NS4]

- **CLEAR**—Used to move past aligned images or other elements. Set to **NONE** (the default; just a normal break), **LEFT** (breaks line and moves down until there is a clear left margin past the aligned element), **RIGHT** (breaks line and moves down until there is a clear right margin past the aligned element), or **ALL** (breaks line and moves down until both margins are clear of the aligned element). [3]

- **COMPACT**—Deprecated. Stand-alone attribute specifying that compact rendering be used. [2, 3, 3.2, 4]
- **DIR**—Gives the direction of directionally neutral text (text that doesn't have inherent direction in which you should read it). Possible values: **LTR**: left-to-right text or table and **RTL**: right-to-left text or table. [4, IE5]
- **ID**—A unique alphanumeric identifier for the tag, which you can use to refer to it. [3, 4, IE4, IE5, NS4]
- **LANG**—Base language used for the tag. [3, 4, IE4, IE5]
- **LANGUAGE**—Scripting language used for the tag. [IE4, IE5]
- **START**—Deprecated. Specifies the first number in the sequence if it's other than 1. [3.2, 4, IE1, IE2, IE3, IE4, IE5, NS1, NS2, NS3, NS4]
- **STYLE**—Inline style indicating how to render the element. [4, IE3, IE4, IE5, NS4]
- **TITLE**—Holds additional information (which might be displayed in tool tips) for the element. [3, 4, IE4, IE5]
- **TYPE**—Deprecated. Specifies the type of list item; for ordered lists, set to **A** (uppercase letters), **a** (lowercase letters), **I** (large roman numerals), **i** (small roman numerals), or **1** (default numbering scheme). [2, 3, 3.2, 4, IE1, IE2, IE3, IE4, IE5, NS1, NS2, NS3, NS4]

You use the **<OL>** element to create ordered lists that display a list of items using ascending numbers or letters. It's easy to make these kinds of lists—just surround the **<LI>** list items in an **<OL>** element as we saw at the beginning of the chapter:

```
<HTML>

    <HEAD>
        <TITLE>
            An Ordered List
        </TITLE>
    </HEAD>

    <BODY>

        <H1 ALIGN=CENTER>
            Creating An Ordered List
        </H1>
```

```
Here are some items to consider when buying a computer:
<OL>
    <LI> Speed
    <LI> Cost
    <LI> RAM
    <LI> Disk space
    <LI> CD ROM speed
</OL>

</BODY>

</HTML>
```

The results of this HTML appear in Figure 5.8. Note that you can also customize ordered lists—see the Immediate Solutions section "Creating Customized Ordered Lists."

Creating Customized Unordered Lists

You can customize unordered lists by setting the **TYPE** attribute to three different values: **DISC** (the default), **SQUARE**, and **CIRCLE**, which set the type of bullet that appears before each list item. Note that these values must be lowercase in Internet Explorer (**disc**, **square**, and **circle**). Here's an example that creates square bullets:

```
<HTML>

    <HEAD>
        <TITLE>
            Customizing An Unordered List
        </TITLE>
    </HEAD>

    <BODY>

        <H1 ALIGN=CENTER>
            Customizing An Unordered List
        </H1>

        Here are some items to consider when buying a computer:
        <UL TYPE=square>
            <LI> Speed
            <LI> Cost
```

```
            <LI> RAM
            <LI> Disk space
            <LI> CD ROM speed
        </UL>

    </BODY>

</HTML>
```

The results of this HTML appear in Figure 5.13, where you can see the square customized bullets.

Note, however, that the **TYPE** attribute is deprecated in HTML 4 in favor of style sheets. So how do you set the type of bullets the new way? We'll see all about how to use style sheets in Chapter 9, but here's a sneak preview—you use the **LIST-STYLE-TYPE** attribute to set the style of list items. For unordered lists, you can set this style to **DISC** (the default), **CIRCLE**, or **SQUARE**. Here's what the previous page looks like using style sheets:

```
<HTML>

    <HEAD>
        <TITLE>
            Customizing An Unordered List
        </TITLE>
    </HEAD>
```

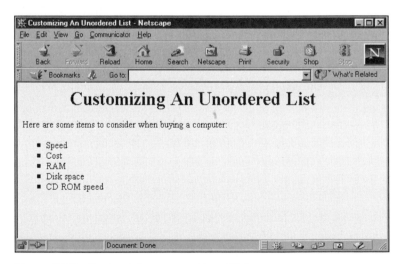

Figure 5.13   Customizing an unordered list.

```
    <STYLE>
        LI {list-style-type: square}
    </STYLE>

    <BODY>

        <H1 ALIGN=CENTER>
            Customizing An Unordered List
        </H1>

        Here are some items to consider when buying a computer:
        <UL>
            <LI> Speed
            <LI> Cost
            <LI> RAM
            <LI> Disk space
            <LI> CD ROM speed
        </UL>

    </BODY>

</HTML>
```

This HTML gives you the same result you saw in Figure 5.13.

Creating Customized Ordered Lists

You can customize the numbering system used in ordered lists by using the **TYPE** attribute, which you can set to these values:

- **1**—default numbering scheme (**1**, **2**, **3**...)
- **A**—uppercase letters (**A**, **B**, **C**...)
- **a**—lowercase letters (**a**, **b**, **c**...)
- **I**—large roman numerals (**I**, **II**, **III**...)
- **i**—small roman numerals (**i**, **ii**, **iii**...)

Here's an example showing how this works. I'll set the list order to A, B, C, and so on by setting the **TYPE** attribute to "A":

```
<HTML>

    <HEAD>
        <TITLE>
```

```
                Customizing An Ordered List
       </TITLE>
   </HEAD>

   <BODY>

       <H1 ALIGN=CENTER>
            Customizing An Ordered List
       </H1>

       Here are some items to consider when buying a computer:
       <OL TYPE="A">
            <LI> Speed
            <LI> Cost
            <LI> RAM
            <LI> Disk space
            <LI> CD ROM speed
       </OL>

   </BODY>

</HTML>
```

The results of this HTML appear in Figure 5.14. You can see the new list order using A, B, C, and so on.

TIP: *To set the number of the first item in an ordered list, use the* **START** *attribute (note that* **START** *is deprecated in HTML 4).*

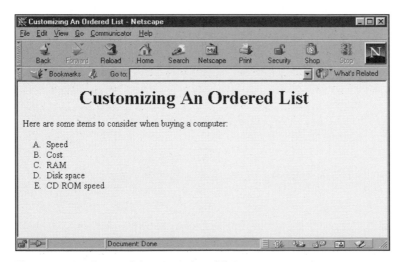

Figure 5.14   Customizing an ordered list.

Note again, that the **TYPE** attribute is deprecated in HTML 4 in favor of style sheets. So how do you set the type of numbering system the new way? We'll see all about how to use style sheets in Chapter 9, but here's a sneak preview—you use the **LIST-STYLE-TYPE** attribute to set the style of list items. For ordered lists, set this style to **DECIMAL** (the default), **LOWER-ROMAN**, **UPPER-ROMAN**, **LOWER-ALPHA**, or **NONE**. Here's what the previous page looks like using style sheets:

```
<HTML>

    <HEAD>
        <TITLE>
            Customizing An Ordered List
        </TITLE>
    </HEAD>

    <STYLE>
        LI {list-style-type: upper-alpha}
    </STYLE>

    <BODY>

        <H1 ALIGN=CENTER>
            Customizing An Ordered List
        </H1>

        Here are some items to consider when buying a computer:
        <OL>
            <LI> Speed
            <LI> Cost
            <LI> RAM
            <LI> Disk space
            <LI> CD ROM speed
        </OL>

    </BODY>

</HTML>
```

This HTML gives you the same result you saw in Figure 5.14.

5. Links And Lists

<DL>, <DT>, And <DD>—Creating Definition Lists

<DL>

Purpose: Creates a definition list. Embed **<DT>** and **<DD>** elements in a **<DL>** element.

Start Tag/End Tag: Required/Required

Supported: [2, 3, 3.2, 4, IE1, IE2, IE3, IE4, IE5, NS1, NS2, NS3, NS4]

Attributes:

- **CLASS**—Class of the element (used for rendering). [3, 4, IE4, IE5, NS4]
- **CLEAR**—Used to move past aligned images or other elements. Set to **NONE** (the default; just a normal break), **LEFT** (breaks line and moves down until there is a clear left margin past the aligned element), **RIGHT** (breaks line and moves down until there is a clear right margin past the aligned element), or **ALL** (breaks line and moves down until both margins are clear of the aligned element). [3]
- **COMPACT**—Deprecated. Stand-alone attribute specifying that compact rendering be used. [2, 3, 3.2, 4, IE4, IE5, NS1, NS2, NS3, NS4]
- **DIR**—Gives the direction of directionally neutral text (text that doesn't have inherent direction in which you should read it). Possible values: **LTR**: left-to-right text or table and **RTL**: right-to-left text or table. [4, IE5]
- **ID**—A unique alphanumeric identifier for the tag, which you can use to refer to it. [3, 4, IE4, IE5, NS4]
- **LANG**—Base language used for the tag. [3, 4, IE4, IE5]
- **LANGUAGE**—Scripting language used for the tag. [IE4, IE5]
- **STYLE**—Inline style indicating how to render the element. [4, IE3, IE4, IE5, NS4]
- **TITLE**—Holds additional information (which might be displayed in tool tips) for the element. [3, 4, IE4, IE5]

<DT>

Purpose: Specifies a definition term used in definition lists. Use inside a **<DL>** element and pair with **<DD>** elements.

Start Tag/End Tag: Required/Optional

Supported: [2, 3, 3.2, 4, IE1, IE2, IE3, IE4, IE5, NS1, NS2, NS3, NS4]

Attributes:

- **CLASS**—Class of the element (used for rendering). [3, 4, IE4, IE5, NS4]

- **CLEAR**—Used to move past aligned images or other elements. Set to **NONE** (the default; just a normal break), **LEFT** (breaks line and moves down until there is a clear left margin past the aligned element), **RIGHT** (breaks line and moves down until there is a clear right margin past the aligned element), or **ALL** (breaks line and moves down until both margins are clear of the aligned element). [3]

- **DIR**—Gives the direction of directionally neutral text (text that doesn't have inherent direction in which you should read it). Possible values: **LTR**: left-to-right text or table and **RTL**: right-to-left text or table. [4, IE5]

- **ID**—A unique alphanumeric identifier for the tag, which you can use to refer to it. [3, 4, IE4, IE5, NS4]

- **LANG**—Base language used for the tag. [3, 4, IE4, IE5]

- **LANGUAGE**—Scripting language used for the tag. [IE4, IE5]

- **STYLE**—Inline style indicating how to render the element. [4, IE3, IE4, IE5, NS4]

- **TITLE**—Holds additional information (which might be displayed in tool tips) for the element. [3, 4, IE4, IE5]

<DD>

Purpose: Specifies a definition description for use in definition lists. Use with **<DT>** elements inside a **<DL>** element.

Start Tag/End Tag: Required/Optional

Supported: [2, 3, 3.2, 4, IE1, IE2, IE3, IE4, IE5, NS1, NS2, NS3, NS4]

Attributes:

- **CLASS**—Class of the element (used for rendering). [3, 4, IE4, IE5, NS4]

- **CLEAR**—Used to move past aligned images or other elements. Set to **NONE** (the default; just a normal break), **LEFT** (breaks line and moves down until there is a clear left margin past the aligned element), **RIGHT** (breaks line and moves down until there is a clear right margin past the aligned element), or **ALL** (breaks line and moves down until both margins are clear of the aligned element). [3]

- **DIR**—Gives the direction of directionally neutral text (text that doesn't have inherent direction in which you should read it). Possible values: **LTR**: left-to-right text or table and **RTL**: right-to-left text or table. [4, IE5]

5. Links And Lists

- **ID**—A unique alphanumeric identifier for the tag, which you can use to refer to it. [3, 4, IE4, IE5, NS4]

- **LANG**—Base language used for the tag. [3, 4, IE4, IE5]

- **LANGUAGE**—Scripting language used for the tag. [IE4, IE5]

- **STYLE**—Inline style indicating how to render the element. [4, IE3, IE4, IE5, NS4]

- **TITLE**—Holds additional information (which might be displayed in tool tips) for the element. [3, 4, IE4, IE5]

Definition lists organize terms and their definitions in pairs (although most browsers can handle these lists if you use terms and definitions separately). You create a definition list with the **<DL>** element. You create items in this list using both the **<DT>** element to define a term and the **<DD>** element to supply the term's definition. The definition usually appears indented under the term being defined. Note, of course, you don't have to use this list for definitions or glossaries only—you can use it for any list that should be annotated.

Here's an example:

```
<HTML>

    <HEAD>
        <TITLE>
            A Definition List
        </TITLE>
    </HEAD>

    <BODY>

        <H1 ALIGN=CENTER>
            Creating A Definition List
        </H1>

        Here are some items to consider when buying a computer:
        <DL>
            <DT>Speed<DD>CPU speed in MHz.
            <DT>Cost<DD>Make sure to keep this down!
            <DT>RAM<DD>Amount of memory in the computer.
            <DT>Disk space<DD>Get plenty of gigabytes.
            <DT>CD ROM speed<DD>Get at least 24X.
        </DL>
```

```
    </BODY>

</HTML>
```

You can see the results of this HTML in Figure 5.15; each annotation is indented under the corresponding term.

TIP: *Some HTML writers use the* ***<DL>*** *tag solely to create indentation in their Web pages.*

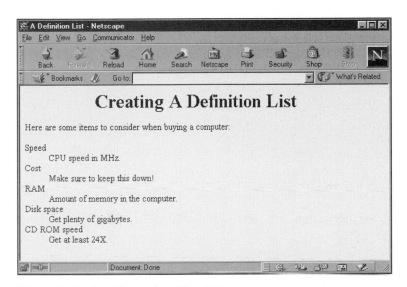

Figure 5.15   Creating a definition list.

Nesting Lists

"Uh oh," the novice programmer says," I need a list *inside* a list. Is there a fancy way to do that? Should I use a **<DIV>** element? Should I use dynamic HTML? How about Java?" You smile and say, "How about straight HTML? Nesting lists is no problem."

You can nest lists inside other lists in HTML, and browsers will know what's going on. In fact, browsers will often provide a visual indication that the list is nested, such as using hollow bullets in a nested unordered list. Here's an example showing how that works. Note that I'm nesting one list inside another here:

```
<HTML>

    <HEAD>
        <TITLE>
            A Nested List
        </TITLE>
    </HEAD>

    <BODY>

        <H1 ALIGN=CENTER>
            Creating A Nested List
        </H1>

        Here are some items to consider when buying a computer:
        <UL>
            <LI> Speed
            <LI> Cost
            <LI> RAM - get one of these:
                <UL>
                    <LI>32 MB
                    <LI>48 MB
                    <LI>64 MB
                    <LI>80 MB
                </UL>
            </LI>
            <LI> Disk space
            <LI> CD ROM speed
        </UL>

    </BODY>

</HTML>
```

The results of this HTML appear in Figure 5.16. As you can see in the figure, one list is nested inside another, and the inner list does indeed have hollow bullets.

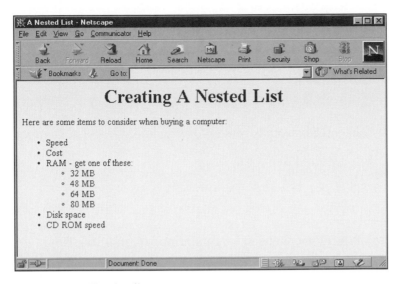

Figure 5.16   Nesting lists.

<DIR> And <MENU>—Deprecated Lists

<DIR>

Purpose: Creates a directory list; usually displayed simply as an unordered list. Deprecated.

Start Tag/End Tag: Required/Required

Supported: [2, 3, 3.2, 4, IE1, IE2, IE3, IE4, IE5, NS1, NS2, NS3, NS4]

Attributes:

- **CLASS**—Class of the element (used for rendering). [4, IE4, IE5, NS4]

- **COMPACT**—Deprecated. Stand-alone attribute specifying that compact rendering be used. [2, 3, 3.2, 4]

- **DIR**—Gives the direction of directionally neutral text (text that doesn't have inherent direction in which you should read it). Possible values: **LTR**: left-to-right text or table and **RTL**: right-to-left text or table. [IE4, IE5]

- **ID**—A unique alphanumeric identifier for the tag, which you can use to refer to it. [4, IE4, IE5, NS4]

- **LANG**—Base language used for the tag. [4, IE4, IE5]

- **LANGUAGE**—Scripting language used for the tag. [IE4, IE5]

- **STYLE**—Inline style indicating how to render the element. [4, IE3, IE4, IE5, NS4]

- **TITLE**—Holds additional information (which might be displayed in tool tips) for the element. [4, IE4, IE5]

\<MENU>

Purpose: Creates a menu list; usually rendered as an unordered list. Deprecated.

Start Tag/End Tag: Required/Required

Supported: [2, 3, 3.2, 4, IE1, IE2, IE3, IE4, IE5, NS1, NS2, NS3, NS4]

Attributes:

- **CLASS**—Class of the element (used for rendering). [4, IE4, IE5, NS4]

- **COMPACT**—Deprecated. Stand-alone attribute specifying that compact rendering be used. [2, 3, 3.2, 4]

- **DIR**—Gives the direction of directionally neutral text (text that doesn't have inherent direction in which you should read it). Possible values: **LTR**: left-to-right text or table and **RTL**: right-to-left text or table. [IE4, IE5]

- **ID**—A unique alphanumeric identifier for the tag, which you can use to refer to it. [4, IE4, IE5, NS4]

- **LANG**—Base language used for the tag. [4, IE4, IE5]

- **LANGUAGE**—Scripting language used for the tag. [IE4, IE5]

- **STYLE**—Inline style indicating how to render the element. [4, IE3, IE4, IE5, NS4]

- **TITLE**—Holds additional information (which might be displayed in tool tips) for the element. [4, IE4, IE5]

Both the **\<DIR>** and **\<MENU>** lists are deprecated. I'm including them here for completeness. In fact, most browsers just display these lists as unordered lists, although they were originally meant to handle short list items (about 20 characters) only. You use the **\<LI>** element to define list items.

Here's an example using the **\<MENU>** element:

```
<HTML>

    <HEAD>
        <TITLE>
            Creating A Menu List
        </TITLE>
    </HEAD>
```

```
<BODY>

    <H1 ALIGN=CENTER>
        Creating A Menu List
    </H1>

    Here are some items to consider when buying a computer:
    <MENU>
        <LI> Speed
        <LI> Cost
        <LI> RAM
        <LI> Disk space
        <LI> CD ROM speed
    </MENU>

    </BODY>

</HTML>
```

Most browsers will render this HTML as a simple unordered list.

Chapter 6

Creating Tables

In Depth

Tables are one of my favorite HTML elements, and, after this chapter, I hope they'll be one of yours too. That's quite a claim, because in fact, HTML tables are the most complex HTML elements that exist (currently anyway). However, their usefulness far outweighs the inconvenience of creating them. Most good HTML editors will make the process of creating tables easy.

The reason tables are so popular has little to do with displaying data in tables; the reason tables are so popular with Web page authors is that they let you arrange the elements of a Web page in such a way that the browser won't rearrange them. Often, it's good to let the browser do the rearranging, as when it reformats text to fit the available display area. However, there are many cases when you want your text to be formatted as specified. These cases often involve a series of images that should be next to each other (as in navigation bars) or text that you want to appear on the side of the page in annotations. Web page authors frequently use tables to structure Web pages using tables, and in fact, if you take a look at pages displayed by large corporations, you'll often find tables in them for just this reason.

The Parts Of A Table

You can see a basic table and its parts in Figure 6.1. Above the table a *caption* appears, which you specify with the **<CAPTION>** element; below the caption and in the table itself are *table headings*, one per column (although headings can span several columns). The rows and columns of the table itself are divided into *cells*, and each cell holds the actual *table data*.

Of course, this table is just a very basic one, but it points out the parts of a table. To see how to create a table like this, we have to dig into the HTML.

Creating A Table

To create a table, you use the **<TABLE>** element, which is the easy part. Then it's up to you to structure the table, using elements like **<TR>** to create a table row, **<TD>** to insert data into the table, and **<TH>** to create table headings.

To make this clearer, I'll go through an example named tables.html, which you'll find on the CD-ROM as well as in Listing 6.1. There you'll find several variations of how to work with tables. I'll also go through them here in the In Depth section of the chapter. And, of course, there's more advanced material in the Immediate Solutions section.

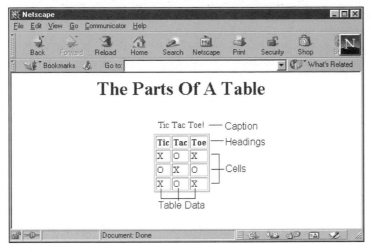

Figure 6.1   A basic table.

I'll start by creating the table you see in Figure 6.2. The table in the figure is a simple one without a border. (To make things easier, the figures discussed in the In Depth section also display the actual HTML used to create those tables.)

To create this table, I begin with the **<TABLE>** element:

```
<TABLE>
    .
    .
    .
</TABLE>
```

You build tables row by row using the **<TR>** element inside the **<TABLE>** element; here's how I create the first (top) row of the table:

```
<TABLE>
    <TR>
        .
        .
        .
    </TR>
    .
    .
    .
</TABLE>
```

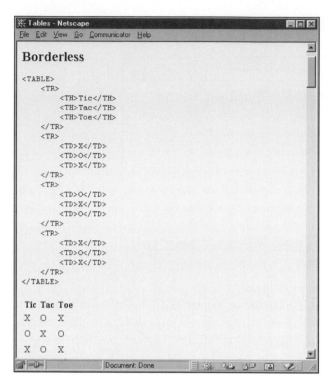

Figure 6.2   A borderless table.

The top row of the table in Figure 6.2 holds headings for each column (heading text is usually displayed in bold and centered both vertically and horizontally)—named "Tic", "Tac", and "Toe". Headings are optional in tables, but I've put them in to show you how to create them with the **<TH>** element. There are three headings here, each in its own column. Note that using three **<TH>** elements (or **<TD>** table data elements) *defines* how many columns the row will have:

```
<TABLE>
    <TR>
        <TH>Tic</TH>
        <TH>Tac</TH>
        <TH>Toe</TH>
    </TR>
        .
        .
        .
</TABLE>
```

Now that I've created the first row of headings, I'll add data to the table, which consists of Xs and Os. I do that by constructing a new row using the **<TR>** element, and then I use the **<TD>** element for the data that should go into each cell (if you don't use **<TH>** elements, the number of **<TD>** elements in a row defines the number of columns in the row):

```
<TABLE>
    <TR>
        <TH>Tic</TH>
        <TH>Tac</TH>
        <TH>Toe</TH>
    </TR>
    <TR>
        <TD>X</TD>
        <TD>O</TD>
        <TD>X</TD>
    <TR>

    .
    .
    .

</TABLE>
```

Finally, I construct the last two rows in the same way:

```
<TABLE>
    <TR>
        <TH>Tic</TH>
        <TH>Tac</TH>
        <TH>Toe</TH>
    </TR>
    <TR>
        <TD>X</TD>
        <TD>O</TD>
        <TD>X</TD>
    </TR>
    <TR>
        <TD>O</TD>
        <TD>X</TD>
        <TD>O</TD>
    </TR>
    <TR>
        <TD>X</TD>
        <TD>O</TD>
        <TD>X</TD>
    </TR>
</TABLE>
```

And that's it—the table is done, and you can see it in Figure 6.2. It's interesting to note that tables have no border by default, indicating the World Wide Web Consortium's (W3C's) understanding that people often use tables to structure a page, not just for simple tables. However, you can add a border to a table easily.

TIP: The **</TR>**, **</TH>**, and **</TD>** tags are actually optional, although this wasn't always so. In fact, some older browsers may have problems if you don't include these tags, so it's probably a good idea to do so.

Adding A Border

To add a border, all you have to do is use the **<TABLE>** element's **BORDER** attribute. In HTML 2, you could use this attribute as a stand-alone attribute and the browser would add a one-pixel border around the table and draw the internal struts that separate each cell (it still works that way in Internet Explorer). Since HTML 3.2, however, you're supposed to specify a value for the **BORDER** attribute in pixels (**BORDER="0"** would turn the border off), so I'll do that here by adding a border two pixels wide:

```
<TABLE BORDER="2">
    <TR>
        <TH>Tic</TH>
        <TH>Tac</TH>
        <TH>Toe</TH>
    </TR>
    <TR>
        <TD>X</TD>
        <TD>O</TD>
        <TD>X</TD>
    </TR>
    <TR>
        <TD>O</TD>
        <TD>X</TD>
        <TD>O</TD>
    </TR>
    <TR>
        <TD>X</TD>
        <TD>O</TD>
        <TD>X</TD>
    </TR>
</TABLE>
```

The results of this HTML appear in Figure 6.3. You can see the table's border and the struts used to separate cells in the figure.

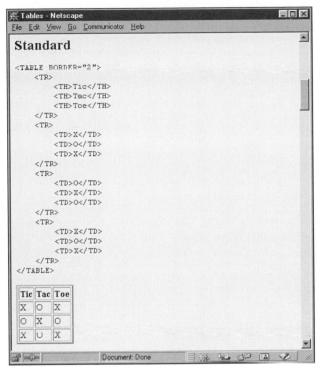

Figure 6.3   Adding a border to a table.

Padding Your Cells

Another formatting option is to specify *cell padding*. To start tailoring your tables the way you want them, you can specify cell padding, which is the amount of space between the edges of the cell and the cell's actual contents. If your tables look too cramped, increasing cell padding is one alternative.

Here's an example where I'm increasing the cell padding to four pixels by assigning that value to the **CELLPADDING** attribute:

```
<TABLE BORDER="2" CELLPADDING = "4">
    <TR>
        <TH>Tic</TH>
        <TH>Tac</TH>
        <TH>Toe</TH>
    </TR>
    <TR>
        <TD>X</TD>
        <TD>O</TD>
        <TD>X</TD>
```

```
    </TR>
    <TR>
        <TD>0</TD>
        <TD>X</TD>
        <TD>0</TD>
    </TR>
    <TR>
        <TD>X</TD>
        <TD>0</TD>
        <TD>X</TD>
    </TR>
</TABLE>
```

You can see the results in Figure 6.4, where the cells have widened somewhat from the previous version shown in Figure 6.3.

TIP: *You can set cell padding to 0, but the cell walls will actually touch the cell contents. This can be useful like when you're aligning images using a table.*

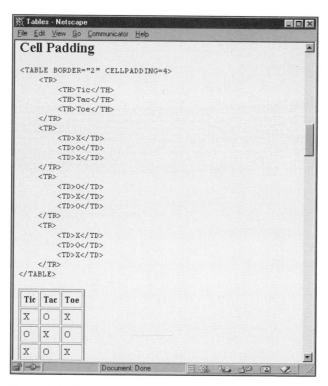

Figure 6.4   Increasing cell padding.

Widening The Cell Spacing

Cell spacing might sound like cell padding, but there's a difference. Cell padding sets the extra space used to separate cell walls from their contents; *cell spacing* sets the space between cells. In this example, I'll set the cell spacing to four pixels using the **CELLSPACING** attribute:

```
<TABLE BORDER="2" CELLSPACING = "4">
    <TR>
        <TH>Tic</TH>
        <TH>Tac</TH>
        <TH>Toe</TH>
    </TR>
    <TR>
        <TD>X</TD>
        <TD>O</TD>
        <TD>X</TD>
    </TR>
    <TR>
        <TD>O</TD>
        <TD>X</TD>
        <TD>O</TD>
    </TR>
    <TR>
        <TD>X</TD>
        <TD>O</TD>
        <TD>X</TD>
    </TR>
</TABLE>
```

You can see the results of this HTML in Figure 6.5. Cell spacing—the widths of the struts that separate each cell—has been expanded.

TIP: Although this example aligned text cell by cell using the **<TD>** element, you can align the text in whole rows horizontally using the **ALIGN** attribute of the **<TR>** element.

Aligning Your Data Horizontally

There are dozens of other formatting options that can be used with tables, of course. You can align your data cell by cell. The default for table data is to center the data vertically and left justify it by using the **ALIGN** attribute, which you set to **RIGHT**, **LEFT**, **JUSTIFY**, **CHAR**, or **CENTER**. In the following HTML, I'm aligning data to the right, left, and center. Note that the **ALIGN** attribute is not deprecated for tables as it is for other elements.

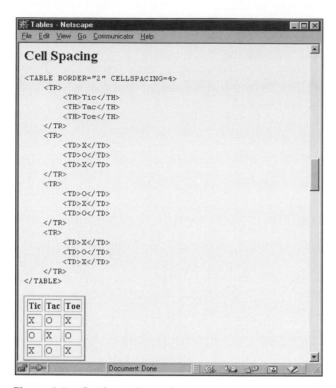

Figure 6.5   Setting cell spacing.

```
<TABLE BORDER="2" WIDTH="200">
    <TR>
        <TH>Tic</TH>
        <TH>Tac</TH>
        <TH>Toe</TH>
    </TR>
    <TR>
        <TD ALIGN = RIGHT>X</TD>
        <TD ALIGN = LEFT>O</TD>
        <TD ALIGN = CENTER>X</TD>
    </TR>
    <TR>
        <TD ALIGN = RIGHT>O</TD>
        <TD ALIGN = LEFT>X</TD>
        <TD ALIGN = CENTER>O</TD>
    </TR>
    <TR>
        <TD ALIGN = RIGHT>X</TD>
        <TD ALIGN = LEFT>O</TD>
        <TD ALIGN = CENTER>X</TD>
    </TR>
</TABLE>
```

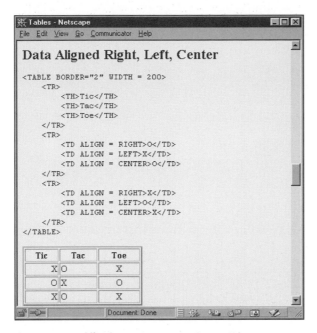

Figure 6.6   Aligning cell data horizontally.

You can see the results of this HTML in Figure 6.6. As you see in the figure, the text in each cell is indeed aligned as we want it to be. Besides aligning your text horizontally, you can also align it vertically.

Aligning Your Data Vertically

To set the vertical alignment of the data in table cells, you can use the **VALIGN** attribute, which you set to **TOP**, **MIDDLE**, **BASELINE**, or **BOTTOM**. Here's an example in which I'm setting the vertical alignment of data in cells using **VALIGN**:

```
<TABLE BORDER="2" HEIGHT = 120>
    <TR>
        <TH>Tic</TH>
        <TH>Tac</TH>
        <TH>Toe</TH>
    </TR>
    <TR>
        <TD VALIGN = TOP>X</TD>
        <TD VALIGN = MIDDLE>O</TD>
        <TD VALIGN = BOTTOM>X</TD>
```

```
    </TR>
    <TR>
        <TD VALIGN = TOP>O</TD>
        <TD VALIGN = MIDDLE>X</TD>
        <TD VALIGN = BOTTOM>O</TD>
    </TR>
    <TR>
        <TD VALIGN = TOP>X</TD>
        <TD VALIGN = MIDDLE>O</TD>
        <TD VALIGN = BOTTOM>X</TD>
    </TR>
</TABLE>
```

You can see the results of this HTML in Figure 6.7. The text in each cell is aligned just as we set it.

TIP: *Although the previous example aligned text cell by cell using the **<TD>** element, you can align the text in whole rows vertically using the **VALIGN** attribute of the **<TR>** element.*

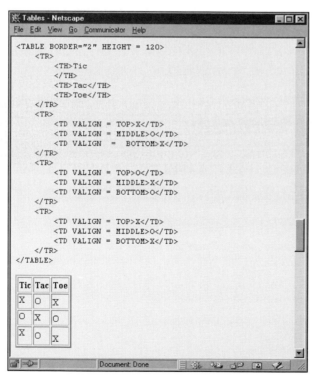

Figure 6.7   Aligning cell data vertically.

Spanning Columns

Of course, there's a great deal more that you can do with tables. For example, you can create cells and headings that *span* columns. A cell or heading that spans two columns stretches across the two columns. Here's an example to make this clearer. In this case, I'll change the headings so that I only have one heading, which spans all three columns. To do that, I use the **COLSPAN** attribute of the **<TH>** and **<TD>** elements like this:

```
<TABLE BORDER="2">
    <TR>
        <TH COLSPAN=3> TicTac Game</TH>
    </TR>
    <TR>
        <TD>X</TD>
        <TD>0</TD>
        <TD>X</TD>
    </TR>
    <TR>
        <TD>0</TD>
        <TD>X</TD>
        <TD>0</TD>
    </TR>
    <TR>
        <TD>X</TD>
        <TD>0</TD>
        <TD>X</TD>
    </TR>
</TABLE>
```

That's all it takes—now the heading spans all three columns as you can see in Figure 6.8. Besides spanning columns, you can also span *rows*.

Spanning Rows

You use the **COLSPAN** attribute to span columns, and you can use the **ROWSPAN** attribute to span rows. Here's an example showing how this looks. I just use the **ROWSPAN** attribute like this:

```
<TABLE BORDER="2">
    <TR>
        <TH ROWSPAN = 3>TicTac<BR>Game</TH>
        <TD>X</TD>
        <TD>0</TD>
```

```
            <TD>X</TD>
        </TR>
        <TR>
            <TD>O</TD>
            <TD>X</TD>
            <TD>O</TD>
        </TR>
        <TR>
            <TD>X</TD>
            <TD>O</TD>
            <TD>X</TD>
        </TR>
    </TABLE>
```

Now the table heading spans all three rows as you can see in Figure 6.9.

TIP: *Spanning rows and columns is a great way to format text in a Web page if you use a borderless table. (You can also use the **<DIV>** elements and style sheets to produce the same effect, however, style sheets are not supported by all browsers.)*

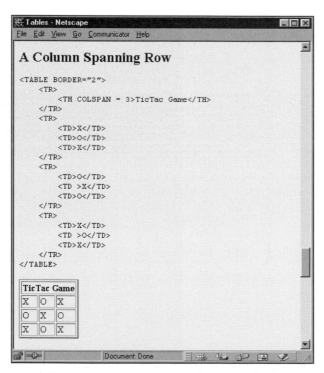

Figure 6.8   Spanning columns.

Figure 6.9   Spanning rows.

Setting Colors

The last topic I'll look at in this In Depth section is how to set colors in tables. To do that, you can use the **BGCOLOR** attributes of the **<TABLE>**, **<TR>**, **<TH>**, and **<TD>** elements (although these attributes have been deprecated in HTML 4 in favor of style sheets—we'll see how to write this example using style sheets in the Immediate Solutions section "Setting Table Colors"). Here's an example where I'm coloring the cells of a table:

```
<TABLE BORDER="2">
    <TR>
        <TH BGCOLOR = "#ff0000">Tic</TH>
        <TH BGCOLOR = "#ff0000">Tac</TH>
        <TH BGCOLOR = "#ff0000">Toe</TH>
    </TR>
    <TR>
        <TD BGCOLOR = "#ffffff">X</TD>
        <TD BGCOLOR = "#000000">
            <FONT COLOR = "#ffffff">O</FONT>
        </TD>
        <TD BGCOLOR = "#ffffff">X</TD>
    </TR>
```

```
<TR>
    <TD BGCOLOR = "#000000">
        <FONT COLOR = "#ffffff">O</FONT>
    <TD BGCOLOR = "#ffffff"/>X</TD>
    <TD BGCOLOR = "#000000">
        <FONT COLOR = "#ffffff">O</FONT>
    </TD>
</TR>
<TR>
    <TD BGCOLOR = "#ffffff"/>X</TD>
    <TD BGCOLOR = "#000000">
        <FONT COLOR = "#ffffff">O</FONT>
    </TD>
    <TD BGCOLOR = "#ffffff"/>X</TD>
</TR>
</TABLE>
```

The results of this HTML, in glorious black and white, appear in Figure 6.10 (the headings are actually red and the table data is presented on a black and white checkerboard).

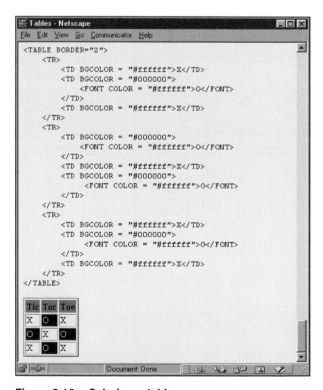

Figure 6.10   Coloring a table.

TIP: *You can also set the background image used for a table with the **BACKGROUND** attribute.*

What we've seen so far is called the *Simple Table Model*. There's also a new *Complex Table Model*, and I'll take a look at that model in this chapter. The Complex Table Model introduces tags like **<COL>**, **<COLGROUP>**, **<THEAD>**, **<TBODY>**, and **<TFOOT>** to let you create column and row groups, and to create a table foot and a table head for your tables.

At this point, our work with tables in the In Depth section gives us a solid foundation—now it's time to turn to the actual HTML in the Immediate Solutions section. You can find the HTML for all the examples discussed in the In Depth section in Listing 6.1.

Listing 6.1   tables.htm displays tables in a number of ways.

```
<HTML>

    <HEAD>
        <TITLE>
            Tables
        </TITLE>
    </HEAD>

    <BODY>

        <CENTER>
            <H1>
                Creating Tables
            </H1>
        </CENTER>

        <BR>
        <H2>Borderless</H2>
        <PRE>
&lt;TABLE&gt;
    &lt;TR&gt;
        &lt;TH&gt;Tic&lt;/TH&gt;
        &lt;TH&gt;Tac&lt;/TH&gt;
        &lt;TH&gt;Toe&lt;/TH&gt;
    &lt;/TR&gt;
    &lt;TR&gt;
        &lt;TD&gt;X&lt;/TD&gt;
        &lt;TD&gt;O&lt;/TD&gt;
        &lt;TD&gt;X&lt;/TD&gt;
    &lt;/TR&gt;
```

```
        &lt;TR&gt;
             &lt;TD&gt;O&lt;/TD&gt;
             &lt;TD&gt;X&lt;/TD&gt;
             &lt;TD&gt;O&lt;/TD&gt;
        &lt;/TR&gt;
        &lt;TR&gt;
             &lt;TD&gt;X&lt;/TD&gt;
             &lt;TD&gt;O&lt;/TD&gt;
             &lt;TD&gt;X&lt;/TD&gt;
        &lt;/TR&gt;
&lt;/TABLE&gt;
             </PRE>

             <TABLE>
                 <TR>
                     <TH>Tic</TH>
                     <TH>Tac</TH>
                     <TH>Toe</TH>
                 </TR>
                 <TR>
                      <TD>X</TD>
                      <TD>O</TD>
                      <TD>X</TD>
                  </TR>
                  <TR>
                         <TD>O</TD>
                         <TD>X</TD>
                         <TD>O</TD>
                 </TR>
                 <TR>
                         <TD>X</TD>
                         <TD>O</TD>
                         <TD>X</TD>
                 </TR>
             </TABLE>


             <BR>
             <BR>
             <H2>Standard</H2>
             <PRE>
&lt;TABLE BORDER="2"&gt;
     &lt;TR&gt;
         &lt;TH&gt;Tic&lt;/TH&gt;
```

```
      &lt;TH&gt;Tac&lt;/TH&gt;
      &lt;TH&gt;Toe&lt;/TH&gt;
   &lt;/TR&gt;
   &lt;TR&gt;
      &lt;TD&gt;X&lt;/TD&gt;
      &lt;TD&gt;O&lt;/TD&gt;
      &lt;TD&gt;X&lt;/TD&gt;
   &lt;/TR&gt;
   &lt;TR&gt;
      &lt;TD&gt;O&lt;/TD&gt;
      &lt;TD&gt;X&lt;/TD&gt;
      &lt;TD&gt;O&lt;/TD&gt;
   &lt;/TR&gt;
   &lt;TR&gt;
      &lt;TD&gt;X&lt;/TD&gt;
      &lt;TD&gt;O&lt;/TD&gt;
      &lt;TD&gt;X&lt;/TD&gt;
   &lt;/TR&gt;
&lt;/TABLE&gt;
   </PRE>

   <TABLE BORDER="2">
      <TR>
         <TH>Tic</TH>
         <TH>Tac</TH>
         <TH>Toe</TH>
      </TR>
      <TR>
         <TD>X</TD>
         <TD>O</TD>
         <TD>X</TD>
      </TR>
      <TR>
         <TD>O</TD>
         <TD>X</TD>
         <TD>O</TD>
      </TR>
      <TR>
         <TD>X</TD>
         <TD>O</TD>
         <TD>X</TD>
      </TR>
   </TABLE>
```

6. Creating Tables

```
            <BR>
            <BR>
            <H2>Cell Padding</H2>

            <PRE>
&lt;TABLE BORDER="2" CELLPADDING=4&gt;
    &lt;TR&gt;
        &lt;TH&gt;Tic&lt;/TH&gt;
        &lt;TH&gt;Tac&lt;/TH&gt;
        &lt;TH&gt;Toe&lt;/TH&gt;
    &lt;/TR&gt;
    &lt;TR&gt;
        &lt;TD&gt;X&lt;/TD&gt;
        &lt;TD&gt;O&lt;/TD&gt;
        &lt;TD&gt;X&lt;/TD&gt;
    &lt;/TR&gt;
    &lt;TR&gt;
        &lt;TD&gt;O&lt;/TD&gt;
        &lt;TD&gt;X&lt;/TD&gt;
        &lt;TD&gt;O&lt;/TD&gt;
    &lt;/TR&gt;
    &lt;TR&gt;
        &lt;TD&gt;X&lt;/TD&gt;
        &lt;TD&gt;O&lt;/TD&gt;
        &lt;TD&gt;X&lt;/TD&gt;
    &lt;/TR&gt;
&lt;/TABLE&gt;
            </PRE>

            <TABLE BORDER="2" CELLPADDING = 4>
                <TR>
                    <TH>Tic</TH>
                    <TH>Tac</TH>
                    <TH>Toe</TH>
                </TR>
                <TR>
                    <TD>X</TD>
                    <TD>O</TD>
                    <TD>X</TD>
                </TR>
                <TR>
                    <TD>O</TD>
                    <TD>X</TD>
                    <TD>O</TD>
                </TR>
```

```
        <TR>
            <TD>X</TD>
            <TD>0</TD>
            <TD>X</TD>
        </TR>
    </TABLE>

    <BR>
    <BR>
    <H2>Wide BORDER="2"</H2>

    <PRE>
&lt;TABLE BORDER="2" CELLSPACING=4&gt;
    &lt;TR&gt;
        &lt;TH&gt;Tic&lt;/TH&gt;
        &lt;TH&gt;Tac&lt;/TH&gt;
        &lt;TH&gt;Toe&lt;/TH&gt;
    &lt;/TR&gt;
    &lt;TR&gt;
        &lt;TD&gt;X&lt;/TD&gt;
        &lt;TD&gt;0&lt;/TD&gt;
        &lt;TD&gt;X&lt;/TD&gt;
    &lt;/TR&gt;
    &lt;TR&gt;
        &lt;TD&gt;0&lt;/TD&gt;
        &lt;TD&gt;X&lt;/TD&gt;
        &lt;TD&gt;0&lt;/TD&gt;
    &lt;/TR&gt;
    &lt;TR&gt;
        &lt;TD&gt;X&lt;/TD&gt;
        &lt;TD&gt;0&lt;/TD&gt;
        &lt;TD&gt;X&lt;/TD&gt;
    &lt;/TR&gt;
&lt;/TABLE&gt;
    </PRE>

    <TABLE BORDER="2" CELLSPACING = 4>
        <TR>
            <TH>Tic</TH>
            <TH>Tac</TH>
            <TH>Toe</TH>
        </TR>
        <TR>
            <TD>X</TD>
            <TD>0</TD>
```

```
                    <TD>X</TD>
                </TR>
                <TR>
                    <TD>O</TD>
                    <TD>X</TD>
                    <TD>O</TD>
                </TR>
                <TR>
                    <TD>X</TD>
                    <TD>O</TD>
                    <TD>X</TD>
                </TR>
            </TABLE>


            <BR>
            <BR>
            <H2>Data Aligned Right, Left, Center</H2>

            <PRE>
    &lt;TABLE BORDER="2" WIDTH = 200&gt;
        &lt;TR&gt;
            &lt;TH&gt;Tic&lt;/TH&gt;
            &lt;TH&gt;Tac&lt;/TH&gt;
            &lt;TH&gt;Toe&lt;/TH&gt;
        &lt;/TR&gt;
        &lt;TR&gt;
            &lt;TD ALIGN = RIGHT&gt;X&lt;/TD&gt;
            &lt;TD ALIGN = LEFT&gt;O&lt;/TD&gt;
            &lt;TD ALIGN = CENTER&gt;X&lt;/TD&gt;
        &lt;/TR&gt;
        &lt;TR&gt;
            &lt;TD ALIGN = RIGHT&gt;O&lt;/TD&gt;
            &lt;TD ALIGN = LEFT&gt;X&lt;/TD&gt;
            &lt;TD ALIGN = CENTER&gt;O&lt;/TD&gt;
        &lt;/TR&gt;
        &lt;TR&gt;
            &lt;TD ALIGN = RIGHT&gt;X&lt;/TD&gt;
            &lt;TD ALIGN = LEFT&gt;O&lt;/TD&gt;
            &lt;TD ALIGN = CENTER&gt;X&lt;/TD&gt;
        &lt;/TR&gt;
    &lt;/TABLE&gt;
            </PRE>
```

```
<TABLE BORDER="2" WIDTH = 200>
    <TR>
        <TH>Tic</TH>
        <TH>Tac</TH>
        <TH>Toe</TH>
    </TR>
    <TR>
        <TD ALIGN = RIGHT>X</TD>
        <TD ALIGN = LEFT>O</TD>
        <TD ALIGN = CENTER>X</TD>
    </TR>
    <TR>
        <TD ALIGN = RIGHT>O</TD>
        <TD ALIGN = LEFT>X</TD>
        <TD ALIGN = CENTER>O</TD>
    </TR>
    <TR>
        <TD ALIGN = RIGHT>X</TD>
        <TD ALIGN = LEFT>O</TD>
        <TD ALIGN = CENTER>X</TD>
    </TR>
</TABLE>


<BR>
<BR>
<H2>Data Aligned Vertically</H2>

<PRE>
&lt;TABLE BORDER="2" HEIGHT = 120&gt;
    &lt;TR&gt;
        &lt;TH&gt;Tic
        &lt;/TH&gt;
        &lt;TH&gt;Tac&lt;/TH&gt;
        &lt;TH&gt;Toe&lt;/TH&gt;
    &lt;/TR&gt;
    &lt;TR&gt;
        &lt;TD VALIGN = TOP&gt;X&lt;/TD&gt;
        &lt;TD VALIGN = MIDDLE&gt;O&lt;/TD&gt;
        &lt;TD VALIGN = BOTTOM&gt;X&lt;/TD&gt;
    &lt;/TR&gt;
    &lt;TR&gt;
        &lt;TD VALIGN = TOP&gt;O&lt;/TD&gt;
        &lt;TD VALIGN = MIDDLE&gt;X&lt;/TD&gt;
        &lt;TD VALIGN = BOTTOM&gt;O&lt;/TD&gt;
```

```
        &lt;/TR&gt;
        &lt;TR&gt;
            &lt;TD VALIGN = TOP&gt;X&lt;/TD&gt;
            &lt;TD VALIGN = MIDDLE&gt;O&lt;/TD&gt;
            &lt;TD VALIGN = BOTTOM&gt;X&lt;/TD&gt;
        &lt;/TR&gt;
    &lt;/TABLE&gt;
        </PRE>

        <TABLE BORDER="2" HEIGHT = 120>
            <TR>
                <TH>Tic</TH>
                <TH>Tac</TH>
                <TH>Toe</TH>
            </TR>
            <TR>
                <TD VALIGN = TOP>X</TD>
                <TD VALIGN = MIDDLE>O</TD>
                <TD VALIGN = BOTTOM>X</TD>
            </TR>
            <TR>
                <TD VALIGN = TOP>O</TD>
                <TD VALIGN = MIDDLE>X</TD>
                <TD VALIGN = BOTTOM>O</TD>
            </TR>
            <TR>
                <TD VALIGN = TOP>X</TD>
                <TD VALIGN = MIDDLE>O</TD>
                <TD VALIGN = BOTTOM>X</TD>
            </TR>
        </TABLE>


        <BR>
        <BR>
        <H2>A Column Spanning Row</H2>
        <PRE>
&lt;TABLE BORDER="2"&gt;
    &lt;TR&gt;
        &lt;TH COLSPAN = 3&gt;TicTac Game&lt;/TH&gt;
    &lt;/TR&gt;
    &lt;TR&gt;
        &lt;TD&gt;X&lt;/TD&gt;
        &lt;TD&gt;O&lt;/TD&gt;
        &lt;TD&gt;X&lt;/TD&gt;
```

```
    &lt;/TR&gt;
    &lt;TR&gt;
        &lt;TD&gt;O&lt;/TD&gt;
        &lt;TD&gt;X&lt;/TD&gt;
        &lt;TD&gt;O&lt;/TD&gt;
    &lt;/TR&gt;
    &lt;TR&gt;
        &lt;TD&gt;X&lt;/TD&gt;
        &lt;TD&gt;O&lt;/TD&gt;
        &lt;TD&gt;X&lt;/TD&gt;
    &lt;/TR&gt;
&lt;/TABLE&gt;
        </PRE>

        <TABLE BORDER="2">
            <TR>
                <TH COLSPAN=3> TicTac Game</TH>
            <TR>
                <TD>X</TD>
                <TD>O</TD>
                <TD>X</TD>
            </TR>
            <TR>
                <TD>O</TD>
                <TD>X</TD>
                <TD>O</TD>
            </TR>
            <TR>
                <TD>X</TD>
                <TD>O</TD>
                <TD>X</TD>
            </TR>
        </TABLE>

        <BR>
        <BR>
        <H2>A Row Spanning Column</H2>

        <PRE>
&lt;TABLE BORDER="2"&gt;
    &lt;TR&gt;
        &lt;TH ROWSPAN = 3&gt;TicTac&lt;BR&gt;Game&lt;/TH&gt;
        &lt;TD&gt;X&lt;/TD&gt;
        &lt;TD&gt;O&lt;/TD&gt;
        &lt;TD&gt;X&lt;/TD&gt;
```

```
        &lt;/TR&gt;
        &lt;TR&gt;
            &lt;TD&gt;O&lt;/TD&gt;
            &lt;TD&gt;X&lt;/TD&gt;
            &lt;TD&gt;O&lt;/TD&gt;
        &lt;/TR&gt;
        &lt;TR&gt;
            &lt;TD&gt;X&lt;/TD&gt;
            &lt;TD&gt;O&lt;/TD&gt;
            &lt;TD&gt;X&lt;/TD&gt;
        &lt;/TR&gt;
    &lt;/TABLE&gt;
        </PRE>

        <BR>
        <TABLE BORDER="2">
            <TR>
                <TH ROWSPAN = 3>TicTac<BR>Game</TH>
                <TD>X</TD>
                <TD>O</TD>
                <TD>X</TD>
            </TR>
            <TR>
                <TD>O</TD>
                <TD>X</TD>
                <TD>O</TD>
            </TR>
            <TR>
                <TD>X</TD>
                <TD>O</TD>
                <TD>X</TD>
            </TR>
        </TABLE>


        <BR>
        <BR>
        <H2>Color</H2>


        <PRE>
&lt;TABLE BORDER="2"&gt;
    &lt;TR&gt;
        &lt;TD BGCOLOR = "#ffffff"&gt;X&lt;/TD&gt;
        &lt;TD BGCOLOR = "#000000"&gt;
            &lt;FONT COLOR = "#ffffff"&gt;O&lt;/FONT&gt;
```

```
      &lt;/TD&gt;
      &lt;TD BGCOLOR = "#ffffff"&gt;X&lt;/TD&gt;
   &lt;/TR&gt;
   &lt;TR&gt;
      &lt;TD BGCOLOR = "#000000"&gt;
          &lt;FONT COLOR = "#ffffff"&gt;O&lt;/FONT&gt;
      &lt;/TD&gt;
      &lt;TD BGCOLOR = "#ffffff"&gt;X&lt;/TD&gt;
      &lt;TD BGCOLOR = "#000000"&gt;
          &lt;FONT COLOR = "#ffffff"&gt;O&lt;/FONT&gt;
      &lt;/TD&gt;
   &lt;/TR&gt;
   &lt;TR&gt;
      &lt;TD BGCOLOR = "#ffffff"&gt;X&lt;/TD&gt;
      &lt;TD BGCOLOR = "#000000"&gt;
          &lt;FONT COLOR = "#ffffff"&gt;O&lt;/FONT&gt;
      &lt;/TD&gt;
      &lt;TD BGCOLOR = "#ffffff"&gt;X&lt;/TD&gt;
   &lt;/TR&gt;
&lt;/TABLE&gt;
      </PRE>


      <TABLE BORDER="2">
         <TR>
             <TH BGCOLOR = "#ff0000">Tic</TH>
             <TH BGCOLOR = "#ff0000">Tac</TH>
             <TH BGCOLOR = "#ff0000">Toe</TH>
         </TR>
         <TR>
             <TD BGCOLOR = "#ffffff">X</TD>
             <TD BGCOLOR = "#000000">
                 <FONT COLOR = "#ffffff">O</FONT>
             </TD>
             <TD BGCOLOR = "#ffffff">X</TD>
         </TR>
         <TR>
             <TD BGCOLOR = "#000000">
                 <FONT COLOR = "#ffffff">O</FONT>
             <TD BGCOLOR = "#ffffff">X</TD>
             <TD BGCOLOR = "#000000">
                 <FONT COLOR = "#ffffff">O</FONT>
             </TD>
         </TR>
         <TR>
             <TD BGCOLOR = "#ffffff">X</TD>
```

```
                    <TD BGCOLOR = "#000000">
                        <FONT COLOR = "#ffffff">O</FONT>
                    </TD>
                    <TD BGCOLOR = "#ffffff">X</TD>
                </TR>
            </TABLE>

        </BODY>

    </HTML>
```

Immediate Solutions

<TABLE>—Creating A Table

Purpose: Creates a table; encloses elements like **<CAPTION>**, **<TR>**, **<TH>**, **<TD>**, **<COLSPAN>**, **<COL>**, **<THEAD>**, **<TBODY>**, and **<TFOOT>**.

Start Tag/End Tag: Required/Required

Supported: [3, 3.2, 4, IE2, IE3, IE4, IE5, NS1, NS2, NS3, NS4]

Attributes:

- **ALIGN**—Specifies the horizontal alignment of the table in the browser window. Set to **LEFT**, **CENTER**, or **RIGHT**. Deprecated. [3, 3.2, 4, IE2, IE3, IE4, IE5, NS2, NS3, NS4]

- **BACKGROUND**—Specifies the URL of a background image to be used as a background for the table. All cell contents are displayed over this image. Note that if the image is smaller than the table, it is tiled to fit the table. Set to a URL. [IE3, IE4, IE5, NS4]

- **BGCOLOR**—Sets the background color of the table cells. You can override this attribute at the row and cell level. Set to a Red, Green, Blue (RGB) triplet color value or a predefined color name. Deprecated. [4, IE2, IE3, IE4, IE5, NS3, NS4]

- **BORDER**—Sets the border width; set to a pixel width. If you set this attribute to 0, no border appears. Although this attribute used to be a stand-alone attribute in HTML 2, as of HTML 3.2, you should assign a number to it.

- **BORDERCOLOR**—Sets the external border color for the entire table. Set to an RGB triplet color value or a predefined color name. [IE2, IE3, IE4, IE5]

- **CELLPADDING**—Sets the spacing between cell walls and cell contents. Set to a pixel size. [3.2, 4, IE2, IE3, IE4, IE5, NS1, NS2, NS3, NS4]

- **CELLSPACING**—Gives the distance between cells (and therefore the width of the struts between cells). Set to pixel values. [3.2, 4, IE2, IE3, IE4, IE5, NS1, NS2, NS3, NS4]

- **CLASS**—Class of the element (used for rendering). [3, 4, IE4, IE5]

- **COLS**—Specifies the number of columns in the table. A Complex Table Model attribute. Set to a positive integer. [IE3, IE4, IE5, NS3, NS4]

- **DATAPAGESIZE**—Sets the number of records displayed in a data-bound repeated table. Set to a positive number. [IE4, IE5]

- **DATASRC**—Gives the URL or ID of the data source object supplying data bound to this element. W3C says this should be a URL, Internet Explorer says it should be a data source ID. [IE4, IE5]

- **DIR**—Gives the direction of directionally neutral text (text that doesn't have inherent direction in which you should read it). Possible values: **LTR**: left-to-right text or table and **RTL**: right-to-left text or table. [4, IE5]

- **FRAME**—Specifies the outer border display of the table. A Complex Table Model attribute. Using this attribute coupled with the **RULES** attribute yields much greater border display control than the older Simple Table Model. Possible values: **VOID** (no borders), **ABOVE** (border on top side only), **BELOW** (border on bottom side only), **HSIDES** (horizontal borders only), **VSIDES** (vertical borders only), **LHS** (border on left side only), **RHS** (border on right side only), **BOX** (border on all four sides), **BORDER** (the default, the same as **BOX**). [4, IE3, IE4, IE5]

- **HEIGHT**—Gives the height of the whole table, in pixels. [IE2, IE3, IE4, IE5, NS1, NS2, NS3, NS4]

- **HSPACE**—Sets the horizontal padding for the whole table, in pixels. [NS1, NS2, NS3, NS4]

- **ID**—Unique alphanumeric identifier for the tag, which you can use to refer to it. [3, 4, IE4, IE5]

- **LANG**—Base language used for the tag. [3, 4, IE4, IE5]

- **LANGUAGE**—Scripting language used for the tag. [IE4, IE5]

- **RULES**—Sets the interior struts in a table. A Complex Table Model attribute. Set to: **NONE** (no interior struts are displayed), **GROUPS** (horizontal struts displayed between table groups created with the **THEAD**, **TBODY**, **TFOOT**, and **COLGROUP** tags), **ROWS** (horizontal struts are displayed between all table rows), **COLS** (vertical struts are displayed between all table columns), and **ALL** (struts displayed between all table cells). [4, IE4, IE5]

- **STYLE**—Inline style indicating how to render the element. [4, IE3, IE4, IE5]

- **SUMMARY**—Sets accessibility information for nonvisual browsers. Set to a text string providing a summary of the table. [4]

- **TITLE**—Holds additional information (which might be displayed in tool tips) for the element. [3, 4, IE4, IE5]

- **VSPACE**—Sets the vertical padding for the whole table, in pixels. [NS1, NS2, NS3, NS4]

- **WIDTH**—Sets the width of the table; set to a pixel value or a percentage of the display area (add a percent sign [%] to such values). [3, 3.2, 4, IE2, IE3, IE4, IE5, NS1, NS2, NS3, NS4]

The novice programmer appears and says, "I want to present my new tic tac toe game in an HTML table—where do I start?" You say, "Start with the **<TABLE>** element." "Great," says the NP, "here's my terminal—can you show me how?"

To create a table, you enclose everything in a **<TABLE>** element like this:

```
<TABLE>
   .
   .
   .
</TABLE>
```

That's all it takes to create a table. But this one is completely empty. So where do you go from here? Now you start building the rows in your table—see the next section.

<TR>—Creating A Table Row

Purpose: Creates a row in a table; encloses **<TH>** and **<TD>** elements.

Start Tag/End Tag: Required/Optional

Supported: [3, 3.2, 4, IE2, IE3, IE4, IE5, NS1, NS2, NS3, NS4]

Attributes:

- **ALIGN**—Specifies the horizontal alignment of the text in this table row. Set to **LEFT**, **CENTER**, or **RIGHT**. Deprecated. [3, 3.2, 4, IE2, IE3, IE4, IE5, NS2, NS3, NS4]

- **BGCOLOR**—Sets the background color of the table cells. You can override this attribute at the row and cell level. Set to an RGB triplet color value or a predefined color name. Deprecated. [4, IE2, IE3, IE4, IE5, NS3, NS4]

- **BORDERCOLOR**—Sets the external border color for the row. Set to an RGB triplet color value or a predefined color name. [IE2, IE3, IE4, IE5]

- **CHAR**—Specifies a character to align text on. Set to an alphanumeric character. [4]

- **CHAROFF**—Sets the alignment offset to the first character to align on, as set with **CHAR**. [4]

- **CLASS**—Class of the element (used for rendering). [3, 4, IE4, IE5]

- **DIR**—Gives the direction of directionally neutral text (text that doesn't have inherent direction in which you should read it). Possible values: **LTR**: left-to-right text or table and **RTL**: right-to-left text or table. [4, IE5]

- **ID**—Unique alphanumeric identifier for the tag, which you can use to refer to it. [3, 4, IE4, IE5]

- **LANG**—Base language used for the tag. [3, 4, IE4, IE5]

- **LANGUAGE**—Scripting language used for the tag. [IE4, IE5]

- **STYLE**—Inline style indicating how to render the element. [4, IE3, IE4, IE5]

- **TITLE**—Holds additional information (which might be displayed in tool tips) for the element. [3, 4, IE4, IE5]

- **VALIGN**—Sets the vertical alignment of the data in this row. Set to **TOP**, **MIDDLE**, **BOTTOM**, or **BASELINE**. [3, 3.2, 4, IE2, IE3, IE4, IE5, NS1, NS2, NS3, NS4]

"OK," says the novice programmer, "I've set up my table with the **<TABLE>** element. What's next?" "Next," you say, "you create the rows in your table with the **<TR>** element."

To create a row in a table, you use the **<TR>** element. The number of these elements that you use specifies the number of rows in your table. Here's how to create a row in a table:

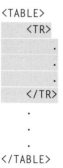

```
<TABLE>
    <TR>
        .
        .
        .
    </TR>
  .
  .
  .
</TABLE>
```

For each row in your table, there's a **<TR>** element; but how does the browser know how many columns you want to use? In the Simple Table Model, it simply checks how many **<TH>** or **<TD>** elements you put into a row. **<TH>** elements create table headings and **<TD>** elements create the table data that appears in the cells of a table. I'll take a look at both of these elements over the next two sections.

TIP: *The **</TR>**, **</TH>**, and **</TD>** tags are actually optional, although this wasn't always so. In fact, some older browsers may have problems if you don't include these tags, so it's probably a good idea to do so. Also, note that Internet Explorer is very tolerant of invalid HTML in tables. So if you're using Internet Explorer, check your HTML in other browsers; they may not be as forgiving.*

<TH>—Creating Table Headings

Purpose: Creates a table heading; just like table data, but usually bold and centered vertically and horizontally.

Start Tag/End Tag: Required/Optional

Supported: [3, 3.2, 4, IE2, IE3, IE4, IE5, NS1, NS2, NS3, NS4]

Attributes:

- **ABBR**—Specifies an abbreviated name for a header cell (the default abbreviation is the actual cell content). Set to alphanumeric characters. [4]

- **ALIGN**—Sets the horizontal alignment of content in the table cell. Set to **LEFT**, **CENTER**, or **RIGHT**. [3, 3.2, 4, IE2, IE3, IE4, IE5, NS1, NS2, NS3, NS4]

- **AXIS**—Specifies a name for a cell and will usually only be applied to table heading cells, allowing the table to be mapped to a tree hierarchy. Set to alphanumeric characters. [3, 4]

- **BACKGROUND**—Specifies the background image for the table cell. All cell contents are displayed over this image. If the image is smaller than the table cell, the image will be tiled. Set to an image's URL. [IE3, IE4, IE5]

- **BGCOLOR**—Sets the background color of the table cells. You can override this attribute at the row and cell level. Set to an RGB triplet color value or a predefined color name. Deprecated. [4, IE2, IE3, IE4, IE5, NS3, NS4]

- **BORDERCOLOR**—Sets the external border color for the cell. Set to an RGB triplet color value or a predefined color name. [IE2, IE3, IE4, IE5]

- **CHAR**—Specifies a character to align text on. Set to an alphanumeric character. [4]

- **CHAROFF**—Sets the alignment offset to the first character to align on, as set with **CHAR**. [4]

- **CLASS**—Class of the element (used for rendering). [3, 4, IE4, IE5]

- **COLSPAN**—Indicates how many cell columns of the table this cell should span. Set to a positive integer (the default is 1). [3, 3.2, 4, IE2, IE3, IE4, IE5, NS1, NS2, NS3, NS4]

- **DIR**—Gives the direction of directionally neutral text (text that doesn't have inherent direction in which you should read it). Possible values: **LTR**: left-to-right text or table and **RTL**: right-to-left text or table. [4, IE5]

- **HEADERS**—Gives the list of header cells that supply header information for the cell. Set to a space separated list of table cell IDs. [4]

- **HEIGHT**—Sets the height of the cell (in general, also sets the height of the whole row). Set to pixel values. Deprecated. [3.2, 4, IE2, IE3, IE4, IE5, NS1, NS2, NS3, NS4]

- **ID**—Unique alphanumeric identifier for the tag, which you can use to refer to it. [3, 4, IE4, IE5]

- **LANG**—Base language used for the tag. [3, 4, IE4, IE5]

- **LANGUAGE**—Scripting language used for the tag. [IE4, IE5]

- **NOWRAP**—Specifies that data in the cell should not be wrapped by the browser, meaning the table cell will be made long enough to fit the contents without line breaks. Deprecated. [3, 3.2, 4, IE2, IE3, IE4, IE5, NS1, NS2, NS3, NS4]

- **ROWSPAN**—Indicates how many rows of the table this cell should span. Set to a positive integer (the default is 1). [3, 3.2, 4, IE2, IE3, IE4, IE5, NS1, NS2, NS3, NS4]

- **SCOPE**—Specifies a set of data cells for which the header cell provides header information. Set to: **ROW** (cell provides header information for the rest of the row that contains it) or **COL** (cell provides header information for the rest of the column), **ROWGROUP** (cell provides header information for the rest of the row group that contains it) or **COLGROUP** (cell provides header information for the rest of the column group that contains it). [4]

- **STYLE**—Inline style indicating how to render the element. [4, IE4, IE5]

- **TITLE**—Holds additional information (which might be displayed in tool tips) for the element. [3, 4,IE4, IE5]

- **VALIGN**—Sets the vertical alignment of the data in this cell. Set to **TOP**, **MIDDLE**, **BOTTOM**, or **BASELINE**. [3, 3.2, 4, IE2, IE3, IE4, IE5, NS1, NS2, NS3, NS4]

- **WIDTH**—Specifies the width of the cell. Set to a pixel width or a percentage of the display area (include a percent sign [%] after percentages). Deprecated. [3.2, 4, IE2, IE3, IE4, IE5, NS1, NS2, NS3, NS4]

"Is it true," the novice programmer wants to know, "that you can use special table cells as table headers?" "Yes indeed," you say, "just use the **<TH>** element." "Great," says the NP, sitting down, "tell me all about it!"

The **<TH>** element gives you an easy way to put a header on top of each column in a table (although you can make headers span several columns). Here's an example in which I'm giving the three columns of a table the headings "Tic", "Tac", and "Toe":

```
<TABLE>
    <TR>
        <TH>Tic</TH>
        <TH>Tac</TH>
        <TH>Toe</TH>
    </TR>
    .
    .
    .
</TABLE>
```

You can see the results of this HTML in Figure 6.3. The text in a table header is usually displayed in bold and centered vertically and horizontally. (In fact, you can have headers that span several columns—see "Spanning Multiple Columns" in the Immediate Solutions section.)

TIP: *The **</TR>**, **</TH>**, and **</TD>** tags are actually optional, although this wasn't always so. In fact, some older browsers may have problems if you don't include these tags, so it's probably a good idea to do so. Also, note that Internet Explorer is very tolerant of invalid HTML in tables. So if you're using Internet Explorer, check your HTML in other browsers; they may not be as forgiving.*

<TD>—Creating Table Data

Purpose: Specifies the data for a table cell. Used inside the **<TR>** element.

Start Tag/End Tag: Required/Optional

Supported: [3, 3.2, 4, IE1, IE2, IE3, IE4, IE5, NS1, NS2, NS3, NS4]

Attributes:

- **ABBR**—Specifies an abbreviated name for a header cell (the default abbreviation is the actual cell content). Set to alphanumeric characters. [4]
- **ALIGN**—Sets the horizontal alignment of content in the table cell. Set to **LEFT**, **CENTER**, or **RIGHT**. [3, 3.2, 4, IE2, IE3, IE4, IE5, NS1, NS2, NS3, NS4]

- **AXIS**—Specifies a name for a cell and will usually only be applied to table heading cells, allowing the table to be mapped to a tree hierarchy. Set to alphanumeric characters. [3, 4]

- **BACKGROUND**—Specifies the background image for the table cell. All cell contents are displayed over this image. If the image is smaller than the table cell, the image will be tiled. Set to an image's URL. [IE3, IE4, IE5]

- **BGCOLOR**—Sets the background color of the table cells. You can override this attribute at the row and cell level. Set to an RGB triplet color value or a predefined color name. Deprecated. [4, IE2, IE3, IE4, IE5, NS3, NS4]

- **BORDERCOLOR**—Sets the external border color for the cell. Set to an RGB triplet color value or a predefined color name. [IE2, IE3, IE4, IE5]

- **CHAR**—Specifies a character to align text on. Set to an alphanumeric character. [4]

- **CHAROFF**—Sets the alignment offset to the first character to align on, as set with **CHAR**. [4]

- **CLASS**—Class of the element (used for rendering). [3, 4, IE4, IE5]

- **COLSPAN**—Indicates how many cell columns of the table this cell should span. Set to a positive integer (the default is 1). [3, 3.2, 4, IE2, IE3, IE4, IE5, NS1, NS2, NS3, NS4]

- **DIR**—Gives the direction of directionally neutral text (text that doesn't have inherent direction in which you should read it). Possible values: **LTR**: left-to-right text or table and **RTL**: right-to-left text or table. [4, IE5]

- **HEADERS**—Gives the list of header cells that supply header information for the cell. Set to a space-separated list of table cell IDs. [4]

- **HEIGHT**—Sets the height of the cell (in general, also sets the height of the whole row). Set to pixel values. Deprecated. [3.2, 4, IE2, IE3, IE4, IE5, NS1, NS2, NS3, NS4]

- **ID**—Unique alphanumeric identifier for the tag, which you can use to refer to it. [3, 4, IE4, IE5]

- **LANG**—Base language used for the tag. [3, 4, IE4, IE5]

- **LANGUAGE**—Scripting language used for the tag. [IE4, IE5]

- **NOWRAP**—Specifies that data in the cell should not be wrapped by the browser, meaning the table cell will be made long enough to fit the contents without line breaks. Deprecated. [3, 3.2, 4, IE2, IE3, IE4, IE5, NS1, NS2, NS3, NS4]

- **ROWSPAN**—Indicates how many rows of the table this cell should span. Set to a positive integer (the default is 1). [3, 3.2, 4, IE2, IE3, IE4, IE5, NS1, NS2, NS3, NS4]

- **SCOPE**—Specifies a set of data cells for which the header cell provides header information. Set to: **ROW** (cell provides header information for the rest of the row that contains it) or **COL** (cell provides header information for the rest of the column), **ROWGROUP** (cell provides header information for the rest of the row group that contains it) or **COLGROUP** (cell provides header information for the rest of the column group that contains it). [4]

- **STYLE**—Inline style indicating how to render the element. [4, IE4, IE5]

- **TITLE**—Holds additional information (which might be displayed in tool tips) for the element. [3, 4, IE4, IE5]

- **VALIGN**—Sets the vertical alignment of the data in this cell. Set to **TOP**, **MIDDLE**, **BOTTOM**, or **BASELINE**. [3, 3.2, 4, IE2, IE3, IE4, IE5, NS1, NS2, NS3, NS4]

- **WIDTH**—Specifies the width of the cell. Set to a pixel width or a percentage of the display area (include a percent sign [%] after percentages). Deprecated. [3.2, 4, IE2, IE3, IE4, IE5, NS1, NS2, NS3, NS4]

"Now I know how to set up a table, how to add rows to it, and how to create a header for each column in a table," the novice programmer says, "but I still don't know how to add data to the table." "That's easy," you say, "just use the **<TD>** element for the data for each cell, and enclose them all in a **<TR>** element." "Wow!" says the NP.

You specify the data for the cells in a table with the **<TD>** element. The browser knows how many columns to create in the table depending on how many **<TD>** or **<TH>** elements you put into a row. Here's an example where I'm adding data to the rows of a table using **<TD>** elements:

```
<TABLE>
    <TR>
        <TH>Tic</TH>
        <TH>Tac</TH>
        <TH>Toe</TH>
    </TR>
    <TR>
        <TD>X</TD>
        <TD>O</TD>
        <TD>X</TD>
    </TR>
    <TR>
        <TD>O</TD>
        <TD>X</TD>
        <TD>O</TD>
```

```
        </TR>
        <TR>
            <TD>X</TD>
            <TD>0</TD>
            <TD>X</TD>
        </TR>
    </TABLE>
```

And that's it—the table is done, and you can see it in Figure 6.3. That's the way it works. You create the structure of a Simple Table Model with **<TABLE>** and **<TR>**, and enter the data in each cell with **<TD>** (and **<TH>** for header text).

You might take a moment to study the table in the previous example—when you have mastered the structure of that table, you will understand all Simple Table Models.

TIP: *The **</TR>**, **</TH>**, and **</TD>** tags are actually optional, although this wasn't always so. In fact, some older browsers may have problems if you don't include these tags, so it's probably a good idea to do so. Also, note that Internet Explorer is very tolerant of invalid HTML in tables. So if you're using Internet Explorer, check your HTML in other browsers; they may not be as forgiving.*

<CAPTION>—Creating A Table Caption

Purpose: Specifies the data for a table cell. Used inside the **<TR>** element.

Start Tag/End Tag: Required/Required

Supported: [3, 3.2, 4, IE1, IE2, IE3, IE4, IE5, NS1, NS2, NS3, NS4]

Attributes:

- **ALIGN**—Sets the horizontal alignment of the caption. Set to **TOP** or **BOTTOM**. Internet Explorer 2 also added settings **LEFT**, **CENTER**, and **RIGHT**. Deprecated. [3, 3.2, 4, IE2, IE3, IE4, IE5, NS1, NS2, NS3, NS4]

- **CLASS**—Class of the element (used for rendering). [3, 4, IE4, IE5]

- **DIR**—Gives the direction of directionally neutral text (text that doesn't have inherent direction in which you should read it). Possible values: **LTR**: left-to-right text or table and **RTL**: right-to-left text or table. [4, IE5]

- **ID**—Unique alphanumeric identifier for the tag, which you can use to refer to it. [3, 4, IE4, IE5]

- **LANG**—Base language used for the tag. [3, 4, IE4, IE5]

- **LANGUAGE**—Scripting language used for the tag. [IE4, IE5]

- **STYLE**—Inline style indicating how to render the element. [4, IE3, IE4, IE5]

- **TITLE**—Holds additional information (which might be displayed in tool tips) for the element. [3, 4, IE4, IE5]

- **VALIGN**—Sets the vertical alignment of the caption. Set to **TOP**, **MIDDLE**, **BOTTOM**, or **BASELINE**. [IE2, IE3, IE4, IE5]

You can give a table, as a whole, a caption using the **<CAPTION>** element. This element goes directly into the **<TABLE>** element. Here's an example showing how this works:

```
<TABLE>
    <CAPTION>How About A Game?</CAPTION>
    <TR>
        <TH>Tic</TH>
        <TH>Tac</TH>
        <TH>Toe</TH>
    </TR>
    <TR>
        <TD>X</TD>
        <TD>O</TD>
        <TD>X</TD>
    </TR>
    <TR>
        <TD>O</TD>
        <TD>X</TD>
        <TD>O</TD>
    </TR>
    <TR>
        <TD>X</TD>
        <TD>O</TD>
        <TD>X</TD>
    </TR>
</TABLE>
```

You can see the results of this HTML in Figure 6.11, including the caption, which appears above the table. Although the **<CAPTION>** element is useful, note that you can create the same effect with simple text or headers like **<H1>** or **<H2>**.

The **ALIGN** attribute is worth taking a look at. In most browsers, you can set this attribute to **TOP** or **BOTTOM** to place the caption at the top or bottom of the table. However, starting in Internet Explorer 2, **ALIGN** takes the values **LEFT**, **RIGHT**, or **CENTER** to align the caption horizontally. To align the caption vertically in Internet Explorer, you use **VALIGN**. The default alignment is centered at the top of the table.

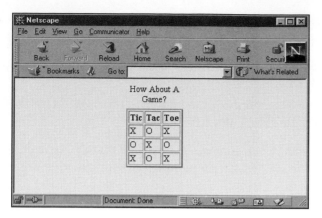

Figure 6.11   Giving a table a caption.

Setting Table Border Widths

You can set the width of table borders with the **<TABLE>** element's **BORDER** attribute, which you set to positive pixel widths (the default is 0). In this example, I'm setting the border width of a table to 10 pixels:

```
<TABLE BORDER="10">
    <TR>
        <TH>Tic</TH>
        <TH>Tac</TH>
        <TH>Toe</TH>
    </TR>
    <TR>
        <TD>X</TD>
        <TD>O</TD>
        <TD>X</TD>
    </TR>
    <TR>
        <TD>O</TD>
        <TD>X</TD>
        <TD>O</TD>
    </TR>
    <TR>
        <TD>X</TD>
        <TD>O</TD>
        <TD>X</TD>
    </TR>
</TABLE>
```

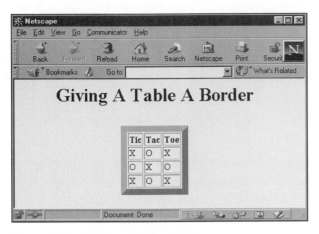

Figure 6.12   Giving a table a border.

The results of this HTML appear in Figure 6.12. To remove the border entirely, set the border width to 0. As you can see in Figure 6.12, most browsers give wider table borders a bevelled look.

Setting Cell Padding

"Your table looks too cramped," says the Web page design czar. "Well," you say, "I could increase the cell padding." "Great!" says the WPDC, "Do that."

The cell padding is the amount of space in pixels between the walls of the cell and its content. Here's an example we saw at the beginning of this chapter, setting the cell padding to 4 pixels:

```
<TABLE BORDER="2" CELLPADDING = "4">
    <TR>
        <TH>Tic</TH>
        <TH>Tac</TH>
        <TH>Toe</TH>
    </TR>
    <TR>
        <TD>X</TD>
        <TD>0</TD>
        <TD>X</TD>
    </TR>
    <TR>
        <TD>0</TD>
        <TD>X</TD>
```

```
            <TD>O</TD>
      </TR>
      <TR>
            <TD>X</TD>
            <TD>O</TD>
            <TD>X</TD>
      </TR>
</TABLE>
```

You can see the results in Figure 6.4. Note that if you set the cell padding to zero, the cell walls will actually touch the content of the cell. If you want to make your tables look less cramped, **CELLPADDING** is an attribute to keep in mind.

Setting Cell Spacing

The cell spacing of a table indicates the amount of space in pixels between each cell—and therefore adjusts the width of the struts between the cells. You set the cell spacing with the **CELLSPACING** attribute. Here's an example we saw at the beginning of the chapter showing how to set the cell spacing to 4 pixels:

```
<TABLE BORDER="2" CELLSPACING = "4">
      <TR>
            <TH>Tic</TH>
            <TH>Tac</TH>
            <TH>Toe</TH>
      </TR>
      <TR>
            <TD>X</TD>
            <TD>O</TD>
            <TD>X</TD>
      </TR>
      <TR>
            <TD>O</TD>
            <TD>X</TD>
            <TD>O</TD>
      </TR>
      <TR>
            <TD>X</TD>
            <TD>O</TD>
            <TD>X</TD>
      </TR>
</TABLE>
```

You can see the results of this HTML in Figure 6.5. As you see in the figure, the cell spacing (and therefore the widths of the struts that separate each cell) has been expanded.

Setting Table And Column Widths

"Uh oh," says the novice programmer, "I'm in trouble now. I designed my new table to display all my data, but I just realized that other people will be using different screen resolutions, and my table might be too wide!" "It's OK," you say, "just tie the width of the table to the width of the display area in the browser." The NP asks, "You can do that?"

You can specify the width of both tables and columns using the **WIDTH** attribute of the **<TABLE>**, **<TH>**, and **<TR>** elements. You can set this attribute to an actual pixel width, which can be a good idea if you have a table of graphics (such as a navigation bar). However, it's often better to set these values to percentages instead. When you set the **<TABLE>** element's **WIDTH** attribute to a percentage, that percentage represents the width of the browser's display area; when you use this attribute with the **<TH>** and **<TR>** elements, the width is a percentage of the table.

Here's an example in which I'm setting the width of a table to 95 percent of the available browser's width, and setting the width of the columns in the table to 40, 35, and 25 percent of the total table width:

```
<TABLE BORDER="2" WIDTH="95%">
    <TR>
        <TH WIDTH="40%">Tic</TH>
        <TH WIDTH="35%">Tac</TH>
        <TH WIDTH="25%">Toe</TH>
    </TR>
    <TR>
        <TD>X</TD>
        <TD>0</TD>
        <TD>X</TD>
    </TR>
    <TR>
        <TD>0</TD>
        <TD>X</TD>
        <TD>0</TD>
    </TR>
    <TR>
```

```
            <TD>X</TD>
            <TD>O</TD>
            <TD>X</TD>
        </TR>
</TABLE>
```

You can see the results of this HTML in Figure 6.13. Note that it's often a good idea to set the size of your tables yourself instead of letting the browser do it. And it's usually better to specify widths in terms of percentages, not absolute pixel measurements (unless you are displaying images or other fixed-width elements).

What happens if the percentages you give for the column widths don't add up to 100 percent? The browser will redistribute the columns using the percentages you've given as relative widths for each column.

TIP: *If the text in a cell is too long, you can always add line breaks with the **
** element.*

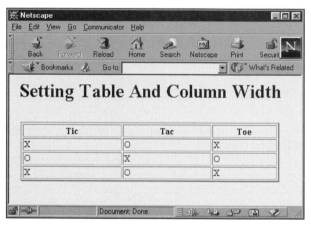

Figure 6.13   Setting table and column widths.

Setting Table Colors

The Web page design czar is back and says, "The table in your Web page is still too drab—you've got to punch it up." "Hm," you say, "I suppose I could add some color to it." "Now *there's* an idea," says the WPDC thoughtfully.

Using the example from the In Depth section of this chapter, we see the color elements of a table:

```
<TABLE BORDER="2">
    <TR>
        <TH BGCOLOR = "#ff0000">Tic</TH>
        <TH BGCOLOR = "#ff0000">Tac</TH>
        <TH BGCOLOR = "#ff0000">Toe</TH>
    </TR>
    <TR>
        <TD BGCOLOR = "#ffffff">X</TD>
        <TD BGCOLOR = "#000000">
            <FONT COLOR = "#ffffff">O</FONT>
        </TD>
        <TD BGCOLOR = "#ffffff">X</TD>
    </TR>
    <TR>
        <TD BGCOLOR = "#000000">
            <FONT COLOR = "#ffffff">O</FONT>
        <TD BGCOLOR = "#ffffff">X</TD>
        <TD BGCOLOR = "#000000">
            <FONT COLOR = "#ffffff">O</FONT>
        </TD>
    </TR>
    <TR>
        <TD BGCOLOR = "#ffffff">X</TD>
        <TD BGCOLOR = "#000000">
            <FONT COLOR = "#ffffff">O</FONT>
        </TD>
        <TD BGCOLOR = "#ffffff">X</TD>
    </TR>
</TABLE>
```

The previous example uses the **BGCOLOR** attribute to set the background color of cells and a **<FONT>** element to set the foreground (text) color. You can see the results of this HTML in Figure 6.10. Note that you can also use the **BGCOLOR** attribute of the table as a whole to set the entire table's background color.

However, both **BGCOLOR** and the **<FONT>** element have been deprecated in favor of style sheets in HTML 4. So how do you set colors in tables now? We'll discuss style sheets in Chapter 9, but here's a sneak preview showing how to convert the HTML in the previous example using inline styles:

```
<TABLE BORDER="2">
    <TR>
        <TH STYLE="background-color: rgb(255, 0, 0)">Tic</TH>
        <TH STYLE="background-color: rgb(255, 0, 0)">Tac</TH>
        <TH STYLE="background-color: rgb(255, 0, 0)">Toe</TH>
```

```
        </TR>
        <TR>
            <TD STYLE="background-color: rgb(255, 255, 255)">X</TD>
            <TD STYLE="background-color: rgb(0, 0, 0); color:
                rgb(255, 255, 255)">
                0
            </TD>
            <TD STYLE="background-color: rgb(255, 255, 255)">X</TD>
        </TR>
        <TR>
            <TD STYLE="background-color: rgb(0, 0, 0); color:
                rgb(255, 255, 255)">
                0
            </TD>
            <TD STYLE="background-color: rgb(255, 255, 255)">X</TD>
            <TD STYLE="background-color: rgb(0, 0, 0); color:
                rgb(255, 255, 255)">
                0
            </TD>
        </TR>
        <TR>
            <TD STYLE="background-color: rgb(255, 255, 255)">X</TD>
            <TD STYLE="background-color: rgb(0, 0, 0); color:
                rgb(255, 255, 255)">
                0
            </TD>
            <TD STYLE="background-color: rgb(255, 255, 255)">X</TD>
        </TR>
</TABLE>
```

TIP: *You can also set the background image for tables and table cells using the* **BACKGROUND** *attribute.*

Aligning Tables In Web Pages

The big boss appears and says, "We need to add this table to the company news-letter. Can you make text flow around tables just as you can with images?" "Sure," you say, "no problem. As long as I get a little raise." "Tell you what," the BB says, "you do this and I won't fire you."

Using the **ALIGN** attribute of the **<TABLE>** element, you can align the table in a Web page by setting this attribute to **RIGHT**, **LEFT**, and **CENTER**. In addition, text will flow around it just as it does with images. Here's an example:

```
<H1 ALIGN="CENTER">Aligning Text And Tables</H1>
<TABLE BORDER="2" ALIGN="RIGHT">
    <TR>
        <TH>Tic</TH>
        <TH>Tac</TH>
        <TH>Toe</TH>
    </TR>
    <TR>
        <TD>X</TD>
        <TD>O</TD>
        <TD>X</TD>
    </TR>
    <TR>
        <TD>O</TD>
        <TD>X</TD>
        <TD>O</TD>
    </TR>
    <TR>
        <TD>X</TD>
        <TD>O</TD>
        <TD>X</TD>
    </TR>
</TABLE>
```
Here's an example in which I'm aligning text to the left of a table.
In this case, the table holds a tic tac toe game, as you can see. In
fact, aligning text and tables works much as aligning text and images.
This text will just keep flowing around the table until it skips to
the line following the table, and then it will resume normally. Here's
how that works; this line follows the table and so goes underneath it.

You can see the results of this HTML in Figure 6.14.

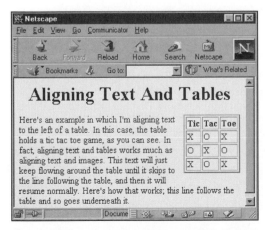

Figure 6.14   Aligning a table in a Web page.

Aligning Cell Text

You can align text in cells using the **<TR>**, **<TH>**, and **<TD>** elements' **ALIGN** and **VALIGN** attributes (not deprecated in HTML 4, although other elements' **ALIGN** attribute is). We saw this example of horizontal alignment in the In Depth section of this chapter:

```
<TABLE BORDER="2" WIDTH = 200>
    <TR>
        <TH>Tic</TH>
        <TH>Tac</TH>
        <TH>Toe</TH>
    </TR>
    <TR>
        <TD ALIGN = RIGHT>X</TD>
        <TD ALIGN = LEFT>O</TD>
        <TD ALIGN = CENTER>X</TD>
    </TR>
    <TR>
        <TD ALIGN = RIGHT>O</TD>
        <TD ALIGN = LEFT>X</TD>
        <TD ALIGN = CENTER>O</TD>
    </TR>
    <TR>
        <TD ALIGN = RIGHT>X</TD>
        <TD ALIGN = LEFT>O</TD>
        <TD ALIGN = CENTER>X</TD>
    </TR>
</TABLE>
```

The results appear in Figure 6.6. You can also align text vertically using the **VALIGN** attribute, as we saw in the following example from the In Depth section of this chapter:

```
<TABLE BORDER="2" HEIGHT = 120>
    <TR>
        <TH>Tic</TH>
        <TH>Tac</TH>
        <TH>Toe</TH>
    </TR>
    <TR>
        <TD VALIGN = TOP>X</TD>
        <TD VALIGN = MIDDLE>O</TD>
        <TD VALIGN = BOTTOM>X</TD>
```

```
      </TR>
      <TR>
          <TD VALIGN = TOP>O</TD>
          <TD VALIGN = MIDDLE>X</TD>
          <TD VALIGN = BOTTOM>O</TD>
      </TR>
      <TR>
          <TD VALIGN = TOP>X</TD>
          <TD VALIGN = MIDDLE>O</TD>
          <TD VALIGN = BOTTOM>X</TD>
      </TR>
</TABLE>
```

The results of this HTML appear in Figure 6.7.

Using Images In Tables

"I want to display images in my tables," says the novice programmer, "can I do that?" "Of course," you say, "just use **<IMG>** elements in the **<TD>** elements." The NP asks, "Really? That easy?"

You can display all kinds of HTML elements in tables, including images. Just include the appropriate **<IMG>** elements in your table as in this example:

```
<TABLE BORDER="2">
    <TR>
        <TH>Tic</TH>
        <TH>Tac</TH>
        <TH>Toe</TH>
    </TR>
    <TR>
        <TD><IMG SRC="x.gif"></TD>
        <TD><IMG SRC="o.gif"></TD>
        <TD><IMG SRC="x.gif"></TD>
    </TR>
    <TR>
        <TD><IMG SRC="o.gif"></TD>
        <TD><IMG SRC="x.gif"></TD>
        <TD><IMG SRC="o.gif"></TD>
    </TR>
    <TR>
        <TD><IMG SRC="x.gif"></TD>
        <TD><IMG SRC="o.gif"></TD>
        <TD><IMG SRC="x.gif"></TD>
```

```
        </TR>
    </TABLE>
```

The results of this HTML appear in Figure 6.15, and as you can see in the figure, I've replaced each X and O with an image of the same.

TIP: In fact, one of the most common uses of tables in HTML is to arrange images in Web pages exactly as you want them. For example, you might want to arrange figures next to explanatory text.

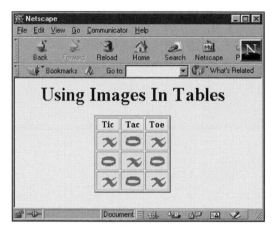

Figure 6.15   Using images in tables.

Nesting Tables

Can you nest tables inside tables? You certainly can. Here's an example in which I nest two tables into one:

```
<TABLE BORDER="2">
    <TR>
        <TD>
            <TABLE BORDER="2">
                <TR>
                    <TH>Tic</TH>
                    <TH>Tac</TH>
                    <TH>Toe</TH>
                </TR>
                <TR>
                    <TD>X</TD>
```

```
                        <TD>0</TD>
                        <TD>X</TD>
                    </TR>
                    <TR>
                        <TD>0</TD>
                        <TD>X</TD>
                        <TD>0</TD>
                    </TR>
                    <TR>
                        <TD>X</TD>
                        <TD>0</TD>
                        <TD>X</TD>
                    </TR>
                </TABLE>
            </TD>
            <TD>
                <TABLE BORDER="2">
                    <TR>
                        <TH>Tic</TH>
                        <TH>Tac</TH>
                        <TH>Toe</TH>
                    </TR>
                    <TR>
                        <TD>X</TD>
                        <TD>0</TD>
                        <TD>X</TD>
                    </TR>
                    <TR>
                        <TD>0</TD>
                        <TD>X</TD>
                        <TD>0</TD>
                    </TR>
                    <TR>
                        <TD>X</TD>
                        <TD>0</TD>
                        <TD>X</TD>
                    </TR>
                </TABLE>
            </TD>
        </TR>
</TABLE>
```

That's all it takes—the results appear in Figure 6.16. In fact, because you can nest tables several levels deep, this capability lets you create very involved structures using tables.

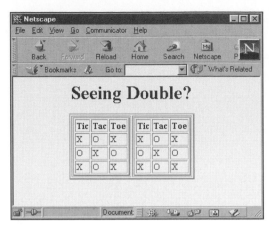

Figure 6.16   Nesting tables.

Spanning Multiple Columns

The novice programmer is back and says, "I have a problem. I'm using column headers, but can't fit all I want to say into the heading on top of one column. Is there any way to *merge* columns together in a row?" "There sure is," you say, "you can use the **COLSPAN** attribute."

You can use the **COLSPAN** attribute in the **<TH>** or **<TD>** elements to indicate that the corresponding cell should span (that is, extend over) several columns. Here's an example we saw in the In Depth section of this chapter:

```
<TABLE BORDER="2">
    <TR>
        <TH COLSPAN=3> TicTac Game</TH>
    </TR>
    <TR>
        <TD>X</TD>
        <TD>O</TD>
        <TD>X</TD>
    </TR>
    <TR>
        <TD>O</TD>
        <TD>X</TD>
        <TD>O</TD>
    </TR>
    <TR>
        <TD>X</TD>
```

```
            <TD>O</TD>
            <TD>X</TD>
        </TR>
</TABLE>
```

The results of this HTML appear in Figure 6.8. As you can see in the figure, the top row spans all three columns. Using **COLSPAN** like this is great if you have a heading that you want to apply to all the data in a table.

Spanning Multiple Rows

"OK," says the novice programmer, "here's the problem—I want to format text so that I can have sidebars, text that appears next to the regular text. No way to do that, huh?" "Sure there is," you say, "use **ROWSPAN** to span a number of rows in a borderless table."

Just as **COLSPAN** lets you span (that is, stretch across) several columns, **ROWSPAN** lets you span several rows. Here's an example that we saw in the In Depth section of this chapter showing how this works:

```
<TABLE BORDER="2">
    <TR>
        <TH ROWSPAN = 3>TicTac<BR>Game</TH>
        <TD>X</TD>
        <TD>O</TD>
        <TD>X</TD>
    </TR>
    <TR>
        <TD>O</TD>
        <TD>X</TD>
        <TD>O</TD>
    </TR>
    <TR>
        <TD>X</TD>
        <TD>O</TD>
        <TD>X</TD>
    </TR>
</TABLE>
```

You can see the results of this code in Figure 6.9. As you see in the figure, **ROWSPAN** is pretty neat in that it allows you to span multiple rows as you like and create some excellent effects.

<COLGROUP> And <COL>—Grouping And Formatting Columns

<COLGROUP>

Purpose: Creates a column group, letting you format columns to your specifications.

Start Tag/End Tag: Required/Optional

Supported: [4, IE3, IE4, IE5]

Attributes:

- **ALIGN**—Specifies alignment of text in the column group. Set to **LEFT**, **CENTER**, or **RIGHT**. [4, IE4, IE5]

- **BGCOLOR**—Specifies the background color. Set to a color value. [IE4, IE5]

- **CHAR**—Specifies a character to align text on. Set to an alphanumeric character. [4]

- **CHAROFF**—Sets the alignment offset to the first character to align on, as set with **CHAR**. [4]

- **CLASS**—Class of the element (used for rendering). [4, IE4, IE5]

- **DIR**—Gives the direction of directionally neutral text (text that doesn't have inherent direction in which you should read it). Possible values: **LTR**: left-to-right text or table and **RTL**: right-to-left text or table. [4, IE5]

- **ID**—Unique alphanumeric identifier for the tag, which you can use to refer to it. [4, IE4, IE5]

- **LANG**—Base language used for the tag. [4, IE4, IE5]

- **SPAN**—Specifies the number of columns this column group includes (the default is 1). Set to positive integers. Note that this attribute is ignored if this element contains **<COL>** elements. [4, IE3, IE4, IE5]

- **STYLE**—Inline style indicating how to render the element. [4, IE4, IE5]

- **TITLE**—Holds additional information (which might be displayed in tool tips) for the element. [4, IE4, IE5]

- **VALIGN**—Sets the vertical alignment of the text. Set to **TOP**, **MIDDLE**, **BOTTOM**, or **BASELINE**. [4, IE4, IE5]

- **WIDTH**—Sets the width of columns in the table. Set to a pixel measurement or percentage, or set to 0* to make the browser display the column in the minimum appropriate width. [4, IE3, IE4, IE5]

<COL>

Purpose: Defines a column structure inside a **<COLGROUP>** element. Using this element is optional in **<COLGROUP>** elements.

Start Tag/End Tag: Required/Omitted

Supported: [4, IE3, IE4, IE5]

Attributes:

- **ALIGN**—Specifies alignment of text in the column group. Set to **LEFT**, **CENTER**, or **RIGHT**. [4, IE4, IE5]

- **BGCOLOR**—Specifies the background color. Set to a color value. [IE4, IE5]

- **CHAR**—Specifies a character to align text on. Set to an alphanumeric character. [4]

- **CHAROFF**—Sets the alignment offset to the first character to align on, as set with **CHAR**. [4]

- **CLASS**—Class of the element (used for rendering). [4, IE4, IE5]

- **DIR**—Gives the direction of directionally neutral text (text that doesn't have inherent direction in which you should read it). Possible values: **LTR**: left-to-right text or table and **RTL**: right-to-left text or table. [4, IE5]

- **ID**—Unique alphanumeric identifier for the tag, which you can use to refer to it. [4, IE4, IE5]

- **LANG**—Base language used for the tag. [4, IE4, IE5]

- **SPAN**—Specifies the number of columns this column group includes (the default is 1). Set to positive integers. [4, IE3, IE4, IE5]

- **STYLE**—Inline style indicating how to render the element. [4, IE4, IE5]

- **TITLE**—Holds additional information (which might be displayed in tool tips) for the element. [4, IE4, IE5]

- **VALIGN**—Sets the vertical alignment of the text. Set to **TOP**, **MIDDLE**, **BOTTOM**, or **BASELINE**. [4, IE4, IE5]

- **WIDTH**—Sets the width of columns in the table. Set to a pixel measurement or percentage, or set to 0* to make the browser display the column in the minimum appropriate width. [4, IE3, IE4, IE5]

The novice programmer has a complaint. "You construct tables row by row," the NP says, "and that seems very row-centric. But what if I want to make things stand out by column, not row?" "In that case," you say, "you can use the new **<COLGROUP>** and **<COL>** elements."

You can group columns together and format them in groups with the new **<COLGROUP>** and **<COL>** elements introduced in HTML 4. However, these elements are only supported in Internet Explorer so far.

NOTE: *The new table model introduced in HTML 4 that uses the **<COLGROUP>**, **<COL>**, **<THEAD>**, **<TBODY>**, and **<TFOOT>** elements is called the Complex Table Model. Using the other table tags, like **<TR>** and **<TD>**, is part of the Simple Table Model.*

Creating Column Groups

As an example of creating column groups, let's say that I want to display a table with three columns, and that I want the first column to take up 40 percent of the width of the table and the next two columns to take up 30 percent each of the table. Let's also say that I want to center the text in the last two columns. I can do that with the **<COLGROUP>** element, which is enclosed in the **<TABLE>** element.

TIP: *One nice aspect of using column groups is that the browser can load and display long tables incrementally.*

To set up a column group consisting only of the first column in the table, and taking 40 percent of the width of the table, I can use this element:

```
<COLGROUP WIDTH="40%">
```

You can also set column width to a pixel value or to 0*, which makes the browser allocate the minimum width needed for the column (if you use 0*, the browser cannot display the table incrementally).

To create a column group of the next two columns, I use the **SPAN** attribute and set it to 2 for the two columns. Then, to center the text in those columns, I use the **ALIGN** attribute:

```
<COLGROUP WIDTH="40%">
<COLGROUP SPAN="2" WIDTH="30%" ALIGN="CENTER">
```

Let's see this at work. Here are those two tags used in a real table:

```
<HTML>

    <HEAD>
        <TITLE>
            Creating Column Groups
        </TITLE>
    </HEAD>
```

```
<BODY>
    <CENTER>
        <H1>Creating Column Groups</H1>

        <TABLE BORDER="2" WIDTH="90%">
            <CAPTION>Horses And Times</CAPTION>
            <COLGROUP WIDTH="40%">
            <COLGROUP SPAN="2" WIDTH="30%" ALIGN="CENTER">
            <TR>
                <TH>Horse</TH>
                <TH>Race</TH>
                <TH>Best Time</TH>
            </TR>
            <TR>
                <TD>Bluebell</TD>
                <TD>Foster Downs</TD>
                <TD>5:33</TD>
            </TR>
            <TR>
                <TD>Sea Breeze</TD>
                <TD>Harness Extra</TD>
                <TD>6:41</TD>
            </TR>
            <TR>
                <TD>No Way O'Shay</TD>
                <TD>Old Bowler</TD>
                <TD>9:29</TD>
            </TR>
        </TABLE>

    </BODY>
</HTML>
```

You can see the results of this HTML in Figure 6.17. As you can see, the table columns do indeed have the relative widths we've specified, and the last two columns are indeed displaying centered text.

Customizing Columns In Column Groups

You can also use the **<COL>** element to specify formatting for every column in a group, if you include these elements inside a **<COLGROUP>** element (in which case the **SPAN** attribute of the **<COLGROUP>** element is ignored).

The first **<COL>** element in a **<COLGROUP>** element sets the formatting (using, for example, the **ALIGN** and **VALIGN** attributes) and style (using the **STYLE** attribute) for the first column. The next **<COL>** element sets the formatting and style for the next column, and so on.

6. Creating Tables

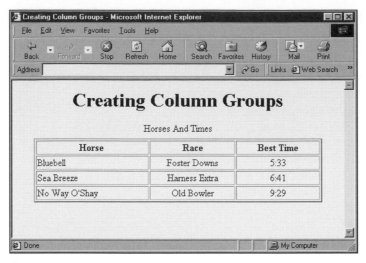

Figure 6.17   Formatting column groups.

In this example, I'm setting the widths of two columns in a column group to different widths, 30 and 15 percent:

```
<HTML>

    <HEAD>
        <TITLE>
            Creating Column Groups
        </TITLE>
    </HEAD>

    <BODY>
        <CENTER>
            <H1>Creating Column Groups</H1>

            <TABLE BORDER="2" WIDTH="90%">
                <CAPTION>Horses And Times</CAPTION>
                <COLGROUP WIDTH="25%">
                <COLGROUP ALIGN="CENTER">
                    <COL SPAN="2" WIDTH="30%">
                    <COL SPAN="1" WIDTH="15%"
                </COLGROUP>
                <TR>
                    <TH>Horse</TH>
                    <TH>Race</TH>
                    <TH>Owner</TH>
                    <TH>Best Time</TH>
```

```
            </TR>
            <TR>
                <TD>Bluebell</TD>
                <TD>Foster Downs</TD>
                <TD>Sad Sam</TD>
                <TD>5:33</TD>
            </TR>
            <TR>
                <TD>Sea Breeze</TD>
                <TD>Harness Extra</TD>
                <TD>Bright Bob</TD>
                <TD>6:41</TD>
            </TR>
            <TR>
                <TD>No Way O'Shay</TD>
                <TD>Old Bowler</TD>
                <TD>Funny Phil</TD>
                <TD>9:29</TD>
            </TR>
        </TABLE>

    </BODY>
</HTML>
```

The results of this HTML appear in Figure 6.18, and you can see that the columns have indeed been formatted as specified. Note that besides working with column groups, you can also create row groups—see the next section for the details.

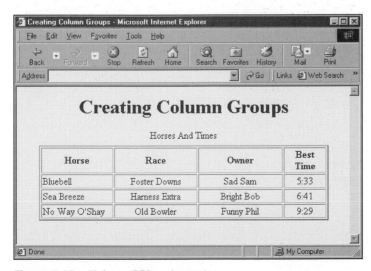

Figure 6.18   Using **<COL>** elements.

<THEAD>, <TBODY>, And <TFOOT>—Grouping And Formatting Rows

<THEAD>

Purpose: Creates a table head when grouping rows.

Start Tag/End Tag: Required/Optional

Supported: [4, IE3, IE4, IE5]

Attributes:

- **ALIGN**—Specifies alignment of text in the group. Set to **LEFT**, **CENTER**, **JUSTIFY**, **CHAR**, or **RIGHT**. [4, IE4, IE5]
- **BGCOLOR**—Sets the background color for the group. Set to an RGB triplet color value or predefined color. [IE4, IE5]
- **CHAR**—Specifies a character to align text on. Set to an alphanumeric character. [4]
- **CHAROFF**—Sets the alignment offset to the first character to align on, as set with **CHAR**. [4]
- **CLASS**—Class of the element (used for rendering). [4, IE4, IE5]
- **DIR**—Gives the direction of directionally neutral text (text that doesn't have inherent direction in which you should read it). Possible values: **LTR**: left-to-right text or table and **RTL**: right-to-left text or table. [4, IE5]
- **ID**—Unique alphanumeric identifier for the tag, which you can use to refer to it. [4, IE4, IE5]
- **LANG**—Base language used for the tag. [4, IE4, IE5]
- **LANGUAGE**—Scripting language used for the tag. [IE4, IE5]
- **STYLE**—Inline style indicating how to render the element. [4, IE4, IE5]
- **TITLE**—Holds additional information (which might be displayed in tool tips) for the element. [4, IE4, IE5]
- **VALIGN**—Sets the vertical alignment of the text. Set to **TOP**, **MIDDLE**, **BOTTOM**, or **BASELINE**. [4, IE4, IE5]

<TBODY>

Purpose: Creates a table body when grouping rows. You can use multiple table bodies, each of which can be separated visually when you use the **FRAMES** and **RULES** attribute of the **<TABLE>** element.

Start Tag/End Tag: Optional/Optional

Supported: [4, IE3, IE4, IE5]

Attributes:

- **ALIGN**—Specifies alignment of text in the group. Set to **LEFT**, **CENTER**, **JUSTIFY**, **CHAR**, or **RIGHT**. [4, IE4, IE5]

- **BGCOLOR**—Sets the background color for the group. Set to an RGB triplet color value or predefined color. [IE4, IE5]

- **CHAR**—Specifies a character to align text on. Set to an alphanumeric character. [4]

- **CHAROFF**—Sets the alignment offset to the first character to align on, as set with **CHAR**. [4]

- **CLASS**—Class of the element (used for rendering). [4, IE4, IE5]

- **DIR**—Gives the direction of directionally neutral text (text that doesn't have inherent direction in which you should read it). Possible values: **LTR**: left-to-right text or table and **RTL**: right-to-left text or table. [4, IE5]

- **ID**—Unique alphanumeric identifier for the tag, which you can use to refer to it. [4, IE4, IE5]

- **LANG**—Base language used for the tag. [4, IE4, IE5]

- **LANGUAGE**—Scripting language used for the tag. [IE4, IE5]

- **STYLE**—Inline style indicating how to render the element. [4, IE4, IE5]

- **TITLE**—Holds additional information (which might be displayed in tool tips) for the element. [4, IE4, IE5]

- **VALIGN**—Sets the vertical alignment of the text. Set to **TOP**, **MIDDLE**, **BOTTOM**, or **BASELINE**. [4, IE4, IE5]

<TFOOT>

Purpose: Creates a table foot when grouping rows.

Start Tag/End Tag: Required/Optional

Supported: [4, IE3, IE4, IE5]

Attributes:

- **ALIGN**—Specifies alignment of text in the group. Set to **LEFT**, **CENTER**, **JUSTIFY**, **CHAR**, or **RIGHT**. [4, IE4, IE5]

- **BGCOLOR**—Sets the background color for the group. Set to an RGB triplet color value or predefined color. [IE4, IE5]

6. Creating Tables

- **CHAR**—Specifies a character to align text on. Set to an alphanumeric character. [4]

- **CHAROFF**—Sets the alignment offset to the first character to align on, as set with **CHAR**. [4]

- **CLASS**—Class of the element (used for rendering). [3, 4, IE4, IE5]

- **DIR**—Gives the direction of directionally neutral text (text that doesn't have inherent direction in which you should read it). Possible values: **LTR**: left-to-right text or table and **RTL**: right-to-left text or table. [4, IE5]

- **ID**—Unique alphanumeric identifier for the tag, which you can use to refer to it. [3, 4, IE4, IE5]

- **LANG**—Base language used for the tag. [3, 4, IE4, IE5]

- **LANGUAGE**—Scripting language used for the tag. [IE4, IE5]

- **STYLE**—Inline style indicating how to render the element. [4, IE4, IE5]

- **TITLE**—Holds additional information (which might be displayed in tool tips) for the element. [3, 4, IE4, IE5]

- **VALIGN**—Sets the vertical alignment of the text. Set to **TOP**, **MIDDLE**, **BOTTOM**, or **BASELINE**. [4, IE4, IE5]

The novice programmer wants to know, "I want to divide my table into groups of rows, setting each one off from the others. Is there any way to do that?" "Sure is," you say, "just create row groups." "Create what?" the NP wants to know.

You can use the **<THEAD>**, **<TBODY>**, and **<TFOOT>** elements to create row groups, just as you use the **<COLGROUP>** and **<COL>** elements to create column groups. All of these elements are new in HTML 4 and, so far, are only supported by Internet Explorer.

NOTE: *The new table model introduced in HTML 4 that uses the **<COLGROUP>**, **<COL>**, **<THEAD>**, **<TBODY>**, and **<TFOOT>** elements is called the Complex Table Model. Using the other table tags, like **<TR>** and **<TD>**, is part of the Simple Table Model.*

Creating Row Groups

To create a row group, you use the **<THEAD>**, **<TBODY>**, and **<TFOOT>** elements. The **<THEAD>** element creates a head for the table, **<TBODY>** creates the body of the table (you can create multiple table bodies, each of which will appear as a row group), and **<TFOOT>** creates a table foot.

In the following example, I'll add a table head to a table with **<THEAD>**. You place the head elements you want in the **<THEAD>** element, one to a column (unless you're spanning multiple columns). You can apply styles as well to the **<THEAD>** element, typically by placing the same elements that you would use in **<TH>** elements in the **<THEAD>** element.

To create a table foot, use the **<TFOOT>** element. This works just like **<THEAD>**, but places its information at the bottom of the table.

If you use **<THEAD>** or **<TFOOT>**, you must also use the **<TBODY>** element. The **<TBODY>** element is what defines a row group, and you can have as many **<TBODY>** elements as you like.

Here's an example in which I create a table with a **<THEAD>** element, a **<TFOOT>** element, and two **<TBODY>** elements:

```
<HTML>

    <HEAD>
        <TITLE>
            Creating Row Groups
        </TITLE>
    </HEAD>

    <BODY>
        <CENTER>
            <H1>Creating Row Groups</H1>

            <TABLE BORDER="2" WIDTH="90%" >
                <CAPTION>Horses And Times</CAPTION>
                <COLGROUP WIDTH="25%">
                <COLGROUP ALIGN="CENTER">
                    <COL SPAN="2" WIDTH="30%">
                    <COL SPAN="1" WIDTH="15%"
                </COLGROUP>

                <THEAD>
                    <TR>
                        <TH>Horse</TH>
                        <TH>Race</TH>
                        <TH>Owner</TH>
                        <TH>Time</TH>
                    </TR>
                </THEAD>

                <TFOOT>
                    <TR>
```

```
                              <TH>Horse</TH>
                              <TH>Race</TH>
                              <TH>Owner</TH>
                              <TH>Time</TH>
                         </TR>
                    </TFOOT>

                    <TBODY>
                    <TR>
                         <TD>Bluebell</TD>
                         <TD>Foster Downs</TD>
                         <TD>Sad Sam</TD>
                         <TD>5:33</TD>
                    </TR>
                    <TR>
                         <TD>Sea Breeze</TD>
                         <TD>Foster Downs</TD>
                         <TD>Bright Bob</TD>
                         <TD>6:41</TD>
                    </TR>
                    </TBODY>

                    <TBODY>
                    <TR>
                         <TD>No Way O'Shay</TD>
                         <TD>Old Bowler</TD>
                         <TD>Funny Phil</TD>
                         <TD>9:29</TD>
                    </TR>
                    <TR>
                         <TD>Crawler</TD>
                         <TD>Old Bowler</TD>
                         <TD>Maudlin Morton</TD>
                         <TD>12:23</TD>
                    </TR>
                    </TBODY>
               </TABLE>

          </BODY>
</HTML>
```

The results of this HTML appear in Figure 6.19. Although you can see the table head and foot in Figure 6.19, the fact that the rows are divided into two groups is not evident. To make it more evident, you can add borders to the row groups.

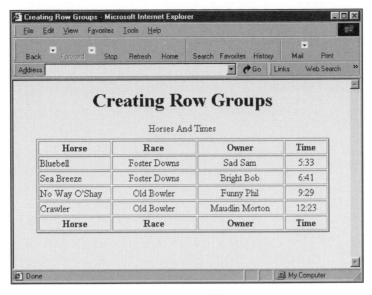

Figure 6.19 Adding table heads and feet.

Configuring Row Group Borders

You can use the **FRAME** and **RULES** Complex Table Model attributes in the **<TABLE>** element to specify the border display of the table. Using the **FRAME** attribute together with the **RULES** attribute gives you much greater border control than the older Simple Table Model. Here are the possible values for **FRAME**:

* **VOID**—No borders.
* **ABOVE**—Border on top side only.
* **BELOW**—Border on bottom side only.
* **HSIDES**—Horizontal borders only.
* **VSIDES**—Vertical borders only.
* **LHS**—Border on left side only.
* **RHS**—Border on right side only.
* **BOX**—Border on all four sides.
* **BORDER**—The default; the same as **BOX**.

The **RULES** Complex Table Model attribute sets the style of the interior struts in a table. Here are the possible values:

* **NONE**—No interior struts are displayed.
* **GROUPS**—Horizontal struts are displayed between table groups created with the **THEAD**, **TBODY**, **TFOOT**, and **COLGROUP** tags.

- **ROWS**—Horizontal struts are displayed between all table rows.

- **COLS**—Vertical struts are displayed between all table columns.

- **ALL**—Struts are displayed between all table cells.

Here's an example adding **FRAME** and **RULES** to the previous table example:

```
<HTML>

    <HEAD>
        <TITLE>
            Creating Row Groups
        </TITLE>
    </HEAD>

    <BODY>
        <CENTER>
            <H1>Creating Row Groups</H1>

            <TABLE BORDER="2" WIDTH="90%" FRAME="HSIDES" RULES="GROUPS">
                <CAPTION>Horses And Times</CAPTION>
                <COLGROUP WIDTH="25%">
                <COLGROUP ALIGN="CENTER">
                    <COL SPAN="2" WIDTH="30%">
                    <COL SPAN="1" WIDTH="15%">
                </COLGROUP>

                <THEAD>
                    <TR>
                        <TH>Horse</TH>
                        <TH>Race</TH>
                        <TH>Owner</TH>
                        <TH>Time</TH>
                    </TR>
                </THEAD>

                <TFOOT>
                    <TR>
                        <TH>Horse</TH>
                        <TH>Race</TH>
                        <TH>Owner</TH>
                        <TH>Time</TH>
```

```
            </TR>
        </TFOOT>

        <TBODY>
        <TR>
            <TD>Bluebell</TD>
            <TD>Foster Downs</TD>
            <TD>Sad Sam</TD>
            <TD>5:33</TD>
        </TR>
        <TR>
            <TD>Sea Breeze</TD>
            <TD>Foster Downs</TD>
            <TD>Bright Bob</TD>
            <TD>6:41</TD>
        </TR>
        </TBODY>

        <TBODY>
        <TR>
            <TD>No Way O'Shay</TD>
            <TD>Old Bowler</TD>
            <TD>Funny Phil</TD>
            <TD>9:29</TD>
        </TR>
        <TR>
            <TD>Crawler</TD>
            <TD>Old Bowler</TD>
            <TD>Maudlin Morton</TD>
            <TD>12:23</TD>
        </TR>
        </TBODY>
    </TABLE>

    </BODY>
</HTML>
```

The results of this HTML appear in Figure 6.20, where you can now see the borders introduced between row groups. As you can see, the Complex Table Model gives you a lot of additional options when it comes to formatting tables.

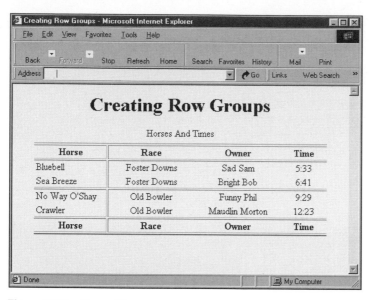

Figure 6.20   Formatting row groups.

Formatting Text With Tables

The novice programmer enters, screaming. "I can't do it! I just can't format this text the way I want it!" "Calm down," you say, "have you tried using tables yet?" "*Tables*?" the NP asks.

One very powerful way of arranging text is with HTML tables. Using tables, you can create a grid of cells that can display text and images. Early on, Web page stylists realized that you could turn the border of a table off making it invisible, which, to their delight, gave them a way of arranging text into columns and rows on a Web page.

Arranging text using HTML tables is a very common thing to do. Here's an example we first saw in Chapter 3. Say that I want to display a large number of hyperlinks in rows and columns. I can do that using a table and even supply text as a caption, spreading the caption over several columns using the **COLSPAN** attribute. Here's how that looks:

```
<TABLE NOBORDER CELLPADDING = 4 WIDTH = 95%>
    <TR>
        <TH COLSPAN = 4>
            <H2>
                Travel to these sites around the world
```

```
            </H2>
        </TH>
    </TR>
    <TR>
        <TH COLSPAN = 4>
            Ever been to a site in Kenya? Russia? China?
            You can travel to those countries now, because
            each tour below is actually at a site in the
            country it describes! <I>Bon Voyage...</I>
        </TH>
    </TR>
    <TR ALIGN = CENTER>
        <TD>
            <A HREF = "http://www.secyt.gov.ar/arg/introi.html">
                Argentina
            </A>
        </TD>
        <TD>
            <A HREF = "http://www.telstra.com.au/meta/australia.html">
                Australia
            </A>
        </TD>
        <TD>
            <A HREF = "http://croco.atnet.at/tourism">
                Austria
            </A>
        </TD>
        <TD>
            <A HREF = "http://canada.gc.ca/canadiana/cdaind_e.html">
                Canada
            </A>
        </TD>
    </TR>
    <TR ALIGN = CENTER>
        <TD>
            <A HREF = "http://sunsite.dcc.uchile.cl/chile/chile.html">
                Chile
            </A>
        </TD>
        <TD>
            <A HREF = "http://www.ihep.ac.cn/tour/china_tour.html">
                China
            </A>
        </TD>
        <TD>
```

```
            <A HREF = "http://www.ciesin.ee/ESTCG/">
                Estonia
            </A>
        </TD>
        <TD>
            <A HREF = "http://www.csc.fi/tiko/finland.html">
                Finland
            </A>
        </TD>
    </TR>
    <TR ALIGN = CENTER>
        <TD>
            <A HREF = "http://www.iway.fr/internet-way/fr/france">
                France
            </A>
        </TD>
        <TD>
            <A HREF = "http://www.chemie.fu-berlin.de/adressen/brd.html">
                Germany
            </A>
        </TD>
        <TD>
            <A HREF = "http://www.culture.gr/2/21/maps/hellas.html">
                Greece
            </A>
        </TD>
        <TD>
            <A HREF = "http://www.arctic.is">
                Iceland
            </A>
        </TD>
    </TR>
    <TR ALIGN = CENTER>
        <TD>
            <A HREF = "http://slarti.ucd.ie/maps/ireland.html">
                Ireland
            </A>
        </TD>
        <TD>
            <A HREF = "http://ece.iisc.ernet.in/india.html">
                India
            </A>
        </TD>
        <TD>
            <A HREF = "http://www.travel.it">
```

```
                Italy
            </A>
        </TD>
        <TD>
            <A HREF = "http://www.recruit.co.jp/Jjapan">
                Japan
            </A>
        </TD>
</TR>
<TR ALIGN = CENTER>
        <TD>
            <A HREF = "http://www.arcc.or.ke">
                Kenya
            </A>
        </TD>
        <TD>
            <A HREF = "http://www.mty.itesm.mx/MexWeb/Info2/">
                Mexico
            </A>
        </TD>
        <TD>
            <A HREF = "http://www.govt.nz/nzinfo.html">
                New Zealand
            </A>
        </TD>
        <TD>
            <A HREF = "http://info.fuw.edu.pl/pl/poland.html">
                Poland
            </A>
        </TD>
</TR>
<TR ALIGN = CENTER>
        <TD>
            <A HREF = "http://indis.ici.ro/romania/romania.html">
                Romania
            </A>
        </TD>
        <TD>
            <A HREF = "http://www.kiae.su/www/wtr">
                Russia
            </A>
        </TD>
        <TD>
            <A HREF = "http://www.technet.sg">
                Singapore
```

```
                    </A>
                </TD>
                <TD>
                    <A HREF = "http://osprey.unisa.ac.za/south-africa/home.html">
                        South Africa
                    </A>
                </TD>
            </TR>
            <TR ALIGN = CENTER>
                <TD>
                    <A HREF = "http://www.uji.es/spain_www.html">
                        Spain
                    </A>
                </TD>
                <TD>
                    <A HREF = "http://www.westnet.se/sweden">
                        Sweden
                    </A>
                </TD>
                <TD>
                    <A HREF = "http://heiwww.unige.ch/switzerland/">
                        Switzerland
                    </A>
                </TD>
                <TD>
                    <A HREF = "http://www.chiangmai.ac.th/thmap.html">
                        Thailand
                    </A>
                </TD>
            </TR>
            <TR ALIGN = CENTER>
                <TD>
                    <A HREF = "http://www.rada.kiev.ua/ukraine.htm">
                        Ukraine
                    </A>
                </TD>
                <TD>
                    <A HREF = "http://www.cs.ucl.ac.uk/misc/uk/intro">
                        United Kingdom
                    </A>
                </TD>
                <TD>
```

```
            <A HREF = "http://www.zamnet.zm/zamnet/zntb.html">
                Zambia
            </A>
        </TD>
        <TD>
            <A HREF = "http://cy.co.za/atg/stbroz.html">
                Zimbabwe
            </A>
        </TD>
    </TR>
</TABLE>
```

The result of this HTML appears in Figure 6.21. As you can see, the hyperlinks appear neatly arranged in rows and columns. In addition, the explanatory text appears neatly centered above it.

You can get more creative, of course, such as flanking an image with two columns of text. Here's a more advanced example, also first introduced in Chapter 3, that uses the **ROWSPAN** attribute to create a nice effect:

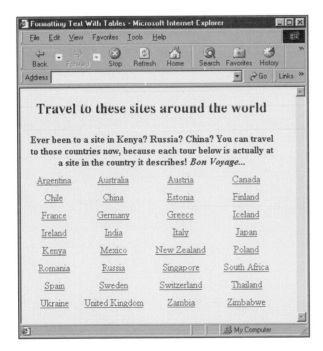

Figure 6.21   Formatting hyperlinks into rows and columns using a table.

```
<TABLE NOBORDER CELLPADDING = 8 WIDTH = 90%>
    <TR ALIGN = CENTER>
        <TH ROWSPAN = 4>
            <H2>
                High
                <BR>
                culture
                <BR>
                on
                <BR>
                demand!
            </H2>
        </TH>
        <TD>
            Download
            <A HREF="darkness.zip">
                Joseph Conrad's Heart of Darkness
            </A>
        </TD>
    </TR>
    <TR ALIGN = CENTER>
        <TD>
            Listen to some of
            <A HREF = "mozart1.mid">
                Mozart's music
            </A>
        </TD>
    </TR>
    <TR ALIGN = CENTER>
        <TD>
            See a
            <A href="chaplin.html">
                Charlie Chaplin movie
            </A>
        </TD>
    </TR>
</TABLE>
```

The results of this HTML appear in Figure 6.22, and as you can see in the figure, you can use tables to format text in a pretty general way in a Web page.

Another popular use of tables is to accentuate Web page elements. Because you can set the background color of the cells in a table, you can surround text in what appears to be colored boxes. Here's another example from Chapter 3:

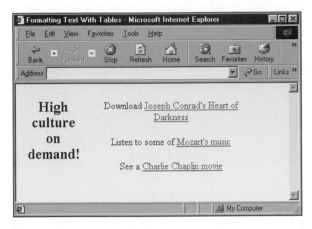

Figure 6.22 Formatting text using a table.

```
<HTML>
    <HEAD>
        <TITLE>
            European Train Travel
        </TITLE>
    </HEAD>

    <BODY>
        <H1>
            European Train Travel
        </H1>
        So you've decided to take the train in Europe!
        Congratulations, you're in for a great time. There are
        a few things you should know that will make
        things a lot easier. Here's an overview:
        <UL>
            <LI>Getting Train Times
            <LI>Getting On The Train
            <LI>Handling Security
        </UL>

        <H2>
            Getting Train Times
        </H2>
        Many train stations are packed with crowds, especially in
        the summer, and you can save yourself a great deal of time
        waiting in lines that can last an hour or more by getting
        a complete train schedule, such as Thomas Cook's European
        Timetable.
        <P>
        <TABLE BGCOLOR="#d0d0d0">
```

```
        <TR>
            <TD>
                TIP: With a complete train schedule, you'll
                also become the most popular person in
                the youth hostel.
            </TD>
        </TR>
    </TABLE>
    <H2>
        Getting On The Train
    </H2>
    In larger stations, you'll find a diagram showing where
    each wagon of the train will stop so if you have a
    reservation for a specific wagon, you can wait in the right
    place with your luggage.
    <P>
    Check the destination of the train, the class of the wagon, and
    whether it's a smoking or non-smoking wagon before getting on. This
    information is displayed on a plaque on the wagon.
    </BODY>
</HTML>
```

You can see the results of this HTML in Figure 6.23. As you can see, tables are good for many text formatting problems—especially when you get creative.

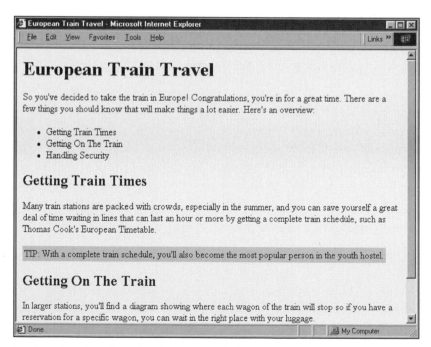

Figure 6.23   Emphasizing text using a table.

Chapter 7

Working With Frames

In Depth

Frames are one of the most powerful aspects of HTML programming, and as such, many people have rigid opinions about them. In fact, many people hate them. But some wouldn't create a Web site without them.

If you've browsed the Web, you know what frames are. They give you the ability to split a browser window into vertical or horizontal, or *both* vertical and horizontal, sections. You can load different pages into the various frames in the browser, creating a multipage display. With frames, you have a significant amount of added control over the browser's layout.

Frames were originally introduced in Netscape Navigator 2, and Internet Explorer added them in version 3 (as well as *inline frames*, which we'll see in the Immediate Solutions section "**<IFRAME>**—Creating Inline Or Floating Frames"). However, many other browsers haven't added support for frames, or if they have, they've done so only recently because frames were not part of the HTML 3.2 specification. They are part of the HTML 4 specification, however (and in fact, so are the inline frames originally introduced in Internet Explorer).

Probably the most common use for frames is to give users an easy way to navigate around a site. For example, you can see two frames in action in Figure 7.1. The frame on the left is acting as a vertical navigation bar, displaying a number of hyperlinks. When the user clicks a hyperlink, the corresponding page is loaded into the frame on the right and displayed. The navigation bar on the left remains visible, however, so the user can click other hyperlinks at will. Frames are customizable, so the user can use the mouse to resize the frames.

You can see another example in Figure 7.2. In this figure, I'm using the other common format for navigation bars using frames—making the navigation bar horizontal and placing it above the rest of the content in the browser. In this case, I've also removed the borders from the page.

We'll discuss everything you can do with frames in HTML in this chapter, including:

- Creating basic frames.
- Handling browsers that don't handle frames.

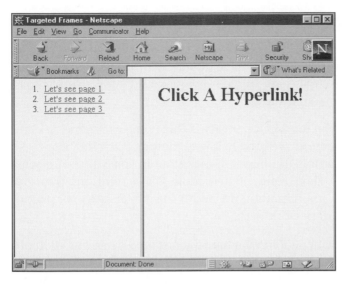

Figure 7.1   A vertical navigation bar.

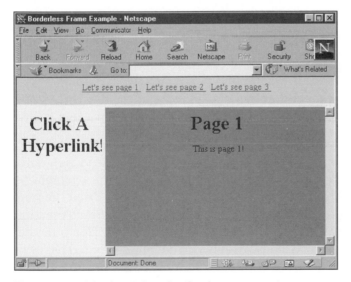

Figure 7.2   A horizontal navigation bar.

- Creating "floating" frames, which can appear in the center of the display, away from the edge of the browser.

- Opening a new browser window on demand.

7. Working With Frames

To Frame Or Not To Frame

As a Web designer, there's one thing to keep in mind—some people really do hate frames. If there are two topics that have significant disapproving populations among Web users, those topics are frames and cookies. I know users who refuse to look at pages that contain frames.

The most common reason for this animosity is that some users, out of choice or necessity, run their screen at a relatively low resolution; they find carelessly designed frames either run off the page or display only small slices of what are supposed to be shown. Then again, some people just hate having their display, where space is always at a premium, divided into smaller sections making the screen too busy and hard to work with.

The best way to work with people who hate frames is to make sure you provide frameless alternatives (and track how many users use each page to see how well your frames are received). At the very least, you should check the appearance of your frames in various screen resolutions and with a variety browsers.

With that warning out of the way, I'll start digging into the HTML now, beginning with creating vertical frames.

Creating Vertical Frames

How do you actually set up frames in a document? You use the **<FRAMESET>** element to indicate how you want to configure the frames, and you use **<FRAME>** elements to create the actual frames.

This is best seen in an example, so I'll create one now that divides the browser window into two vertical frames, with each taking up half of the available display area. To do that, I start by using the **<FRAMESET>** element. From the frameset point of view, dividing the browser into two vertical frames means creating two columns using the **<FRAMESET>** element's **COLS** attribute. You indicate how many columns you want to create by assigning a comma separated list of values to the **COLS** attribute with the appropriate column widths. You can assign actual pixel values to **COLS**, although it's not advisable usually when working with frames. In most cases, it is far better to assign percentages of the available display to each column and let the browser set the columns to match the space it has to work with.

Here's how I create two column frames, each of which take 50 percent of the available horizontal display area:

```
<HTML>

    <HEAD>
        <TITLE>
            Creating Frames
        </TITLE>
    </HEAD>

    <FRAMESET COLS = "50%, 50%">
        .
        .
        .
    </FRAMESET>

</HTML>
```

There are two important points to consider when working with **<FRAMESET>**. The first is that the **<FRAMESET>** element actually takes the place of the **<BODY>** element in a document that displays frames (this makes sense because the frames take the place of the document's body). The second is that, although I've said it's not a good idea usually when working with frames to specify actual pixel dimensions for frames, there is one technique that can help—you can use an asterisk (*) to represent the rest of the space available in the browser window. For example, **COLS="145, *"** will create one column 145 pixels in width and assign the remaining horizontal width to the other column. In this way, if you really need to have a frame of a particular width or height (this happens most commonly when you're displaying images of fixed dimensions), you can do it and still let the browser arrange the other frame or frames as appropriate for the amount of space it has available. If you use more than one asterisk, the browser will give each asterisk-designated frame as much space as it can, dividing the space equally among those frames.

Now that I've set up the *frameset* for the page, it's time to set up the frames themselves with the **<FRAME>** element. In this case, I'll load a page into each of these frames. You do that with the **<FRAME>** element's **SRC** attribute, as you can see in the following example. I'm loading frame1.htm into the frame on the left and frame2.htm into the frame on the right. Note that you can set the **SRC** attribute to a full URL, not just a relative one as I've used here:

```
<HTML>

    <HEAD>
        <TITLE>
```

```
                    Creating Frames
            </TITLE>
        </HEAD>

        <FRAMESET COLS = "50%, 50%">
            <FRAME SRC="frame1.htm">
            <FRAME SRC="frame2.htm">
        </FRAMESET>

    </HTML>
```

We're going to need some pages to load into the frames, so I'll put together some pages that simply announce which page they are: page one, page two, or page three (using various colored backgrounds). Here's page one:

```
<HTML>

    <HEAD>
        <TITLE>
            Page 1
        </TITLE>
    </HEAD>

    <BODY BGCOLOR="RED">

        <CENTER>
        <H1>
            Page 1
        </H1>

            This is page 1!
        </CENTER>
    </BODY>

</HTML>
```

Here's page two:

```
<HTML>

    <HEAD>
        <TITLE>
            Page 2
        </TITLE>
    </HEAD>
```

```
<BODY BGCOLOR="YELLOW">

    <CENTER>
    <H1>
        Page 2
    </H1>

        This is page 2!
    </CENTER>
</BODY>

</HTML>
```

And here's page three:

```
<HTML>

    <HEAD>
        <TITLE>
            Page 3
        </TITLE>
    </HEAD>

    <BODY BGCOLOR="PINK">

        <CENTER>
        <H1>
            Page 3
        </H1>

            This is page 3!
        </CENTER>
    </BODY>

</HTML>
```

You can see page one, which actually has a red background in Figure 7.3. The other pages look the same, except for the page number and color.

Now that the pages displayed in the frames are ready, we can take a look at the actual frames by loading the frameset page into the browser. You can see two vertical frames in Figure 7.4, each displaying a page.

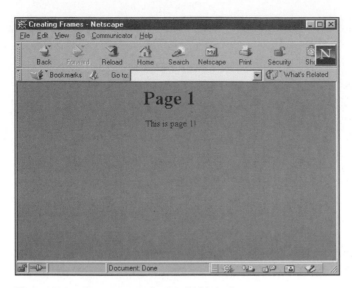

Figure 7.3   Page one to be loaded into frames.

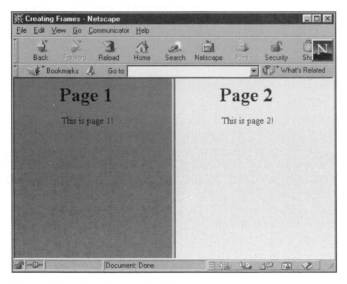

Figure 7.4   Creating vertical frames.

But what if the user's browser doesn't support frames? In that case, the user will see nothing because the browser will ignore the **<FRAMESET>** and **<FRAME>** elements. However, there is a way around this, and we'll discuss the solution in the next section.

What If The Browser Doesn't Do Frames?

You might think that it would be hard to find a graphical browser that doesn't handle frames today, but that's not necessarily true. For example, Microsoft Word can now display HTML documents—but it doesn't handle frames. How do you handle browsers that don't handle frames? You use the **<NOFRAMES>** element.

The **<NOFRAMES>** element is ignored by browsers that handle frames, and in fact, it's also ignored by browsers that don't handle frames, but in a different way. If a browser doesn't understand a tag, it'll just treat the tag's contents as plain text. Browsers that handle frames will ignore that text, so you can place text in the **<NOFRAMES>** element to indicate to users that they're missing something. In other words, you can use the **<NOFRAMES>** element in any kind of browser, those that handle frames and those that don't, and it'll do the right thing. Here's an example. Note that the **<NOFRAMES>** element goes inside the **<FRAMESET>** element:

```
<HTML>

    <HEAD>
        <TITLE>
            Creating Frames
        </TITLE>
    </HEAD>

    <FRAMESET COLS = "50%, 50%">
        <NOFRAMES>Your browser does not support frames...</NOFRAMES>
        <FRAME SRC="frame1.htm">
        <FRAME SRC="frame2.htm">
    </FRAMESET>

</HTML>
```

You can see the result in Figure 7.5 in Microsoft Word. As you see, Microsoft Word doesn't support frames in Web pages, so the user is notified of that fact.

TIP: *It's good to include a hyperlink to the frameless version of your page in the text of the **<NOFRAMES>** element. In fact, you can include the entire frameless version of your page in the **<NOFRAMES>** element.*

Creating Horizontal Frames

We've learned how to create vertical frames by using the **COLS** attribute of the **<FRAMESET>** element to set up the document, and to create each frame with the **<FRAME>** element. What about creating horizontal frames?

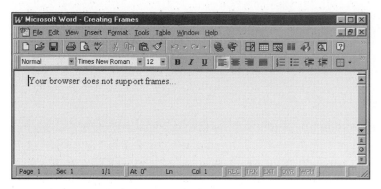

Figure 7.5   Handling browsers that don't handle frames.

As you might expect, there's another attribute of the **<FRAMESET>** element we can use—**ROWS**. For example, converting the previous example to horizontal instead of vertical frames is easy. Here's what it looks like:

```
<HTML>

    <HEAD>
        <TITLE>
            Creating Frames
        </TITLE>
    </HEAD>

    <FRAMESET ROWS = "50%, 50%">
        <FRAME SRC="frame1.htm">
        <FRAME SRC="frame2.htm">
    </FRAMESET>

</HTML>
```

You can see the results of this HTML in Figure 7.6, where there are now two horizontal frames instead of vertical frames.

We're on a roll—so how do we create horizontal *and* vertical frames in the same document? That's coming up in the next section.

Creating Horizontal And Vertical Frames

To create both horizontal and vertical frames in a document, you can use nested **<FRAMESET>** elements. In one element, you set up the rows, and in the other element, you set up the columns. In this example, I'm using an outer **<FRAMESET>** element to divide the display into two columns:

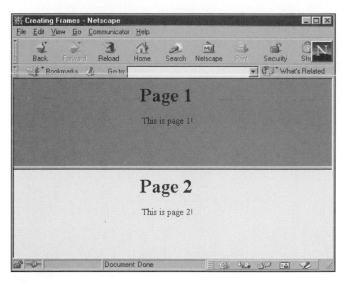

Figure 7.6 Creating horizontal frames.

```
<HTML>

    <HEAD>
        <TITLE>Row And Column Frames</TITLE>
    </HEAD>

    <FRAMESET COLS = "50%, 50%">
        <NOFRAMES>Your browser does not support frames...</NOFRAMES>
            .
            .
            .
    </FRAMESET>

</HTML>
```

Now I add two inner **<FRAMESET>** elements to create three rows of various
heights in each column:

```
<HTML>

    <HEAD>
        <TITLE>Row And Column Frames</TITLE>
    </HEAD>

    <FRAMESET COLS = "50%, 50%">
        <NOFRAMES>Your browser does not support frames...</NOFRAMES>
```

```
<FRAMESET ROWS = "25%, 50%, 25%">
    <FRAME SRC="frame1.htm">
    <FRAME SRC="frame2.htm">
    <FRAME SRC="frame3.htm">
</FRAMESET>

<FRAMESET ROWS = "25%, 25%, 50%">
    <FRAME SRC="frame1.htm">
    <FRAME SRC="frame2.htm">
    <FRAME SRC="frame3.htm">
</FRAMESET>

  </FRAMESET>

</HTML>
```

You can see the result of this HTML in Figure 7.7. As you can see, once you've created columns, you can break them up into rows as you like with nested **<FRAMESET>** elements. If you prefer, you can set up the rows first, and then divide each row into columns.

You don't have to have the same number of rows in each column. In this example, I have no rows in the left-hand frame and three in the right:

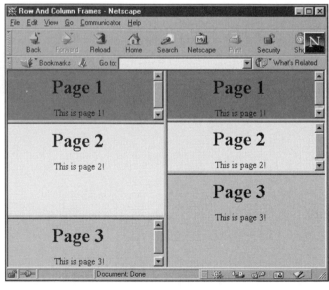

Figure 7.7   Creating horizontal and vertical frames.

```
<HTML>

    <HEAD>
        <TITLE>Row And Column Frames</TITLE>
    </HEAD>

    <FRAMESET COLS = "30%, 70%">
        <NOFRAMES>Your browser does not support frames...</NOFRAMES>

        <FRAME SRC="frame1.htm">

        <FRAMESET ROWS = "25%, 25%, 50%">
            <FRAME SRC="frame1.htm">
            <FRAME SRC="frame2.htm">
            <FRAME SRC="frame3.htm">
        </FRAMESET>

    </FRAMESET>

</HTML>
```

You can see the results of this HTML in Figure 7.8. Working with frames is a lot like working with tables—you have to experiment with the HTML and frequently look at the results in your browser to get things just right.

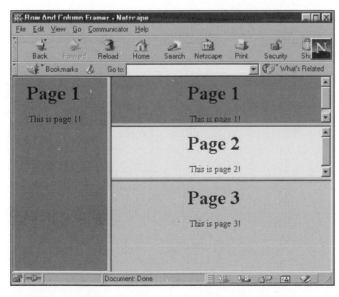

Figure 7.8   Creating a new layout with horizontal and vertical frames.

TIP: *You can use the **ROWS** and **COLS** attributes in the same **<FRAMESET>** element—see "Creating Both Horizontal And Vertical Frames" in the Immediate Solutions section of this chapter.*

Named Frames

One important aspect of working with frames is using *named frames*. When you give a frame a name, you can use it as a *target* to load new pages into (thus supporting the navigation bars I discussed in the Immediate Solutions section "Creating Navigation Bars" in Chapter 5).

In this example, I'm dividing the display into a vertical navigation bar and a display frame, naming that frame "display":

```
<HTML>

    <HEAD>
        <TITLE>
            Targeted Frames
        </TITLE>
    </HEAD>

    <FRAMESET COLS = "40%, 60%">
        <FRAME SRC = menu.htm >
        <FRAME SRC = default.htm NAME = "display">
    </FRAMESET>

</HTML>
```

In the navigation bar, I'll display a page named menu.htm, and in the display frame, I'll show a default welcoming page named default.htm. The navigation bar, menu.htm, has a list of hyperlinks to pages that, when clicked by the user, will show in the display frame. How do we get those pages into the display frame when a hyperlink is clicked? All you have to do is use the **<A>** tag's **TARGET** attribute to specify a frame to load those pages into, like this in menu.htm:

```
<HTML>
    .
    .
    .
    <BODY>
    <OL>
        <LI>
            <A HREF = "frame1.htm" TARGET = "display">
```

```
            Let's see page 1
            </A>
        </LI>
        <LI>
            <A HREF = "frame2.htm" TARGET = "display">
            Let's see page 2
            </A>
        </LI>
        <LI>
            <A HREF = "frame3.htm" TARGET = "display">
            Let's see page 3
            </A>
        </LI>
    </OL>
    </BODY>
</HTML>
```

Before any of the linked-to pages are displayed, however, a default page, default.htm, is shown in the display frame. The default page looks like this:

```
<HTML>

    <HEAD>
        <TITLE>
            Default Frame
        </TITLE>
    </HEAD>

    <BODY>

        <CENTER>
        <H1>
            Click A Hyperlink!
        </H1>
        </CENTER>
    </BODY>

</HTML>
```

You can see the results of this HTML in Figure 7.9. As you see in the figure, the navigation bar, menu.htm, appears on the left, and the default display page, default.htm, appears on the right.

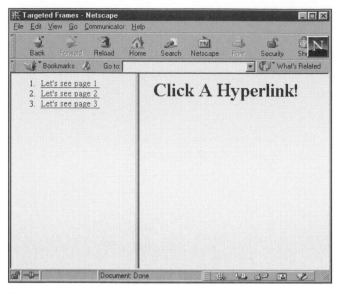

Figure 7.9   Creating a vertical navigation bar.

When the user clicks a hyperlink in the navigation bar, the appropriate page is loaded into the hyperlink's target frame, the display frame, as you see in Figure 7.10. And that's all there is to it.

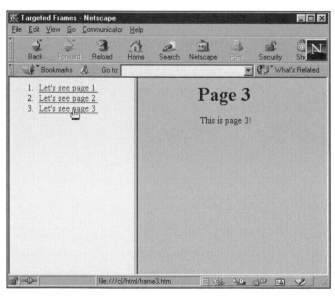

Figure 7.10   Using a navigation bar.

Opening New Browser Windows

What if you specify the name of a target frame that doesn't exist in the hyperlink? In that case, the browser will open a new window to display the linked-to page. This technique is useful if you want to link to a different site, but don't want the user to leave your site.

In the following example, I'll let the user open a new browser window each time a hyperlink is clicked by giving the hyperlinks the targets named "a", "b", and "c", which are *not* named frames in the document:

```
<HTML>
    .
    .
    .
    <BODY>
    <OL>
        <LI>
            <A HREF = "frame1.htm" TARGET = "a">
            Let's see page 1
            </A>
        </LI>
        <LI>
            <A HREF = "frame2.htm" TARGET = "b">
            Let's see page 2
            </A>
        </LI>
        <LI>
            <A HREF = "frame3.htm" TARGET = "c">
            Let's see page 3
            </A>
        </LI>
    </OL>
    </BODY>
</HTML>
```

Now when the user clicks one of the hyperlinks in the navigation bar, the browser will display the linked-to page in a new browser window, as you see in Figure 7.11.

It's worth noting that the browser will keep track of the name you've given the new display window. This allows you to use a navigation bar in one window to load pages into another window if you always refer to that display window using the same name. In the next example, I'm using the same name for the new display window in all hyperlinks. Now, each time the user clicks a hyperlink, the new page will be displayed in the same new browser window:

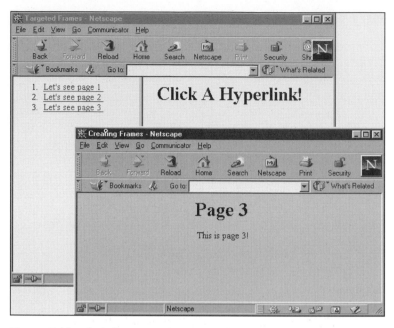

Figure 7.11   Opening a new browser window.

```html
<HTML>
     .
     .
     .
     <BODY>
     <OL>
         <LI>
             <A HREF = "frame1.htm" TARGET = "newwindow">
             Let's see page 1
             </A>
         </LI>
         <LI>
             <A HREF = "frame2.htm" TARGET = "newwindow">
             Let's see page 2
             </A>
         </LI>
         <LI>
             <A HREF = "frame3.htm" TARGET = "newwindow">
             Let's see page 3
```

```
            </A>
        </LI>
    </OL>
    </BODY>
</IITML>
```

This technique allows you to use the original page as a table of contents, and to open new pages as required in the new browser window.

All the information up to this point in the chapter has given us a good start with frames. We've created horizontal frames, vertical frames, and both horizontal and vertical frames. We've used named frames as the target for hyperlinks and opened new browser windows. It's time to turn to the Immediate Solutions section for more details and more topics.

7. Working With Frames

Immediate Solutions

<FRAMESET>—Creating Frames

Purpose: Structures a document using frames. Replaces the **<BODY>** element and uses the **ROWS** and/or **COLS** attribute to set up the frame. Use the **<FRAME>** element to specify the content and name of individual frames.

Start Tag/End Tag: Required/Required

Supported: [4, IE3, IE4, IE5, NS2, NS3, NS4]

Attributes:

- **BORDER**—Use this attribute in the outermost **FRAMESET** tag to set the border thickness for all frames within the **FRAMESET**. Set to positive integers indicating the pixel space between frames; set to 0 to set the **FRAMEBORDER** to **NO**. [IE4, IE5, NS3, NS4]

- **BORDERCOLOR**—Sets the color of the borders for all frames in the frameset. (Can be overriden in the **FRAME** tag for individual frames.) Set to a Red, Green, Blue (RGB) triplet color value or a predefined color. [IE4, IE5, NS3, NS4]

- **CLASS**—Class of the element (used for rendering). [4, IE4, IE5]

- **COLS**—Sets the number of columns (vertical framed bands) in the frameset. Separate the values assigned to this attribute with commas; each value represents the width of a column. The values you use should add up to the total display width available. Set to pixel values, percentages (include a percent sign [%] after the value), or use an asterisk (*) to specify that the browser should give the column or columns the remaining space. [4, IE3, IE4, IE5, NS2, NS3, NS4]

- **FRAMEBORDER**—Sets whether or not borders surround the frames in the **FRAMESET** (you can override this setting for individual frames with the **<FRAME>** element). For Netscape Navigator, set to **YES** (the default) and **NO**; for Internet Explorer lists, set to 1 (the default) and 0 (no border). [IE3, IE4, IE5, NS3, NS4]

- **FRAMESPACING**—Sets the pixel spacing between frames (you can override this setting for individual frames with the **<FRAME>** element). Set to positive integers. [IE3, IE4, IE5]

- **ID**—Unique alphanumeric identifier for the tag, which you can use to refer to it. [4, IE4, IE5]

- **LANG**—Base language used for the tag. [IE4, IE5]

- **LANGUAGE**—Scripting language used for the tag. [IE4, IE5]

- **ROWS**—Sets the number of rows (horizontal framed bands) in the frameset. Separate the values assigned to this attribute with commas; each value represents the height of a row. The values you use should add up to the total display height available. Set to pixel values, percentages (include a percent sign [%] after the value), or use an asterisk (*) to specify that the browser should give the column or columns the remaining space. [4, IE3, IE4, IE5, NS2, NS3, NS4]

- **STYLE**—Inline style indicating how to render the element. [4]

- **TITLE**—Holds additional information (which might be displayed in tool tips) for the element. [4, IE4, IE5]

The novice programmer appears and says, "I want to create frames in my new Web pages, and I figure it'll be pretty easy. You start with the **<FRAME>** element, right?" "Sorry," you say, "you start with the **<FRAMESET>** element."

As discussed in the In Depth section of this chapter, you use the **<FRAMESET>** element to format a page into frames. This element takes the place of the **<BODY>** element in documents that display frames. To actually create the frames themselves, you use the **<FRAME>** element (see the next section).

You can use the **ROWS** or **COLS** attribute of the **<FRAMESET>** element to divide the document into rows or columns. You specify the number of rows or columns by supplying their heights or widths in a comma separated list. Here's an example from the beginning of the chapter, which creates two columns—that is, two vertical frames—each of which take up half the available width:

```
<HTML>

    <HEAD>
        <TITLE>
            Creating Frames
        </TITLE>
    </HEAD>

    <FRAMESET COLS = "50%, 50%">
        .
```

```
                   .
                   .
        </FRAMESET>
```

```
</HTML>
```

You can assign actual pixel values to the **ROWS** and **COLS** attributes, although it's not usually a good idea when working with frames. In most cases, it's better to assign percentages of the available display width to each column and let the browser set the column widths to match the space it has to work with.

You can use an asterisk (*) to represent the remaining available space. For example, **COLS="180, *"** will create one column of 180 pixels in width and assign the remaining horizontal width to the other column. Using values allows you to have a frame of a specific width or height (for example, when you're displaying images of fixed dimensions), and still let the browser arrange the other frame or frames appropriately to the amount of space it has available. If you use more than one asterisk, it's an indication to the browser that it should divide the remaining space among all such frames.

TIP: *There is no limit to the number of **<FRAMESET>** tags you use in a document. In fact, you can load framed windows into frames. Keep in mind that too many frames will make your display surfaces too small to work with.*

As you see from the attributes listed for this tag, there are many options available to you when working with the **<FRAMESET>** element—such as setting borders and border colors. I'll take a look at more of these options in the coming sections.

<FRAME>—Creating Frames

Purpose: Creates a frame. Use inside the **<FRAMESET>** element.

Start Tag/End Tag: Required/Omitted. This element contains no content.

Supported: [4, IE3, IE4, IE5, NS2, NS3, NS4]

Attributes:

- **BORDERCOLOR**—Sets the color used for the frame border. This setting overrides the color specified in the surrounding **<FRAMESET>** element. Set to an RGB triplet color value or predefined color name. [IE4, IE5, NS3, NS4]
- **CLASS**—Class of the element (used for rendering). [4, IE4, IE5]

- **DATAFLD**—Name of the column of the data source object that supplies the bound data. Set to alphanumeric characters. [IE4, IE5]

- **DATASRC**—Gives the URL or ID of the data source object supplying data bound to this element. The World Wide Web Consortium (W3C) says this should be a URL; IE says it should be a data source ID. [IE4, IE5]

- **FRAMEBORDER**—Sets whether or not borders surround the frame. For Netscape Navigator, set to **YES** (the default) and **NO**; for Internet Explorer lists, set to 1 (the default) and 0 (no border). [IE3, IE4, IE5, NS3, NS4]

- **ID**—Unique alphanumeric identifier for the tag, which you can use to refer to it. [4, IE4, IE5]

- **LANG**—Base language used for the tag. [IE4, IE5]

- **LANGUAGE**—Scripting language used for the tag. [IE4, IE5]

- **LONGDESC**—Indicates the URL for a longer description of the frame contents. Set to a URL. [4]

- **MARGINHEIGHT**—Sets the size of the top and bottom margins used in the frame. Set to a pixel height. [4, IE3, IE4, IE5, NS2, NS3, NS4]

- **MARGINWIDTH**—Sets the size of the right and left margins used in the frame. Set to a pixel width. [4, IE3, IE4, IE5, NS2, NS3, NS4]

- **NAME**—Sets the name of the frame. You can use named frames as target destinations for **<A>**, **<AREA>**, **<BASE>**, and **<FORM>** elements. Set to a text string. [4, IE3, IE4, IE5, NS2, NS3, NS4]

- **NORESIZE**—Stand-alone attribute indicating that the frame may not be resized. The default is that frames may be resized by dragging the border. [4, IE3, IE4, IE5, NS2, NS3, NS4]

- **SCROLLING**—Determines scrollbar action; possible values: **AUTO** (the default; lets the browser decide when to display scrollbars), **YES** (always show a scrollbar), or **NO** (never show a scrollbar). [4, IE3, IE4, IE5, NS2, NS3, NS4]

- **SRC**—Specifies the URL of the frame document. If you don't specify a URL, the frame will appear blank. Set to a URL. Required. [4, IE3, IE4, IE5, NS2, NS3, NS4]

- **STYLE**—Inline style indicating how to render the element. [4]

- **TITLE**—Holds additional information (which might be displayed in tool tips) for the element. [4, IE4, IE5]

"OK," says the novice programmer, "I've created a **<FRAMESET>** element—now I can use **<FRAME>** elements to actually create the frames I want, right?" "Exactly," you say, "one **<FRAME>** element to a frame, and you're all set!"

You use the **<FRAME>** element inside a **<FRAMESET>** element to create a frame. The reason this element exists is so you can specify the document that is displayed in a URL. In fact, one attribute of this element must be set to a value—**SRC**, which holds the URL of the document the frame is to display.

Here's an example from the beginning of this chapter showing how to use the **<FRAME>** element to create two frames inside a frameset that renders them as vertical frames:

```
<HTML>

    <HEAD>
        <TITLE>
            Creating Frames
        </TITLE>
    </HEAD>

    <FRAMESET COLS = "50%, 50%">
        <FRAME SRC="frame1.htm">
        <FRAME SRC="frame2.htm">
    </FRAMESET>

</HTML>
```

The result of this HTML appears in Figure 7.4. As you can see in the list of attributes for this element, there's a lot of options here too. I'll be exploring this element and **<FRAMESET>** throughout the rest of the chapter.

Creating Vertical Frames

The big boss appears and says, "I want to divide our company Web page into two vertical frames, consolidating the content that's there now into one frame, and displaying something different in the other." "OK," you say, "I can use the **<FRAMESET>** and **<FRAME>** tags for that. What's going to be in the new frame?" "A picture of me, of course," says the BB.

To divide a document into vertical frames, you use the **COLS** attribute of the **<FRAMESET>** element. You assign this attribute a comma separated list of values indicating the width of the columns you want to create (in pixel measurements, with percentages, or by using an asterisk [*] to indicate that the frame or frames should be given the remaining available space).

Here's an example from the beginning of this chapter. In this case, I'm creating two vertical frames:

```
<HTML>

    <HEAD>
        <TITLE>
            Creating Frames
        </TITLE>
    </HEAD>

    <FRAMESET COLS = "50%, 50%">
        <FRAME SRC="frame1.htm">
        <FRAME SRC="frame2.htm">
    </FRAMESET>

</HTML>
```

You can see the results of this HTML in Figure 7.4. If I had wanted to create three columns with widths of 35, 35, and 30 percent, I could have done this:

```
<HIML>

    <HEAD>
        <TITLE>
            Creating Frames
        </TITLE>
    </HEAD>

    <FRAMESET COLS = "35%, 35%, 30%">
        <FRAME SRC="frame1.htm">
        <FRAME SRC="frame2.htm">
        <FRAME SRC="frame3.htm">
    </FRAMESET>

</HTML>
```

Of course, these are pretty basic examples—the following sections discuss examples of more complexity.

Creating Horizontal Frames

"No, no, no," the big boss says, "I've changed my mind. I don't want to divide the company Web page into two vertical frames, I want to create two *horizontal* frames." "Hm," you say, "looks like it's time to use the **ROWS** attribute."

When creating frame layouts, you use the **COLS** attribute of the **<FRAMESET>** element to create vertical frames and the **ROWS** attribute to create horizontal frames. You assign these attributes a comma separated list of values indicating the width of the columns or the height of the rows you want to create (in pixel measurements, with percentages, or by using an asterisk [*] character to indicate that the frame or frames should be given the remaining space).

Here's an example from the beginning of this chapter, where I'm creating two horizontal frames:

```
<HTML>

    <HEAD>
        <TITLE>
            Creating Frames
        </TITLE>
    </HEAD>

    <FRAMESET ROWS = "50%, 50%">
        <FRAME SRC="frame1.htm">
        <FRAME SRC="frame2.htm">
    </FRAMESET>

</HTML>
```

You can see the results of this HTML in Figure 7.6. If you wanted to divide the page into three rows, taking 35, 35, and 30 percent of the vertical display area, you could do that like this:

```
<HTML>

    <HEAD>
        <TITLE>
            Creating Frames
        </TITLE>
    </HEAD>

    <FRAMESET ROWS = "35%, 35%, 30%">
        <FRAME SRC="frame1.htm">
        <FRAME SRC="frame2.htm">
        <FRAME SRC="frame3.htm">
    </FRAMESET>

</HTML>
```

These are still pretty elementary examples. See the next section for information about how to create both rows and columns in the same document.

Creating Both Horizontal And Vertical Frames

"OK," says the big boss, "I've got it now. I want to break the company Web page into two columns, each with three rows." "You're sure that's what you want?" you ask. "Probably," says the BB.

You can nest **<FRAMESET>** elements to first create columns, then rows—or rows, and then columns—in a document. Here's an example from the beginning of this chapter. In this example, I'm creating two columns, each with three rows of different sizes:

```
<HTML>

    <HEAD>
        <TITLE>Row And Column Frames</TITLE>
    </HEAD>

    <FRAMESET COLS = "50%, 50%">
        <NOFRAMES>Your browser does not support frames...</NOFRAMES>
        <FRAMESET ROWS = "25%, 50%, 25%">
            <FRAME SRC="frame1.htm">
            <FRAME SRC="frame2.htm">
            <FRAME SRC="frame3.htm">
        </FRAMESET>

        <FRAMESET ROWS = "25%, 25%, 50%">
            <FRAME SRC="frame1.htm">
            <FRAME SRC="frame2.htm">
            <FRAME SRC="frame3.htm">
        </FRAMESET>

    </FRAMESET>

</HTML>
```

The result of this HTML appears in Figure 7.7. You don't have to have the same number of rows in each column. Here's an example, where there are no rows in the left-hand frame and three in the right:

```
<HTML>

    <HEAD>
        <TITLE>Row And Column Frames</TITLE>
    </HEAD>

    <FRAMESET COLS = "30%, 70%">
        <NOFRAMES>Your browser does not support frames...</NOFRAMES>

        <FRAME SRC="frame1.htm">

        <FRAMESET ROWS = "25%, 25%, 50%">
            <FRAME SRC="frame1.htm">
            <FRAME SRC="frame2.htm">
            <FRAME SRC="frame3.htm">
        </FRAMESET>

    </FRAMESET>

</HTML>
```

The results of this HTML appear in Figure 7.8.

TIP: *You can actually specify **ROWS** and **COLS** in the same **FRAMESET** element. If you do, the nested **FRAME** references are assigned sequentially to the **COLS** and then the **ROWS** specification.*

Using Named Frames As Hyperlink Targets

"Well," says the novice programmer proudly, "I've finished my novel. Now I want to use frames to display it. I'll provide hyperlinks to each chapter in one frame and the chapter itself in the other frame. Good idea, eh?" "Sounds good," you say, "but how will you display a chapter when the user clicks a hyperlink?" "Hm," says the NP.

As discussed in the In Depth section of this chapter, you can give names to frames, and when you do, you can use those names as the targets of hyperlinks in the **<A>**, **<AREA>**, **<BASE>**, and **<FORM>** elements.

Here's an example from the beginning of this chapter, which appears in Figure 7.9. In this case, I'm creating a vertical navigation bar of hyperlinks in the left frame and displaying the documents they are linked to in the frame on the right.

When the user clicks a hyperlink, the associated page is loaded into the browser in the frame on the right, as you see in Figure 7.10. The following code is what the HTML for the main document looks like. Note that I'm setting up the vertical navigation bar, menu.htm, in the left frame, and displaying a default introductory page, default.htm (which you can see in Figure 7.9), in the right frame—I'm naming that frame "display":

```
<HTML>

    <HEAD>
        <TITLE>
            Targeted Frames
        </TITLE>
    </HEAD>

    <FRAMESET COLS = "40%, 60%">
        <FRAME SRC = menu.htm >
        <FRAME SRC = default.htm NAME = "display">
    </FRAMESET>
</HTML>
```

The following HTML is the menu.htm file, which includes the hyperlink for the navigation bar. Note that I'm assigning the **<A>** element's **TARGET** attribute the name of the frame I want to display pages in, like this:

```
<HTML>
    .
    .
    .
    <BODY>
    <OL>
        <LI>
            <A HREF = "frame1.htm" TARGET = "display">
            Let's see page 1
            </A>
        </LI>
        <LI>
            <A HREF = "frame2.htm" TARGET = "display">
            Let's see page 2
            </A>
        </LI>
        <LI>
            <A HREF = "frame3.htm" TARGET = "display">
            Let's see page 3
            </A>
```

```
            </LI>
        </OL>
        </BODY>
    </HTML>
```

Because I've given a frame in the document the name "display" and set up the hyperlinks to load to that frame, any pages that these hyperlinks load into the browser will be sent to that frame. In this way, you can create navigation bars easily, letting the user move around your site at will.

TIP: *There are a number of predefined target names available. For instance, **_blank**, which opens a new, unnamed browser window. Take a look at the next section for more details.*

Using Predefined Target Names

There are several predefined target names that you can assign to the **TARGET** attribute of the **<A>**, **<AREA>**, **<BASE>**, and **<FORM>** elements. The following list contains predefined target names and what they mean:

- **_blank**—Opens documents in a new, unnamed browser window.
- **_self**—Opens documents in the same window or frame.
- **_parent**—Opens documents in the **<FRAMESET>** parent of the current document. (If there is no parent, **_self** is used.)
- **_top**—Replaces the current document when the linked-to document is opened. This is the same as **_self** except it replaces the entire top-level document, not just the current frame if there is one.

TIP: *When you want to replace the entire current document, for instance, when linking to another site, set **TARGET="_top"**.*

Handling Browsers That Don't Handle Frames

The novice programmer enters and says, "I'm using my favorite Web browser, *SuperDuperWebProKing* 5.3, patch level 97, which may be a little nonstandard, and I'm afraid it doesn't support frames. What the heck can I do?" "One thing you can do," you say, "is to include a **<NOFRAMES>** element. That's what you do when a browser can't handle frames." "Hm," says the NP, " tell me all about it."

Older browsers can't handle frames. Frames were first introduced in Netscape Navigator 2 followed by Internet Explorer 3. You use the **<NOFRAMES>** element to handle them in older browsers. Browsers that handle frames will ignore the content of this element; browsers that don't handle frames will display the content directly. This means you can place a hyperlink to a frameless version of your page in the **<NOFRAMES>** element. In fact, you can include the entire HTML of the frameless version of your page in the **<NOFRAMES>** element.

We saw this example in the beginning of this chapter:

```
<HTML>

    <HEAD>
        <TITLE>
            Creating Frames
        </TITLE>
    </HEAD>

    <FRAMESET COLS = "50%, 50%">
        <NOFRAMES>Your browser does not support frames...</NOFRAMES>
        <FRAME SRC="frame1.htm">
        <FRAME SRC="frame2.htm">
    </FRAMESET>

</HTML>
```

You can see the results of this HTML in a browser that does not support frames—Microsoft Word, which can open rudimentary Web pages. See Figure 7.5.

Opening New Browser Windows

"Wow," the novice programmer says, "I just saw something neat. When I clicked a link, my browser opened a whole new, separate window and displayed the new page in it." "That's an easy one," you say, "you just set the hyperlink's **TARGET** attribute to a new window name, one that doesn't match any named frame."

To open a new browser window when the user clicks a hyperlink, you can set the **TARGET** attribute of the **<A>**, **<AREA>**, **<BASE>**, and **<FORM>** elements to the name you select for a new window.

Here's an example from the beginning of this chapter:

```
<HTML>
    .
    .
    .
    <BODY>
    <OL>
        <LI>
            <A HREF = "frame1.htm" TARGET = "a">
            Let's see page 1
            </A>
        </LI>
        <LI>
            <A HREF = "frame2.htm" TARGET = "b">
            Let's see page 2
            </A>
        </LI>
        <LI>
            <A HREF = "frame3.htm" TARGET = "c">
            Let's see page 3
            </A>
        </LI>
    </OL>
    </BODY>
</HTML>
```

In the previous example, I'm opening new, freestanding browser windows each time the user clicks a hyperlink by supplying different target names—"a", "b", and "c"—to each hyperlink. These target names do not correspond to any named frames in the document.

Note that the browser remembers the name you've given to the new browser window, so you can send all hyperlinked documents to the same new window by using the same target name like this:

```
<HTML>
    .
    .
    .
    <BODY>
    <OL>
        <LI>
            <A HREF = "frame1.htm" TARGET = "newwindow">
            Let's see page 1
```

```
            </A>
        </LI>
        <LI>
            <A HREF = "frame2.htm" TARGET = "newwindow">
            Let's see page 2
            </A>
        </LI>
        <LI>
            <A HREF = "frame3.htm" TARGET = "newwindow">
            Let's see page 3
            </A>
        </LI>
    </OL>
    </BODY>
</HTML>
```

Creating Borderless Frames

"No, no, no," says the big boss, "we don't have the right look at all on the company Web site. Take a look at our competitor's Web site; their frames don't have any borders between them and they look a lot slicker." "Hm," you say, "I can remove the borders from our frames." "You're hired," says the BB. "I already work here," you say.

To remove the borders around frames, you can use the **FRAMEBORDER** attribute of the **<FRAME>** and **<FRAMESET>** elements, and the **FRAMESPACING** attribute of the **<FRAMESET>** element in Internet Explorer, or **BORDER** in the Netscape Navigator. To remove the borders around a frame, set the corresponding **<FRAME>** element's **FRAMEBORDER** attribute to 0 in Internet Explorer or **NO** in Netscape Navigator; to remove the border around all frames, set the enclosing **<FRAMESET>** element's **FRAMEBORDER** and **FRAMESPACING** elements to 0.

Here's an example showing how to remove borders:

```
<HTML>
<HEAD>
<TITLE>Borderless Frame Example</TITLE>
</HEAD>

<FRAMESET ROWS = "110, *" FRAMEBORDER = 0 FRAMESPACING = 0>
        <FRAME SRC = "frame1.htm" SCROLLING = "no" NORESIZE>
```

```
<FRAMESET COLS = "145, *">
    <FRAME NAME = "frame2" SRC = "frame2.htm" SCROLLING = "no"
        NORESIZE>
    <FRAME NAME = "frame3" SRC = "frame3.htm" SCROLLING = "yes"
        NORESIZE>
</FRAMESET>
</FRAMESET>

</HTML>
```

You can see the results of this HTML in Figure 7.12 in Internet Explorer, where, as you see, there are no borders between the frames. Also note that I've used the **SCROLLING** attribute to set the scrolling behavior of the frames and the **NORESIZE** attribute to specify that the frames may not be resized.

TIP: *Netscape Navigator doesn't place frames right next to each other when requested, leaving a thin white line between frames. You can fix this by setting **BORDER** to 0 in the **<FRAMESET>** element or using a table instead of frames, setting **CELLSPACING** and **CELLPADDING** to 0.*

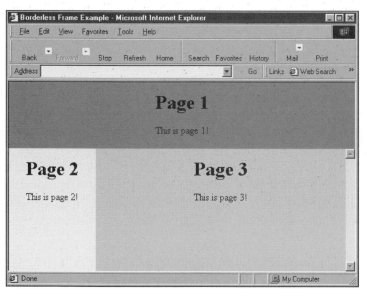

Figure 7.12   Creating borderless frames.

Creating Navigation Bars

The big boss is back and says, "We need navigation bars that will always stay visible to the users as they move through our site. I've been getting complaints that our site is too hard to use." "OK," you say, "what about creating a navigation bar using frames?" "Let's see it," the BB says, "and then I'll let you know."

Here's an example using borderless named frames to create a horizontal navigation bar at the top of the browser's display area:

```
<HTML>

    <HEAD>
        <TITLE>
            Borderless Frame Example
        </TITLE>
    </HEAD>

    <FRAMESET ROWS = "50, *" FRAMEBORDER = 0 FRAMESPACING = 0>

        <FRAME SRC = "menu.htm" SCROLLING = "no" NORESIZE>

        <FRAMESET COLS = "165, *">

            <FRAME NAME = "frame2" SRC = "default.htm"
                SCROLLING = "no" NORESIZE>
            <FRAME NAME = "display" SRC = "frame3.htm"
                SCROLLING = "yes" NORESIZE>

        </FRAMESET>

    </FRAMESET>

</HTML>
```

And here's the page with the hyperlinks in it, menu.htm (note that I'm including nonbreaking spaces whose character entities are ** ** to add spaces between the hyperlinks; see the Immediate Solutions section "Displaying Special Characters: Character Entities" in Chapter 2 for more on character entities):

```
<HTML>
    <BODY BGCOLOR="LIGHTGREEN">
        <CENTER>
```

```
                <A HREF = "frame1.htm" TARGET = "display">
                    Let's see page 1
                </A>

                 

                <A HREF = "frame2.htm" TARGET = "display">
                    Let's see page 2
                </A>

                 

                <A HREF = "frame2.htm" TARGET = "display">
                    Let's see page 3
                </A>
            </CENTER>
        </BODY>
</HTML>
```

You can see the results of this HTML in Figure 7.13 in Internet Explorer (in Netscape Navigator, set **BORDER** to 0 in the **<FRAMESET>** element to get the same results). The borderless navigation bar does indeed appear at the top of the browser window. When the user clicks a hyperlink, the browser loads the corresponding page into the display area under the navigation bar. Note that using images in your hyperlinks would improve the appearance of pages like this one.

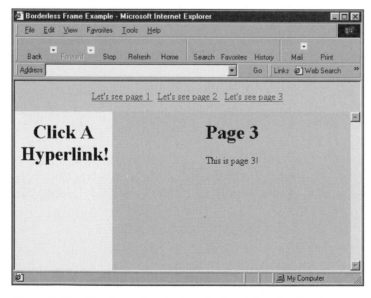

Figure 7.13   Creating a borderless horizontal navigation bar.

Here's another example; this time, the navigation bar is on the left side:

```
<HTML>

    <HEAD>
        <TITLE>
            Targeted Frames
        </TITLE>
    </HEAD>

    <FRAMESET COLS = "40%, 60%">
        <FRAME SRC = menu.htm >
        <FRAME SRC = default.htm NAME = "display">
    </FRAMESET>

</HTML>
```

Here's the new version of menu.htm, the document I'm using to hold the hyperlinks:

```
<HTML>
    .
    .
    .
    <BODY>
    <OL>
        <LI>
            <A HREF = "frame1.htm" TARGET = "display">
            Let's see page 1
            </A>
        </LI>
        <LI>
            <A HREF = "frame2.htm" TARGET = "display">
            Let's see page 2
            </A>
        </LI>
        <LI>
            <A HREF = "frame3.htm" TARGET = "display">
            Let's see page 3
            </A>
        </LI>
    </OL>
    </BODY>
</HTML>
```

You can see the results of this HTML in Figure 7.10.

Enabling And Disabling Scrolling

"Consistency, that's what we want"; says the Web page design czar, "some of our frames have scrollbars, some don't." "That's because the browser decides whether or not there are scrollbars for frames, which it does by default," you say. "All of our frames should have scrollbars"; the WPDC says, "see to it." "Hm," you say.

You can turn scrolling on or off in frames with the **<FRAME>** element's **SCROLLING** attribute. The following list contains the possible settings for this attribute:

- **AUTO**—Lets the browser display scrollbars as needed.
- **NO**—Never display scrollbars.
- **YES**—Always display scrollbars.

In this next example, I'm displaying scrollbars in two of the three frames, like this:

```
<HTML>
    <HEAD>
        <TITLE>
            Borderless Frame Example
        </TITLE>
    </HEAD>

    <FRAMESET ROWS = "80, *" FRAMEBORDER = 0 FRAMESPACING = 0>

        <FRAME SRC = "frame1.htm" SCROLLING = "YES" NORESIZE>

        <FRAMESET COLS = "200, *">
            <FRAME NAME = "frame2" SRC = "frame2.htm"
             SCROLLING = "NO" NORESIZE>
            <FRAME NAME = "frame3" SRC = "frame3.htm"
             SCROLLING = "YES" NORESIZE>
        </FRAMESET>

    </FRAMESET>

</HTML>
```

You can see the results in Figure 7.14 in Internet Explorer (to get the same results in Netscape Navigator, set **BORDER** to 0 in the **<FRAMESET>** element).

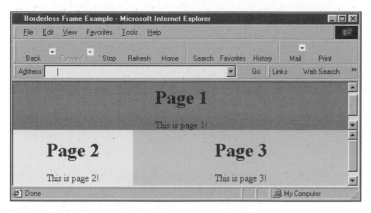

Figure 7.14   Enabling and disabling scrollbars.

Stopping Frames From Being Resized

By default, the user can resize frames in a browser just by dragging them with the mouse. You can, however, disable this feature by using the **NORESIZE** attribute in the **<FRAME>** element. Here's an example from the previous section showing how this works:

```
<HTML>
    <HEAD>
        <TITLE>
            Borderless Frame Example
        </TITLE>
    </HEAD>

    <FRAMESET ROWS = "110, *" FRAMEBORDER = 0 FRAMESPACING = 0 BORDER = 0>
        <FRAME SRC = "frame1.htm" SCROLLING = "no" NORESIZE>
        <FRAMESET COLS = "145, *">
            <FRAME NAME = "frame2" SRC = "frame2.htm"
            SCROLLING = "no" NORESIZE>
            <FRAME NAME = "frame3" SRC = "frame3.htm"
            SCROLLING = "yes" NORESIZE>
        </FRAMESET>
    </FRAMESET>

</HTML>
```

7. Working With Frames

411

Setting Frame Border Thickness

You can set the thickness of frame borders using the **<FRAMESET>** element's **FRAMESPACING** attribute in Internet Explorer. Here's an example, where I'm setting the thickness of the borders of frames to 10 pixels:

```
<HTML>
    <HEAD>
        <TITLE>
            Border Example
        </TITLE>
    </HEAD>

    <FRAMESET ROWS = "110, *" FRAMEBORDER="1" FRAMESPACING="10">
        <FRAME SRC = "frame1.htm" SCROLLING = "no" NORESIZE>
        <FRAMESET COLS = "145, *">
            <FRAME NAME = "frame2" SRC = "frame2.htm"
            SCROLLING = "no" NORESIZE>
            <FRAME NAME = "frame3" SRC = "frame3.htm"
            SCROLLING = "yes" NORESIZE>
        </FRAMESET>
    </FRAMESET>

</HTML>
```

The results of this HTML appear in Figure 7.15.

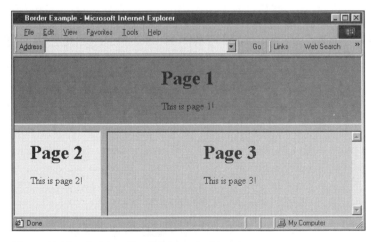

Figure 7.15   Setting the thickness of borders.

Setting Frame Color

You can set the color of frames with the **\<FRAMESET\>** and **\<FRAME\>** elements' **BORDERCOLOR** attribute. Here's an example in which I'm making the borders of the frames red:

```
<HTML>
    <HEAD>
        <TITLE>
            Border Example
        </TITLE>
    </HEAD>

    <FRAMESET ROWS = "110, *" FRAMEBORDER="1" BORDERCOLOR="RED">

        <FRAME SRC = "frame1.htm" SCROLLING = "no" NORESIZE>

        <FRAMESET COLS = "145, *">

            <FRAME NAME = "frame2" SRC = "frame2.htm"
             SCROLLING = "no" NORESIZE>
            <FRAME NAME = "frame3" SRC = "frame3.htm"
             SCROLLING = "yes" NORESIZE>

        </FRAMESET>

    </FRAMESET>

</HTML>
```

The results of this HTML appear in Figure 7.16.

NOTE: *You can set the **BORDERCOLOR** attribute of both the **\<FRAMESET\>** and the **\<FRAME\>** elements. What if you set both and there's a conflict? Here's what happens: The attributes in the outermost element have the lowest precedence; attributes are overridden by attributes in nested **\<FRAMESET\>** elements; and finally, attributes in the current **\<FRAME\>** element take precedence over attributes in the enclosing **\<FRAMESET\>** element.*

---

7. Working With Frames

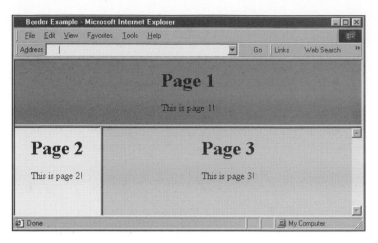

Figure 7.16   Setting frame colors.

<IFRAME>—Creating Inline Or Floating Frames

Purpose: Creates an inline or floating frame.

Start Tag/End Tag: Required/Required

Supported: [4, IE3, IE4, IE5]

Attributes:

- **ALIGN**—Specifies alignment of text following on the screen, much as you align text with images. Possible values: **LEFT**, **RIGHT**, **TOP**, **MIDDLE**, and **BOTTOM**.

- **CLASS**—Class of the element (used for rendering). [4, IE4, IE5]

- **DIR**—Gives the direction of directionally neutral text (text that doesn't have inherent direction in which you should read it). Possible values: **LTR**: left-to-right text or table and **RTL**: right-to-left text or table. [IE5]

- **FRAMEBORDER**—Sets whether or not borders surround the frame. For Netscape Navigator, set to **YES** (the default) and **NO**; for Internet Explorer lists, set to 1 (the default) and 0 (no border). [4, IE3, IE4, IE5]

- **HEIGHT**—Sets the height of the frame in pixels. As with images, you can set aside the appropriate space in the page for the frame using the **HEIGHT** and **WIDTH** properties. Set to positive integers. [4, IE3, IE4, IE5]

- **HSPACE**—Specifies horizontal spacing around the frame in pixels. Set to positive integers. [IE3, IE4, IE5]

- **ID**—Unique alphanumeric identifier for the tag, which you can use to refer to it. [4, IE4, IE5]

- **LANG**—Base language used for the tag. [IE4, IE5]

- **LANGUAGE**—Scripting language used for the tag. [IE4, IE5]

- **LONGDESC**—Indicates the URL for a longer description of the frame contents. Set to a URL. [4]

- **MARGINHEIGHT**—Sets the size of the top and bottom margins used in the frame. Set to a pixel height. [4, IE3, IE4, IE5]

- **MARGINWIDTH**—Sets the size of the right and left margins used in the frame. Set to a pixel width. [4, IE3, IE4, IE5]

- **NAME**—Sets the name of the frame. You can use named frames as target destinations for **<A>**, **<AREA>**, **<BASE>**, and **<FORM>** elements. Set to a text string. [4, IE3, IE4, IE5]

- **SCROLLING**—Determines scrollbar action; possible values: **AUTO** (the default; lets the browser decide when to display scrollbars), **YES** (always show a scrollbar), or **NO** (never show a scrollbar). [4, IE3, IE4, IE5]

- **SRC**—Specifies the URL of the frame document. If you don't specify a URL, the frame will appear blank. Set to a URL. Required. [4, IE3, IE4, IE5]

- **STYLE**—Inline style indicating how to render the element. [4, IE4, IE5]

- **TITLE**—Holds additional information (which might be displayed in tool tips) for the element. [4, IE4, IE5]

- **VSPACE**—Specifies the vertical spacing around the frame in pixels. Set to positive integers. [IE3, IE4, IE5]

- **WIDTH**—Sets the width of the frame in pixels. As with images, you can set aside the appropriate space in the page for the frame using the **HEIGHT** and **WIDTH** properties. Set to positive integers. [4, IE3, IE4, IE5]

The novice programmer wants to know, "Why do frames have to be right up against the edge of the browser? Can't they be in the middle?" "In the middle?" asks the Web page design czar, "What an idea!" You smile and say, "It's perfectly possible."

Internet Explorer supports *inline frames*, also called *floating frames*. Inline frames can appear wherever you want them, including in the middle of the page. All you have to do is specify the height and width of the frame and the HTML page to load into it, and you're set. Inline frames are supported with the **<IFRAME>** element, which in many ways is Internet Explorer's answer to Netscape Navigator's **<LAYER>** element. You can use inline frames to display a number of pages in one, and if you turn the borders off (see the next section in this chapter), the result can be much like using the **<LAYER>** element.

7. Working With Frames

Here's an example showing how to create two inline frames:

```
<HTML>
    <HEAD>
        <TITLE>
            Inline Frames!
        </TITLE>
    </HEAD>

    <BODY BGCOLOR="BLACK">

        <CENTER>
            <BR>
            <BR>

            <IFRAME WIDTH = 50% HEIGHT = 25% NAME = frame1
                SRC="frame1.htm">
            </IFRAME>

            <IFRAME WIDTH = 50% HEIGHT = 25% NAME = frame2
                SRC="frame2.htm">
            </IFRAME>

            <BR>
            <BR>

        </CENTER>

    </BODY>

</HTML>
```

You can see the results in Figure 7.17. Note that it's up to the browser to place these frames, much like other elements, such as images.

NOTE: Some versions of Internet Explorer, prior to the late beta versions of Internet Explorer 3, used extensions to the **<FRAME>** element to create inline frames; so it's possible you might run into this.

TIP: Internet Explorer lists a **BORDER** attribute for the **<IFRAME>** element, but it actually appears to add padding, like **HSPACE** and **VSPACE**, around the frames, not an actual border.

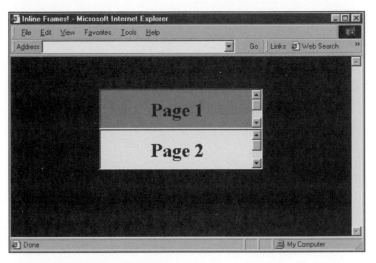

Figure 7.17   Using inline frames.

Creating Borderless Inline Frames

You can make inline frames borderless, and in fact, you do so just as you would with standard frames. Use the **FRAMEBORDER** attribute to make the frame border invisible (by setting this attribute to 0) and the **SCROLLING** attribute to turn off the scrollbars (by setting this attribute to **NO**).

Here's an example showing how to display borderless inline frames:

```
<HTML>
    <HEAD>
        <TITLE>
            Inline Frames!
        </TITLE>
    </HEAD>

<BODY BGCOLOR="BLACK">

        <CENTER>
            <BR>
            <BR>

            <IFRAME WIDTH = 50% HEIGHT = 25% NAME = frame1
                SRC="frame1.htm" FRAMEBORDER="0" SCROLLING="NO">
            </IFRAME>
```

```
        <IFRAME WIDTH = 50% HEIGHT = 25% NAME = frame2
            SRC="frame2.htm" FRAMEBORDER="0" SCROLLING="NO">
        </IFRAME>

        <BR>
        <BR>

    </CENTER>

  </BODY>

</HTML>
```

The results of this HTML appear in Figure 7.18, where you can see that each inline frame is now borderless.

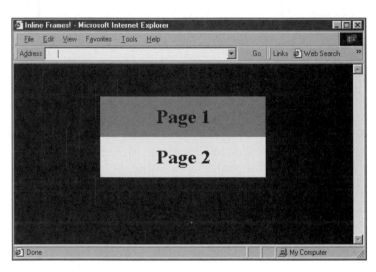

Figure 7.18   Creating borderless inline frames.

Chapter 8

Working With Multimedia

In Depth

There are plenty of multimedia sources out there in the world—CDs, video players, televisions, DVD players, and more. If the Web is going to compete with all of these media, it has to provide the same kind of multimedia support and even improve on it. As you know, the Web is reacting to this challenge. You now find Web pages with inline video, sound, and Shockwave presentations everywhere, and there's more coming all the time. I'll take a look at how multimedia has been developing on the Web and in Web browsers in this chapter.

There are two main ways of handling multimedia in a Web browser—as inline or external data, similar to working with images. Inline multimedia refers to files and data that are handled as part of the page, which play when the page is visible. You can embed video and sound in pages in many ways. You can also link to external files using hyperlinks. For example, when the user clicks a hyperlink, the browser asks if it should download the corresponding file and when it does, it *launches* (that is, starts playing) that file with an external application, such as the Windows Media Player.

How does the browser know which application can handle the multimedia data? It can check the file extension if there is one, such as .jpg or .gif or .avi. If it can match the extension with an application (which might be the Web browser itself), it can open the file. Also, when data is sent from the Web server, the server notifies the browser of the type of data it is using by sending the data's Multipurpose Internet Mail Extension (MIME) type. There are a variety of available MIME types, and I'll list them in this chapter; see the Immediate Solutions section "What MIME Types Are Available?"

NOTE: *You don't usually have to worry about MIME types yourself unless you're doing something like sending binary data streams from programs on your Web server, as you can with Perl scripts. You will also need to be familiar with MIME types if your Web server can't handle the format of data you want to transfer through it because it doesn't know that data's MIME type, or if you're using the **<OBJECT>** element.*

Netscape Navigator is able to handle multimedia in various formats with *plug-ins*. A plug-in is an application that fits smoothly into Netscape Navigator and handles data that the browser itself doesn't, often displaying multimedia inline in the Web page. If a plug-in that you don't have is needed, Netscape Navigator will ask you if the plug-in, which it can usually find from netscape.com, should be installed. You can find a complete list of available plug-ins at **http://home.netscape.com/plugins/index.html**. Here are some of the more popular plug-ins:

- *Crescendo*—Displays a CD-like control panel to let you stream Musical Instrument Digital Interface (MIDI) music. Written by LiveUpdate, see **www.liveupdate.com/crescendo.html**.

- *Flash Player*—Lets you *stream* animations directly to the browser (as does Shockwave). Streaming is useful because your browser can play the animations as it gets data without having to wait for all the data to be downloaded. For more information, take a look at Macromedia's site, see **www.macromedia.com**.

- *mBED*—Lets you display animations, sounds, interactive video, and RealAudio. Written by mBED Software, see **www.mbed.com**.

- *Shockwave*—Handles Macromedia Director movies. Macromedia Director is very popular among multimedia CD developers, and many multimedia presentations and games are written using it. Because of the power of Macromedia Director in creating terrific animations, Shockwave has become very popular. For more about Macromedia Director, see **www.macromedia.com**.

- *Sizzler*—Lets you view and interact with Web pages and supports animation streaming. Written by Totally Hip Software, see **www.totallyhip.com/Products/Products.html**.

TIP: *Some plug-ins, like the Shockwave plug-in, come with Netscape Navigator (although you can elect not to install them when you install Netscape Navigator), but others do not. When you rely on a plug-in, it's often a good idea to be sure that the users of your page have the plug-in they'll need (you can do that in JavaScript by checking the special Netscape Navigator plugins collection).*

As of version 3, Internet Explorer supports the **<EMBED>** element as well. Microsoft's preference, however, is to use ActiveX controls (often stored in Windows systems as the \Windows\System directory and files with the extension .ocx), which you embed with the **<OBJECT>** element to handle data in various multimedia formats.

If Internet Explorer finds it needs an ActiveX control not already installed on your machine, it will ask you before downloading and installing it (you can specify the location of the ActiveX control with a URL in the **<OBJECT>** element's **CODEBASE** attribute). There is good multimedia support already built into Internet Explorer as we'll see throughout this chapter, but you can augment that support with ActiveX controls. I'll take a look at that here as well; see Immediate Solutions sections like "**<OBJECT>** And **<PARAM>**—Placing An Object Into A Web Page."

I'll start digging into the details of handling multimedia in the next section. There are two main multimedia categories: sound and video. I'll concentrate on both and take a look at 3D multimedia as well.

Multimedia Sound

Using sound is one of the most popular uses of multimedia on the Web today because most computers are equipped to play sound. In fact, you can even add background music to Web pages, although that's becoming less and less popular as Web authors seem to realize how annoying it can be (and even dangerous if you're just browsing the Web and the big boss is in the next cubicle). I've seen page after page add and then remove background sounds. On the other hand, sound that you actually ask to hear is getting more and more popular, including *streaming* sound formats like RealAudio (also called Web radio), which let you play sounds in realtime as they're downloaded.

To convert sounds to digital files, computers take *samples* of those sounds. Each sample records the current amplitude of the sound wave. The more frequently you sample the sound wave, the better the reproduction of the sound. What's actually stored in the sound file are the sample measurements, usually compressed to take up less space. The software that plays back the sound uses those measurements to reproduce the sound wave.

NOTE: *Typical sampling rates today are 11kHz, 22kHz, and 44kHz. Samples are typically stored in 8-bit or 16-bit format, which is why you see software that boasts it can handle 16-bit sound.*

There are a number of sound formats available, each with plusses and minuses. I'll take a look at the popular ones in the following sections.

μ-Law (AU) Sound Format

Probably the most popular sound format is the μ-Law, or AU, format (the m is the Greek letter mu) because of its cross-platform capabilities (even the European version, called A-law, is in the same format). Sun and NeXT computer corporations use this sound format as their standard. When you see the extension .au on a sound file, you'll know you're dealing with a μ-Law format sound file.

In fact, the sampling rate of the μ-Law sound format is quite low, only 8kHz (although there are some nonstandard higher sampling rate versions). In addition, this sound is mono, not stereo, and it stores samples in 8-bit format only. The upshot to using this sound format is that you'll be pretty sure users will be able to play it.

AIFF/AIFC Sound Format

Audio Interchange File Format (AIFF) was developed by Apple Computer and is used mostly on the Macintosh. This format has built-in compression, 8-bit or 16-bit sampling, and mono or stereo sound. The extensions on files in this format are .aiff or .aif.

The compression algorithm used with AIFF is called Macintosh Audio Compression/Expansion (MACE), which comes in two versions, 3 to 1 compression, MACE3, and 6 to 1 compression, MACE6. Both compression schemes lose some sound fidelity.

Although this is a good format, it is usually limited to the Macintosh.

Macintosh SND Sound Format

The SND (short for sound) format is the basic Macintosh sound recording format. It is used for internal files on the Macintosh. Because these files are usually Macintosh-only and relatively low fidelity, you won't find them on the Web very often. However, this format casily converts into other formats.

Windows WAV Sound Format

The WAV (short for waveform) format was developed by Microsoft and IBM, and because it was part of Windows 3.1, it's become a popular format. WAV files are quite flexible and can use various compression schemes as well as being able to handle samples of just about any size, rate, and number of channels. You'll often find .wav format files on the Web and in Usenet, but it's not truly a cross-platform format.

MPEG Audio Sound Format

The Moving Pictures Experts Group (MPEG) format has become popular for sound files, especially with the introduction of the MP2 and MP3 formats. The MPEG format was originally developed for video. Because video usually includes sound tracks, MPEG handles sound too, and with good fidelity.

8. Working With Multimedia

Although the sound and sampling rates are very good for MPEG audio, the chief attraction to this format is that these files remain well compressed while reproducing quality sound. The upshot of using this format is that it provides small files that sound terrific. MPEG audio players are widespread and will probably be built into browsers one day.

RealAudio Sound Format

A relatively new, but exciting sound format called RealAudio lets you stream audio to the browser in realtime. You need a 14.4K modem, at least, or a 28.8K modem for better sound. Although RealAudio files are usually smaller than other formats, the sound quality is correspondingly not as good.

MIDI Sound Format

MIDI is another popular sound format (see **www.midi.org**). The files compressed in this format have the extension .midi or .mid. The MIDI format is becoming increasingly cross-platform and it is very flexible, offering a range of sampling rates, sampling sizes, and sound fidelity.

So how can you find some free sounds to add to your pages? Just search the Web. For example, a search for "MIDI" turns up more than three million matches, which seems overwhelming, but if you scan the Web page titles, you'll see endless listings containing MIDI archives, collections, libraries, and more. Just check the copyrights to make sure they're okay to use.

Multimedia Video

Video is even more popular than multimedia sound. There are quite a few video formats to choose, but these are currently the big four:

- MPEG Video format
- QuickTime Video format
- Shockwave Video format
- Video For Windows format

MPEG Video Format

The MPEG video standard may be the most popular format used today. Actually, there are three MPEG standards: MPEG video (pictures only), MPEG audio, and MPEG systems (audio and video). It's expensive to encode MPEG files, and in fact, it's slow to decompress them. So slow that there are many hardware boards you can buy to assist with the decompression process. However, picture quality is good. Although MPEG hardware encoders are very expensive, you can usually find companies that will do the work for you. The files in MPEG format use the extensions .mpg or .mpeg.

QuickTime Video Format

QuickTime was created by Apple Computer for the Macintosh, but it's become a fairly cross-platform format with QuickTime players standard in Windows as well. On the Macintosh, QuickTime plays in MoviePlayer or SimplePlayer. On the PC, QuickTime plays in the QuickTime for Windows application. The QuickTime format supports many different types of encodings and is quite flexible. Files in QuickTime format have the extension .qt or .mov.

TIP: *QuickTime movies made for the Macintosh must be specially prepared through a process called flattening for other platforms, so you can't assume that if it plays on the Macintosh it'll also play on the PC.*

Shockwave Video Format

As mentioned earlier, the Shockwave format brings Macromedia's Director to the Web. Director is a famous authoring product for multimedia presentations on CD-ROMs. Courseware, games, and interactive presentations of all kinds have been created with Director. Shockwave is available as a plug-in for Netscape Navigator and as an ActiveX control for the Internet Explorer.

Video For Windows (AVI) Format

Video For Windows was created by Microsoft and has become popular for Windows platforms. These files are also called Audio Video Interleave (AVI) files because they use the .avi extension. Although AVI is popular in the Windows world, there is relatively little cross-platform support for other operating systems.

TIP: *Don't need all the power of full video? See how to create animated GIFs in the In Depth section of Chapter 4.*

Multimedia 3D

Also available is Virtual Reality Modeling Language (VRML), which is a text-based language that lets you model and display 3D interactive graphics. Since its introduction in 1994, VRML has become more and more popular, although it has yet to take the Web by storm.

8. Working With Multimedia

You can model 3D images using VRML, but you'll need a VRML-enabled browser to view them. ActiveX controls that display VRML are now also available for Internet Explorer and plug-ins for Netscape Navigator. Both browsers will load the ActiveX control or plug-in automatically when you start working with pages that include VRML.

For VRML resources, search the Web to find VRML examples and browsers (a search of the Web using the term VRML turns up nearly one million matches). Also check out **www.vrml.org** and the VRML repository at **www.web3d.org/vrml/ vrml.htm**.

Creating Your Own Multimedia

So far, I've just looked at the consumer side of multimedia, but in case you actually want to produce your own multimedia for the Web, it's worth taking a look at the producer side too. It's no secret that creating multimedia for the Web can be a very, very costly affair, although prices are coming down. The software alone can cost tens of thousands of dollars, and that's not counting hardware boards you might have to buy to connect video cameras to your computer.

Here's a sampler of sites and software available to help you produce your own multimedia projects:

- *3DSite (**www.3dsite.com**)*—Lists lots of resources for 3D Web design. Also includes online resources, mostly for the Macintosh.

- *Asymetrix Multimedia Toolbook (**www.asymetrix.com**)*—Provides tools usually used for training and education. Lets you create interactive courseware, 3D images, and digital videos. Expensive.

- *Autodesk/Kinetix's 3D Studio Max (**www.ktx.com**)*—Lets you create studio-quality 3D animations and videos. Photo-realistic animations with many tools and aids are also available. Expensive, but very powerful.

- *GoldWave (**www.goldwave.com**)*—Provides a shareware sound recorder and editor for Windows.

- *Macromedia (**www.macromedia.com**)*—Provides the famous Shockwave, which brings Macromedia Director, the basis of so many commercial CD multimedia products, to the Web. Here you'll find Director Multimedia Studio, Authorware Interactive Studio, as well as many other products, some with free trials. Expensive, but if you have the resources, it's hard to beat.

- *MacWorld (**www.macworld.com**)*—Provides a number of multimedia authoring software products for the Macintosh, some of which are reviewed on the site.

- *Movie Cleaner Pro (**www.terran-int.com**)*—Compresses and cleans videos for the best results. For the Macintosh.

- *Noteworthy Composer (**www.ntworthy.com**)*—Lets you compose your own MIDI files. A Windows product.

- *PCWorld (**www.pcworld.com**)*—Offers a lot of software for the PC including multimedia authoring products. Similar to the MacWorld site for the Macintosh.

- *Personal AVI Editor (**www.flickerfree.com**)*—Provides a Windows editor for AVI files.

- *RealAudio and RealVideo (**www.realaudio.com**)*—Supports what amounts to Web radio and (slow-scan) TV. Free and commercial plug-ins are available. You can also pick up their server package here, which, although expensive, can put you in the RealAudio and RealVideo business.

- *Sound Forge (**www.sfoundry.com**)*—Provides a sound editor that is a high-end tool for assembling your own sound tracks. Also available in a less-costly edition.

- *ZDNet's Hotfiles Software Library (**www.hotfiles.com/graphics.html**)*—Provides a large collection of reviewed shareware and trial software. Cross-platform selection.

TIP: *On Windows systems, you can create your own sound recordings using a microphone, a sound card, and the Windows utility called Sound Recorder. The Macintosh can also record sounds using its Sound utility in the control panel. Of course, there's a great deal of software out there to help you record and process sounds—in fact, sound cards often come with software applications, so you might want to check out your sound card's CD.*

As mentioned earlier, there are two ways of presenting multimedia in your Web pages: inline and as external files. I'll discuss external files in the next section.

Connecting To External Multimedia Files

Multimedia files can be very large, so most of the time you won't want to include them in a Web page directly. You really don't want users, who don't want to see them, to have to wait for them to download. Instead, you can link to the multimedia files and allow users to download these files by clicking the appropriate link when they want to.

These hyperlinks will link to the actual multimedia file, such as mozart1.mid, which you'll see in the next example. When the hyperlink is clicked, the browser determines what type of file to download by checking its MIME type (as sent by the Web server) or file extension. If the browser recognizes an application (which may be the browser itself) that handles that type of multimedia on the user's system, such as Windows Media Player, it opens the file in that application. If the type of data is unfamiliar to the browser, it'll ask users if they want to download and store the file on disk.

In this example, I'm creating a page with links to two sound files and one video file:

```
<HTML>

    <HEAD>
        <TITLE>
            Linking To External Multimedia Files
        </TITLE>
    </HEAD>

    <BODY>

        <H1>
            Linking To External Multimedia Files
        </H1>

        <TABLE BORDER CELLPADDING = 8 WIDTH = 90%>

            <TR ALIGN = CENTER>
                <TH ROWSPAN = 3>
                    <H2>High<BR>culture<BR>on<BR>demand</H2>
                </TH>
                <TD>
                    Listen to some of <A href = "mozart1.mid">
                    Mozart's music</A> (127K)
                </TD>
            </TR>

            <TR ALIGN = CENTER>
                <TD>
                    Listen to some <I>more</I> of
                    <A href = "mozart2.wav"> Mozart's music</A> (122K)
                </TD>
            </TR>

            <TR ALIGN = CENTER>
                <TD>
```

```
                      See a <A HREF=
                      "http://www.starpowder.com/steve/chaplin.avi">
                      Charlie Chaplin short movie</a> (173K)
            </TD>
         </TR>

      </TABLE>

   </BODY>

</HTML>
```

You can see the results of this HTML in Figure 8.1.

In Figure 8.2, I've downloaded a sound file, and Netscape Navigator has opened it in a sound player. Netscape calls such applications *helper applications*. You can find out which helper application Navigator uses for different file types by selecting Edit|Preferences; then open the Navigator node in the Category box and click the Applications entry.

Creating Inline Sound

You can also present multimedia inline as part of a page. For example, Internet Explorer includes the **<BGSOUND>** element, which lets you set background music for a page. Here's an example showing how to use this element:

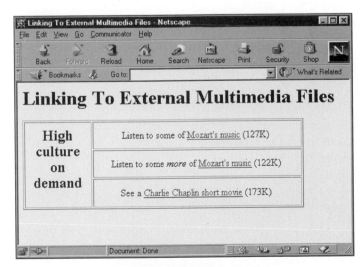

Figure 8.1   Linking to external multimedia files.

```
<HTML>

    <HEAD>
        <TITLE>
            Using Background Music
        </TITLE>
    </HEAD>

    <BODY>

        <H1>
            Playing Background Music
        </H1>

        <BGSOUND SRC="mozart.wav" LOOP="INFINITE">

    </BODY>

</HTML>
```

However, background music can be annoying. You can turn it off or use the **<BGSOUND>** element's **VOLUME** attribute to make the music softer. A better choice might be to use a helper application that lets the user control the volume of the music.

TIP: To turn off sounds in Internet Explorer, select Tools\|Internet Options, click the Advanced tab, then deselect the Play Sounds item under the Multimedia heading in the Settings box.

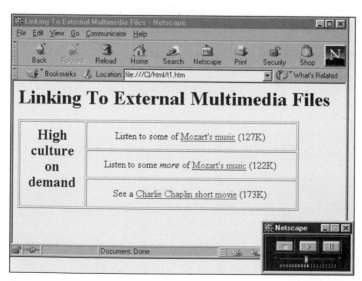

Figure 8.2   Netscape Navigator using a helper application.

You can make Internet Explorer or Netscape Navigator display a sound application in your Web page using the **<EMBED>** element. Here's an example:

```
<HTML>

    <HEAD>
        <TITLE>
            Creating Inline Sound
        </TITLE>
    </HEAD>

    <BODY>
        <CENTER>

            <H1>
                Creating Inline Sound
            </H1>

            <EMBED SRC="mozart.wav" WIDTH=145 HEIGHT=60>

        </CENTER>
    </BODY>

</HTML>
```

The results of this HTML appear in Figure 8.3, where you can see a control panel the user can use to control the sound playback.

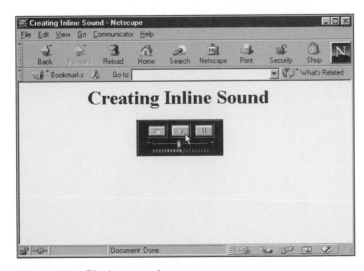

Figure 8.3   Playing sounds.

TIP: *You can also use the* **<OBJECT>** *element to play sounds and videos as we'll see in "* **<OBJECT>** *And* **<PARAM>** *—Placing An Object Into A Web Page" in the Immediate Solutions section.*

Creating Inline Video

You can also include videos in your Web pages. One way to do this in Internet Explorer is with the **<IMG>** element, if you include the **DYNSRC** attribute. Here, I'm adding a Charlie Chaplin movie to a Web page:

```
<HTML>
    <HEAD>
        <TITLE>
            Video With the &lt;IMG&gt; Element
        </TITLE>
    </HEAD>

    <BODY>

        <CENTER>
            <H1>
                Video With the &lt;IMG&gt; Element
            </H1>
            <BR>
            <BR>
            <IMG DYNSRC="chaplin.avi" ALIGN="TOP">
            <BR>
            <BR>
        </CENTER>

    </BODY>

</HTML>
```

The results of this HTML appear in Internet Explorer in Figure 8.4.

You can also use the **<EMBED>** element in Internet Explorer or Netscape Navigator to play videos. Here's an example:

```
<HTML>
    <HEAD>
        <TITLE>
            Video With the &lt;EMBED&gt; Element
        </TITLE>
```

```
    </HEAD>

    <BODY>

        <CENTER>
            <H1>
                Video With the &lt;EMBED&gt; Element
            </H1>

            <EMBED SRC="chaplin.avi">

        </CENTER>

    </BODY>

</HTML>
```

The results of this HTML appear in Figure 8.5. As you can see, the short movie is playing.

TIP: You can also use the **<OBJECT>** element to play sounds and videos as we'll see in "**<OBJECT>** And **<PARAM>**—Placing An Object Into A Web Page" in the Immediate Solutions section.

That's it for the introduction. We've gotten a good start with multimedia, and it's time to turn to the Immediate Solutions for more details and more topics.

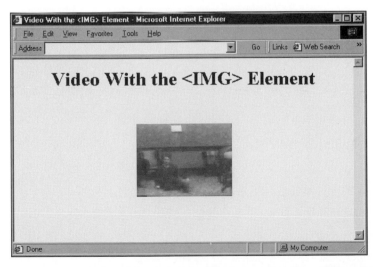

Figure 8.4   Playing video in Internet Explorer using the **<IMG>** element.

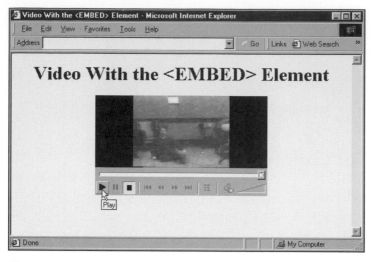

Figure 8.5   Playing video using the **<EMBED>** element.

Immediate Solutions

Creating Links To External Multimedia Files

"Darn," says the novice programmer, "ever since I added a video to my home page, everyone hates it." "Hm," you say, "how long is the video file?" "About twelve megabytes," says the NP. "Ah," you say, "how about providing a link to that file instead of embedding it in your page? That would save a lot of download time."

To avoid long download times for large multimedia files, you can treat them as external files in your Web page and include a hyperlink to them. We saw an example of this in the beginning of this chapter:

```
<HTML>

    <HEAD>
        <TITLE>
            Linking To External Multimedia Files
        </TITLE>
    </HEAD>

    <BODY>

        <H1>
            Linking To External Multimedia Files
        </H1>

        <TABLE BORDER CELLPADDING = 8 WIDTH = 90%>

            <TR ALIGN = CENTER>
                <TH ROWSPAN = 3>
                    <H2>High<BR>culture<BR>on<BR>demand</H2>
                </TH>
                <TD>
                    Listen to some of <A href = "mozart1.mid">
                    Mozart's music</A> (127K)
                </TD>
            </TR>
```

```
        <TR ALIGN = CENTER>
            <TD>
                Listen to some <I>more</I> of
                <A href = "mozart2.wav"> Mozart's music</A> (122K)
            </TD>
        </TR>

        <TR ALIGN = CENTER>
            <TD>
                See a <A HREF=
                "http://www.starpowder.com/steve/chaplin.avi">
                Charlie Chaplin short movie</a> (173K)
            </TD>
        </TR>

    </TABLE>

    </BODY>

</HTML>
```

You can see the results of this HTML in Figure 8.1. Note in particular that I list the size of each multimedia file so the user will have an idea of how long it will take to download. When I download a sound file, Netscape Navigator opens it in a helper application as you see in Figure 8.2.

As discussed in the In Depth section of this chapter, it's up to the browser to handle files it downloads. If it can find a helper application (which might actually be the browser itself if it's registered to handle the type of file you're downloading), it'll open the file in the application. Otherwise, the browser will usually ask users if they want to store the file on disk or, if it's an executable file, if they want to open and run it.

How does the browser know what type of file it is downloading? It can check the file's extension, if there is one, or the MIME information from the Web server. For more on MIME types, see the next section.

What MIME Types Are Available?

There are many data types on the Web, and each recognized data format is given its own MIME type. If your Web server doesn't know how to handle some data's MIME type, it'll typically convert it to text. Browsers use the MIME type of data to figure out how to handle data and to figure out which helper application to use with it. You specify the MIME type of data in certain elements, like the **<OBJECT>** element.

So what MIME types are available? There are many types, such as image/gif (for GIF files) or text/html (for HTML Web pages). You'll find a long list of all MIME media types, as assigned by the Internet Assigned Number Authority (IANA), in Table 8.1. To create a MIME type matching the type of data you want, separate the type from the subtype using a forward slash (/) as in text/plain. Even though this is a long list, you'll likely find yourself referring back to this table as your Web expertise grows.

Table 8.1   MIME media types assigned by the IANA.

Type	Subtype
application	
	activemessage
	andrew-inset
	applefile
	atomicmail
	batch-SMTP
	cals-1840
	commonground
	cybercash
	dca-rft
	dec-dx
	EDI-Consent
	EDIFACT
	EDI-X12
	eshop
	http
	hyperstudio
	iges
	index
	index.cmd
	index.obj
	index.response

(continued)

Table 8.1   MIME media types assigned by the IANA (continued).

Type	Subtype
	index.vnd
	ipp
	mac-binhex40
	macwriteii
	marc
	mathematica
	msword
	news-message-id
	news-transmission
	ocsp-request
	ocsp-response
	octet-stream
	oda
	pdf
	pgp-encrypted
	pgp-keys
	pgp-signature
	pkcs7-mime
	pkcs7-signature
	pkcs10
	pkix-cert
	pkixcmp
	pkix-crl
	postscript
	prs.alvestrand.titrax-sheet
	prs.cww
	prs.nprend
	remote-printing
	riscos
	rtf
	sdp

(continued)

Table 8.1   MIME media types assigned by the IANA (continued).

Type	Subtype
	set-payment
	set-payment-initiation
	set-registration
	set-registration-initiation
	sgml
	sgml-open-catalog
	slate
	vemmi
	vnd.$commerce_battelle
	vnd.3M.Post-it-Notes
	vnd.accpac.simply.aso
	vnd.accpac.simply.imp
	vnd.acucobol
	vnd.anser-web-certificate-issue-initiation
	vnd.anser-web-funds-transfer-initiation
	vnd.audiograph
	vnd.businessobjects
	vnd.claymore
	vnd.commonspace
	vnd.comsocaller
	vnd.cups-postscript
	vnd.cups-raster
	vnd.cups-raw
	vnd.cybank
	vnd.dna
	vnd.dpgraph
	vnd.dxr
	vnd.ecdis-update
	vnd.ecowin.chart
	vnd.ecowin.filerequest
	vnd.ecowin.fileupdate

(continued)

Table 8.1   MIME media types assigned by the IANA (continued).

Type	Subtype
	vnd.ecowin.series
	vnd.ecowin.seriesrequest
	vnd.ecowin.seriesupdate
	vnd.enliven
	vnd.epson.msf
	vnd.epson.quickanime
	vnd.epson.salt
	vnd.epson.ssf
	vnd.fdf
	vnd.ffsns
	vnd.FloGraphlt
	vnd.framemaker
	vnd.fujitsu.oasys
	vnd.fujitsu.oasys2
	vnd.fujitsu.oasys3
	vnd.fujitsu.oasysgp
	vnd.fujitsu.oasysprs
	vnd.fujixerox.docuworks
	vnd.fut-misnet
	vnd.hp-HPGL
	vnd.hp-hpid
	vnd.hp-hps
	vnd.hp-PCL
	vnd.hp-PCLXL
	vnd.ibm.MiniPay
	vnd.ibm.modcap
	vnd.intercon.formnet
	vnd.intertrust.digibox
	vnd.intertrust.nncp
	vnd.intu.qbo
	vnd.intu.qfx

(continued)

Table 8.1   MIME media types assigned by the IANA (continued).

Type	Subtype
	vnd.is-xpr
	vnd.japannet-directory-service
	vnd.japannet-jpnstore-wakeup
	vnd.japannet-payment-wakeup
	vnd.japannet-registration
	vnd.japannet-registration-wakeup
	vnd.japannet-setstore-wakeup
	vnd.japannet-verification
	vnd.japannet-verification-wakeup
	vnd.koan
	vnd.lotus-1-2-3
	vnd.lotus-approach
	vnd.lotus-freelance
	vnd.lotus-notes
	vnd.lotus-organizer
	vnd.lotus-screencam
	vnd.lotus-wordpro
	vnd.mediastation.cdkey
	vnd.meridian-slingshot
	vnd.mif
	vnd.minisoft-hp3000-save
	vnd.mitsubishi.misty-guard.trustweb
	vnd.Mobius.DAF
	vnd.Mobius.DIS
	vnd.Mobius.MSL
	vnd.Mobius.PLC
	vnd.Mobius.TXF
	vnd.motorola.flexsuite
	vnd.motorola.flexsuite.adsi
	vnd.motorola.flexsuite.fis
	vnd.motorola.flexsuite.gotap

(continued)

Table 8.1   MIME media types assigned by the IANA (continued).

Type	Subtype
	vnd.motorola.flexsuite.kmr
	vnd.motorola.flexsuite.ttc
	vnd.motorola.flexsuite.wem
	vnd.ms-artgalry
	vnd.ms-asf
	vnd.ms-excel
	vnd.ms-powerpoint
	vnd.ms-project
	vnd.ms-tnef
	vnd.ms-works
	vnd.musician
	vnd.music-niff
	vnd.netfpx
	vnd.noblenet-directory
	vnd.noblenet-sealer
	vnd.noblenet-web
	vnd.novadigm.EDM
	vnd.novadigm.EDX
	vnd.novadigm.EXT
	vnd.osa.netdeploy
	vnd.pg.format
	vnd.pg.osasli
	vnd.powerbuilder6
	vnd.powerbuilder6-s
	vnd.powerbuilder7
	vnd.powerbuilder7-s
	vnd.powerbuilder75
	vnd.powerbuilder75-s
	vnd.previewsystems.box
	vnd.publishare-delta-tree
	vnd.rapid

(continued)

***Table 8.1   MIME media types assigned by the IANA** (continued).*

Type	Subtype
	vnd.seemail
	vnd.shana.informed.formdata
	vnd.shana.informed.formtemplate
	vnd.shana.informed.interchange
	vnd.shana.informed.package
	vnd.street-stream
	vnd.svd
	vnd.swiftview-ics
	vnd.triscape.mxs
	vnd.truedoc
	vnd.ufdl
	vnd.uplanet.alert
	vnd.uplanet.alert-wbxml
	vnd.uplanet.bearer-choice
	vnd.uplanet.bearer-choice-wbxml
	vnd.uplanet.cacheop
	vnd.uplanet.cacheop-wbxml
	vnd.uplanet.channel
	vnd.uplanet.channel-wbxml
	vnd.uplanet.list
	vnd.uplanet.list-wbxml
	vnd.uplanet.listcmd
	vnd.uplanet.listcmd-wbxml
	vnd.uplanet.signal
	vnd.vcx
	vnd.visio
	vnd.wap.wbxml
	vnd.wap.wmlc
	vnd.wap.wmlscriptc
	vnd.webturbo
	vnd.wrq-hp3000-labelled

(continued)

8. Working With Multimedia

Table 8.1   MIME media types assigned by the IANA (continued).

Type	Subtype
	vnd.wt.stf
	vnd.xara
	vnd.xfdl
	vnd.yellowriver-custom-menu
	wita
	wordperfect5.1
	x400-bp
	xml
	zip
audio	
	32kadpcm
	basic
	L16
	vnd.cns.anp1
	vnd.cns.inf1
	vnd.digital-winds
	vnd.lucent.voice
	vnd.nortel.vbk
	vnd.octel.sbc
	vnd.qcelp
	vnd.rhetorex.32kadpcm
	vnd.vmx.cvsd
image	
	cgm
	g3fax
	gif
	ief
	jpeg
	naplps
	png
	prs.btif

(continued)

***Table 8.1   MIME media types assigned by the IANA** (continued).*

Type	Subtype
	prs.pti
	tiff
	vnd.cns.inf2
	vnd.dwg
	vnd.dxf
	vnd.fastbidsheet
	vnd.fpx
	vnd.mix
	vnd.net-fpx
	vnd.svf
	vnd.wap.wbmp
	vnd.xiff
message	
	delivery-status
	disposition-notification
	external-body
	http
	news
	partial
	s-http
model	
	iges
	mesh
	vnd.dwf
	vnd.flatland.3dml
	vnd.gtw
	vrml
multipart	
	alternative
	appledouble
	byteranges

(continued)

Table 8.1   MIME media types assigned by the IANA (continued).

Type	Subtype
	digest
	encrypted
	form-data
	header-set
	mixed
	parallel
	related
	report
	signed
	voice-message
text	
	calendar
	css
	directory
	enriched
	html
	plain
	prs.lines.tag
	rfc822-headers
	richtext
	rtf
	sgml
	tab-separated-values
	uri-list
	vnd.abc
	vnd.fly
	vnd.fmi.flexstor
	vnd.in3d.3dml
	vnd.in3d.spot
	vnd.latex-z
	vnd.motorola.reflex

(continued)

Table 8.1   MIME media types assigned by the IANA (continued).

Type	Subtype
	vnd.wap.wml
	vnd.wap.wmlscript
	xml
video	
	mpeg
	quicktime
	vnd.motorola.video
	vnd.motorola.videop
	vnd.vivo

<BGSOUND>—Adding Background Sounds

Purpose: Plays background sound from AU, MIDI, or WAV files while the user is viewing a page.

Start Tag/End Tag: Required/Omitted. This element contains no content.

Supported: [IE4, IE5]

Attributes:

- **BALANCE**—Sets the stereophonic balance. Setting this attribute to -10,000 creates left-only balance, and setting it to 10,000 represents right-only balance. Setting it to 0 (the default) results in balanced output between the two stereo output devices. [IE4, IE5]

- **CLASS**—Class of the element (used for rendering). [IE4, IE5]

- **ID**—Unique alphanumeric identifier for the tag, which you can use to refer to it. [IE4, IE5]

- **LANG**—Base language used for the tag. [IE4, IE5]

- **LOOP**—Sets the number of times the sound should play. Set to positive integers, or -1, which means the sound will play continuously until the page is unloaded or sound is turned off in the browser. [IE3, IE4, IE5]

- **SRC**—Indicates the URL of the audio file to play; can be WAV, AU, or MIDI format. [IE3, IE4, IE5]

- **VOLUME**—Sets the volume of the output device. Setting this to 0 (the default) results in full volume; -10,000 results in zero volume. [IE4, IE5]

The novice programmer appears with a dented hat and says, "The big boss didn't appreciate the change I made to the company Web page." "What was it?" you ask. "Well," the NP says, "I made it play Row, Row, Row Your Boat at full volume continuously."

We saw how to use this element in the In Depth section of this chapter. Here's the example in which I'm playing a sound file over and over:

```
<HTML>

    <HEAD>
        <TITLE>
            Using Background Music
        </TITLE>
    </HEAD>

    <BODY>

        <H1>
            Playing Background Music
        </H1>

        <BGSOUND SRC="mozart.wav" LOOP=-1>

    </BODY>

</HTML>
```

You can also do the same thing in Internet Explorer or Netscape Navigator with the **<EMBED>** element by setting the **HIDDEN** attribute to **TRUE** to hide the sound player (see "**<EMBED>**—Embedding Multimedia And Plug-ins In A Web Page" in the Immediate Solutions section of this chapter for more details):

```
<HTML>

    <HEAD>
        <TITLE>
            Using Background Music
        </TITLE>
    </HEAD>

    <BODY>

        <H1>
            Playing Background Music
```

```
        </H1>

            <EMBED SRC="mozart.wav" WIDTH=145 HEIGHT=60 HIDDEN="TRUE">

        </BODY>

    </HTML>
```

Note that playing background sounds can be annoying, and the practice is on the decline.

TIP: *You can also use the **<OBJECT>** element to play sounds and videos as we'll see in "**<OBJECT>** And **<PARAM>**—Placing An Object Into A Web Page" in the Immediate Solutions section.*

<EMBED>—Embedding Multimedia And Plug-Ins In A Web Page

Purpose: Lets you embed a plug-in in a Web page to play multimedia inline or anything else a plug-in can do. There are three required attributes: **HEIGHT**, **WIDTH**, and **SRC**.

Start Tag/End Tag: Required/Optional

Supported: [IE3, IE4, IE5, NS2, NS3, NS4]

Attributes:

- **ACCESSKEY**—Sets the access key for the embedded component, which the user can use with a platform-specific key, like the Alt key in Windows, to give the component the focus. [IE5]

- **ALIGN**—Sets the text alignment around the embedded component. Possible values for Internet Explorer: **ABSBOTTOM**, **ABSMIDDLE**, **BASELINE**, **BOTTOM**, **LEFT**, **MIDDLE**, **RIGHT**, **TEXTTOP**, or **TOP**. Possible values for Netscape Navigator: **LEFT**, **RIGHT**, **TOP**, and **BOTTOM**. [IE4, IE5, NS2, NS3, NS4]

- **ALT**—Sets the alternate text for the component, which is displayed if the component can't be loaded. Set to alphanumeric text. [IE3, IE4, IE5]

- **BORDER**—Sets the border width; set to positive pixel widths. [NS2, NS3, NS4]

- **CLASS**—Class of the element (used for rendering). [IE4, IE5]

- **CODE**—Specifies the code for the component; set to a URL. [IE3, IE4, IE5]

- **DIR**—Gives the direction of directionally neutral text (text that doesn't have inherent direction in which you should read it). Possible values: **LTR**: left-to-right text or table and **RTL**: right-to-left text or table. [IE5]

- **FRAMEBORDER**—Sets the border. [NS3, NS4]

- **HEIGHT**—Gives the height of the embedded component in the page. Set to a pixel measurement or a percentage of the available display height. Required. [IE3, IE4, IE5, NS2, NS3, NS4]

- **HIDDEN**—Indicates if the embedded component should be visible or not. Set to **TRUE** (the default) or **FALSE**. [NS2, NS3, NS4]

- **HSPACE**—Sets the horizontal padding around the element. [IE3, IE4, IE5, NS2, NS3, NS4]

- **ID**—Unique alphanumeric identifier for the tag, which you can use to refer to it. [IE4, IE5]

- **LANG**—Base language used for the tag. [IE4, IE5]

- **LANGUAGE**—Scripting language used for the tag. [IE4, IE5]

- **PALETTE**—Sets the color palette to use in the component; set to **FOREGROUND** or **BACKGROUND**. [NS2, NS3, NS4]

- **PLUGINSPAGE**—Provides the URL for the associated plug-in. [IE3, IE4, IE5, NS2, NS3, NS4]

- **PLUGINURL**—Provides the URL for the associated plug-in. [NS4]

- **SRC**—Sets the URL of the multimedia file. Required. [IE3, IE4, IE5, NS2, NS3, NS4]

- **STYLE**—Inline style indicating how to render the element. [IE4, IE5]

- **TITLE**—Sets the element's title. [IE4, IE5]

- **TYPE**—Sets the MIME type for the component. [NS2, NS3, NS4]

- **UNITS**—Sets the height and width units of the component. [IE3, IE4, IE5, NS2, NS3, NS4]

- **VSPACE**—Sets the vertical padding around the element. [IE3, IE4, IE5, NS2, NS3, NS4]

- **WIDTH**—Gives the width of the embedded component in the page. Set to a pixel measurement or a percentage of the available display width. Required. [IE3, IE4, IE5, NS2, NS3, NS4]

The **<EMBED>** element lets you embed a plug-in in a page. Although the World Wide Web Consortium (W3C) says this element should now be replaced with the

<OBJECT> element, there's no doubt that **<EMBED>** will be around for some time to come.

There are all types of plug-ins available (you can find a complete list of available plug-ins at **http://home.netscape.com/plugins/index.html**), and many come with Netscape Navigator. If the browser needs a plug-in you don't have, it will ask you before downloading and installing it.

Here's an example we saw using the **<EMBED>** element in the beginning of this chapter; here, I'm playing a sound with that element:

```
<HTML>

    <HEAD>
        <TITLE>
            Creating Inline Sound
        </TITLE>
    </HEAD>

    <BODY>
        <CENTER>

            <H1>
                Creating Inline Sound
            </H1>

            <EMBED SRC="mozart.wav" WIDTH=145 HEIGHT=60>
            </EMBED>

        </CENTER>
    </BODY>

</HTML>
```

TIP: *You can also use the **<OBJECT>** element to play sounds and videos as we'll see in "**<OBJECT>** And **<PARAM>**—Placing An Object Into A Web Page" in the Immediate Solutions section.*

You can see the results of this HTML in Figure 8.3. If you're using a plug-in available on the Web, you can specify the plug-in's URL as well as the data's URL like this:

```
<EMBED PLUGINURL=PLUGINURL SRC=DATAURL WIDTH=PIXELSX HEIGHT=PIXELSY>
</EMBED>
```

<NOEMBED>—Handling Browsers That Don't Handle Embedding

Purpose: Displays text (including hyperlinks) or HTML that doesn't use embedded components. For browsers that don't handle the **<EMBED>** element.

Start Tag/End Tag: Required/Required

Supported: [IE3, IE4, IE5, NS2, NS3, NS4]

Attributes:

• None

You use the **<NOEMBED>** element to display text, hyperlinks, and nonembedded HTML if a browser doesn't support the **<EMBED>** element. In fact, you can include an entire alternate page in this element, one that is the same as the original page but doesn't rely on embeds.

TIP: *Now that the **<EMBED>** element has been superceded by the **<OBJECT>** element, the **<NOEMBED>** element's task has been taken over by placing text or HTML in the **<OBJECT>** element.*

Here's an example showing how to use this element:

```
<HTML>

    <HEAD>
        <TITLE>
            Creating Inline Sound
        </TITLE>
    </HEAD>

    <BODY>
        <CENTER>

            <H1>
                Creating Inline Sound
            </H1>

            <EMBED SRC="mozart.wav" WIDTH=145 HEIGHT=60>
                <NOEMBED>
                    Sorry, your browser doesn't handle embeds!
                </NOEMBED>
            </EMBED>
```

```
            </CENTER>
        </BODY>

    </HTML>
```

Creating Inline Sounds

"I've finally got my favorite song in a MIDI file!" the novice programmer exults, "But how can I add it to my Web page?" "Well," you say, "you can use the **<EMBED>** element. There are other elements that you can use, like the **<OBJECT>** element, but **<EMBED>** is probably easier." "Just what I'm looking for!" says the NP.

Using the **<EMBED>** element, you can embed inline sounds in your Web pages, complete with a console to let the user play those sounds. Here's an example we saw in the beginning of this chapter using the **<EMBED>** element:

```
<HTML>

    <HEAD>
        <TITLE>
            Creating Inline Sound
        </TITLE>
    </HEAD>

    <BODY>
        <CENTER>

            <H1>
                Creating Inline Sound
            </H1>

            <EMBED SRC="mozart.wav" WIDTH=145 HEIGHT=60>

        </CENTER>
    </BODY>

</HTML>
```

You can see the results of this HTML in Figure 8.3. If you prefer, you can hide the console by setting the **<EMBED>** element's **HIDDEN** attribute to **TRUE**.

In the next example, I'm creating some inline sound with the **<OBJECT>** element. According to W3C, the **<EMBED>** element has now been superceded by **<OBJECT>** (see the "**<OBJECT>** And **<PARAM>**—Placing An Object Into A Web Page" section coming up next):

```
<HTML>

    <HEAD>
        <TITLE>
            Creating Inline Sound
        </TITLE>
    </HEAD>

    <BODY>
        <CENTER>
            <H1>
                Creating Inline Sound
            </H1>

            <OBJECT DATA="mozart.mid" TYPE="audio/midi">

        </CENTER>

    </BODY>

</HTML>
```

<OBJECT> And <PARAM>—Placing An Object Into A Web Page

<OBJECT>

Purpose: Embeds objects, such as ActiveX controls, in Web pages. Can also handle the tasks of the **<APPLET>**, **<EMBED>**, **<BGSOUND>**, **<SOUND>**, and **<IMG>** elements.

Start Tag/End Tag: Required/Required

Supported: [4, IE3, IE4, IE5]

Attributes:

- **ACCESSKEY**—Sets the access key for the embedded component, which the user can use with a platform-specific key, like the Alt key in Windows, to give the component the focus. [IE5]

- **ALIGN**—Sets the text alignment around the embedded component. Possible values for Internet Explorer: **ABSBOTTOM**, **ABSMIDDLE**, **BASELINE**, **BOTTOM**, **LEFT**, **MIDDLE**, **RIGHT**, **TEXTTOP**, or **TOP**. Possible values for Netscape Navigator: **LEFT**, **RIGHT**, **TOP**, and **BOTTOM**. [4, IE4, IE5, NS2, NS3, NS4]

- **CLASS**—Class of the element (used for rendering). [4, IE4, IE5]

- **CLASSID**—Set to the class ID for the object. Set to a class ID value as set in the Windows Registry or a URL. [4, IE3, IE4, IE5, NS4]

- **CODE**—Holds a URL pointing to the object's code or class. Required. [4, IE3, IE4, IE5]

- **CODEBASE**—Specifies where to find the code for the object. [4, IE3, IE4, IE5, NS4]

- **CODETYPE**—Indicates the MIME type of the code referred to by the **CLASSID** attribute. Set to an alphanumeric MIME type. [4, IE3, IE4, IE5]

- **DATA**—Specifies the URL of the object's data. If you didn't specify a value for the **CLASSID** attribute, the MIME type of the data sets a default value for the **CLASSID** attribute. [4, IE3, IE4, IE5, NS4]

- **DATAFLD**—Name of the column of the data source object that supplies the bound data. Set to alphanumeric characters. [IE4, IE5]

- **DATASRC**—Gives the URL or ID of the data source object supplying data bound to this element. W3C says this should be a URL; Internet Explorer says it should be a data source ID. [IE4, IE5]

- **DECLARE**—Indicates that the object should not be created or instantiated until needed (called *late binding*). Stand-alone attribute. [4]

- **DIR**—Gives the direction of directionally neutral text (text that doesn't have inherent direction in which you should read it). Possible values: **LTR**: left-to-right text or table and **RTL**: right-to-left text or table. [IE5]

- **HEIGHT**—Specifies the height of the object in pixels. [4, IE3, IE4, IE5, NS4]

- **HSPACE**—Sets the horizontal spacing around objects in pixels. Set to pixel values. [4, IE3, IE4, IE5]

- **ID**—Unique alphanumeric identifier for the tag, which you can use to refer to it. [4, IE4, IE5, NS4]

- **LANG**—Base language used for the tag. [IE4, IE5]

- **LANGUAGE**—Scripting language used for the tag. [IE4, IE5]

- **NAME**—Gives the object a name so you can use it with forms and scripts. [4, IE3, IE4, IE5]

- **STANDBY**—Sets a text string for the browser to display while it loads the object. Set to alphanumeric text. [4, IE3, IE4, IE5]

- **STYLE**—Inline style indicating how to render the element. [4, IE4, IE5]

- **TABINDEX**—Sets the tab index of the object. Using the Tab key, the user can tab around the elements of the Web page. Set to positive or negative integers. [4, IE4, IE5]

- **TITLE**—Holds additional information (which might be displayed in tool tips) for the element. [4, IE4, IE5]

- **TYPE**—Specifies the MIME type of the data referenced in the **DATA** attribute. [4, IE3, IE4, IE5, NS4]

- **USEMAP**—Specifies the URL; usually in the same document of a client-side image map to be used with the object. [4, IE3, IE4, IE5]

- **VSPACE**—Specifies the vertical spacing around objects in pixels (top and bottom padding). Set to positive integer pixel values. [4, IE3, IE4, IE5]

- **WIDTH**—Sets the width of the object in pixels. [4, IE3, IE4, IE5, NS4]

<PARAM>

Purpose: Supplies parameters to the object specified by the enclosing **<OBJECT>** or **<APPLET>** element.

Start Tag/End Tag: Required/Omitted. This element contains no content.

Supported: [3.2, 4, IE3, IE4, IE5, NS2, NS3, NS4]

Attributes:

- **DATAFLD**—Name of the column of the data source object that supplies the bound data. Set to alphanumeric characters. [IE4, IE5]

- **DATAFORMATAS**—Specifies if bound data is plain text or HTML. Set to **HTML**, **PLAINTEXT**, or **TEXT**. [IE4, IE5]

- **DATASRC**—Gives the URL or ID of the data source object supplying data bound to this element. W3C says this should be a URL; Internet Explorer says it should be a data source ID. [IE4, IE5]

- **ID**—Unique alphanumeric identifier for the tag, which you can use to refer to it. [4]

- **NAME**—Specifies the name of the parameter. Set to an alphanumeric string. Required. [3.2, 4, IE3, IE4, IE5, NS2, NS3, NS4]

- **TYPE**—Sets the MIME type of the parameter. [4]

- **VALUE**—Specifies the value of the parameter. Set to alphanumeric values. [3.2, 4, IE3, IE4, IE5, NS2, NS3, NS4]

- **VALUETYPE**—Sets the MIME type of the value. [4]

The **<OBJECT>** element, originally introduced by Microsoft in Internet Explorer 3 and now adopted by W3C in HTML 4, is designed to handle all inline elements. Created to embed ActiveX controls in Web pages, it can now handle the tasks of the **<APPLET>**, **<EMBED>**, **<BGSOUND>**, **<SOUND>**, and **<IMG>** elements.

NOTE: *If you're looking for coverage of the **<SOUND>** element in this chapter, you won't find it. This element is the same as the **<BGSOUND>** element, but it's only supported by the NCSA Mosaic browser, which has not been supported since 1997, and is not a part of the HTML specification.*

You can use the **<OBJECT>** element to display videos in Internet Explorer, like this:

```
<HTML>
    <HEAD>
        <TITLE>
            Videos With the &lt;OBJECT&gt; Element
        </TITLE>
    </HEAD>

    <BODY>

        <CENTER>
            <H1>
                Videos With the &lt;OBJECT&gt; Element
            </H1>
            <BR>
            <BR>
            <OBJECT DATA="chaplin.avi" TYPE="video/msvideo"
                WIDTH=120
                HEIGHT=160>
            </OBJECT>
            <BR>
            <BR>
        </CENTER>
```

```
        </BODY>

</HTML>
```

In this example, I'm creating some inline sound with the **<OBJECT>** element in Internet Explorer:

```
<HTML>

    <HEAD>
        <TITLE>
            Creating Inline Sound
        </TITLE>
    </HEAD>

    <BODY>
        <CENTER>
            <H1>
                Creating Inline Sound
            </H1>

            <OBJECT DATA="mozart.mid" TYPE="audio/midi">

        </CENTER>

    </BODY>

</HTML>
```

Here's how you use the **<OBJECT>** element to display simple graphics files in Internet Explorer:

```
<HTML>
    <HEAD>
        <TITLE>
            Images With the &lt;OBJECT&gt; Element
        </TITLE>
    </HEAD>

    <BODY>

        <CENTER>
            <H1>
                Images With the &lt;OBJECT&gt; Element
            </H1>
```

```
        <BR>
        <BR>
        <OBJECT DATA="image.gif" TYPE="image/gif"
            WIDTH=200
            HEIGHT=360>
        </OBJECT>
        <BR>
        <BR>
    </CENTER>

</BODY>

</HTML>
```

TIP: *To see what MIME types you can use in the **<OBJECT>** element, see "What MIME Types Are Available?" at the beginning of the Immediate Solutions section in this chapter. You can also use nested **<OBJECT>** elements to handle browsers that might not recognize your preferred data format. For example, if the browser can't handle the QuickTime file format in an **<OBJECT>** element, the browser will ignore the tag, and you might have a nested **<OBJECT>** element inside that element with another format, such as AVI, which the browser will be able to handle.*

In fact, the **<OBJECT>** element is now intended to supercede elements like **<EMBED>** and **<APPLET>**, which you use to embed Java applets. We'll see a great deal more about Java applets later in Chapter 16. Executable applet files have the extension .class, and you can now set the **<OBJECT>** element's **CLASSID** attribute like this: **<OBJECT CLASSID="java:***filename.class***">**. W3C also suggests providing the appropriate MIME type for the applet like this: **<OBJECT CLASSID="java:***filename.class***" CODETYPE="application/ octet-stream">**. If your applet is in another location, you can specify that location with the **CODEBASE** attribute like this: **<OBJECT CLASSID= "java:***filename.class***" CODETYPE="application/octet-stream" CODEBASE="***URL***">**.

In this example, I'm loading a Java applet named "button.class" into a Web page using the **<OBJECT>** element:

```
<HTML>
    <HEAD>
        <TITLE>
            Java Applets With the &lt;OBJECT&gt; Element
        </TITLE>
    </HEAD>
```

```
<BODY>

    <CENTER>
        <H1>
            Java Applets With the &lt;OBJECT&gt; Element
        </H1>
        <BR>
        <BR>
        <OBJECT CODETYPE="application/octet-stream"
            CLASSID="java:button.class"
            WIDTH=200 HEIGHT=200 >
            Your browser does not handle Java...
        </OBJECT>
        <BR>
        <BR>
    </CENTER>

    </BODY>

</HTML>
```

You can see the results of this HTML in Figure 8.6.

There are a great many ActiveX controls that you can use to create multimedia with the **<OBJECT>** element. For example, one ActiveX control that comes with Internet Explorer is the structured graphics control, and to use it, you must supply its *class ID* in the **<OBJECT>** element.

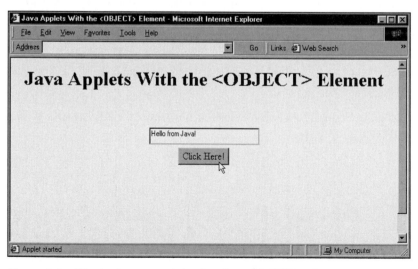

Figure 8.6   Displaying an applet using the **<OBJECT>** element.

NOTE: *Each ActiveX control has its own class ID, which you can find in its documentation or in the Windows Registry if you use a tool like RegEdit, the Registry Editor (usually stored as C:\WINDOWS\REGEDIT.EXE).*

The structured graphics control needs you to tell it what to draw. You do this with **<PARAM>** elements in the **<OBJECT>** element, which pass parameter names and values to the control (and also to Java applets). Here's how that looks in an example:

```
<HTML>

    <HEAD>
        <TITLE>
            Creating Structured Graphics
        </TITLE>
    </HEAD>

    <BODY>

        <CENTER>
            <H1>
                Creating Structured Graphics
            </H1>

            <OBJECT ID="graphics"
                CLASSID="CLSID:369303C2-D7AC-11d0-89D5-00A0C90833E6"
                STYLE="WIDTH:150; HEIGHT:150">
                <PARAM NAME="Line0001" VALUE="SetLineColor(255, 0, 0)">
                <PARAM NAME="Line0002" VALUE="SetFillColor(0, 0, 255)">
                <PARAM NAME="Line0003" VALUE="SetFillStyle(1)">
                <PARAM NAME="Line0004" VALUE="Oval(-75, -75, 80, 80, 0)">
                <PARAM NAME="Line0005" VALUE="SetFillColor(255, 0, 0)">
                <PARAM NAME="Line0006" VALUE="Pie(-75, -75, 80, 80, 0,
                    90, 0)">
                <PARAM NAME="Line0007" VALUE="Pie(-75, -75, 80, 80, 0,
                    90, 180)">
            </OBJECT>

        </CENTER>

    </BODY>
</HTML>
```

This HTML just tells the structured graphics control to draw the image you see in Figure 8.7.

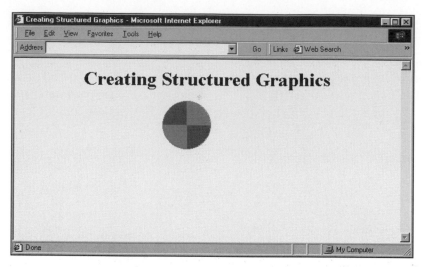

Figure 8.7   Displaying structured graphics using the **<OBJECT>** element.

You can get as elaborate and complex as you like using objects in Web pages. The next example uses JavaScript, which we'll see later in Chapters 10 and 11, with Internet Explorer's **DirectAnimation** control to draw a graphics shape that moves and twists around on top of the content of a Web page:

```
<HTML>

    <HEAD>

        <TITLE>
            Using DirectAnimation
        </TITLE>

        <SCRIPT LANGUAGE = JavaScript>
        <!--

        document.write("<CENTER>")
        document.write("<FORM NAME = form2>")
        document.write("<INPUT TYPE = BUTTON VALUE =
            'Click here for a little animation!' onClick = 'animate()'>")
        document.write("</FORM>")
        document.write("</CENTER>")

        function animate()
        {
            var MeterLibrary = DirectAnimationControl.MeterLibrary
```

```
        var surface = MeterLibrary.NewDrawingSurface()

        surface.FillColor(MeterLibrary.ColorRgb(1, 0, 0))
        surface.FillPath(MeterLibrary.Polyline(Array(0, 0, 400, 0,
            400, 400, 0, 400, 0, 0)))

        surface.FillColor(MeterLibrary.ColorRgb(1, 0, 0))
        surface.FillPath(MeterLibrary.Polyline(Array(200, 0, 0,
            400, 400, 400, 200, 0)))

        surface.FillColor(MeterLibrary.ColorRgb(1, 0, 0))
        surface.FillPath(MeterLibrary.Polyline(Array(0, 0, -400,
            0, -400, -400, 0, -400, 0, 0)))

        surface.FillColor(MeterLibrary.ColorRgb(1, 0, 0))
        surface.FillPath(MeterLibrary.Polyline(Array(-200, -400,
            -400, 0, 0, 0, -200, -400)))

        var axis = MeterLibrary.Vector3(20, 20, 20)
        var start = MeterLibrary.Point2(-2000, 0)
        var end = MeterLibrary.Point2(4000, 0)

        var Sweep = MeterLibrary.FollowPath(MeterLibrary.Line(start,
            end), 10)

        var Twist = MeterLibrary.Rotate3RateDegrees(axis,
            180).Duration(10).ParallelTransform2()

        DirectAnimationControl.Image =
            surface.Image.Transform(Twist).
            Transform(Sweep).Transform(MeterLibrary.
            Scale2(1./30000., 1./30000.))

        DirectAnimationControl.Start()
    }

    //-->

    </SCRIPT>

</HEAD>

<BODY>

    <CENTER>
```

```
<H1>
     Using DirectAnimation
</H1>

<OBJECT ID="DirectAnimationControl"
     STYLE = "POSITION:ABSOLUTE; LEFT:10%; TOP:150;
     WIDTH:90%; HEIGHT:80%"
     CLASSID="CLSID:B6FFC24C-7E13-11D0-9B47-00C04FC2F51D">
</OBJECT>

<BR>
<BR>
<BR>
<BR>
<BR>
<H2>
     Animated graphics that moves over the text in your Web page!
</H2>

</CENTER>

</BODY>

</HTML>
```

You can see the results of this HTML in Figure 8.8. When you click the button, a red figure appears and twists over the text in the Web page while moving to the right.

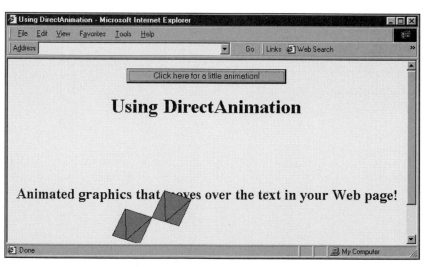

Figure 8.8   Using **DirectAnimation** and an **<OBJECT>** element.

Creating Inline Video

The big boss appears and says, "We need to add some video in our Web page; all the competitors are doing it." "What kind of video would you like?" you ask. "Why," the BB says, startled, "a video of me, of course."

We saw how to use the **<IMG>** element and the **<EMBED>** element to produce inline video in the In Depth section of this chapter. You can use the **<IMG>** element's **DYNSRC** attribute in Internet Explorer to display videos. Here's the example we saw in the beginning of this chapter:

```
<HTML>
    <HEAD>
        <TITLE>
            Video With the &lt;IMG&gt; Element
        </TITLE>
    </HEAD>

    <BODY>

        <CENTER>
            <H1>
                Video With the &lt;IMG&gt; Element
            </H1>
            <BR>
            <RR>
            <IMG DYNSRC="chaplin.avi" ALIGN="TOP" WIDTH="160" HEIGHT="120">
            <BR>
            <BR>
        </CENTER>

    </BODY>

</HTML>
```

You can see the results of this HTML, which plays a Charlie Chaplin video in Figure 8.4. In addition to using the **<IMG>** element's **DYNSRC** attribute in Internet Explorer, you can use the **<EMBED>** element in either Internet Explorer or Netscape Navigator to display inline video, like this:

```
<HTML>
    <HEAD>
        <TITLE>
```

```
                            Video With the &lt;EMBED&gt; Element
                    </TITLE>
            </HEAD>

            <BODY>

                <CENTER>
                    <H1>
                        Video With the &lt;EMBED&gt; Element
                    </H1>

                    <EMBED SRC="chaplin.avi" BORDER="0" AUTOSTART="TRUE"
                        LOOP="TRUE" WIDTH="160" HEIGHT="120">

                </CENTER>

            </BODY>

    </HTML>
```

You can see the results of this HTML in Figure 8.5. According to W3C, **<EMBED>** has been superceded by **<OBJECT>**, so you can use the **<OBJECT>** element to display inline videos, like this:

```
<HTML>
    <HEAD>
        <TITLE>
            Videos With the &lt;OBJECT&gt; Element
        </TITLE>
    </HEAD>

    <BODY>

        <CENTER>
            <H1>
                Videos With the &lt;OBJECT&gt; Element
            </H1>
            <BR>
            <BR>
            <OBJECT DATA="chaplin.avi" TYPE="video/msvideo"
                    WIDTH=120
                    HEIGHT=160>
            </OBJECT>
            <BR>
            <BR>
```

```
        </CENTER>

    </BODY>

</HTML>
```

See "**<OBJECT>** And **<PARAM>**—Placing An Object Into A Web Page" in the Immediate Solutions section of this chapter for more details.

Displaying Loading Images For Inline Video

Sometimes it takes a long time to download video files. In Internet Explorer, you can display an image containing a message to inform the user that the video is in the process of being downloaded. You do this with the **<IMG>** element's **SRC** attribute, which holds the image to display while the video is loading. Here's an example:

```
<HTML>
    <HEAD>
        <TITLE>
            Displaying A Wait Image
        </TITLE>
    </HEAD>

    <BODY>

        <CENTER>
            <H1>
                Displaying A Wait Image
            </H1>
            <BR>
            <BR>
            <IMG DYNSRC="chaplin.avi" SRC="wait.gif" ALIGN="TOP">
            <BR>
            <BR>
        </CENTER>

    </BODY>

</HTML>
```

You can see the image that this HTML displays in Figure 8.9.

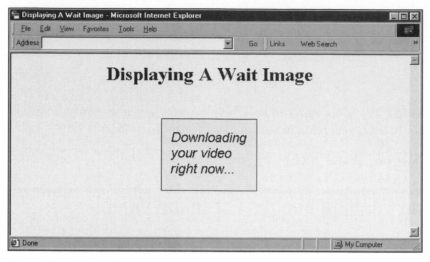

Figure 8.9   Displaying an image while downloading a video.

Using Scrolling Marquees

In Chapter 3, we discussed the use of scrolling marquees in Internet Explorer to display moving text. See "**<MARQUEE>**—Displaying Text In A Scrolling Marquee" in the Immediate Solutions section in Chapter 3 for the details.

Here's an example showing the various **<MARQUEE>** options at work:

```
<HTML>
    <HEAD>
        <TITLE>
            Using the &lt;MARQUEE&gt; tag
        </TITLE>
    </HEAD>

    <BODY>

        <MARQUEE ALIGN="TOP" LOOP="INFINITE" BEHAVIOR="BOUNCE"
            BGCOLOR="#00FF00" DIRECTION="RIGHT">
            <H2>
                Here's a marquee!
            </H2>
        </MARQUEE>
```

```
<CENTER>
    <H1>
        Using Marquees
    </H1>
</CENTER>

<MARQUEE ALIGN="LEFT" LOOP="INFINITE" BEHAVIOR="SCROLL"
    BGCOLOR="#FF0000" HEIGHT=40 WIDTH=300 DIRECTION="DOWN">
    <H2>
        Here's another marquee!
    </H2>
</MARQUEE>

<MARQUEE ALIGN="TOP" LOOP="INFINITE" BEHAVIOR="SLIDE"
    BGCOLOR="#00FFFF" WIDTH=100% DIRECTION="RIGHT">
    <H2>
        And one more!
    </H2>
</MARQUEE>

    </BODY>
</HTML>
```

The results of this HTML appear in Figure 8.10.

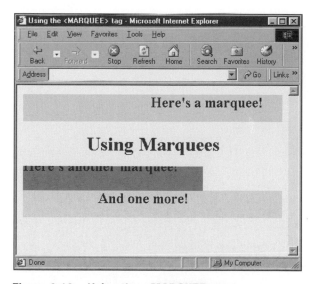

Figure 8.10   Using the **<MARQUEE>** tag.

Using Internet Explorer's Multimedia Controls

As of version 4, Internet Explorer comes with a number of controls that Microsoft calls the multimedia controls. We'll cover these when discussing dynamic HTML in Chapter 13, but here's a short overview of these controls and their functions:

- *Behaviors*—Creates special behaviors for elements in the page.
- *Effects*—Lets you apply graphics filters to the page.
- *Hot Spot*—Converts regions of the screen into clickable regions.
- *Mixer*—Mixes WAV files.
- *Path*—Moves elements along a path, creating animation.
- *Sequencer*—Provides control for timing events.
- *Sprite*—Creates sprite-based animations.
- *Sprite Buttons*—Creates sprite-based animated buttons.
- *Structured Graphics*—Creates powerful graphics.

You can find an example of the structured graphics control in "**<OBJECT>** And **<PARAM>**—Placing An Object Into A Web Page" in the Immediate Solutions section of this chapter. Here's an example using the effects control to show how to apply a shadow filter to text:

```
<HTML>

    <HEAD>
        <TITLE>
            Using Filters
        </TITLE>
    </HEAD>

    <BODY>

        <CENTER>
            <H1>
                Using Filters
            </H1>

            <input value="Click Me" type=button
                onclick="Div1.style.filter =
                'shadow(color=#550055, direction=300, enabled=1)'">

            <P>
```

```
        <DIV ID=Div1 style ="WIDTH:95%"
            style="font-size:24pt;font-family:verdana;font-style:bold">
            Here's some text showing what the shadow filter does.
        </DIV>

    </CENTER>

  </BODY>

</HTML>
```

You can see the results of this HTML in Figure 8.11, where you see a shadow applied to the text in that figure.

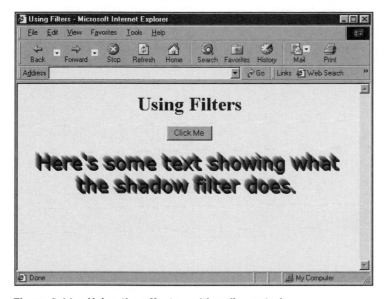

Figure 8.11   Using the effects multimedia control.

Chapter 9

Working With Style Sheets

In Depth

As you know, part of the onward and upward march of HTML has involved replacing style tags and attributes with cascading style sheets. In this chapter, we're going to cover the details of how cascading style sheets work.

One thing you should know is that many people find working with style sheets somewhat involved and difficult. I'll try to make the subject as clear as possible, but there's a fair bit of syntax to learn when applying styles, and in fact, there are three different ways to apply styles in Web pages. The upshot is that this topic takes some patience and investment of time to master. In fact, it's a huge topic and entire books have been devoted to it.

What Are Style Sheets All About?

Style sheets represent the World Wide Web Consortium's (W3C's) effort to improve on the tag- and attribute-based style of formatting. The idea is that style sheets provide a way of customizing whole pages at once and in much richer detail than the simple use of tags and attributes. For that reason, most style attributes (such as **ALIGN**) and many style tags (such as **<U>** for underlined text) have been deprecated. Instead, you can specify the style for the elements in a page all at once as in this next example, where I'm assigning styles for the **<BODY>**, **<A>**, and **<H1>** elements in the **<STYLE>** element, which goes in a page's head:

```
<HTML>
    <HEAD>
        <TITLE>
            Welcome
        </TITLE>

        <STYLE type="text/css">
            BODY {background: white; color: black}
            A:link {color: red}
            A:visited {color: blue}
            A:active {color: green}
            H1 {font-size: 36pt}
        </STYLE>

    </HEAD>
```

```
<BODY>
    Welcome to my page!
    If you don't like it, you can go to
    <A HREF="http://www.w3.org">W3C</A>.
</BODY>
</HTML>
```

Now the **<BODY>**, **<A>**, and **<H1>** elements will appear as we have styled them throughout the page. An expression like **H1 {font-size: 36pt}** is called a *rule*, and in this case, it sets the font size of **<H1>** elements to 36 points. The term **font-size** is called a *property*. This is the way style sheets work—you set a certain style, such as the size of a font, by assigning a value to the corresponding property and enclosing the assignment in curly braces (use a colon, not an equal sign to assign that value to the property). There are hundreds of properties to choose from—you'll find lists of them throughout this chapter. You assign values to properties in style rules: Style sheets themselves are just lists of rules.

In fact, you can create styles in three ways:

- *Embedded style sheets*—Styles are specified in the **<STYLE>** element, like the one in the previous example.

- *External style sheets*—Useful when you want all the pages on your Web site to adhere to the same style.

- *Inline styles*—**STYLE** attribute of the tags you want to style is used, instead of the **<STYLE>** element.

We'll use all three techniques in this chapter.

Style sheets themselves are implemented with the Cascading Style Sheet (CSS) specification, which is now in its second version. The first CSS specification is known as CSS1 and the second as CSS2. CSS2 implements CSS1 and adds a great deal to it.

TIP: *There are more styles in CSS2—such as aural style sheets—than I can possibly include in this chapter. See* **www.w3.org/TR/REC-CSS2/** *for all the details.*

So what should you learn, CSS1 or the expanded and improved version CSS2? It all depends on your browser because most browsers have only implemented part of each specification (these specifications are so large that one can easily imagine the browser programming teams being overwhelmed). I can't stress this enough—test your code in as many browsers as you can. It is the most important thing you can do because style sheet implementation varies a great deal from browser to browser.

In this example, I'll take a look at the same page in two different browsers, Internet Explorer and Netscape Navigator. Here's the HTML:

```
<HTML>

    <HEAD>
        <TITLE>
            Style Differences
        </TITLE>
    </HEAD>

    <BODY>

        <CENTER>
            <H1>Style Differences</H1>
        </CENTER>

        <SPAN STYLE="letter-spacing: 20px">letter-spacing: 20px</SPAN>
        <BR>
        vertical-align:<SPAN STYLE="vertical-align: super">super</SPAN>
        <BR>
        <SPAN STYLE="text-decoration: underline">
            text-decoration: underline
        </SPAN>
        <BR>
        <SPAN STYLE="margin-left: 20%">margin-left: 20%</SPAN>
        <BR>
        <SPAN STYLE="text-indent: 20px">text-indent: 20px</SPAN>
        <BR>
        <SPAN STYLE="text-decoration: overline">
            text-decoration: overline
        </SPAN>

    </BODY>

</HTML>
```

You can see the results of this same HTML in the two browsers in Figures 9.1 and 9.2. As you can see, there's quite a difference. Of course, I'm emphasizing the difference by choosing styles that these browsers implement differently, but the point is an important one—browsers do indeed implement styles in ways that can differ significantly.

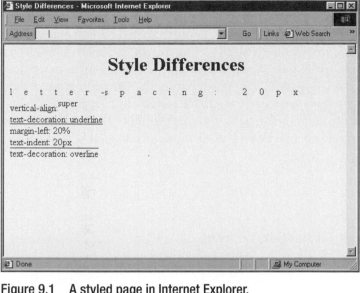

Figure 9.1   A styled page in Internet Explorer.

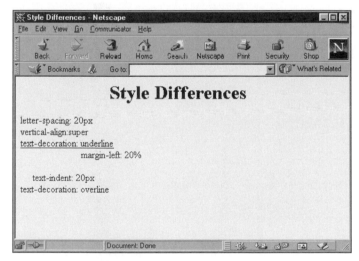

Figure 9.2   A styled page in Netscape Navigator.

Much of this chapter will list the properties that you use to set styles, discuss what elements those properties apply to, and show their possible settings because that's what you need to know before working with style sheets. However, before we get to those details, there's more information we should cover. For example, I said that there are three different ways to implement styles: external style sheets, embedded style sheets, and inline styles, so I'll take a look at how those work now.

External Style Sheets

External style sheets are just that—style sheets that are stored separately from your Web page. These are useful if you're setting the styles for an entire Web site, meaning all the pages in the site. When you change the styles in an external style sheet, you change the styles of all the pages that use it. To specify that your page uses an external style sheet, you use the **<LINK>** element introduced in Chapter 5, setting its **HREF** attribute to the name of the style sheet (which has the extension .css for CSS style sheets). Here's an example—note that the **<LINK>** element goes in the page's head:

```
<HTML>
    <HEAD>
        <TITLE>
            Using An External Style Sheet
        </TITLE>

        <LINK REL="stylesheet" HREF="style.css">

    </HEAD>

    <BODY>

        <CENTER>

            <H1>
                Using An External Style Sheet
            </H1>

            <P>
            This page uses an external style sheet.
        </CENTER>

    </BODY>
</HTML>
```

The style sheet itself simply contains CSS rules, one per line. Here's an example of style.css, which is a plain text file with the following contents:

```
BODY {background-color: #FFFFCC; font-family: Arial}
A:link {color: #0000FF}
A:visited {color: #FFFF00}
A:hover {color: #00FF00}
A:active {color: #FF0000}
P {font-style: italic}
```

In the previous example, I'm setting the background color of the Web page by setting the background color property of the **<BODY>** element as well as setting the font it uses. In addition, I'm setting the colors used for the **<A>** element, setting the colors used for the hyperlinks, and making sure that paragraph text in the **<P>** element appears in italics. You can see the results in Figure 9.3.

As you can see from this example, working with styles is largely a matter of knowing what properties are available and what kinds of values they can take, which is why a large part of this chapter is arranged in a reference style, listing properties and values for easier access.

NOTE: *There's one more point to mention—when setting the styles of hyperlinks, visited hyperlinks, hyperlinks with the mouse hovering over them, and active hyperlinks that are being clicked, you use a slight variation in syntax. You need to follow the **A** element with a colon (:) and one of the following terms, **link**, **visited**, **hover**, **active**. See "Applying Styles To Hyperlinks" in the Immediate Solutions section of this chapter for all the details.*

Embedded Style Sheets

On the other hand, embedded style sheets are part of a Web page itself. They're useful because they collect the styles applied throughout the page and put them into one place—the **<STYLE>** element in the page's head.

Here's an example—notice that the rules look just as they do in external style sheets and that the **<STYLE>** element does indeed appear in the page's head:

```
<HTML>
    <HEAD>
        <TITLE>
```

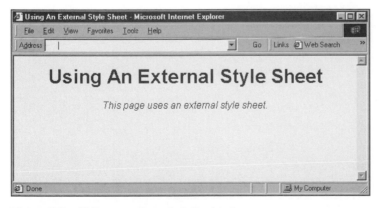

Figure 9.3   Using an external style sheet.

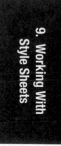

```
            This is a Web page!
       </TITLE>

       <STYLE TYPE="text/css">
            BODY {background: white; color: black}
            A:link {color: red}
            A:visited {color: blue}
            A:active {color: green}
            P {font-style: italic}
       </STYLE>

   </HEAD>

   <BODY>
       Welcome to my page!
       <P>
            If you don't like it, you can go to
            <A HREF="http://www.w3c.org">W3C</A>.
   </BODY>
</HTML>
```

NOTE: *The style type in the previous example is specified as text/css, which is often not necessary because browsers will default to that type. It does serve to distinguish this style sheet from JavaScript style sheets, which type is text/javascript.*

You can see the results of this HTML in Figure 9.4. Using embedded style sheets is one of the most common ways of working with style sheets, but there is another way—using inline styles.

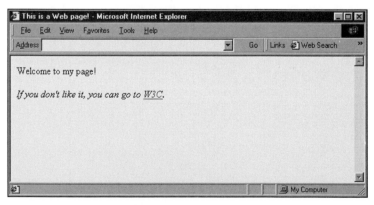

Figure 9.4   Using an embedded style sheet.

Inline Styles

One gets the strong feeling that style sheet purists would like to confine all styles to well-defined style sheets. However this idea creates a problem—what if you want to deviate briefly from those styles, such as making a word italic? To handle such cases, HTML tags include a **STYLE** attribute (which is different from the **STYLE** tag), which you can use to set styles for the corresponding element.

Here's an example that we first saw in Chapter 6. In this case, I'm setting the colors of table cells one by one:

```
<TABLE BORDER="2">
    <TR>
        <TH STYLE="background-color: rgb(255, 0, 0)">Tic</TH>
        <TH STYLE="background-color: rgb(255, 0, 0)">Tac</TH>
        <TH STYLE="background-color: rgb(255, 0, 0)">Toe</TH>
    </TR>
    <TR>
        <TD STYLE="background-color: rgb(255, 255, 255)">X</TD>
        <TD STYLE="background-color: rgb(0, 0, 0); color:
            rgb(255, 255, 255)">
            O
        </TD>
        <TD STYLE="background-color: rgb(255, 255, 255)">X</TD>
    </TR>
    <TR>
        <TD STYLE="background-color: rgb(0, 0, 0); color:
            rgb(255, 255, 255)">
            O
        </TD>
        <TD STYLE="background-color: rgb(255, 255, 255)">X</TD>
        <TD STYLE="background-color: rgb(0, 0, 0); color:
            rgb(255, 255, 255)">
            O
        </TD>
    </TR>
    <TR>
        <TD STYLE="background-color: rgb(255, 255, 255)">X</TD>
        <TD STYLE="background-color: rgb(0, 0, 0); color:
            rgb(255, 255, 255)">
            O
        </TD>
        <TD STYLE="background-color: rgb(255, 255, 255)">X</TD>
    </TR>
</TABLE>
```

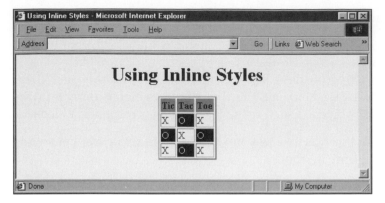

Figure 9.5   Using inline styles.

You can see the results of this HTML in Figure 9.5.

So, as you can see, there are three ways to apply styles: using external style sheets, using embedded style sheets with the **<STYLE>** element, and using inline styles with the **STYLE** attribute. What happens if they conflict? There's a well-defined precedence here: External styles can be overridden by embedded styles, and embedded styles can be overridden by inline styles.

In view of the fact that style purists have had to accept the ill-favored **STYLE** attribute and the resulting decentralization of style definitions, the CSS specification introduced style *classes* to ease the situation.

Creating Style Classes

A style class is a new style that you can apply to various elements throughout your page. When you create a class, you centralize the class's style definition with the rest of the styles in the **<STYLE>** element or external style sheet.

In this next example, I'm creating a class named **BIG**, which can only be applied to **<P>** elements and a style named **RED**, which can be applied to any element. Note the syntax: To make sure you can only use **BIG** with **<P>** elements, you define it as **P.BIG**. To let the **RED** class be used with any element that can display foreground colors, you define it as **.RED** (the dot in front indicates that you're creating a universally applicable class). Here's the HTML:

```
<HTML>
    <HEAD>
        <TITLE>Using Style Classes</TITLE>
        <STYLE type="text/css">
            BODY {background: white; color: black}
```

```
            A:link {color: red}
            A:visited {color: blue}
            A:active {color: green}
            P.BIG {font-size: 18pt}
            .RED {color: red}
        </STYLE>
    </HEAD>
      .
      .
      .
```

Now I apply these classes to various elements using the **CLASS** attribute that most displayable tags have. Here's how the example continues:

```
<HTML>
    <HEAD>
        <TITLE>Using Style Classes</TITLE>
        <STYLE type="text/css">
            BODY {background: white; color: black}
            A:link {color: red}
            A:visited {color: blue}
            A:active {color: green}
            P.BIG {font-size: 18pt}
            .RED {color: red}
        </STYLE>
    </HEAD>

    <BODY>
        <CENTER>
            <H1>
                Using Style Classes
            </H1>
        </CENTER>

        Welcome to my page!
        If you don't like it, you can go to
        <A HREF="http://www.w3.org">W3C</A>.

        <P>
        Here's some normal paragraph text.

        <P CLASS="BIG">
        Here's some bigger paragraph text.
```

```
        <P>
        Here's some <SPAN CLASS="RED">text in red</SPAN>.
    </BODY>
</HTML>
```

Note that I use the **<SPAN>** element to mark the text I want to apply the **RED** class to. That's what **<SPAN>** is really for, to mark small sections of your page and allow you to apply a style. The results of this HTML appear in Figure 9.6. The **<DIV>** element works much the same way, except that you use **<DIV>** to mark whole text blocks, not individual words.

The idea behind classes is that you can put all the style definitions in the same place, and then just use classes in various elements as needed. This technique can be more useful than using the **STYLE** attribute if the style you're applying is long and involved.

TIP: In fact, you can also specify styles targeted to the ID you give to an element; see "Specifying Styles By Element ID" in the Immediate Solutions section of this chapter for the details.

There are still a few more points to clarify before moving to the Immediate Solutions section for details. For example, HTML styles are called *cascading styles*. What does that mean? We'll discuss cascading styles in the next section.

Cascading Styles

Cascading styles are called cascading because a child element (that is, an element enclosed in another element) can inherit the styles of its parent. In this example, I'm applying a style (setting indentation and font size) to a **<DIV>**

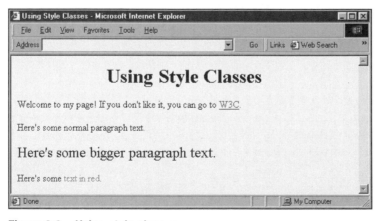

Figure 9.6   Using style classes.

element. Another **<DIV>** element inside the first **<DIV>** element will inherit those styles:

```
<HTML>

    <HEAD>
        <TITLE>
            Using Style Inheritance
        </TITLE>

        <STYLE>
            DIV.indentlarge {font-size: 24pt; margin-left: 10%}
        </STYLE>
    </HEAD>

    <BODY>

        <CENTER>
            <H1>Using Style Inheritance</H1>
        </CENTER>

        <DIV CLASS="indentlarge">
            This is the outer &lt;DIV&gt;.
            <BR>
            <BR>

            <DIV>
                This is the inner &lt;DIV&gt;, which
                has inherited its style from the outer &lt;DIV&gt;.
            </DIV>

        </DIV>

    </BODY>

</HTML>
```

Notice how this works—I'm applying the style to the outer **<DIV>** element only, not the inner one, but the inner **<DIV>** inherits the style from its parent. You can see the results of this HTML in Figure 9.7.

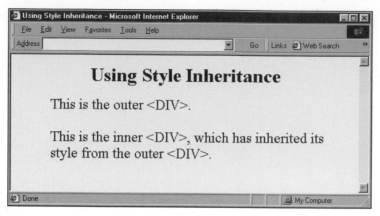

Figure 9.7   Using style inheritance.

Organizing Styles

As you become more familiar with working with styles, you'll appreciate the fact that style rules can take on various shortcut forms. For example, you can collapse all these rules:

```
H4 {font-weight: bold}
H4 {font-size: 12pt}
H4 {font-family: Arial}
H4 {font-style: normal}
```

into one, like this (note that you separate each property assignment with a semicolon):

```
H4 {
    font-weight: bold;
    font-size: 12pt;
    font-family: Arial;
    font-style: normal
}
```

You can specify that a style applies to more than one element in this way:

```
H1, H2, H3, H4 {
    font-weight: bold;
    font-size: 12pt;
    font-family: Arial;
    font-style: normal
}
```

You can also use *shorthand* properties. As you'll see in the reference material in the Immediate Solutions section of this chapter, using some properties, like the **font** property, allows you to handle assignments for a number of other properties at the same time, such as **font-family**, **font-size**, and **font-weight**. Here's an example; this rule:

```
BODY {font-family: arial, helvetica; font-size: 10pt; font-weight: bold}
```

is the same as this rule:

```
BODY {font: bold 10pt arial, helvetica}
```

Understanding Style Specifications

If you actually look at the style specifications in the W3C documents, you'll find that the syntax used is a little complex. However, it's the standard way to specify the syntax used for styles, and I've used it in the reference material throughout this chapter. For example, here's how the style specification for the **background-color** property looks:

background-color

CSS1: **<color>|transparent**

CSS2: **inherit**

Initial: **transparent**

Applies to: All elements

Inherited: No

Supported: [IE4, IE5, NS4]

This syntax is worth getting to know—or at least it's worth knowing that you can refer back to the following list if things get confusing. Here is how the various syntax elements of the style specifications you'll find in this chapter work:

- Terms in angle brackets (**<**) and (**>**) indicate units for values (see Table 9.1) or properties.
- Values separated with a pipe (**I**) indicate alternatives, only one of which may be used.
- Values separated with a double pipe (**II**) indicate options, one or more of which must be used in any order.

- Brackets ([) and (]) group statements that are evaluated much like mathematical statements.
- An asterisk (*) means the preceding term occurs zero or more times.
- A plus sign (+) means the preceding term occurs one or more times.
- A question mark (?) means the preceding term is optional.
- Curly braces ({) and (}) surround pairs of numbers giving the minimum and maximum number of times a term may occur (for example, {1, 4}).

Using this list, you can decipher the **background-color** property specification. Next, I'm listing the values that this style can take in the CSS1 specification, **<color>** or **transparent**, first, and then the values that CSS2 adds, which in this case is just the value **inherit**:

background-color

CSS1: <color>|transparent

CSS2: inherit

Initial: transparent

Applies to: All elements

Inherited: No

Supported: [IE4, IE5, NS4]

Although you can use the terms **transparent** and **inherit** directly (like this: {**background-color: transparent**}), expressions in angle brackets, like **<color>**, use a specific format. You'll find these formats in Table 9.1. There you'll see that **<color>** can be set to a Red, Green, Blue (RGB) triplet value or a predefined color, which means you can assign a color to the **background-color** property like this: {**background-color: "#FFFF00"**}.

Note that in the specification of all properties, I indicate if the property can inherit values from its parent element and what elements the property applies to, as well as the initial setting of the property. I also indicate what version of what browser supports each property (note, however, that although a browser may support a property, it may not support all possible values listed for that property).

Table 9.1 Predefined units in the CSS2 specification.

Unit Measurement	Means
<absolute-size>	Absolute font sizes; may be **xx-small**, **x-small**, **small**, **medium**, **large**, **x-large**, **xx-large**.
<angle>	Angles; may be **deg**, **grad**, or **rad**.
<border-style>	Border of box; may be **none**, **dotted**, **dashed**, **solid**, **double**, **groove**, **ridge**, **inset**, or **outset**.
<border-width>	Width of a border; may be **thin**, **medium**, **thick**, or an explicit length.
<color>	Color; may be specified with a predefined color value or RGB triplet color value.
<family-name>	Name of a font family, such as Arial, Times New Roman, or Courier.
<frequency>	Frequency values; units may be Hz or kHz.
<generic-family>	Generic names for fonts that you use as a last resort if the browser can't find a specific font. Examples are **serif** (browser should choose a serif font), **sans-serif** (browser should choose from the sans-serif family), **monospace** (browser should choose a monospace font).
<generic-voice>	Aural voices; may be **male**, **female**, or **child**.
<integer>	Standard integer values.
<length>	Length; may start with a **+** or **-** followed by a number, which may include a decimal point followed by a unit identifier, which may be **em** (font size of the relevant font), **ex** (the x-height of the font), **px** (pixels as specified relative to the viewing device), **pt** (points, 1/72 of an inch), **in** (inches), **cm** (centimeters), **mm** (millimeters), **pc** (picas, 1/6 of an inch).
<number>	Number; may include a sign and a decimal point.
<percentage>	Number; which may include a sign followed by a percent sign (**%**).
<relative-size>	Font size relative to the parent element; may be either larger or smaller.
<shape>	Rectangle only at present, like this: **rect (<top> <right> <bottom> <left>)**.
<time>	Time units specified as a number followed immediately by **ms** (for milliseconds) or **s** (for seconds).
<uri>	Uniform Resource Indicator (URI), the Web address of a page element, such as an image.

9. Working With Style Sheets

background-color

CSS1: **<color>|transparent**

CSS2: **inherit**

Initial: **transparent**

Applies to: All elements

Inherited: No

Supported: [IE3, IE4, IE5, NS4]

Before we start going into more details in the Immediate Solutions section, there are two property values that you should know about: **auto** and the new CSS2 value **inherit**. Assigning the **auto** value to a property means that the browser should set the property (the actual setting usually depends on context, such as the color of surrounding text). Assigning the **inherit** value to a property means that it should inherit this setting from its parent element, if there is one.

You should also know one more term—*box*. As far as style sheets are concerned, each element in your page is rendered in its own box. For that reason, many of the style specifications refer to the element's box, which is the invisible rectangle that surrounds the element. Boxes have borders, padding, and margins surrounding their content.

That's how style specifications work. Now it's time to start listing them and putting them to work. As mentioned earlier in this chapter, learning to work with styles means knowing what properties are available for what elements and knowing what values they can take. Much of this chapter is written as a reference, making it easier and faster for you to find the information you need. It's time to turn to the Immediate Solutions section for the details now.

NOTE: *The style specifications I'll refer to in the Immediate Solutions section come from the official CSS2 specification—bear in mind that the way your browser uses these styles may differ.*

Immediate Solutions

Using External Style Sheets

The novice programmer says, "I've got two hundred Web pages that I want to format in the same way—what a job!" "Not really," you say, "just use external style sheets and apply the same style sheet to each page."

As mentioned in the In Depth section of this chapter, you can specify styles using external style sheets, which you connect to a page using the **<LINK>** element like this:

```
<HTML>
    <HEAD>
        <TITLE>
            Using An External Style Sheet
        </TITLE>

        <LINK REL="stylesheet" HREF="style.css">

    </HEAD>

    <BODY>

        <CENTER>

            <H1>
                Using An External Style Sheet
            </H1>

            <P>
            This page uses an external style sheet.
        </CENTER>

    </BODY>
</HTML>
```

This HTML links the Web page to an external style sheet named style.css. Here's how that style sheet looks:

```
BODY {background-color: #FFFFCC; font-family: Arial}
A:link {color: #0000FF}
A:visited {color: #FFFF00}
A:hover {color: #00FF00}
A:active {color: #FF0000}
P {font-style: italic}
```

Note the syntax here, as discussed in the In Depth section of this chapter. You create style rules for the various elements you're styling. In this case, I'm creating a style for the **<BODY>** and **<P>** elements as well as setting the colors for hyperlinks, visited hyperlinks, hyperlinks when the mouse is over them, and hyperlinks as they're being clicked. You can see the results of this HTML in Figure 9.3.

<STYLE>—Using Embedded Style Sheets

Purpose: Creates styles.

Start Tag/End Tag: Required/Required

Supported: [3, 3.2, 4, IE3, IE4, IE5, NS4]

Attributes:

- **DIR**—Gives the direction of directionally neutral text (text that doesn't have inherent direction in which you should read it). Possible values: **LTR**: left-to-right text or table and **RTL**: right-to-left text or table. [4]

- **DISABLED**—Specifies that the styles should not be applied initially. Stand-alone attribute. [IE4, IE5]

- **LANG**—Base language used for the tag. [4]

- **MEDIA**—Sets the media for style sheet definitions (multiple destinations are given delimited by commas). Possible values: **SCREEN** (the default), **PRINT**, **PROJECTION**, **BRAILLE**, **SPEECH**, and **ALL**. [4, IE4, IE5]

- **TITLE**—Allows the browser to build a menu of alternative style sheets. Set to alphanumeric values. [4]

- **TYPE**—Indicates the MIME type of the **STYLE** element content. Set to text/css or text/javascript. Required. [4, IE4, IE5, NS4]

The novice programmer says, "I don't want to have to fuss with external style sheets—can't I put everything into the same Web page?" "You certainly can," you say, "and that's exactly what the **<STYLE>** element is for." "Yes?" the NP asks.

As discussed in the In Depth section of this chapter, you can use the **<STYLE>** element to set styles for an entire Web page. This element goes in a Web page's head as in this next example, which we saw in the beginning of the chapter:

```
<HTML>
    <HEAD>
        <TITLE>This is a Web page!</TITLE>
        <STYLE TYPE="text/css">
            BODY {background: white; color: black}
            A:link {color: red}
            A:visited {color: blue}
            A:active {color: green}
            P {font-style: italic}
        </STYLE>
    </HEAD>

    <BODY>
        Welcome to my page!
        <P>
            If you don't like it, you can go to
            <A HREF="http://www.w3.org">W3C</A>.
    </BODY>
</HTML>
```

As with other style sheets, I'm applying the various styles here to Web page elements by listing the style rules, such as **BODY {background: white; color: black}**. You can see the results of this HTML in Figure 9.4.

Using Inline Styles

"Uh oh," says the novice programmer, "now I've got a problem. I want to apply a style to just a single word, making it italic. How can I do that with a style sheet?" "There are two ways," you say, "you can use style classes, or you can use inline styles."

As discussed in the In Depth section of this chapter, you can create inline styles, where you apply styles to one HTML element only. You create inline styles with the **STYLE** attribute that most HTML elements have. Here's an example we saw in the beginning of this chapter:

```
<TABLE BORDER="2">
    <TR>
```

```
        <TH STYLE="background-color: rgb(255, 0, 0)">Tic</TH>
        <TH STYLE="background-color: rgb(255, 0, 0)">Tac</TH>
        <TH STYLE="background-color: rgb(255, 0, 0)">Toe</TH>
    </TR>
    <TR>
        <TD STYLE="background-color: rgb(255, 255, 255)">X</TD>
        <TD STYLE="background-color: rgb(0, 0, 0); color:
            rgb(255, 255, 255)">
            0
        </TD>
        <TD STYLE="background-color: rgb(255, 255, 255)">X</TD>
    </TR>
    <TR>
        <TD STYLE="background-color: rgb(0, 0, 0); color:
            rgb(255, 255, 255)">
            0
        </TD>
        <TD STYLE="background-color: rgb(255, 255, 255)">X</TD>
        <TD STYLE="background-color: rgb(0, 0, 0); color:
            rgb(255, 255, 255)">
            0
        </TD>
    </TR>
    <TR>
        <TD STYLE="background-color: rgb(255, 255, 255)">X</TD>
        <TD STYLE="background-color: rgb(0, 0, 0); color:
            rgb(255, 255, 255)">
            0
        </TD>
        <TD STYLE="background-color: rgb(255, 255, 255)">X</TD>
    </TR>
</TABLE>
```

The results of this HTML appear in Figure 9.5.

TIP: *Inline styles are best used for short applications, for instance, when you italicize a single word. For more lengthy applications, it's a good idea to use style classes. See the next section "Creating And Using Style Classes."*

Creating And Using Style Classes

"Uh oh," says the novice programmer, "my styles are getting really long now, and it's hard to use them as inline styles because they're doubling the size of my Web page's HTML." "Hm," you say, "how about using style classes?"

As discussed in the In Depth section of this chapter, you can create style classes and apply the styles in those classes to HTML elements by using the **CLASS** attribute of those elements. Here's an example we saw at the beginning of this chapter. In this case, I'm creating a class named **BIG** for use with **<P>** elements only, which displays larger text and a class named **RED** for use with any element that changes the foreground color to red (the dot in front of **RED** indicates that **RED** is a class, not an HTML element):

```
<HTML>
    <HEAD>
        <TITLE>This is a Web page!</TITLE>
        <STYLE type="text/css">
            BODY {background: white; color: black}
            A:link {color: red}
            A:visited {color: blue}
            A:active {color: green}
            P.BIG {font-size: 18pt}
            .RED {color: red}
        </STYLE>
    </HEAD>

    <BODY>
        Welcome to my page!
        If you don't like it, you can go to
        <A HREF="http://www.w3c.org">W3C</A>.
        <P>
        Here's some normal paragraph text.
        <P CLASS="BIG">
        Here's some bigger paragraph text.
        <P>
        Here's some <SPAN CLASS="RED">text in red</SPAN>.
    </BODY>
</HTML>
```

You can see the results of this HTML in Figure 9.6. Here's another example where I'm creating a new class named **underlinedText**, which uses the **text-decoration** property to underline text:

```
<HTML>

    <HEAD>
        <TITLE>
            Using Style Classes
        </TITLE>
```

```
        <STYLE>
            .underlinedText {text-decoration: underline}
        </STYLE>
    </HEAD>

    <BODY>
        <CENTER>
            <H1>
                Using Style Classes
            </H1>

            <BR>

            <H1 CLASS="underlinedText">
                This text is underlined.
            </H1>

        </CENTER>

    </BODY>

</HTML>
```

You can see the results of this HTML in Figure 9.8.

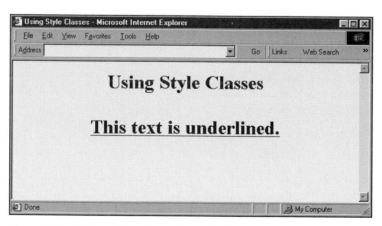

Figure 9.8   Using style classes to underline text.

Specifying Styles By Element ID

If you want to create a number of styles for a certain HTML element, such as a paragraph, it won't work to list a style simply for the **<P>** element because you can create only one style for the **<P>** element that way. Classes—see the previous section—give you a way around this by allowing you to use different classes for different paragraphs in the document. There's also another way. You can set styles by element ID. To do this, you give an element an ID by using its **ID** attribute, then refer to that ID in the style sheet by prefacing it with a pound sign (**#**).

Here's an example where I'm styling the paragraph with the **ID PARA2** to be different than the other paragraphs in the document:

```
<HTML>
    <HEAD>
        <TITLE>
            Using IDs To Style Elements
        </TITLE>

        <STYLE TYPE="text/css">
            BODY {background: white; color: black}
            A:link {color: red}
            A:visited {color: blue}
            A:active {color: green}
            P {font-style: italic}
            #PARA2 {font-style: normal; color: red}
        </STYLE>
    </HEAD>

    <BODY>
        <H1>
            Using IDs To Style Elements
        </H1>
        <P>
            Here's a paragraph.
        <P ID="PARA2">
            Here's a paragraph.
    </BODY>
</HTML>
```

What Background And Color Properties Are Available?

There are a huge number of style properties available. What follows are the background and color properties in CSS1 and CSS2.

background

CSS1: [<background-color>||<background-image>||<background-repeat>||<background-attachment>||<background-position>]

CSS2: inherit

Initial: Not defined

Applies to: All elements

Inherited: No

Supported: [IE3, IE4, IE5, NS4]

Sets the specific background properties (such as **background-color**, **background-image**, **background-repeat**, **background-attachment**, and **background-position**) at the same time. This background property is a shorthand property.

background-attachment

CSS1: scroll|fixed

CSS2: inherit

Initial: scroll

Applies to: All elements

Inherited: No

Supported: [IE4, IE5]

Sets whether a background image is fixed or scrolls when the user scrolls the rest of the page.

background-color

CSS1: <color>|transparent

CSS2: inherit

Initial: transparent

Applies to: All elements

Inherited: No

Supported: [IE4, IE5, NS4]

Specifies the background color of an element using either a **<color>** value or the keyword **transparent**, which makes the underlying color shine through.

background-image

CSS1: **<uri>**|none

CSS2: **inherit**

Initial: None

Applies to: All elements

Inherited: No

Supported: [IE4, IE5, NS4]

Specifies the background image of an element.

TIP: *When setting a background image, you should also specify a background color that will be used when the image is unavailable.*

---

background-position

CSS1: **[[<percentage>|<length>]{1,2}|[[top|center|bottom]||[left|center|right]]]**

CSS2: **inherit**

Initial: 0% 0%

Applies to: Block-level and replaced elements

Inherited: No

Supported: [IE4, IE5]

Specifies a background image's initial position.

background-repeat

CSS1: **repeat|repeat-x|repeat-y|no-repeat**

CSS2: **inherit**

Initial: **repeat**

Applies to: All elements

Inherited: No

9. Working With Style Sheets

Supported: [IE4, IE5]

Specifies if the background image is tiled (repeated), and if so, how.

color

CSS1: **<color>**

CSS2: **inherit**

Initial: Browser dependent

Applies to: All elements

Inherited: Yes

Supported: [IE3, IE4, IE5, NS4]

Sets the foreground color of elements that display text.

TIP: *You'll find a complete listing of the CSS1 specification at **www.w3.org/TR/REC-CSS1** and a complete listing of the CSS2 specification at **www.w3.org/TR/REC-CSS2/***.

What Positioning And Block Properties Are Available?

One of the major uses for style sheets is to set the position of elements in a Web page. I'll take a look at how to position elements in the Immediate Solutions sections "Positioning Elements Using Styles: Absolute Positioning" and "Positioning Elements Using Styles: Relative Positioning". You'll find that these specifications refer to the terms *box* and *block* quite a bit. As mentioned in the In Depth section of this chapter, an element's box is the rectangle it is drawn in. A block simply refers to a block of elements as marked with a **<DIV>** or other enclosing element.

What follows are the positioning and block properties in CSS1 and CSS2.

bottom, top, left, right

CSS2: **<length>|<percentage>|auto|inherit**

Initial: **auto**

Applies to: All elements

Inherited: No

Supported: [IE3, IE4, IE5, NS4]

Indicates how far a box's bottom, top, left, or right content edge should be offset from the corresponding edge of the box's containing area. These are the properties that position the box.

direction

CSS1: **ltr|rtl**

CSS2: **inherit**

Initial: **ltr**

Applies to: All elements

Inherited: Yes

Supported: [IE5]

Indicates the base writing direction of HTML blocks as well as the direction of embeddings and overrides for the Unicode bidirectional algorithm.

display

CSS1: **inline|block|list-item**

CSS2: **run-in|compact|marker|table|inline-table|table-row-group|table-header-group|table-footer-group|table-row|table-column-group|table-column|table-cell|table-caption|none|inherit**

Initial: **inline**

Applies to: All elements

Inherited: No

Supported: [IE4, IE5]

Specifies how the contents of a block should be created.

float

CSS1: **left|right|none**

CSS2: **inherit**

Initial: None

Applies to: All but positioned elements

Inherited: No

Supported: [IE4, IE5, NS4]

Indicates if a box should float to the left, right, or not at all.

position
CSS2: **staticlrelativelabsolutelfixedlinherit**

Initial: **static**

Applies to: All elements, but not generated content

Inherited: No

Supported: [IE4, IE5, NS4]

Specifies which positioning algorithm to use, which makes a difference when you specify properties like left and right.

unicode-bidi
CSS2: **normallembedlbidi-overridelinherit**

Initial: **normal**

Applies to: All elements

Inherited: No

Supported: [IE5]

Handles embedded elements with reversed Unicode order.

z-index
CSS2: **autol<integer>linherit**

Initial: **auto**

Applies to: Positioned elements

Inherited: No

Supported: [IE4, IE5, NS4]

Specifies the stacking level of the box in the stacking order for positioned boxes.

TIP: *You'll find a complete listing of the CSS1 specification at **www.w3.org/TR/REC-CSS1** and a complete listing of the CSS2 specification at **www.w3.org/TR/REC-CSS2/**.*

What HTML Element Box Properties Are Available?

An element's box is the rectangle it is drawn in; boxes have borders, margins, padding, and content. You can affect those parts of a box with the styles listed here.

border

CSS1: [**<border-width>||<border-style>||<color>**]

CSS2: **inherit**

Initial: Varies

Applies to: All elements

Inherited: No

Supported: [IE4, IE5, NS4]

Sets the width, style, and color for all four borders of a box at once. This **border** property is a shorthand property.

border-top, border-right, border-bottom, border-left

CSS1: [**<border-top/right/bottom/left-width>||<border-style>||<color>**]

CSS2: **inherit**

Initial: Varies

Applies to: All elements

Inherited: No

Supported: [IE4, IE5]

Sets the width, style, and color of the top, right, bottom, and left border of a box.

border-color

CSS1: **<color>{1,4}|transparent**

CSS2: **inherit**

Initial: Varies

Applies to: All elements

Inherited: No

Supported: [IE4, IE5, NS4]

Sets the color of the four borders of a box.

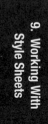

9. Working With
Style Sheets

border-top-color, border-right-color, border-bottom-color, border-left-color

CSS1: <color>

CSS2: **inherit**

Initial: Varies

Applies to: All elements

Inherited: No

Supported: [IE4, IE5]

Sets the color of a specific border of a box.

border-style

CSS1: <border-style>{1,4}

CSS2: **inherit**

Initial: **aries**

Applies to: All elements

Inherited: No

Supported: [IE4, IE5, NS4]

Specifies the style of the four borders of a box. Can have from one to four values (the values will be set on the different sides of the box).

border-top-style, border-right-style, border-bottom-style, border-left-style

CSS1: <border-style>

CSS2: **inherit**

Initial: None

Applies to: All elements

Inherited: No

Supported: [IE4, IE5]

Sets the style of a specific border of a box.

border-width

CSS1: **<border-width>{1,4}**

CSS2: **inherit**

Initial: Not defined

Applies to: All elements

Inherited: No

Supported: [IE4, IE5, NS4]

Sets the **border-top-width**, **border-right-width**, **border-bottom-width**, and **border-left-width** properties at the same time. This **border-width** property is a shorthand property.

border-top-width, border-right-width, border-bottom-width, border-left-width

CSS1: **<border-width>**

CSS2: **inherit**

Initial: **medium**

Applies to: All elements

Inherited: No

Supported: [IE4, IE5, NS4]

Sets the border widths of a box's various sides.

clear

CSS1: None**|left|right|both**

CSS2: **inherit**

Initial: None

Applies to: Block-level elements

Inherited: No

Supported: [IE4, IE5, NS4]

Specifies that the sides of an element's boxes may not be adjacent to an earlier floating box.

height, width

CSS1: **<length>l<percentage>lauto**

CSS2: **inherit**

Initial: **auto**

Applies to: All elements except inline elements, table columns, and column groups

Inherited: No

Supported: [IE4, IE5, NS4]

Gives the content height or width of boxes.

margin

CSS1: **<margin-width>{1,4}**

CSS2: **inherit**

Initial: Not defined

Applies to: All elements

Inherited: No

Supported: [IE3, IE4, IE5, NS4]

Sets the **margin-top**, **margin-right**, **margin-bottom**, and **margin-left** proper-ties at the same time. This **margin** property is a shorthand property.

margin-top, margin-right, margin-bottom, margin-left

CSS1: **<margin-width>**

CSS2: **inherit**

Initial: 0

Applies to: All elements

Inherited: No

Supported: [IE3, IE4, IE5, NS4]

Sets the top, right, bottom, and left margin of a box.

max-height, max-width

CSS2: **<length>l<percentage>lnonelinherit**

Initial: None

Applies to: All elements except nonreplaced inline elements and table elements

Inherited: No

Supported: [IE4, IE5]

Lets you constrain box heights to a certain range.

min-height

CSS2: **<length>|<percentage>|inherit**

Initial: 0

Applies to: All elements except nonreplaced inline elements and table elements

Inherited: No

Supported: [None]

Allows authors to constrain box heights and widths to a certain range.

min-width

CSS2: **<length>|<percentage>|inherit**

Initial: 0

Applies to: All elements except nonreplaced inline elements and table elements

Inherited: No

Supported: [None]

Allows authors to constrain box heights and widths to a certain range.

padding

CSS1: **<length>|<percentage>**

CSS2: **inherit**

Initial: Not defined

Applies to: All elements

Inherited: No

Supported: [IE4, IE5, NS4]

Sets the **padding-top**, **padding-right**, **padding-bottom**, and **padding-left** properties at the same time. This **padding** property is a shorthand property.

padding-top, padding-right, padding-bottom, padding-left

CSS1: <length>|<percentage>

CSS2: **inherit**

Initial: 0

Applies to: All elements

Inherited: No

Supported: [IE4, IE5, NS4]

Specifies the top, right, bottom, and left padding of a box.

TIP: *You'll find a complete listing of the CSS1 specification at **www.w3.org/TR/REC-CSS1** and a complete listing of the CSS2 specification at **www.w3.org/TR/REC-CSS2/**.*

What Font Properties Are Available?

The font properties in CSS1 and CSS2 are listed here.

font

CSS1: **[[<font-style>||<font-variant>||<font-weight>]?<font-size>[/<line-height>]?<font-family>**

CSS2: **caption|icon|menu|message-box|small-caption|status-bar|inherit**

Initial: Varies

Applies to: All elements

Inherited: Yes

Supported: [IE3, IE4, IE5]

Sets **font-style**, **font-variant**, **font-weight**, **font-size**, **line-height**, and **font-family** properties (in that order and without commas between them, except between font families) at the same time. This **font** property is a shorthand property.

font-family

CSS1: **[[<family-name>|<generic-family>],]*[<family-name>|<generic-family>]**

CSS2: **inherit**

Initial: Depends on the browser

Applies to: All elements

Inherited: Yes

Supported: [IE3, IE4, IE5, NS4]

Indicates a list of font family names and/or generic family names. Because not all fonts are available on all systems, this property allows you to specify a list of fonts. The browser will use the first one it can find, starting with the first item in the list. Generic families refer to font characteristics the browser should try to match, like serif or monospace.

font-size

CSS1: **<absolute-size>|<relative-size>|<length>|<percentage>**

CSS2: **inherit**

Initial: **medium**

Applies to: All elements

Inherited: Yes

Supported: [IE3, IE4, IE5, NS4]

Describes the size of a font.

font-stretch

CSS2: **normal|wider|narrower|ultra-condensed|extra-condensed| condensed|semi-condensed|semi-expanded|expanded|extra-expanded| ultra-expanded|inherit**

Initial: **normal**

Applies to: All elements

Inherited: Yes

Supported: [None]

Specifies a normal, condensed, or extended font face.

font-style

CSS1: **normal|italic|oblique**

CSS2: **inherit**

Initial: **normal**

Applies to: All elements

Inherited: Yes

Supported: [IE3, IE4, IE5, NS4]

Specifies normal (also called Roman or upright), italic, and oblique font faces.

font-variant

CSS1: **normal|small-caps**

CSS2: **inherit**

Initial: **normal**

Applies to: All elements

Inherited: Yes

Supported: [IE4, IE5]

Specifies whether or not a font is a small-caps font.

font-weight

CSS1: **normal|bold|bolder|lighter|100|200|300|400|500|600|700|800|900**

CSS2: **inherit**

Initial: **normal**

Applies to: All elements

Inherited: Yes

Supported: [IE3, IE4, IE5, NS4]

Indicates the weight of a font, such as normal or bold.

TIP: *You'll find a complete listing of the CSS1 specification at **www.w3.org/TR/REC-CSS1** and a complete listing of the CSS2 specification at **www.w3.org/TR/REC-CSS2/**.*

What List Properties Are Available?

There are a huge number of style properties available. Here are the properties that you use with lists in CSS1 and CSS2.

list-style

CSS1: [**<list-style-type>||<list-style-position>||<list-style-image>**]

CSS2: **inherit**

Initial: Not defined

Applies to: List items

Inherited: Yes

Supported: [IE4, IE5]

Sets the **list-style-type**, **list-style-image**, and **list-style-position** properties at the same time. This **list-style** property is a shorthand property.

list-style-image

CSS1: **<uri>**|none

CSS2: **inherit**

Initial: None

Applies to: List items

Inherited: Yes

Supported: [IE4, IE5]

Sets the image that will be used as the list item marker.

list-style-position

CSS1: **inside|outside**

CSS2: **inherit**

Initial: **outside**

Applies to: List items

Inherited: Yes

Supported: [IE4, IE5]

Indicates the position of the list item marker.

list-style-type

CSS1: **disc|circle|square|decimal|decimal-leading-zero|lower-roman|upper-roman|lower-alpha|upper-alpha|**none

CSS2: **lower-greek|lower-latin|upper-latin|hebrew|armenian|georgian|cjk-ideographic|hiragana|katakana|hiragana-iroha|katakana-iroha|inherit**

Initial: **disc**

Applies to: List items

Inherited: Yes

Supported: [IE4, IE5, NS4]

Indicates the appearance of the list item marker if the **list-style-image** property has the value **none** (the default) or if the image pointed to by the URI in that property cannot be displayed.

TIP: *You'll find a complete listing of the CSS1 specification at **www.w3.org/TR/REC-CSS1** and a complete listing of the CSS2 specification at **www.w3.org/TR/REC-CSS2/**.*

What Text Properties Are Available?

One of the main reasons people use styles is to format text. There are a number of style properties available for text, and they are listed here.

letter-spacing

CSS1: **normal|<length>**

CSS2: **inherit**

Initial: **normal**

Applies to: All elements

Inherited: Yes

Supported: [IE4, IE5]

Sets the spacing behavior between text characters.

line-height

CSS1: normal|<number>|<length>|<percentage>

CSS2: inherit

Initial: normal

Applies to: All elements

Inherited: Yes

Supported: [IE3, IE4, IE5, NS4]

Specifies the minimal height of the element's box.

text-align

CSS1: left|right|center|justify

CSS2: <string>|inherit

Initial: Varies

Applies to: Block-level elements

Inherited: Yes

Supported: [IE3, IE4, IE5, NS4]

Sets how the content of a block is aligned: left, right, center, or justified. In CSS2, you can specify a string to align the text on.

text-decoration

CSS1: None|[underline||overline||line-through||blink]

CSS2: inherit

Initial: None

Applies to: All elements

Inherited: No

Supported: [IE3, IE4, IE5, NS4]

Sets the decorations that are added to the text of an element, such as underlining, overlining, and line-through (that is, strikethrough).

text-indent

CSS1: <length>l<percentage>

CSS2: inherit

Initial: 0

Applies to: Block-level elements

Inherited: Yes

Supported: [IE3, IE4, IE5, NS4]

Sets the indentation of the first line of text in a block.

text-shadow

CSS2: Nonel[<color>ll<length><length><length>?,]*[<color>ll<length> <length><length>?]linherit

Initial: None

Applies to: All elements

Inherited: No

Supported: [IE5]

Specifies a (comma separated) list of shadow effects that should be applied to text in the element.

vertical-align

CSS1: **baselinelsublsuperltopltext-toplmiddlelbottomltext-bottoml** **<percentage>l<length>**

CSS2: **inherit**

Initial: **baseline**

Applies to: Inline-level and table cell elements

Inherited: No

Supported: [IE4, IE5]

Sets the vertical positioning of text in the element.

white-space

CSS1: **normal|pre|nowrap**

CSS2: **inherit**

Initial: **normal**

Applies to: Block-level elements

Inherited: Yes

Supported: [NS4]

Sets how white space inside the element is handled.

word-spacing

CSS1: **normal|<length>**

CSS2: **inherit**

Initial: **normal**

Applies to: All elements

Inherited: Yes

Supported: [None]

Sets the spacing behavior between words.

TIP: *You'll find a complete listing of the CSS1 specification at **www.w3.org/TR/REC-CSS1** and a complete listing of the CSS2 specification at **www.w3.org/TR/REC-CSS2/**.*

What Table Properties Are Available?

You can apply CSS styles to tables as of CSS2. The table properties follow.

border-collapse

CSS2: **collapse|separate|inherit**

Initial: **collapse**

Applies to: Table and inline table elements

9. Working With
Style Sheets

Inherited: Yes

Supported: [IE5]

Sets a table's border model.

border-spacing

CSS2: **<length><length>?|inherit**

Initial: 0

Applies to: Table and inline table elements

Inherited: Yes

Supported: [None]

Sets the distance that separates adjacent cell borders.

column-span, row-span

CSS2: **<integer>|inherit**

Initial: 1

Applies to: Table cells, table columns, and table-column-group elements

Inherited: No

Supported: [None]

Sets the number of columns or rows spanned by a cell.

empty-cells

CSS2: **show|hide|inherit**

Initial: **show**

Applies to: Table cell elements

Inherited: Yes

Supported: [None]

Controls the drawing of borders around cells that have no visible content.

table-layout

CSS2: **auto|fixed|inherit**

Initial: **auto**

Applies to: Table and inline table elements

Inherited: No

Supported: [IE5]

Sets the algorithm used to lay out table cells, rows, and columns.

TIP: *You'll find a complete listing of the CSS1 specification at **www.w3.org/TR/REC-CSS1** and a complete listing of the CSS2 specification at **www.w3.org/TR/REC-CSS2/**.*

What Visual Effects Properties Are Available?

Visual effects are new in CSS2 and describe how elements are drawn. The visual effects properties in CSS2 are listed here.

clip

CSS2: **<shape>|auto|inherit**

Initial: **auto**

Applies to: Block-level and replaced elements

Inherited: No

Supported: [IE5]

Sets the clipping region of an element (the clipping region specifies what part of an element is visible).

overflow

CSS2: **visible|hidden|scroll|auto|inherit**

Initial: **visible**

Applies to: Block-level and replaced elements

Inherited: No

Supported: [IE5]

Indicates if the content of a block-level element is clipped when it overflows the element's box.

9. Working With Style Sheets

visibility

CSS2: **visible|hidden|collapse|inherit**

Initial: **inherit**

Applies to: All elements

Inherited: No

Supported: [IE5]

Indicates if the element is displayed.

TIP: *You'll find a complete listing of the CSS1 specification at **www.w3.org/TR/REC-CSS1** and a complete listing of the CSS2 specification at **www.w3.org/TR/REC-CSS2/**.*

Using **<SPAN>** To Apply Styles

Often you want to apply styles not to whole blocks like paragraphs, but rather to just a word or a few words. To mark an inline part of the page to apply styles to, you can use the **<SPAN>** element (introduced in Chapter 3), which supports both the **STYLE** and **CLASS** attributes. Here's an example showing how to use **<SPAN>**:

```
<HTML>
    <HEAD>
        <TITLE>
            Styling Text
        </TITLE>

        <STYLE>
            P {font-size: 18pt; font-style: italic; font-family:
                Arial, Helvetica; text-align: center}
        </STYLE>
    </HEAD>

    <BODY>
        <CENTER>
            <H1>
                Styling Text
            </H1>
        </CENTER>
```

```
        <P>
                Here is some text displayed in italics and
                <SPAN STYLE="font-weight: bold">bold</SPAN>,
                as well as
                <SPAN STYLE="text-decoration: underline">
                underlined</SPAN>, in Arial font.
    </BODY>
</HTML>
```

See the next section to see how to use the **<DIV>** element to select HTML blocks (as opposed to the inline selections you use with **<SPAN>**).

Using **<DIV>** To Apply Styles

You can use **<SPAN>** to mark smaller, inline sections of HTML (see the previous section), but for longer blocks of HTML, you usually use **<DIV>** (introduced in Chapter 3). The **<DIV>** element supports the **STYLE** and **CLASS** attributes you need for styles; here's an example showing how to use **<DIV>**:

```
<HTML>
    <HEAD>
        <TITLE>
            Using the &lt;DIV&gt; tag
        </TITLE>
    </HEAD>

    <BODY>

        <DIV ALIGN="LEFT">
            Manager
            <BR>
            SlowPoke Products, Inc.
            <BR>
            Languid, TX
        </DIV>

        <P>
            Dear You:
        <DIV ALIGN="CENTER" STYLE="color: red; font-style: italic">
            When are you going to ship my order?
        </DIV>
```

```
<DIV ALIGN="RIGHT">
    <P>
    President
    <BR>
    NeedItNow, Inc.
    <BR>
    Speedy, CO
</DIV>

</BODY>
</HTML>
```

Applying Styles To Text: Bold, Italic, And Underlined

"Arrgh," says the novice programmer, "I just can't get my text displayed in bold! You use the **font-style** property to do that, don't you?" "Sorry," you say, " use the **font-weight** property." "Well, then," the NP says, "underlining—you use **font-style** for underlining, right?" "Sorry," you say, "use **text-decoration**." "Arrgh!" says the NP.

Setting text styles is one of the more important aspects of cascading style sheets, but the process is not straightforward. For instance, in the following example, you'll notice that you use:

- **font-family**—To set the font face.

- **font-size**—To set the font size.

- **font-style**—To make text italic.

- **font-weight**—To make text bold.

- **text-align**—To center the text.

- **text-decoration**—To underline the text.

Here's what the example looks like:

```
<HTML>
    <HEAD>
        <TITLE>
            Styling Text
        </TITLE>

        <STYLE>
            P {font-size: 18pt; font-style: italic; font-family:
                Arial, Helvetica; text-align: center}
```

```
            </STYLE>
    </HEAD>

    <BODY>
        <CENTER>
            <H1>
                Styling Text
            </H1>
        </CENTER>
        <P>
            Here is some text displayed in italics and
            <SPAN STYLE="font-weight: bold">bold</SPAN>,
            as well as
            <SPAN STYLE="text-decoration: underline">
            underlined</SPAN>, in Arial font.
    </BODY>
</HTML>
```

You can see the results of this HTML in Figure 9.9.

TIP: By the way, if you don't like underlined hyperlinks, just set **text-decoration** to **none**.

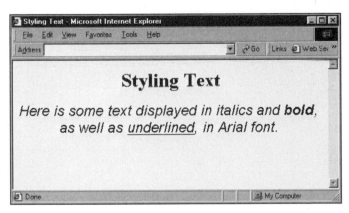

Figure 9.9   Applying styles to text.

Applying Styles To Fonts: Font, Font Size, Font Style, Font Weight

"Hm," says the novice programmer, "I just can't get this business about setting font properties right. How do you do it?" "Better pull up a chair," you say, "and get some coffee." "Uh oh," says the NP.

Here are the properties you use with fonts:

- **font-family**—Specifies the actual font, like Arial or Helvetica. If you want to list alternative fonts in case the target computer is missing your first choice, specify them as a comma separated list (for example, **{font-family: Arial, Helvetica}**).

- **font-size**—Refers to the size of the font.

- **font-stretch**—Indicates the desired amount of condensing or expansion in the letters used to draw the text.

- **font-style**—Specifies whether the text is to be rendered using a normal, italic, or oblique face.

- **font-variant**—Indicates if the text is to be rendered using the normal letters for lowercase characters or rendered using small-cap letters for lowercase characters.

- **font-weight**—Refers to the boldness or lightness of the glyphs used to render the text, relative to other fonts in the same font family.

- **line-height**—Indicates the height given to each line.

Here's an example putting font properties to work:

```
<HTML>
    <HEAD>
        <TITLE>
            Setting Font Styles
        </TITLE>
        <STYLE type="text/css">
            BODY {font-style: italic; font-variant: normal;
            font-weight: bold; font-size: 12pt;
            line-height: 10pt; font-family: arial, helvetica;
            text-align: center}
        </STYLE>
    </HEAD>

    <BODY>
        <H1>Setting Font Styles</H1>
        <BR>
        This text has been styled!
    </BODY>
</HTML>
```

The results of this HTML appear in Figure 9.10.

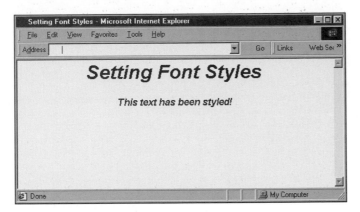

Figure 9.10   Applying styles to fonts.

There's a shortcut property you can use to set the **font-family, font-size, font-style**, **font-variant**, **font-weight**, and **line-height** properties all once—the **font** property. You just specify values for all of these properties in this order separating the **font-size** and **line-height** values with a forward slash (/) and listing all values without commas (except between font family names if you list more than one). Here's how the previous example looks using the **font** shorthand property:

```
<HTML>
    <HEAD>
        <TITLE>
            Setting Font Styles
        </TITLE>
        <STYLE type="text/css">
            BODY {font: italic normal bold 12pt/10pt arial,
            helvetica; text-align: center}
        </STYLE>
    </HEAD>

    <BODY>
        <H1>Setting Font Styles</H1>
        <BR>
        This text has been styled!
    </BODY>
</HTML>
```

In fact, you don't have to specify all values because the **font** property will leave the defaults intact for those properties you don't assign. Most browsers can also tolerate the list of values out of order. For example, this HTML:

```
<HTML>
    <HEAD>
        <TITLE>
            Setting Font Styles
        </TITLE>
        <STYLE type="text/css">
            BODY {font-family: arial, helvetica;
            font-size: 10pt; font-weight: bold}
        </STYLE>
    </HEAD>

    <BODY>
        <H1>Setting Font Styles</H1>
        <BR>
        This text has been styled!
    </BODY>
</HTML>
```

gives the same result as this HTML:

```
<HTML>
    <HEAD>
        <TITLE>
            Setting Font Styles
        </TITLE>
        <STYLE type="text/css">
            BODY {font: bold 10pt arial, helvetica}
        </STYLE>
    </HEAD>

    <BODY>
        <H1>Setting Font Styles</H1>
        <BR>
        This text has been styled!
    </BODY>
</HTML>
```

TIP: *As a last resort, you can assign a generic font family to **font-family** to use in case the user's computer doesn't have the one you specified. The browser will select a font family that's similar. Generic font families include **serif**, **sans-serif**, **cursive**, **fantasy**, and **monospace**.*

Setting Colors And Backgrounds

"Darn," says the novice programmer, "all I want to do is create headings that are white on black instead of black on white. How can I do it?" "It's not hard," you say, "sit down and we'll go through it."

Here are the properties you use to set color and backgrounds:

- **color**—Sets the foreground color.
- **background-color**—Sets the background color.
- **background-image**—Sets the background image.
- **background-repeat**—Specifies if the background image should be tiled.
- **background-attachment**—Specifies if the background scrolls with the rest of the document.
- **background-position**—Sets the initial position of the background.

In this next example, I'm styling both the background and foreground of a document:

```
<IITML>
    <HEAD>
        <TITLE>
            Using the &lt;DIV&gt; tag
        </TITLF>
    </HEAD>

    <BODY STYLE="background-color: #AAFFFF">

        <DIV ALIGN="LEFT">
            Manager
            <BR>
            SlowPoke Products, Inc.
            <BR>
            Languid, TX
        </DIV>

        <P>
            Dear You:
            <DIV ALIGN="CENTER" STYLE="color: red; font-style: italic">
                When are you going to ship my order?
            </DIV>

            <DIV ALIGN="RIGHT">
```

```
              <P>
              President
              <BR>
              NeedItNow, Inc.
              <BR>
              Speedy, CO
           </DIV>

     </BODY>
</HTML>
```

Here's another example that we saw in the beginning of this chapter:

```
<TABLE BORDER="2">
    <TR>
        <TH STYLE="background-color: rgb(255, 0, 0)">Tic</TH>
        <TH STYLE="background-color: rgb(255, 0, 0)">Tac</TH>
        <TH STYLE="background-color: rgb(255, 0, 0)">Toe</TH>
    </TR>
    <TR>
        <TD STYLE="background-color: rgb(255, 255, 255)">X</TD>
        <TD STYLE="background-color: rgb(0, 0, 0); color:
           rgb(255, 255, 255)">
           0
        </TD>
        <TD STYLE="background-color: rgb(255, 255, 255)">X</TD>
    </TR>
    <TR>
        <TD STYLE="background-color: rgb(0, 0, 0); color:
           rgb(255, 255, 255)">
           0
        </TD>
        <TD STYLE="background-color: rgb(255, 255, 255)">X</TD>
        <TD STYLE="background-color: rgb(0, 0, 0); color:
           rgb(255, 255, 255)">
           0
        </TD>
    </TR>
    <TR>
        <TD STYLE="background-color: rgb(255, 255, 255)">X</TD>
        <TD STYLE="background-color: rgb(0, 0, 0); color:
           rgb(255, 255, 255)">
           0
        </TD>
```

```
            <TD STYLE="background-color: rgb(255, 255, 255)">X</TD>
        </TR>
</TABLE>
```

You can see the results of this HTML in Figure 9.5. Here's another example. In this case, I'm styling **<H1>** elements to have a white foreground and a black background:

```
<HTML>
    <HEAD>
        <TITLE>
            Setting Colors And Backgrounds
        </TITLE>
        <STYLE type="text/css">
            H1 {background: black; color: white; text-align: center}
        </STYLE>
    </HEAD>

    <BODY>
        <H1>Setting Colors And Backgrounds</H1>
    </BODY>
</HTML>
```

You can see the results in Figure 9.11, which shows the box for the **<H1>** element quite clearly.

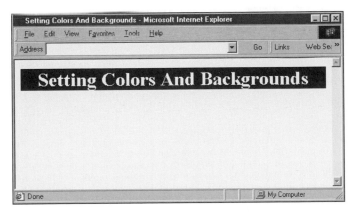

Figure 9.11   Applying background styles to text.

Applying Styles To Margins, Indentations, And Alignments

"Jeez," says the novice programmer, "I just can't get this text indented. How do I do it?" "With properties like **margin-left**," you say, "and a few others."

Here are the properties you use to work with margins, indentations, and alignments:

- **margin-left**—Sets the left margin.
- **margin-right**—Sets the right margin.
- **margin-top**—Sets the top margin.
- **text-indent**—Sets the indentation of text.
- **text-align**—Sets the alignment of text.

And here's an example showing how to put some of these properties to work:

```
<HTML>
    <HEAD>
        <TITLE>
            Setting Margins And Alignments
        </TITLE>

        <STYLE type="text/css">
            BODY {margin-left: 10px}
            H1 {text-align: center}
            P {text-indent: 40px}
        </STYLE>

    </HEAD>

    <BODY>
        <H1>Setting Margins And Alignments</H1>
        <P>
            This text has been indented!
    </BODY>
</HTML>
```

You can see the result of this HTML in Figure 9.12.

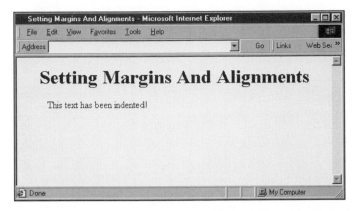

Figure 9.12   Applying alignment and indentation styles to text.

Applying Styles To Hyperlinks

"What about hyperlinks?" the novice programmer asks, "How can you style them? You can't just style the **<A>** element with one entry, can you? What about visited links, what about active links? It's impossible!" "Take it easy, NP," you say, "there's a way; you just use properties like **A:link** and **A:visited**."

You can specify styles for hyperlinks using these terms:

• **A:link**—Hyperlinks as they originally appear.

• **A:visited**—Hyperlinks that have been visited.

• **A:hover**—Hyperlinks that have the mouse over them (Internet Explorer only).

• **A:active**—Hyperlinks that are active, that is, being clicked.

Here's an example. In this case, I'm setting the color of hyperlinks to red, visited links to blue, links with the mouse over them to yellow, and active links to green:

```
<HTML>
    <HEAD>
        <TITLE>This is a Web page!</TITLE>
        <STYLE type="text/css">
            BODY {background: white; color: black}
            A:link {color: red}
            A:visited {color: blue}
            A:hover {color: yellow}
            A:active {color: green}
```

9. Working With Style Sheets

```
            </STYLE>
    </HEAD>

    <BODY>
        Welcome to my page!
        If you don't like it, you can go to
        <A HREF="http://www.w3c.org">W3C</A>.
    </BODY>
</HTML>
```

Applying Styles To Lists

Here are the properties you typically use with lists:

- **list-style-image**—Sets the image that will be used as the list item marker. Internet Explorer only.

- **list-style-type**—Sets the appearance of the list item marker, such as disc, circle, square, decimal, lowercase Roman, uppercase Roman, and others.

In this example, I'm setting the marker in front of each list item in an unordered list to a square using **list-style-type**:

```
<HTML>

    <HEAD>
        <TITLE>
            Setting List Styles
        </TITLE>

        <STYLE>
            LI {list-style-type: square}
        </STYLE>
    </HEAD>

    <BODY>

        <H1 ALIGN=CENTER>
            Setting List Styles
        </H1>

        Here are some items to consider when buying a computer:
        <UL>
            <LI> Speed
```

```
            <LI> Cost
            <LI> RAM
            <LI> Disk space
            <LI> CD ROM speed
        </UL>

    </BODY>

</HTML>
```

You can see the results of this HTML in Figure 9.13.

Here's another example; this time, I'm making an ordered list use uppercase letters using **list-style-type**:

```
<HTML>

    <HEAD>
        <TITLE>
            Setting Ordered List Styles
        </TITLE>

        <STYLE>
            LI {list-style-type: upper-alpha}
        </STYLE>
    </HEAD>

    <BODY>

        <H1 ALIGN=CENTER>
            Setting Ordered List Styles
```

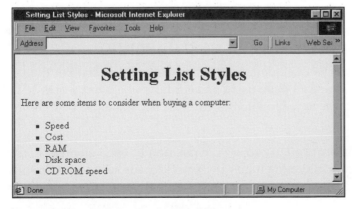

Figure 9.13   Setting an unordered list style.

```
    </H1>

    Here are some items to consider when buying a computer:
    <OL>
        <LI> Speed
        <LI> Cost
        <LI> RAM
        <LI> Disk space
        <LI> CD ROM speed
    </OL>

    </BODY>

</HTML>
```

You can see the results of this HTML in Figure 9.14.

Figure 9.14   Setting an ordered list style.

Positioning Elements Using Styles: Absolute Positioning

The novice programmer is back and asks, "I understand you can set the actual position of elements in a Web page using styles—how does that work?" "There are two main ways," you say knowingly, "you can use absolute positioning or relative positioning."

You can use the **position** property to set the position of each element in a Web page. I'll take a look at positioning items absolutely in this section and relatively in the next section. Here are the properties you usually use when working with positioning:

- **position**—Can hold values like **absolute** and **relative**.
- **top**—Offset of the top of the element's box.
- **bottom**—Offset of the bottom of the element's box.
- **left**—Offset of the left edge of the element's box.
- **right**—Offset of the right edge of the element's box.

In this example, I set **position** to **absolute**, and then specify the **top** and **left** properties for three **<DIV>** elements, each of which has an image and text:

```
<HTML>

    <HEAD>
        <TITLE>
            Absolute Positioning
        </TITLE>
    </HEAD>

    <BODY>

        <H1 ALIGN="CENTER">
            Absolute Positioning
        </H1>

        <DIV STYLE=
            "position:absolute; left:50; top:60; border-width: thick">
            <IMG SRC="FLOWER1.JPG" WIDTH=85 HEIGHT=129>
            <BR>
            Flower 1
        </DIV>


        <DIV STYLE=
            "position:absolute; left:200; top:90; border-width: thick">
            <IMG SRC="FLOWER2.JPG" WIDTH=85 HEIGHT=129>
            <BR>
            Flower 2
        </DIV>


        <DIV STYLE="position:absolute; left:350; top:120;
            border-width: thick">
            <IMG SRC="FLOWER3.JPG" WIDTH=85 HEIGHT=129>
            <BR>
            Flower 3
        </DIV>
```

```
        </BODY>

</HTML>
```

You can see the results of this HTML in Figure 9.15. As you can see, I've positioned the **<DIV>** elements and given them a border. You can also position elements in a relative way—see the next section.

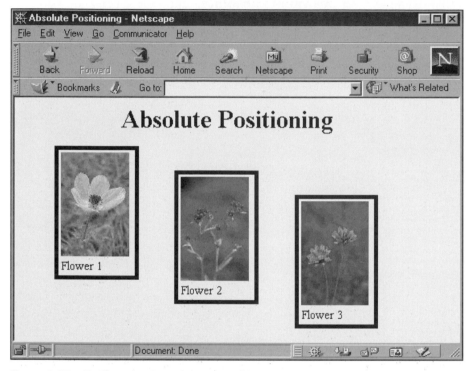

Figure 9.15   Setting absolute element positions.

Positioning Elements Using Styles: Relative Positioning

In addition to absolute positioning—see the previous section—you can also use relative positioning. When you use relative positioning, elements are positioned relative to the location they would have had in the normal flow of elements in the Web browser.

Here are the properties you usually use when working with positioning:

- **position**—Can hold values like **absolute** and **relative**.

- **top**—Offset of the top of the element's box.

- **bottom**—Offset of the bottom of the element's box.

- **left**—Offset of the left edge of the element's box.

- **right**—Offset of the right edge of the element's box.

To position items in a relative way, you set **position** to **relative**. You can also set the other properties to indicate the new relative position. In this example, I'm moving some text up five pixels and other text down five pixels from the normal position at which the browser would place this text:

```
<HTML>

    <HEAD>
        <TITLE>
            Relative Positioning
        </TITLE>
    </HEAD>

    <BODY>

        <H1 ALIGN="CENTER">
            Relative Positioning
        </H1>
        This text goes
        <SPAN STYLE="position: relative; top: -5">up</SPAN>and
        <SPAN STYLE="position: relative; top: 5">down</SPAN>,
        as you can see.

    </BODY>

</HTML>
```

You can see the results of this HTML in Figure 9.16, where, as you can see, some of the text is positioned higher and some lower than the rest, just as we designed it.

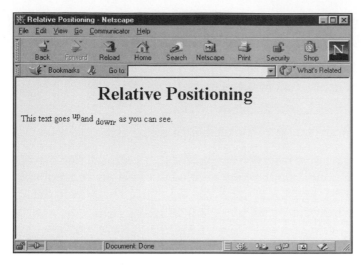

Figure 9.16   Setting relative element positions.

Chapter 10

Essential JavaScript

In Depth

These days, knowing how to use JavaScript is becoming more and more of a necessity for HTML programmers, especially with the introduction of dynamic HTML, which relies on it. This chapter and Chapter 11 are all about JavaScript and using it to make your Web pages come alive.

What Is JavaScript?

JavaScript, originally supported by Netscape Navigator, is the most popular Web scripting language today. JavaScript lets you embed programs right in your Web pages and run these programs using the Web browser. You place these programs in a **<SCRIPT>** element, usually within the **<HEAD>** element. If you want the script to write directly to the Web page, place it in the **<BODY>** element.

In this example, I'm writing the text "Welcome to JavaScript!" directly into a Web page when that Web page is first displayed by the browser (we'll see more about how this works in Chapter 11):

```
<HTML>
    <HEAD>
        <TITLE>
            Welcome To JavaScript
        </TITLE>


    </HEAD>

<BODY>
        <SCRIPT LANGUAGE="JavaScript">
        <!--
            document.writeln("Welcome to JavaScript!")
        //-->
        </SCRIPT>

        <CENTER>
            <H1>
                Welcome To JavaScript!
            </H1>
```

```
        </CENTER>

    </BODY>

</HTML>
```

You can see the results of this HTML in Figure 10.1. The JavaScript program wrote the text you see in the upper-left corner. As you can see, one thing JavaScript lets you do is write your Web pages on the fly, which is a powerful feature.

So what's going on in the previous example? First, I use the **<SCRIPT>** element to embed the JavaScript program into the page. Note that I set the **<SCRIPT>** element's **LANGUAGE** attribute to "JavaScript" to indicate to the browser which scripting language I'm using:

```
<HTML>
    <HEAD>
        <TITLE>
            Welcome To JavaScript
        </TITLE>

    </HEAD>

    <BODY>

        <SCRIPT LANGUAGE="JavaScript">
        .
        .
        .
        </SCRIPT>
```

Figure 10.1   Our first JavaScript example.

```
            <CENTER>
                <H1>
                    Welcome To JavaScript!
                </H1>
            </CENTER>

        </BODY>

</HTML>
```

Next, I'll enclose the actual JavaScript in an HTML comment. Why is this a good idea? Recall that browsers that can't handle an HTML tag just display the contents of the tag as plain text in a Web page. If a browser can't handle JavaScript, it'll display the JavaScript code directly in the Web page. To avoid this, place the actual JavaScript in the **<SCRIPT>** element in an HTML comment like this:

```
<HTML>
    <HEAD>
        <TITLE>
            Welcome To JavaScript
        </TITLE>

    </HEAD>

    <BODY>

        <SCRIPT LANGUAGE="JavaScript">
        <!--
            .
            .
            .
        //-->
        </SCRIPT>

        <CENTER>
            <H1>
                Welcome To JavaScript!
            </H1>
        </CENTER>

    </BODY>

</HTML>
```

Now I'm ready to add the actual JavaScript. In this case, I'll use the JavaScript expression **document.writeln** to write the text "Welcome to JavaScript!" to the Web page:

```
<HTML>
    <HEAD>
        <TITLE>
            Welcome To JavaScript
        </TITLE>

    </HEAD>

    <BODY>

        <SCRIPT LANGUAGE="JavaScript">
        <!--
            document.writeln("Welcome to JavaScript!")
        //-->
        </SCRIPT>

        <CENTER>
            <H1>
                Welcome To JavaScript!
            </H1>
        </CENTER>

    </BODY>

</HTML>
```

And that's all it takes; that's our first line of JavaScript: **document. writeln("Welcome to JavaScript!")**. As you can see, JavaScript is just embedded text in the Web page—the Web browser reads, interprets, and runs that script.

Despite its name, JavaScript is different from Java both in syntax and in use. Java is a separate language that you compile to create *bytecode* files, and those files, which the browser can run, are stored separately from Web pages. JavaScript, on the other hand, is stored directly as text in the Web page, making it very easy to work with. In this chapter and Chapter 11, we're going to see how to write JavaScript in Web pages.

Because JavaScript is implemented in Web browsers, you might expect, knowing the big two, that the actual implementation of JavaScript in each might differ, and you'd be quite right. Netscape Navigator's implementation of JavaScript is a pure one, and you can find documentation about Netscape Navigator's JavaScript at **http://developer.netscape.com/tech/javascript/index.html**. In fact, Netscape is helping to pioneer server-side JavaScript, which actually runs on the server, not in the Web browser. You can find Netscape's documentation for server-side JavaScript at **http://developer.netscape.com/docs/manuals/enterprise/wrijsap/index.htm**.

On the other hand, Microsoft's implementation of JavaScript differs slightly and extends the Netscape standards. In fact, Internet Explorer's implementation of JavaScript is actually called JScript. You can find the documentation for JScript at **http://msdn.microsoft.com/scripting/default.htm?/scripting/jscript/techinfo/jsdocs.htm**.

NOTE: *Microsoft also has a competing scripting language, VBScript, which runs in Web browsers and is based on Microsoft's Visual Basic language. However, VBScript hasn't gained much popularity over the years, at least not yet. JavaScript rules in this arena. You can find more about VBScript, which is only supported in Internet Explorer, at **www.microsoft.com/vbscript/us/techinfo/vbsdocs.htm**.*

Isn't there a JavaScript standard that will settle the dispute between browsers? Actually, there is, and it was created by the European Computer Manufacturers Association (ECMA) in Geneva, Switzerland. You can find the current standard for JavaScript at **www.ecma.ch/stand/ecma-262.htm** and **www.ecma.ch/stand/ecma-290.htm**. In fact, many people treat the official name of JavaScript as ECMAScript, but that name hasn't quite caught on. Netscape Navigator's version of JavaScript is ECMA compliant.

As you might expect, there is an incredible number of JavaScript resources on the Web—just search for the word JavaScript and you'll be deluged with information. Here's a set of resources to get you started:

- *http://home.netscape.com/eng/mozilla/3.0/handbook/javascript/index.html*—Netscape's guide to JavaScript
- *http://javascript.internet.com*—Cut-and-paste scripts

- ***www.infohiway.com/javascript/***—Ready-to-use scripts

- ***www.jsworld.com***—Examples and archives of JavaScript

- ***www.webteacher.com/javascript/***—Tutorial of JavaScript

Before actually digging into JavaScript programming, it's a good idea to get an overview of where we're going, so I'll take a look at the bigger picture now.

JavaScript Objects

JavaScript is an *object-oriented* language. The term object-oriented might make you nervous, but in fact using objects makes JavaScript programming tremendously easier. As far as we're concerned here, an object just refers to some aspect of the Web browser, which gives us access to that aspect.

For example, JavaScript comes with a number of predefined objects, such as the **document** object we saw in the first example in this chapter. The **document** object refers to the body of the current page in the browser, giving you an easy way to access the HTML in that page. In fact, I used the **writeln** (*write line*) *method* of that object to write the text "Welcome to JavaScript" to the current Web page like this:

```
<SCRIPT LANGUAGE="JavaScript">
<!--
    document.writeln("Welcome to JavaScript!")
//-->
</SCRIPT>
```

You use a method of an object to perform some *action* with that object. In the previous example, I'm writing a line of text to the document. Other methods let you display message boxes, navigate to new pages, and submit data to the Web server.

So what objects are available for use in JavaScript and what do they stand for? Here's a list of some JavaScript objects you have access to in your code:

- **document**—Corresponds to the current Web page's body. Using this object, you have access to the HTML of the page itself, including all the links, images, and anchors in it.

- **form**—Holds information about HTML forms in the current page; forms can contain buttons, text fields, and all kinds of other HTML elements. I'll take a look at these in Chapter 12.

- **frame**—Refers to a frame in the browser window.

- **history**—Holds the record of the sites the Web browser has visited before reaching the current page. Gives you access to methods that let you move back to previous pages.

- **location**—Holds information about the location of the current Web page, such as its URL, the domain name, path, server port, and more.

- **navigator**—Refers to the browser itself, letting you determine what browser the user has.

- **window**—Refers to the current browser window.

TIP: *There are more JavaScript objects, and you can create your own objects as well. There's far more to JavaScript than we can cover in two chapters—for all the details, check out a few good JavaScript books.*

These objects come ready for you to use, but there are also other objects that you can create yourself using JavaScript's predefined *classes*. A class is like a cookie cutter for an object—it defines the object's type. We'll see how to use the **new** operator to create objects from JavaScript classes in the Immediate Solutions section "Creating JavaScript Objects". There are many other utility classes, like the **Date** and **Math** classes in which you have to create your own objects from before you can use them. We'll see how that works in the Immediate Solutions section "Creating JavaScript Objects".

There are two aspects of objects that you have to know about to be able to get anywhere in JavaScript—methods, which we've already seen, and *properties*.

Object Properties And Methods

We've seen that the **document** object refers to the current page, but how do you actually *use* such an object? Well, we've already seen one way, which is to use object methods, such as the **writeln** method to write text to the Web page. You use a method of an object by giving the object's name a dot (**.**) followed by the method name, such as **document.writeln**. Here are a few examples of methods:

- **document.write**—Writes text to the current Web page.

- **document.writeln**—Writes text to the current Web page and adds a carriage return.

- **history.go**—Navigates the Web browser to a location in the browser's history.

- **window.alert**—Displays an alert dialog box.

- **window.open**—Opens a new browser window.

As you can see, these methods provide a lot of ready-made power for you to work with the browser interactively. Besides performing actions with objects using methods, you can also read and change settings in those objects using *properties*. A property holds some setting of an object. For example, the **document.linkcolor** property holds the color of unvisited hyperlinks in the current Web page, and by changing the **document.linkcolor** property, you can change that color. Here are some example properties and the objects they belong to:

- **document.bgcolor**—Background color of the current page.
- **document.fgcolor**—Foreground color of the current page.
- **document.lastmodified**—Date the page was last modified.
- **document.title**—Title of the current page.
- **location.hostname**—Name of the Internet Service Provider (ISP) host.
- **navigator.appName**—Name of the browser, which you can use to determine what browser the user has.

Object properties and methods give you access to what's going on in the browser, letting you change just about everything under programmatic control. In this chapter, we're going to master the basics of JavaScript programming, and in Chapter 11, we'll work with the built-in objects.

Besides properties and methods, there is one more very important concept in JavaScript: *events*, and that's the next topic in our JavaScript survey.

JavaScript Events

Dynamic HTML makes your Web pages come alive and allows you to respond to the user's actions. But how do you know when such an action has occurred? For example, what if you want to change the color of a Web page when the user clicks that page? To inform you when something's happened, JavaScript uses events, such as mouse clicks. When the user clicks the page, a mouse down event occurs. To handle that event, many HTML tags now support events. You use the **onMouseDown** event attribute when the mouse is clicked in a Web page's body. Here's an example showing one way of responding to such events. In this case, I'll change the document's background color to red when the mouse is clicked:

```
<HTML>

    <HEAD>
        <TITLE>
            JavaScript Event Example
        </TITLE>
```

```
        </HEAD>

        <BODY onMouseDown="document.bgColor='red'">

            <CENTER>

                <H1>
                    Click this page to turn it red!
                </H1>

            </CENTER>
        </BODY>

    </HTML>
```

I've indicated that I want to assign the predefined color red to **document.bgcolor** when the user clicks the mouse, and I do that with the JavaScript assignment **document.bgColor='red'**. The equal sign in the assignment means that I want to set **document.bgColor** to **red** (much like the way we've assigned values to attributes throughout the book). The results of this page appear in Figure 10.2 in the Internet Explorer.

TIP: *The previous example is a particularly simple one because the actual JavaScript code is in the **<BODY>** element itself. For code longer than one line, you'll usually store the code in the **<SCRIPT>** element instead, and call that code from elements like **<BODY>**. We'll see how that works in the Immediate Solutions section "Creating Functions."*

What event attributes are available? Here are the common ones—note that support for these attributes varies by browser and by tag:

- **onAbort**—Occurs when an action is aborted.
- **onBlur**—Occurs when an element loses the input focus.
- **onChange**—Occurs when data in a control, like a text field, changes.
- **onClick**—Occurs when an element is clicked.
- **onDblClick**—Occurs when an element is double-clicked.
- **onDragDrop**—Occurs when a drag-and-drop operation is undertaken.
- **onError**—Occurs when there's been a JavaScript error.
- **onFocus**—Occurs when an element gets the focus.
- **onKeyDown**—Occurs when a key goes down.
- **onKeyPress**—Occurs when a key is pressed and the key code is available.
- **onKeyUp**—Occurs when a key goes up.

- **onLoad**—Occurs when the page loads.
- **onMouseDown**—Occurs when a mouse button goes down.
- **onMouseMove**—Occurs when the mouse moves.
- **onMouseOut**—Occurs when the mouse leaves an element.
- **onMouseOver**—Occurs when the mouse moves over an element.
- **onMouseUp**—Occurs when a mouse button goes up.
- **onMove**—Occurs when an element is moved.
- **onReset**—Occurs when the user clicks the Reset button.
- **onResize**—Occurs when an element or page is resized.
- **onSelect**—Occurs when a selection takes place.
- **onSubmit**—Occurs when the user clicks the Submit button.
- **onUnload**—Occurs when a page is unloaded.

You can find out which HTML tags support what event attributes in Table 10.1 for Internet Explorer and Table 10.2 for Netscape Navigator.

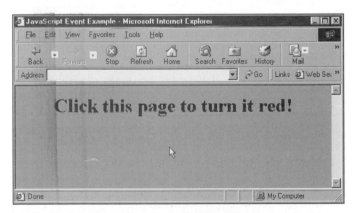

Figure 10.2   Using an event in JavaScript.

Table 10.1   Event attributes of Internet Explorer elements.

Element	Event Attributes
A	onbeforecopy, onbeforecut, onbeforeeditfocus, onbeforefocusenter, onbeforefocusleave, onbeforepaste, onblur, onclick, oncontextmenu, oncontrolselect, oncopy, oncut, ondblclick, ondrag, ondragend, ondragenter, ondragleave, ondragover, ondragstart, ondrop, onfocus, onfocusenter,

(continued)

Table 10.1   Event attributes of Internet Explorer elements (continued).

Element	Event Attributes
	onfocusleave, onhelp, onkeydown, onkeypress, onkeyup, onlosecapture, onmousedown, onmouseenter, onmouseleave, onmousemove, onmouseout, onmouseover, onmouseup, onpaste, onpropertychange, onreadystatechange, onresize, onresizeend, onresizestart, onselectstart
BODY	onafterprint, onbeforecut, onbeforefocusenter, onbeforefocusleave, onbeforepaste, onbeforeprint, onbeforeunload, onclick, oncontextmenu, oncontrolselect, oncut, ondblclick, ondrag, ondragend, ondragenter, ondragleave, ondragover, ondragstart, ondrop
BUTTON	onbeforecut, onbeforeeditfocus, onbeforefocusenter, onbeforefocusleave, onbeforepaste, onblur, onclick, oncontextmenu, oncontrolselect, oncut, ondblclick, ondragenter, ondragleave, ondragover, ondrop, onfilterchange, onfocus, onfocusenter, onfocusleave, onhelp, onkeydown, onkeypress, onkeyup, onlosecapture, onmousedown, onmouseenter, onmouseleave, onmousemove, onmouseout, onmouseover, onmouseup, onpaste, onpropertychange, onreadystatechange, onresize, onresizeend, onresizestart, onselectstart
DIV	onbeforecopy, onbeforecut, onbeforeeditfocus, onbeforefocusenter, onbeforefocusleave, onbeforepaste, onblur, onclick, oncontextmenu, oncontrolselect, oncopy, oncut, ondblclick, ondrag, ondragend, ondragenter, ondragleave, ondragover, ondragstart, ondrop, onfilterchange, onfocus, onfocusenter, onfocusleave, onhelp, onkeydown, onkeypress, onkeyup, onlayoutcomplete, onlosecapture, onmousedown, onmouseenter, onmouseleave, onmousemove, onmouseout, onmouseover, onmouseup, onpaste, onpropertychange, onreadystatechange, onresize, onresizeend, onresizestart, onscroll, onselectstart
FORM	onbeforecopy, onbeforecut, onbeforefocusenter, onbeforefocusleave, onbeforepaste, onblur, onclick, oncontextmenu, oncontrolselect, oncopy, oncut, ondblclick, ondrag, ondragend, ondragenter, ondragleave, ondragover, ondragstart, ondrop, onfocus, onfocusenter, onfocusleave, onhelp, onkeydown, onkeypress, onkeyup, onlosecapture, onmousedown, onmouseenter, onmouseleave, onmousemove, onmouseout, onmouseover, onmouseup, onpaste, onpropertychange, onreadystatechange, onreset, onresize, onresizeend, onresizestart, onselectstart, onsubmit

(continued)

Table 10.1   *Event attributes of Internet Explorer elements* (continued).

Element	Event Attributes
FRAME	onbeforefocusenter, onbeforefocusleave, onblur, oncontrolselect, onfocus, onfocusenter, onfocusleave, onresize, onresizeend, onresizestart
IFRAME	onbeforefocusenter, onbeforefocusleave, onblur, oncontrolselect, onfocus, onfocusenter, onfocusleave, onresizeend, onresizestart
IMG	onabort, onbeforecopy, onbeforecut, onbeforefocusenter, onbeforefocusleave, onbeforepaste, onblur, onclick, oncontextmenu, oncontrolselect, oncopy, oncut, ondblclick, ondrag, ondragend, ondragenter, ondragleave, ondragover, ondragstart, ondrop, onerror, onfilterchange, onfocus, onfocusenter, onfocusleave, onhelp, onload, onlosecapture, onmousedown, onmouseenter, onmouseleave, onmousemove, onmouseout, onmouseover, onmouseup, onpaste, onpropertychange, onreadystatechange, onresize, onresizeend, onresizestart, onselectstart
INPUT (button)	onbeforecut, onbeforeeditfocus, onbeforefocusenter, onbeforefocusleave, onbeforepaste, onblur, onclick, oncontextmenu, oncontrolselect, oncut, ondblclick, ondrag, ondragend, ondragenter, ondragleave, ondragover, ondragstart, ondrop, onfilterchange, onfocus, onfocusenter, onfocusleave, onhelp, onkeydown, onkeypress, onkeyup, onlosecapture, onmousedown, onmouseenter, onmouseleave, onmousemove, onmouseout, onmouseover, onmouseup, onpaste, onpropertychange, onreadystatechange, onresize, onresizeend, onresizestart, onselectstart
INPUT (checkbox)	onbeforecut, onbeforeeditfocus, onbeforefocusenter, onbeforefocusleave, onbeforepaste, onblur, onclick, oncontextmenu, oncontrolselect, oncut, ondblclick, ondrag, ondragend, ondragenter, ondragleave, ondragover, ondragstart, ondrop, onfilterchange, onfocus, onfocusenter, onfocusleave, onhelp, onkeydown, onkeypress, onkeyup, onlosecapture, onmousedown, onmouseenter, onmouseleave, onmousemove, onmouseout, onmouseover, onmouseup, onpaste, onpropertychange, onreadystatechange, onresizeend, onresizestart, onselectstart
INPUT (radio button)	onbeforecut, onbeforeeditfocus, onbeforefocusenter, onbeforefocusleave, onbeforepaste, onblur, onclick, oncontextmenu, oncontrolselect, oncut, ondblclick, ondrag,

(continued)

Table 10.1   Event attributes of Internet Explorer elements (continued).

Element	Event Attributes
	ondragend, ondragenter, ondragleave, ondragover, ondragstart, ondrop, onfilterchange, onfocus, onfocusenter, onfocusleave, onhelp, onkeydown, onkeypress, onkeyup, onlosecapture, onmousedown, onmouseenter, onmouseleave, onmousemove, onmouseout, onmouseover, onmouseup, onpaste, onpropertychange, onreadystatechange, onresizeend, onresizestart, onselectstart
INPUT (Submit button)	onbeforecut, onbeforeeditfocus, onbeforefocusenter, onbeforefocusleave, onbeforepaste, onblur, onclick, oncontextmenu, oncontrolselect, oncut, ondblclick, ondrag, ondragend, ondragenter, ondragleave, ondragover, ondragstart, ondrop, onfilterchange, onfocus, onfocusenter, onfocusleave, onhelp, onkeydown, onkeypress, onkeyup, onlosecapture, onmousedown, onmouseenter, onmouseleave, onmousemove, onmouseout, onmouseover, onmouseup, onpaste, onpropertychange, onreadystatechange, onresize, onresizeend, onresizestart, onselectstart
INPUT (text field)	onafterupdate, onbeforecut, onbeforeeditfocus, onbeforefocusenter, onbeforefocusleave, onbeforepaste, onbeforeupdate, onblur, onchange, onclick, oncontextmenu, oncontrolselect, oncut, ondblclick, ondrag, ondragend, ondragenter, ondragleave, ondragover, ondragstart, ondrop, onerrorupdate, onfilterchange, onfocus, onfocusenter, onfocusleave, onhelp, onkeydown, onkeypress, onkeyup, onlosecapture, onmousedown, onmouseenter, onmouseleave, onmousemove, onmouseout, onmouseover, onmouseup, onpaste, onpropertychange, onreadystatechange, onresize, onresizeend, onresizestart, onselect, onselectstart
LI	onbeforecopy, onbeforecut, onbeforefocusenter, onbeforefocusleave, onbeforepaste, onblur, onclick, oncontextmenu, oncontrolselect, oncopy, oncut, ondblclick, ondrag, ondragend, ondragenter, ondragleave, ondragover, ondragstart, ondrop, onfocus, onfocusenter, onfocusleave, onhelp, onkeydown, onkeypress, onkeyup, onlayoutcomplete, onlosecapture, onmousedown, onmouseenter, onmouseleave, onmousemove, onmouseout, onmouseover, onmouseup, onpaste, onpropertychange, onreadystatechange, onresize, onresizeend, onresizestart, onselectstart

(continued)

Table 10.1   Event attributes of Internet Explorer elements (continued).

Element	Event Attributes
MARQUEE	onbeforecut, onbeforeeditfocus, onbeforefocusenter, onbeforefocusleave, onbeforepaste, onblur, onbounce, oncontextmenu, oncontrolselect, oncut, ondblclick, ondrag, ondragend, ondragenter, ondragleave, ondragover, ondragstart, ondrop, onfilterchange, onfinish, onfocus, onfocusenter, onfocusleave, onhelp, onkeydown, onkeypress, onkeyup, onlosecapture, onmousedown, onmouseenter, onmouseleave, onmousemove, onmouseout, onmouseover, onmouseup, onpaste, onpropertychange, onreadystatechange, onresize, onresizeend, onresizestart, onscroll, onselectstart, onstart
OBJECT	onbeforeeditfocus, onbeforefocusenter, onbeforefocusleave, onblur, oncellchange, onclick, oncontrolselect, ondataavailable, ondatasetchanged, ondatasetcomplete, ondblclick, ondrag, ondragend, ondragenter, ondragleave, ondragover, ondragstart, ondrop, onerror, onfocus, onfocusenter, onfocusleave, onkeydown, onkeypress, onkeyup, onlosecapture, onpropertychange, onreadystatechange, onresize, onresizeend, onresizestart, onrowenter, onrowexit, onrowsdelete, onrowsinserted, onscroll, onselectstart
P	onbeforecopy, onbeforecut, onbeforefocusenter, onbeforefocusleave, onbeforepaste, onblur, onclick, oncontextmenu, oncontrolselect, oncopy, oncut, ondblclick, ondrag, ondragend, ondragenter, ondragleave, ondragover, ondragstart
PRE	onbeforecopy, onbeforecut, onbeforefocusenter, onbeforefocusleave, onbeforepaste, onblur, onclick, oncontextmenu, oncontrolselect, oncopy, oncut, ondblclick, ondrag, ondragend, ondragenter, ondragleave, ondragover, ondragstart, ondrop, onfocus, onfocusenter, onfocusleave, onhelp, onkeydown, onkeypress, onkeyup, onlosecapture, onmousedown, onmouseenter, onmouseleave, onmousemove, onmouseout, onmouseover, onmouseup, onpaste, onpropertychange, onreadystatechange, onresize, onresizeend, onresizestart, onselectstart
SELECT	onbeforecut, onbeforeeditfocus, onbeforefocusenter, onbeforefocusleave, onbeforepaste, onblur, onchange, onclick, oncontextmenu, oncontrolselect, oncut, ondblclick, ondragenter, ondragleave, ondragover, ondrop, onfocus, onfocusenter,

(continued)

Table 10.1   *Event attributes of Internet Explorer elements* (continued).

Element	Event Attributes
	onfocusleave, onhelp, onkeydown, onkeypress, onkeyup, onlosecapture, onmousedown, onmouseenter, onmouseleave, onmousemove, onmouseout, onmouseover, onmouseup, onpaste, onpropertychange, onreadystatechange, onresize, onresizeend, onresizestart, onscroll, onselectstart
SPAN	onbeforecopy, onbeforecut, onbeforeeditfocus, onbeforefocusenter, onbeforefocusleave, onbeforepaste, onblur, onclick, oncontextmenu, oncontrolselect, oncopy, oncut, ondblclick, ondrag, ondragend, ondragenter, ondragleave, ondragover, ondragstart, ondrop, onfilterchange, onfocus, onfocusenter, onfocusleave, onhelp, onkeydown, onkeypress, onkeyup, onlosecapture, onmousedown, onmouseenter, onmouseleave, onmousemove, onmouseout
TABLE	onbeforecut, onbeforeeditfocus, onbeforefocusenter, onbeforefocusleave, onbeforepaste, onblur, onclick, oncontextmenu, oncontrolselect, oncut, ondblclick, ondrag, ondragend, ondragenter, ondragleave, ondragover, ondragstart, ondrop, onfilterchange, onfocus, onfocusenter, onfocusleave, onhelp, onkeydown, onkeypress, onkeyup, onlosecapture, onmousedown, onmouseenter, onmouseleave, onmousemove, onmouseout, onmouseover, onmouseup, onpaste, onpropertychange, onreadystatechange, onresize, onresizeend, onresizestart, onscroll, onselectstart
TD	onbeforecopy, onbeforecut, onbeforeeditfocus, onbeforefocusenter, onbeforefocusleave, onbeforepaste, onblur, onclick, oncontextmenu, oncontrolselect, oncopy, oncut, ondblclick, ondrag, ondragend, ondragenter, ondragleave, ondragover, ondragstart, ondrop, onfilterchange, onfocus, onfocusenter, onfocusleave, onhelp, onkeydown, onkeypress, onkeyup, onlosecapture, onmousedown, onmouseenter, onmouseleave, onmousemove, onmouseout, onmouseover, onmouseup, onpaste, onpropertychange, onreadystatechange, onresizeend, onresizestart, onselectstart
TEXTAREA	onafterupdate, onbeforecopy, onbeforecut, onbeforeeditfocus, onbeforefocusenter, onbeforefocusleave, onbeforepaste, onbeforeupdate, onblur, onchange, onclick, oncontextmenu, oncontrolselect, oncut, ondblclick, ondrag,

(continued)

Table 10.1   *Event attributes of Internet Explorer elements* (continued).

Element	Event Attributes
	ondragend, ondragenter, ondragleave, ondragover, ondragstart, ondrop, onerrorupdate, onfilterchange, onfocus, onfocusenter, onfocusleave, onhelp, onkeydown, onkeypress, onkeyup, onlosecapture, onmousedown, onmouseenter, onmouseleave, onmousemove, onmouseout, onmouseover, onmouseup, onpaste, onpropertychange, onreadystatechange, onresize, onresizeend, onresizestart, onscroll, onselect, onselectstart

Table 10.2   *Event attributes of Netscape Navigator elements.*

Element	Event Attributes
A	onclick, onmouseout, onmouseover
BODY	onblur, onfocus, onload, onunload
DIV	none
EMBED	none
FORM	onreset, onsubmit
FRAME	none
ILAYER	none
IMG	onabort, onerror, onload
INPUT (button)	onclick
INPUT (checkbox)	onclick
INPUT (radio button)	onclick
INPUT (Submit button)	onclick
INPUT (text field)	onblur, onchange, onfocus, onselect
LAYER	onblur, onfocus, onload, onmouseout, onmouseover
LI	none
OBJECT	none
P	none
PRE	none
SELECT	onblur, onchange, onclick, onfocus
SPAN	none
TABLE	none
TD	none
TEXTAREA	onblur, onchange, onfocus, onselect

We'll see how to handle events like these when we deal with dynamic HTML in Chapter 13; for now, we'll just concentrate on the basics.

JavaScript Programming

Our overview of JavaScript has given us a hint of the power available in its use. However, we'll need a good foundation to work from, so the remainder of this chapter is all about JavaScript programming basics.

In this chapter, I'll concentrate on what you need to write JavaScript itself. In Chapter 11, we'll boost the power of JavaScript by using the built-in objects we've already seen. In the next chapter, we'll see how to work with HTML *controls*, like buttons, text fields (which you type text into), radio buttons, and more. After that, we'll launch directly into working with HTML forms and dynamic HTML.

At this point, let's look at essential JavaScript programming. For example, one of the most important parts of programming is to make decisions based on your data—in JavaScript, you can use the **if** statement to do so. In this next example, I'm comparing the numbers 5 and 3 using the **if** statement. If 5 is greater than 3, the code will display the message "Yes, 5 is greater than 3!" in a Web page:

```
<HTML>

    <HEAD>
        <TITLE>
            Using The if Statement
        </TITLE>

    </HEAD>

    <BODY>

        <SCRIPT LANGUAGE="JavaScript">

            if(5 > 3){
                document.writeln("Yes, 5 is greater than 3!")
            }

        </SCRIPT>

        <CENTER>
            <H1>
                Using The if Statement
            </H1>
```

```
        </CENTER>

    </BODY>

</HTML>
```

You can see the results in Figure 10.3, where we find that 5 is indeed greater than 3.

TIP: *If you make a mistake while developing your JavaScript code, Internet Explorer will display a dialog box indicating what the problem is, but Netscape Navigator just will not run your code. To see what the problem with the code is in Netscape Navigator, type "javascript:" in the Location box and press Enter; the browser will open a new window telling you what's wrong with the code.*

We'll see how to use statements like **if** in the Immediate Solutions section "Creating **if...else** Statements" in this chapter—and put them to work in Chapter 11. It's time to start the Immediate Solutions section, so I'll do that right now.

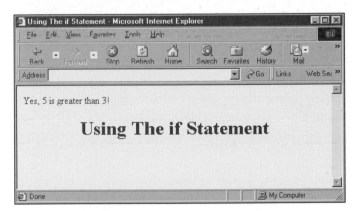

Figure 10.3   Using the JavaScript **if** statement.

Immediate Solutions

<SCRIPT>—Creating A Script

Purpose: Embeds a script, such as those written in JavaScript, JScript, or VBScript in a Web page. This element is usually included in a page's head, except when the script writes to the Web page, in which case it should go into the page's body.

Start Tag/End Tag: Required/Required

Supported: [3.2, 4, IE3, IE4, IE5, NS1, NS2, NS3, NS4]

Attributes:

- **CHARSET**—Specifies the character encoding of the script contents. Set to a Request for Comments (RFC) 2045 language character set string (the default is ISO-8859-1). [4]

- **CLASS**—Class of the element (used for rendering). [IE4, IE5]

- **DEFER**—Indicates to the browser that the script is not going to generate any document content (which means the browser can continue parsing and drawing the page). Stand-alone attribute. [4, IE4, IE5]

- **EVENT**—Gives the event the script is written for. Set to an event name. [IE4, IE5]

- **FOR**—Indicates which element is bound to the script. Set to an HTML element or element ID. [IE4, IE5]

- **ID**—Unique alphanumeric identifier for the tag, which you can use to refer to it. [IE4, IE5]

- **LANGUAGE**—Sets the scripting language. This attribute is required if the **SRC** attribute is not set and is optional otherwise. Set to the name of a scripting language, such as JavaScript or VBScript. [4, IE3, IE4, IE5, NS3, NS4]

- **SRC**—Gives an external source for the script code. Set to a URL. [4, IE3, IE4, IE5, NS3, NS4]

- **TITLE**—Holds additional information (which might be displayed in tool tips) for the element. [IE4, IE5]

- **TYPE**—Indicates the Multipurpose Internet Mail Extension (MIME) type of the scripting code. Set to an alphanumeric MIME type. [4, IE4, IE5]

The novice programmer says, "This is great! I can actually control what goes in my Web page using JavaScript. Where do I start?" You smile and say, "Probably with the **<SCRIPT>** element."

You embed JavaScript in Web pages using the **<SCRIPT>** element, which you usually place in the **<HEAD>** element, unless the script writes directly to the Web page, in which case you place it in the body of the document. We already saw this example in the In Depth section of this chapter, which writes "Welcome to JavaScript!" to the current page:

```
<HTML>
    <HEAD>
        <TITLE>
            Welcome To JavaScript
        </TITLE>

    </HEAD>

    <BODY>

        <SCRIPT LANGUAGE="JavaScript">
        <!--
            document.writeln("Welcome to JavaScript!")
        //-->
        </SCRIPT>

        <CENTER>
            <H1>
                Welcome To JavaScript!
            </H1>
        </CENTER>

    </BODY>

</HTML>
```

You can see the results of this HTML in Figure 10.1. Note that I'm specifying the type of language as JavaScript using the **<SCRIPT>** element's **LANGUAGE** attribute. Browsers are usually smart enough to figure out what scripting language you're using, but it's good practice to assign the actual name, "JavaScript", to the **LANGUAGE** attribute.

Although the **<SCRIPT>** element can contain JavaScript, what about browsers that don't handle JavaScript? See the next section for the details.

<NOSCRIPT>—Handling Browsers That Don't Handle JavaScript

Purpose: Used to add HTML for browsers that don't use JavaScript or other scripting languages.

Start Tag/End Tag: Required/Required

Supported: [4, IE4, IE5, NS3, NS4]

Attributes:

- **CLASS**—Class of the element (used for rendering). [4]

- **DIR**—Gives the direction of directionally neutral text (text that doesn't have inherent direction in which you should read it). Possible values: **LTR**: left-to-right text or table and **RTL**: right-to-left text or table. [4]

- **ID**—Unique alphanumeric identifier for the tag, which you can use to refer to it. [4, IE4, IE5]

- **LANG**—Base language used for the tag. [4]

- **STYLE**—Inline style indicating how to render the element. [4]

- **TITLE**—Holds additional information (which might be displayed in tool tips) for the element. [4]

The novice programmer says, "I'm using my favorite Web browser, Super DuperWebProKing 5.3, patch level 97, and it has a problem with JavaScript—all my scripting code appears in the page itself! My browser may be a little nonstandard." "I'll say," you reply, "looks like you'll have to hide the JavaScript from your browser."

As discussed in the In Depth section, some browsers can't handle JavaScript, so they ignore the **<SCRIPT>** tag, which means your script will appear directly in the browser as plain text. To avoid this, place your script inside an HTML comment like this:

```
<HTML>
    <HEAD>
        <TITLE>
            Welcome To JavaScript
        </TITLE>

    </HEAD>

    <BODY>
```

```
        <SCRIPT LANGUAGE="JavaScript">
        <!--
            document.writeln("Welcome to JavaScript!")
        //-->
        </SCRIPT>

        <CENTER>
            <H1>
                Welcome To JavaScript!
            </H1>
        </CENTER>

    </BODY>

</HTML>
```

NOTE: *You must make the closing comment tag a JavaScript comment by starting it with two forward slashes (//) or even JavaScript-enabled browsers will ignore your script.*

This technique takes care of hiding the script from the browser. But what if you want to indicate to users that they're missing something? You use the **<NOSCRIPT>** element. JavaScript-enabled browsers will ignore this element, but the text in it will be displayed in browsers that can't handle JavaScript. Here's how you use it:

```
<HTML>
    <HEAD>
        <TITLE>
            Welcome To JavaScript
        </TITLE>

    </HEAD>

    <BODY>

        <SCRIPT LANGUAGE="JavaScript">
        <!--
            document.writeln("Welcome to JavaScript!")
        //-->
        </SCRIPT>

        <NOSCRIPT>
            Sorry, your browser doesn't support JavaScript!
        </NOSCRIPT>
```

```
    <CENTER>
        <H1>
            Welcome To JavaScript!
        </H1>
    </CENTER>

</BODY>

</HTML>
```

TIP: It's a good idea to include a hyperlink to a non-JavaScript version of the page in the **<NOSCRIPT>** element. In fact, it's an even better idea to include the entire non-JavaScript version of the page itself in the **<NOSCRIPT>** element. Also, some browsers might not display text from elements in the **<HEAD>** element, so you might want to place **<NOSCRIPT>** outside the **<HEAD>** element.

<SERVER>—Running Server-Side JavaScript Scripts

Purpose: Embeds server-side scripts in a Web page. You use this element instead of **<SCRIPT>** for server-side scripts.

Start Tag/End Tag: Required/Required

Supported: Not applicable

Attributes:

• None

This element holds server-side JavaScript code, which is code that runs on the server. You can find Netscape's documentation for server-side JavaScript at **http://developer.netscape.com/docs/manuals/enterprise/wrijsap/index.htm**.

I'm going to stick to client-side JavaScript in this chapter, but here's a server-side example:

```
<HTML>
    <HEAD>
        <TITLE>
            Server-Side JavaScript
        </TITLE>

    </HEAD>
```

```
<BODY>

      Hello - your server's IP address is
      <SERVER>
          write(request.ip)
      </SERVER>

      <CENTER>
          <H1>
              Using Server-Side JavaScript
          </H1>
      </CENTER>

  </BODY>

</HTML>
```

Commenting Your JavaScript

Similar to HTML, you can add comments to JavaScript code using the double forward slash (*//*) notation. The JavaScript interpreter in your browser will stop reading anything on a line past *//*, so you can comment your code like this:

```
<HTML>
    <HEAD>
        <TITLE>
            Welcome To JavaScript
        </TITLE>

    </HEAD>

    <BODY>

        <SCRIPT LANGUAGE="JavaScript">
        <!--
            //Write "Welcome to JavaScript!" in the page.
            document.writeln("Welcome to JavaScript!")
        //-->
        </SCRIPT>

        <NOSCRIPT>
            Sorry, your browser doesn't support JavaScript!
        </NOSCRIPT>
```

```
<CENTER>
    <H1>
        Welcome To JavaScript!
    </H1>
</CENTER>

</BODY>

</HTML>
```

Working With Data In JavaScript

"OK," says the novice programmer, "I've gotten JavaScript to display a welcome message, but that's not too powerful. How can I start storing some data?" "Pull up a chair," you say, "and we'll go through it."

JavaScript recognizes several types of data: numbers, Boolean values, text strings, functions, and objects. Boolean data holds values of true or false, we'll discuss functions in the Immediate Solution's "Creating Functions" section, and we've already seen objects. JScript, on the other hand, recognizes six types of data: numbers, text strings, objects, Boolean values, null, and undefined. The null type simply holds a value of 0, and the undefined type indicates that the data has not been assigned a value.

So how do you store data values in JavaScript? As with other programming languages, you use *variables*. A variable is simply the name of a memory location in which you can store data and access it later. To create a variable in JavaScript, you use the **var** statement. After you've created the variable, you can store data of the type JavaScript can handle in that variable.

In this example, I'm creating a variable named **number** with the **var** statement. Next, I'm assigning that variable the value of 366 with the *assignment operator* (**=**). Now when I use the name **number**, JavaScript will replace it with the value in that variable, so I can display the number of days in the year 2000 like this:

```
<HTML>

    <HEAD>

        <TITLE>
            Creating Variables In JavaScript
        </TITLE>
```

```
    </HEAD>

    <BODY>

        <SCRIPT LANGUAGE="JavaScript">
            var number
            number = 366
            document.writeln("There are " +  number +
                " days in the year 2000.")
        </SCRIPT>

        <CENTER>
            <H1>
                Creating Variables In JavaScript
            </H1>
        </CENTER>

    </BODY>

</HTML>
```

I'm using the addition JavaScript operator (**+**) to join the value in **number** into the middle of a text string (see "Working With JavaScript Operators" in the Immediate Solutions section of this chapter). You can see the results of this code in Figure 10.4, and as you see, 366 was indeed stored in our variable.

There's a shorthand technique you should know about—you can also create a variable and assign a value to it at the same time, as in this next example:

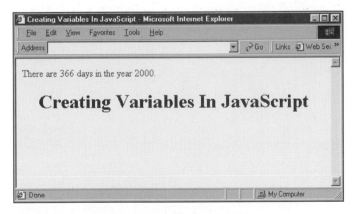

Figure 10.4   Using a variable in JavaScript.

```
var number = 366
document.writeln("There are " +  number +
    " days in the year 2000.")
```

You can store other types of data that JavaScript recognizes in variables too, such as text strings (just make sure the text string is enclosed in quotation marks). Here's an example where I'm setting the variable **greeting** to "Welcome to JavaScript!":

```
<HTML>
    <HEAD>
        <TITLE>
            Welcome To JavaScript
        </TITLE>

    </HEAD>

    <BODY>

        <SCRIPT LANGUAGE="JavaScript">
        <!--
            var greeting
            greeting = "Welcome to JavaScript!"
            document.writeln(greeting)
        //-->
        </SCRIPT>

        <CENTER>
            <H1>
                Welcome To JavaScript!
            </H1>
        </CENTER>

    </BODY>

</HTML>
```

This code produces the same display as you see in Figure 10.1.

The JavaScript convention is to use lowercase letters for variable names if they are single words, like **counter** or **index**. However, if you form a variable name by putting more than one word together, the JavaScript convention is to capitalize the first letter of each word after the first word, such as **theNumber**, **countLeftUntilCompletion**, **numberOfImages**, or **aReallyReallyReallyLong VariableName**.

Working With JavaScript Operators

"Now that I can store data in variables," the novice programmer says, "how can I work with that data? I want to do something!" You smile and say, "A good place to start is with the JavaScript operators."

Say that you wanted to add two numbers, 2 plus 2. How could you do that in JavaScript? You can use the *addition operator* (+). Here's an example showing how this works:

```
<HTML>

    <HEAD>

        <TITLE>
            Using Operators In JavaScript
        </TITLE>

    </HEAD>

    <BODY>

        <SCRIPT LANGUAGE="JavaScript">
            var number
            number = 2 + 2
            document.writeln("2 + 2 = " + number)
        </SCRIPT>

        <CENTER>
            <H1>
                Using Operators In JavaScript
            </H1>
        </CENTER>

    </BODY>

</HTML>
```

You can see the results of this code in Figure 10.5.

There are many operators available in JavaScript besides the addition operator. For instance, the increment operator (++), which adds 1 to the value in a variable. For example, if **number** holds 100, then after you've applied the increment operator to **number** like this: **number++**, **number** will hold 101.

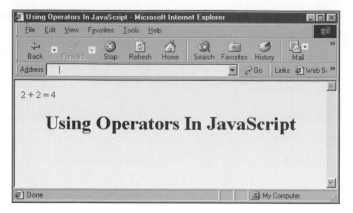

Figure 10.5   Using operators in JavaScript.

Here's the list of JavaScript operators—we'll be seeing these operators throughout this and the next few chapters:

- *Addition operator* (**+**)—Sums two numbers or concatenates two strings.

- *Assignment operator* (**=**)—Assigns a value to a variable.

- *Bitwise AND operator* (**&**)—Performs a bitwise AND on two expressions.

- *Bitwise left shift operator* (**<<**)—Shifts the bits of an expression to the left.

- *Bitwise NOT operator* (**~**)—Performs a bitwise NOT (negation) on an expression.

- *Bitwise OR operator* (l)—Performs a bitwise OR on two expressions.

- *Bitwise right shift operator* (**>>**)—Shifts the bits of an expression to the right, maintaining sign.

- *Bitwise XOR operator* (**^**)—Performs a bitwise exclusive OR on two expressions.

- *Comma operator* (**,**)—Causes two expressions to be executed sequentially.

- *Conditional (trinary) operator* (**?:**)—Executes one of two expressions depending on a condition.

- *Decrement operator* (--)—Decrements a variable by 1.

- *Division operator* (*/*)—Divides two numbers and returns a numeric result.

- *Equality operator* (**==**)—Compares two expressions to determine if they are equal.

- *Greater than operator* (**>**)—Compares two expressions to determine if one is greater than the other.

- *Greater than or equal to operator* (**>=**)—Compares two expressions to determine if one is greater than or equal to the other.

- *Identity operator* (**===**)—Compares two expressions to determine if they are equal in value and of the same data type.

- *Increment operator* (**++**)—Increments a variable by 1.

- *Inequality operator* (**!=**)—Compares two expressions to determine if they are unequal.

- *Less than operator* (**<**)—Compares two expressions to determine if one is less than the other.

- *Less than or equal to operator* (**<=**)—Compares two expressions to determine if one is less than or equal to the other.

- *Logical AND operator* (**&&**)—Performs a logical conjunction on two expressions.

- *Logical NOT operator* (**!**)—Performs logical negation on an expression.

- *Logical OR operator* (**||**)—Performs a logical disjunction on two expressions.

- *Modulus operator* (**%**)—Divides two numbers and returns the remainder.

- *Multiplication operator* (*****)—Multiplies two numbers.

- *New operator* (**new**)—Creates a new object.

- *Nonidentity operator* (**!==**)—Compares two expressions to determine if they are not equal in value or of the same data type.

- *Subtraction operator* (**-**)—Performs subtraction of two expressions.

- *Typeof operator* (**typeof**)—Returns a string that identifies the data type of an expression.

- *Unary negation operator* (**-**)—Indicates the negative value of a numeric expression.

- *Unsigned right shift operator* (**>>>**)—Performs an unsigned right shift of the bits in an expression.

There are also a number of combination assignment operators that combine assignment with another operation, such as **+=**, which adds a value and then assigns the result to the original value. For example, **variable1 += 2** adds 2 to the value in **variable1**. These operators are: **+=, -=, *=, /=, %=, &=, |=, ^=, <<=, >>=,** and **>>>=**.

A number of important operators are the *comparison operators*, such as equality (**==**) and greater than (**>**). These operators let you compare values and make decisions based on the results. How does this work? Take a look at the section coming up next for some examples.

Creating **if** Statements

The big boss appears and says, "I need a secret Web page, which I can use to check to see if the budget is still in the black." "OK," you say, "I'll use the JavaScript **if** statement." "Just make sure we're solvent," says the BB.

You use the **if** statement in JavaScript to construct a test, executing the code in the statement only if the test turns out to be true. Here's what the **if** statement looks like formally:

```
if (condition) {
    code
}
```

In this statement, *condition* is a situation that you want to check, and *code* is the code you want to execute if the condition is true. Note that you must enclose the code to execute in curly braces, **{** and **}**.

So how do you create a condition to check? You use the comparison operators, such as **<** (less than), **>** (greater than), **==** (is equal to), **<=** (is less than or equal to), or **>=** (is greater than or equal to). Here's an example showing how to check if the value in a variable named **budget** is greater than 0:

```
<HTML>

    <HEAD>

        <TITLE>
            Using The if Statement In JavaScript
        </TITLE>

    </HEAD>

    <BODY>

        <SCRIPT LANGUAGE="JavaScript">
            var budget
            budget = 52.16
            if (budget > 0) {
                document.writeln("The value in budget > 0, so the " +
                    "budget is still in the black")
            }
        </SCRIPT>
```

```
<CENTER>
    <H1>
        Using The if Statement In JavaScript
    </H1>
</CENTER>

</BODY>

</HTML>
```

You can see the results of this code in Figure 10.6.

Here are some other **if** statement examples:

```
if (number == 5) {
    document.writeln("The number is equal to 5.")
}

if (price > 2000.00) {
    document.writeln("WARNING: Price is over $2000.00.")
}
```

You can also use the AND operator (**&&**) and OR operator (**||**) to combine conditions. Here's an example:

```
if (day == 29 && month == "February") {
    document.writeln("Happy Leap Year!")
}
```

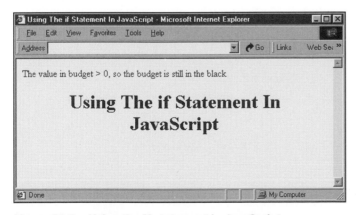

Figure 10.6   Using the **if** statement in JavaScript.

In the previous case, *both* **day == 29** *and* **month == "February"** must be true for the code in the **if** statement to be executed because I'm using the AND operator (**&&**). On the other hand, take a look at this example:

```
if (hour < 8 || hour > 17) {
    document.writeln("Sorry, we're closed.")
}
```

Here, I'm using the OR operator. If the value in **hour** is less than 8 *or* greater than 17 (using a 24-hour clock), this code displays the message "Sorry, we're closed."

Creating **if...else** Statements

You can elaborate **if** statements to include an **else** clause, and the code in the **else** statement will be executed if the condition in the **if** statement is *false*, not true. Here's how the **if...else** statement looks in general:

```
if (condition) {
    code executed if condition is true
}
else {
    code executed if condition is true
}
```

In this next example, I'm checking the value in a variable named **budget**; if it's greater than zero, the code displays the message, "The value in budget > 0, so the budget is still in the black". Otherwise, the code displays the message, "The value in budget < 0. Uh oh!":

```
<HTML>

    <HEAD>

        <TITLE>
            Using The if...else Statement In JavaScript
        </TITLE>

    </HEAD>

    <BODY>

        <SCRIPT LANGUAGE="JavaScript">
```

```
        var budget
        budget = -200000.03
        if (budget > 0) {
            document.writeln("The value in budget > 0, so the " +
                "budget is still in the black")
        }
        else {
            document.writeln("The value in budget < 0. Uh oh!")
        }
    </SCRIPT>

    <CENTER>
        <H1>
            Using The if...else Statement In JavaScript
        </H1>
    </CENTER>

    </BODY>

</HTML>
```

You can see the results of this code in Figure 10.7.

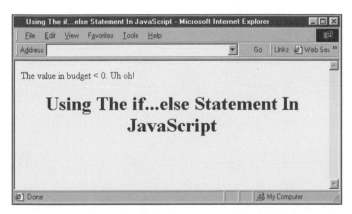

Figure 10.7   Using the **if...else** statement in JavaScript.

Creating **switch** Statements

"Jeez," says the novice programmer, "I have so many nested **if...else** statements in my code just to test for one value that I hardly know what's going on anymore." "What you need," you say judiciously, "is a **switch** statement."

The JavaScript **switch** statement is a powerful one, and appropriate if you have a lot of test cases and don't want to have to construct a long ladder of **if...else** statements. The **switch** statement lets you compare a test expression to a number of values, and if one of those values matches, the corresponding code is executed until it finds a statement named **break**. Here's what this statement looks like in general:

```
switch(test){
    case value1:
        .
        .
        .
        code executed if test matches value1
        .
        .
        .
        break;
    case value2:
        .
        .
        .
        code executed if test matches value2
        .
        .
        .
        break;
    case value3:
        .
        .
        .
        code executed if test matches value3
        .
        .
        .
        break;
    default:
        .
        .
        .
        code executed if test doesn't match any case
        .
        .
        .
        break;
}
```

Note that you list each possible value using the **case** statement. There's also a **default** statement that always matches the value you're testing, which you can use to ensure you've handled all possible test expressions.

In this next example, I'm checking a string the user typed in, which is stored in the variable **userResponse**, against various possible strings and displaying an appropriate response:

```
switch(userResponse){
    case "GO":
        document.writeln("Do you want to navigate to a new URL?")
        break;
    case "PANIC!":
        document.writeln("Do not panic, just reboot your computer.")
        break;
    case "QUIT":
        document.writeln("Are you sure you want to quit?")
        break;
    default:
        document.writeln("Sorry, did not understand your response!")
        break;
}
```

TIP: *If you omit a **break** statement, program execution will continue with the code in the next **case** statement. This is usually undesirable, but at times it's useful to create a cascading effect, allowing each case to fall through to the code in the cases following it.*

Creating **for** Loop Statements

The novice programmer appears and says, "Help! The big boss wants a table of factorials quickly!" "OK," you say, "you can use JavaScript to create one." "Great," says the NP, "what's a factorial?"

A *factorial* is the product of all the positive integers from 1 to a number you specify. For example, 6 factorial, which is written as 6!, is 6×5×4×3×2×1 = 720. To create a table of factorials, we'll have to perform many successive multiplication operations for which the **for** loop statement is renown. Here's an example showing what this statement looks like in general:

```
for (initialization; test; increment) {
    code
}
```

Using loops, you can execute code as many times as you want. Here's how it works—place a statement in the *initialization* part of the **for** loop (which typically initializes a variable to 0, also called a *loop index variable*), then test a condition in the *test* part of the loop each time the code in the loop has been executed. If the test is false, the loop ends (typically you're checking to see if the value in the loop index exceeds a specified value). On the other hand, if the test is true, the body of the loop is executed and the code in the *increment* part of the loop is executed to get the loop ready for the next iteration (typically by incrementing the loop index).

Here's an example to make this clear. In this case, I'm just setting a loop index variable, **loopIndex** to 1, printing the HTML "Hello from JavaScript
" to the Web page, then testing to make sure the value in **loopIndex** is less than or equal to 10. If it is, that value increments by 1 using the handy JavaScript increment operator (**++**), which just adds 1 to the value in the variable you apply it to. Here's what the code looks like:

```
<HTML>
    <HEAD>

        <TITLE>
            Using The for Statement
        </TITLE>

    </HEAD>

    <BODY>

        <SCRIPT LANGUAGE = JavaScript>
            for(var loopIndex = 1; loopIndex <= 10; loopIndex++){
                document.writeln("Hello from JavaScript!<BR>")
            }
        </SCRIPT>

        <CENTER>
            <H1>
                Using The for Statement
            </H1>
        </CENTER>

    </BODY>

</HTML>
```

Note that since **loopIndex** is a variable in this code, I have to declare it, so I'm using a JavaScript shortcut declaring **loopIndex** with a **var** statement right inside the initialization part of the **for** loop. This is a common practice, and I'm including it here because you'll see it often. The results of this code, which displays "Hello from JavaScript" 10 times in the Web page, appear in Figure 10.8.

Here's the example that the big boss wanted; this code displays a table of factorials. It's easy to understand if you bear in mind that **loopIndex**, the loop index variable, is just another variable in the code, which means you have access to the value in it just by referring to it by name:

```
<HTML>
    <HEAD>

        <TITLE>
            Using The for Statement
        </TITLE>

    </HEAD>

    <BODY>

        <SCRIPT LANGUAGE = JavaScript>
            var factorial = 1

            for(var loopIndex = 1; loopIndex <= 10; loopIndex++){
```

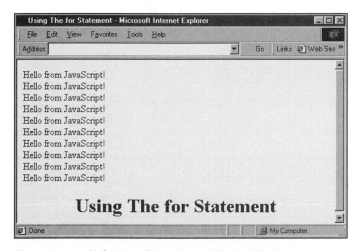

Figure 10.8   Using the **for** statement in JavaScript.

```
                    factorial = factorial * loopIndex
                    document.writeln(loopIndex + "! = " + factorial + "<BR>")
            }

        </SCRIPT>

        <CENTER>
            <H1>
                Using The for Statement
            </H1>
        </CENTER>

    </BODY>

</HTML>
```

You can see the results of this code in Figure 10.9.

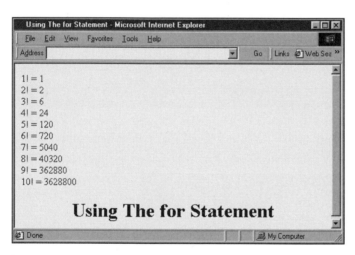

Figure 10.9 Using a **for** statement to compute factorials.

Creating **while** Loop Statements

In addition to the **for** loop, another powerful loop in JavaScript is the **while** loop. This loop tests a logical condition and, while the condition is true, executes the code in the statement. Here's how this statement looks in general:

```
while (condition){
    code
}
```

In this next example, I use a **while** loop to store the value 2001 in a variable the hard way—by incrementing the value in the number, starting from 0:

```
var number = 0

while(number <= 2001){
    number++
}
```

Here's an example that converts the **for** loop in the previous section to use a **while** loop:

```
<HTML>

    <HEAD>

        <TITLE>
            Using The while Statement
        </TITLE>

    </HEAD>

    <BODY>

        <SCRIPT LANGUAGE = JavaScript>
            var factorial = 1
            var loopIndex = 1

            while(loopIndex <= 10){
                factorial = factorial * loopIndex
                document.writeln(loopIndex + "! = " + factorial + "<BR>")
                loopIndex++
            }

        </SCRIPT>

        <CENTER>
            <H1>
                Using The while Statement
            </H1>
        </CENTER>

    </BODY>

</HTML>
```

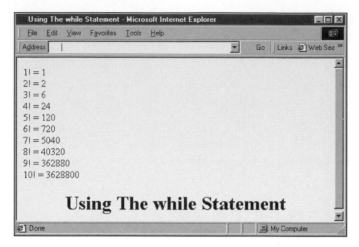

Figure 10.10   Using a **while** statement to compute factorials.

You can see the results of this code in Figure 10.10.

Creating **do...while** Loop Statements

A variation of the **while** loop is the **do...while** loop. They're actually the same loop, except that the **while** loop tests its condition at the beginning of the loop and the **do...while** loop tests its condition at the end of the loop. Here's what the **do...while** loop looks like in general:

```
do {
    code
} while (condition)
```

Testing the condition at the beginning or the end makes a difference because, unlike the **while** loop, the code in a **do...while** loop is always executed at least once. Take a look at this next portion of code—no matter whether the value in condition is **"RED"** or not, this code will always display "PANIC!" at least once (and probably make the user somewhat uncomfortable):

```
do {
    document.writeln("PANIC!<BR>")
} while (condition = "RED")
```

A better choice would be to use the **while** loop, which won't display "PANIC!" unless the value in condition is actually **RED**:

```
while (condition = "RED") {
    document.writeln("PANIC!<BR>")
}
```

On the other hand, if you need to execute the body of the loop before testing to see if the loop should continue, using the **do...while** loop is the best solution.

Creating Functions

"Hm," says the novice programmer, "I need to determine the time of day in many places in my script. I guess that means I'll have to duplicate a lot of code, once for each place." "Not at all," you say, "just create a new function."

Functions are very important in Java programming. You can wrap code into a discrete programming construct called a *function*, and you can *call* that function to execute the code in it. You create functions with the **function** statement, which looks like this in general:

```
function functionname([argument1 [, argument2 [, ...argumentn]]])
{
    code
}
```

To return a value from a function, you use the **return** statement. To see how this works, I'll create a function named **getCurrentTime** in the next example. Note the syntax of the **function** statement, and note that I place an empty pair of parentheses after the name of the function (I do this because the function takes no arguments—see the next section for more details):

```
function getCurrentTime()
{
    var time = new Date
    var returnValue = "The current time is " +
        time.getHours() + ":" + time.getMinutes()
    return(returnValue)
}
```

I'm using the built-in JavaScript **Date** class to find the time. You create an object of this class with the **new** operator (see "Creating JavaScript Objects" in the Immediate Solutions section of this chapter for all the details), and then you can use the object's **getHours** and **getMinutes** methods to obtain the current time. Note that after I get the current time and place it in a text string in the variable named

returnValue, I return that value from the **getCurrentTime** function using the **return** statement. You can now call this function from other parts of your script; JavaScript will run the code in the function and substitute the returned value for the name of the function.

In this next example, I'm calling **getCurrentTime** to get a string with the current time and display that time in a Web page (note that if you place code in a **<SCRIPT>** element, but not inside a function, that code is run automatically when the page is loaded; however, code inside functions is *not* run until that function is called):

```
<HTML>
    <HEAD>
        <TITLE>
            Using Functions In JavaScript
        </TITLE>

    </HEAD>

    <BODY>

        <SCRIPT LANGUAGE = JavaScript>
            document.writeln(getCurrentTime())

            function getCurrentTime()
            {
                var time = new Date
                var returnValue = "The current time is " +
                    time.getHours() + ":" + time.getMinutes()
                return(returnValue)
            }
        </SCRIPT>

        <CENTER>
            <H1>
                Using Functions In JavaScript
            </H1>

        </CENTER>

    </BODY>

</HTML>
```

The result of this code appears in Figure 10.11. As you can see, the current time is calculated in the **getCurrentTime** function, returned from that function, and displayed in the page.

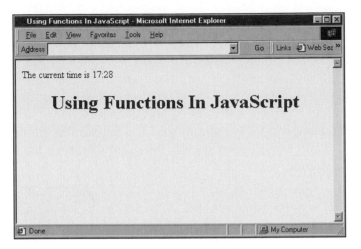

Figure 10.11   Creating and calling functions.

You might also notice that I've included an empty pair of parentheses after the name of the function when calling the function. These parentheses are empty because I'm not passing any *arguments* to this function. However, if you want to pass data to the function to work on, you can do so by passing that data as arguments—see the next section for the details.

TIP: *Methods in JavaScript are just functions that are built into objects.*

Passing Arguments To Functions

"Arggh!" says the novice programmer, "I need to determine the minimum of two numbers in about a million places in my script, so I have to duplicate the code to find the minimum in all those places." "Not at all," you say, "just write a function, *pass* the two numbers to the function, and return the minimum. Then all you have to do is call the function each time you need it." "Oh," says the NP.

You can pass data as *arguments* to a function, and that data will become available inside the function for you to work on. When you create a function, you indicate what arguments will be passed to the function in an argument list, which you place in parentheses like this:

```
function min(value1, value2)
{
    .
    .
    .
}
```

Inside the function, you can now refer to the values passed to your function using the names you've given them in the argument list. Here's how I return the minimum of the two passed values:

```
function min(value1, value2)
{
    if (value1 < value2) {
        return(value1)
    }
    else {
        return(value2)
    }
}
```

TIP: *The built-in JavaScript **Math** object actually has a **min** method. Using the **min** method would eliminate the need for the previous code.*

To pass values to the **min** function, you enclose them in parentheses following the function name when you call that function. Here's how I can call the **min** function with two values, 1 and 2:

```
<HTML>
    <HEAD>
        <TITLE>
            Using Function Arguments In JavaScript
        </TITLE>

    </HEAD>

    <BODY>

        <SCRIPT LANGUAGE = JavaScript>

            document.writeln("The minimum of 1 and 2 is " +  min(1, 2))

            function min(value1, value2)
```

```
                {
                    if (value1 < value2) {
                        return(value1)
                    }
                    else {
                        return(value2)
                    }
                }

        </SCRIPT>

        <CENTER>
            <H1>
                Using Function Arguments In JavaScript
            </H1>

        </CENTER>

    </BODY>

</HTML>
```

You can see the results of this code in Figure 10.12. As you can see, the values 1 and 2 were passed to the **min** function, which determined which of the two values was the minimum value, and then returned that value to be displayed in the Web page.

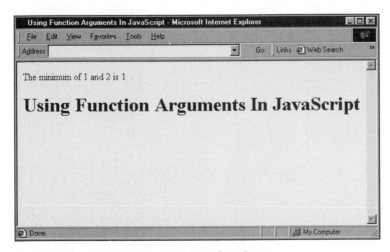

Figure 10.12   Passing arguments to functions.

TIP: *You can actually call a function with fewer arguments than you've declared the function with. This is okay as long as you don't try to read values from arguments that were not passed. You can also pass more arguments to a function than the function is set up to take. To read such arguments, you can use the arguments array, which is available in every function (we'll see how arrays work later in the Immediate Solutions section "Creating Arrays With The **Array** Class"). The first argument passed to the function is the first entry in the arguments array, and you refer to it as* **functionName.arguments[0]***, the second argument is referred to as* **functionName.arguments[1]***, and so on (using square brackets this way is how you use arrays).*

NOTE: *By default in JavaScript, the items that are really passed to functions are copies of the arguments you pass, not the arguments themselves. This is referred to as calling by value.*

Creating JavaScript Objects

Some objects have been created and are ready for you to use in JavaScript, such as the **document**, **location**, **navigator**, and **history** objects. However, JavaScript comes with many utility classes, like the **Date** and **Math** classes, which you can use to create objects. Obviously, these objects aren't available until you create them.

As mentioned in the In Depth section of this chapter, a class is like a cookie cutter for an object; you can think of a class as an object's *type*. Using a class, you can create an object with the **new** operator. In fact, we've already seen one such example in this chapter, which used the **Date** class. In this next example, I create a new JavaScript **Date** object from the **Date** class, store it in a variable named **time**, and then use the **getHours** and **getMinutes** methods of that object, like this:

```
<HTML>
    <HEAD>
        <TITLE>
            Using Functions In JavaScript
        </TITLE>

    </HEAD>

    <BODY>

        <SCRIPT LANGUAGE = JavaScript>
            document.writeln(getCurrentTime())
```

```
        function getCurrentTime()
        {
            var time = new Date
            var returnValue = "The current time is " +
                time.getHours() + ":" + time.getMinutes()
            return(returnValue)
        }
    </SCRIPT>

    <CENTER>
        <H1>
            Using Functions In JavaScript
        </H1>

    </CENTER>

  </BODY>

</HTML>
```

To create objects, you use the **new** operator as we've seen with the **Date** class:

```
var time = new Date
```

The **new** operator actually uses the **Date** class's *constructor*, which is a special method of the class that creates objects of that class. In the previous example, I didn't pass any arguments to the **Date** class's constructor, which means the **Date** object created will correspond to the current time. On the other hand, you can pass a specified date to the **Date** class's constructor to create a **Date** object for that time like this:

```
var time = new Date("9/2/2000")
```

The kind of data you can pass to class constructors in JavaScript varies by class—see the JavaScript documentation for the details. You can also find another example using constructors in the next section, where I'm working with the JavaScript **String** object.

Using JavaScript **String** Objects

The JavaScript **String** class is a useful one and is designed to hold text strings and let you work on them. You'll find the JavaScript methods of this class in Table 10.3 and the JScript methods of this class in Table 10.4.

Table 10.3   Methods of the JavaScript String class.

Methods			
anchor	big	blink	bold
charAt	charCodeAt	concat	fixed
fontcolor	fontsize	indexOf	italics
lastIndexOf	link	match	replace
search	slice	small	split
strike	sub	substr	substring
sup	toLowerCase	toSource	toUpperCase
toString	valueOf		

Table 10.4   Methods of the JScript String object.

Methods			
anchor	big	blink	bold
charAt	charCodeAt	concat	fixed
fontcolor	fontsize	fromCharCode	indexOf
italics	lastIndexOf	link	match
replace	search	slice	small
split	strike	sub	substr
substring	sup	toLowerCase	toString
toUpperCase	valueOf		

In this next example, I'm creating an object of the JavaScript **String** class, using that object's **bold** method to make the string bold, and then using its **length** property to determine its length:

```
<HTML>
    <HEAD>
        <TITLE>
            Using The JavaScript String Class
        </TITLE>

    </HEAD>

    <BODY>

        <SCRIPT LANGUAGE = JavaScript>
```

```
        var newString = new String("This is a JavaScript string")

        document.writeln("This string, " + newString.bold() +
        ", is exactly " + newString.length + " characters long.")
    </SCRIPT>

    <CENTER>
        <H1>
            Using The JavaScript String Class
        </H1>
    </CENTER>
</BODY>

</HTML>
```

Note that I pass the text for the string in parentheses after the word **String** in this code. I do this because I'm passing that text as an argument to the **String** class's constructor, which is a special method with the same name as the class (which is **String** here) that creates objects (see the previous section for more details). The results of this code appear in Figure 10.13.

It's worth mentioning that JavaScript treats the **String** class in a special way, allowing you to create objects of this class without the **new** operator because it's such a common thing to do. Here's an example that creates a new **String** object simply when you enclose text in quotation marks:

```
<HTML>
    <HEAD>
        <TITLE>
            Using The JavaScript String Class
```

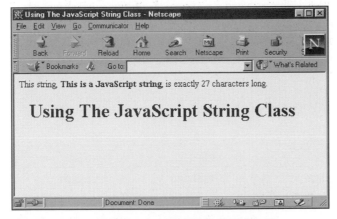

Figure 10.13   Creating JavaScript **String** objects.

```
        </TITLE>

    </HEAD>

    <BODY>

        <SCRIPT LANGUAGE = JavaScript>
            var newString = "This is a JavaScript string"

            document.writeln("This string, " + newString.bold() +
            ", is exactly " + newString.length + " characters long.")
        </SCRIPT>

        <CENTER>
            <H1>
                Using The JavaScript String Class
            </H1>
        </CENTER>
    </BODY>

</HTML>
```

Creating Arrays With The **Array** Class

"Hm," says the novice programmer, "I want to work with a whole set of data at once, and a **for** loop would be great. But how should I store the data?" "Sounds like you need an array," you say. "Let's try the JavaScript **Array** class."

Arrays can hold whole sets of data, allowing you to access each data item by specifying a numeric index. This makes arrays perfect for working with loops because you can use the loop index to successively iterate through each item in the array. To create arrays in JavaScript, you use the JavaScript **Array** class. You can find the methods of this class in Table 10.5 and the methods of the JScript **Array** class in Table 10.6.

Table 10.5   Methods of the JavaScript Array class.

concat	join	pop	push
reverse	shift	slice	splice
sort	toSource	toString	unshift
valueOf			

Table 10.6   Methods of the JScript Array class.

concat	join	reverse	slice
sort	toString	valueOf	

Here's an example where I create an array, place data into the array, and then use a **for** loop to find the average value of that data. I start by creating the new array named **data** and a variable I'll use to hold the total of all the data items in the array:

```
var data = new Array
var total = 0
    .
    .
    .
```

Now I'm free to store data in the array, arranging it by using a numeric index. Arrays in JavaScript start with an index of 0 (although they didn't in earlier versions). You refer to a data item in an array like this, **data[1]**, which refers to the second item in the array named **data** (**data[0]** is the first element). To fill the new array with data, I execute this code:

```
var data = new Array
var total = 0

data[0] = 1
data[1] = 2
data[2] = 3
data[3] = 4
data[4] = 5
data[5] = 6
data[6] = 7
    .
    .
    .
```

All I need to do now is loop over this array with a **for** loop, adding all the data items together, and then dividing the result by the total number of elements in the array. There's an easy way to find the number of elements in an array—use its **length** property. Here's the final code, already in place in a Web page:

```
<HTML>

    <HEAD>
```

```
        <TITLE>
            An Array Example
        </TITLE>

    </HEAD>

    <BODY>

        <SCRIPT LANGUAGE = JavaScript>
            var data = new Array
            var total = 0

            data[0] = 1
            data[1] = 2
            data[2] = 3
            data[3] = 4
            data[4] = 5
            data[5] = 6
            data[6] = 7

            for(var loopIndex = 0; loopIndex < data.length; loopIndex++){
                total = total + data[loopIndex]
            }

            document.write("The average value of your data is " +
                total / data.length)
        </SCRIPT>

        <CENTER>
            <H1>
                Using JavaScript Arrays
            </H1>
        </CENTER>

    </BODY>

</HTML>
```

The results of this code appear in Figure 10.14, where you can see that the average value of the items in the array is 4.

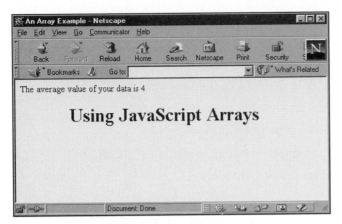

Figure 10.14   Creating JavaScript **Array** objects.

Handling Events In Browsers

As discussed in the In Depth section of this chapter, much of dynamic HTML has to do with using JavaScript for handling events, such as mouse clicks or key presses. Here are the common events that JavaScript can handle. Each one is an event attribute that you can use in an HTML tag:

- **onAbort**—Occurs when an action is aborted.
- **onBlur**—Occurs when an element loses the input focus.
- **onChange**—Occurs when data in a control, like a text field, changes.
- **onClick**—Occurs when an element is clicked.
- **onDblClick**—Occurs when an element is double-clicked.
- **onDragDrop**—Occurs when a drag-and-drop operation is undertaken.
- **onError**—Occurs when there's been a JavaScript error.
- **onFocus**—Occurs when an element gets the focus.
- **onKeyDown**—Occurs when a key goes down.
- **onKeyPress**—Occurs when a key is pressed and the key code is available.
- **onKeyUp**—Occurs when a key goes up.
- **onLoad**—Occurs when the page loads.
- **onMouseDown**—Occurs when a mouse button goes down.
- **onMouseMove**—Occurs when the mouse moves.
- **onMouseOut**—Occurs when the mouse leaves an element.

- **onMouseOver**—Occurs when the mouse moves over an element.
- **onMouseUp**—Occurs when a mouse button goes up.
- **onMove**—Occurs when an element is moved.
- **onReset**—Occurs when the user clicks the Reset button.
- **onResize**—Occurs when an element or page is resized.
- **onSelect**—Occurs when a selection takes place.
- **onSubmit**—Occurs when the user clicks the Submit button.
- **onUnload**—Occurs when a page is unloaded.

These event attributes have been added to many HTML elements, and you can assign a JavaScript function to be called to one of these event attributes. Table 10.1 contains a list of event attributes for many HTML elements in Internet Explorer. A list of event attributes for many HTML elements in Netscape Navigator can be found in Table 10.2.

Here's an example using two HTML controls, which we'll see in Chapter 12—text fields and buttons. You create these controls with the **<INPUT>** element, setting the **TYPE** attribute to **text** to create a text field and **button** to create a button. When the user clicks the button, the code will display a message in the text field. As you'll see in the code, the **<INPUT>** element must be used inside an HTML **<FORM>** element. Here's how I create the text field and button (the **VALUE** attribute of the button sets the button's caption):

```
<FORM name = "form1">

    <H1>
        Handling JavaScript Events
    </H1>
    <BR>
    <H2>
        Click the button!
    </H2>
    <BR>
    <INPUT TYPE = "text" NAME = "Text" SIZE = 60>
    <BR>
    <BR>
    <INPUT TYPE="button" VALUE="Click Me">

</FORM>
```

To connect the button to a JavaScript function named **clickHandler**, so that **clickHandler** is called when the button is clicked, I set the button's **onClick** event attribute to **clickHandler( )**:

```
<FORM name = "form1">

    <H1>
        Handling JavaScript Events
    </H1>
    <BR>
    <H2>
        Click the button!
    </H2>
    <BR>
    <INPUT TYPE = "text" NAME = "Text" SIZE = 60>
    <BR>
    <BR>
    <INPUT TYPE="button" VALUE="Click Me"
        onClick="clickHandler()">

</FORM>
```

Now I just create a JavaScript function named **clickHandler** that places the message, "You clicked the button!", in the text field. As we'll see in Chapter 12, I can access the text field, which I've named "Text", using the document object called **document.form1.Text**. Here's what the code looks like:

```
<HTML>

    <HEAD>
        <TITLE>
            Handling JavaScript Events
        </TITLE>

    <SCRIPT LANGUAGE= "JavaScript">
        function clickHandler(e)
        {
            document.form1.Text.value = "You clicked the button!"
        }
    </SCRIPT>

    </HEAD>


    <BODY>

        <CENTER>
            <FORM name = "form1">
```

```
<H1>
    Handling JavaScript Events
</H1>
<BR>
<H2>
    Click the button!
</H2>
<BR>
<INPUT TYPE = "text" name = "Text" SIZE = 60>
<BR>
<BR>
<INPUT TYPE="button" VALUE="Click Me"
    onClick="clickHandler()">

        </FORM>

    </CENTER>

</BODY>

</HTML>
```

That's all it takes—now when the user clicks the button, the message is displayed
in the text field, as you can see in Figure 10.15.

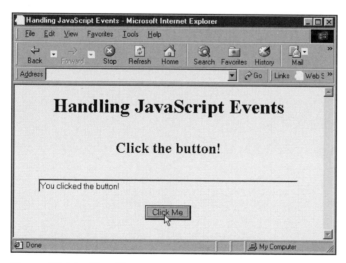

Figure 10.15   Handling events with JavaScript.

Why did I declare the event handler **clickHandler** as **clickHandler(e)** in the code in the previous example? I did so because when an event occurs, an object of the **event** class (which I'm naming **e** here) is passed to event handlers in Netscape Navigator. You'll find the properties of this event for Netscape Navigator in Table 10.7.

On the other hand, no object is passed to event handlers in Internet Explorer (but JavaScript is flexible enough so you can still declare **clickHandler** as though it does take one argument, **clickHandler(e)**, so the same function works with both browsers). Instead, you use the **window.event** object, which is accessible at any point in your code, to get data about the event. You'll find the properties of the **window.event** for Internet Explorer in Table 10.8.

Table 10.7   Netscape Navigator's event object properties.

Property	Means
data	Array of strings containing the URLs of the dropped objects, used with the **dragdrop** event
height	Height associated with event
layerX	Cursor's horizontal position in pixels, relative to the layer in which the event occurred
layerY	Cursor's vertical position in pixels, relative to the layer in which the event occurred
modifiers	Modifier keys associated with a mouse or key event; possible values: **ALT_MASK**, **CONTROL_MASK**, **SHIFT_MASK**, and **META_MASK**
pageX	Cursor's horizontal position in pixels, relative to the page
pageY	Cursor's vertical position in pixels, relative to the page
screenX	Cursor's horizontal position in pixels, relative to the screen
screenY	Cursor's vertical position in pixels, relative to the screen
type	Type of event
which	Mouse button that was pressed or the ASCII value of a pressed key
width	Width associated with event

Table 10.8   Internet Explorer's window.event object properties.

Property	Means
altKey	True if the Alt key was down
altLeft	True if the left Alt key is down
button	Specifies which mouse button, if any, is pressed
cancelBubble	Indicates if this event should move up the event hierarchy
clientX	x coordinate with respect to the client area

(continued)

595

Table 10.8   Internet Explorer's window.event object properties (continued).

Property	Means
clientY	y coordinate with respect to the client area
ctrlKey	True if the Ctrl key was down
ctrlLeft	True if the left Ctrl key was down
fromElement	Specifies element being moved
keyCode	Code of struck key
offsetX	Container relative x position
offsetY	Container relative y position
reason	Disposition of data transfer
returnValue	Specifies the return value from the event
screenX	x coordinate relative to physical screen size
screenY	y coordinate relative to physical screen size
shiftKey	True if the Shift key was down
shiftLeft	True if the left Shift key was down
srcElement	Element that caused the event
srcFilter	Filter event if this is a **filterChange** event
toElement	Specifies element being moved to
type	Returns event type as a string
x	x position of the event in context
y	y position of the event in context

For an example that uses the event objects in Tables 10.7 and 10.8, see the next section.

Event Handling: Mouse Events

In this section, I'm going to put the JavaScript mouse events to work to give you an idea of what a full-scale JavaScript program handling events looks like. Here are the JavaScript events this program will use:

- **onMouseDown**—Occurs when a mouse button goes down in the page.

- **onMouseOut**—Occurs when the mouse leaves a hyperlink in the page.

- **onMouseOver**—Occurs when the mouse moves over a hyperlink in a page.

- **onMouseUp**—Occurs when a mouse button goes up in the page.

You can use the mouse in the Web page itself, and the code will report the location of the mouse when an event occurs and whether the Ctrl, Shift, or Alt key is down. I'll add a hyperlink to the page as well to show how the **onMouseOver** (occurs when the mouse is over an element) and **onMouseOut** (occurs when the mouse leaves an element) events work.

As discussed in the previous section, you get event data in different ways for the two browsers, so I'll need to write the code to handle both Internet Explorer and Netscape Navigator. I'll determine what browser the user has with a technique we'll discuss in Chapter 11, which checks the **navigator** object's **appName** property to determine the name of the browser.

There's one more point that should be mentioned—you would normally connect event handlers for **onMouseDown** and **onMouseUp** to the Web page using the **<BODY>** element like this:

```
<BODY onMouseDown = "mouseDownFunction()" onMouseUp = "mouseUpFunction()">
```

However, in Netscape Navigator, the **<BODY>** element does not support the **onMouseDown** and **onMouseUp** event attributes. Instead, you assign the name of the event handler functions you want to use to the **document** object's **onMouseDown** and **onMouseUp** properties like I have done here in the **<SCRIPT>** element:

```
<SCRIPT LANGUAGE= "JavaScript">

//Added for Netscape Navigator
document.onMouseDown = mouseDownFunction
document.onMouseUp = mouseUpFunction

    .
    .
    .
```

The remainder of the code follows what we've already accomplished in this chapter. You can see this example at work in Figure 10.16. The entire code, entitled mouse.htm, is shown in Listing 10.1. Take a look at the code if you're so inclined—it's a pretty good example of event handling in the two browsers.

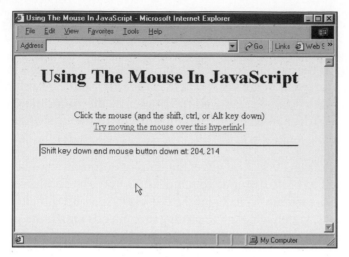

Figure 10.16   Handling mouse events with JavaScript.

Listing 10.1   mouse.htm displays information about mouse events.

```
<HTML>

    <HEAD>

    <TITLE>
        Using The Mouse In JavaScript
    </TITLE>

    <SCRIPT LANGUAGE= "JavaScript">

    //Added for Netscape Navigator
    document.onMouseDown = mouseDownFunction
    document.onMouseUp = mouseUpFunction

    function mouseOverFunction(e)
    {
        if (navigator.appName == "Microsoft Internet Explorer") {

            if(window.event.shiftKey && window.event.ctrlKey){
                document.form1.Textbox.value =
                "Shift and Ctrl keys down and mouse over at: " +
                window.event.x + ", " + window.event.y
                return
            }
```

```
        if(window.event.shiftKey)
        {
            document.form1.Textbox.value =
            "Shift key down and mouse over at: " +
            window.event.x + ", " + window.event.y
            return
        }

        if(window.event.ctrlKey)
        {
            document.form1.Textbox.value =
            "Ctrl key down and mouse over at: " +
            window.event.x + ", " + window.event.y
            return
        }

        if(window.event.altKey)
        {
            document.form1.Textbox.value =
            "Alt key down and mouse over at: " +
            window.event.x + ", " + window.event.y
            return
        }

        document.form1.Textbox.value = "Mouse over at: " +
            window.event.x + ", " + window.event.y
    }

    if(navigator.appName == "Netscape") {

        document.form1.Textbox.value = "Mouse over"
    }
}

function mouseOutFunction(e)
{
    if (navigator.appName == "Microsoft Internet Explorer") {

        if(window.event.shiftKey && window.event.ctrlKey){
            document.form1.Textbox.value =
            "Shift and Ctrl keys down and mouse out at: " +
            window.event.x + ", " + window.event.y
            return
        }
```

```
                            if(window.event.shiftKey)
                            {
                                document.form1.Textbox.value =
                                "Shift key down and mouse out at: " +
                                window.event.x + ", " + window.event.y
                                return
                            }

                            if(window.event.ctrlKey)
                            {
                                document.form1.Textbox.value =
                                "Ctrl key down and mouse out at: " +
                                window.event.x + ", " + window.event.y
                                return
                            }

                            if(window.event.altKey)
                            {
                                document.form1.Textbox.value =
                                "Alt key down and mouse out at: " +
                                window.event.x + ", " + window.event.y
                                return
                            }

                            document.form1.Textbox.value = "Mouse out at: " +
                                window.event.x + ", " + window.event.y
                        }

                    if(navigator.appName == "Netscape") {
                        document.form1.Textbox.value = "Mouse out"
                    }


                }
                function mouseDownFunction(e)
                {
                    if (navigator.appName == "Microsoft Internet Explorer") {

                        if(window.event.shiftKey && window.event.ctrlKey){
                            document.form1.Textbox.value =
                            "Shift and Ctrl keys down and mouse button down at: " +
                            window.event.x + ", " + window.event.y
                            return
                        }
```

```
        if(window.event.shiftKey)
        {
            document.form1.Textbox.value =
            "Shift key down and mouse button down at: " +
            window.event.x + ", " + window.event.y
            return
        }

        if(window.event.ctrlKey)
        {
            document.form1.Textbox.value =
            "Ctrl key down and mouse button down at: " +
            window.event.x + ", " + window.event.y
            return
        }

        if(window.event.altKey)
        {
            document.form1.Textbox.value =
            "Alt key down and mouse button down at: " +
            window.event.x + ", " + window.event.y
            return
        }

        document.form1.Textbox.value = "Mouse button down at: " +
            window.event.x + ", " + window.event.y
    }

    if(navigator.appName == "Netscape") {

        switch(e.modifiers){
            case 0:
                document.form1.Textbox.value = "Mouse button down at: "
                    + e.pageX + ", " + e.pageY
                break
            case 2:
                document.form1.Textbox.value =
                "Ctrl key down and mouse button down at: " +
                e.pageX + ", " + e.pageY
                break
            case 4:
                document.form1.Textbox.value =
                "Shift key down and mouse button down at: " +
                e.pageX + ", " + e.pageY
                break
```

```
                    case 6:
                        document.form1.Textbox.value =
                            "Shift and Ctrl keys down and mouse button down "
                            + "at: " +
                            e.pageX + ", " + e.pageY
                        break
                    case 1:
                        document.form1.Textbox.value =
                        "Alt key down and mouse button down at: " +
                        e.pageX + ", " + e.pageY
                        break
            }
        }
    }


    function mouseUpFunction(e)
    {
        if (navigator.appName == "Microsoft Internet Explorer") {

            if(window.event.shiftKey && window.event.ctrlKey){
                document.form1.Textbox.value =
                "Shift and Ctrl keys down and mouse button up at: " +
                window.event.x + ", " + window.event.y
                return
            }

            if(window.event.shiftKey)
            {
                document.form1.Textbox.value =
                "Shift key down and mouse button up at: " +
                window.event.x + ", " + window.event.y
                return
            }

            if(window.event.ctrlKey)
            {
                document.form1.Textbox.value =
                "Ctrl key down and mouse button up at: " +
                window.event.x + ", " + window.event.y
                return
            }
```

```
        if(window.event.altKey)
        {
            document.form1.Textbox.value =
            "Alt key down and mouse button up at: " +
            window.event.x + ", " + window.event.y
            return
        }

        document.form1.Textbox.value = "Mouse button up at: " +
            window.event.x + ", " + window.event.y
    }

    if(navigator.appName == "Netscape") {
        switch(e.modifiers){
            case 0:
                document.form1.Textbox.value = "Mouse button up at: "
                    + e.pageX + ", " + e.pageY
                break
            case 2:
                document.form1.Textbox.value =
                "Ctrl key down and mouse button up at: " +
                e.pageX + ", " + e.pageY
                break
            case 4:
                document.form1.Textbox.value =
                "Shift key down and mouse button up at: " +
                e.pageX + ", " + e.pageY
                break
            case 6:
                document.form1.Textbox.value =
                "Shift and Ctrl keys down " +
                "and mouse button up at: " + e.pageX + ", " + e.pageY
                break
            case 1:
                document.form1.Textbox.value =
                "Alt key down and mouse button up at: " +
                e.pageX + ", " + e.pageY
                break
        }
    }
}
```

```
        </SCRIPT>

    </HEAD>

    <BODY onMouseDown = "mouseDownFunction()" onMouseUp =
        "mouseUpFunction()">

        <CENTER>
            <FORM name = "form1">

            <H1>
                Using The Mouse In JavaScript
            </H1>

            <BR>
            Click the mouse (and the shift, ctrl, or Alt key down)
            <BR>

            <A HREF="mouse.htm" name="mouseLink"
            onMouseOver="mouseOverFunction()"
            onMouseOut="mouseOutFunction()">
                Try moving the mouse over this hyperlink!
            </A>
            <BR>
            <BR>
            <INPUT TYPE = "text" name = "Textbox" SIZE = 60>
            </FORM>

        </CENTER>

    </BODY>

</HTML>
```

Chapter 11

Putting JavaScript To Work

In Depth

In the previous chapter, we worked through a lot of JavaScript syntax, and in this chapter, it's time to put it to work by creating self-modifying Web pages, displaying Alert dialog boxes, writing to the status bar, navigating to past pages, and even creating cookies.

After getting a good foundation in JavaScript syntax, you'll find that most JavaScript programming revolves around the predefined objects available to you in the browser. This chapter is about working with the principal objects: the **document**, **window**, **location**, and **history** objects. To put these objects in perspective, I'll start with an overview of what objects are available, and what objects contain what other objects in Internet Explorer and Netscape Navigator.

JavaScript Objects In Overview

Before you even start working in JavaScript, the Web browser has created many objects for you to work with. These objects can also contain other objects. For example, in the previous chapter, we saw that the **window** object contains an **event** object in Internet Explorer. To access the **event** object inside the **window** object, you refer to it as **window.event**. In this way, you can access a whole hierarchy of objects. Here's what that hierarchy looks like for objects in Internet Explorer (not all objects are represented here as it would be very lengthy):

```
window
    |
    |--event
    |
    |--frames
    |
    |--history
    |
    |--location
    |
    |--navigator
    |
   --document
             |
             |--links
             |
             |--anchors
```

```
    |
    |--images
    |
    |--forms
    |
    |--applets
    |
    |--embeds
    |
    |--frames
    |˙
    |--scripts
    |
    |--all
    |
    |--selection
    |
    |--body
    |
    |--anchor
    |
    |--applet
    |
    |--image
    |
    |--link
    |
     --form
          |
          |--elements
          |
          |--button
          |
          |--checkbox
          |
          |--fileUpload
          |
          |--hidden
          |
          |--option
          |
          |--password
          |
          |--radio
          |
          |--select
          |
```

```
                        |--submit
                        |
                        |--text
                        |
                      --textarea
```

Here's the corresponding object hierarchy in Netscape Navigator (again, not all objects are listed):

```
|
|--navigator
|       |
|         --plugins
|
 --window
        |
        |--location
        |
        |--history
        |
        |--frame
        |
        |--frames
        |
         --document
                |
                |--links
                |
                |--anchors
                |
                |--images
                |
                |--forms
                |
                |--applets
                |
                |--embeds
                |
                |--layers
                |
                |--anchor
                |
                |--applet
                |
                |--image
                |
                |--link
```

```
       |
       |--plugin
       |
        --form
            |
            |--button
            |
            |--checkbox
            |
            |--fileUpload
            |
            |--hidden
            |
            |--option
            |
            |--password
            |
            |--radio
            |
            |--select
            |
            |--submit
            |
            |--text
            |
             --textarea
```

In this chapter, I'm going to put four of these objects—the most popular ones—to work:

- **document**—This object corresponds to a Web page, and you can use it to gain access to all elements in the page. You can also use it to write in a Web page and to use cookies.

- **window**—This object corresponds to the Web browser window, and you can display all kinds of dialog boxes with it, among other things.

- **location**—This object holds or sets the current location, and using it, you can navigate to a new URL.

- **history**—This object holds the "history" of the browser, recording where the user has been, and letting you navigate back there if you wish.

These are the main objects used in JavaScript, and I'll take a look at each of these important objects in more detail in the next few sections. For reference, I'm going to list the properties, methods, and events of these objects. It's worth taking a moment to work through the corresponding tables to see what's available.

The document Object

The **document** object has been available in Netscape Navigator since version 2 and in Internet Explorer since version 3. This object corresponds to a Web page, and using it, you can access all the elements of that page, such as its hyperlinks, images, and HTML forms. For example, in "Reloading Images At Runtime" in the Immediate Solutions section of this chapter, I'll create a form (see Chapter 12 for more on forms) named **FORM1** with an **<IMG>** element named **IMG1** in it. I can then access the **SRC** attribute of that element like this:

```
function reloadImage()
{
    document.FORM1.IMG1.src = "gif/image2.gif"
}
```

We'll see more about working with the elements in a page when discussing dynamic HTML in Chapter 13. As we've seen in Chapter 10, you can also use the **document** object's **writeln** method to write to a Web page as it's being loaded. Furthermore, you can use this object to create and read cookies, as we'll see at the end of this chapter.

As with any other object, the document object is full of properties, methods, and events. You can study this object using JavaScript itself to find the setting of a property by using the expression **document.[*propertyname*]**, where *propertyname* is the name of the property you want to check. In fact, JavaScript can help out even more here with its **for...in** construct, which loops over all the members of an object automatically. Here's an example showing how this works. I'm listing all the properties of the **document** object and their settings:

```
<HTML>
    <HEAD>
        <TITLE>
            Document Object Properties
        </TITLE>

    </HEAD>

    <BODY>
        <SCRIPT LANGUAGE = JavaScript>

        document.writeln(
            "<H1>Here are the properties of the document object:</H1>"
        )
```

```
        for(var property in document){
            document.writeln(property +
            " = " + document[property] + "<BR>")
        }
```

```
    </SCRIPT>

    <CENTER>
        <H1>
            Document Object Properties
        </H1>
    </CENTER>

    </BODY>

</HTML>
```

You can see the results of this code in Figure 11.1. As you can see, there are many properties in this object—many more than can fit into the browser window. What are all these properties and what do they mean? You'll find Internet Explorer's **document** object properties in Table 11.1. In addition, you'll find the methods of this object in Table 11.2 and its events in Table 11.3. Internet Explorer's **document** object also has a number of *collections*, which are arrays of other objects; you'll find them in Table 11.4.

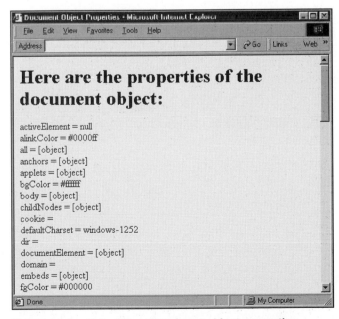

Figure 11.1 Examining **document** object properties.

Table 11.1   Properties of the *document* object in Internet Explorer.

Property	Means
activeElement	Gets the object that has the current focus.
aLinkColor	Specifies or retrieves the color of all active links.
bgColor	Specifies or retrieves the background color for the **document** object.
body	Marks the beginning and end of the body of the document.
contentEditable	Indicates if the user can edit the content of the object.
cookie	Holds the string corresponding to a cookie.
defaultCharset	Specifies or retrieves the default character set of the document.
designMode	Indicates if the document can be edited.
documentElement	Holds a reference to the root node.
domain	Specifies or retrieves security domain for the document.
expando	Indicates if variables can be created in the **document** object.
fgColor	Specifies or retrieves the foreground color for the document.
fileCreatedDate	Gets the date the document was created.
fileModifiedDate	Gets the date the document was last modified.
fileSize	Gets the file size.
hideFocus	Specifies if the object visibly indicates the focus.
lastModified	Gets the date the document was last modified.
linkColor	Specifies or retrieves the color of the document links.
location	Has the location of the current URL.
media	Indicates the type of media to display a document.
parentWindow	Gets a reference to the container of the window.
protocol	Specifies or retrieves the protocol part of a URL.
readyState	Gets the current state of the **document** object while it is being downloaded.
referrer	Holds the URL that referred the browser to this page.
selection	Specifies the active selection in the document.
title	Holds the title of the document.
uniqueID	Gets a unique identifier that specifies the **document** object.
URL	Specifies or retrieves the URL of this document.
vlinkColor	Specifies or retrieves the color of links that the browser has already visited.

Table 11.2 *Methods of the **document** object in Internet Explorer.*

Method	Means
attachEvent	Binds a function to an event occuring in the **document** object.
clear	Clears the document.
clearAttributes	Clears the **document** object of all attributes and values.
close	Closes a stream of output.
createElement	Creates an element object for the given tag.
createEventObject	Creates an event object for handling event context information in the **fireEvent** method.
createStyleSheet	Gets a style sheet.
createTextNode	Gets a text string.
detachEvent	Detaches the given function from an event.
elementFromPoint	Gets the element for the given coordinates.
execCommand	Executes a command.
focus	Makes a control receive the focus.
getElementById	Gets a reference to the object with the given **ID**.
getElementsByName	Gets a collection of objects as specified by name.
getElementsByTagName	Gets a collection of objects as specified by tag name.
hasFocus	Indicates whether the object has the focus.
mergeAttributes	Copies attributes to the indicated element.
open	Opens a document.
queryCommandEnabled	Indicates whether the command can be executed with **execCommand**.
queryCommandIndeterm	Indicates if the given command is indeterminate.
queryCommandState	Indicates the state of the specified command.
queryCommandSupported	Indicates if the command is supported.
queryCommandValue	Gets the value of the given command.
recalc	Recalculates all properties in the document.
releaseCapture	Releases mouse capture.
setActive	Sets the indicated object as the active object.
write	Writes HTML to a document in the given window.
writeln	Writes HTML and then a carriage return to a document in the given window.

11. Putting JavaScript To Work

Table 11.3   Events of the *document* object in Internet Explorer.

Event	Means
onbeforecut	Happens before the selection is deleted.
onbeforeeditfocus	Happens before the edit focus event.
onbeforefocusenter	Happens before the object gets the focus.
onbeforefocusleave	Happens before the object loses the focus.
onbeforepaste	Happens before the selection is pasted into the document.
onclick	Happens when the user clicks the mouse.
oncontextmenu	Happens when the right mouse button is clicked to open a context menu.
oncontrolselect	Happens when the user selects a control.
oncut	Happens when the selection is cut.
ondblclick	Happens when the user double-clicks.
ondrag	Happens during a mouse drag operation.
ondragend	Happens when a drag operation ends.
ondragenter	Happens when the user drags the document into a drop target.
ondragleave	Happens when the mouse moves out of a drop target.
ondragover	Happens while the document is dragged over a drop target.
ondragstart	Happens when a drag operation starts.
ondrop	Happens when the mouse button is released, dropping a dragged object.
onfocusenter	Happens when the object gets the focus.
onfocusleave	Happens when the object loses the focus.
onhelp	Happens when the F1 key is pressed.
onkeydown	Happens when a key is pressed.
onkeypress	Happens when an alphanumeric key is pressed.
onkeyup	Happens when a key is released.
onmousedown	Happens when a mouse button is pressed.
onmousemove	Happens when the mouse is moved.
onmouseout	Happens when the mouse is moved out of the **document** object.
onmouseover	Happens when the mouse is moved over the **document** object.
onmouseup	Happens when a mouse button is released.
onpaste	Happens when data is pasted.
onpropertychange	Happens when a property changes.

(continued)

*Table 11.3   Events of the **document** object in Internet Explorer (continued).*

Event	Means
onreadystatechange	Happens when the state of the **document** object changes.
onresizeend	Happens when a resize operation ends.
onresizestart	Happens when a resize operation starts.
onselectiontypechange	Happens when the type of a selection changes.
onstop	Happens when the Stop button is clicked.

*Table 11.4   Collections of the **document** object in Internet Explorer.*

Collection	Means
all	Gets the collection of elements in **document** object.
anchors	Contains all **A** objects that have a name and/or ID property.
applets	Contains all **APPLET** objects in the document.
childNodes	Contains all descendent elements of the **document** object.
children	Contains all descendent elements of the **document** object.
embeds	Contains all **EMBED** objects in the document.
forms	Contains all **FORM** objects in the document.
frames	Contains all frames in the document.
images	Contains the **IMG** objects in the document.
lInks	Contains the **A** objects with a **href** property, as well as all **AREA** objects.
namespaces	Contains the **NAMESPACE** objects.
scripts	Contains the **SCRIPT** objects in the document.
styleSheets	Contains the **styleSheet** objects for each **LINK** or **STYLE** object.

Netscape Navigator's **document** object properties appear in Table 11.5, its methods in Table 11.6, and its events in Table 11.7.

*Table 11.5   Properties of the **document** object in Netscape Navigator.*

Property	Means
alinkColor	Specifies the **ALINK** attribute.
anchors	Refers to an array holding the anchors in the document.
applets	Refers to an array holding the applets in the document.
bgColor	Specifies the **BGCOLOR** attribute.
classes	Creates **Style** objects with a given **CLASS** attribute.

(continued)

Table 11.5   Properties of the *document* object in Netscape Navigator (continued).

Property	Means
cookie	Holds a cookie.
domain	Specifies the domain name of the document.
embeds	Refers to an array holding all plug-ins in the document.
fgColor	Indicates the **TEXT** attribute.
formName	Refers to each form in the document.
forms	Refers to an array containing each form in the document.
height	Refers to the pixel height of the document.
ids	Creates a **Style** object to hold the style of HTML tags.
images	Refers to an array holding all images.
lastModified	Indicates the last modified date of the document.
layers	Refers to an array holding all layers in the document.
linkColor	Indicates the **LINK** attribute.
links	Indicates the array holding all links.
plugins	Indicates the array holding all plug-ins.
referrer	Indicates the URL of the referring document.
tags	Creates a **Style** object to specify HTML tags.
title	Indicates the contents of the **TITLE** tag.
URL	Indicates the complete URL of the document.
vlinkColor	Indicates the **VLINK** attribute.
width	Refers to the pixel width of the document.

Table 11.6   Methods of the *document* object in Netscape Navigator.

Method	Means
close	Closes an output stream.
open	Opens a stream for the **write** or **writeln** methods.
write	Writes HTML to a document.
writeln	Writes HTML to a document, followed with a **newline** character.

As you can see, there's a lot to the **document** object—even though it differs radically by browser. We'll put this object to work in this chapter.

*Table 11.7 Events of the **document** object in Netscape Navigator.*

Event	Means
onClick	Click event.
onDblClick	Double-click event.
onKeyDown	Key went down.
onKeyPress	Key was interpreted.
onKeyUp	Key went up.
onMouseDown	Mouse went down.
onMouseUp	Mouse went up.

The window Object

The **window** object has been available in Netscape Navigator since version 2 and in Internet Explorer since version 3. This object corresponds to the current browser window, which may contain a page or a number of pages in frames. The **document** object is a part of the **window** object, so the proper name of the **document** object is **window.document** (although you can omit the "window" part here and JavaScript will still know that you want to access the **window.document** object). In fact, the **window** object is the top object in Internet Explorer's hierarchy and nearly the top object in Netscape Navigator.

So what's available in the **window** object? The **document** object is the most often used browser object in JavaScript programming, but there's plenty of power in the **window** object as well. You'll find Internet Explorer's **window** object properties in Table 11.8, its methods in Table 11.9, its events in Table 11.10, and its collections in Table 11.11.

*Table 11.8 Properties of the **window** object in Internet Explorer.*

Property	Means
clipboardData	Returns clipboard formats.
closed	Indicates if the window is closed.
defaultStatus	Holds the message in the status bar.
dialogArguments	Gets arguments passed to a modal dialog window.
dialogHeight	Specifies or retrieves the height of the dialog window.
dialogLeft	Specifies or retrieves the left coordinate of the dialog window.
dialogTop	Specifies or retrieves the top coordinate of the dialog window.
dialogWidth	Specifies or retrieves the width of the dialog window.

(continued)

*Table 11.8   Properties of the **window** object in Internet Explorer (continued).*

Property	Means
document	Indicates the document in the browser.
event	Indicates the state of an event.
frameElement	Gets the **FRAME** or **IFRAME** object hosting the window.
hideFocus	Indicates whether the object indicates the focus.
history	Holds the history of URLs visited.
length	Gets the number of objects in a collection.
location	Holds the location and additional information about the current URL.
name	Specifies or retrieves the name of the window or frame name.
navigator	Indicates the object referring to the Web browser.
offscreenBuffering	Indicates if objects are drawn offscreen before being drawn on the screen.
opener	Specifies or retrieves the window that created the current window.
parent	Gets the parent of the current window.
returnValue	Specifies or retrieves the return value of the dialog window.
screen	Holds data about the client's screen capabilities.
screenLeft	Gets the x-coordinate of the upper-left corner of the client area of the browser.
screenTop	Gets the y-coordinate of the top corner of the client area of the browser.
self	Gets the current window or the current frame.
status	Specifies or retrieves the text in the status bar.
top	Gets the topmost window.

*Table 11.9   Methods of the **window** object in Internet Explorer.*

Method	Means
alert	Makes visible an Alert dialog box displaying a message.
attachEvent	Attaches a function to an event that occurs in the **window** object.
blur	Makes an object lose the focus.
clearInterval	Clears the interval started with the **setInterval** method.
clearTimeout	Clears a time-out set with the earlier **setTimeout** method.
close	Closes the browser window.
confirm	Shows a Confirmation dialog box.
createPopup	Creates a popup.
detachEvent	Detaches the given function from an event.

(continued)

Table 11.9 *Methods of the **window** object in Internet Explorer* (continued).

Method	Means
execScript	Executes a script.
focus	Makes a control receive the focus.
moveBy	Moves the window by the specified x and y values.
moveTo	Moves the upper-left corner of the window.
navigate	Navigates to the indicated URL.
open	Opens a window.
print	Prints the document.
prompt	Displays a Prompt dialog box.
resizeBy	Resizes the window.
resizeTo	Resizes the window to the indicated width and length.
scroll	Scrolls the window.
scrollBy	Scrolls the window relative to the current position.
scrollTo	Scrolls the window to an x- and y-offset.
setActive	Makes the current object the active object.
setInterval	Sets a timer interval.
setTimeout	Evaluates an expression after a timer interval has elapsed.
showHelp	Shows a Help file.
showModalDialog	Shows a dialog box.
showModelessDialog	Shows a Modeless dialog box.

Table 11.10 *Events of the **window** object in Internet Explorer.*

Event	Means
onafterprint	Happens after the document is printed.
onbeforefocusenter	Happens before the object gets the focus.
onbeforefocusleave	Happens before the object loses the focus.
onbeforeprint	Happens before the document is printed.
onbeforeunload	Happens before a page is unloaded.
onblur	Happens when the **window** loses the focus.
oncontrolselect	Happens when a control is selected.
onerror	Happens when there's an error while a **window** object is loading.
onfocus	Happens when the **window** object gets the focus.

(continued)

11. Putting JavaScript To Work

Table 11.10   Events of the *window* object in Internet Explorer (continued).

Event	Means
onfocusenter	Happens when the object gets the focus.
onfocusleave	Happens when the object loses the focus.
onhelp	Happens when the F1 key is pressed.
onload	Happens after the browser loads a **window** object.
onresize	Happens when the **window** object is resized.
onresizeend	Happens when a resize operation ends.
onresizestart	Happens when a resize operation starts.
onunload	Happens before the **window** object is unloaded.

Table 11.11   Collections of the *window* object in Internet Explorer.

Collection	Means
frames	Holds all window objects in the frames of the document.

You'll find Netscape Navigator's **window** object properties in Table 11.12, its methods in Table 11.13, and its events in Table 11.14.

Table 11.12   Properties of the *window* object in Netscape Navigator.

Property	Means
closed	Indicates if a window was closed.
crypto	Provides access to Navigator's encryption capabilities.
defaultStatus	Holds the default message in the status bar.
document	Holds data about the current document, makes methods for displaying HTML accessible.
frames	Refers to an array holding the frames in the window.
history	Holds data about the URLs the client has visited.
innerHeight	Gives the vertical height of the window's content area in pixels.
innerWidth	Gives the horizontal width of the window's content area in pixels.
length	Refers to the number of frames in the window.
location	Holds data specifying the current URL.
locationbar	Refers to the object corresponding to the location bar.
menubar	Refers to the object corresponding to the menu bar.
name	Refers to the name of this window.

(continued)

Table 11.12   Properties of the _window_ object in Netscape Navigator (continued).

Property	Means
offscreenBuffering	Specifies if rendering updates are performed off screen.
opener	Specifies the name of the calling document.
outerHeight	Gives the height of the window in pixels.
outerWidth	Gives the width of the window in pixels.
pageXOffset	Gives the x-position of a window's page in pixels.
pageYOffset	Gives the y-position of a window's page in pixels.
parent	Refers to the window (or frame) that contains the current frame.
personalbar	Corresponds to the browser window's personal bar.
screenX	Gives the x-coordinate of the window's left edge.
screenY	Gives the y-coordinate of the window's top edge.
scrollbars	Corresponds to the window's scrollbars.
self	Corresponds to the current window.
status	Holds a message in the status bar.
statusbar	Corresponds to the window's status bar.
toolbar	Corresponds to the window's toolbar.
top	Refers to the topmost browser window.
window	Corresponds to the current window.

Table 11.13   Methods of the _window_ object in Netscape Navigator.

Method	Means
alert	Shows an Alert dialog box.
atob	Decodes string data encoded with base-64 encoding.
back	Moves back one history step.
blur	Releases the focus.
btoa	Codes a string using base-64 encoding.
captureEvents	Captures all events of the specified type.
clearInterval	Clears a timeout earlier set using the **setInterval** method.
clearTimeout	Clears a timeout earlier set with the **setTimeout** method.
close	Closes a window.
confirm	Makes visible a Confirmation dialog box.
crypto.random	Returns a pseudorandom text string.

(continued)

Table 11.13   Methods of the *window* object in Netscape Navigator (continued).

Method	Means
crypto.signText	Returns an encoded text string corresponding to a signed object.
disableExternalCapture	Disables external event capturing.
enableExternalCapture	Enables external event capturing.
find	Locates the specified text string in a window.
focus	Assigns the focus to the specified object.
forward	Moves forward in the history list.
handleEvent	Calls an event handler.
home	Navigates to the user's home page.
moveBy	Moves the window.
moveTo	Moves the top-left corner of the window.
open	Opens a new browser window.
print	Prints out the window or frame.
prompt	Shows a Prompt dialog box.
releaseEvents	Releases event capture.
resizeBy	Resizes a window.
resizeTo	Resizes a window to the specified width and height.
routeEvent	Sends an event to the event hierarchy.
scroll	Scrolls a window.
scrollBy	Scrolls a window by the amount indicated.
scrollTo	Scrolls a window to the coordinates indicated.
setHotKeys	Enables or disables hot keys if the window does not support menus.
setInterval	Evaluates code every specified interval.
setResizable	Specifies if a window can be resized.
setTimeout	Sets the number of milliseconds between calls to specified code.
setZOptions	Returns a window's z-order behavior.
stop	Ends a download.

Table 11.14   Events of the *window* object in Netscape Navigator.

Event	Means
onBlur	Lost focus.
onDragDrop	Occurrence of a drag and drop operation.
onError	Occurrence of an error.

(continued)

*Table 11.14   Events of the **window** object in Netscape Navigator* (continued).

Event	Means
onFocus	Gained focus.
onLoad	Loaded page.
onMove	Moved window.
onResize	Resized window.
onUnload	Unloaded page.

As you can see, the **window** object is another big one in JavaScript, and we'll put it to work in this chapter.

The location Object

The **location** object has been available in Netscape Navigator since version 2 and in Internet Explorer since version 3. This object is part of the **window** object (its real name is **window.location**) and represents the complete URL of the page in the current window. By setting this object to a new URL, you can navigate to that URL. Here's an example; when you call this function, the Web browser will navigate to the World Wide Web Consortium (W3C) site:

```
function goW3C()
{
    window.location = "http://www.W3C.org"
}
```

So what's available in the **location** object? You'll find Internet Explorer's **location** object properties in Table 11.15 and its methods in Table 11.16 (it has no events or collections). As you can see in these tables, you can dissect the current browser's location very easily using this object.

*Table 11.15   Properties of the **location** object in Internet Explorer.*

Property	Means
hash	Holds the part of the **href** property following the # mark.
host	Specifies or retrieves the hostname and port of the current URL.
hostname	Specifies or retrieves the hostname.
href	Specifies or retrieves the URL, returned as a string.
pathname	Specifies or retrieves the file name corresponding to the **location** object.
port	Specifies or retrieves the URL's port number.
protocol	Specifies or retrieves the URL's protocol.
search	Specifies or retrieves the part of the URL following the question mark.

Table 11.16   Methods of the location object in Internet Explorer.

Method	Means
assign	Navigates to a new document.
reload	Reloads a page.
replace	Loads a new document, replacing the current one.

Table 11.17   Properties of the location object in Netscape Navigator.

Property	Means
hash	Refers to an anchor name as extracted from the URL.
host	Refers to the network host's name and domain name (or IP address).
hostname	Refers to the URL's host:port part.
href	Refers to the URL.
pathname	Refers to the path part of the URL.
port	Refers to the server's port.
protocol	Refers to the protocol of the URL.
search	Refers to a query.

Table 11.18   Methods of the location object in Netscape Navigator.

Method	Means
reload	Reloads the current document in the window.
replace	Replaces the current document with a new one.

You'll find Netscape Navigator's **location** object properties in Table 11.17 and its methods in Table 11.18.

The last object I'll take a detailed look at in this chapter is the **history** object.

The history Object

The **history** object has been available in Netscape Navigator since version 2 and in Internet Explorer since version 3. Anyone familiar with the back button in browsers knows about browser history. The history corresponds to an ordered list of the URLs the user has been to before the current page (and possibly after the current page, if the user has already clicked the back button to move back to the current page).

You can use the **forward**, **back**, and **go** methods of the **window.history** object to navigate around the browser's history list. The **forward** method navigates the browser forward one page in the history list, the **back** button navigates back one page, and the **go** method lets you specify how many pages to move by passing it a positive or negative integer.

What's in the **history** object? You'll find Internet Explorer's **history** object properties in Table 11.19 and its methods in Table 11.20 (it has no events or collections).

You'll find Netscape Navigator's **history** object properties in Table 11.21 and its methods in Table 11.22.

As you've seen from all the tables in this chapter so far, there's a great deal of material here. In the Immediate Solutions section of this chapter, I'm going to take a look at the best of what these objects have to offer. In fact, I'm going to start with an entirely different object—the **navigator** object (which is part of the **window** object in Internet Explorer, but a top-level object in the Netscape Navigator) because that object can tell you what browser, and what browser version, you're working with. A glance at the tables in this chapter can tell you how important it is because the implementation of JavaScript and the scripting object model is very different in the two browsers. It's time to turn to the Immediate Solutions section for the details now.

*Table 11.19   Properties of the **history** object in Internet Explorer.*

Property	Means
length	Indicates how many objects exist in a collection.

*Table 11.20   Methods of the **history** object in Internet Explorer.*

Method	Means
back	Moves back in the **history** list.
forward	Moves forward in the **history** list.
go	Goes to a URL in the **history** list.

*Table 11.21   Properties of the **history** object in Netscape Navigator.*

Property	Means
current	Refers to the **history** object's current URL.
length	Refers to the **history** list's number of items.
next	Refers to the next **history** item's URL.
previous	Refers to the previous **history** item's URL.

*Table 11.22   Methods of the **history** object in Netscape Navigator.*

Method	Means
back	Goes back one entry in the **history** list.
forward	Goes forward in the **history** list.
go	Goes to a URL in the **history** list.

Immediate Solutions

Determining Browser Type In Code

"Darn," says the novice programmer, "I want to use Netscape layers, but they're not available in Internet Explorer." "That's why they're called Netscape layers," you say wisely. "So how can I tell if someone is using Netscape Navigator or not?" the NP asks. "You can check the **navigator.AppName** property," you say.

So much HTML work differs by browser that it's sometimes very important to know what browser you're working with. To determine the browser type, check the **navigator.AppName** property in your script. If it's "Microsoft Internet Explorer", you're working with Internet Explorer; if it's "Netscape", your script is executing in Netscape Navigator. You can also check the version of the browser with the **navigator.AppVersion** property.

TIP: In Internet Explorer, the **navigator** object is part of the **window** object, so its real name is **window.navigator**, but in Netscape Navigator, it's a top-level object, so its name is just **navigator**. However, JavaScript is usually very tolerant if you omit the beginning of a full name of a browser object, as long as it can uniquely identify the object you want. This means you can refer to the **navigator** object simply by using this name in JavaScript in both browsers.

Here's an example that will tell you which of the two browsers you're running, and what version:

```
<HTML>

    <HEAD>
        <TITLE>
            Checking Your Browser Type
        </TITLE>

    </HEAD>

    <BODY>
        <SCRIPT LANGUAGE = JavaScript>

            if (navigator.appName == "Microsoft Internet Explorer") {
                document.write("<B><CENTER>")
                document.write("You have Microsoft Internet Explorer " +
```

```
                    navigator.appVersion)
            document.write("</B></CENTER>")
    }

    if(navigator.appName == "Netscape") {
        document.write("<B><CENTER>")
        document.write("You have Netscape Navigator " +
            navigator.appVersion)
        document.write("</B></CENTER>")
    }

</SCRIPT>

<CENTER>
    <H1>
        Checking Your Browser Type
    </H1>
</CENTER>

</BODY>

</HTML>
```

The results of this code appear in Figure 11.2, where you can see the browser type and version.

NOTE: *See how useful this is—not only can you use different JavaScript code for each browser now, but, using* **document.writeln**, *you can also write entirely different Web pages, each one suited to the browser it appears in.*

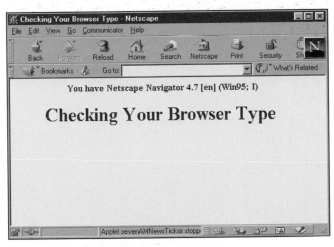

Figure 11.2   Examining browser type.

Creating A Self-Modifying Web Page

"Jeez," says the novice programmer, "people are avoiding my Web page just because I have an image in it that's 1024×1024 pixels in 16.7 million colors. Of course, it can take about ten minutes to download." "Hm," you say, "why not *ask* the users if they want to download huge images before doing so?" "How do you mean?" the NP asks.

Using the document object's **write** and **writeln** (write line) methods, you can modify Web pages. In this next example, I'm using a Confirmation dialog box from JavaScript (see "Creating Confirmation Dialog Boxes" in the Immediate Solutions section of this chapter for the details on Confirmation dialog boxes) to ask the users if they want to download the large graphics image. This dialog box will display the message "View graphics intensive page?", and if the user clicks the OK button, the code will write an **<IMG>** element to download the large graphics file. However, if the user clicks the Cancel button, it will download a smaller version of the file. Here's what the code looks like:

```
<HTML>
    <HEAD>
        <TITLE>
            Creating A Self-Modifying Web Page
        </TITLE>
    </HEAD>

    <BODY>
        <CENTER>
            <H1>
                Creating A Self-Modifying Web Page
            </H1>

            <SCRIPT LANGUAGE="JavaScript">
                if(confirm("View graphics intensive page?")) {
                    document.write("<BR><IMG WIDTH=1024 HEIGHT=1024 " +
                    "SRC='gif/image1.gif'></IMG>")
                }
                else {
                    document.write("<BR><IMG WIDTH=120 HEIGHT=120 " +
                    "SRC='gif/image1small.gif'></IMG>")
                }
            </SCRIPT>

        </CENTER>

    </BODY>

</HTML>
```

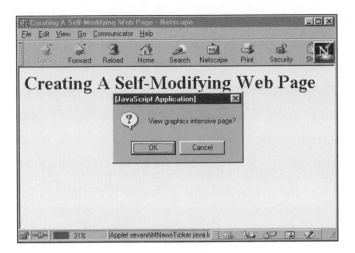

Figure 11.3   Creating a self-modifying Web page.

You can see the results in Figure 11.3, where the Confirmation dialog box is visible.

TIP: *Note that I put the **<SCRIPT>** element in the **<BODY>** element in the previous example. I did this because the script is run when it is encountered, and I wanted the beginning of the page to show before displaying the Confirmation dialog box. (The usual rule of putting the **<SCRIPT>** element in the **<HEAD>** element is to make sure that all code is in place before any element in the page itself needs to refer to it, but that doesn't apply in this case.)*

Here's an important note— you often only use **document.write** or **document. writeln** when a page is first loaded, to write the page as it's loading. But you can also rewrite the page after it's been loaded. Take a look at this next example; when the user clicks the page, the whole page is replaced by the text "This is a new page!" (this example will only work in Internet Explorer):

```
<HTML>

    <HEAD>
        <TITLE>
            Using document.writeln
        </TITLE>

        <SCRIPT>
            function rewrite()
            {
```

```
                    document.writeln("This is a new page!")
                }
        </SCRIPT>
    </HEAD>


    <BODY onMouseDown="rewrite()">

        <CENTER>

        <H1>
            Click this page to rewrite it!
        </H1>

    </BODY>


</HTML>
```

In Netscape Navigator, you need to open the document for writing and then close it as well. Note that you also need the line **document.onMouseDown = rewrite** to connect the **rewrite** function to the **mousedown** event in the document in Netscape Navigator. Here's how is looks:

```
<HTML>

    <HEAD>
        <TITLE>
            Using document.writeln
        </TITLE>

    </HEAD>

    <BODY onMouseDown="rewrite()">

        <SCRIPT>
            document.onMouseDown = rewrite

            function rewrite()
            {
                document.open()
                document.writeln("This is a new page!")
                document.close()
            }
        </SCRIPT>

        <CENTER>
```

```
        <H1>
            Click this page to rewrite it!
        </H1>

    </BODY>

</HTML>
```

TIP: *We'll see other ways of rewriting Web pages when discussing dynamic HTML in Chapter 13.*

Here's another example. This page presents a menu to the user displaying the breakfast, lunch, or dinner menus automatically, based on the time of day (which is found using the JavaScript **Date** object):

```
<HTML>
    <HEAD>
        <TITLE>
            The JavaScript Menu Example
        </TITLE>
    </HEAD>

    <BODY>
        <SCRIPT LANGUAGE="JavaScript">
            var dateNow = new Date()
            var hourNow = dateNow.getHours()
            document.write( "<CENTER>")
            document.write( "<H1>")
            document.write( "Welcome To Our Restaurant")
            document.write( "</H1>")
            document.write( "</CENTER>")

            if (hourNow < 5 || hourNow > 23){
                document.write( "<CENTER>")
                document.write( "<H1>")
                document.write( "Sorry, We Are Closed." )
                document.write( "</H1>")
                document.write( "</CENTER>")
            }

            if (hourNow > 6 && hourNow < 12 ) {
                document.write( "<CENTER>")
                document.write( "<TABLE BORDER>")
                document.write(
```

```
            "<TR><TH COLSPAN = 2>Breakfast</TH></TR>")
        document.write(
            "<TR><TD>Pancakes</TD><TD>$2.00</TD></TR>")
        document.write(
            "<TR><TD>Eggs</TD><TD>$2.50</TD></TR>")
        document.write(
            "<TR><TD>Waffles</TD><TD>$1.50</TD></TR>")
        document.write(
            "<TR><TD>Oatmeal</TD><TD>$1.00</TD></TR>")
        document.write( "</TABLE>")
        document.write( "</CENTER>")
    }

    if ( hourNow >= 12 && hourNow < 17 ) {
        document.write( "<CENTER>")
        document.write( "<TABLE BORDER>")
        document.write(
            "<TR><TH COLSPAN = 2>Lunch</TH></TR>")
        document.write(
            "<TR><TD>Ham Sandwich</TD><TD>$3.50</TD></TR>")
        document.write(
            "<TR><TD>Chicken Sandwich</TD><TD>$3.50</TD></TR>")
        document.write(
            "<TR><TD>Cheese Sandwich</TD><TD>$3.00</TD></TR>")
        document.write(
            "<TR><TD>Lobster Nuggets</TD><TD>$5.00</TD></TR>")
        document.write(
            "<TR><TD>Peacock</TD><TD>$4.50</TD></TR>")
        document.write(
            "<TR><TD>Chili</TD><TD>$2.00</TD></TR>")
        document.write(
            "<TR><TD>Chicken Soup</TD><TD>$1.50</TD></TR>")
        document.write( "</TABLE>")
        document.write( "</CENTER>")
    }

    if ( hourNow >= 17 && hourNow < 22 ) {
        document.write( "<CENTER>")
        document.write( "<TABLE BORDER>")
        document.write(
            "<TR><TH COLSPAN = 2>Dinner</TH></TR>")
        document.write(
            "<TR><TD>Lobster</TD><TD>$7.50</TD></TR>")
```

```
          document.write(
              "<TR><TD>Filet Mignon</TD><TD>$8.00</TD></TR>")
          document.write(
              "<TR><TD>Flank Steak</TD><TD>$7.00</TD></TR>")
          document.write(
              "<TR><TD>Tube Steak</TD><TD>$3.50</TD></TR>")
          document.write(
              "<TR><TD>Salad</TD><TD>$2.50</TD></TR>")
          document.write(
              "<TR><TD>Potato</TD><TD>$1.50</TD></TR>")
          document.write(
              "<TR><TD>Eggplant</TD><TD>$1.50</TD></TR>")
          document.write( "</TABLE>")
          document.write( "</CENTER>")
      }

  </SCRIPT>
</BODY>

</HTML>
```

You can see the results of this code in Figure 11.4.

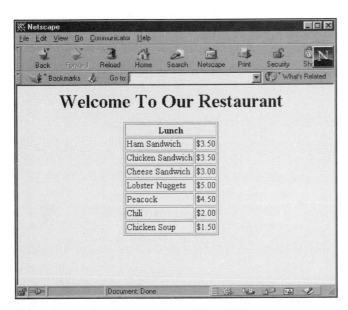

Figure 11.4   Creating a self-modifying Web page based on time of day.

Setting A Page's Background Color

Here are some useful **document** object properties:

- **document.bgcolor**—Background color of the current page.
- **document.fgcolor**—Foreground color of the current page.
- **document.lastmodified**—Date the page was last modified.
- **document.title**—Title of the current page.

You can set these properties at runtime; here's an example page that turns red when you click it in Internet Explorer:

```
<HTML>

    <HEAD>
        <TITLE>
            Setting Background Color With JavaScript
        </TITLE>
    </HEAD>

    <BODY onMouseDown="document.bgColor='red'">

        <CENTER>

        <H1>
            Click this page to turn it red!
        </H1>

    </BODY>

</HTML>
```

Reloading Images At Runtime

"Hm," says the novice programmer, "the big boss wants me to put the photos of the company picnic online, but there are two thousand of them. Am I going to have to create a new page for each image?" "Not at all," you say, "you can use JavaScript to load new images into the same page interactively." The NP says, "Huh?"

You can use the **document** object to reach the elements in a Web page if you give those elements names. In this case, I'm going to reload an image in an **<IMG>**

element when the user clicks a button. I'll give the **<IMG>** element the name **IMG1**, and it will be in the same HTML form as the button (we'll cover forms in Chapter 12). The form's name is "FORM1", and it's an element in the document, so I can reach it as **document.FORM1**. I can then refer to the **<IMG>** element as **document.FORM1.IMG1** and the actual **SRC** attribute of that image element as **document.FORM1.IMG1.src**. This means I can reload the image by resetting the **SRC** attribute of the **<IMG>** element like this:

```
<HTML>
    <HEAD>
        <TITLE>
            Reloading Images At Run Time
        </TITLE>

        <SCRIPT LANGUAGE = Javascript>
            function reloadImage()
            {
                document.FORM1.IMG1.src = "gif/image2.gif"
            }
        </SCRIPT>
    </HEAD>

    <BODY>
        <CENTER>
            <FORM NAME = FORM1>
                <IMG NAME = "IMG1" SRC = "gif/image1.gif"
                    WIDTH = 236 HEIGHT = 118>
            <BR>
            <BR>
            <INPUT TYPE = BUTTON Value = "Load new image"
                onClick = "reloadImage()">
            </FORM>
        </CENTER>

    </BODY>

</HTML>
```

That's it; when the user clicks the button in this example, the Web browser will load a new image, replacing the old one. We'll see a great deal more about working with the elements in a Web page like this when discussing dynamic HTML in Chapter 13.

Opening A New Browser Window

The novice programmer has a problem and says, "I want to let people who read my online novel open a glossary defining various terms—how do I open a new window when the user clicks a button?" "No problem," you say, "just use the **window** object's **open** method."

You can use the **window** object's **open** method to open new browser windows and to configure those windows. Here's how to use **window.open** in Netscape Navigator (optional arguments appear in brackets, **[** and **]**):

```
newWindow = window.open(URL, Name [, Features])
```

URL is the URL of the new page to open, *Name* is the name you want to give the new window, and the *Features* argument lets you configure the window including hiding toolbars and status bars. The possible settings for the *Features* argument appear in Table 11.23. You place the features you want in a comma separated list, enclose that list in quotes like this, "height=200,width=400,status=no, toolbar=no,menubar=no,location=no", and pass that string as the *Features* argument.

NOTE: Do not include spaces in the list in the *Features* string. Internet Explorer doesn't have a problem if you do, but Netscape Navigator won't be able to understand what you want if you include spaces.

Table 11.23   Window features in Netscape Navigator.

Feature	Means
alwaysLowered	Set to **yes** to create a new window below other windows.
alwaysRaised	Set to **yes** to create a new window on top of other windows.
dependent	Set to **yes** to create a new window, a child of the current window.
directories	Set to **yes** to create the standard browser directory buttons.
height	Refers to the height of the window measured in pixels.
hotkeys	Set to **no** or 0 to disable most hotkeys in new windows that have no menu bar.
innerHeight	Refers to the height of the window's content area as measured in pixels.
innerWidth	Refers to the width of the window's content area as measured in pixels. When you want to create a window smaller than 100x100 pixels, use this feature.
location	Set to **yes** to create a **location** entry field.

(continued)

Table 11.23   Window features in Netscape Navigator (continued).

Feature	Means
menubar	Set to **yes** to create a menu bar at the top of the window.
outerHeight	Refers to the height, in pixels, of the outside edge of the window.
personalbar	Set to **yes** to create the Personal Toolbar.
resizable	Set to **yes** to allow a user to resize the window.
screenX	Refers to the distance a new window should be set from the left side of the screen.
screenY	Refers to the distance a new window should be set from the top of the screen.
scrollbars	Set to **yes** to create horizontal and vertical scrollbars that appear when needed.
status	Set to **yes** to create a status bar, which is displayed at the bottom of the window.
titlebar	Set to **yes** to create a title bar.
toolbar	Set to **yes** to create the standard browser toolbar.
width	Refers to the width of the window, measured in pixels.
z-lock	Set to **yes** to create a window that does not move above other windows when becoming active.

In Internet Explorer, you use **window.open** like this:

```
newWindow = window.open([URL] [, Name] [, Features] [, Replace])
```

As before, **URL** is the URL of the new page to open, **Name** is the name you want to give the new window, and the **Features** argument lets you configure the window. The possible settings for the **Features** argument appear in Table 11.24. The **Replace** argument specifies whether the URL that is loaded into the new page should create a new entry in the window's browsing history or replace the current entry in the browsing history. If this argument is set to true, no new history entry is created for the new page.

Table 11.24   Window features in Internet Explorer.

Feature	Means
channelmode	Specifies whether the window should be displayed in theater mode. By default, set to **no**. Can be **yes**, **no**, 1, or 0.
directories	Specifies whether to display directory buttons. By default, set to **yes**. Can be **yes**, **no**, 1, or 0.

(continued)

11. Putting JavaScript To Work

Table 11.24 Window features in Internet Explorer (continued).

Feature	Means
fullscreen	Specifies whether to display the browser in a full-screen or normal window. By default, set to **no** (which displays the browser as a normal window). Can be **yes**, **no**, 1, or 0.
height	Specifies the height of the window, as measured in pixels. Note that the minimum possible value is 100 pixels.
left	Specifies the left location in pixels.
location	Specifies whether or not to show the location box in the browser. By default, set to **yes**. Can be **yes**, **no**, 1, or 0.
menubar	Specifies whether or not the menu bar should be visible. By default, set to **yes**. Can be **yes**, **no**, 1, or 0.
resizable	Specifies whether to let the new window be resizeable. By default, set to **yes**. Can be **yes**, **no**, 1, or 0.
scrollbars	Specifies whether or not the new window should display horizontal and vertical scrollbars. By default, set to **yes**. Can be **yes**, **no**, 1, or 0.
status	Specifies whether or not the new window should display a status bar. By default, set to **yes**. Can be **yes**, **no**, 1, or 0.
titlebar	Specifies whether or not the new window should display a title bar. By default, set to **yes**. Can be **yes**, **no**, 1, or 0.
toolbar	Specifies whether or not the new window should display a browser toolbar. By default, set to **yes**. Can be **yes**, **no**, 1, or 0.
top	Specifies the top location in pixels.
width	Specifies the width of the new window, as measured in pixels. Note that the minimum possible value is 100.

TIP: *Although you can open a browser in full-screen mode, be careful. Because this mode hides the browser's title bar and menus, you should always provide a button to help the user close the window. Note that ALT+F4 also closes the new window.*

In this example, I'm opening a glossary page, glossary.htm, when the user clicks a button:

```
<HTML>

    <HEAD>
        <TITLE>
            Opening A New Window With JavaScript
        </TITLE>
```

```
        <SCRIPT LANGUAGE = JavaScript>
            function showGlossary()
            {
                window.open("glossary.htm")
            }
        </SCRIPT>
    </HEAD>

    <BODY>

        <FORM>
            <CENTER>
                <BR>
                <H1>
                    Opening A New Window With JavaScript
                </H1>
                <BR>
                <BR>
                <INPUT TYPE = BUTTON Value = "See Glossary"
                onClick = "showGlossary()">
            </CENTER>
        </FORM>

    </BODY>

</HTML>
```

Here's the page I use for the glossary, glossary.htm:

```
<HTML>
    <HEAD>
        <TITLE>
            Glossary
        </TITLE>
    </HEAD>

    <BODY>
        <CENTER>
            <BR>
            <H1>
                Glossary
            </H1>
        </CENTER>
        <BR>
        <UL>
```

```
              <LI>HTML: HyperText Markup Language
              <LI>JavaScript: a fun scripting language
              <LI>W3C: The World Wide Web Consortium
        </UL>
    </BODY>

</HTML>
```

The results of this code appear in Figure 11.5. For a more involved example show-ing how to configure and write in a new window using **window.open**, see the next section.

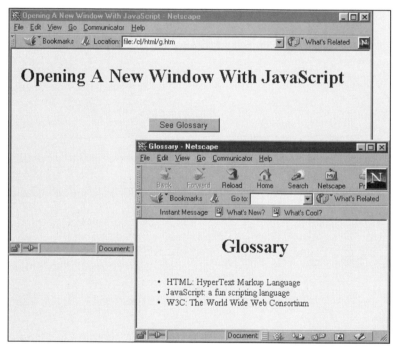

Figure 11.5   Opening a new window.

Configuring And Writing To A New Window

The big boss appears and says, "When someone navigates to our site, can we open a new browser window without toolbars or status bars, to display advertis-ing?" "You can," you say, "but that's kind of cheesy." "But will it bring in more sales?" the BB wants to know. You say, "It'll probably bring in more complaints than sales."

Using the **window.open** method (see the previous section), you can configure new windows as you open them. In this example, I'll create a window of a certain size without any toolbars or status bars to show how it's done.

To do this, I just use the **window.open** method, specifying the way I want the new window, and then I write to the new window using the **document.write** method like this:

```
<HTML>
    <HEAD>
        <TITLE>
            Creating A New Window
        </TITLE>

        <SCRIPT LANGUAGE = JavaScript>

            function createNewWindow()
            {
                var newWindow = window.open("window.htm", null,
                "height=200,width=400,status=no," +
                "toolbar=no,menubar=no,location=no")

                newWindow.document.write(
                "<BR><BR><CENTER><H1>This window " +
                "has just been created!</H1></CENTER>")
            }
        </SCRIPT>

    </HEAD>

    <BODY>
        <CENTER>
            <BR>
            <H1>
                Creating A New Window
            </H1>
            <BR>
            <BR>
            <FORM>
                <INPUT TYPE = BUTTON Value = "Create New Window"
                    onClick = "createNewWindow()">
            </FORM>
        </CENTER>
```

```
        </BODY>

</HTML>
```

Here's the page I use for the opened window, window.htm:

```
<HTML>
    <HEAD>
        <TITLE>
            This Is A New Window
        </TITLE>

    </HEAD>

    <BODY>
    </BODY>
</HTML>
```

And that's all it takes—the results of this code appear in Figure 11.6. Now you know how to remove toolbars and status bars from a browser window.

Figure 11.6   Opening and configuring a new window.

Creating Alert Dialog Boxes

The novice programmer says, "I need some way of strongly warning users. I need some way of grabbing their attention. I need some way of..." "Alert dialog boxes," you say, "what you need is an Alert dialog box."

When you want to bring a strong message to the attention of the users and make sure they notice it before continuing, you can use the **window** object's Alert dialog box. This dialog box displays a message and an OK button; users must click the OK button before they can continue browsing.

Here's an example. In this case, I'm checking the URL of a Web page using the **location** object's **href** property, and if the page is not where it should be, the code will display an Alert box with the message "Hey! You copied my page without permission!" like this:

```
<HTML>
    <HEAD>
        <TITLE>
            Using An Alert Dialog Box
        </TITLE>
    </HEAD>

    <BODY>
        <SCRIPT LANGUAGE = JavaScript>

        if (location.href !=
        "http://www.starpowder.com/steve/index.html") {
            window.alert("Hey! You copied my page without permission!")
        }
        else {
            document.writeln("Welcome to my Web page!")
        }

    </SCRIPT>
    </BODY>

</HTML>
```

You can see the results of this HTML in Figure 11.7; this page works in both Internet Explorer and Netscape Navigator.

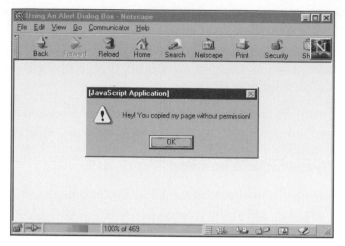

Figure 11.7   Using an Alert dialog box.

Creating Confirmation Dialog Boxes

"Hm," says the novice programmer, "Alert dialog boxes are nice, but I want an actual response from the user before continuing. Is there some way to get that?" "Well," you say, "you can try a Confirmation dialog box."

The **window** object's **confirm** method displays a Confirmation dialog box with two buttons: OK and Cancel. This method returns a Boolean value of **true** if users click the OK button and **false** if they click Cancel.

Here's an example putting **window.confirm** to work. In this case, the code displays a message saying "Your total comes to $34.23. Click OK to complete the order.". If the user clicks OK, the page continues with the message "Thanks for your purchase.", and if the user clicks Cancel, the page displays "Would you like to order something else?". This page works in both Internet Explorer and Netscape Navigator:

```
<HTML>
    <HEAD>
        <TITLE>
            Using A Confirmation Dialog Box
        </TITLE>
    </HEAD>

    <BODY>
        <CENTER>
```

```
<H1>
    Using A Confirmation Dialog Box
</H1>

<SCRIPT LANGUAGE="JavaScript">
if(confirm(
"Your total comes to $34.23. Click OK to complete the order.")
)
{
    document.write("<BR>Thanks for your purchase.")
}
else
{
    document.write
    (
        "<BR>Would you like to order something else?"
    )
}
</SCRIPT>

    </CENTER>

</BODY>

</HTML>
```

You can see the results of this code in Figure 11.8.

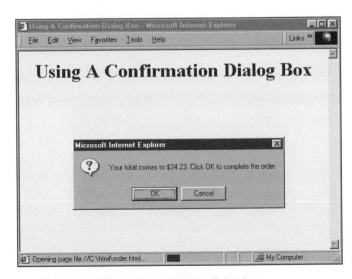

Figure 11.8   Using a Confirmation dialog box.

Creating Prompt Dialog Boxes

The novice programmer is perplexed and says, "I really need to have the user type something in, which means I can't use Alert or Confirmation dialog boxes. Am I stuck?" "By no means," you say suavely, "just use a Prompt dialog box."

You can use the **window** object's **prompt** method to display a dialog box that will display a prompt to the user and accept a typed string back. The return value of this method will be the typed string.

In this next example, I'm letting the user type text directly into a Web page by using a Prompt dialog box. Note that you can specify two arguments to **window.prompt**—the prompt to display and some default text, which will appear in the text field in the Prompt dialog box. Here, I'm setting the prompt to "Enter the text you want in this page", and the default text to "Hi there!":

```
<HTML>
    <HEAD>
        <TITLE>
            Creating A Prompt Dialog Box
        </TITLE>
    </HEAD>

    <BODY>
        <SCRIPT LANGUAGE = JavaScript>
            var text = prompt("Enter the text you want in this page",
                "Hi there! ")

            if (text == "") {
                alert("You didn't enter anything.")
            }
            else {
                document.writeln("<CENTER><H1>" + text + "</H1></CENTER>")
            }
        </SCRIPT>
    </BODY>

</HTML>
```

You can see the results of this code in Figure 11.9. As you can see, the Prompt dialog box is displaying its prompt, and I've entered the text "Greetings!" in the text field. When I click the OK button, the Prompt dialog box disappears and "Greetings!" appears in the Web page, which you can see in Figure 11.10. It's a nice effect—users get the impression they've written directly to the HTML of your Web page, and in fact, that is exactly what's happened.

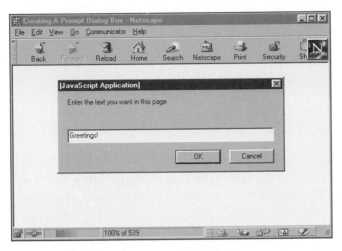

Figure 11.9   Creating a Prompt dialog box.

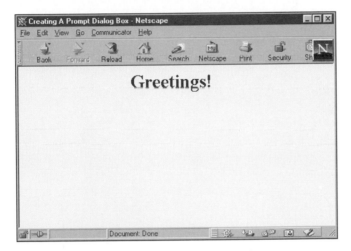

Figure 11.10   Writing a Web page at load time.

Writing To The Browser's Status Bar

You can use the **window** object's **defaultStatus** property to display text in the Web browser's status bar. In this example, I'm using a JavaScript *timer* event to call a function named **showMessage** once every two tenths of a second, allowing the code to scroll a message ("Welcome!") around in the status bar:

```
<HTML>
    <HEAD>
```

```
<TITLE>
    Writing To The Browser's Status Bar
</TITLE>

<SCRIPT LANGUAGE = JavaScript>
    var position = 0
    var message = "Welcome!"
    timerID = setInterval('showMessage()', 200)

    function showMessage()
    {
        if (position > 20){
            position = 0
        }

        var text = " "
        for (var loopIndex = 0; loopIndex <= position;
            loopIndex++) {
            text = text + " "
        }

        text = text + message
        window.defaultStatus = text
        position++
    }

</SCRIPT>

</HEAD>

<BODY>

    <CENTER>
        <H1>
            Writing To The Browser's Status Bar
        </H1>
    </CENTER>
</BODY>

</HTML>
```

Note how the **setInterval** method works—you pass it the JavaScript you want executed periodically and the interval between calls. In the previous example, I'm just calling the **showMessage** function every 200 milliseconds, and that

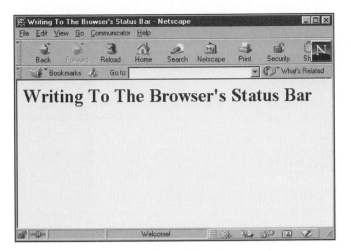

Figure 11.11   Writing to the browser's status bar.

function will display the message as needed. The results appear in Figure 11.11. This is a common effect seen in JavaScript-enabled Web pages: scrolling text in the status bar. It can be fun, but can also look a little cutesy.

Navigating With The **location** Object

"Well," the big boss says, "why can't we take control of what happens when users browse around our site? Let's send them directly to the page with the big photo of me." "Well," you say, "I can use the **location** object to do that, but…" "Great," says the BB, "do it."

When you set **window.location** to a new URL, the browser will navigate to that URL. In this example, I'm letting users enter a new URL in a text field and click a button marked Navigate. When they do, the browser navigates to the new URL. Here's the example:

```html
<HTML>
    <HEAD>
        <TITLE>
            Navigating To A New URL Using JavaScript
        </TITLE>

        <SCRIPT LANGUAGE = JavaScript>

            function goTo()
```

```
                {
                    window.location = document.form1.Textbox.value
                }

        </SCRIPT>

    </HEAD>

    <BODY>
        <CENTER>
            <H1>
                Navigating To A New URL Using JavaScript
            </H1>

            <FORM NAME = form1>
                <BR>
                <INPUT TYPE = TEXT NAME = "Textbox" SIZE = 60>
                <BR>
                <BR>
                <INPUT TYPE = BUTTON Value = "Navigate" onClick = "goTo()">
            </FORM>

        </CENTER>

    </BODY>

</HTML>
```

You can see the results of this code in Figure 11.12. When the user enters a URL and clicks the Navigate button, the browser navigates to that URL.

In fact, you can redirect a browser to a new page immediately by using this technique, saving you the trouble of writing an http redirection header. This technique is commonly used when you've created a new Web page and want to direct people from the old URL to the new one. Here's an example that redirects users to the W3C Web site as soon as they open this page:

```
<HTML>
    <HEAD>
        <TITLE>
            Navigating To A New URL Using JavaScript
        </TITLE>

        <SCRIPT LANGUAGE = JavaScript>
```

```
            window.location = "http://www.W3C.org"

        </SCRIPT>

    </HEAD>

    <BODY>
        <CENTER>
            <H1>
                Redirecting To A New URL Using JavaScript
            </H1>
            My page is down right now. Redirecting you now...
        </CENTER>

    </BODY>

</HTML>
```

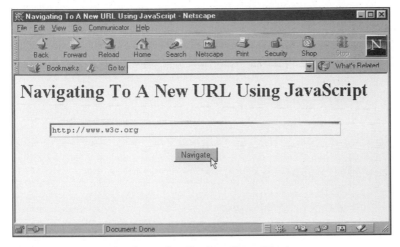

Figure 11.12   Navigating using the **location** object.

Navigating With The **history** Object

"Hmm," says the novice programmer, "using the **location** object, I can navigate to a new URL, but it's too bad I can't create a back button in a Web page—I'd have a browser within a browser!" You smile and say, "Not only can you create a Back button, you can create a Forward button too!"

You can use the **forward**, **back**, and **go** methods of the **window.history** object to navigate around the browser's history list. The **forward** method navigates the browser forward one page in the **history** list, the **back** button navigates back one page, and the **go** method lets you specify how many pages to move by passing it a positive or negative integer.

Here's an example putting the **history** object to work. In this case, I'll create Forward and Back buttons and also Forward Two Pages and Back Two Pages buttons:

```
<HTML>
    <HEAD>
        <TITLE>
            Using The history Object
        </TITLE>

        <SCRIPT LANGUAGE = JavaScript>

            function goBack()
            {
                window.history.back()
            }

            function goForward()
            {
                window.history.forward()
            }

            function goBackTwo()
            {
                window.history.go(-2)
            }

            function goForwardTwo()
            {
                window.history.go(2)
            }

        </SCRIPT>

    </HEAD>

    <BODY>

        <CENTER>
```

```
<H1>
    Using The history Object
</H1>

<FORM>
    <BR>
    Navigate using the history object!
    <BR>
    <BR>
    <INPUT TYPE = BUTTON Value = "< Back One Page"
        onClick = "goBack()">
    <INPUT TYPE = BUTTON Value = "Forward One Page >"
        onClick = "goForward()">
    <BR>
    <BR>
    <INPUT TYPE = BUTTON Value = "<< Back Two Pages"
        onClick = "goBackTwo()">
    <INPUT TYPE = BUTTON Value = "Forward Two Pages >>"
        onClick = "goForwardTwo()">
    </FORM>
</CENTER>

</BODY>

</HTML>
```

You can see the results in Figure 11.13. The user can click the buttons in that page to move forward or back by one or by two pages. You don't need buttons to navigate, of course; you can do it directly from code.

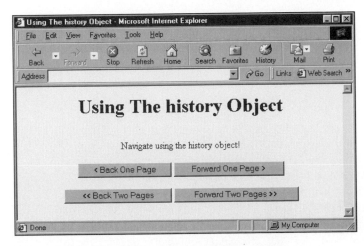

Figure 11.13   Navigating using the **history** object.

Creating JavaScript URLs: Improving Image Maps

The Web page design czar is worried and says, "Our image maps lack pizazz. They should do something." "They *do* do something," you say, "but I could make them do more with a little JavaScript." The WPDC says, "Now you're talking!"

You can create JavaScript URLs that don't jump to a new page—they jump to a JavaScript function. To do that, you use the protocol, **javascript:** instead of **http:**, and you provide the name of a JavaScript function, not a URL. Here's an example. When the user clicks this link, the JavaScript function **displayWarning** is called; this function might display a Confirmation dialog box, and if users click OK, they navigate onto the appropriate URL:

```
If you dare, you can go to my
<A HREF="javascript:displayWarning()">dangerous page</A>!
```

Here's another example, modifying the image map example from Chapter 5. In this case, I'll assume the guest book part of the Web site is down, so when the user clicks the guest book region in the image map, I'll display an Alert dialog box with a message that indicates the guest book is not working:

```
<HTML>
    <HEAD>
        <TITLE>
            Using A Client Side Image Map
        </TITLE>

        <SCRIPT LANGUAGE="JavaScript">
            function sorry()
            {
                alert("Sorry, the guestbook is not working right now.")
            }
        </SCRIPT>
    </HEAD>

<BODY BGCOLOR="BLACK">

    <CENTER>
        <IMG WIDTH=528 HEIGHT=137 SRC="mainmenu.jpg"
            BORDER=0 ALT="Image Map" USEMAP="#IMAP">
        <MAP NAME="IMAP">
            <AREA NAME="LINK1" SHAPE=RECT COORDS="16,39 127,61"
                HREF="http://www.reuters.com" ALT="News">
            <AREA NAME="LINK2" SHAPE=RECT COORDS="62,71 173,93"
```

```
                HREF="http://www.starpowder.com/steve/search.html"
                ALT="Web search">
            <AREA NAME="LINK3" SHAPE=RECT COORDS="98,104 209,126"
                HREF="http://www.nnic.noaa.gov" ALT="Weather">
            <AREA NAME="LINK4" SHAPE=RECT COORDS="411,35 522,57"
                HREF="javascript:sorry()"
                ALT="Guest book">
            <AREA NAME="LINK5" SHAPE=RECT COORDS="360,67 471,89"
                HREF="http://www.yahoo.com/Guides_and_Tutorials/"
                ALT="Create a Web page">
            <AREA NAME="LINK6" SHAPE=RECT COORDS="328,98 439,120"
                HREF="http://www.web21.com/services/hot100/index.html"
                "Hottest 100 sites">
            <AREA NAME="DEFAULT" SHAPE=DEFAULT
                HREF=
                "http://www.starpowder.com/steve/index.html#mainmenu"
                ALT="Image map">
        </MAP>
    </CENTER>

    </BODY>
</HTML>
```

You can see the results in Figure 11.14. When the user clicks the guest book URL, the Alert dialog box appears with the message that the guest book is out of commission. As you can imagine, this technique need not only be applied to image maps; you can create a graphical interface for nearly any purpose, including games, and tie it to JavaScript this way.

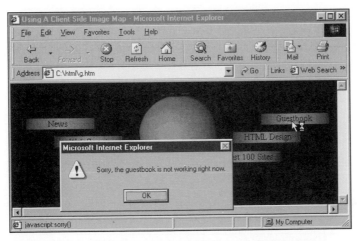

Figure 11.14   Adding a JavaScript URL to an image map.

Creating Cookies With JavaScript

The novice programmer races up and asks breathlessly, "Is it true? Can I really create cookies with JavaScript?" "Sure is," you say, "and it's easy." "Wow," cries the NP, "tell me how!"

Cookies are both loved and hated (so be careful before using them), and you can indeed set them using JavaScript. A cookie is text that the browser stores on the local machine, and which you can access at a later date. A common use of cookies is to store shopping cart information, that is, a user's purchases, while he or she browses around a commercial site. If you're experienced with the Web, you know about cookies.

TIP: You should be aware that cookies really annoy some people (I almost count myself among them), so be judicious in using them if you have to. Also, you should know that most browsers set limits on the maximum number of cookies they'll store, such as 200, so don't set too many. I wish all Web authors were so considerate—I've seen a single page attempt to set nearly one hundred cookies.

The **cookie** property of a page's **document** object holds the actual cookie text, and unless you make special preparations, you'll only see the cookie text that was stored for the current Web page or for other pages stored in the same directory on the server. I'll create an example here that creates a cookie when the user clicks a button and retrieves the cookie's text when the user clicks another button (of course, you can retrieve the cookie at a later time by reloading this example and clicking the retrieve button again). In this case, I'll set the cookie to expire in one day.

Creating A Cookie

To create a cookie, all you need to do is set **document.cookie** to a string containing keyword/value pairs, separated by semicolons. For instance, I'll call the cookie in this example "greatCookie" and give it the text "This is the cookie text." To make the cookie expire on September 2, 2000 (that is, set a date for when the browser will delete the cookie), I would use the **expires** keyword and set **document.cookie** to "greatCookie=This is the cookie text.;expires=MON, 02-Sep-00 12:00:00 GMT".

Here are the possible keywords you can use in **document.cookie** (all of them are optional):

- **domain=*domainname***—This makes the cookie accessible to other pages at the same site.

- **expires=*date***—The date the cookie expires; must end with GMT for Netscape Navigator (here's the format: MON, 02-Sep-00 12:00:00 GMT).

- **name=*cookiename***—The name of the cookie, which you use to refer to it.

- **path=*pathname***—The directory to use for the cookie; pages with cookies in the same directory can read each other's cookies.

- **secure**—This cookie must only be used with a secure (https:) server.

TIP: *In a very early version of Netscape Navigator, version 1.1, you must set the **PATH** attribute to something, at least a forward slash (/), if you set an **expires** keyword, or the cookie will not be stored.*

To create the cookie in this example, I'll write a function named **setCookie**. In this function, I'll create a new **Date** object to set the time this cookie expires. I want to make the cookie expire in one day, so I use the **Date** object's **getTime** method, which returns the time in milliseconds and add 24×60×60×1000 milliseconds to that time. Then I'll convert the new date to GMT using the JavaScript **toGMTString** function, display an Alert dialog box announcing that the cookie was created, and so create the new cookie like this:

```
function setCookie()
{
    var cookieDate = new Date()
    cookieDate.setTime(cookicDate.getTime() + 24 * 60 * 60 *
        1000)

    document.cookie =
        "greatCookie=This is the cookie text.;expires="
        + cookieDate.toGMTString()

    window.alert("Cookie created!")
}
```

Now it's time to retrieve the newly set cookie.

Retrieving A Cookie

To read the cookie, you only need to search the text in **document.cookie** (which is automatically loaded) for the beginning of the cookie text. In this case, the cookie text begins with "greatCookie=", so I'll search for that using the JavaScript **String** class's **indexOf** method, which returns the location at which "greatCookie=" appears in the text. Next, I'll use the **String** class's **substring** method to retrieve the actual cookie text, like this, in a function named **getCookie.** Note that if you have more than one cookie set, you should search for the end of the cookie you're looking for as well, because they're all stored in one long string, and the following code will return everything after the location at which **greatCookie=** appears:

```
function getCookie()
{
    var cookieData = new String(document.cookie)
    var cookieHeader = "greatCookie="

    var cookieStart = cookieData.indexOf(cookieHeader)

    if (cookieStart != -1){

        document.form1.Text.value =
            cookieData.substring(cookieStart
            + cookieHeader.length)
    }
    else{
        document.form1.Text.value = "Did not find the cookie."
    }
}
```

If the cookie was indeed found, I display the text of the cookie in a text field (this text is what you'd use in your code if you were making use of the cookie to store data, such as shopping cart purchases). Here's the whole example in place in a Web page:

```
<HTML>
    <HEAD>
        <TITLE>
            Working With Cookies
        </TITLE>

        <SCRIPT LANGUAGE="JavaScript">

            function setCookie()
            {

                var cookieDate = new Date()
                cookieDate.setTime(cookieDate.getTime() + 24 * 60 * 60 *
                    1000)

                document.cookie =
                    "greatCookie=This is the cookie text.;expires="
                    + cookieDate.toGMTString()

                window.alert("Cookie created!")
            }
```

```
        function getCookie()
        {

            var cookieData = new String(document.cookie)
            var cookieHeader = "greatCookie="

            var cookieStart = cookieData.indexOf(cookieHeader)

            if (cookieStart != -1){

                document.form1.Text.value =
                    cookieData.substring(cookieStart
                    + cookieHeader.length)
            }
            else{
                document.form1.Text.value = "Did not find the cookie."
            }
        }
    </SCRIPT>
</HEAD>

<BODY>
    <CENTER>
        <H1>
            Working With Cookies In JavaScript
        </Il1>
    </CENTER>

    <FORM NAME = form1>

        <CENTER>
            <INPUT TYPE="TEXT" NAME="Text" SIZE="30">
            <BR>
            <BR>
            <INPUT TYPE = BUTTON Value = "Create the cookie"
                onClick = "setCookie()">
            <BR>
            <BR>
            <INPUT TYPE = BUTTON Value = "Retrieve the cookie"
                onClick = "getCookie()">
        </CENTER>

    </FORM>

</BODY>

</HTML>
```

Figure 11.15   Creating and retrieving a cookie.

You can see the results in Figure 11.15. When the user clicks the Create The Cookie button, the cookie is created and stored. When the user clicks the Retrieve The Cookie button (or reloads the page within one day and clicks this button), the cookie text is retrieved and displayed. That's it—now you're working with cookies.

NOTE: *No one I know knows for sure why cookies are called cookies. Some people say it's because of the Unix fortune program, which types out a fortune cookie message when you run it. My own preference is to believe that the name comes from the infamous cookie program I remember from the MIT Artificial Intelligence Lab. When you ran this program, it would startle someone by printing out at their terminal, "Would you give me a cookie?" If the person ignored it, the program would become more and more insistent over time, finally printing out the message "I WANT A COOKIE!" in letters one screen high. All you had to do was type "cookie" and the program would thank you politely and quit.*

Chapter 12

Creating HTML Forms
And HTML Controls

In Depth

In the previous two chapters, we worked through a lot of JavaScript syntax, and in this chapter, it's time to put it to work with the original and still primary way of making your Web pages interactive—HTML *forms*. Using forms, we'll be able to handle HTML *controls*, like buttons, checkboxes, radio buttons, select controls (much like a drop-down list box), text areas, and more. We'll learn about all these uses and more in this chapter.

What's A Form?

There's no denying the popularity of HTML buttons, checkboxes, text fields, and other controls in modern Web pages. Everywhere you look it seems some Web page is asking you to enter your email address (be wary) or your credit card number (be even warier). Other pages are studded with buttons and checkboxes that let you work with them much as you'd work with a program on your own computer. To use HTML controls like these, you must enclose them in HTML forms.

Why do you need to enclose controls in forms before you can use them? Forms were originally intended to let the user send data back to the server, for instance, when you type your email address into an HTML text field (called a text box in other programs) and click a Submit button to subscribe to an email list. By clicking the Submit button in a form, all the data in the controls in the form is gathered together and sent to the server. You can use code on the server to decipher that data and act on what the user has sent you. In this way, a form packages all the data from a group of controls, and all the data is then sent to the server.

TIP: *Although you need to enclose controls in a form in Netscape Navigator (or they won't appear), you don't actually need to enclose them in a form in Internet Explorer. However, if you want to send data from a particular set of controls back to a program on the server, you must enclose them in a form, even in Internet Explorer.*

We'll learn more about how to handle data sent to a Web server from a form when we discuss Common Gateway Interface (CGI) programming later in this book (and a little in this chapter; see Chapter 20 for all the details). However, it's becoming more and more common not to send anything back to the server at all, but instead, use controls in a Web page to make that page come alive—that's a large part of what dynamic HTML is all about (which we'll work with starting in

Chapter 13). For example, you might let the user customize the appearance of a page interactively by using buttons and text fields in a page (and you can even store the new settings using a JavaScript cookie). To work with dynamic HTML, it's essential to be able to handle HTML controls, and to handle these controls, you need to work with forms.

Despite their name, forms are not visible objects on the screen—they are purely logical inventions that you create with the **<FORM>** element to group controls together. In fact, you can have multiple forms on a page (although it's not legal to nest forms—at least not yet).

Here are some online resources that can help you learn more about creating and using forms:

- *http://developer.netscape.com/docs/manuals/htmlguid/tags10.htm*— Netscape Navigator documentation on forms.

- *http://dir.yahoo.com/Computers_and_Internet/Internet/ World_Wide_Web/Programming/Forms/*—Yahoo's HTML forms pages.

- *http://ecco.bsee.swin.edu.au/text/form-tut/ft.1.html*—Carlos' forms tutorial.

- *www.utoronto.ca/webdocs/HTMLdocs/NewHTML/forms.html*—The Information Commons introduction to HTML Forms.

- *www.webcom.com/~webcom/html/tutor/forms/*—Webcom's tutorial on forms.

People use forms to display HTML controls, and that raises the question: Just what controls are available to us? I'll take a look at that now.

What Controls Are Available?

There are plenty of controls available in HTML, and as you might expect, we'll take a look at all of them in this chapter. Here's the current list of the HTML controls and the HTML element you use to create them—note that many HTML controls are created with the **<INPUT>** element, using a different value for the **TYPE** attribute to create the various controls.

- *Buttons* (**<INPUT TYPE=BUTTON>**)—Are the standard clickable buttons you see on so many Web pages these days.

- *Checkboxes* (**<INPUT TYPE=CHECKBOX>**)—Displayed usually as a small box with a checkmark in it. The user can toggle the checkmark on or off by clicking the checkbox.

- *Customizable buttons* (**<BUTTON>**)—Display images and other HTML inside itself. A relatively new element.

- *File uploading controls* (**<INPUT TYPE=FILE>**)—Allow the user to upload files to the server.

- *Hidden controls* (**<INPUT TYPE=HIDDEN>**)—Store data that is not visible to users (unless they view the Web page's HTML source).

- *Image controls* (**<INPUT TYPE=IMAGE>**)—Are like Submit buttons except they are images the user can click. The actual location that the user clicks in the image is also sent to the server with the rest of the data from the form.

- *Password controls* (**<INPUT TYPE=PASSWORD>**)—Are like a text field, but this control masks each typed character by simply displaying an asterisk (*) instead of the character itself. This control is valuable for typing in passwords because, if someone is peeking over your shoulder, he or she can't read your password on the screen. (Watching your fingers on the keyboard is, of course, another matter.)

- *Radio buttons* (**<INPUT TYPE=RADIO>**)—Displayed usually as a circle, which, when selected, displays a dot in the middle. These controls act much like checkboxes except that they work in mutually exclusive groups in which only one radio button may be selected at a time.

- *Reset buttons* (**<INPUT TYPE=RESET>**)—Allow the user to clear all the data they've entered and start over. When the user clicks the Reset button, all the controls in the form are returned to their original state, displaying the data they had when they first appeared. Great for complex forms.

- *Selection lists* (**<SELECT>**)—Work much like drop-down list boxes. Also called select controls.

- *Submit buttons* (**<INPUT TYPE=SUBMIT>**)—Used to be the most important control in forms because when you clicked this button, all the data in the form (that is, all the data in the controls in the form) was sent to a Web server for more processing. However, more and more forms are appearing that handle all the processing they need without sending anything back to a Web server, and the Submit button is omitted.

- *Text areas* (**<TEXTAREA>**)—Are two-dimensional text fields, allowing the user to enter more than one line of text. Text areas can also support text wrapping.

- *Text fields* (**<INPUT TYPE=TEXT>**)—Allow the user to enter and edit a line of text. Called text boxes in other programs.

So just how do you create a form and add controls to it? I'll take a look at how this works next.

Creating A Form And Adding HTML Controls

To create a form, you use the **<FORM>** element. After you've created a form, you can fill it with controls and make those controls active with JavaScript or another scripting language.

Here's how it works. In this example, I'll add a button and a text field to a Web page, and when the user clicks the button, the code will display the message "Hello from HTML!" in the text field. To use controls like this in a Web page, I'll start with a form in the page like this:

```
<HTML>
    <HEAD>
        <TITLE>
            Creating HTML Forms
        </TITLE>
    </HEAD>

    <BODY>

        <CENTER>
            <H1>Creating HTML Forms</H1>

            <FORM Name = form1>
                        .
                        .
                        .
            </FORM>
        </CENTER>

    </BODY>
</HTML>
```

Note that I've given this new form a name, **form1**. I've done that because we'll need to refer to the form when working with the controls in it from JavaScript (also note that if you have a number of forms in the same page, you should definitely give them names to keep them straight).

Next, I'll add the two controls; we'll use a text field and a button. I'll start by creating the text field, which you do with the **<INPUT>** element. In fact, you create nearly all HTML controls using the **<INPUT>** element (although now the World Wide Web Consortium (W3C) is breaking away from the exclusive use of this element to create controls and supports other elements to create controls as well; we'll see this in the next section). You create controls, like buttons, text fields, checkboxes, radio buttons, and more with the **<INPUT>** element's **TYPE** attribute. To create a text field, you set **TYPE** to **TEXT**. I'll also give the text field a width of 25 characters using the **SIZE** attribute and name it **"textfield"** with the **NAME** attribute like this:

```
<HTML>
    <HEAD>
        <TITLE>
            Creating HTML Forms
        </TITLE>
    </HEAD>

    <BODY>

        <CENTER>
            <H1>Creating HTML Forms</H1>
            <FORM Name = form1>
                <INPUT TYPE = TEXT NAME = "textfield" SIZE = 25>
                    .
                    .
                    .
            </FORM>
        </CENTER>

    </BODY>
</HTML>
```

Now I'll create the button we'll need. To create a normal HTML button, you use the **<INPUT>** element with the **TYPE** attribute set to **BUTTON**. In this case, the code will display its message in the text field when the user clicks this button, so I will also add the caption "Display Message" to the button using the **<INPUT>** element's **VALUE** attribute. Here's how it looks in HTML:

```
<HTML>
    <HEAD>
        <TITLE>
            Creating HTML Forms
        </TITLE>
    </HEAD>

    <BODY>

        <CENTER>
            <H1>Creating HTML Forms</H1>
            <FORM Name = form1>
```

```
                    <INPUT TYPE = TEXT NAME = "textfield" SIZE = 25>
                    <BR>
                    <BR>
                    <INPUT TYPE = BUTTON Value = "Display Message">
              </FORM>
        </CENTER>

    </BODY>
</HTML>
```

TIP: *The* **<INPUT>** *element's* **VALUE** *attribute has different meanings for different controls. For example, although it sets the caption of buttons, it also sets the default text contents of text fields. Refer to the Immediate Solutions section of this chapter for more control-by-control information.*

So far we've just displayed a text field and a button with nothing happening when the user clicks the button. To make the button active, we can use its events, just as we have with other HTML elements in the previous two chapters. In this case, all I need to do is connect the button's **onClick** event to the JavaScript code that will display the message in the text field. I'll place that code in a JavaScript function named **displayMessage** and connect that function to the button's **onClick** event this way:

```
<HTML>
    <HEAD>
        <TITLE>
            Creating HTML Forms
        </TITLE>
    </HEAD>

    <BODY>

        <CENTER>
            <H1>Creating HTML Forms</H1>
            <FORM Name = form1>
                <INPUT TYPE = TEXT NAME = "textfield" SIZE = 25>
                <BR>
                <BR>
                <INPUT TYPE = BUTTON Value = "Display Message"
                    onClick = "displayMessage()">
            </FORM>
        </CENTER>

    </BODY>
</HTML>
```

All that remains is to write the JavaScript **displayMessage** function, which is called when the user clicks the button:

```
<HTML>
    <HEAD>
        <TITLE>
            Creating HTML Forms
        </TITLE>

        <SCRIPT LANGUAGE = JavaScript>
            function displayMessage()
            {
                    .
                    .
                    .
            }
        </SCRIPT>
    </HEAD>

    <BODY>

        <CENTER>
            <H1>Creating HTML Forms</H1>
            <FORM Name = form1>
                <INPUT TYPE = TEXT NAME = "textfield" SIZE = 25>
                <BR>
                <BR>
                <INPUT TYPE = BUTTON Value = "Display Message"
                    onClick = "displayMessage()">
            </FORM>
        </CENTER>

    </BODY>
</HTML>
```

The code in the function **displayMessage** must be able to place the message "Hello from HTML!" in the text field we've named **textfield**. But how can we access that text field? Recall that the **document** object represents the current Web page, and you can access all elements in the page using that object. Because the text field is in the form we've named **form1**, it's easy to refer to this text field—you simply call it **document.form1.textfield**. To display text in this text field, you simply need to set its **VALUE** attribute, which you can do by working with its **value** property in JavaScript as **document.form1.textfield.value**. Here's what the final HTML looks like:

```
<HTML>
    <HEAD>
        <TITLE>
            Creating HTML Forms
        </TITLE>

        <SCRIPT LANGUAGE = JavaScript>
            function displayMessage()
            {
                document.form1.textfield.value = "Hello from HTML!"
            }
        </SCRIPT>
    </HEAD>

    <BODY>

        <CENTER>
            <H1>Creating HTML Forms</H1>
            <FORM Name = form1>
                <INPUT TYPE = TEXT NAME = "textfield" SIZE = 25>
                <BR>
                <BR>
                <INPUT TYPE = BUTTON Value = "Display Message"
                    onClick = "displayMessage()">
            </FORM>
        </CENTER>

    </BODY>
</HTML>
```

That's all it takes. You can see the results of this HTML in Figure 12.1. When the user clicks the button, the message is indeed displayed in the text field. Congratulations, you've just created an HTML form.

Element Attributes Become JavaScript Properties

Using the JavaScript **value** property of the text field brings up an important point—most HTML element attributes are now accessible from JavaScript as JavaScript properties. For example, the **VALUE** attribute is accessible as the **value** property. As we'll see in this chapter, the **CHECKED** attribute of checkboxes and radio buttons is accessible as the **checked** property. In the previous chapter, we saw that you can use an image element's **src** property to set its **SRC** attribute, and in Chapter 13, we'll see that the **STYLE** attribute is accessible as the **style** property. By making most attributes available as properties, JavaScript lets you interact immediately with the elements in a Web page. When you decide which attribute you

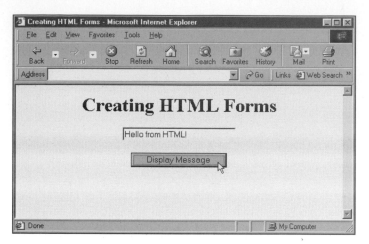

Figure 12.1   Creating and using HTML forms and controls.

want to work with, you automatically know the property you need to work with in JavaScript because the property has the same name.

TIP: *Although HTML attributes usually have the same name as JavaScript properties, translating certain HTML attributes to the corresponding JavaScript properties can be unpredictable; for example, the HTML style **font-size** becomes the JavaScript property **fontSize**. You can find all the details about what properties are available for what elements in the documentation for Netscape Navigator's JavaScript at **http://developer.netscape.com/tech/ javascript/index.html**. You can find the documentation for Microsoft's JScript at **http://msdn.microsoft.com/ scripting/default.htm?/scripting/jscript/techinfo/jsdocs.htm**.*

Referring To Controls In A Form In Code

Another thing to bear in mind—note that in the previous code, I refer to controls in a form from code in a script as **document.formname.control**. That is, the **document** object contains all other objects, including the form you want to use, and the form contains the control you want to reach, so to refer to a control from code, you supply its full name: **document.formname.control**.

To set an attribute of a control, then, you set the corresponding JavaScript property like this: **document.formname.control.property**. To call a JavaScript method of the control, you use this syntax: **document.formname.control. method(*arguments*)**. As you can see in the previous example, I set the **value** property of a text field, which holds the text in the text field like this: **document.form1.textfield.value = "Hello from HTML!"**. We'll discuss what attributes each HTML control has in this chapter, and as a result, what properties you can set in JavaScript.

Submitting Data From Forms

In the previous section, we saw how you can use JavaScript to make something happen when you use controls in a page without sending anything to the server. However, I've mentioned sending data from a form back to the server, which was originally what forms were all about. You may be wondering how this works. The actual details will have to wait until we discuss CGI programming in Chapter 20, but we can take a look at an example now.

There are two ways for forms to send data to code on a Web server: using the GET or POST methods.

NOTE: *When you send data using the GET method, a question mark (**?**) and the form data is appended to the target URL of the code on the server, which can point to a CGI file. For example, say that the URL of the CGI file to handle the data from your form is **http://www.starpowder.com/steve/cgi/cgidata.cgi**. If you had a text field named "name" and one named "ID", the data from these text fields would be appended to the URL like this (note that spaces will be converted to plus signs [**+**]): **http://www.starpowder.com/steve/cgi/cgidata.cgi?name=Steve+Hoizner&ID=1000**. On the other hand, with the POST method, data from the form is sent as environment variables that are accessible to the CGI script.*

I'll use the POST method in the next example. I'll create a form that accepts the user's name and then echoes it back from a CGI script. To use the POST method, you set the **METHOD** attribute of the **<FORM>** element to **POST**. In addition, you set the **ACTION** attribute of the form to the URL you want the data to be sent to, so I'll use the URL **http://www.starpowder.com/steve/cgi/cgidata.cgi**. Here's what the form looks like—note that I'm including a Submit button. When the user clicks this button, the data in the text field will be posted to the URL in the **ACTION** attribute:

```
<HTML>
    <HEAD>
        <TITLE>
            CGI Example
        </TITLE>
    </HEAD>

    <BODY>
        <FORM METHOD="POST"
            ACTION="http://www.starpowder.com/steve/cgi/cgidata.cgi">

            Please enter your name:
            <INPUT TYPE="text" NAME="text" VALUE="">
            <P>
            <CENTER>
                <INPUT TYPE="submit" NAME="Submit" VALUE="Submit">
```

```
                         <INPUT TYPE="reset">
                    </CENTER>
             </FORM>
      </BODY>
</HTML>
```

The results of this HTML appear in Figure 12.2. All you have to do is enter your name and click the Submit button to send it to the waiting CGI script, which will echo back what you typed.

What does the CGI script look like? I'll use the most popular CGI scripting language—Perl (although C++ and now server-side JavaScript are becoming popular). Here's a sneak peek at what the Perl code for this example looks like:

```
#!/usr/local/bin/perl

use CGI;

$co = new CGI;

print $co->header,

$co->start_html(
    -title=>'CGI Example',
    -author=>'Steve',
    -meta=>{'keywords'=>'CGI Perl'},
),

$co->hr;
```

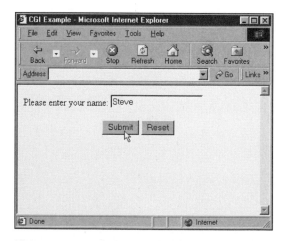

Figure 12.2   Creating an HTML form that will post data.

```
if ($co->param()) {
    print
        "Your name is: ",$co->em($co->param('text')), ".";
}

print $co->hr;

print $co->end_html;
```

This CGI script is installed on the server as we'll see in Chapter 20. When the name the user has typed into the text field in Figure 12.2 is sent, it immediately creates a Web page and sends it back to the browser, displaying the name that was typed, which is what you see in Figure 12.3.

There's one more topic to take a look at in this overview—using **<FIELDSET>**, **<LEGEND>**, and **<LABEL>**.

Using <FIELDSET>, <LEGEND>, And <LABEL>

The **<FIELDSET>**, **<LEGEND>**, and **<LABEL>** elements are relatively new and let you group controls in a form visually. Use the **<FIELDSET>** element to group elements in a form together in a box (although the actual rendering is left to the browser, this element is only supported in Internet Explorer as far as I know, and it comes up as a box), the **<LEGEND>** element to add a caption to the box, and the **<LABEL>** element to label the elements in the form. Here's an example:

```
<HTML>
    <HEAD>
        <TITLE>
            Using &lt;FIELDSET&gt;, &lt;LEGEND&gt;, And &lt;LABEL&gt;
```

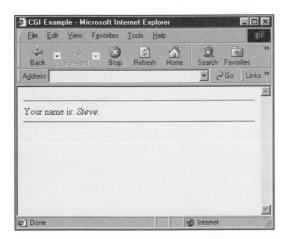

Figure 12.3   Using a CGI script to echo data sent to it.

```
                    </TITLE>
            </HEAD>

            <BODY>

                <CENTER>
                    <H1>Using &lt;FIELDSET&gt;, &lt;LEGEND&gt;, And
                        &lt;LABEL&gt;</H1>
                    <FORM Name = form1>
                        <FIELDSET>
                            <LEGEND ACCESSKEY=C TABINDEX=1>Color</LEGEND>
                            <LABEL ACCESSKEY=Y>
                                <INPUT TYPE=RADIO NAME=COLOR VALUE=YELLOW>Yellow
                            </LABEL>
                            <BR>
                            <LABEL ACCESSKEY=W>
                                <INPUT TYPE=RADIO NAME=COLOR VALUE=ORANGE>Orange
                            </LABEL>
                        </FIELDSET>
                    </FORM>
                </CENTER>
            </BODY>
    </HTML>
```

You can see the results in Figure 12.4. As you can see in the figure, the controls in the **<FIELDSET>** element are wrapped in a box, which has the caption we've given it with the **<LEGEND>** element, and the controls have the captions we've given them with the **<LABEL>** element.

That's all the introduction to forms and controls we need—it's time to dig into the details now, and I'll do that in the Immediate Solutions section.

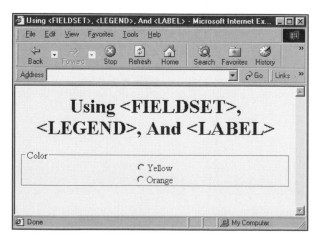

Figure 12.4   Using **<FIELDSET>**, **<LEGEND>**, and **<LABEL>**.

Immediate Solutions

<FORM>—Creating HTML Forms

Purpose: Creates an HTML form; used to enclose HTML controls, like buttons and text fields.

Start Tag/End Tag: Required/Required

Supported: [2, 3, 3.2, 4, IE1, IE2, IE3, IE4, IE5, NS1, NS2, NS3, NS4]

Attributes:

- **ACCEPT**—Specifies a comma separated list of content types that a server processing this form will handle correctly. [4]

- **ACCEPT-CHARSET**—Indicates a list of possible language character sets for the form data. Set to a space separated or comma separated list of language character sets. [4]

- **ACTION**—Gives the URL that will handle the form data. Note that although this attribute is listed as required, you can omit it, and if you do, its default is the base URL of the document itself. Set to a URL. [2, 3, 3.2, 4, IE1, IE2, IE3, IE4, IE5, NS1, NS2, NS3, NS4]

- **AUTOCOMPLETE**—Set to **TRUE** (the default) if you want Internet Explorer to automatically complete data in controls like text fields based on what the user has entered before. [IE5]

- **CLASS**—Class of the element. [4, IE4, IE5]

- **CONTENTEDITABLE**—Set to **TRUE** if the content of the form is editable. [IE5]

- **DIR**—Gives the direction of directionally neutral text (text that doesn't have inherent direction in which you should read it). Possible values: **LTR**: left-to-right text or table and **RTL**: right-to-left text or table. [4, IE5]

- **DISABLED**—Set to **TRUE** if the form should be disabled. [IE5]

- **ENCTYPE**—Sets the Multipurpose Internet Mail Extension (MIME) type used to encode the name/value pairs when sent to the action URL. The default is "application/x-www-form-urlencoded", but you can also use "multipart/form-data", which is for **<INPUT TYPE=FILE>** elements. [2, 3, 3.2, 4, IE1, IE2, IE3, IE4, IE5, NS1, NS2, NS3, NS4]

- **ID**—Unique alphanumeric identifier for the tag, which you can use to refer to it. [4, IE4, IE5]

- **LANG**—Base language used for the tag. [3, 4, IE4, IE5]

- **LANGUAGE**—Scripting language used for the tag. [IE4, IE5]

- **METHOD**—Indicates a method or protocol for sending data to the target action URL. The GET method is the default. This method sends all form name/value pair information in an URL that looks like: *URL?name=value&name=value&name=value*. On the other hand, using the POST method, the contents of the form are encoded as with the GET method, but are sent in environment variables. Set to **GET** (the default) or **POST**. [2, 3, 3.2, 4, IE1, IE2, IE3, IE4, IE5, NS1, NS2, NS3, NS4]

- **NAME**—Gives a name to the form so you can reference it in code. Set to an alphanumeric string. [4, IE3, IE4, IE5, NS2, NS3, NS4]

- **STYLE**—Inline style indicating how to render the element. [4, IE4, IE5]

- **TABINDEX**—Sets a tab index for the form in the page. [IE5]

- **TARGET**—Indicates a named frame for the browser to display the form results in. [4, IE3, IE4, IE5, NS2, NS3, NS4]

- **TITLE**—Holds additional information (which might be displayed in tool tips) for the element. [4, IE4, IE5]

Events:

- *Internet Explorer*—**onbeforecopy, onbeforecut, onbeforefocusenter, onbeforefocusleave, onbeforepaste, onblur, onclick, oncontextmenu, oncontrolselect, oncopy, oncut, ondblclick, ondrag, ondragend, ondragenter, ondragleave, ondragover, ondragstart, ondrop, onfocus, onfocusenter, onfocusleave, onhelp, onkeydown, onkeypress, onkeyup, onlosecapture, onmousedown, onmouseenter, onmouseleave, onmousemove, onmouseout, onmouseover, onmouseup, onpaste, onpropertychange, onreadystatechange, onreset, onresize, onresizeend, onresizestart, onselectstart, onsubmit**

- *Netscape Navigator*—**onsubmit, onreset**

The novice programmer enters breathlessly and cries, "I want to use HTML controls in my Web page!" "Hold on there," you say, laughing, "you need to start by creating an HTML form first." "I knew there would be a catch," the NP says. "It's no catch," you say, "and besides, it's easy."

To use controls in a Web page, you should enclose them in an HTML form. Netscape Navigator insists that you use a form to display controls, and although Internet Explorer does not, you must still use forms if you want to collect and send data back to the Web server. We already saw this example of using a form in the In Depth section of this chapter:

```html
<HTML>
    <HEAD>
        <TITLE>
            Creating HTML Forms
        </TITLE>

        <SCRIPT LANGUAGE = JavaScript>
            function displayMessage()
            {
                document.form1.textfield.value = "Hello from HTML!"
            }
        </SCRIPT>
    </HEAD>

    <BODY>

        <CENTER>
            <H1>Creating HTML Forms</H1>
            <FORM Name = form1>
                <INPUT TYPE = TEXT NAME = "textfield" SIZE = 25>
                <BR>
                <BR>
                <INPUT TYPE = BUTTON Value = "Display Message"
                    onClick = "displayMessage()">
            </FORM>
        </CENTER>

    </BODY>
</HTML>
```

You can see the results of this HTML in Figure 12.1. This Web page is self-contained and sends nothing back to the server, but of course, you can also use forms to send data back to code on the server. There are two ways for forms to send data to code on a Web server—using the GET or POST methods.

As mentioned in the In Depth section of this chapter, when you send data using the GET method, a question mark (**?**) followed by the form data is added to the target URL of the code on the server, which points to a CGI file. Say that the URL of the CGI file to handle the data from your form is **http://www.starpowder.com/ steve/cgi/cgidata.cgi**. If you had a text field named "name" and one named "ID", the data from these text fields would be appended to the URL like this (note that

spaces will be converted to plus signs [+]): **http://www.starpowder.com/steve/
cgi/cgidata.cgi?name=Steve+Holzner&ID=1000**. On the other hand, with the
POST method, data from the form is sent as environment variables, which are
accessible to the CGI script.

I'll use the POST method in an example. In this case, I'll create a form that accepts the user's name and then echoes it back from a CGI script. To use the POST
method, you set the **METHOD** attribute of the **<FORM>** element to **POST**. In
addition, you set the **ACTION** attribute of the form to the URL you want the data
to be sent to, so I'll use the URL **http://www.starpowder.com/steve/cgi/
cgidata.cgi** here. If you omit the **ACTION** attribute, the data is sent back to the
same URL as the current document.

Here's what the form looks like—note that I'm including a Submit button, so when
the user clicks the button, the data in the text field will be posted to the URL in
the **ACTION** attribute (note also that unless you supply a caption for the Submit
button with the **VALUE** attribute, most browsers, including Netscape Navigator
and Internet Explorer, will give the button a caption of Submit Query):

```
<HTML>
    <HEAD>
        <TITLE>
            CGI Example
        </TITLE>
    </HEAD>

    <BODY>
        <FORM METHOD="POST"
            ACTION="http://www.starpowder.com/steve/cgi/cgidata.cgi">

            Please enter your name:
            <INPUT TYPE="text" NAME="text" VALUE="">
            <P>
            <CENTER>
                <INPUT TYPE="submit" NAME="Submit" VALUE="Submit">
                <INPUT TYPE="reset">
            </CENTER>
        </FORM>
    </BODY>
</HTML>
```

We saw the CGI script that will handle data from this form in the In Depth section
of this chapter; the results appear in Figures 12.2 and 12.3.

TIP: *You have to be careful with forms and the **<LAYER>** and **<ILAYER>** elements. If a **<LAYER>** or **<ILAYER>** element is nested inside a **<FORM>** element, and any controls for the form are inside the layer, they will not be drawn.*

<INPUT TYPE=BUTTON>—Creating Buttons

Purpose: Creates an HTML button in a form.

Start Tag/End Tag: Required/Omitted

Supported: [4, IE3, IE4, IE5, NS1, NS2, NS3, NS4]

Attributes:

- **ACCESSKEY**—Keyboard shortcut key; a single character is used as the value of this attribute. The user can type a platform-dependent key (such as Alt) with the **ACCESSKEY** character to trigger the active field. Set to an alphanumeric character. [4, IE4, IE5]

- **CLASS**—Class of the element. [4, IE4, IE5]

- **DATAFLD**—Name of the column of the data source object that supplies the bound data. Set to alphanumeric characters. [IE4, IE5]

- **DATAFORMATAS**—Specifies if bound data is plain text or HTML. Set to **HTML**, **PLAINTEXT**, or **TEXT**. [IE4, IE5]

- **DATASRC**—Gives the URL or ID of the data source object supplying data bound to this element. W3C says this should be a URL; Internet Explorer says it should be a data source ID. [IE4, IE5]

- **DIR**—Gives the direction of directionally neutral text (text that doesn't have inherent direction in which you should read it). Possible values: **LTR**: left-to-right text or table and **RTL**: right-to-left text or table. [4, IE5]

- **DISABLED**—Specifies that the element is disabled when first displayed. Stand-alone attribute. [4, IE4, IE5]

- **ID**—Unique alphanumeric identifier for the tag, which you can use to refer to it. [4, IE4, IE5]

- **LANG**—Base language used for the tag. [4, IE4, IE5]

- **LANGUAGE**—Scripting language used for the tag. [IE4, IE5]

- **NAME**—Gives the element a name. Set to alphanumeric characters. Required. [4, IE3, IE4, IE5, NS1, NS2, NS3, NS4]

- **SIZE**—Sets the size. [4, IE3, IE4, IE5]

- **STYLE**—Inline style indicating how to render the element. [4, IE4, IE5]

- **TABINDEX**—Sets the tab index of the element, which locates it in the tab order of the form, allowing the user to press the Tab key and navigate from element to element. Set to positive or negative integers. [4, IE4, IE5]

- **TITLE**—Holds additional information (which might be displayed in tool tips) for the element. [4, IE4, IE5]

- **TYPE**—Specifies the type of the element. [4, IE3, IE4, IE5, NS1, NS2, NS3, NS4]

- **VALUE**—Sets the caption of the element. Set to alphanumeric characters. [4, IE3, IE4, IE5, NS1, NS2, NS3, NS4]

Events:

- *Internet Explorer*—**onbeforecut, onbeforeeditfocus, onbeforefocusenter, onbeforefocusleave, onbeforepaste, onblur, onclick, oncontextmenu, oncontrolselect, oncut, ondblclick, ondrag, ondragend, ondragenter, ondragleave, ondragover, ondragstart, ondrop, onfilterchange, onfocus, onfocusenter, onfocusleave, onhelp, onkeydown, onkeypress, onkeyup, onlosecapture, onmousedown, onmouseenter, onmouseleave, onmousemove, onmouseout, onmouseover, onmouseup, onpaste, onpropertychange, onreadystatechange, onresize, onresizeend, onresizestart, onselectstart**

- *Netscape Navigator*—**onclick**

"OK," says the novice programmer, "I've created a form; now how do I add a button to it?" "One way," you say, "is with the **<INPUT>** element, setting the **TYPE** attribute to **BUTTON**."

There are now two ways to create buttons in HTML—with the **<INPUT TYPE=BUTTON>** element and with the **<BUTTON>** element. I'll look at the first way in this section. We already saw an example showing how to use **<INPUT TYPE=BUTTON>** in the In Depth section of this chapter—you use the **VALUE** attribute to set the caption of the button and connect its **onClick** event to code like this:

```
<HTML>
    <HEAD>
        <TITLE>
            Creating HTML Forms
        </TITLE>

        <SCRIPT LANGUAGE = JavaScript>
            function displayMessage()
```

```
            {
                document.form1.textfield.value = "Hello from HTML!"
            }
        </SCRIPT>
    </HEAD>

    <BODY>

        <CENTER>
            <H1>Creating HTML Forms</H1>
            <FORM Name = form1>
                <INPUT TYPE = TEXT NAME = "textfield" SIZE = 25>
                <BR>
                <BR>
                <INPUT TYPE = BUTTON Value = "Display Message"
                    onClick = "displayMessage()">
            </FORM>
        </CENTER>

    </BODY>
</HTML>
```

You can see the results of this code in Figure 12.1.

Here's another example. In this case, I'm creating a button that will reload the current Web page, just as the Reload button in the browser would. To reload the page, you can use the **reload** method of the **location** object like this:

```
<HTML>
    <HEAD>
        <TITLE>
            Reloading A Web Page
        </TITLE>
    </HEAD>

    <BODY>

        <CENTER>
            <FORM Name = form1>
                <BR>
                <INPUT TYPE = BUTTON Value = "Reload this page"
                    onClick = "location.reload()">
            </FORM>
        </CENTER>

    </BODY>

</HTML>
```

Supplying a reload button like this can be useful if you have many images in your page and the user's browser times out before loading them all. Just have the user click the reload button, and the browser will only download the remaining images that aren't already in its cache.

TIP: Internet Explorer 4 and later uses all white space and carriage returns you place in the **VALUE** attribute for this element, displaying them "as is." Note, however, that other browsers (and earlier Internet Explorer versions) do not do so.

`<INPUT TYPE=CHECKBOX>`—Creating Checkboxes

Purpose: Creates a checkbox in a form.

Start Tag/End Tag: Required/Omitted

Supported: [2, 3, 3.2, 4, IE1, IE2, IE3, IE4, IE5, NS1, NS2, NS3, NS4]

Attributes:

- **ACCESSKEY**—Keyboard shortcut key; a single character is used as the value of this attribute. The user can type a platform-dependent key (such as Alt) with the **ACCESSKEY** character to trigger the active field. Set to an alphanumeric character. [4, IE4, IE5]

- **CHECKED**—Indicates if the checkbox should appear checked initially or not. Stand-alone attribute. [2, 3, 3.2, 4, IE1, IE2, IE3, IE4, IE5, NS1, NS2, NS3, NS4]

- **CLASS**—Class of the element. [3, 4, IE4, IE5]

- **DATAFLD**—Name of the column of the data source object that supplies the bound data. Set to alphanumeric characters. [IE4, IE5]

- **DATASRC**—Gives the URL or ID of the data source object supplying data bound to this element. W3C says this should be a URL; Internet Explorer says it should be a data source ID. [IE4, IE5]

- **DIR**—Gives the direction of directionally neutral text (text that doesn't have inherent direction in which you should read it). Possible values: **LTR**: left-to-right text or table and **RTL**: right-to-left text or table. [4, IE5]

- **DISABLED**—Specifies that the element is disabled when first displayed. Stand-alone attribute. [3, 4, IE4, IE5]

- **ID**—Unique alphanumeric identifier for the tag, which you can use to refer to it. [3, 4, IE4, IE5]

- **LANG**—Base language used for the tag. [3, 4, IE4, IE5]

- **LANGUAGE**—Scripting language used for the tag. [IE4, IE5]

- **NAME**—Gives the element a name. Set to alphanumeric characters. Required. [2, 3, 3.2, 4, IE1, IE2, IE3, IE4, IE5, NS1, NS2, NS3, NS4]

- **SIZE**—Sets the size. [4, IE3, IE4, IE5]

- **STYLE**—Inline style indicating how to render the element. [4, IE4, IE5]

- **TABINDEX**—Sets the tab index of the element, which locates it in the tab order of the form, allowing the user to press the Tab key and navigate from element to element. Set to positive or negative integers. [4, IE4, IE5]

- **TITLE**—Holds additional information (which might be displayed in tool tips) for the element. [2, 3, 4, IE4, IE5]

- **TYPE**—Specifies the type of the element. [2, 3, 3.2, 4, IE1, IE2, IE3, IE4, IE5, NS1, NS2, NS3, NS4]

- **VALUE**—Represents the result of the checkbox when clicked, which is passed to the form's action URL. Set to alphanumeric characters. Required. [2, 3, 3.2, 4, IE1, IE2, IE3, IE4, IE5, NS1, NS2, NS3, NS4]

Events:

- *Internet Explorer*—**onbeforecut, onbeforeeditfocus, onbeforefocusenter, onbeforefocusleave, onbeforepaste, onblur, onclick, oncontextmenu, oncontrolselect, oncut, ondblclick, ondrag, ondragend, ondragenter, ondragleave, ondragover, ondragstart, ondrop, onfilterchange, onfocus, onfocusenter, onfocusleave, onhelp, onkeydown, onkeypress, onkeyup, onlosecapture, onmousedown, onmouseenter, onmouseleave, onmousemove, onmouseout, onmouseover, onmouseup, onpaste, onpropertychange, onreadystatechange, onresizeend, onresizestart, onselectstart**

- *Netscape Navigator*—**onclick**

"Darn," says the novice programmer, "I wish there was a button that, when clicked, would *stay* clicked. I'm trying to let the user select options like spell checking in my Web page." "You can use a checkbox," you say, "and by the way, how does your Web page do spell checking?" "I haven't got that part worked out yet," admits the NP.

A checkbox is much like a button; when clicked, it stays clicked. Checkboxes are usually drawn as small squares (although this is platform dependent). When clicked, a checkmark appears in the box, and when clicked again, the checkmark disappears. The checkmark toggles on and off as the user clicks the checkbox.

You create checkboxes with the **<INPUT TYPE = CHECKBOX>** element, and similar to HTML buttons, checkboxes have an **onClick** event. Here's an example displaying five checkboxes and indicating which one was clicked:

```
<HTML>

    <HEAD>
        <TITLE>Using Check Boxes</TITLE>

        <SCRIPT LANGUAGE = JavaScript>

            function check1Clicked()
            {
                document.form1.textfield.value = "You clicked check box 1."
            }

            function check2Clicked()
            {
                document.form1.textfield.value = "You clicked check box 2."
            }

            function check3Clicked()
            {
                document.form1.textfield.value = "You clicked check box 3."
            }

            function check4Clicked()
            {
                document.form1.textfield.value = "You clicked check box 4."
            }

            function check5Clicked()
            {
                document.form1.textfield.value = "You clicked check box 5."
            }

        </SCRIPT>

    </HEAD>

    <BODY>

        <CENTER>
            <H1>
                Using Check Boxes
```

```
        </H1>

        <FORM NAME = form1>
            <TABLE BORDER BGCOLOR = CYAN WIDTH = 200>
            <TR><TD>
            <INPUT TYPE = CHECKBOX NAME = check1 onClick =
                check1Clicked()>Check 1
            </TD></TR>
            <TR><TD>
                <INPUT TYPE = CHECKBOX NAME = check2 onClick =
                    check2Clicked()>Check 2
            </TD></TR>
            <TR><TD>
                <INPUT TYPE = CHECKBOX NAME = check3 onClick =
                    check3Clicked()>Check 3
            </TD></TR>
            <TR><TD>
                <INPUT TYPE = CHECKBOX NAME = check4 onClick =
                    check4Clicked()>Check 4
            </TD></TR>
            <TR><TD>
                <INPUT TYPE = CHECKBOX NAME = check5 onClick =
                    check5Clicked()>Check 5
            </TD></TR>
            </TABLE>
            <BR>
                <INPUT TYPE  =  TEXT NAME  =  "textfield" SIZE  =  25>
        </FORM>
    </CENTER>

    </BODY>

</HTML>
```

The result of this HTML appears in Figure 12.5, and as you can see, when the user clicks a checkbox, the code indicates which one was checked.

In fact, the code in this example is longer than it needs to be. Rather than having a separate function for each checkbox, you can use the same function for all checkboxes and examine each checkbox's **checked** property (for example, **document.form1.check1.checked**) to see if the checkbox is displaying a checkmark or not. You can also set this property to **true** or **false** to select or clear the checkbox.

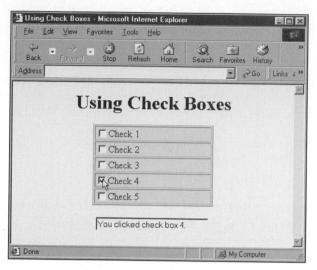

Figure 12.5   Using checkboxes.

<INPUT TYPE=FILE>—Creating File Input For A Form

Purpose: Lets the user upload files.

Start Tag/End Tag: Required/Omitted

Supported: [3, 3.2, 4, IE4, IE5, NS2, NS3, NS4]

Attributes:

- **ACCEPT**—Sets the MIME type of the file transfer. Set to a MIME type, or a space separated or comma separated list of MIME types. [4]

- **ACCESSKEY**—Keyboard shortcut key; a single character is used as the value of this attribute. The user can type a platform-dependent key (such as Alt) with the **ACCESSKEY** character to trigger the active field. Set to an alphanumeric character. [4, IE4, IE5]

- **CLASS**—Class of the element. [4, IE4, IE5]

- **DATAFLD**—Name of the column of the data source object that supplies the bound data. Set to alphanumeric characters. [IE4, IE5]

- **DATASRC**—Gives the URL or ID of the data source object supplying data bound to this element. W3C says this should be a URL; Internet Explorer says it should be a data source ID. [IE4, IE5]

- **DIR**—Gives the direction of directionally neutral text (text that doesn't have inherent direction in which you should read it). Possible values: **LTR**: left-to-right text or table and **RTL**: right-to-left text or table. [4, IE5]

- **DISABLED**—Specifies that the element is disabled when first displayed. Stand-alone attribute. [3, 4, IE4, IE5]

- **ID**—Unique alphanumeric identifier for the tag, which you can use to refer to it. [4, IE4, IE5]

- **LANG**—Base language used for the tag. [4, IE4, IE5]

- **LANGUAGE**—Scripting language used for the tag. [IE4, IE5]

- **NAME**—Gives the element a name. Set to alphanumeric characters. Required. [4, IE3, IE4, IE5, NS2, NS3, NS4]

- **SIZE**—Sets the size. [4, IE3, IE4, IE5]

- **STYLE**—Inline style indicating how to render the element. [4, IE4, IE5]

- **TABINDEX**—Sets the tab index of the element, which locates it in the tab order of the form, allowing the user to press the Tab key and navigate from element to element. Set to positive or negative integers. [4, IE4, IE5]

- **TITLE**—Holds additional information (which might be displayed in tool tips) for the element. [4, IE4, IE5]

- **TYPE**—Specifies the type of the element. [3, 3.2, 4, IE4, IE5, NS2, NS3, NS4]

- **VALUE**—Sets the default contents of the element. Set to alphanumeric characters. [3, 3.2, 4, IE4, IE5, NS2, NS3, NS4]

Events:

- *Internet Explorer*—**onbeforecut, onbeforeeditfocus, onbeforefocusenter, onbeforefocusleave, onbeforepaste, onblur, onclick, oncontextmenu, oncontrolselect, oncut, ondblclick, ondrag, ondragend, ondragenter, ondragleave, ondragover, ondragstart, ondrop, onfilterchange, onfocus, onfocusenter, onfocusleave, onhelp, onkeydown, onkeypress, onkeyup, onlosecapture, onmousedown, onmouseenter, onmouseleave, onmousemove, onmouseout, onmouseover, onmouseup, onpaste, onpropertychange, onreadystatechange, onresize, onresizeend, onresizestart, onselectstart**

- *Netscape Navigator*—none

The big boss appears and says, "We need to automate things now that we're displaying advertising on our Web site. What I want is one page that lets our operators enter the number of paid hits for each ad banner and also uploads the banner image itself." "No problem," you say, "I'll just use **<INPUT TYPE=FILE>**." "Whatever," says the BB.

You can upload files with the **<INPUT TYPE=FILE>** element. You need to add code on the server to handle any file that's been uploaded, so I'll do this with a

CGI script (see Chapters 19 and 20 on Perl later in the book to decipher what's going on here). One item to note is that if you use **<INPUT TYPE=FILE>**, you also need to set the **<FORM>** element's **ENCTYPE** attribute to **multipart/form-data**.

In this case, I'll create a Web page that will upload files and display their contents. I'll use a file named, originally enough, file.txt, which has this content:

```
Here is some text!
```

Here's the actual Perl CGI script that will create the file upload control:

```perl
#!/usr/local/bin/perl

use CGI;

$co = new CGI;

if (!$co->param())
{
    print $co->header,
        $co->start_html('CGI File Upload Example'),
        $co->center(
        $co->br,
        $co->center($co->h1('CGI File Upload Example')),
        $co->start_multipart_form,
        $co->filefield(-name=>'filename', -size=>30),
        $co->br,
        $co->submit(-value=>'Upload'),
        $co->reset,
        $co->end_form
    ),
    $co->hr;

} else {
    print
        $co->header,
        $co->start_html('CGI File Upload Example'),
        $co->center($co->h1('CGI File Upload Example'));

    $file = $co->param('filename');

    @data = <$file>;

    foreach (@data) {
```

```
        s/\n/<br>/g;
    }

    print
        $co->center($co->h2("Here's the contents of $file...")),
        "@data";
}

print $co->end_html;
```

Here's the HTML created by this CGI script (note that I haven't added an **ACTION** attribute to the **<FORM>** element here, so data is sent back to the same CGI script when the user clicks the Submit button, or in this case, the Upload button):

```
<HTML>
    <HEAD>
        <TITLE>
            CGI File Upload Example
        </TITLE>
    </HEAD>

    <BODY>
        <CENTER>
            <BR>
            <H1>
                CGI File Upload Example
            </H1>

            <FORM METHOD="POST"  ENCTYPE="multipart/form-data">
                <INPUT TYPE="FILE" NAME="filename" VALUE="" SIZE=30>
                <BR>
                <INPUT TYPE="submit" NAME="submit" VALUE="Upload">
                <INPUT TYPE="reset">
            </FORM>
        </CENTER>
        <HR>

    </BODY>
</HTML>
```

You can see this page in Figure 12.6, where you see that the file upload control is actually two controls—a text field and a browse button. If users click the browse button, they can browse their disks to find the file to upload. In this case, I've just entered that file's path and name directly into the text field.

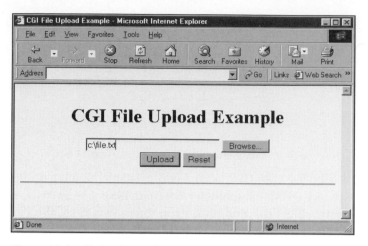

Figure 12.6   Uploading a file.

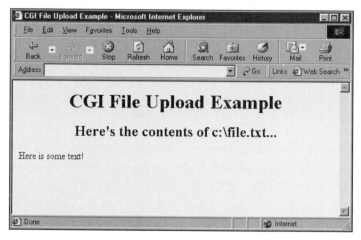

Figure 12.7   Displaying the contents of the uploaded file.

When the user clicks the Upload button (which is just a Submit button with the caption "Upload"), the contents of the file is sent to the CGI script, which then displays the contents in a Web page, as you see in Figure 12.7.

<INPUT TYPE=HIDDEN>—Creating Hidden Data

Purpose: Stores hidden data; data is not visible to users unless they view the page source.

Start Tag/End Tag: Required/Omitted

Supported: [2, 3, 3.2, 4, IE1, IE2, IE3, IE4, IE5, NS1, NS2, NS3, NS4]

Attributes:

- **CLASS**—Class of the element. [4, IE4, IE5]

- **DATAFLD**—Name of the column of the data source object that supplies the bound data. Set to alphanumeric characters. [IE4, IE5]

- **DATASRC**—Gives the URL or ID of the data source object supplying data bound to this element. W3C says this should be a URL; Internet Explorer says it should be a data source ID. [IE4, IE5]

- **DIR**—Gives the direction of directionally neutral text (text that doesn't have inherent direction in which you should read it). Possible values: **LTR**: left-to-right text or table and **RTL**: right-to-left text or table. [4]

- **ID**—Unique alphanumeric identifier for the tag, which you can use to refer to it. [4, IE4, IE5]

- **LANG**—Base language used for the tag. [4, IE4, IE5]

- **LANGUAGE**—Scripting language used for the tag. [IE4, IE5]

- **NAME**—Gives the element a name. Set to alphanumeric characters. Required. [4, IE3, IE4, IE5, NS1, NS2, NS3, NS4]

- **STYLE**—Inline style indicating how to render the element. [4, IE4, IE5]

- **TITLE**—Holds additional information (which might be displayed in tool tips) for the element. [4]

- **TYPE**—Specifies the type of the element. [2, 3, 3.2, 4, IE1, IE2, IE3, IE4, IE5, NS1, NS2, NS3, NS4]

- **VALUE**—Sets the caption of the element. Set to alphanumeric characters. [2, 3, 3.2, 4, IE1, IE2, IE3, IE4, IE5, NS1, NS2, NS3, NS4]

Events:

- *Internet Explorer*—**onbeforeeditfocus, onbeforefocusenter, onbeforefocusleave, oncontrolselect, onfocus, onfocusenter, onfocusleave, onlosecapture, onpropertychange, onreadystatechange, onresizeend, onresizestart**

- *Netscape Navigator*—none

"I'm creating a Web word game," the novice programmer says, "and I don't want to have to keep track of the secret word on the server. Is there any way to store the secret word in the Web page that users see, but make sure they can't see that word?" "Sure," you say, "use an **<INPUT TYPE=HIDDEN>** control. The control holds hidden text that users won't see in the Web page. Problem solved."

You can store invisible text in a hidden control in a Web page, which you create with the **<INPUT TYPE=HIDDEN>** element. Hidden controls just store text that you can read later and can be very useful by providing, for example, an alternative to cookies.

In this next example, I'll display the text "Hello from HTML!" in a text field and store it in a hidden control. The user can edit the text in the text field, and then restore it from the hidden control just by clicking a button. Here's the HTML:

```
<HTML>

    <HEAD>
        <TITLE>
            Using Hidden Controls
        </TITLE>
        <SCRIPT LANGUAGE = JavaScript>
            function restoreText()
            {
                document.form1.Textbox.value = document.form1.backup.value
            }
        </SCRIPT>
    </HEAD>

    <BODY>

        <CENTER>

            <H1>
                Edit the text, then click the "Restore text" button
                to restore it.
            </H1>

            <BR>

            <FORM NAME = form1>
                <INPUT TYPE = TEXT VALUE="Hello from HTML!"
                    NAME = "Textbox" SIZE = 25>
                <BR>
                <BR>
                <INPUT TYPE = BUTTON Value = "Restore text"
                    onClick = restoreText()>
                <INPUT TYPE = HIDDEN NAME = backup VALUE =
                    "Hello from HTML!">
            </FORM>
        </CENTER>
```

```
    </BODY>

</HTML>
```

You can see the results of this HTML in Figure 12.8. When the user edits the text and then clicks the "Restore text" button, the original text is restored from the hidden control to the text field.

TIP: *Note that storing text in a hidden control is not secure, if you're worried about security. The user can always view what's in the hidden control simply by viewing the source HTML in the browser.*

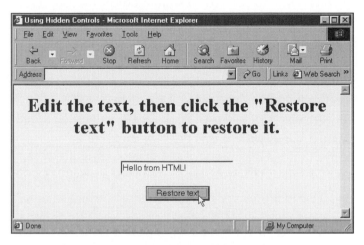

Figure 12.8   Restoring data from a hidden control.

<INPUT TYPE=IMAGE>—Creating Image Submit Buttons

Purpose: Indicates an image users can click much as they would a Submit button. The mouse coordinates in the image are also passed to the form's action URL.

Start Tag/End Tag: Required/Omitted

Supported: [2, 3, 3.2, 4, IE1, IE2, IE3, IE4, IE5, NS1, NS2, NS3, NS4]

Attributes:

• **ACCESSKEY**—Keyboard shortcut key; a single character is used as the value of this attribute. The user can type a platform-dependent key (such as

Alt) with the **ACCESSKEY** character to trigger the active field. Set to an alphanumeric character. [4, IE4, IE5]

- **ALIGN**—Sets the alignment of text following the image. Set to **LEFT**, **RIGHT**, **TOP** (the default), **TEXTTOP**, **MIDDLE**, **ABSMIDDLE**, **BASELINE**, **BOTTOM**, or **ABSBOTTOM**. [2, 3, 3.2, 4, IE1, IE2, IE3, IE4, IE5, NS1, NS2, NS3, NS4]

- **ALT**—Sets the text that should be displayed for browsers that cannot handle images. Set to an alphanumeric string. [4, IE4, IE5]

- **CLASS**—Class of the element. [3, 4, IE4, IE5]

- **DATAFLD**—Name of the column of the data source object that supplies the bound data. Set to alphanumeric characters. [IE4, IE5]

- **DATASRC**—Gives the URL or ID of the data source object supplying data bound to this element. W3C says this should be a URL; Internet Explorer says it should be a data source ID. [IE4, IE5]

- **DIR**—Gives the direction of directionally neutral text (text that doesn't have inherent direction in which you should read it). Possible values: **LTR**: left-to-right text or table and **RTL**: right-to-left text or table. [4, IE5]

- **DISABLED**—Specifies that the element is disabled when first displayed. Stand-alone attribute. [3, 4, IE4, IE5]

- **ID**—Unique alphanumeric identifier for the tag, which you can use to refer to it. [3, 4, IE4, IE5]

- **LANG**—Base language used for the tag. [3, 4, IE4, IE5]

- **LANGUAGE**—Scripting language used for the tag. [IE4, IE5]

- **NAME**—Gives the element a name. Set to alphanumeric characters. Required. [2, 3, 3.2, 4, IE1, IE2, IE3, IE4, IE5, NS1, NS2, NS3, NS4]

- **SRC**—Specifies the URL of the image. Set to a URL. [2, 3, 3.2, 4, IE1, IE2, IE3, IE4, IE5, NS1, NS2, NS3, NS4]

- **SIZE**—Sets the size. [4, IE3, IE4, IE5]

- **STYLE**—Inline style indicating how to render the element. [4, IE4, IE5]

- **TABINDEX**—Sets the tab index of the element, which locates it in the tab order of the form, allowing the user to press the Tab key and navigate from element to element. Set to positive or negative integers. [4, IE4, IE5]

- **TITLE**—Holds additional information (which might be displayed in tool tips) for the element. [3, 4, IE4, IE5]

- **TYPE**—Specifies the type of the element. [2, 3, 3.2, 4, IE1, IE2, IE3, IE4, IE5, NS1, NS2, NS3, NS4]

- **USEMAP**—Sets the URL of the client-side image map specification to be used. If you begin the **USEMAP** value with a pound sign (**#**), the image map is in the same document as the **<INPUT TYPE=IMAGE>** element. Set to a URL. [4]

- **VALUE**—Indicates the symbolic result of the field when activated that is passed to the form processing script. [2, 3, 3.2, 4, IE1, IE2, IE3, IE4, IE5, NS1, NS2, NS3, NS4]

Events:

- *Internet Explorer*—**onbeforecut, onbeforeeditfocus, onbeforefocusenter, onbeforefocusleave, onbeforepaste, onblur, onclick, oncontextmenu, oncontrolselect, oncut, ondblclick, ondrag, ondragend, ondragenter, ondragleave, ondragover, ondragstart, ondrop, onfilterchange, onfocus, onfocusenter, onfocusleave, onhelp, onkeydown, onkeypress, onkeyup, onlosecapture, onmousedown, onmouseenter, onmouseleave, onmousemove, onmouseout, onmouseover, onmouseup, onpaste, onpropertychange, onreadystatechange, onresize, onresizeend, onresizestart, onselectstart**

- *Netscape Navigator*—none

There's an easy way to use an image as a Submit button in a form—just use the **<INPUT TYPE=IMAGE>** element. To indicate what image to use, you set the **SRC** attribute.

Here's an example using an image, submit.gif, as a Submit button:

```
<HTML>
    <HEAD>
        <TITLE>
            CGI Example
        </TITLE>
    </HEAD>

    <BODY>
        <CENTER>
            <H1>
                Using An Image Control
            </H1>
            <FORM METHOD="POST"
                ACTION="http://www.starpowder.com/steve/cgi/cgidata.cgi">
                    Please enter your name:
                    <INPUT TYPE="text" NAME="text">
                    <P>
```

```
                          <INPUT TYPE="IMAGE" SRC="submit.gif"
                          NAME="Submit" VALUE="Submit">
            </FORM>
        </CENTER>
    </BODY>
</HTML>
```

You can see the results of this HTML in Figure 12.9.

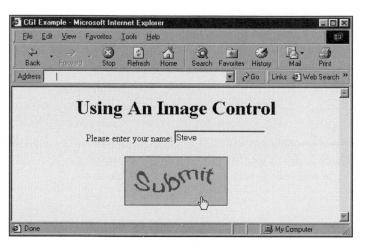

Figure 12.9   Using an image Submit button.

<INPUT TYPE=PASSWORD>—Creating Password Controls

Purpose: Creates a password text field, which masks typed input.

Start Tag/End Tag: Required/Omitted

Supported: [2, 3, 3.2, 4, IE1, IE2, IE3, IE4, IE5, NS1, NS2, NS3, NS4]

Attributes:

- **ACCESSKEY**—Keyboard shortcut key; a single character is used as the value of this attribute. The user can type a platform-dependent key (such as Alt) with the **ACCESSKEY** character to trigger the active field. Set to an alphanumeric character. [4, IE4, IE5]

- **AUTOCOMPLETE**—Set to **TRUE** (the default) if you want Internet Explorer to automatically complete data typed into the control based on what the user has entered before. [IE5]

- **CLASS**—Class of the element. [3, 4, IE4, IE5]

- **CONTENTEDITABLE**—Set to **TRUE** if you want the content of the control to be editable. [IE5]

- **DATAFLD**—Name of the column of the data source object that supplies the bound data. Set to alphanumeric characters. [IE4, IE5]

- **DATASRC**—Gives the URL or ID of the data source object supplying data bound to this element. W3C says this should be a URL; Internet Explorer says it should be a data source ID. [IE4, IE5]

- **DIR**—Gives the direction of directionally neutral text (text that doesn't have inherent direction in which you should read it). Possible values: **LTR**: left-to-right text or table and **RTL**: right-to-left text or table. [4, IE5]

- **DISABLED**—Specifies that the element is disabled when first displayed. Stand-alone attribute. [3, 4, IE4, IE5]

- **ID**—Unique alphanumeric identifier for the tag, which you can use to refer to it. [3, 4, IE4, IE5]

- **LANG**—Base language used for the tag. [3, 4, IE4, IE5]

- **LANGUAGE**—Scripting language used for the tag. [IE4, IE5]

- **MAXLENGTH**—Sets the maximum length of the data in the control, in characters. [NS2, NS3, NS4, IE3, IE4, IE5]

- **NAME**—Gives the element a name. Set to alphanumeric characters. Required. [2, 3, 3.2, 4, IE1, IE2, IE3, IE4, IE5, NS1, NS2, NS3, NS4]

- **READONLY**—Set to **TRUE** if you want the control to be read-only. [IE4, IE5]

- **SIZE**—Specifies the size. [4, IE3, IE4, IE5]

- **STYLE**—Inline style indicating how to render the element. [4, IE4, IE5]

- **TABINDEX**—Sets the tab index of the element, which locates it in the tab order of the form, allowing the user to press the Tab key and navigate from element to element. Set to positive or negative integers. [4, IE4, IE5]

- **TITLE**—Holds additional information (which might be displayed in tool tips) for the element. [2, 3, 4, IE4, IE5]

- **TYPE**—Specifies the type of the element. [2, 3, 3.2, 4, IE1, IE2, IE3, IE4, IE5, NS1, NS2, NS3, NS4]

- **VALUE**—Sets the default contents of the element. Set to an alphanumeric string. [2, 3, 3.2, 4, IE1, IE2, IE3, IE4, IE5, NS1, NS2, NS3, NS4]

Events:

- *Internet Explorer*—**onbeforecut, onbeforeeditfocus, onbeforefocusenter, onbeforefocusleave, onbeforepaste, onblur,**

onclick, oncontextmenu, oncontrolselect, oncut, ondblclick, ondrag, ondragend, ondragenter, ondragleave, ondragover, ondragstart, ondrop, onfilterchange, onfocus, onfocusenter, onfocusleave, onhelp, onkeydown, onkeypress, onkeyup, onlosecapture, onmousedown, onmouseenter, onmouseleave, onmousemove, onmouseout, onmouseover, onmouseup, onpaste, onpropertychange, onreadystatechange, onresize, onresizeend, onresizestart, onselectstart

• *Netscape Navigator*—**onselect**

"Uh oh," says the novice programmer, "that darn Johnson was looking over my shoulder as I entered my password. Now what?" "Well," you say, "the first thing to do is to use a password control in your Web page from now on." "Thanks a lot," says the NP.

Password controls are just like text fields except that each character you enter appears as an asterisk (*), not as the actual character you typed. This hides what you actually did type, so you can enter passwords even if someone is looking. The password "open sesame!" will be displayed as "************". In script, you can get the actual value of the password just by using the control's **value** property.

Here's an example. In this case, the user enters a password in a password control, and when the button is clicked, the actual text in the password control appears in a text field:

```
<HTML>

    <HEAD>
        <TITLE>
            Using Password Controls
        </TITLE>

        <SCRIPT LANGUAGE = JavaScript>
        function showPassword()
        {
            document.form1.textfield.value = "Password:" +
                document.form1.password.value
        }
        </SCRIPT>
    </HEAD>

    <BODY>

        <CENTER>
```

```
<H1>
    Enter a password in the password field and click the button.
</H1>

<FORM NAME = form1>
    <INPUT TYPE = PASSWORD NAME = "password" SIZE = 25>
    <BR>
    <BR>
    <INPUT TYPE = TEXT NAME = "textfield" SIZE = 25>
    <BR>
    <BR>
    <INPUT TYPE = BUTTON Value = "Show Password"
            onClick = "showPassword()">
</FORM>
        </CENTER>

    </BODY>

</HTML>
```

The results of this HTML appear in Figure 12.10, and as you can see, entering a password results in a string of asterisks, but you can access the actual password in your script.

TIP: Would-be miscreants might try to select the text in the password control and paste it into another control to see what that actual text is, but you don't have to worry—when you copy text from a password control (as when you press Ctrl+C in Windows), all you'll get are asterisks.

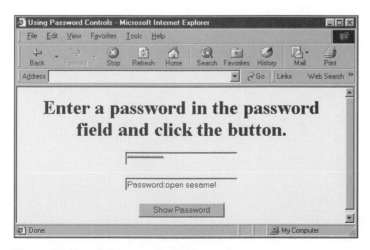

Figure 12.10   Using a password control.

699

<INPUT TYPE=RADIO>—Creating Radio Buttons

Purpose: Creates a radio button in a form.

Start Tag/End Tag: Required/Omitted

Supported: [2, 3, 3.2, 4, IE1, IE2, IE3, IE4, IE5, NS1, NS2, NS3, NS4]

Attributes:

- **ACCESSKEY**—Keyboard shortcut key; a single character is used as the value of this attribute. The user can type a platform-dependent key (such as Alt) with the **ACCESSKEY** character to trigger the active field. Set to an alphanumeric character. [4, IE4, IE5]

- **CHECKED**—Indicates if the radio button should appear checked initially or not. Stand-alone attribute. [2, 3, 3.2, 4, IE1, IE2, IE3, IE4, IE5, NS1, NS2, NS3, NS4]

- **CLASS**—Class of the element. [3, 4, IE4, IE5]

- **DATAFLD**—Name of the column of the data source object that supplies the bound data. Set to alphanumeric characters. [IE4, IE5]

- **DATASRC**—Gives the URL or ID of the data source object supplying data bound to this element. W3C says this should be a URL; Internet Explorer says it should be a data source ID. [IE4, IE5]

- **DIR**—Gives the direction of directionally neutral text (text that doesn't have inherent direction in which you should read it). Possible values: **LTR**: left-to-right text or table and **RTL**: right-to-left text or table. [4, IE5]

- **DISABLED**—Specifies that the element is disabled when first displayed. Stand-alone attribute. [4, IE4, IE5]

- **ID**—Unique alphanumeric identifier for the tag, which you can use to refer to it. [3, 4, IE4, IE5]

- **LANG**—Base language used for the tag. [3, 4, IE4, IE5]

- **LANGUAGE**—Scripting language used for the tag. [IE4, IE5]

- **NAME**—Gives the element a name. Set to alphanumeric characters. Required. [2, 3, 3.2, 4, IE1, IE2, IE3, IE4, IE5, NS1, NS2, NS3, NS4]

- **STYLE**—Inline style indicating how to render the element. [4, IE4, IE5]

- **SIZE**—Sets the control's size. [4, IE3, IE4, IE5]

- **TABINDEX**—Sets the tab index of the element, which locates it in the tab order of the form, allowing the user to press the Tab key and navigate from element to element. Set to positive or negative integers. [4, IE4, IE5]

- **TITLE**—Holds additional information (which might be displayed in tool tips) for the element. [2, 3, 4, IE4, IE5]

- **TYPE**—Specifies the type of the element. [2, 3, 3.2, 4, IE1, IE2, IE3, IE4, IE5, NS1, NS2, NS3, NS4]

- **VALUE**—Represents the result of the radio button when clicked that is passed to the form's action URL. Set to alphanumeric characters. Required. [2, 3, 3.2, 4, IE1, IE2, IE3, IE4, IE5, NS1, NS2, NS3, NS4]

Events:

- *Internet Explorer*—**onbeforecut, onbeforeeditfocus, onbeforefocusenter, onbeforefocusleave, onbeforepaste, onblur, onclick, oncontextmenu, oncontrolselect, oncut, ondblclick, ondrag, ondragend, ondragenter, ondragleave, ondragover, ondragstart, ondrop, onfilterchange, onfocus, onfocusenter, onfocusleave, onhelp, onkeydown, onkeypress, onkeyup, onlosecapture, onmousedown, onmouseenter, onmouseleave, onmousemove, onmouseout, onmouseover, onmouseup, onpaste, onpropertychange, onreadystatechange, onresizeend, onresizestart, onselectstart**

- *Netscape Navigator*—**onclick**

"Uh oh," says the novice programmer, "I have a problem. The user is supposed to enter the day of the week by clicking a checkbox, but sometimes they leave two checkboxes clicked, and my code gets all messed up." "That's an easy one," you say, "just use radio buttons instead of checkboxes."

Radio buttons can be selected and unselected just as checkboxes can be, but you can *group* radio buttons together so that only one radio button in the group may be selected at one time (if the user clicks a new radio button, the previously selected one is automatically deselected).

Like checkboxes, radio buttons have an **onClick** event you can use to connect them to code. To create a group of mutually exclusive radio buttons, you give them all the same name (using the **NAME** attribute—note that you can have multiple groups of radio buttons in the same page). Here's an example that displays five radio buttons in a group and displays which one the user clicked:

```
<HTML>

    <HEAD>
        <TITLE>
            Using Radio Buttons
        </TITLE>
```

```
<SCRIPT LANGUAGE = JavaScript>

    function radio1Clicked()
    {
        document.form1.TextBox.value =
            "You clicked radio button 1."
    }

    function radio2Clicked()
    {
        document.form1.TextBox.value =
            "You clicked radio button 2."
    }

    function radio3Clicked()
    {
        document.form1.TextBox.value =
            "You clicked radio button 3."
    }

    function radio4Clicked()
    {
        document.form1.TextBox.value =
            "You clicked radio button 4."
    }

    function radio5Clicked()
    {
        document.form1.TextBox.value =
            "You clicked radio button 5."
    }
</SCRIPT>

</HEAD>

<BODY>

<FORM NAME = "form1">

    <CENTER>
        <H1>
            Using Radio Buttons
        </H1>
```

```
<TABLE BORDER BGCOLOR = CYAN WIDTH = 200>
<TR><TD>
<INPUT TYPE = RADIO NAME = RadioButtons
    onClick = radio1Clicked()>Radio 1
</TD></TR>
<TR><TD>
<INPUT TYPE = RADIO NAME = RadioButtons
    onClick = radio2Clicked()>Radio 2
</TD></TR>
<TR><TD>
<INPUT TYPE = RADIO NAME = RadioButtons
    onClick = radio3Clicked()>Radio 3
</TD></TR>
<TR><TD>
<INPUT TYPE = RADIO NAME = RadioButtons
    onClick = radio4Clicked()>Radio 4
</TD></TR>
<TR><TD>
<INPUT TYPE = RADIO NAME = RadioButtons
    onClick = radio5Clicked()>Radio 5
</TD></TR>
</TABLE>
<BR>
<INPUT TYPE  =  TEXT NAME  =  TextBox SIZE  =  35>
</CENTER>

</FORM>

</BODY>

</HTML>
```

You can see the results in Figure 12.11. When the user clicks one radio button, it's selected and all the others are deselected, making radio buttons a good idea when you want to let the user select from a set of mutually exclusive options, such as days of the week.

In fact, the code in this example is longer than it needs to be. Rather than having a separate function for each radio button, you can use the same function for all radio buttons and examine each radio button's **checked** property (for example, **document.form1.radio1**) to see if the radio button is selected or not. You can also set this property to **true** or **false** to select or deselect the radio button.

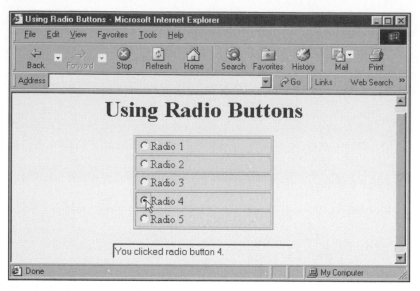

Figure 12.11   Using radio buttons.

<INPUT TYPE=RESET>—Creating Reset Buttons

Purpose: Creates a reset button in a form that resets all fields to their original values.

Start Tag/End Tag: Required/Omitted

Supported: [2, 3, 3.2, 4, IE1, IE2, IE3, IE4, IE5, NS1, NS2, NS3, NS4]

Attributes:

- **ACCESSKEY**—Keyboard shortcut key; a single character is used as the value of this attribute. The user can type a platform-dependent key (such as Alt) with the **ACCESSKEY** character to trigger the active field. Set to an alphanumeric character. [4, IE4, IE5]

- **CLASS**—Class of the element. [3, 4, IE4, IE5]

- **DATAFLD**—Name of the column of the data source object that supplies the bound data. Set to alphanumeric characters. [IE4, IE5]

- **DATASRC**—Gives the URL or ID of the data source object supplying data bound to this element. W3C says this should be a URL; Internet Explorer says it should be a data source ID. [IE4, IE5]

- **DIR**—Gives the direction of directionally neutral text (text that doesn't have inherent direction in which you should read it). Possible values: **LTR**: left-to-right text or table and **RTL**: right-to-left text or table. [4, IE5]

- **DISABLED**—Specifies that the element is disabled when first displayed. Stand-alone attribute. [3, 4, IE4, IE5]

- **ID**—Unique alphanumeric identifier for the tag, which you can use to refer to it. [3, 4, IE4, IE5]

- **LANG**—Base language used for the tag. [3, 4, IE4, IE5]

- **LANGUAGE**—Scripting language used for the tag. [IE4, IE5]

- **NAME**—Gives the element a name. Set to alphanumeric characters. [2, 3, 3.2, 4, IE1, IE2, IE3, IE4, IE5, NS1, NS2, NS3, NS4]

- **SIZE**—The size for the control. [4, IE3, IE4, IE5]

- **STYLE**—Inline style indicating how to render the element. [4, IE4, IE5]

- **TABINDEX**—Sets the tab index of the element, which locates it in the tab order of the form, allowing the user to press the Tab key and navigate from element to element. Set to positive or negative integers. [4, IE4, IE5]

- **TITLE**—Holds additional information (which might be displayed in tool tips) for the element. [2, 3, 4, IE4, IE5]

- **TYPE**—Specifies the type of the element. [2, 3, 3.2, 4, IE1, IE2, IE3, IE4, IE5, NS1, NS2, NS3, NS4]

- **VALUE**—Gives this button another label besides the default, Reset. Set to alphanumeric characters. [2, 3, 3.2, 4, IE1, IE2, IE3, IE4, IE5, NS1, NS2, NS3, NS4]

Events:

- *Internet Explorer*—**onbeforecut, onbeforeeditfocus, onbeforefocusenter, onbeforefocusleave, onbeforepaste, onblur, onclick, oncontextmenu, oncontrolselect, oncut, ondblclick, ondrag, ondragend, ondragenter, ondragleave, ondragover, ondragstart, ondrop, onfilterchange, onfocus, onfocusenter, onfocusleave, onhelp, onkeydown, onkeypress, onkeyup, onlosecapture, onmousedown, onmouseenter, onmouseleave, onmousemove, onmouseout, onmouseover, onmouseup, onpaste, onpropertychange, onreadystatechange, onresize, onresizeend, onresizestart, onselectstart**

- *Netscape Navigator*—**onclick**

A Reset button clears all the controls in a form, restoring them to the original contents they displayed when they first appeared. Using a Reset button is useful in case you have a complex form and at some point users decide they'd like to start over. You'll find an example using this element in the next section on the Submit button.

TIP: *Internet Explorer 4 and later uses all white space and carriage returns you place in the **VALUE** attribute for this element, displaying them "as is." Note, however, that other browsers (and earlier Internet Explorer versions) do not do so.*

<INPUT TYPE=SUBMIT>—Creating Submit Buttons

Purpose: Creates a Submit button that the user can click to send data in the form back to the Web server.

Start Tag/End Tag: Required/Omitted

Supported: [2, 3, 3.2, 4, IE1, IE2, IE3, IE4, IE5, NS1, NS2, NS3, NS4]

Attributes:

- **ACCESSKEY**—Keyboard shortcut key; a single character is used as the value of this attribute. The user can type a platform-dependent key (such as Alt) with the **ACCESSKEY** character to trigger the active field. Set to an alphanumeric character. [4, IE4, IE5]

- **CLASS**—Class of the element. [3, 4, IE4, IE5]

- **DATAFLD**—Name of the column of the data source object that supplies the bound data. Set to alphanumeric characters. [IE4, IE5]

- **DATASRC**—Gives the URL or ID of the data source object supplying data bound to this element. W3C says this should be a URL; Internet Explorer says it should be a data source ID. [IE4, IE5]

- **DIR**—Gives the direction of directionally neutral text (text that doesn't have inherent direction in which you should read it). Possible values: **LTR**: left-to-right text or table and **RTL**: right-to-left text or table. [4, IE5]

- **DISABLED**—Specifies that the element is disabled when first displayed. Stand-alone attribute. [3, 4, IE4, IE5]

- **ID**—Unique alphanumeric identifier for the tag, which you can use to refer to it. [3, 4, IE4, IE5]

- **LANG**—Base language used for the tag. [3, 4, IE4, IE5]

- **LANGUAGE**—Scripting language used for the tag. [IE4, IE5]

- **NAME**—Gives the element a name. Set to alphanumeric characters. [2, 3, 3.2, 4, IE1, IE2, IE3, IE4, IE5, NS1, NS2, NS3, NS4]

- **SIZE**—Specifies a size for the control. [4, IE3, IE4, IE5]

- **STYLE**—Inline style indicating how to render the element. [4, IE4, IE5]

- **TABINDEX**—Sets the tab index of the element, which locates it in the tab order of the form, allowing the user to press the Tab key and navigate from element to element. Set to positive or negative integers. [4, IE4, IE5]

- **TITLE**—Holds additional information (which might be displayed in tool tips) for the element. [2, 3, 4, IE4, IE5]

- **TYPE**—Specifies the type of the element. [2, 3, 3.2, 4, IE1, IE2, IE3, IE4, IE5, NS1, NS2, NS3, NS4]

- **VALUE**—Gives this button another label besides the default, Submit Query. Set to alphanumeric characters. [2, 3, 3.2, 4, IE1, IE2, IE3, IE4, IE5, NS1, NS2, NS3, NS4]

Events:

- *Internet Explorer*—**onbeforecut**, **onbeforeeditfocus**, **onbeforefocusenter**, **onbeforefocusleave**, **onbeforepaste**, **onblur**, **onclick**, **oncontextmenu**, **oncontrolselect**, **oncut**, **ondblclick**, **ondrag**, **ondragend**, **ondragenter**, **ondragleave**, **ondragover**, **ondragstart**, **ondrop**, **onfilterchange**, **onfocus**, **onfocusenter**, **onfocusleave**, **onhelp**, **onkeydown**, **onkeypress**, **onkeyup**, **onlosecapture**, **onmousedown**, **onmouseenter**, **onmouseleave**, **onmousemove**, **onmouseout**, **onmouseover**, **onmouseup**, **onpaste**, **onpropertychange**, **onreadystatechange**, **onresize**, **onresizeend**, **onresizestart**, **onselectstart**

- *Netscape Navigator*—none.

"OK," says the novice programmer, "my form is all set; now how do I send its data back to the server?" "That's an easy one," you say, "just add a Submit button."

When the user clicks the Submit button in a form, the data in the controls in the form is sent to the URL given by the form's **ACTION** attribute. In other words, if you're sending data back to the server, the Submit button will be valuable to you. For an example showing how to send data to the server, see the In Depth section of this chapter.

TIP: *Unless you supply a caption for the Submit button with the **VALUE** attribute, most browsers, including Netscape Navigator and Internet Explorer, will give that button a caption of Submit Query.*

Note that there's a very useful event you can use with the Submit button—**onSubmit**, which is an event of the **<FORM>** element. Code executed in this event's handler function can check the form and return a value of **true** if the data should be sent to the server, and **false** otherwise, in which case the data simply is not sent to the server. Here's an example. If the user doesn't enter a name when asked, the code displays an alert box and refuses to send the data from the form to the server:

```
<HTML>

    <HEAD>
        <TITLE>
            Using Submit And Reset Buttons
        </TITLE>
        <SCRIPT LANGUAGE = JavaScript>
            function checkData()
            {
                if (document.form1.name.value == ""){
                    alert("Enter your name, please.")
                    return false
                }
                else{
                    return true
                }
            }
        </SCRIPT>
    </HEAD>

    <BODY>

        <CENTER>
            <H1>
                Using Submit And Reset Buttons
            </H1>

            <TABLE BORDER CELLPADDING = 6>
            <TR ALIGN= CENTER>
            <TD BGCOLOR = cyan>
            Sign the guestbook!
            <BR>

            <P>
            <FORM NAME = form1 onSubmit = "return checkData()" METHOD=POST
                ACTION="http://www.starpowder.com//guestbook.cgi">
                Name: <INPUT TYPE="text" NAME="name" SIZE=30 MAXLENGTH=30>

            <P>
                Email: <INPUT TYPE="text" NAME="address" SIZE=30
                    MAXLENGTH=30>
```

```
        <P>
              <TEXTAREA ROWS=5 COLS=60 NAME="body"></TEXTAREA>
              <BR>
              <BR>

              <INPUT TYPE=submit VALUE="Submit">
              <INPUT TYPE=reset VALUE="Reset">
          </FORM>
        </TD>
        </TR>
        </TABLE>

    </CENTER>

  </BODY>
</HTML>
```

You can see the result of this HTML in Figure 12.12. If users don't enter anything in the Name field and then click Submit, the code will ask them to provide a name. They can enter a name and click Submit again to submit the data to the server.

TIP: *Internet Explorer 4 and later uses all white space and carriage returns you place in the **VALUE** attribute for this element, displaying them "as is." Note, however, that other browsers (and earlier Internet Explorer versions) do not do so.*

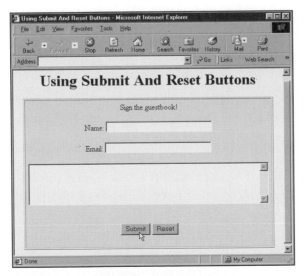

Figure 12.12   Creating a Submit button.

\<INPUT TYPE=TEXT\>—Creating Text Fields

Purpose: Creates a text field that the user can enter or edit text in.

Start Tag/End Tag: Required/Omitted

Supported: [2, 3, 3.2, 4, IE1, IE2, IE3, IE4, IE5, NS1, NS2, NS3, NS4]

Attributes:

- **ACCESSKEY**—Keyboard shortcut key; a single character is used as the value of this attribute. The user can type a platform-dependent key (such as Alt) with the **ACCESSKEY** character to trigger the active field. Set to an alphanumeric character. [4, IE4, IE5]

- **AUTOCOMPLETE**—Completes text in the control based on previously entered text. [IE5]

- **CLASS**—Class of the element. [3, 4, IE4, IE5]

- **DATAFLD**—Name of the column of the data source object that supplies the bound data. Set to alphanumeric characters. [IE4, IE5]

- **DATASRC**—Gives the URL or ID of the data source object supplying data bound to this element. W3C says this should be a URL; Internet Explorer says it should be a data source ID. [IE4, IE5]

- **DIR**—Gives the direction of directionally neutral text (text that doesn't have inherent direction in which you should read it). Possible values: **LTR**: left-to-right text or table and **RTL**: right-to-left text or table. [4, IE5]

- **DISABLED**—Specifies that the element is disabled when first displayed. Stand-alone attribute. [3, 4, IE4, IE5]

- **ID**—Unique alphanumeric identifier for the tag, which you can use to refer to it. [3, 4, IE4, IE5]

- **LANG**—Base language used for the tag. [3, 4, IE4, IE5]

- **LANGUAGE**—Scripting language used for the tag. [IE4, IE5]

- **MAXLENGTH**—Sets the maximum number of characters that can be entered into the text field. Note that if **MAXLENGTH** is larger than the value of the **SIZE** attribute, the text field will scroll as needed. Set to positive integers. [2, 3, 3.2, 4, IE1, IE2, IE3, IE4, IE5, NS1, NS2, NS3, NS4]

- **NAME**—Gives the element a name. Set to alphanumeric characters. Required. [2, 3, 3.2, 4, IE1, IE2, IE3, IE4, IE5, NS1, NS2, NS3, NS4]

- **READONLY**—Indicates that the content of the text field may not be modified. Stand-alone attribute. [4, IE4, IE5]

- **SIZE**—Sets the size of the text field in characters. Set to positive integers. [2, 3, 3.2, 4, IE1, IE2, IE3, IE4, IE5, NS1, NS2, NS3, NS4]

- **STYLE**—Inline style indicating how to render the element. [4, IE4, IE5]

- **TABINDEX**—Sets the tab index of the element, which locates it in the tab order of the form, allowing the user to press the Tab key and navigate from element to element. Set to positive or negative integers. [4, IE4, IE5]

- **TITLE**—Holds additional information (which might be displayed in tool tips) for the element. [2, 3, 4, IE4, IE5]

- **TYPE**—Specifies the type of the element. [2, 3, 3.2, 4, IE1, IE2, IE3, IE4, IE5, NS1, NS2, NS3, NS4]

- **VALUE**—Holds the initial text in the text field. Set to alphanumeric characters. [2, 3, 3.2, 4, IE1, IE2, IE3, IE4, IE5, NS1, NS2, NS3, NS4]

Events:

- *Internet Explorer*—**onafterupdate, onbeforecut, onbeforeeditfocus, onbeforefocusenter, onbeforefocusleave, onbeforepaste, onbeforeupdate, onblur, onchange, onclick, oncontextmenu, oncontrolselect, oncut, ondblclick, ondrag, ondragend, ondragenter, ondragleave, ondragover, ondragstart, ondrop, onerrorupdate, onfilterchange, onfocus, onfocusenter, onfocusleave, onhelp, onkeydown, onkeypress, onkeyup, onlosecapture, onmousedown, onmouseenter, onmouseleave, onmousemove, onmouseout, onmouseover, onmouseup, onpaste, onpropertychange, onreadystatechange, onresize, onresizeend, onresizestart, onselect, onselectstart**

- *Netscape Navigator*—**onblur, onchange, onfocus, onselect**

"Say," asks the novice programmer, "just how do I create text fields? There's no **<TEXTFIELD>** element." "You just use **<INPUT TYPE=TEXT>**," you say, "no problem."

You can create a text field (referred to as a text box in other programming environments) with the **<INPUT TYPE=TEXT>** element. You can set the size of the text field in characters with the **SIZE** attribute and the maximum length of text (the text field will scroll if the maximum length is greater than its size) with the **MAXLENGTH** attribute. Here's an example:

```
<HTML>
    <HEAD>
        <TITLE>Using Text Fields</TITLE>
    </HEAD>
```

```
<BODY>
    <FORM NAME="form1">
        <CENTER>
            <BR>
            <H1>Using Text Fields</H1>
            <BR>
            <BR>
            <INPUT TYPE = TEXT NAME = textfield SIZE = 40 MAXLENGTH=60>
        </CENTER>
    </FORM>
</BODY>
</HTML>
```

You can see the text field in Figure 12.13, and you can enter and edit text in it. From a programming point of view, you can refer to the text in a text field using the JavaScript **value** property like this: **document.form1.textfield.value= "Hello from HTML!"**. See the examples in the In Depth section of this chapter for more information.

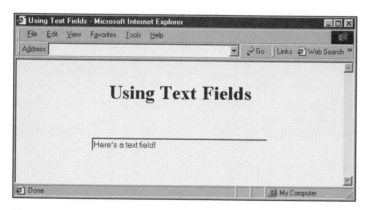

Figure 12.13   Creating a text field.

<TEXTAREA>—Creating Text Areas

Purpose: Creates a text area, much like a two-dimensional text field.

Start Tag/End Tag: Required/Required

Supported: [2, 3, 3.2, 4, IE1, IE2, IE3, IE4, IE5, NS1, NS2, NS3, NS4]

Attributes:

- **ACCESSKEY**—Keyboard shortcut key; a single character is used as the value of this attribute. The user can type a platform-dependent key (such as Alt) with the **ACCESSKEY** character to trigger the active field. Set to an alphanumeric character. [4, IE4, IE5]

- **COLS**—Specifies number of columns visible in the control. Set to a positive integer. Required. [2, 3, 3.2, 4, IE1, IE2, IE3, IE4, IE5, NS1, NS2, NS3, NS4]

- **CLASS**—Class of the element. [3, 4, IE4, IE5]

- **DATAFLD**—Name of the column of the data source object that supplies the bound data. Set to alphanumeric characters. [IE4, IE5]

- **DATASRC**—Gives the URL or ID of the data source object supplying data bound to this element. W3C says this should be a URL; Internet Explorer says it should be a data source ID. [IE4, IE5]

- **DIR**—Gives the direction of directionally neutral text (text that doesn't have inherent direction in which you should read it). Possible values: **LTR**: left-to-right text or table and **RTL**: right-to-left text or table. [4, IE5]

- **DISABLED**—Specifies that the element is disabled when first displayed. Stand-alone attribute. [3, 4, IE4, IE5]

- **ID**—Unique alphanumeric identifier for the tag, which you can use to refer to it. [3, 4, IE4, IE5]

- **LANG**—Base language used for the tag. [3, 4, IE4, IE5]

- **LANGUAGE**—Scripting language used for the tag. [IE4, IE5]

- **NAME**—Gives the element a name. Set to alphanumeric characters. [2, 3, 3.2, 4, IE1, IE2, IE3, IE4, IE5, NS1, NS2, NS3, NS4]

- **READONLY**—Indicates that the content of the text field may not be modified. Stand-alone attribute. [4, IE4, IE5]

- **ROWS**—Specifies the number of rows in the control. Set to positive integers. Required. [2, 3, 3.2, 4, IE1, IE2, IE3, IE4, IE5, NS1, NS2, NS3, NS4]

- **STYLE**—Inline style indicating how to render the element. [4, IE4, IE5]

- **TABINDEX**—Sets the tab index of the element, which locates it in the tab order of the form, allowing the user to press the Tab key and navigate from element to element. Set to positive or negative integers. [4, IE4, IE5]

- **TITLE**—Holds additional information (which might be displayed in tool tips) for the element. [2, 3, 4, IE4, IE5]

- **WRAP**—Determines the word wrap behavior for the control. Set to **OFF** (no word wrapping, the default), **SOFT** (text is wrapped, but the wrapping is not transmitted back to the server as return/linefeed characters), or **HARD** (text is wrapped, and the wrapping is preserved when the data is submitted back to the server). [IE4, IE5, NS2, NS3, NS4]

Events:

- *Internet Explorer*—**onafterupdate, onbeforecopy, onbeforecut, onbeforeeditfocus, onbeforefocusenter, onbeforefocusleave, onbeforepaste, onbeforeupdate, onblur, onchange, onclick, oncontextmenu, oncontrolselect, oncut, ondblclick, ondrag, ondragend, ondragenter, ondragleave, ondragover, ondragstart, ondrop, onerrorupdate, onfilterchange, onfocus, onfocusenter, onfocusleave, onhelp, onkeydown, onkeypress, onkeyup, onlosecapture, onmousedown, onmouseenter, onmouseleave, onmousemove, onmouseout, onmouseover, onmouseup, onpaste, onpropertychange, onreadystatechange, onresize, onresizeend, onresizestart, onscroll, onselect, onselectstart**

- *Netscape Navigator*—**onblur, onchange, onfocus, onselect**

"I can't fit all I want to say in the Suggestions box in your Web page," the big boss says. "Well," you say, "I can use a text area there instead of a text field, I suppose." The BB hurries off to enter more suggestions on how you can improve yourself. You think, "Great."

Text areas are like two-dimensional text fields, and you create them with the **<TEXTAREA>** element, not the **<INPUT>** element. One reason there is a separate **<TEXTAREA>** element is because any text you enter in this element appears in the text area (unlike the **<INPUT>** element, you must use a closing **</TEXTAREA>** tag with the **<TEXTAREA>** element). You must also set the number of rows and columns you want in the text area using the **ROWS** and **COLS** attributes. Here's an example:

```
<HTML>
    <HEAD>
        <TITLE>Using Text Areas</TITLE>
    </HEAD>

    <BODY>
        <FORM NAME="form1">
            <CENTER>
                <BR>
                <H1>Using Text Areas</H1>
                <BR>
                <TEXTAREA NAME = textarea ROWS = 10 COLS = 30>
```

```
                    Hello from HTML!
                </TEXTAREA>
            </CENTER>
        </FORM>
    </BODY>
</HTML>
```

You can see the results of this HTML in Figure 12.14, where you see the text "Hello from HTML!" displayed in the text area.

TIP: *You can turn text wrapping on and off with the* **WRAP** *attribute in Internet Explorer and Netscape Navigator.*

From a programming point of view, you can refer to the text in a text area using the JavaScript **value** property like this: **document.form1.textarea.value="Hello from HTML!"**, just as you would with a text field. See the examples in the In Depth section of this chapter for more information.

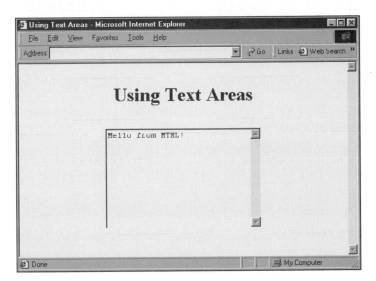

Figure 12.14   Creating a text area.

<BUTTON>—Creating A Customizable Button

Purpose: Creates a customizable button.

Start Tag/End Tag: Required/Required

Supported: [4, IE4, IE5]

Attributes:

- **ACCESSKEY**—Keyboard shortcut key; a single character is used as the value of this attribute. The user can type a platform-dependent key (such as Alt) with the **ACCESSKEY** character to trigger the active field. Set to an alphanumeric character. [4, IE4, IE5]

- **CLASS**—Class of the element. [4, IE4, IE5]

- **DATAFLD**—Name of the column of the data source object that supplies the bound data. Set to alphanumeric characters. [IE4, IE5]

- **DATAFORMATAS**—Specifies if bound data is plain text or HTML. Set to **HTML**, **PLAINTEXT**, or **TEXT**. [IE4, IE5]

- **DATASRC**—Gives the URL or ID of the data source object supplying data bound to this element. W3C says this should be a URL; Internet Explorer says it should be a data source ID. [IE4, IE5]

- **DIR**—Gives the direction of directionally neutral text (text that doesn't have inherent direction in which you should read it). Possible values: **LTR**: left-to-right text or table and **RTL**: right-to-left text or table. [4, IE5]

- **DISABLED**—Specifies that the element is disabled when first displayed. Stand-alone attribute. [3, 4, IE4, IE5]

- **ID**—Unique alphanumeric identifier for the tag, which you can use to refer to it. [4, IE4, IE5]

- **LANG**—Base language used for the tag. [4, IE4, IE5]

- **LANGUAGE**—Scripting language used for the tag. [IE4, IE5]

- **NAME**—Gives the element a name. Set to alphanumeric characters. [4, IE4, IE5]

- **STYLE**—Inline style indicating how to render the element. [4, IE4, IE5]

- **TABINDEX**—Sets the tab index of the element, which locates it in the tab order of the form, allowing the user to press the Tab key and navigate from element to element. Set to positive or negative integers. [4, IE4, IE5]

- **TITLE**—Holds additional information (which might be displayed in tool tips) for the element. [4, IE4, IE5]

- **TYPE**—Specifies the purpose that the button will fulfill—that of the traditional Submit, Reset, or multipurpose button. Set to **SUBMIT**, **RESET**, or **BUTTON**. [4, IE4, IE5]

- **VALUE**—Represents the result of the button when clicked. Set to alphanumeric characters. [4, IE4, IE5]

Events:

- *Internet Explorer*—**onbeforecut, onbeforeeditfocus,
  onbeforefocusenter, onbeforefocusleave, onbeforepaste, onblur,
  onclick, oncontextmenu, oncontrolselect, oncut, ondblclick,
  ondragenter, ondragleave, ondragover, ondrop, onfilterchange,
  onfocus, onfocusenter, onfocusleave, onhelp, onkeydown, onkeypress,
  onkeyup, onlosecapture, onmousedown, onmouseenter, onmouseleave,
  onmousemove, onmouseout, onmouseover, onmouseup, onpaste,
  onpropertychange, onreadystatechange, onresize, onresizeend,
  onresizestart, onselectstart**

- *Netscape Navigator*—not applicable

"Wow," says the novice programmer, "I have a great idea. You know how you can
display HTML in Web pages? Well, what if you could do the same thing for the
caption of a button? I'm going to patent this idea." "Too late," you say, "it already
exists—and it's called the **<BUTTON>** element."

You can customize the appearance of buttons using HTML (including images) in
the caption of a **<BUTTON>** control, which has been supported in Internet Explorer since version 4 (but not in Netscape). And you can use this control as a
Submit, Reset, or standard button—just set the **TYPE** attribute to **SUBMIT**,
RESET, or **BUTTON**. Here's an example showing how to use **<BUTTON>**:

```
<HTML>
    <HEAD>
        <TITLE>
            Using &lt;BUTTON&gt;
        </TITLE>
    </HEAD>

    <BODY>
        <CENTER>
            <H1>
                Using &lt;BUTTON&gt;
            </H1>
            <FORM METHOD="POST"
                ACTION="http://www.starpowder.com/steve/cgi/cgidata.cgi">

                Please enter your name:
                <INPUT TYPE="text" NAME="text" VALUE="">
                <P>
                <BUTTON TYPE=SUBMIT NAME=HELPBUTTON>
                    <IMG SRC="SUBMIT.GIF" ALIGN=MIDDLE> Click
```

```
                  <STRONG>here</STRONG> to send the data.
              </BUTTON>
          </FORM>
       </CENTER>
   </BODY>
</HTML>
```

You can see the results of this HTML in Figure 12.15.

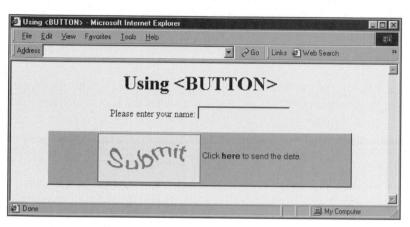

Figure 12.15 Creating a **<BUTTON>** control.

<SELECT>, **<OPTION>**, And **<OPTGROUP>**—Creating A Select Control

<SELECT>

Purpose: Displays a select control, much like a drop-down list box.

Start Tag/End Tag: Required/Required

Supported: [2, 3, 3.2, 4, IE1, IE2, IE3, IE4, IE5, NS1, NS2, NS3, NS4]

Attributes:

- **ACCESSKEY**—Keyboard shortcut key; a single character is used as the value of this attribute. The user can type a platform-dependent key (such as Alt) with the **ACCESSKEY** character to trigger the active field. Set to an alphanumeric character. [4, IE4, IE5]

- **ALIGN**—Gives the alignment of the contents of the **SELECT**. Set to **LEFT**, **RIGHT**, **TOP**, **MIDDLE**, or **BOTTOM**. [IE4, IE5]

- **CLASS**—Class of the element. [3, 4, IE4, IE5]

- **DISABLED**—Specifies that the element is disabled when first displayed. Stand-alone attribute. [3, 4, IE4, IE5]

- **DATAFLD**—Name of the column of the data source object that supplies the bound data. Set to alphanumeric characters. [IE4, IE5]

- **DATASRC**—Gives the URL or ID of the data source object supplying data bound to this element. W3C says this should be a URL; Internet Explorer says it should be a data source ID. [IE4, IE5]

- **DIR**—Gives the direction of directionally neutral text (text that doesn't have inherent direction in which you should read it). Possible values: **LTR**: left-to-right text or table and **RTL**: right-to-left text or table. [4, IE5]

- **DISABLED**—Specifies that the element is disabled when first displayed. Stand-alone attribute. [3, 4, IE4, IE5]

- **ID**—Unique alphanumeric identifier for the tag, which you can use to refer to it. [3, 4, IE4, IE5]

- **LANG**—Base language used for the tag. [3, 4, IE4, IE5]

- **LANGUAGE**—Scripting language used for the tag. [IE4, IE5]

- **MULTIPLE**—Indicates that more than one option can be selected at a time. Stand-alone attribute. [2, 3, 3.2, 4, IE1, IE2, IE3, IE4, IE5, NS1, NS2, NS3, NS4]

- **NAME**—Gives the element a name. Set to alphanumeric characters. [2, 3, 3.2, 4, IE1, IE2, IE3, IE4, IE5, NS1, NS2, NS3, NS4]

- **SIZE**—Gives the number of items visible in the list. Set to a positive integer. [2, 3.2, 4, IE1, IE2, IE3, IE4, IE5, NS1, NS2, NS3, NS4]

- **STYLE**—Inline style indicating how to render the element. [4, IE4, IE5]

- **TABINDEX**—Sets the tab index of the element, which locates it in the tab order of the form, allowing the user to press the Tab key and navigate from element to element. Set to positive or negative integers. [4, IE4, IE5]

- **TITLE**—Holds additional information (which might be displayed in tool tips) for the element. [2, 3, 4, IE4, IE5]

Events:

- *Internet Explorer*—**onbeforecut, onbeforeeditfocus, onbeforefocusenter, onbeforefocusleave, onbeforepaste, onblur, onchange, onclick, oncontextmenu, oncontrolselect, oncut, ondblclick, ondragenter, ondragleave, ondragover, ondrop, onfocus, onfocusenter,**

onfocusleave, onhelp, onkeydown, onkeypress, onkeyup, onlosecapture, onmousedown, onmouseenter, onmouseleave, onmousemove, onmouseout, onmouseover, onmouseup, onpaste, onpropertychange, onreadystatechange, onresize, onresizeend, onresizestart, onscroll, onselectstart

- *Netscape Navigator*—**onblur, onchange, onclick, onfocus**

\<OPTION>

Purpose: Specifies a list item in the list of a **SELECT** control.

Start Tag/End Tag: Required/Optional

Supported: [2, 3, 3.2, 4, IE1, IE2, IE3, IE4, IE5, NS1, NS2, NS3, NS4]

Attributes:

- **CLASS**—Class of the element. [3, 4, IE4, IE5]

- **DIR**—Gives the direction of directionally neutral text (text that doesn't have inherent direction in which you should read it). Possible values: **LTR**: left-to-right text or table and **RTL**: right-to-left text or table. [4, IE5]

- **DISABLED**—Specifies that the element is disabled when first displayed. Stand-alone attribute. [3, 4, IE5]

- **ID**—Unique alphanumeric identifier for the tag, which you can use to refer to it. [3, 4, IE4, IE5]

- **LABEL**—Holds a short label that should be used when using **OPTGROUP** elements to create a hierarchy of list values. Set to alphanumeric characters. [4]

- **LANG**—Base language used for the tag. [3, 4, IE4, IE5]

- **LANGUAGE**—Scripting language used for the tag. [IE4, IE5]

- **SELECTED**—Indicates that the item should appear selected at first. Stand-alone attribute. [2, 3, 3.2, 4, IE1, IE2, IE3, IE4, IE5, NS1, NS2, NS3, NS4]

- **STYLE**—Inline style indicating how to render the element. [4]

- **TABINDEX**—Sets the tab index of the element, which locates it in the tab order of the form, allowing the user to press the Tab key and navigate from element to element. Set to positive or negative integers. [4]

- **VALUE**—Holds the value to be sent to the server if the item is chosen. The default is the content of the **OPTION** element. Set to an alphanumeric string. [2, 3, 3.2, 4, IE1, IE2, IE3, IE4, IE5, NS1, NS2, NS3, NS4]

Events:

- *Internet Explorer*—**onlayoutcomplete, onlosecapture, onpropertychange, onreadystatechange, onselectstart**

- *Netscape Navigator*—none

<OPTGROUP>

Purpose: Groups selection list choices into a hierarchy.

Start Tag/End Tag: Required/Required

Supported: [4]

Attributes:

- **CLASS**—Class of the element. [4]

- **DISABLED**—Specifies that the element is disabled when first displayed. Stand-alone attribute. [4]

- **DIR**—Gives the direction of directionally neutral text (text that doesn't have inherent direction in which you should read it). Possible values: **LTR**: left-to-right text or table and **RTL**: right-to-left text or table. [4]

- **DISABLED**—Specifies that the element is disabled when first displayed. Stand-alone attribute. [4]

- **ID**—Unique alphanumeric identifier for the tag, which you can use to refer to it. [4]

- **LABEL**—Holds a short label that should be used when using **OPTGROUP** elements to create a hierarchy of list values. Set to alphanumeric characters. [4]

- **LANG**—Base language used for the tag. [4]

- **STYLE**—Inline style indicating how to render the element. [4]

You can use select controls to display a drop-down list in a Web page. You create a select control with the **<SELECT>** element, and create each of the items in the drop-down list with the **<OPTION>** element. Here's an example in which I'm adding five items to a select control—note that I'm adding code to the **onChange** event to display the selections the user makes:

```
<HTML>

    <HEAD>
        <TITLE>
            Using Select Controls
```

12. Creating HTML Forms
And HTML Controls

```
        </TITLE>

        <SCRIPT LANGUAGE = JavaScript>
            function reportSelection()
            {
                document.form1.textfield.value = "You chose item " +
                    (document.form1.Select1.selectedIndex + 1)
            }
        </SCRIPT>
    </HEAD>

    <BODY>

        <FORM NAME = form1>
            <CENTER>
                <H1>
                    Using Select Controls
                </H1>
                <INPUT NAME = textfield TYPE = Text SIZE = 20>
                <BR>
                <BR>
                <SELECT NAME = Select1 onChange = reportSelection()>
                    <OPTION>Item 1
                    <OPTION>Item 2
                    <OPTION>Item 3
                    <OPTION>Item 4
                    <OPTION>Item 5
                </SELECT>
            </CENTER>
        </FORM>

    </BODY>

</HTML>
```

You can see the results of this HTML in Figure 12.16. When the user makes a selection, that selection is reported in the text field.

You can also support multiple selections in a **SELECT** control if you use the **MULTIPLE** attribute. Here's an example that allows you to do just that—you hold down the Ctrl key to select a number of items or the Shift key to select a range of items (note that whichever key you use is platform dependent). Here's the HTML (the **with** JavaScript statement is a shortcut statement that sets the default object for the code in the code block that follows):

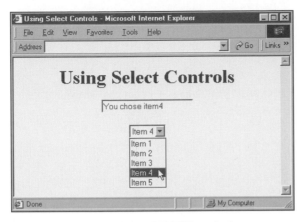

Figure 12.16   Creating a **SELECT** control.

```
<HTML>
    <HEAD>
        <TITLE>
            Multiple Selection Example
        </TITLE>

        <SCRIPT LANGUAGE = JavaScript>
            function reportSelection()
            {
                document.form1.textarea.value = ""

                with(document.form1.select1){
                    for(var loopIndex = 0; loopIndex < length;
                        loopIndex++){
                        if (options[loopIndex].selected){
                            document.form1.textarea.value =
                                document.form1.textarea.value
                                + options[loopIndex].text + "\r\n"
                        }
                    }
                }
            }
        </SCRIPT>
    </HEAD>

    <BODY>
        <CENTER>
            <H1>
                Multiple Selection Example
            </H1>
```

```
<BR>
<FORM NAME = form1>
    <TEXTAREA NAME = textarea COLS = 20 ROWS = 5></TEXTAREA>
    <BR>
    <BR>
    <SELECT NAME = select1 onChange = reportSelection()
        MULTIPLE>
        <OPTION>Item 1
        <OPTION>Item 2
        <OPTION>Item 3
        <OPTION>Item 4
        <OPTION>Item 5
    </SELECT>
</FORM>

</CENTER>

</BODY>

</HTML>
```

Every time the user makes a selection, the loop in the code checks the **selected** property of each item in the **SELECT** control; if that property is **true**, the item is selected, and the code reports it as selected in the Web page's text area. You can see this code at work in Figure 12.17.

The **<OPTGROUP>** element lets you group selection choices into a hierarchy. Browsers may implement this as a collapsible hierarchy list—as yet, no major browser implements this element.

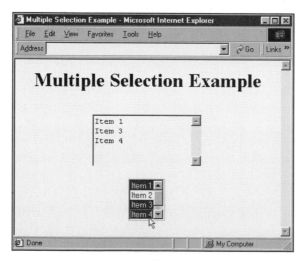

Figure 12.17 Making multiple selections in a **SELECT** control.

<FIELDSET>, **<LEGEND>**, And **<LABEL>**—Grouping And Labeling Form Elements

<FIELDSET>

Purpose: Groups elements in an HTML form.

Start Tag/End Tag: Required/Required

Supported: [4, IE4, IE5]

Attributes:

- **ACCESSKEY**—Sets the access key for the element. [IE5]
- **ALIGN**—Gives the alignment of the contents of the **FIELDSET**. Set to **LEFT**, **CENTER**, or **RIGHT**. [IE4, IE5]
- **CLASS**—Class of the element. [4, IE4, IE5]
- **CONTENTEDITABLE**—Set to **TRUE** if the content is editable. [IE5]
- **DIR**—Gives the direction of directionally neutral text (text that doesn't have inherent direction in which you should read it). Possible values: **LTR**: left-to-right text or table and **RTL**: right-to-left text or table. [4, IE5]
- **DISABLED**—Set to **TRUE** if the element is disabled. [IE4, IE5]
- **ID**—Unique alphanumeric identifier for the tag, which you can use to refer to it. [4, IE4, IE5]
- **LANG**—Base language used for the tag. [4, IE4, IE5]
- **LANGUAGE**—Scripting language used for the tag. [IE4, IE5]
- **STYLE**—Inline style indicating how to render the element. [4, IE4, IE5]
- **TABINDEX**—Sets the tab index for the element. [IE3, IE4, IE5]
- **TITLE**—Holds additional information (which might be displayed in tool tips) for the element. [4, IE4, IE5]

Events:

- *Internet Explorer*—**onbeforecopy, onbeforecut, onbeforeeditfocus, onbeforefocusenter, onbeforefocusleave, onbeforepaste, onblur, onclick, oncontextmenu, oncontrolselect, oncopy, oncut, ondblclick, ondrag, ondragend, ondragenter, ondragleave, ondragover, ondragstart, ondrop, onfilterchange, onfocus, onfocusenter, onfocusleave, onhelp, onkeydown, onkeypress, onkeyup, onlosecapture, onmousedown, onmouseenter, onmouseleave, onmousemove, onmouseout, onmouseover, onmouseup, onpaste,**

12. Creating HTML Forms And HTML Controls

onpropertychange, **onreadystatechange**, **onresize**, **onresizeend**, **onresizestart**, **onselectstart**

- *Netscape Navigator*—not applicable

<LEGEND>

Purpose: Adds a legend to a **FIELDSET**.

Start Tag/End Tag: Required/Required

Supported: [4, IE4, IE5]

Attributes:

- **ACCESSKEY**—Keyboard shortcut key; a single character is used as the value of this attribute. The user can type a platform-dependent key (such as Alt) with the **ACCESSKEY** character to trigger the active field. Set to an alphanumeric character. [4, IE4, IE5]

- **ALIGN**—Gives the alignment of the contents of the **FIELDSET**. Set to **LEFT**, **CENTER**, or **RIGHT**. [4, IE4, IE5]

- **CLASS**—Class of the element. [4, IE4, IE5]

- **CONTENTEDITABLE**—Indicates if the content is editable. [IE4, IE5]

- **DIR**—Gives the direction of directionally neutral text (text that doesn't have inherent direction in which you should read it). Possible values: **LTR**: left-to-right text or table and **RTL**: right-to-left text or table. [4, IE5]

- **DISABLED**—Indicates if the element is disabled. [IE4, IE5]

- **ID**—Unique alphanumeric identifier for the tag, which you can use to refer to it. [4, IE4, IE5]

- **LANG**—Base language used for the tag. [4, IE4, IE5]

- **LANGUAGE**—Scripting language used for the tag. [IE4, IE5]

- **STYLE**—Inline style indicating how to render the element. [4, IE4, IE5]

- **TABINDEX**—Holds the tab index for the element. [IE4, IE5]

- **TITLE**—Holds additional information (which might be displayed in tool tips) for the element. [4, IE4, IE5]

Events:

- *Internet Explorer*—**onbeforecopy**, **onbeforecut**, **onbeforefocusenter**, **onbeforefocusleave**, **onbeforepaste**, **onblur**, **onclick**, **oncontextmenu**, **oncontrolselect**, **oncopy**, **oncut**, **ondblclick**, **onfocus**, **onfocusenter**, **onfocusleave**, **onhelp**, **onkeydown**, **onkeypress**, **onkeyup**, **onlosecapture**, **onmousedown**, **onmouseenter**, **onmouseleave**,

onmousemove, **onmouseout**, **onmouseover**, **onmouseup**, **onpaste**, **onpropertychange**, **onreadystatechange**, **onresize**, **onresizeend**, **onresizestart**

- *Netscape Navigator*—not applicable

<LABEL>

Purpose: Adds a label to an element in a **FIELDSET**.

Start Tag/End Tag: Required/Required

Supported: [4, IE4, IE5]

Attributes:

- **ACCESSKEY**—Keyboard shortcut key; a single character is used as the value of this attribute. The user can type a platform-dependent key (such as Alt) with the **ACCESSKEY** character to trigger the active field. Set to an alphanumeric character. [4, IE4, IE5]

- **CLASS**—Class of the element. [4, IE4, IE5]

- **CONTENTEDITABLE**—Indicates if the content of the element is editable. [IE5]

- **DATAFLD**—Name of the column of the data source object that supplies the bound data. Set to alphanumeric characters. [IE4, IE5]

- **DATAFORMATAS**—Specifies if bound data is plain text or HTML. Set to **HTML**, **PLAINTEXT**, or **TEXT**. [IE4, IE5]

- **DATASRC**—Gives the URL or ID of the data source object supplying data bound to this element. W3C says this should be a URL; Internet Explorer says it should be a data source ID. [IE4, IE5]

- **DIR**—Gives the direction of directionally neutral text (text that doesn't have inherent direction in which you should read it). Possible values: **LTR**: left-to-right text or table and **RTL**: right-to-left text or table. [4, IE5]

- **DISABLED**—Indicates if the element is disabled. [IE5]

- **FOR**—Indicates which form element the **LABEL** is for. If you don't use this attribute, the label is associated with its contents. Set to an ID of a form element. [4, IE4, IE5]

- **ID**—Unique alphanumeric identifier for the tag, which you can use to refer to it. [4, IE4, IE5]

- **LANG**—Base language used for the tag. [4, IE4, IE5]

- **LANGUAGE**—Scripting language used for the tag. [IE4, IE5]

- **STYLE**—Inline style indicating how to render the element. [4, IE4, IE5]

- **TABINDEX**—Holds the element's tab index. [IE5]

- **TITLE**—Holds additional information (which might be displayed in tool tips) for the element. [4, IE4, IE5]

Events:

- *Internet Explorer*—**onbeforecopy, onbeforecut, onbeforefocusenter, onbeforefocusleave, onbeforepaste, onblur, onclick, oncontextmenu, oncontrolselect, oncut, ondblclick, ondrag, ondragend, ondragenter, ondragleave, ondragover, ondragstart, ondrop, onfocus, onfocusenter, onfocusleave, onhelp, onkeydown, onkeypress, onkeyup, onlosecapture, onmousedown, onmouseenter, onmouseleave, onmousemove, onmouseout, onmouseover, onmouseup, onpaste, onpropertychange, onreadystatechange, onresize, onresizeend, onresizestart, onselectstart**

- *Netscape Navigator*—not applicable

"Darn," says the novice programmer, "the form in my Web page is becoming pretty confusing—I've got 73 groups of radio buttons, and even I can't keep things straight anymore." "Well," you smile, "why not break them up into visual groups with the **<FIELDSET>** element?" "How's that work?" the NP wants to know.

You use the **<FIELDSET>** element to group elements in a form together in a box (although the actual rendering is left to the browser, this element is only supported in Internet Explorer so far, and it uses boxes), the **<LEGEND>** element to add a caption to the box, and the **<LABEL>** element to label the elements in the form. Here's the example we saw in the In Depth section at the beginning of this chapter showing how this works:

```
<HTML>
    <HEAD>
        <TITLE>
            Using &lt;FIELDSET&gt;, &lt;LEGEND&gt;, And &lt;LABEL&gt;
        </TITLE>
    </HEAD>

    <BODY>

        <CENTER>
            <H1>Using &lt;FIELDSET&gt;, &lt;LEGEND&gt;, And
                &lt;LABEL&gt;</H1>
            <FORM Name = form1>
```

```
              <FIELDSET>
                  <LEGEND ACCESSKEY=C TABINDEX=1>Color</LEGEND>
                  <LABEL ACCESSKEY=Y>
                      <INPUT TYPE=RADIO NAME=COLOR VALUE=YELLOW>Yellow
                  </LABEL>
                  <BR>
                  <LABEL ACCESSKEY=W>
                      <INPUT TYPE=RADIO NAME=COLOR VALUE=ORANGE>Orange
                  </LABEL>
              </FIELDSET>
          </FORM>
      </CENTER>
  </BODY>
</HTML>
```

You can see the results in Figure 12.4. As you can see, grouping elements visually like this can be a great aid for organizing your page visually.

<ISINDEX>—Using An Index

Purpose: Indicates that the browser should let the user search an index by entering keywords. This element is deprecated.

Start Tag/End Tag: Required/Omitted

Supported: [2, 3, 3.2, 4, IE1, IE2, IE3, IE4, IE5, NS1, NS2, NS3, NS4]

Attributes:

- **ACTION**—Gives the URL of code to process the **ISINDEX** data. Set to a URL. [IE1, IE2, IE3, IE4, IE5]

- **ACCESSKEY**—Sets an access key. [IE5]

- **CLASS**—Class of the element. [4, IE4, IE5]

- **CONTENTEDITABLE**—Set to **TRUE** if the content is editable. [IE5]

- **DIR**—Gives the direction of directionally neutral text (text that doesn't have inherent direction in which you should read it). Possible values: **LTR**: left-to-right text or table and **RTL**: right-to-left text or table. [4]

- **DISABLED**—Set to **TRUE** to disable the index. [IE4, IE5]

- **ID**—Unique alphanumeric identifier for the tag, which you can use to refer to it. [4, IE4, IE5]

12. Creating HTML Forms
And HTML Controls

729

- **LANG**—Base language used for the tag. [4, IE4, IE5]

- **LANGUAGE**—Scripting language used for the tag. [IE4, IE5]

- **PROMPT**—Specifies an alternate string that should be used to query the user. Set to alphanumeric text. [3, 3.2, 4, IE1, IE2, IE3, IE4, IE5, NS1, NS2, NS3, NS4]

- **STYLE**—Sets the style for this element. [IE4, IE5]

- **TABINDEX**—Sets the tab index for this element. [IE4, IE5]

The **<ISINDEX>** element was an early form of a text input field and was used to let users search an index by entering keywords. However, this element is now strongly deprecated; I'm only including it here for completeness. This element is usually found in the **<HEAD>** section of a page like this:

```
<HTML>
    <HEAD>
        <TITLE>
            Using &lt;ISINDEX&gt;
        </TITLE>

        <ISINDEX PROMPT="Enter your name: ">

    </HEAD>

    <BODY>
        <CENTER>
            <H1>
                Using &lt;ISINDEX&gt;
            </H1>
            <BR>
        </CENTER>

    </BODY>

</HTML>
```

You can see the results of this HTML in Figure 12.18.

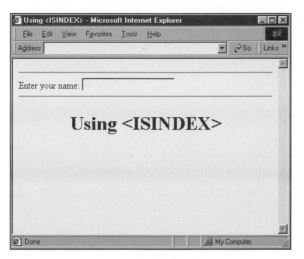

Figure 12.18   Using <ISINDEX>.

<KEYGEN>—Processing Secure Transactions

Purpose: Processes secure transactions in Netscape Navigator.

Start Tag/End Tag: Required/Omitted

Supported: [NS3, NS4]

Attributes:

- **CHALLENGE**—Specifies the challenge string that will be packaged with the public key for verification of the form submission. Set to alphanumeric characters. [NS3, NS4]

- **NAME**—Paired with the challenge string. Set to alphanumeric characters. Required. [NS3, NS4]

The **<KEYGEN>** element is only available in Netscape Navigator and is used to handle security transactions with Web-based certificate management systems. It's an advanced element that is used in an HTML form to construct a certificate request, which involves generating a key and submitting a public key. The transaction results in a signed certificate, which the form can use to generate a challenge string paired with the **<KEYGEN>** element's **NAME** attribute. The

<KEYGEN> element displays a menu of choices that the user can choose from to set key size. When the form contents are submitted, a key of the specified size is generated by the browser. If you are a developer and want to dig deeper into this element, here are some resources you can explore:

- *http://developer.netscape.com/docs/manuals/htmlguid/ tags10.htm#1615503*—Netscape's documentation on the **<KEYGEN>** element.

- *http://home.netscape.com/eng/security/cert-exts.html*—Developer-oriented documentation about **<KEYGEN>** interaction with servers.

- *http://home.netscape.com/eng/security/downloadcert.html*—Netscape's certificate download specification.

Here's an example showing how the **<KEYGEN>** element generates the menu of key sizes:

```
<HTML>
    <HEAD>
        <TITLE>
            Using &lt;KEYGEN&gt;
        </TITLE>

    </HEAD>

    <BODY>
        <CENTER>
            <H1>
                Using &lt;KEYGEN&gt;
            </H1>
            <BR>
            <FORM METHOD="POST"
                ACTION="http://www.starpowder/cgi/secure.cgi"
                ENCTYPE="application/x-www-form-urlencoded">
                <KEYGEN NAME="SECUREKEY" CHALLENGE="12345678">
                <INPUT TYPE=TEXT VALUE="Data">
                <INPUT TYPE=SUBMIT VALUE="Submit">
            </FORM>
        </CENTER>

    </BODY>

</HTML>
```

You can see the results of this HTML in Figure 12.19.

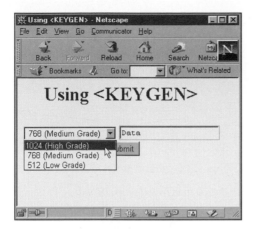

Figure 12.19   Using **<KEYGEN>**.

Chapter 13

Dynamic HTML: Changing Web Pages On The Fly

In Depth

In this chapter, I'll start looking at the huge topic known as dynamic HTML. It's a good thing we've gotten JavaScript under our belts in the previous few chapters because we'll need it here. As you've seen in Chapter 12, you can use a scripting language like JavaScript to make the controls in your Web page, such as buttons and checkboxes, come alive. With dynamic HTML, there are no limits, and just about every element in a Web page can come alive in the same way by being scripted to handle events.

Here's an example we saw in Chapter 11 when working with the **document** object. In that example, I used the **<BODY>** element's **bgColor** property to change the background color of a Web page to red:

```
<HTML>

    <HEAD>
        <TITLE>
            Setting Background Color With JavaScript
        </TITLE>
    </HEAD>

    <BODY onMouseDown="document.bgColor='red'">

    <CENTER>

        <H1>
            Click this page to turn it red!
        </H1>

    </CENTER>
    </BODY>

</HTML>
```

When you click this page, it changes to red before your very eyes—in Internet Explorer, anyway. As it stands, this code won't work in Netscape Navigator, pointing out a very big issue when it comes to dynamic HTML—it means different things to different browsers. Isn't there some standard? What does the World Wide Web Consortium (W3C) have to say on the issue? Let's take a look.

W3C And Dynamic HTML

You can find W3C's comments about dynamic HTML at **www.w3.org/DOM**, and here's an excerpt:

> 'Dynamic HTML' is a term used by some vendors to describe the combination of HTML, style sheets, and scripts that allows documents to be animated. W3C has received several submissions from members' companies on the way in which the object model of HTML documents should be exposed to scripts. These submissions do not propose any new HTML tags or style sheet technology. The W3C DOM WG is working hard to make sure interoperable and scripting-language neutral solutions are agreed upon.

Unfortunately, that's as far as W3C has gotten, which means that the browser companies have been free to develop in different directions. And they have. It must be said that although dynamic HTML is a term used by both Microsoft and Netscape, the dynamic HTML implementation in Internet Explorer is far more comprehensive than what you'll find in Netscape Navigator. I'll take a look at what dynamic HTML means in Internet Explorer first, then take a look at what it means in Netscape Navigator.

Dynamic HTML In Internet Explorer

You can find information about Microsoft's dynamic HTML at the following Web site: **www.msdn.microsoft.com/workshop/c-frame.htm#/workshop/author/default.asp**. Dynamic HTML in Internet Explorer is extensive, virtually turning Web pages into entire applications that run in the browser without any round-trips to the server.

TIP: *In fact, Microsoft has invested heavily in the idea that Web pages can indeed be applications that run in your browser. You can develop applications with packages like Microsoft Visual Basic, which include executable files that run in the browser as active documents, as would other Visual Basic applications. You can also use Visual Basic's built-in dynamic HTML editor to create extensive dynamic HTML pages that will run in Internet Explorer. Making Web pages into applications allows a unique form of distributed computing, where, for example, agents in the field can open the latest form of the software they need simply by navigating to a URL.*

The following list contains the key features of dynamic HTML in Internet Explorer:

- *Absolute positioning*—Using cascading style sheet positioning, you can change the location of elements in a page to create animated effects.

- *Behaviors*—Represents Microsoft's attempt to separate code from data in Web pages and let you specify how elements in your Web page work. We'll learn more about behaviors in Chapter 14.

- *Data binding*—Writes Web pages that display, sort, and filter, as well as update data in a database from the browser.

- *Document Object Model (DOM)*—Using Microsoft's dynamic HTML, all page elements are represented as objects. From the Web author's point of view, this means that page elements can be manipulated easily in code.

- *Dynamic content*—Using dynamic HTML, Web page content can be added, deleted, or changed on the fly. For example, a Web page can display a headline that's updated without refreshing the page from the server.

- *Dynamic styles*—Changes the style of elements, such as color and font, without a server roundtrip. For instance, text can change color or size when a mouse pointer passes over it.

- *Scriptlets*—Refers to scripts that function as components in Web applications.

- *Special ActiveX controls*—Supports many visual effects, such as animation, filtering, and visual transitions that appear when you move to a new page.

As you can see, the support for dynamic HTML is extensive in Internet Explorer. I'll take a look at what's available in Netscape Navigator next.

Dynamic HTML In Netscape Navigator

Netscape's implementation of dynamic HTML is more limited than Microsoft's. See **http://developer.netscape.com/docs/manuals/communicator/dynhtml/index.htm** for information.

The following list contains the key elements of Netscape's version of dynamic HTML:

- *Absolute positioning*—You can update cascading style sheet positioning coordinates in a page at any time to create animated effects, and you can also use layers to do the same thing.

- *DOM*—Netscape's dynamic HTML provides an object model for HTML, just as Microsoft's does. However, as we've seen in previous chapters, Netscape's DOM is more limited.

- *Downloadable fonts*—You can download fonts from the Internet and install them in your Web pages.

- *Dynamic content*—You can change the content of a page in Netscape Navigator at any time, adding or deleting items.

As you can see, Netscape's implementation of dynamic HTML is more restricted than Microsoft's. For us, this means that nearly all the topics in this chapter and

Chapter 14 will apply to Internet Explorer only, although I'll try to mimic Internet Explorer's dynamic HTML effects in Netscape Navigator when I can.

TIP: *Because dynamic HTML varies so much by browser, it's crucial to know which browser your page is being viewed in. See the Immediate Solutions section "Determining Browser Type In Code" in Chapter 11 to see how to make that determination.*

It's worth taking a look at some of the most popular aspects of dynamic HTML in overview before digging into the details, so I'll do that now.

Dynamic Styles: Setting Styles On The Fly

Because you can now set attributes on the fly in Internet Explorer, you can set the styles of elements dynamically. Here's an example where I set the font size of some displayed text to 48 points when the mouse moves over it—note the JavaScript keyword **this**, which refers to the current element:

```
<HTML>
    <HEAD>
        <TITLE>
            Using Dynamic Styles
        </TITLE>
    </HEAD>

    <BODY>
        <CENTER>
            <H1>
                Using Dynamic Styles.
            </H1>
            <SPAN onmouseover="this.style.fontSize = '48'">
                This text gets bigger when you move the mouse over it!
            </SPAN>
        </CENTER>
    </BODY>
</HTML>
```

You can see the results in Figure 13.1. When the mouse moves over the text in the page, its style changes to 48-point text. Dynamically changing styles opens the door to many possibilities—now your Web page can react to users as they move the mouse around.

Another feature of dynamic HTML in Internet Explorer is that by using the **document** object's **styleSheets** collection, you can now toggle style sheets on and off, selecting which style sheet you want to apply on the fly. See the

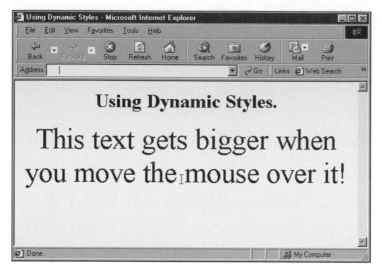

Figure 13.1   Using dynamic styles.

Immediate Solutions section "Toggling Style Sheets On And Off" in this chapter for the details.

Dynamic Content: Changing Web Pages On The Fly

The archetypal way of changing a Web page on the fly is to use the **document.write** method. Here's an example we first saw in Chapter 11 when working with the **document** object, which rewrites a Web page as it's being loaded, depending on which button the user clicks in an HTML Confirmation dialog box. If the user so directs, the code writes HTML to display a large image in the page; otherwise, it writes HTML to display a small image:

```
<HTML>
    <HEAD>
        <TITLE>
            Creating A Self-Modifying Web Page
        </TITLE>
    </HEAD>

    <BODY>
        <CENTER>
            <H1>
                Creating A Self-Modifying Web Page
            </H1>
```

```
<SCRIPT LANGUAGE="JavaScript">
    if(confirm("View graphics intensive page?")) {
        document.write("<BR><IMG WIDTH=1024 HEIGHT=1024 " +
        "SRC='gif/image1.gif'>")
    }
    else {
        document.write("<BR><IMG WIDTH=120 HEIGHT=120 " +
        "SRC='gif/image1small.gif'>")
    }
</SCRIPT>

</CENTER>

</BODY>

</HTML>
```

Because this code writes the Web page as it's being loaded, it works with both Netscape Navigator and Internet Explorer. However, you can also modify a Web page using the **document.write** method *after* a Web page has been loaded. Here's another example from Chapter 11. In this case, the code rewrites the entire page (to just the text "This is a new page!") in the Internet Explorer when the user clicks the page:

```
<HTML>

    <HEAD>
        <TITLE>
            Using document.writeln
        </TITLE>

        <SCRIPT>
            function rewrite()
            {
                document.writeln("This is a new page!")
            }
        </SCRIPT>
    </HEAD>

    <BODY onMouseDown="rewrite()">

        <CENTER>

            <H1>
```

```
              Click this page to rewrite it!
         </H1>

      </CENTER>

   </BODY>

</HTML>
```

In Netscape Navigator, you can do the same thing, but you have to connect the
mousedown event to the code, as well as explicitly opening and closing the document like this (this page will also work in Internet Explorer):

```
<HTML>

   <HEAD>
      <TITLE>
         Using document.writeln
      </TITLE>

      <SCRIPT>
         document.onmousedown = rewrite

         function rewrite()
         {
            document.open()
            document.writeln("This is a new page!")
            document.close()
         }
      </SCRIPT>
   </HEAD>

   <BODY onMouseDown="rewrite()">

      <CENTER>

         <H1>
            Click this page to rewrite it!
         </H1>

      </CENTER>

   </BODY>

</HTML>
```

There's often more than one way to do things in Internet Explorer, and in addition to **document.write**, you can rewrite a Web page on the fly using the following methods, all of which I'll take a look at in this chapter:

- **innerHTML**—Changes the contents of the element between the start and end tags; can include HTML.

- **innerText**—Lets you change the text between the start and end tags of an element.

- **insertAdjacentHTML**—Lets you insert new HTML (which the browser will read and handle as HTML) into a page.

- **insertAdjacentText**—Lets you insert new text into a page.

- **outerHTML**—Contains the contents of an element, including start and end tags; treats text as HTML.

- **outerText**—Lets you change all the element's text including the start and end tags.

- **pasteHTML**—Used with text ranges to paste HTML into a document.

These methods are more precise than **document.write** because they let you work with specific parts of a Web page, not the whole thing at once. Here's an example using the **outerHTML** property. I'll use the **outerHTML** method of an **<H1>** element to rewrite that element entirely as a **<MARQUEE>** element when the user clicks the element:

```
<HTML>

    <HEAD>
        <TITLE>
            Changing HTML on the fly
        </TITLE>

        <SCRIPT LANGUAGE = "JavaScript">
            function changeHeader()
            {
                Header.outerHTML =
                    "<MARQUEE STYLE='font-size: 54;'>" +
                    "This marquee was just created!</MARQUEE>"
            }
        </SCRIPT>

    </HEAD>

    <BODY>
```

```
<CENTER>
    <H1 ID = Header onClick = "changeHeader()">Dynamic HTML</H1>

    Click the above header to change it....
</CENTER>

</BODY>

</HTML>
```

You can see the results in Figure 13.2 after the user has clicked the **<H1>** element. In this case, I've rewritten just a single HTML element in a Web page, changing the content of the Web page dynamically.

Creating mouseover Effects

Dynamic HTML has been out for several years now, and undoubtedly its biggest use is for **mouseover** effects. You've probably seen these effects—when you move the mouse, a hyperlink or other text changes when the mouse is over it. The change can involve making text larger, displaying a new image, or any of dozens of other effects. There are many ways to implement such effects in Internet Explorer, some simple and some complex, and I'll take a look at them in the Immediate Solutions section of this chapter. Here's an example using the **mouseover** and **mouseout** events in Internet Explorer that changes the color of a header from black to red when the mouse is over it and changes it back to black when the mouse moves away:

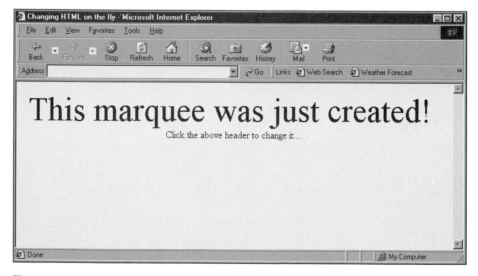

Figure 13.2   Rewriting an HTML element.

```
<HTML>

    <HEAD>
        <TITLE>
            Using Dynamic Styles
        </TITLE>
    </HEAD>

    <BODY>

        <CENTER>
            <H1 onmouseover="this.style.color = 'red';"
                onmouseout="this.style.color = 'black';">
                Turn me red with the mouse.
            </H1>
        </CENTER>

    </BODY>

</HIML>
```

In this next example, I'll swap images when the mouse moves over an image. The second image is the same as the first, but lighter in color, so it appears that the image is highlighted when the mouse is over it (again, this won't work in Netscape Navigator):

```
<HTML>
    <HEAD>
        <TITLE>
            Mouseover Image Handling
        </TITLE>
    </HEAD>

    <BODY>
        <CENTER>
            <H1>
                Mouseover Image Handling
            </H1>

            <IMG SRC="flower.jpg"
                onmouseover="this.src='flower2.jpg'"
                onmouseout="this.src='flower.jpg'">
        </CENTER>
    </BODY>
</HTML>
```

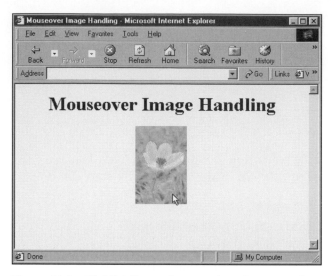

Figure 13.3   Highlighting an image when the mouse is over it.

You can see the results in Figure 13.3. When the user moves the mouse over the image, a lighter version of the same image is displayed, making the image appear to be highlighted.

Here's an example creating **mouseover** effects using layers in Netscape Navigator. In this case, I set the background of the text to cyan when the mouse is over it:

```
<HTML>
    <HEAD>
        <TITLE>
            Mouseover Effects Using Layers
        </TITLE>

    </HEAD>

    <BODY>
        <LAYER BGCOLOR="white" TOP=40 LEFT=40
            onmouseover="setcolor('cyan')" onmouseout="setcolor('white')" >
            <SCRIPT LANGUAGE=JavaScript>
                function setcolor(color)
                {
                    bgColor=color
                }
            </SCRIPT>
            <H1>
                Mouseover Effects Using Layers
```

```
                    </H1>
            </LAYER>

        </BODY>
</HTML>
```

The results appear in Figure 13.4. When the user moves the mouse over the text in the Web page, a box appears behind it highlighting it.

We'll also learn how to handle animation, downloadable fonts, visual filters and transitions, and more, coming right up in this chapter. I'll start the Immediate Solutions section now.

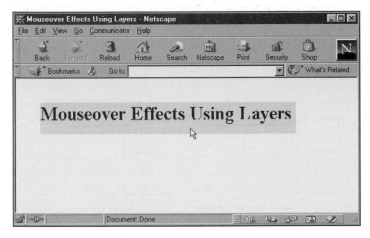

Figure 13.4   Using layers for **mouseover** effects.

Immediate Solutions

Using Dynamic Styles

The novice programmer wants to know, "Where's a good place to start with dynamic HTML?" "Well," you say, "one good place to make your Web pages come alive is to make your styles dynamic, modifying how things appear in response to user actions." "Give me an example," the NP says. You smile and say, "I can give you several."

You can change styles on the fly in Internet Explorer (but not in Netscape Navigator) in several ways. Here's an example from the In Depth section of this chapter. In this case, I'm changing the color of text from black to red and then back to black again when the mouse moves over it—note the JavaScript keyword **this**, which refers to the current element:

```
<HTML>

    <HEAD>
        <TITLE>
            Using Dynamic Styles
        </TITLE>
    </HEAD>

    <BODY>

        <CENTER>
            <H1 onmouseover="this.style.color = 'red';"
                onmouseout="this.style.color = 'black';">
                Turn me red with the mouse.
            </H1>
        </CENTER>

    </BODY>

</HTML>
```

Here's another example, also from the In Depth section of this chapter. Here, I'm changing the font size of text when you move the mouse over it:

```
<HTML>
    <HEAD>
        <TITLE>
            Using Dynamic Styles
        </TITLE>
    </HEAD>

    <BODY>
        <CENTER>
            <H1>
                Using Dynamic Styles.
            </H1>
            <SPAN onmouseover=" this.style.fontSize = '48'">
                This text gets bigger when you move the mouse over it!
            </SPAN>
        </CENTER>
    </BODY>
</HTML>
```

You can see the results of this HTML in Figure 13.1. Here's another example. This time I'm changing the mouse cursor from an arrow to a hand when the mouse is over a header, and then back to the arrow when the mouse moves away. To do this, I set the **cursor** style:

```
<HTML>

    <HEAD>
        <TITLE>
            Using Dynamic Styles
        </TITLE>
    </HEAD>

    <BODY>

        <CENTER>
            <H1 onmouseover="this.style.cursor = 'hand';"
                onmouseout="this.style.cursor = 'default';">
                Change the cursor with the mouse.
            </H1>
        </CENTER>

    </BODY>

</HTML>
```

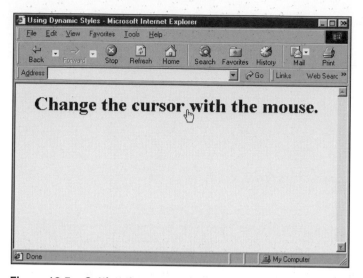

Figure 13.5   Setting the mouse cursor in response to mouse location.

You can see the results of this HTML in Figure 13.5. When the mouse cursor is over the header, the cursor changes to a hand. This is a great effect to show the user what's clickable in your page and what's not.

Here's another example in which I'm using classes to change styles dynamically. In this case, I'm assigning a whole new class to an element in response to mouse movements:

```
<HTML>
    <HEAD>
        <TITLE>
            Dynamic Styles Using Classes
        </TITLE>
        <STYLE>
            .red {color:red}
            .blue {color:blue}
        </STYLE>
    </HEAD>

    <BODY>
        <CENTER>
            <H1 class=blue onmouseover="this.className='red'"
                onmouseout="this.className='blue'">
                Move the mouse here to change colors.
            </H1>
        </CENTER>
    </BODY>
</HTML>
```

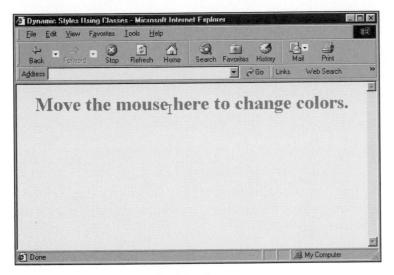

Figure 13.6 Using dynamic style classes.

You can see the results in Figure 13.6. When the mouse is moved over the header in the page, the code switches the style class and as a result the text appears in red, not blue.

Toggling Style Sheets On And Off

"It's no use," the novice programmer says, "I just can't decide. Should I use my normal style sheet or the dramatic one in my Web page?" "Why not let the user decide?" you ask. The NP says, "Huh?"

You can now determine which style sheet to apply to a page in Internet Explorer when the page is actually being viewed. To do that, you use the **styleSheets** collection of the **document** object. To select which style sheet applies to the page, you simply disable all other style sheets, setting their disabled property to true.

Here's an example. In this case, I'll add two style sheets to a Web page, giving them the names **NORMAL** and **DRAMATIC**:

```
<HTML>
    <HEAD>
        <STYLE ID=DRAMATIC>
            body
```

```
                     {font-family: verdana; color: white; background-color: black}
          </STYLE>

          <STYLE ID=NORMAL DISABLED=TRUE>
               body {font-family: 'times new roman'; color: black;
                    background-color: white}
          </STYLE>
          .
          .
          .
```

Next, I'll add a function named **setStyle** to which you pass the name of the style sheet you want to make active. This function just disables all style sheets except the one you want to use:

```
<HTML>
    <HEAD>
        <STYLE ID=DRAMATIC>
            body
                {font-family: verdana; color: white; background-color: black}
        </STYLE>

        <STYLE ID=NORMAL DISABLED=TRUE>
            body {font-family: 'times new roman'; color: black;
                background-color: white}
        </STYLE>

        <SCRIPT LANGUAGE="JAVASCRIPT">
            function setStyle(styleName)
            {
                var sheet
                for (var loopIndex = 0; loopIndex <
                    document.styleSheets.length; loopIndex++) {
                    sheet = document.styleSheets[loopIndex]
                    sheet.disabled = true
                    if (sheet.id == styleName) {
                        sheet.disabled = false
                    }
                }
            }
        </SCRIPT>

    </HEAD>
        .
        .
        .
```

All that's left to do is add two buttons to let users decide which style sheet they want to use:

```
<HTML>
    <HEAD>
        <STYLE ID=DRAMATIC>
            body
                {font-family: verdana; color: white; background-color: black}
        </STYLE>

        <STYLE ID=NORMAL DISABLED=TRUE>
            body {font-family: 'times new roman'; color: black;
                background-color: white}
        </STYLE>

        <SCRIPT LANGUAGE="JAVASCRIPT">
            function setStyle(styleName)
            {
                var sheet
                for (var loopIndex = 0; loopIndex <
                    document.styleSheets.length; loopIndex++) {
                    sheet = document.styleSheets[loopIndex]
                    sheet.disabled = true
                    if (sheet.id == styleName) {
                        sheet.disabled = false
                    }
                }
            }
        </SCRIPT>

    </HEAD>

    <BODY>
        <H1>
            Toggling Style Sheets
        </H1>

        <CENTER>
            <INPUT TYPE=BUTTON VALUE="Normal Style"
                onclick="setStyle('NORMAL')">
            <INPUT TYPE=BUTTON VALUE="Dramatic Style"
                onclick="setStyle('DRAMATIC')">
        </CENTER>

        <P>
```

```
                    You can set the style sheet for the entire document just
                    by clicking a button.

            </BODY>

    </HTML>
```

That's it. The results appear in Figure 13.7. When the user clicks the Normal Style button, the **NORMAL** style sheet is used in the page; when the user clicks the Dramatic Style button, the **DRAMATIC** style sheet is used. In this way, you can change style sheets on the fly, producing some amazing effects.

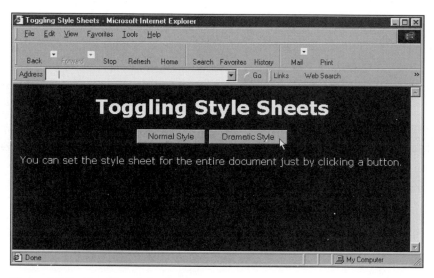

Figure 13.7   Toggling style sheets.

Dynamic Content: **document.write**

Using the **document** object's **write** and **writeln** (write line) methods, you can modify Web pages on the fly. We discussed **document.write** in Chapter 11, but I'll review it here for reference.

Here's an example from Chapter 11, which was also discussed briefly in the In Depth section of this chapter. In this case, I'm using a Confirmation dialog box from JavaScript to ask users if they want to download the large graphics image. This dialog box will display the message "View graphics intensive page?" and if users click OK, the code will write an **<IMG>** element to download the large graphics file; but if users click Cancel, it will download a smaller version of the file. Here's what the code looks like:

```
<HTML>
    <HEAD>
        <TITLE>
            Creating A Self-Modifying Web Page
        </TITLE>
    </HEAD>

    <BODY>
        <CENTER>
            <H1>
                Creating A Self-Modifying Web Page
            </H1>

            <SCRIPT LANGUAGE="JavaScript">
                if(confirm("View graphics intensive page?")) {
                    document.write("<BR><IMG WIDTH=1024 HEIGHT=1024 " +
                    "SRC='gif/image1.gif'>")
                }
                else {
                    document.write("<BR><IMG WIDTH=120 HEIGHT=120 " +
                    "SRC='gif/image1small.gif'>")
                }
            </SCRIPT>

        </CENTER>

    </BODY>

</HTML>
```

You can see the results in Chapter 11, in Figure 11.3, where the Confirmation dialog box is visible.

Take a look at this next example, also from the In Depth section of this chapter. When the user clicks the page, the whole page is replaced by the text "This is a new page!":

```
<HTML>

    <HEAD>
        <TITLE>
            Using document.writeln
        </TITLE>

        <SCRIPT>
```

```
            function rewrite()
            {
                    document.writeln("This is a new page!")
            }
        </SCRIPT>
    </HEAD>

    <BODY onMouseDown="rewrite()">

        <CENTER>

            <H1>
                Click this page to rewrite it!
            </H1>

        </CENTER>

    </BODY>

</HTML>
```

In Netscape Navigator, you can do the same thing, but you have to connect the **mousedown** event to the code, as well as explicitly opening and closing the document, like this (this page will also work in Internet Explorer):

```
<HTML>

    <HEAD>
        <TITLE>
            Using document.writeln
        </TITLE>

        <SCRIPT>
            document.onmousedown = rewrite

            function rewrite()
            {
                document.open()
                document.writeln("This is a new page!")
                document.close()
            }
        </SCRIPT>
    </HEAD>

    <BODY onMouseDown="rewrite()">
```

```
        <CENTER>

            <H1>
                Click this page to rewrite it!
            </H1>

        </CENTER>

    </BODY>

</HTML>
```

Using **document.write**, you can tailor your Web pages to the time of day. Here's another example. In this case, the page presents a menu to the user, displaying the breakfast, lunch, or dinner menus automatically, based on the time of day:

```
<HTML>
    <HEAD>
        <TITLE>
            Welcome to our restaurant
        </TITLE>
    </HEAD>

    <BODY>
        <SCRIPT LANGUAGE="JavaScript">
            var dateNow = new Date()
            var hourNow = dateNow.getHours()
            document.write( "<CENTER>")
            document.write( "<H1>")
            document.write( "Welcome To Our Restaurant")
            document.write( "</H1>")
            document.write( "</CENTER>")

            if (hourNow < 5 || hourNow > 23){
                document.write( "<CENTER>")
                document.write( "<H1>")
                document.write( "Sorry, We Are Closed." )
                document.write( "</H1>")
                document.write( "</CENTER>")
            }

            if (hourNow > 6 && hourNow < 12 ) {
                document.write( "<CENTER>")
                document.write( "<TABLE BORDER>")
```

```
            document.write(
                "<TR><TH COLSPAN = 2>Breakfast</TH></TR>")
            document.write(
                "<TR><TD>Pancakes</TD><TD>$2.00</TD></TR>")
            document.write(
                "<TR><TD>Eggs</TD><TD>$2.50</TD></TR>")
            document.write(
                "<TR><TD>Waffles</TD><TD>$1.50</TD></TR>")
            document.write(
                "<TR><TD>Oatmeal</TD><TD>$1.00</TD></TR>")
            document.write( "</TABLE>")
            document.write( "</CENTER>")
            document.write( "</TABLE>")
            document.write( "</CENTER>")
        }

        if ( hourNow >= 12 && hourNow < 17 ) {
            document.write( "<CENTER>")
            document.write( "<TABLE BORDER>")
            document.write(
                "<TR><TH COLSPAN = 2>Lunch</TH></TR>")
            document.write(
                "<TR><TD>Ham Sandwich</TD><TD>$3.50</TD></TR>")
            document.write(
                "<TR><TD>Chicken Sandwich</TD><TD>$3.50</TD></TR>")
            document.write(
                "<TR><TD>Cheese Sandwich</TD><TD>$3.00</TD></TR>")
            document.write(
                "<TR><TD>Lobster Nuggets</TD><TD>$5.00</TD></TR>")
            document.write(
                "<TR><TD>Peacock</TD><TD>$4.50</TD></TR>")
            document.write(
                "<TR><TD>Chili</TD><TD>$2.00</TD></TR>")
            document.write(
                "<TR><TD>Chicken Soup</TD><TD>$1.50</TD></TR>")
            document.write( "</TABLE>")
            document.write( "</CENTER>")
        }

        if ( hourNow >= 17 && hourNow < 22) {
            document.write( "<CENTER>")
            document.write( "<TABLE BORDER>")
            document.write(
                "<TR><TH COLSPAN = 2>Dinner</TH></TR>")
            document.write(
```

```
                    "<TR><TD>Lobster</TD><TD>$7.50</TD></TR>")
                document.write(
                    "<TR><TD>Filet Mignon</TD><TD>$8.00</TD></TR>")
                document.write(
                    "<TR><TD>Flank Steak</TD><TD>$7.00</TD></TR>")
                document.write(
                    "<TR><TD>Tube Steak</TD><TD>$3.50</TD></TR>")
                document.write(
                    "<TR><TD>Salad</TD><TD>$2.50</TD></TR>")
                document.write(
                    "<TR><TD>Potato</TD><TD>$1.50</TD></TR>")
                document.write(
                    "<TR><TD>Eggplant</TD><TD>$1.50</TD></TR>")
                document.write( "</TABLE>")
                document.write( "</CENTER>")
            }

        </SCRIPT>
    </BODY>

</HTML>
```

You can see the results of this code in Chapter 11, in Figure 11.4.

Dynamic Content: The **insertAdjacentHTML** and **insertAdjacentText** Methods

"Hey," says the novice programmer, "I don't want to rewrite a whole Web page with **document.write**; I just want to insert a new control when the user wants one. How do I do that?" "There are a couple of ways," you say, "and one of the best ways is to use the **insertAdjacentHTML** and **insertAdjacentText** methods."

The **insertAdjacentHTML** and **insertAdjacentText** methods give you finer control over placement of inserted HTML in pages in Internet Explorer than **document.write**. The **insertAdjacentHTML** method lets you insert HTML next to an element that already exists, and the **insertAdjacentText** method lets you insert text (which will not be parsed as HTML by the browser) in the same way. You can determine where the new text or HTML will go with respect to the existing element by passing the constants **BeforeBegin**, **AfterBegin**, **BeforeEnd**, or **AfterEnd** to **insertAdjacentHTML** and **insertAdjacentText**.

In this next example, I'll write code using **insertAdjacentHTML** to insert a new text field after a **<DIV>** element when the user clicks a button. Here's what the HTML looks like:

```
<HTML>
    <HEAD>
        <TITLE>
            Using insertAdjacentHTML
        </TITLE>

        <SCRIPT LANGUAGE="JavaScript">
            function showMore()
            {
                div1.insertAdjacentHTML("AfterEnd",
                "<P>A new text field: <input type=text VALUE='Hello!'>");
            }
        </SCRIPT>
    </HEAD>

    <BODY>

        <CENTER>
            <H1>
                Using insertAdjacentHTML
            </H1>
        </CENTER>

        <DIV ID=div1>
            <INPUT TYPE=BUTTON VALUE="Click Me!" onclick="showMore()">
        </DIV>

    </BODY>
</HTML>
```

Now when the user clicks the button, the code in the page adds a new text field right after the **<DIV>** element. Clicking the button several times adds several text fields, as you can see in Figure 13.8.

TIP: *There's another way to add elements to a Web page; see the Immediate Solutions section "Dynamic Content: Using The **createElement** Method" in this chapter.*

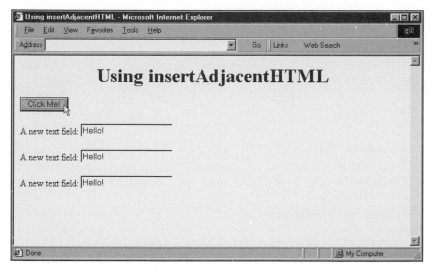

Figure 13.8   Using **insertAdjacentHTML**.

Dynamic Content: The **innerText**, **outerText**, **innerHMTL**, and **outerHTML** Properties

"OK," says the novice programmer, "I can insert new HTML into a Web page with the **insertAdjacentHTML** method, but isn't there a way to modify elements that already exist in a Web page?" "There sure is," you say, "you can use the **innerText**, **outerText**, **innerHTML**, and **outerHTML** properties of virtually every element in Internet Explorer." "To do what?" the NP wants to know.

You can modify the HTML of existing elements in a Web page in Internet Explorer using the **innerText**, **outerText**, **innerHTML**, and **outerHTML** properties of almost every element. The following list describes these properties—note the difference between text and HTML; text is not treated as HTML by the browser, and is simply inserted "as is" into the page:

- **innerText**—Lets you change the text between the start and end tags.
- **outerText**—Lets you change all the text including the start and end tags.
- **innerHTML**—Changes contents of elements between the start and end tags; treats text as HTML.
- **outerHTML**—Changes contents of an element including the start and end tags; treats text as HTML.

Here's an example using the **innerText** property. This property lets you change the text content of an element. I'll change the text in a header from "Dynamic HTML" to "This is the new header" like this:

```
<HTML>

    <HEAD>
        <TITLE>
            Changing HTML on the fly
        </TITLE>

        <SCRIPT LANGUAGE = "JavaScript">
            function changeHeader()
            {
                Header.innerText = "This is the new header"
            }
        </SCRIPT>

    </HEAD>

    <BODY>

        <CENTER>
            <H1 ID = Header onClick = "changeHeader()">Dynamic HTML</H1>

            Click the above header to change it....
        </CENTER>

    </BODY>

</HTML>
```

You can see the results of this HTML after the user has clicked the header in Figure 13.9. When the header is clicked, the text changes to what you see in the figure.

On the other hand, if I used the **innerHTML** property, I could change the text content of the header to something the browser will interpret as HTML. For example, I can change the original text "Dynamic HTML" in the **<H1>** header to a **<MARQUEE>** element. Note that because I'm using **innerHTML**, the outer **<H1>** tag is preserved, so the text in the marquee is styled by the enclosing **<H1>** header:

```
<HTML>

    <HEAD>
```

13: Dynamic HTML: Changing Web Pages On The Fly

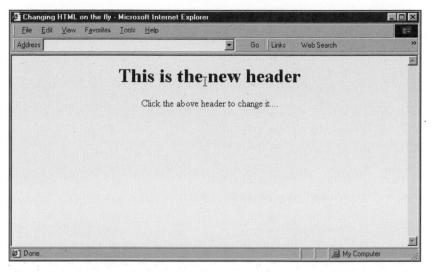

Figure 13.9 Using the **innerText** property.

```
<TITLE>
    Changing HTML on the fly
</TITLE>

<SCRIPT LANGUAGE = "JavaScript">

    function changeHeader()
    {
        Header.innerHTML =
            "<MARQUEE>This marquee was just created!</MARQUEE>"
    }
</SCRIPT>

</HEAD>

<BODY>

    <CENTER>
        <H1 ID = Header onClick = "changeHeader()">Dynamic HTML</H1>

        Click the above header to change it....
    </CENTER>

</BODY>

</HTML>
```

If you want to replace the element entirely, including the surrounding **<H1>** tag, you can use the **outerHTML** property like this:

```
<HTML>

    <HEAD>
        <TITLE>
            Changing HTML on the fly
        </TITLE>

        <SCRIPT LANGUAGE = "JavaScript">
            function changeHeader()
            {
                Header.outerHTML =
                    "<MARQUEE STYLE='font-size: 54;'>" +
                    "This marquee was just created!</MARQUEE>"
            }
        </SCRIPT>

    </HEAD>

    <BODY>

        <CENTER>
            <H1 ID = Header onClick = "changeHeader()">Dynamic HTML</H1>

            Click the above header to change it....
        </CENTER>

    </BODY>

</HTML>
```

Now when the user clicks the header, the entire header is rewritten as a marquee with 54-point font size. You can see the results in Figure 13.2.

Dynamic Content: Using Text Ranges

Another way to modify a Web page on the fly in Internet Explorer is to use a **TextRange** object. Using text ranges, you can select, copy, and replace text in a Web page in a general way.

Here's an example in which I create a text range with the **createTextRange** method, select the text of an element with the **moveToElementText** method, and replace that text with the **pasteHTML** method:

```
<HTML>
    <HEAD>
        <TITLE>
            Using the TextRange Object
        </TITLE>

        <SCRIPT LANGAUGE="JavaScript">
            function replaceText()
            {
                var range = document.body.createTextRange()
                range.moveToElementText(Text1)
                range.pasteHTML("Here is the new text.")
            }
        </SCRIPT>
    </HEAD>

    <BODY>
        <CENTER>
            <H1>
                Using the TextRange Object
            </H1>
        </CENTER>

        <INPUT TYPE=BUTTON VALUE="Click Me" onclick="replaceText()">

        <BR>
        <BR>

        <DIV ID=Text1 STYLE=
            "font-family:Arial, sans-serif; font-weight:bold">
            Click the button to replace all this text at once.
        </DIV>

    </BODY>
</HTML>
```

When you display this page in Internet Explorer, you see the text "Click the button to replace all this text at once." When you click the button, that text is selected and replaced by the text "Here is the new text.", as you can see in Figure 13.10.

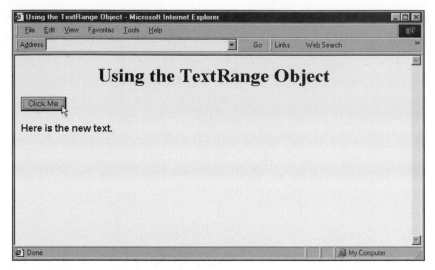

Figure 13.10   Using the **TextRange** object to modify a Web page on the fly.

Dynamic Content: Using The **createElement** Method

The novice programmer says, "I can rewrite elements in a Web page in Internet Explorer using various properties and methods, but isn't there a way that is dedicated only to creating new Web page elements?" "Yes," you say, "there is. You can use the **createElement** method." "Tell me how!" the NP says.

As of Internet Explorer 5, you can use the **createElement** method to create new Web page elements and use methods like **insertBefore** and **insertAfter** to insert those elements into a Web page. In this example, I'm mimicking the example shown in "Dynamic Content: The **insertAdjacentHTML** and **insertAdjacent Text** Methods" in the Immediate Solutions section, where I added text fields to a Web page. However, this time, I'm using **createElement** to create the new elements and **insertBefore** to insert them into a Web page. I'm also using the **createTextNode** method to create new text in the Web page. Here's what the example looks like:

```
<HTML>
    <HEAD>
        <TITLE>
```

```
                Using createElement To Create New Elements
        </TITLE>

        <SCRIPT LANGUAGE="JavaScript">
            function showMore()
            {
                var newDiv, newTextfield, newText;

                newDiv = document.createElement("DIV");
                newDiv.id = "NewDIV";

                newTextfield = document.createElement("INPUT");
                newTextfield.type = "TEXT";
                newTextfield.value = "Hello!"

                newText = document.createTextNode("A new text field: ");

                newDiv.insertBefore(newText, null);
                newDiv.insertBefore(newTextfield, null);

                document.body.insertBefore(newDiv, null);
            }
        </SCRIPT>
    </HEAD>

    <BODY>
        <CENTER>
            <H1>
                Using createElement To Create New Elements
            </H1>
        </CENTER>

        <DIV ID=InitialDIV>
            <INPUT TYPE=BUTTON VALUE="Click Me" ONCLICK="showMore()">
        </DIV>

    </BODY>
</HTML>
```

You can see the results of this HTML in Figure 13.11. When the user clicks the button, the code uses the **createElement** method to create new elements and insert them in the Web page on the fly.

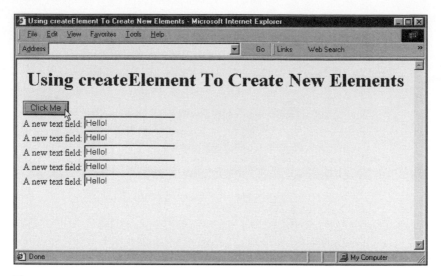

Figure 13.11   Using **createElement** to create new HTML elements.

Dynamic Content: Creating Dynamic Tables

"Say," says the novice programmer, "I'm having some trouble making HTML tables dynamic. I can rewrite the whole table, but I can't seem to access just one cell at a time." "Tables are special unto themselves in Internet Explorer," you say, "and there's special methods to deal with them to make them dynamic." "It figures," says the NP.

The **<TABLE>** and **<TR>** elements have their own set of methods to make them dynamic in Internet Explorer. The following list contains the methods for the **<TABLE>** element:

- **object.deleteRow(index)**—Deletes a row. The **index** value indicates the row index of the row to delete.

- **object.insertRow(index)**—Inserts a new row. Returns the inserted **<TR>** element (which will be empty) or null for failure. If **index** isn't supplied, then the **<TR>** element will be inserted at the end.

- **object.rows(index)**—Returns a collection (array) of the rows in the table.

And the following list contains the methods for **<TR>** elements:

- **object.cells(index)**—Returns a collection (array) of the cells in the row.

- **object.deleteCell(index)**—Deletes a cell. The **index** value indicates the position in the cell collection to delete.

- **object.insertCell(index)**—Inserts a new cell and returns the inserted **<TD>** element (which will be empty) or null for failure. If **index** isn't supplied, then the **<TD>** element will be inserted at the end of the row.

- **object.rowIndex**—Returns the row index of the row. Useful for inserting and deleting rows.

Here's an example showing how to create a dynamic table in Internet Explorer. In this case, I'll insert a new row in a table using the **insertRow** method, then insert three cells into the new row with the **insertCell** method, and set the contents of the cell with the **innerText** property. Here's the HTML:

```
<HTML>
    <HEAD>
        <TITLE>
            Creating Dynamic Tables
        </TITLE>

        <SCRIPT LANGUAGE="JAVASCRIPT">
            function addem()
            {
                var newRow = table1.insertRow(3)
                var newCell = newRow.insertCell(0)
                newCell.innerText = "X"
                newCell = newRow.insertCell(1)
                newCell.innerText = "O"
                newCell = newRow.insertCell(2)
                newCell.innerText = "X"
            }
        </SCRIPT>
    </HEAD>

    <BODY>
        <CENTER>
            <H1>
                Creating Dynamic Tables
            </H1>

                <TABLE ID="table1" BORDER="2">
                    <TR>
                        <TH>Tic</TH>
                        <TH>Tac</TH>
                        <TH>Toe</TH>
                    </TR>
                    <TR>
```

```
                              <TD>X</TD>
                              <TD>O</TD>
                              <TD>X</TD>
                          </TR>
                          <TR>
                              <TD>O</TD>
                              <TD>X</TD>
                              <TD>O</TD>
                          </TR>
                          <TR>
                              <TD>X</TD>
                              <TD>O</TD>
                              <TD>X</TD>
                          </TR>
                     </TABLE>

                  <INPUT TYPE="BUTTON" VALUE="Add Row" onclick="addem()">

             </CENTER>
        </BODY>
   </HTML>
```

This Web page appears in Figure 13.12. When the user clicks the button, a new row, complete with Xs and Os, appears in the table.

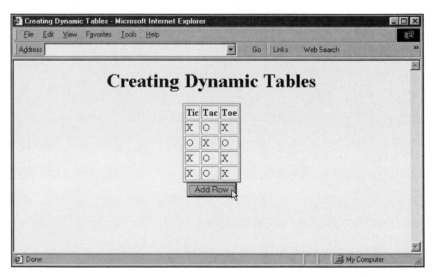

Figure 13.12   Creating a dynamic table.

Dynamic Content: Using Conditional Comments To Set Content On The Fly

There's one additional way to set Web page content on the fly—using conditional comments. In Internet Explorer, conditional comments take the form **<!--[*condition*]>**, where ***condition*** is a logical condition, such as the comment **<!--[if IE 5]>**, which checks if the browser is Internet Explorer 5, or simply the comment **<!--[if IE]>**, which checks if the browser is Internet Explorer. Here's an example targeted to Internet Explorer:

```
<HTML>
    <HEAD>
        <TITLE>
            Using Conditional Comments
        </TITLE>
    </HEAD>

    <BODY>
        <CENTER>
            <H1>
                Using Conditional Comments
            </H1>

            <!--[if IE ]>
                Welcome to Internet Explorer.
            <![endif]>

            <!--[if IE 5]>
                In fact, welcome to Internet Explorer 5!
            <![endif]-->

            <!--[if ! IE 5]>
                Please upgrade to Internet Explorer 5.
            <![endif]>

    </BODY>
</HTML>
```

You can see the results of this HTML in Figure 13.13.

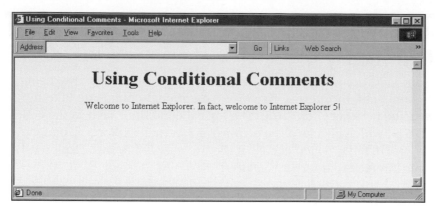

Figure 13.13   Using conditional comments in Internet Explorer.

Creating Amazing **mouseover** Effects

The novice programmer appears and says, "I wonder if I can use dynamic HTML to make my Web page respond when the user moves the mouse over it?" You laugh heartily and say, "That may be the most common use of dynamic HTML these days."

There are many ways to use dynamic HTML to let a Web page react as the user moves the mouse over it—and most of these require using Internet Explorer. I'll take a look at them in this section as well as one way of working with layers in Netscape Navigator to create **mouseover** effects.

One easy way to create **mouseover** effects in Internet Explorer using hyperlinks is to use the **HOVER** attribute, which was created for just this purpose. Here's an example in which I'm setting the style of hyperlinks to bold, red, and a large font size when the mouse hovers over them:

```
<HTML>
    <HEAD>
        <TITLE>
            Using The HOVER Attribute
        </TITLE>
        <STYLE>
            A {font-family: verdana; font-weight: normal; color: blue}
            A:hover {font-weight: bold; color: red; font-size: 24}
            A:active {font-weight: bold; color: red;
            background-color: darkgray}
            A:visited {font-weight: bold; color: gray;
```

```
              background-color: darkgray}
        </STYLE>
    </HEAD>

    <BODY>
        <CENTER>
            <H1>
                Using The HOVER Attribute
            </H1>
        </CENTER>

            <A href="http://www.starpowder.com">
                Move the mouse over Me
            </A>
            <A href="http://www.starpowder.com">
                Now over me!
            </A>
    </BODY>
</HTML>
```

You can see the results of this HTML in Figure 13.14. When the user moves the mouse over a hyperlink, the new style takes effect, as you can see in the figure, and when the mouse moves away, the original hyperlink style is restored.

Here's another example in Internet Explorer, here I'm changing the style of a header to red when the mouse is over it and back to black when the mouse moves away:

```
<HTML>

    <HEAD>
        <TITLE>
```

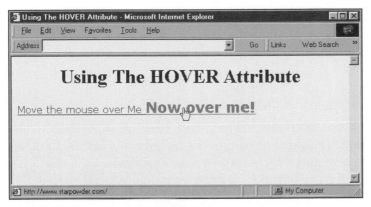

Figure 13.14   Using the HOVER attribute for mouseover effects.

```
                    Using Dynamic Styles
            </TITLE>
        </HEAD>

        <BODY>

            <CENTER>
                <H1 onmouseover="this.style.color = 'red';"
                    onmouseout="this.style.color = 'black';">
                    Turn me red with the mouse.
                </H1>
            </CENTER>

        </BODY>

</HTML>
```

And here's another example, which we saw in the In Depth section of this chapter, which uses dynamic styles to create **mouseover** effects:

```
<HTML>
    <HEAD>
        <TITLE>
            Using Dynamic Styles
        </TITLE>
    </HEAD>

    <BODY>
        <CENTER>
            <H1>
                Using Dynamic Styles.
            </H1>
            <SPAN onmouseover="this.style.fontSize = '48'">
                This text gets bigger when you move the mouse over it!
            </SPAN>
        </CENTER>
    </BODY>
</HTML>
```

You can see the results of this HTML in Figure 13.1. Here's another example, which we saw in the Immediate Solutions section "Using Dynamic Styles" in this chapter. In this case, I'm changing the cursor to a hand shape when the cursor moves over a header—note the use of the JavaScript term **this**, which refers to the current element:

```
<HTML>

    <HEAD>
        <TITLE>
            Using Dynamic Styles
        </TITLE>
    </HEAD>

    <BODY>

        <CENTER>
            <H1 onmouseover="this.style.cursor = 'hand';"
                onmouseout="this.style.cursor = 'default';">
                Change the cursor with the mouse.
            </H1>
        </CENTER>

    </BODY>

</HTML>
```

You can see the results of this HTML in Figure 13.5. Here's another example, this time I'm using style classes to change text from blue to red when the mouse moves over it:

```
<HTML>
    <HEAD>
        <TITLE>
            Dynamic Styles Using Classes
        </TITLE>
        <STYLE>
            .red {color:red}
            .blue {color:blue}
        </STYLE>
    </HEAD>

    <BODY>
        <CENTER>
            <H1 class=blue onmouseover="this.className='red'"
                onmouseout="this.className='blue'">
                Move the mouse here to change colors.
            </H1>
        </CENTER>
    </BODY>
</HTML>
```

Here's an example from the In Depth section of this chapter that uses layers in Netscape Navigator to create a **mouseover** effect. In this case, I set the background color of the layer when the mouse moves over it, creating a **mouseover** effect much like that in Internet Explorer:

```
<HTML>
    <HEAD>
        <TITLE>
            Mouseover Effects Using Layers
        </TITLE>

    </HEAD>

    <BODY>
        <LAYER BGCOLOR="white" TOP=40 LEFT=40
            ONMOUSEOVER="setcolor('cyan')" ONMOUSEOUT="setcolor('white')" >
            <SCRIPT LANGUAGE=JavaScript>
                function setcolor(color)
                {
                    bgColor=color
                }
            </SCRIPT>
            <H1>
                Mouseover Effects Using Layers
            </H1>
        </LAYER>

    </BODY>
</HTML>
```

You can see the results of this HTML in Figure 13.4. Here's another example for Internet Explorer. In this case, I'll use the **SRC** attribute of an image to display a new image when the mouse moves over it. The new image is the same as the original image except that it's lighter, giving the impression that moving the mouse over the image selects it:

```
<HTML>
    <HEAD>
        <TITLE>
            Mouseover Image Handling
        </TITLE>
    </HEAD>

    <BODY>
```

```
        <CENTER>
            <H1>
                Mouseover Image Handling
            </H1>

            <IMG SRC="flower.jpg"
                 onmouseover="this.src='flower2.jpg'"
                 onmouseout="this.src='flower.jpg'">
        </CENTER>
    </BODY>
</HTML>
```

You can see the results of this HTML in Figure 13.3.

Positioning Elements Using Styles

One more aspect of dynamic HTML is to position elements in a Web page. We first saw this in Chapter 9; I'll take another look at it here.

You use the **position** style property to set the position of elements in a Web page. The following list contains the properties you usually use when you work with positioning:

- **position**—Can hold values like **absolute** and **relative**.
- **top**—Offset of the top of the element's box.
- **bottom**—Offset of the bottom of the element's box.
- **left**—Offset of the left edge of the element's box.
- **right**—Offset of the right edge of the element's box.

In this next example, I set **position** to **absolute**, and then specify the **top** and **left** properties for three **<DIV>** elements, each of which has an image and text:

```
<HTML>

    <HEAD>
        <TITLE>
            Absolute Positioning
        </TITLE>
    </HEAD>

    <BODY>
```

```
<H1 ALIGN="CENTER">
    Absolute Positioning
</H1>

<DIV STYLE=
    "position:absolute; left:50; top:60; border-width: thick">
    <IMG SRC="FLOWER1.JPG" WIDTH=85 HEIGHT=129>
    <BR>
    Flower 1
</DIV>

<DIV STYLE=
    "position:absolute; left:200; top:90; border-width: thick">
    <IMG SRC="FLOWER2.JPG" WIDTH=85 HEIGHT=129>
    <BR>
    Flower 2
</DIV>

<DIV STYLE="position:absolute; left:350; top:120;
    border-width: thick">
    <IMG SRC="FLOWER3.JPG" WIDTH=85 HEIGHT=129>
    <BR>
    Flower 3
</DIV>

</BODY>

</HTML>
```

In addition to absolute positioning, you can also use relative positioning. What are elements positioned relative *to*? They're positioned relative to the location they would have had in the normal flow of elements in the Web browser.

To position items in a relative way, you set **position** to **relative,** and then set the other properties to indicate the new relative position. In this example, I'm moving some text up five pixels and other text down five pixels from the normal position at which the browser would place that text:

```
<HTML>

    <HEAD>
        <TITLE>
            Relative Positioning
        </TITLE>
    </HEAD>
```

```
<BODY>

    <H1 ALIGN="CENTER">
        Relative Positioning
    </H1>
    This text goes
    <SPAN STYLE="position: relative; top: -5">up</SPAN> and
    <SPAN STYLE="position: relative; top: 5">down</SPAN>,
    as you can see.

</BODY>

</HTML>
```

I'll apply this idea of element positioning in the next section on animation.

Creating Animation

The novice programmer appears and says, "I thought dynamic HTML would be dynamic. What about creating animation in a Web page?" "No sooner said than done," you say.

You can reset the position of Web page elements using dynamic styles—see the previous section for more details. You can set the location of elements using the JavaScript style properties **posLeft** and **posTop**. Here's an example where I'm moving three **<DIV>** elements around the page using JavaScript—note that I'm relating the location of the second and third **<DIV>** elements to the position of the first **<DIV>** with the **expression** keyword, which lets you calculate an expression in the **STYLE** attribute:

```
<HTML>
    <HEAD>
        <TITLE>
            Animation Using Dynamic Properties
        </TITLE>
        <SCRIPT LANGUAGE="JavaScript">
            var increment = 1;
            function setPosition()
            {
                text1.style.posLeft = text1.style.posLeft + increment;
                if (text1.style.posLeft >= 600 || text1.style.posLeft < 0)
                {
```

```
                    increment = -1 * increment;
            }
        }
        setInterval ("setPosition()", 50)
    </SCRIPT>
</HEAD>

<BODY>
    <CENTER>
        <H1>
            Animation Using Dynamic Properties
        </H1>
    </CENTER>

    <DIV ID=text1 STYLE=
        "position: absolute; top: 80; left: 0; height: 30;
        width: 100; background: cyan; font-size: 16">
        Hello from dynamic HTML!
    </DIV>

    <DIV ID=text2 STYLE="position: absolute; top: 140; left:
        expression(text1.style.posLeft * 0.75); height: 30;
        width: 100; background: pink; font-size: 16">
        Hello again from dynamic HTML!
    </DIV>

    <DIV ID=text2 STYLE="position: absolute; top: 200; left:
        expression(text1.style.posLeft * 0.5); height: 30;
        width: 100; background: yellow; font-size: 16">
        Hello once again from dynamic HTML!
    </DIV>

</BODY>

</HTML>
```

You can see the results of this HTML in Figure 13.15. In this page, the three **<DIV>** elements move from left to right and back again, and the second **<DIV>** moves three-quarters as fast as the top **<DIV>**, while the third element moves only half as fast.

Note that you cannot use dynamic styles in Netscape Navigator yet, however, you can use layers to support animation—see the next section.

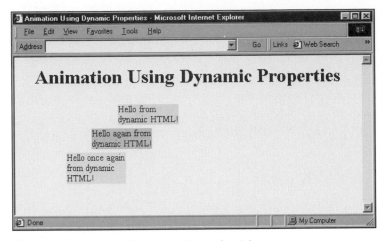

Figure 13.15   Animation using dynamic styles.

Creating Animation With Layers

The novice programmer stomps in and says, "I'm using Netscape Navigator. How can I create animation in a Web page using this browser?" "With layers," you say. "Ah," says the NP, "of course."

You can move layers around in Netscape Navigator by using the **left** and **top** properties. Here's an example where I display one layer on top of another, and then move one layer over to the left, uncovering the other layer steadily:

```
<HTML>
    <HEAD>
        <TITLE>
            Animation With Layers
        </TITLE>

        <SCRIPT LANGUAGE="JavaScript">
            function handleTransition()
            {
                document.layers['layer1'].left =
                    document.layers['layer1'].left - 5

                if (document.layers['layer1'].left > -256) {
                    setTimeout('handleTransition()',50)
                }
            }
        </SCRIPT>
```

```
        </HEAD>

        <BODY>
            <CENTER>
                <H1>
                    Animation Using Layers
                </H1>
            </CENTER>

            <DIV STYLE="POSITION:absolute;TOP:60;LEFT:0">
                <IMG SRC="image1.jpg">
            </DIV>

            <LAYER NAME=layer1 left=0 top = 60><IMG SRC="image2.jpg"></LAYER>

            <DIV STYLE="POSITION:absolute;TOP:340;LEFT:40">
                <FORM>

                <INPUT TYPE="BUTTON" NAME="startTrans" VALUE="Start Transition"
                    onclick="handleTransition()">
                </FORM>
            </DIV>
        </BODY>
    </HTML>
```

You can see the results of this HTML in Figure 13.16. When the user clicks the button in this page, the animation begins, and the top layer slides off to the right.

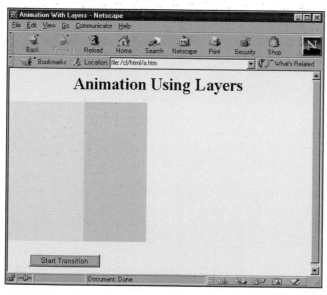

Figure 13.16   Creating animation using layers.

Using Vector Markup Language (VML)

There's a way to draw figures in Internet Explorer that's worth mentioning—Vector Markup Language (VML). VML is implemented as a *behavior* in Internet Explorer, and we'll see how behaviors work in detail in Chapter 14. Here's an example showing how to draw ovals, rectangles, and polylines with VML:

```
<HTML xmlns:v="urn:schemas-microsoft-com:vml">

    <HEAD>
        <TITLE>
            Using Vector Markup Language
        </TITLE>

        <STYLE>
        v\:* {behavior: url(#default#VML);}
        </STYLE>
    </HEAD>

    <BODY>
        <CENTER>
            <H1>
                Using Vector Markup Language
            </H1>
        </CENTER>
        <P>
        <v:oval STYLE='width:100pt; height:75pt' fillcolor="yellow">
        </v:oval>
        <P>
        <v:rect STYLE='width:100pt; height:75pt' fillcolor="blue"
            strokecolor="red" STROKEWEIGHT="2pt"/>
        <P>
        <v:polyline POINTS="20pt,55pt,100pt,-10pt,180pt,65pt,260pt,25pt"
            strokecolor="red" STROKEWEIGHT="2pt"/>
    </BODY>
</HTML>
```

The result of this HTML appears in Figure 13.17.

TIP: *To learn more about VML, take a look at **http://msdn.microsoft.com/standards/vml/ref/**.*

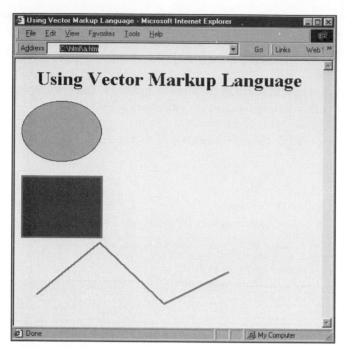

Figure 13.17   Using VML in Internet Explorer.

Setting Element Visibility

"Now I've got another problem," the novice programmer says, "because I want to make some controls in my Web page visible at times and invisible at others. What can I do?" "There are a few ways to handle that in Internet Explorer," you say. "Great!" says the NP.

In Internet Explorer, you can make elements visible or invisible using two style properties: **visibility** and **display**. Here's an example using the **visibility** property, which you can set to either **hidden** or **visible**. In this case, when the user clicks a button, previously hidden text is displayed.

```
<HTML>
    <HEAD>
        <TITLE>
            Making Elements Visible With The visibility Property
        </TITLE>

        <SCRIPT LANGUAGE="JAVASCRIPT">
            function showMore()
```

```
            {
                div1.style.visibility = "visible"
            }
        </SCRIPT>
    </HEAD>

    <BODY>

        <CENTER>
            <H1>
                Making Elements Visible With The visibility Property
            </H1>
        </CENTER>

        <INPUT TYPE=BUTTON VALUE="Click Me" ONCLICK="showMore()">
        <P>
        <DIV ID=div1 STYLE="visibility:hidden">
            Here's some newly-visible text!
        </DIV>
    </BODY>
</HTML>
```

You can see the results after the user clicks the button, and the text has been made visible in Figure 13.18.

Here's the same example rewritten to use the **display** property, which you can set to an empty string to display the element or set to **none** to hide the element:

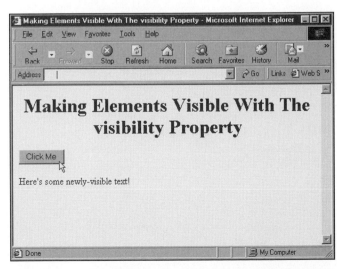

Figure 13.18   Making elements visible with the **visibility** property in Internet Explorer.

```
<HTML>
    <HEAD>
        <TITLE>
            Making Elements Visible With The display Property
        </TITLE>

        <SCRIPT LANGUAGE="JavaScript">
            function showMore()
            {
                div1.style.display = ""
            }
        </SCRIPT>
    </HEAD>

    <BODY>
        <CENTER>
            <H1>
                Making Elements Visible With The display Property
            </H1>
        </CENTER>

        <INPUT TYPE=BUTTON VALUE="Click Me" ONCLICK="showMore()">
        <P>
        <DIV ID=div1 STYLE="display: none">
            Here's some newly-visible text!
        </DIV>
    </BODY>
</HTML>
```

The results of this HTML appear in Figure 13.19.

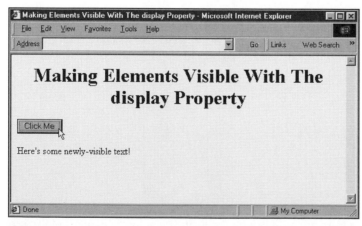

Figure 13.19   Making elements visible with the **display** property in Internet Explorer.

Printing Web Pages

The big boss is upset and says, "What if users want a hard copy of the Web page that has my picture on it? How can we do that?" "No problem," you say, "as of Internet Explorer 5, I can use the **window.print** method to print the page out at the click of a button." "Hm," says the BB, "better make the printing automatic so it prints as soon as the page appears."

As of Internet Explorer 5, you can use the **window.print** method to print a Web page. In fact, you can control the placement of page breaks in your documents by using the **page-break-before** and **page-break-after** style properties. These properties indicate when to break to a new page when printing the document.

Here's an example. When the user clicks the button, the page is printed. I've also set the page up so a page break occurs before the **<P>** element:

```
<HTML>
    <HEAD>
        <TITLE>
            Printing Web Pages
        </TITLE>

        <SCRIPT LANGUAGE="JAVASCRIPT">
            function showMore()
            {
                window.print()
            }
        </SCRIPT>

        <STYLE>
            P {page-break-before: always}
        </STYLE>

    </HEAD>

    <BODY>

        <CENTER>
            <H1>
                Printing Web Pages
            </H1>
        </CENTER>

        <INPUT TYPE=BUTTON VALUE="Print Page" ONCLICK="showMore()">
        <P>
```

```
        Here's some text!
    </BODY>
</HTML>
```

When the user clicks the Print Page button, a Print dialog box opens, and if the user wants to, the page is printed with a page break before the **<P>** element.

Using Dynamic Fonts

One aspect of dynamic HTML in Netscape Navigator is using dynamic fonts, which you can download from the Internet. To indicate that you want to download a font, you use the **<LINK>** element, setting the **REL** attribute to **FONTDEF** and the **SRC** attribute to the URL of the dynamic font like this:

```
<LINK REL=FONTDEF SRC="font.pfr">
```

Here's an example in which I'll download the Chianti font from Bitstream, Inc. and use it in a Web page. To find out more about the dynamic fonts Bitstream, Inc. offers, take a look at **www.truedoc.com/webpages/intro/**.

Here's the HTML:

```
<HTML>
    <HEAD>
        <TITLE>
            Using Dynamic Fonts
        </TITLE>

        <LINK REL=FONTDEF SRC="http://www.truedoc.com/webpages/chianti.pfr">

    </HEAD>

    <BODY>
        <CENTER>
            <H1>
                Using Dynamic Fonts
            </H1>
        </CENTER>

        <P>
            <FONT FACE="Chianti BT" SIZE="5" COLOR="#000000">
                Chianti ROMAN
```

```
          </FONT>

    <P>
          <FONT FACE="Chianti It BT" SIZE="5" COLOR="#000000">
               Chianti ITALIC
          </FONT>

    <P>
          <FONT FACE="Chianti BT" SIZE="5" COLOR="#000000">
               <B>Chianti BOLD</B>
          </FONT>

    <P>
          <FONT FACE="Chianti BdIt BT" SIZE="5" COLOR="#000000">
               Chianti BOLD ITALIC
          </FONT>

    <P>
          <FONT FACE="Chianti XBd BT" SIZE="5" COLOR="#000000">
               Chianti EXTRA BOLD
          </FONT>

    </BODY>
</HTML>
```

You can see the results of this HTML in Figure 13.20 where you can see the dynamic font loaded and in use.

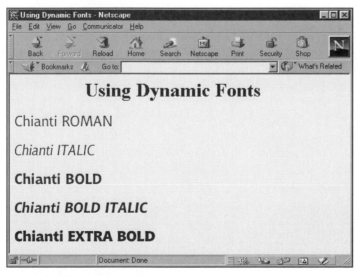

Figure 13.20   Using dynamic fonts.

Visual Effects: Filters

"I've heard that you can use visual filters in Internet Explorer," says the novice programmer, "How does that work?" "It's easy," you say, "just pull up a chair and we'll go through it."

Internet Explorer lets you apply the following various visual *filters* to HTML elements:

- Alpha (Sets opacity, 0 percent equals transparent, 100 percent equals fully opaque)
- Blur
- Chroma
- Drop shadow
- Flip horizontal
- Flip vertical
- Glow
- Gray
- Invert
- Mask
- Shadow
- Wave
- XRay

You apply these filters to Web page elements using the **filter** property of the **style** object of an element. In this next example, I'll let the user select a filter for a **<DIV>** element that displays some text. When the user clicks a button that displays the caption "Apply Filter", the code will apply the selected filter. Here's the HTML—note that I let the user set the opacity of the Alpha filter with a text field:

```
<HTML>
    <HEAD>
        <TITLE>
            Using Visual Filters
        </TITLE>

        <SCRIPT LANGUAGE="JavaScript">

            function useFilter()
```

```
        {
        div1.style.filter=""

        if (radio01.checked)
            div1.style.filter = "fliph(enabled=1)"
        if (radio02.checked)
            div1.style.filter = "flipv(enabled=1)"
        if (radio03.checked)
            div1.style.filter = "gray(enabled=1)"
        if (radio04.checked)
            div1.style.filter = "invert(enabled=1)"
        if (radio05.checked)
            div1.style.filter = "xray(enabled=1)"
        if (radio06.checked){
            var newOpacity
            newOpacity = Opacity.value
            div1.style.filter = "alpha(opacity=" + newOpacity +
                ", enabled=1)"
        }
        if (radio07.checked)
            div1.style.filter =
                "blur(direction=45, strength=15, add=0, enabled=1)"
        if (radio08.checked)
            div1.style.filter = "chroma(color=#FFFF00, enabled=1)"
        if (radio09.checked)
            div1.style.filter = "dropshadow(offx=5, offy=9, " +
                "color=#008fff, enabled=1)"
         if (radio10.checked)
            div1.style.filter = "glow(strength=5, color=#ffff00, "
            + "enabled=1) "
        if (radio11.checked)
            div1.style.filter = "mask(color=#FF0000 ,enabled=1)"
        if (radio12.checked)
            div1.style.filter =
            "shadow(color=#FF0088,direction=315,enabled=1)"
        if (radio13.checked)
            div1.style.filter = "wave(freq=2, strength=6,
            phase=0, " + "lightstrength=0, add=0, enabled=1)"
        }
    </SCRIPT>
</HEAD>

<BODY>
    <CENTER>
        <H1>
```

```
        Using Filters
    </H1>
    <INPUT TYPE="RADIO" NAME="RADIOS" ID="radio01">Flip Horizontal
    <INPUT TYPE="RADIO" NAME="RADIOS" ID="radio02">Flip Vertical
    <INPUT TYPE="RADIO" NAME="RADIOS" ID="radio03">Gray
    <INPUT TYPE="RADIO" NAME="RADIOS" ID="radio04">Invert
    <INPUT TYPE="RADIO" NAME="RADIOS" ID="radio05">XRay
    <BR>
    <BR>
    <INPUT TYPE="RADIO" NAME="RADIOS" ID="radio07">Blur
    <INPUT TYPE="RADIO" NAME="RADIOS" ID="radio08">Chroma
    <INPUT TYPE="RADIO" NAME="RADIOS" ID="radio09">Drop Shadow
    <INPUT TYPE="RADIO" NAME="RADIOS" ID="radio10">Glow
    <INPUT TYPE="RADIO" NAME="RADIOS" ID="radio11">Mask
    <BR>
    <BR>
    <INPUT TYPE="RADIO" NAME="RADIOS" ID="radio12">Shadow
    <INPUT TYPE="RADIO" NAME="RADIOS" ID="radio13">Wave
    <INPUT TYPE="RADIO" NAME="RADIOS"
        ID="radio06">
        Alpha   Opacity: 
    <INPUT TYPE="TEXT" ID="Opacity" VALUE="50" SIZE="3"
        MAXLENGTH="3">
    <P>
    <INPUT TYPE="SUBMIT" NAME="startFilter" VALUE="Apply Filter"
        onclick="useFilter()">
</CENTER>

<DIV ID="div1" STYLE="POSITION:absolute; WIDTH:300; HEIGHT:80;
    TOP:250; LEFT:30%; font-size:24pt;font-family:verdana;
    font-style:bold; color:blue;">
    Filter this text!
</DIV>

</BODY>
</HTML>
```

You can see the result of this HTML in Figure 13.21 where I've applied the shadow filter to the text in the **<DIV>** element. To get a feeling for the various filters, you can play around with this page—all it takes is two clicks per filter and you see the results immediately.

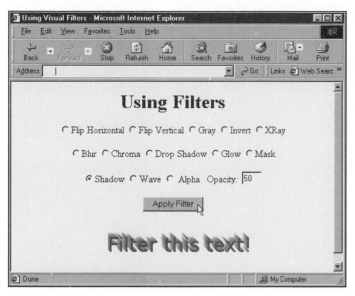

Figure 13.21   Using visual filters.

Visual Effects: Transitions

"Visual filters are nice," says the novice programmer, "but what about *transitions*? Can't you use all kinds of transitions when showing or hiding elements in Internet Explorer?" "You sure can," you say, "get some coffee and we'll take a look."

There are all kinds of visual transitions you can use when showing or hiding an element in Internet Explorer. The following list contains the possible transitions:

- Box in
- Box out
- Checkerboard across
- Checkerboard down
- Circle in
- Circle out
- Horizontal blinds
- Random
- Random bars horizontal

- Random bars vertical
- Random dissolve
- Split horizontal in
- Split horizontal out
- Strips left down
- Strips left up
- Strips right down
- Strips right up
- Split vertical in
- Split vertical out
- Vertical blinds
- Wipe down
- Wipe left
- Wipe right
- Wipe up

Transitions happen when you switch an element's **visibility** property from **hidden** to **visible**. You select a transition with the **Transition** property and make it occur with the **play** method. Here's an example to show how this works. In this case, the user can select which transition to make with a select control, and then click a button with the caption "Start Transition" to make the transition happen. Here, I'll add display images, one of which is pure yellow and the other is pure cyan, in a **<DIV>** element. To show how elements appear and disappear in transitions, I'll make one image disappear when the other is appearing and vice versa. Here's the HTML:

```
<HTML>
    <HEAD>
        <TITLE>
            Using Visual Transitions
        </TITLE>

        <SCRIPT LANGUAGE="JavaScript">
            var transitionDuration
            var transitionDirection
            var transitionHappening

            transitionDirection = 0
            transitionDuration = 3
```

```
        function filterChange()
        {
            transitionHappening = false
        }

        function handleTransition()
        {
            if (transitionHappening)
                return

            div1.filters.item(0).apply()

            if (transitionDirection == 1){
                transitionDirection = 2
                Image2.style.visibility = "visible"
                Image1.style.visibility = "hidden"
            }
            else {
                transitionDirection = 1
                Image1.style.visibility = "visible"
                Image2.style.visibility = "hidden"
            }
            div1.filters.item(0).Transition = select1.selectedIndex
            div1.filters(0).play(transitionDuration)
            transitionHappening = true
        }

    </SCRIPT>
</HEAD>

<BODY>
    <CENTER>
        <H1>
            Using Visual Transitions
        </H1>
    </CENTER>

    <DIV STYLE="POSITION:absolute;TOP:270;LEFT:25%">
        <SELECT ID="select1">
            <OPTION>Box In Transition</OPTION>
            <OPTION>Box Out Transition</OPTION>
            <OPTION>Circle In Transition</OPTION>
            <OPTION>Circle Out Transition</OPTION>
            <OPTION>Wipe Up Transition</OPTION>
```

795

```
                    <OPTION>Wipe Down Transition</OPTION>
                    <OPTION>Wipe Right Transition</OPTION>
                    <OPTION>Wipe Left Transition</OPTION>
                    <OPTION>Vertical Blinds Transition</OPTION>
                    <OPTION>Horizontal Blinds Transition</OPTION>
                    <OPTION>Checker Board Across Transition</OPTION>
                    <OPTION>Checker Board Down Transition</OPTION>
                    <OPTION>Random Dissolve Transition</OPTION>
                    <OPTION>Split Vertical In Transition</OPTION>
                    <OPTION>Split Vertical Out Transition</OPTION>
                    <OPTION>Split Horizontal In Transition</OPTION>
                    <OPTION>Split Horizontal Out Transition</OPTION>
                    <OPTION>Strips Left Down Transition</OPTION>
                    <OPTION>Strips Left Up Transition</OPTION>
                    <OPTION>Strips Right Down Transition</OPTION>
                    <OPTION>Strips Right Up Transition</OPTION>
                    <OPTION>Random Bars Horizontal Transition</OPTION>
                    <OPTION>Random Bars Vertical Transition</OPTION>
                    <OPTION>Random Transition</OPTION>
                </SELECT>

                <INPUT TYPE="SUBMIT" NAME="startTrans" VALUE="Start Transition"
                    onclick="handleTransition()">
            </DIV>

            <DIV ID="div1" STYLE="POSITION:absolute; WIDTH:450; HEIGHT:210;
                TOP:60; LEFT:15%; FILTER:revealTrans(Duration=1.0,
                Transition=1)"
                    OnFilterChange="filterChange()">
                <IMG ID="Image1" STYLE=
                    "Position:absolute;Width:200;height:200;visibility:hidden"
                    SRC="image1.jpg" WIDTH="256" HEIGHT="256">
                <IMG ID="Image2" STYLE=
                    "Position:absolute;Width:200;height:200;left:210"
                    SRC="image2.jpg" WIDTH="256" HEIGHT="256">
            </DIV>

        </BODY>
</HTML>
```

You can see the results of this HTML in Figure 13.22. When the user selects a transition in the select control and clicks the Start Transition button, the transition begins. For example, you can see the circle in transition occurring in Figure 13.22. The cyan image on the left is appearing as the transition circle becomes smaller and smaller, and the yellow image on the right is disappearing at the same

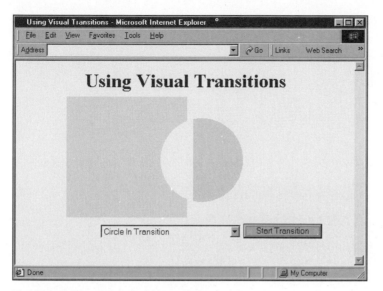

Figure 13.22   Using visual transitions.

timc. If you click the button again, the cyan image will disappear and the yellow image will appear.

Using transitions in Web pages can truly add a touch of professionalism to your Web pages—give it a try.

Visual Effects: Transitions Using Layers

You can't use transition effects using filters—see the previous section—in Netscape Navigator, but you can use layers instead. We saw this example from the Immediate Solutions section "Creating Animation With Layers" of this chapter:

```
<HTML>
    <HEAD>
        <TITLE>
            Visual Transitions With Layers
        </TITLE>

        <SCRIPT LANGUAGE="JavaScript">
            function handleTransition()
            {
                document.layers['layer1'].left =
                    document.layers['layer1'].left - 5
```

```
                    if (document.layers['layer1'].left > -256) {
                        setTimeout('handleTransition()',50)
                    }
                }
        </SCRIPT>

    </HEAD>

    <BODY>
        <CENTER>
            <H1>
                Visual Transitions With Layers
            </H1>
        </CENTER>

        <DIV STYLE="POSITION:absolute;TOP:60;LEFT:0">
            <IMG SRC="image1.jpg">
        </DIV>

        <LAYER NAME=layer1 left=0 top = 60><IMG SRC="image2.jpg"></LAYER>

        <DIV STYLE="POSITION:absolute;TOP:340;LEFT:40">
            <FORM>

            <INPUT TYPE="BUTTON" NAME="startTrans" VALUE="Start Transition"
                onclick="handleTransition()">
            </FORM>
        </DIV>
    </BODY>
</HTML>
```

This code simply displays one layer on top of another, and when the user clicks the button, slides the top layer off to the right. You can see the results of this HTML in Figure 13.16.

Chapter 14

Dynamic HTML: Drag And Drop, Data Binding, And Behaviors

In Depth

In this chapter, I'm going to take a look at some advanced dynamic HTML topics: dragging and dropping, data binding, and behaviors. Netscape Navigator does not support these topics, unfortunately, except for dragging and dropping, and of course you implement it differently than you would in Internet Explorer. The upshot is that this chapter is almost exclusively an Internet Explorer chapter except where I implement dragging and dropping using layers.

I'm going to start our overview of these topics with dragging and dropping.

Dragging And Dropping

There are two ways to implement dragging and dropping in Internet Explorer—first, simple dragging and dropping using absolute positioning with styles, and second, dragging and dropping data. Simple dragging and dropping involves using the mouse and setting an element's position to match mouse movements. Dragging and dropping data, on the other hand, involves specialized data transfer; you can even drag and drop data across applications. In Netscape Navigator, you use layers to implement dragging and dropping. It's not as easy as it sounds because you have to make sure the layer captures mouse events correctly (see the Immediate Solutions section "Dragging And Dropping Using Layers" later in this chapter).

I'll take a look at how to implement simple dragging and dropping in Internet Explorer first to get us started. In Figure 14.1, a Web page displays two images, both of which you can drag around using the mouse. Just press the mouse button when the mouse cursor is over an image, and drag that image around while holding the mouse button down.

The dragging operation begins when the mouse button is pressed when the mouse is over an image. Because there are two images, the code needs to determine which one is being dragged, and I do that with the event object's **srcElement** property. Note that I also check to make sure that the type of element being dragged is indeed an image before allowing it to be dragged, and then I store the dragged image's ID in a variable named **draggingID**:

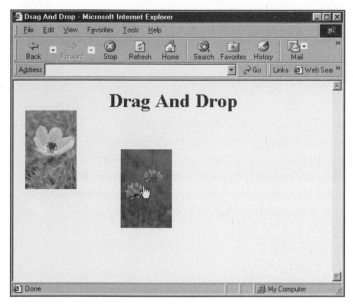

Figure 14.1   Dragging and dropping in Internet Explorer.

```
function mouseDownEvent()
{
    if (event.srcElement.tagName == "IMG"){

        draggingID = event.srcElement.id
        .
        .
        .
    }
}
```

Also note that because there are two images, I have to set their z order—that is,
their stacking order—so the image that's being dragged will ride over the stationary image like this:

```
function mouseDownEvent()
{
    if (event.srcElement.tagName == "IMG"){

        draggingID = event.srcElement.id

        if (draggingID == "IMG1"){
            document.all["IMG1"].style.zIndex = 1
```

```
            document.all["IMG2"].style.zIndex = 0
        }
        else {
            document.all["IMG1"].style.zIndex = 0
            document.all["IMG2"].style.zIndex = 1
        }
    }
}
```

Next, when the mouse moves, I make sure there is an image being dragged by checking **draggingID** in a new function, **mouseMoveEvent**. If an image is indeed being dragged, I set the location of the image to the new mouse location using the style properties **pixelLeft** and **pixelTop** like this:

```
function mouseMoveEvent()
{
    if (draggingID != null && event.srcElement.tagName == "IMG"){
        document.all[draggingID].style.pixelLeft = event.x -
            document.all[draggingID].width/2
        document.all[draggingID].style.pixelTop = event.y -
            document.all[draggingID].height/2

        event.returnValue = false
    }
}
```

Note also that at the end of this code, I set the return value of the **event** object to **false** to indicate that we've handled the event.

TIP: *It's worth noting that you can support events in hierarchies of elements in Internet Explorer. In Internet Explorer, events bubble, which means that if one element doesn't handle the event, it propagates up to the element's parent element to see if that element can handle the event. In the previous example, events would bubble from the images to their parent, the **document** object itself. The idea is that you can provide one event handler for the parent element instead of separate event handlers for each child element. If you want to prevent event bubbling from happening, you can set the event object's **cancelBubble** property to **true** (**event.cancelBubble = true**) to cancel event bubbling.*

When the mouse button is released, I place the image in its final position, set the **draggingID** variable to **null**, and set the event object's return value to **false** to indicate we've handled the event in one final function, **mouseUpEvent**:

```
function mouseUpEvent()
{
    if (draggingID != null  && event.srcElement.tagName == "IMG"){
        document.all[draggingID].style.pixelLeft = event.x -
```

```
            document.all[draggingID].width/2
        document.all[draggingID].style.pixelTop = event.y -
            document.all[draggingID].height/2

        draggingID = null
        event.returnValue = false
    }
}
```

That's what the JavaScript for this example looks like. You'll find the full Web page in the Immediate Solutions section "Dragging And Dropping" of this chapter. You can see the results in Figure 14.1.

Data Binding

Another important aspect of dynamic HTML in Internet Explorer is *data binding*. Using data binding, you can connect HTML elements in a Web page to a data source. There are two aspects to this process—using data source objects (DSOs) and binding to HTML elements.

TIP: *You can find information about data binding in Internet Explorer at* ***http://msdn.microsoft.com/workshop/c-frame.htm#/workshop/author/default.asp***.

Data Source Objects

There are a variety of DSOs in Internet Explorer, including the Microsoft HTML (MSHTML) control, the tabular data control (TDC), and the Extensible Markup Language (XML) data source control. I'll take a look at all of them in this chapter. I'll also take a look at the more complex remote data service (RDS) DSO, which you use to connect to database applications on Web servers. In this chapter, I'll use RDS to connect to the Microsoft SQL Server on a Web server.

DSOs are invisible in the Web page, but you can bind them to HTML elements and control their behavior with buttons and other controls. Using the MSHTML control makes this process easy. For example, say that you have a Web page with data about various employees, employee.htm, which looks like the following example where a **<SPAN>** element is used to identify the fields of your database—**NAME**, **ID**, **HIRE_DATE**, and **DEPARTMENT**—each group of such elements forms a *record*:

```
<HTML>
    <HEAD>
        <TITLE>
```

```
            Data Page
        </TITLE>
    </HEAD>

    <BODY>
        <H1>
            This page holds data.
        </H1>
        Name: <SPAN ID="NAME">Tony</SPAN><BR>
        ID: <SPAN ID="ID">1234</SPAN><BR>
        Hire Date: <SPAN ID="HIRE_DATE">
            4-1-2001</SPAN><BR>
        Department: <SPAN ID="DEPARTMENT">
            Shipping</SPAN><BR>
        Title: <SPAN ID="TITLE">Packer</SPAN><BR>
        Name: <SPAN ID="NAME">Ed</SPAN><BR>
        ID: <SPAN ID="ID">1235</SPAN><BR>
        Hire Date: <SPAN ID="HIRE_DATE">
            4-1-2001</SPAN><BR>
        Department: <SPAN ID="DEPARTMENT">
            Programming</SPAN><BR>
        Title: <SPAN ID="TITLE">Programmer</SPAN><BR>
        Name: <SPAN ID="NAME">Francis</SPAN><BR>
        ID: <SPAN ID="ID">1236</SPAN><BR>
        Hire Date: <SPAN ID="HIRE_DATE">
            4-1-2001</SPAN><BR>
        Department: <SPAN ID="DEPARTMENT">
            Shipping</SPAN><BR>
        Title: <SPAN ID="TITLE">Packer</SPAN><BR>
        Name: <SPAN ID="NAME">Linda</SPAN><BR>
        ID: <SPAN ID="ID">1237</SPAN><BR>
        Hire Date: <SPAN ID="HIRE_DATE">
            4-1-2001</SPAN><BR>
        Department: <SPAN ID="DEPARTMENT">
            Shipping</SPAN><BR>
        Title: <SPAN ID="TITLE">Packer</SPAN><BR>
        Name: <SPAN ID="NAME">Louise</SPAN><BR>
        ID: <SPAN ID="ID">1238</SPAN><BR>
        Hire Date: <SPAN ID="HIRE_DATE">
            4-1-2001</SPAN><BR>
        Department: <SPAN ID="DEPARTMENT">
            Shipping</SPAN><BR>
        Title: <SPAN ID="TITLE">Packer</SPAN><BR>
    </BODY>
</HTML>
```

The MSHTML control can read this HTML and assemble it into an internal database, called a *record set*, which you can bind to HTML elements. Here's how you would create an MSHTML control in a Web page with the name **dsoEmployees** and a connection to employee.htm:

```
<OBJECT ID="dsoEmployees" DATA="employee.htm" HEIGHT=0 WIDTH=0>
</OBJECT>
```

You can use the DSO's **Recordset** property to access methods and properties of the record set, and I'll do that throughout this chapter. Some common methods are **MoveFirst**, **MoveLast**, **MoveNext**, and **MovePrevious**, which let you navigate from record to record in the record set. I'll put those methods to work throughout this chapter. To actually display the data from this DSO, you can bind it to HTML elements.

HTML Bound Tags

Many tags in Internet Explorer now support properties that you can bind to data sources; to bind these tags to a data source, you use their **DATASRC** and **DATAFLD** attributes. The **DATASRC** attribute points to the DSO, and the **DATAFLD** attribute points to the field in the database you want to bind to (such as **NAME** or **ID** in this example). The HTML element then displays the data supplied by the DSO. For example, if the current record in a DSO is the first record in employee.htm, and you have a text field bound to the **NAME** field, the text field would display the word "Tony". When you make the DSO move to the next record, the text field would display the word "Ed".

The following is a list of HTML tags showing what property is actually bound when you use the **DATASRC** and **DATAFLD** attributes:

- **A**—Binds to the **href** property; does not update data.
- **APPLET**—Binds to the **param** property; updates data.
- **BUTTON**—Binds to the **value** property; does not update data.
- **DIV**—Binds to the **innerText** and **innerHTML** properties; does not update data.
- **FRAME**—Binds to the **src** property; does not update data.
- **IFRAME**—Binds to the **src** property; does not update data.
- **IMG**—Binds to the **src** property; does not update data.
- **INPUT TYPE=BUTTON**—Binds to the **value** property; does not update data.

- **INPUT TYPE=CHECKBOX**—Binds to the **checked** property; updates data.

- **INPUT TYPE=HIDDEN**—Binds to the **value** property; updates data.

- **INPUT TYPE=PASSWORD**—Binds to the **value** property; updates data.

- **INPUT TYPE=RADIO**—Binds to the **checked** property; updates data.

- **INPUT TYPE=TEXT**—Binds to the **value** property; updates data.

- **LABEL**—Binds to the **value** property; does not update data.

- **MARQUEE**—Binds to the **innerText** and **innerHTML** properties; does not update data.

- **OBJECT**—Binds to the **objects** property; updates data.

- **PARAM**—Binds to the **param** property; updates data.

- **SELECT**—Binds to the **text** property of an option; updates data.

- **SPAN**—Binds to the **innerText** and **innerHTML** properties; does not update data.

- **TABLE**—Constructs an entire table; does not update data.

- **TEXTAREA**—Binds to the **value** property; updates data.

In addition, HTML tags have certain events that you use with data bindings:

- **onafterupdate**—Occurs after the data in the tag is sent to the DSO.

- **onbeforeunload**—Occurs before the page is unloaded.

- **onbeforeupdate**—Occurs when the data in the tag is sent to the DSO.

- **onerrorupdate**—Occurs if there was an error that stops data being sent to the DSO.

Here's how you put the MSHTML DSO and text fields to work. I'll use the **DATASRC** and **DATAFLD** attributes of the text fields to connect to the **dsoEmployees** DSO as well as connect the **MoveFirst**, **MoveLast**, **MoveNext**, and **MovePrevious** methods to buttons to let the user navigate around the record set (for details on how this code works, see the Immediate Solutions section "Using The MSHTML Data Source Control" in this chapter):

```
<HTML>
    <HEAD>
        <TITLE>
            Using The MSHTML Control
        </TITLE>
    </HEAD>

    <BODY>
```

```
<CENTER>
    <H1>
        Using The MSHTML Control
    </H1>

    <OBJECT ID="dsoEmployees" DATA="employee.htm" HEIGHT=0 WIDTH=0>
    </OBJECT>

    Name: <INPUT TYPE="TEXT" DATASRC="#dsoEmployees"
        DATAFLD="NAME" SIZE=10>
    <P>
    ID: <INPUT TYPE="TEXT" DATASRC="#dsoEmployees"
        DATAFLD="ID" SIZE=5>
    <P>
    Hire date: <SPAN DATASRC="#dsoEmployees"
        DATAFLD="HIRE_DATE"></SPAN>
    <P>
    Title: <SPAN DATASRC="#dsoEmployees" DATAFLD="TITLE">
    </SPAN>
    <P>
    Department: <SELECT DATASRC="#dsoEmployees"
        DATAFLD="DEPARTMENT" SIZE=1>
        <OPTION VALUE="Shipping">Shipping
        <OPTION VALUE="Programming">Programming
        <OPTION VALUE="Editing">Editing
        <OPTION VALUE="Writing">Writing
    </SELECT>
    <P>

    <BUTTON ONCLICK=
        "dsoEmployees.recordset.MoveFirst()" >&lt;&lt;</BUTTON>
    <BUTTON ONCLICK="if (!dsoEmployees.recordset.BOF)
        dsoEmployees.recordset.MovePrevious()" >&lt;</BUTTON>
    <BUTTON ONCLICK="if (!dsoEmployees.recordset.EOF)
        dsoEmployees.recordset.MoveNext()" >&gt;</BUTTON>
    <BUTTON ONCLICK=
        "dsoEmployees.recordset.MoveLast()">&gt;&gt;</BUTTON>
    </CENTER>
  </BODY>
</HTML>
```

The results of this HTML appear in Figure 14.2 where you can see one record from the record set displayed in the text fields of the Web page. The user can navigate from record to record by simply clicking the buttons in the page.

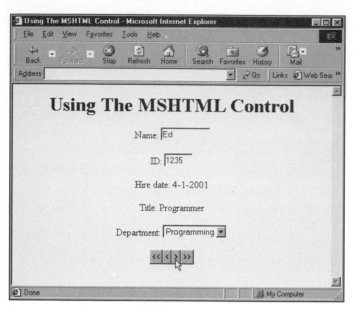

Figure 14.2   Using the MSHTML data source control.

There is a great deal of depth in this topic. For example, you can bind a DSO to a table and see all the data in the database at once or even connect to a SQL database on a server using the RDS. I'll take a look at these topics as well in this chapter; see the Immediate Solutions section "Using The RDS Control" for more details.

Internet Explorer Behaviors

As of Internet Explorer 5, dynamic HTML supports *behaviors*. As the name indicates, behaviors set the behavior of HTML elements. For example, you can create a behavior that applies a different filter to HTML elements each time it's invoked. You can think of behaviors much like styles, which you can code using JavaScript or other scripting languages.

TIP: *You can find information about behaviors in Internet Explorer at **http://msdn.microsoft.com/workshop/ c-frame.htm#/workshop/author/default.asp**.*

To create a behavior, you write an *HTML component* (HTC), which is a separate HTML file that holds the script for the behavior. Microsoft's motivation in creating HTCs was to separate code from data, which has become a big movement in HTML programming these days (and it's one of the reasons the World Wide Web Consortium [W3C] wouldn't make the **<LAYER>** element into an official element).

An HTC file is nothing but an HTML file saved with the extension .htc, which contains scripts and a set of HTC-specific custom elements that expose properties, methods, and events that define the component. As an HTML file, an HTC provides the same access as dynamic HTML to all elements on the page. In other words, within an HTC, all HTC elements are accessible from script as objects using their **ID** attributes. This allows all attributes and methods of HTC elements to be manipulated through script as properties and methods of objects.

You can use HTCs to implement behaviors that do the following:

- *Access the containing page's Dynamic HTML Object Model*—You can use the **element** object in HTCs to access the actual element that has the behavior attached. Using this object, you can access properties, methods, and events of the containing document.

- *Expose custom events*—You can create events with the **EVENT** element. These events will be sent to the containing page with the element's **fire** method.

- *Expose properties and methods*—You can create properties and methods with the **PROPERTY** and **METHOD** elements, respectively.

- *Receive notifications*—You can use the **ATTACH** element to make sure that the browser will pass on standard events to the HTC.

Here's an example. In this case, I'll create an HTC called glow.htc that will make HTML elements glow (using the glow filter we saw in Chapter 13) when the mouse is over them, as you see in Figure 14.3.

Figure 14.3   Using a behavior in Internet Explorer.

To apply a behavior, you can create a style—I'll call that style *glow* here—and use the **behavior** keyword to provide the URL of the associated HTC like this:

```
<HTML>
    <HEAD>
        <TITLE>
            Using Behaviors
        </TITLE>

        <STYLE>
            .glow {font-size:40pt; font-weight:bold;
            color:white; position:absolute; cursor:default;
            filter:glow(color=yellow, strength=6, enabled=0);
            behavior:url(glow.htc);}
        </STYLE>
    </HEAD>
        .
        .
        .
```

Now I'll apply the **glow** style to a **<DIV>** element like this:

```
<HTML>
    <HEAD>
        <TITLE>
            Using Behaviors
        </TITLE>

        <STYLE>
            .glow {font-size:40pt; font-weight:bold;
            color:white; position:absolute; cursor:default;
            filter:glow(color=yellow, strength=6, enabled=0);
            behavior:url(glow.htc);}
        </STYLE>
    </HEAD>

    <BODY STYLE="background-color: black">
        <CENTER>
            <H1 STYLE="color: white;">
                Using Behaviors
            </H1>
        </CENTER>
        <DIV class="glow" style="top:100; left:40">
            Behaviors are cool!
        </DIV>
```

```
    </BODY>
</HTML>
```

The next step is to create glow.htc, which makes HTML elements glow when the mouse passes over them. HTCs start with the **<PUBLIC:COMPONENT>** element. To attach this behavior to the **onmouseover** and **onmouseout** events for an event, you use the **<ATTACH>** element. With the **<ATTACH>** element, you can use the XML-style shortcut for a closing tag (we'll learn about this in detail when we discuss XML in Chapters 17 and 18), which just uses a forward slash at the end of the element and avoids the necessity of an additional closing tag. Here's how this works:

```
<PUBLIC:COMPONENT>

    <ATTACH EVENT="onmouseover" FOR="element" HANDLER="showGlow" />
    <ATTACH EVENT="onmouseout" FOR="element" HANDLER="hideGlow" />
        .
        .
        .
```

Now, I've tied the function **showGlow** to the **onmouseover** event of elements that use this behavior and the function **hideGlow** to their **onmouseout** events. To complete the HTC, I just implement those functions like this (note that you can refer to the element the behavior is connected to simply as **element** in the HTC):

```
<PUBLIC:COMPONENT>

    <ATTACH EVENT="onmouseover" FOR="element" HANDLER="showGlow" />
    <ATTACH EVENT="onmouseout" FOR="element" HANDLER="hideGlow" />

    <SCRIPT language="JScript">

        function showGlow()
        {
                element.filters.glow.color = (65536 * 255) + (256 * 255)
                element.filters.glow.enabled = true;
        }

        function hideGlow()
        {
            element.filters.glow.enabled = false;
        }
```

```
    </SCRIPT>
</PUBLIC:COMPONENT>
```

And that's all there is to it. Now the new behavior is connected to the HTML element you specified, and the results appear in Figure 14.3.

Besides attaching behaviors to events, you can also create properties, methods, and custom events with behaviors. I'll do that throughout this chapter. In fact, it's time to turn to the Immediate Solutions section of the chapter now and dig into the details.

Immediate Solutions

Dragging And Dropping

"Drag and drop, drag and drop," the novice programmer says, "all I hear about is drag and drop. So how can I implement it in a Web page?" "There are several ways," you say, "and the simplest involves just setting an element's absolute position to match the mouse."

You can implement dragging and dropping of Web page elements by setting those elements' absolute position when the mouse moves. Because you can't set absolute position in Netscape Navigator after a page has fully loaded, this example is for Internet Explorer only. We worked through the JavaScript for this example in the In Depth section of this chapter, and here's the full page (note that I'm setting the mouse cursor to a hand when it's over a draggable image):

```
<HTML>
    <HEAD>
        <TITLE>
            Drag And Drop
        </TITLE>

        <SCRIPT LANGUAGE="JavaScript">
            var draggingID = null;

            function mouseDownEvent()
            {
                if (event.srcElement.tagName == "IMG"){

                    draggingID = event.srcElement.id

                        if (draggingID == "IMG1"){
                            document.all["IMG1"].style.zIndex = 1
                            document.all["IMG2"].style.zIndex = 0
                        }
                        else {
                            document.all["IMG1"].style.zIndex = 0
                            document.all["IMG2"].style.zIndex = 1
                        }
```

```
                    }
                }

            function mouseMoveEvent()
            {
                if (draggingID != null && event.srcElement.tagName ==
                    "IMG"){
                    document.all[draggingID].style.pixelLeft = event.x -
                        document.all[draggingID].width/2
                    document.all[draggingID].style.pixelTop = event.y -
                        document.all[draggingID].height/2

                    event.returnValue = false
                }
            }

            function mouseUpEvent()
            {
                if (draggingID != null  && event.srcElement.tagName ==
                    "IMG"){
                    document.all[draggingID].style.pixelLeft = event.x -
                        document.all[draggingID].width/2
                    document.all[draggingID].style.pixelTop = event.y -
                        document.all[draggingID].height/2

                    draggingID = null
                    event.returnValue = false
                }
            }

        document.onmousedown=mouseDownEvent
        document.onmousemove=mouseMoveEvent
        document.onmouseup=mouseUpEvent
    </SCRIPT>

</HEAD>

<BODY>
    <CENTER>
        <H1>
            Drag And Drop
        </H1>
    </CENTER>

    <IMG ID="IMG1" SRC="flower.jpg"
```

```
        STYLE="position:absolute; top=50; left=20; width=85; height=130;
        zindex: 0" onmouseover="this.style.cursor = 'hand';"
            onmouseout="this.style.cursor = 'default';">
    <IMG ID="IMG2" SRC="flower3.jpg"
      STYLE="position:absolute; top=50; left=220; width=85; height=130;
        zindex: 0" onmouseover="this.style.cursor = 'hand';"
            onmouseout="this.style.cursor = 'default';">
</BODY>
</HTML>
```

You can see the results of this HTML in Figure 14.1. This certainly implements drag and drop operations in the way most people think of them, allowing you to use the mouse to drag and drop elements in a Web page. However, there's also a more complex version of dragging and dropping that Internet Explorer supports—dragging and dropping data.

Dragging And Dropping Data

You can use the **dataTransfer** object of the **event** object in Internet Explorer to implement drag and drop operations that also transfer data. Here's an example showing how this works. In this case, I'll let the user drag and drop the same image I used in the example in the previous section, but this time I'll add some data to the drag and drop operation.

When the dragging operation starts, the code will call a function named **startDrag**, which contains the **dataTransfer** object's **setData** method to add the text, "The data reached the target!" to the drag operation and the **effectAllowed** property to indicate that the drag and drop operation should copy the item being dragged:

```
function startDrag()
{
    event.dataTransfer.setData("Text",
        "The data reached the target!");
    event.dataTransfer.effectAllowed = "copy"
}
```

Now when users drag the image, they can drag it to another application, such as Microsoft Word or Word Pad, and drop it into that application. To actually retrieve the text associated with the image, however, we'll need to add a little more code. To show how this works, I'll add a **<DIV>** element to the Web page and make it into a *drop target*, giving it the ID **DROPTARGET**:

```
<DIV ID=DROPTARGET
    style="background:cyan; width:300; height:100;">
    Drop the image here!
</DIV>
```

To allow items to be dropped into the **<DIV>** element, I connect that element's **ondrop** event to the function **endDrag**, which looks like this:

```
function endDrag()
{
    event.returnValue = false
    event.dataTransfer.dropEffect = "copy"
    DROPTARGET.innerHTML =
        event.dataTransfer.getData("Text")
}
```

In this case, I'm indicating that the **<DIV>** element can act as a drop target, and by using the **getData** method to get the text associated with the dropped image, display it in the **<DIV>**. When the user drags the image, the mouse cursor will change to a circle with a slash through it unless the cursor is over a drop target, in which case, it'll turn into an arrow with a plus sign (**+**) next to it indicating that you can drop the dragged item there. To indicate that the **<DIV>** element can handle drops, I connect its **ondragenter** and **ondragover** events to the **dragOver** function:

```
function dragOver()
{
    event.returnValue = false
    event.dataTransfer.dropEffect = "copy"
}
```

All that's left to do is connect the **<DIV>** element itself to the functions we've defined, and you do that with the **ondragenter**, **ondrop**, and **ondragover** event attributes like this:

```
<DIV ID=DROPTARGET
    style="background:cyan; width:300; height:100;"
    ondragenter="dragOver()" ondrop="endDrag()"
    ondragover="dragOver()">
    Drop the image here!
</DIV>
```

And that's all we need. Here's the whole page:

```
<HTML>

    <HEAD>
        <TITLE>
            Dragging And Dropping Data
        </TITLE>

        <SCRIPT>

            function startDrag()
            {
                event.dataTransfer.setData("Text",
                    "The data reached the target!");
                event.dataTransfer.effectAllowed = "copy"
            }

            function endDrag()
            {
                event.returnValue = false
                event.dataTransfer.dropEffect = "copy"
                DROPTARGET.innerHTML =
                    event.dataTransfer.getData("Text")
            }

            function dragOver()
            {
                event.returnValue = false
                event.dataTransfer.dropEffect = "copy"
            }

        </SCRIPT>
    </HEAD>

    <BODY>
        <CENTER>
            <H1>
                Dragging And Dropping Data
            </H1>
            <IMG ID=IMG1 SRC="flower.jpg" ondragstart="startDrag()">
            <DIV ID=DROPTARGET
                style="background:cyan; width:300; height:100;"
            ondragenter="dragOver()" ondrop="endDrag()"
                ondragover="dragOver()">
                Drop the image here!
            </DIV>
```

```
            </CENTER>
         </BODY>

</HTML>
```

The results of this HTML after the user has dropped the image into the **<DIV>** element appear in Figure 14.4. As you can see, the **<DIV>** element's text has changed to the data that was dropped—"The data reached the target!". This example is a success; now we're dragging and dropping data.

Figure 14.4   Dragging and dropping data.

Dragging And Dropping Using Layers

"Ugh," says the novice programmer, "I'd like to implement dragging and dropping, but I'm using Netscape Navigator and can't use absolute positioning after the page has loaded. What can I do?" "Well," you say, "you can use layers instead." "Hm," says the NP, "that's an idea."

You can indeed use layers to implement dragging and dropping in Netscape Navigator. To show how this works, I'll let users drag around the same image they dragged around in the previous two sections. I start by creating a layer in JavaScript when the page first loads, place the image in that layer, assign that layer to a variable, **draglayer**, and make sure that layer captures the **mousedown** event with the **captureEvents** method. I also connect the **mousedown** event to the function **mouseDown**:

```
var draglayer

document.write("<layer name=layer1 left=100 top=100>" +
    "<IMG SRC='flower.jpg'></layer>")
draglayer=document.layers.layer1
draglayer.captureEvents(Event.MOUSEDOWN);
draglayer.onmousedown=mouseDown

    .
    .
    .
```

In the **mouseDown** function, I capture the **mousemove** and **mouseup** events and connect the functions **mouseDrag** and **mouseUp** functions to them:

```
function mouseDown(e)
{
    draglayer.offX=e.pageX-draglayer.pageX
    draglayer.offY=e.pageY-draglayer.pageY
    window.captureEvents(Event.MOUSEMOVE|Event.MOUSEUP)
    window.onmousemove=mouseDrag
    window.onmouseup=mouseUp
    return false
}
```

In the **mouseDrag** function, called when the user wants to drag the layer, I set the position of the dragged layer to the new mouse position:

```
function mouseDrag(e)
{
    draglayer.pageX=e.pageX-draglayer.offX
    draglayer.pageY=e.pageY-draglayer.offY
    return false
}
```

Finally, in the **mouseUp** function, all I have to do is release the **mousemove** and **mouseup** events like this:

```
function mouseUp ()
{
    window.releaseEvents(Event.MOUSEMOVE | Event.MOUSEUP)
    return false
}
```

And that's it. Here's the full page:

```
<HTML>
    <HEAD>
        <TITLE>
            Drag And Drop With Layers
        </TITLE>

        <SCRIPT LANGUAGE="JavaScript">

            var draglayer

            document.write("<layer name=layer1 left=100 top=100>" +
                "<IMG SRC='flower.jpg'></layer>")
            draglayer=document.layers.layer1
            draglayer.captureEvents(Event.MOUSEDOWN);
            draglayer.onmousedown=mouseDown

            function mouseDown(e)
            {
                draglayer.offX=e.pageX-draglayer.pageX
                draglayer.offY=e.pageY-draglayer.pageY
                window.captureEvents(Event.MOUSEMOVE|Event.MOUSEUP)
                window.onmousemove=mouseDrag
                window.onmouseup=mouseUp
                return false
            }

            function mouseDrag(e)
            {
                draglayer.pageX=e.pageX-draglayer.offX
                draglayer.pageY=e.pageY-draglayer.offY
                return false
            }

            function mouseUp ()
            {
                window.releaseEvents(Event.MOUSEMOVE | Event.MOUSEUP)
                return false
            }
        </SCRIPT>
    </HEAD>

    <BODY>
        <CENTER>
```

```
        <H1>
            Drag And Drop With Layers
        </H1>
    </CENTER>
  </BODY>
</HTML>
```

You can see the results of this HTML in Figure 14.5 where I'm dragging around the image using layers in Netscape Navigator. As you can see, using these techniques you can indeed support dragging and dropping in Netscape Navigator.

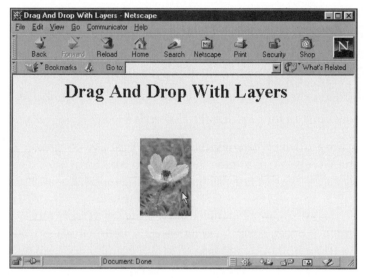

Figure 14.5   Dragging and dropping using layers.

Using The MSHTML Data Source Control

The big boss appears and says, "All of our agents in the field need the latest pricing information. What's the easiest way of getting it to them?" "Well," you say, "we can put a database on the Web server and display its data in Web pages. When do you need it?" "Is it done yet?" the BB asks.

As discussed in the In Depth section of this chapter, you can use DSOs in Internet Explorer (as of version 4) to connect to databases, and you can bind HTML elements to DSOs to display the data in the database.

The first DSO I'll take a look at is the MSHTML data source control. Using this control as a DSO is easy. You just use the **<OBJECT>** element in a Web page, giving the MSHTML data source control the ID you want to use to refer to it in the rest of the page, designate the height and width as 0, and set the tag's **DATA** attribute to the HTML page you want to use as the actual source of the data, like this:

```
<OBJECT ID="dsoEmployees" DATA="employee.htm" HEIGHT=0 WIDTH=0>
</OBJECT>
```

The following list contains the events of this DSO:

- **onDataAvailable**—Occurs each time a batch of data is downloaded.

- **onDatasetChanged**—Occurs when the data set was changed.

- **onDatasetComplete**—Occurs when the data is downloaded and ready for use.

- **onReadyStateChange**—Occurs when the **ReadyState** property changes.

- **onRowEnter**—Occurs when the a new record becomes the current one.

- **onRowExit**—Occurs just before exiting the current record.

To use the MSHTML DSO, I'll start by constructing the database. It turns out that you can construct the Web page that holds the data in a free-form way, using all kinds of tags, as long as the type of tag you use has both an opening and closing tag (for example, **<H1>** and **</H1>**) as well as an **ID** attribute. The MSHTML control will open and read through the data page, treating the **ID** attribute values as fields and successive groupings of fields as records. You can then treat the values you set for the **ID** attributes as fields in a database and bind them to other HTML tags using the **DATAFLD** attribute.

Here's an example of setting up a small database of employee records that we saw in the In Depth section of this chapter. In this case, I'm using the **<SPAN>** element to define fields in records. Note also that the MSHTML control ignores tags that do not have their **ID** attribute set, so you can add other tags to the page as you like:

```
<HTML>
    <HEAD>
        <TITLE>
            Data Page
        </TITLE>
    </HEAD>

    <BODY>
        <H1>
            This page holds data.
```

```
        </H1>
        Name: <SPAN ID="NAME">Tony</SPAN><BR>
        ID: <SPAN ID="ID">1234</SPAN><BR>
        Hire Date: <SPAN ID="HIRE_DATE">
            4-1-2001</SPAN><BR>
        Department: <SPAN ID="DEPARTMENT">
            Shipping</SPAN><BR>
        Title: <SPAN ID="TITLE">Packer</SPAN><BR>
        Name: <SPAN ID="NAME">Ed</SPAN><BR>
        ID: <SPAN ID="ID">1235</SPAN><BR>
        Hire Date: <SPAN ID="HIRE_DATE">
            4-1-2001</SPAN><BR>
        Department: <SPAN ID="DEPARTMENT">
            Programming</SPAN><BR>
        Title: <SPAN ID="TITLE">Programmer</SPAN><BR>
        Name: <SPAN ID="NAME">Francis</SPAN><BR>
        ID: <SPAN ID="ID">1236</SPAN><BR>
        Hire Date: <SPAN ID="HIRE_DATE">
            4-1-2001</SPAN><BR>
        Department: <SPAN ID="DEPARTMENT">
            Shipping</SPAN><BR>
        Title: <SPAN ID="TITLE">Packer</SPAN><BR>
        Name: <SPAN ID="NAME">Linda</SPAN><BR>
        ID: <SPAN ID="ID">1237</SPAN><BR>
        Hire Date: <SPAN ID="HIRE_DATE">
            4-1-2001</SPAN><BR>
        Department: <SPAN ID="DEPARTMENT">
            Shipping</SPAN><BR>
        Title: <SPAN ID="TITLE">Packer</SPAN><BR>
        Name: <SPAN ID="NAME">Louise</SPAN><BR>
        ID: <SPAN ID="ID">1238</SPAN><BR>
        Hire Date: <SPAN ID="HIRE_DATE">
            4-1-2001</SPAN><BR>
        Department: <SPAN ID="DEPARTMENT">
            Shipping</SPAN><BR>
        Title: <SPAN ID="TITLE">Packer</SPAN><BR>
        </BODY>
</HTML>
```

I'll call this database page employee.htm. Now that we have an HTML database, I'll put it to work with the MSHTML control. Because the MSHTML control is built into Internet Explorer, we can put it to work without any additional preparation, connecting it to the employee.htm data page. I'll start by using the **<OBJECT>** element to point the MSHTML control at the data page, employee.htm, and name this new DSO **dsoEmployees**:

```
<HTML>
    <HEAD>
        <TITLE>
            Using The MSHTML Control
        </TITLE>
    </HEAD>

    <BODY>

        <CENTER>
            <H1>
                Using The MSHTML Control
            </H1>

            <OBJECT ID="dsoEmployees" DATA="employee.htm" HEIGHT=0 WIDTH=0>
            </OBJECT>
            .
            .
            .
```

To display the data in the database, I can connect text fields to the new DSO by setting their **DATASRC** attribute to **#dsoEmployees** and their **DATAFLD** attributes to the field I want to display (such as **NAME** or **ID**):

```
<HTML>
    <HEAD>
        <TITLE>
            Using The MSHTML Control
        </TITLE>
    </HEAD>

    <BODY>

        <CENTER>
            <H1>
                Using The MSHTML Control
            </H1>

            <OBJECT ID="dsoEmployees" DATA="employee.htm" HEIGHT=0 WIDTH=0>
            </OBJECT>

            Name: <INPUT TYPE="TEXT" DATASRC="#dsoEmployees"
                DATAFLD="NAME" SIZE=10>
            <P>
            ID: <INPUT TYPE="TEXT" DATASRC="#dsoEmployees"
```

```
            DATAFLD="ID" SIZE=5>
    <P>
    Hire date: <SPAN DATASRC="#dsoEmployees"
            DATAFLD="HIRE_DATE"></SPAN>
    <P>
    Title: <SPAN DATASRC="#dsoEmployees" DATAFLD="TITLE">
    </SPAN>
    <P>
    Department: <SELECT DATASRC="#dsoEmployees"
            DATAFLD="DEPARTMENT" SIZE=1>
            <OPTION VALUE="Shipping">Shipping
            <OPTION VALUE="Programming">Programming
            <OPTION VALUE="Editing">Editing
            <OPTION VALUE="Writing">Writing
    </SELECT>
    <P>
        .
        .
        .
```

Finally, as discussed in the In Depth section of this chapter, I'll use the **MoveFirst**, **MoveLast**, **MoveNext**, and **MovePrevious** methods of the DSO's **Recordset** object to let the user navigate through the record set. These methods are methods of the DSO's **Recordset** object. I can also check the **Recordset** object's **BOF** (Beginning Of File) and **EOF** (End Of File) properties to see if we've reached the beginning or end of the record set, respectively:

```
<HTML>
    <HEAD>
        <TITLE>
            Using The MSHTML Control
        </TITLE>
    </HEAD>

    <BODY>

        <CENTER>
            <H1>
                Using The MSHTML Control
            </H1>

            <OBJECT ID="dsoEmployees" DATA="employee.htm" HEIGHT=0 WIDTH=0>
            </OBJECT>

            Name: <INPUT TYPE="TEXT" DATASRC="#dsoEmployees"
```

```
                    DATAFLD="NAME" SIZE=10>
            <P>
            ID: <INPUT TYPE="TEXT" DATASRC="#dsoEmployees"
                DATAFLD="ID" SIZE=5>
            <P>
            Hire date: <SPAN DATASRC="#dsoEmployees"
                DATAFLD="HIRE_DATE"></SPAN>
            <P>
            Title: <SPAN DATASRC="#dsoEmployees" DATAFLD="TITLE">
            </SPAN>
            <P>
            Department: <SELECT DATASRC="#dsoEmployees"
                DATAFLD="DEPARTMENT" SIZE=1>
                <OPTION VALUE="Shipping">Shipping
                <OPTION VALUE="Programming">Programming
                <OPTION VALUE="Editing">Editing
                <OPTION VALUE="Writing">Writing
            </SELECT>
            <P>

            <BUTTON ONCLICK=
                "dsoEmployees.recordset.MoveFirst()" >&lt;&lt;</BUTTON>
            <BUTTON ONCLICK="if (!dsoEmployees.recordset.BOF)
                dsoEmployees.recordset.MovePrevious()" >&lt;</BUTTON>
            <BUTTON ONCLICK="if (!dsoEmployees.recordset.EOF)
                dsoEmployees.recordset.MoveNext()" >&gt;</BUTTON>
            <BUTTON ONCLICK=
                "dsoEmployees.recordset.MoveLast()">&gt;&gt;</BUTTON>
        </CENTER>
    </BODY>
</HTML>
```

And that's it. You can see the results of this HTML in Figure 14.2. Note that the user can navigate through the database with the buttons in that Web page, and that the text fields in the page display the data from each record.

Besides using buttons to navigate through the record set, you can also display all the data in a record set at once using tables, and I'll take a look at this in the next section.

Creating Tables With The MSHTML Control

The big boss appears and says, "I don't like the way you've set up the data in the company's Web page. I want to see it all at once." "No problem," you say, "I'll just bind a DSO to a table." The BB asks, "Huh?"

To show how to display a whole database table at once, I'll create a new page that will use the MSHTML control to display the data in employee.htm in an HTML table. To do this, I just include the MSHTML DSO as in the previous section. Next, I create a **<TABLE>** element, setting its **DATASRC** attribute to the DSO, setting the **DATAFLD** attribute of each cell to the corresponding field in the database, and setting the **DATAFORMATAS** attribute of each cell to HTML like this:

```
<HTML>
    <HEAD>
        <TITLE>
            Using The MSHTML Control And Tables
        </TITLE>
    </HEAD>

    <BODY>

        <CENTER>
            <H1>
                Using The MSHTML Control And Tables
            </H1>

            <OBJECT ID="dsoEmployees" DATA="employee.htm"
                HEIGHT=0 WIDTH=0></OBJECT>


            <TABLE DATASRC="#dsoEmployees" CELLSPACING=10>
                <THEAD>
                    <TR>
                        <TH>Name</TH>
                        <TH>ID</TH>
                        <TH>Hire Date</TH>
                        <TH>Department</TH>
                    </TR>
                </THEAD>
                <TBODY>
                    <TR>
                    <TD><SPAN DATAFLD="NAME"
                        DATAFORMATAS="HTML"></SPAN></TD>
                    <TD><SPAN DATAFLD="ID" DATAFORMATAS="HTML"></SPAN></TD>
                    <TD><SPAN DATAFLD="HIRE_DATE"
                        DATAFORMATAS="HTML"></SPAN></TD>
                    <TD><SPAN DATAFLD="DEPARTMENT"
                        DATAFORMATAS="HTML"></SPAN></TD>
                    </TR>
                </TBODY>
            </TABLE>
```

```
        </CENTER>
      </BODY>
   </HTML>
```

And that's it, the table will be filled with data from the database automatically; the results appear in Figure 14.6. As you can see in the figure, using HTML tables like this makes life very easy—all the data in the record set is displayed at once for viewing.

Besides the MSHTML control, another control comes with Internet Explorer, and I'll take a look at it in the next section.

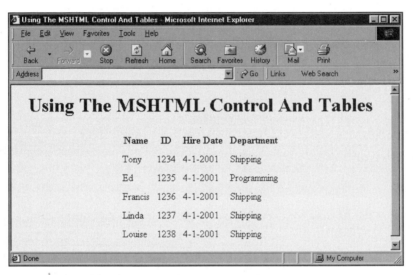

Figure 14.6   Using the MSHTML control to display a table of data.

Using The Tabular Data Control

"I understand that you can use the MSHTML data source control to bind databases to HTML elements," the novice programmer says, "but my database isn't in HTML format, it's in text format. Guess I'll have to spend a few days converting it." "Not at all," you say, "you can use the Tabular Data Control." "The what?" the NP asks.

The MSHTML control is great when you want to work with data stored in a Web page, but you can also work with data stored in text files using the Tabular Data Control ([TDC], but at times it is incorrectly called the Text Data Control). You can use this control to work with delimited text files (that is, text files where the fields are delimited with a certain character, such as commas or semicolons; a common format used for interchange of data between database formats is called comma separated value [CSV] format).

Here's how you place the TDC in a Web page using the **<OBJECT>** element (the TDC is registered on your system when you install Internet Explorer):

```
<OBJECT
    CLASSID="clsid:333C7BC4-460F-11D0-BC04-0080C7055A83"
    ID=dsoEmployees WIDTH=0 HEIGHT=0>
    <PARAM NAME="DataURL" VALUE="employees.csv">
</OBJECT>
```

Note that I'm using an element that we'll see in Chapter 16, the **<PARAM>** element. This element passes parameter data to Web page objects and applets as we saw in Chapter 8. In this case, the **DataURL** parameter is a property specific to the TDC; you use this property to specify the data that should get loaded along with the page. The following list contains the names of the **<PARAM>** elements you can use with the TDC:

- **AppendData**—Determines if new data is appended or replaces existing data.
- **CaseSensitive**—Indicates if the TDC distinguishes characters in the data set based upon their case.
- **CharSet**—Identifies the character set of the data file.
- **DataURL**—Specifies the location of the data file.
- **EscapeChar**—Specifies the character used to escape special characters.
- **FieldDelim**—Specifies the character used to mark the end of data fields.
- **Filter**—Specifies the criteria to use for filtering the data.
- **Language**—Specifies the language of the data file including numerical and date formats.
- **Recordset**—Retrieves the record set if the object is a data provider.
- **RowDelim**—Specifies the character used to mark the end of each row.
- **Sort**—Identifies the columns to be sorted in ascending or descending sort order.
- **TextQualifier**—Specifies the optional character that surrounds a field.
- **UseHeader**—Specifies whether the first line of the data file contains header information.

The TDC has one method called **Reset**, which causes the control to filter or sort its data based on new settings.

14. Dynamic HTML: Drag And Drop, Data Binding, And Behaviors

The TDC also supports these events:

- **onDataAvailable**—Occurs each time a batch of data is downloaded.

- **onDatasetChanged**—Occurs when the data set was changed.

- **onDatasetComplete**—Occurs when the data is downloaded and ready for use.

- **onReadyStateChange**—Occurs when the **ReadyState** property changes.

- **onRowEnter**—Occurs when the new record becomes the current one.

- **onRowExit**—Occurs just before exiting the current record.

I'll take a look at an example now to make this more concrete. In this case, I'll store the employee data from employee.htm, which we saw in the In Depth section of this chapter, in a text file, employee.txt. Note the format here; I start with a header line naming each field and giving its type (**String**, **Int** for integer, or **Date** for a date), then supply one line of text for each record:

```
NAME:String;ID:Int;HIRE_DATE:Date;DEPARTMENT:String;TITLE:String
Tony;1234;4-1-2001;Shipping;Packer
Ed;1235;4-1-2001;Programming;Programmer
Francis;1236;4-1-2001;Shipping;Packer
Linda;1237;4-1-2001;Shipping;Packer
Louise;1238;4-1-2001;Shipping;Packer
```

Now I can use the TDC to read this database, similar to the way I used the MSHTML control earlier in this chapter (see the Immediate Solutions section "Using The MSHTML Data Source Control")—the only difference is that I have to use the **<OBJECT>** element differently. In this case, I'll use the parameter **DataURL** to indicate the URL of the database text file, the parameter **FieldDelim** to indicate the delimited character between fields in the database (in this case a semicolon [**;**]), the parameter **UseHeader** to indicate that the database file has a one-line header, and the parameter **Sort** to indicate that the database should be sorted:

```
<HTML>
    <HEAD>
        <TITLE>
            Using The Tabular Data Control
        </TITLE>
    </HEAD>

    <BODY>
        <CENTER>
```

```
<H1>
    Using the Tabular Data Control
</H1>

<OBJECT CLASSID="clsid:333C7BC4-460F-11D0-BC04-0080C7055A83"
    ID="dsoEmployees" WIDTH=0 HEIGHT=0>
    <PARAM NAME="DataURL" VALUE="employee.txt">
    <PARAM NAME="FieldDelim" VALUE=";">
    <PARAM NAME="UseHeader" VALUE="True">
    <PARAM NAME="Sort" VALUE="ID">
</OBJECT>

Name: <INPUT TYPE="TEXT" DATASRC="#dsoEmployees"
    DATAFLD="NAME" SIZE=10><P>
ID: <INPUT TYPE="TEXT" DATASRC="#dsoEmployees"
    DATAFLD="ID" SIZE=5><P>
Department: <SELECT DATASRC="#dsoEmployees"
    DATAFLD="DEPARTMENT" SIZE=1>

<OPTION VALUE="Shipping">Shipping
<OPTION VALUE="Programming">Programming
<OPTION VALUE="Editing">Editing
<OPTION VALUE="Writing">Writing
</SELECT><P>

Hire date: <SPAN DATASRC="#dsoEmployees"
    DATAFLD="HIRE_DATE"></SPAN><P>
Title: <SPAN DATASRC="#dsoEmployees" DATAFLD="TITLE"></SPAN><P>

<BUTTON ONCLICK="dsoEmployees.recordset.MoveFirst()" >
    &lt;&lt;
</BUTTON>
<BUTTON ONCLICK="if (!dsoEmployees.recordset.BOF)
    dsoEmployees.recordset.MovePrevious()" >
    &lt;
</BUTTON>
<BUTTON ONCLICK="if (!dsoEmployees.recordset.EOF)
    dsoEmployees.recordset.MoveNext()" >
    &gt;
</BUTTON>
<BUTTON ONCLICK="dsoEmployees.recordset.MoveLast()">
    &gt;&gt;
</BUTTON>
    </CENTER>
  </BODY>
</HTML>
```

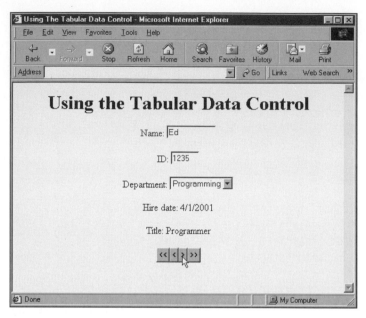

Figure 14.7 Using the TDC control to navigate through data.

You can see the results in Figure 14.7. As with the MSHTML control, the user can navigate through the record set using the buttons that appear in the page. In fact, you can also bind the TDC to tables—see the next section.

Creating Tables With TDC

In the previous section, we saw how to connect the TDC to HTML elements like text fields in a Web page. You can also use the TDC to present data in a table. To do this, you just bind the TDC to a table; see the Immediate Solutions section "Creating Tables With The MSHTML Control" earlier in this chapter. Here's an example showing how this works; I just add a TDC to a Web page and bind it to a table like this:

```
<HTML>
    <HEAD>
        <TITLE>
            Using the Tabular Data Control With Tables
        </TITLE>
    </HEAD>
```

```
<BODY>
    <CENTER>
        <H1>
            Using the Tabular Data Control With Tables
        </H1>

        <OBJECT CLASSID="clsid:333C7BC4-460F-11D0-BC04-0080C7055A83"
            ID="dsoEmployees" WIDTH=0 HEIGHT=0>
            <PARAM NAME="DataURL" VALUE="employee.txt">
            <PARAM NAME="FieldDelim" VALUE=";">
            <PARAM NAME="UseHeader" VALUE="True">
            <PARAM NAME="Sort" VALUE="ID">
        </OBJECT>

        <TABLE DATASRC="#dsoEmployees" CELLSPACING=10>
            <THEAD>
                <TR>
                    <TH>Name</TH>
                    <TH>ID</TH>
                    <TH>Hire Date</TH>
                    <TH>Department</IH>
                </TR>
            </THEAD>

            <TBODY>
                <TR>
                    <TD><SPAN DATAFLD="NAME" DATAFORMATAS="HTML">
                        </SPAN></TD>
                    <TD><SPAN DATAFLD="ID" DATAFORMATAS="HTML">
                        </SPAN></TD>
                    <TD><SPAN DATAFLD="HIRE_DATE"
                        DATAFORMATAS="HTML">
                        </SPAN></TD>
                    <TD><SPAN DATAFLD="DEPARTMENT"
                        DATAFORMATAS="HTML"></SPAN></TD>
                </TR>
            </TBODY>
        </TABLE>
    </CENTER>
</BODY>
</HTML>
```

That's all it takes. The results appear in Figure 14.8. As you can see, you can bind the TDC to tables just as easily as binding tables to the MSHTML control.

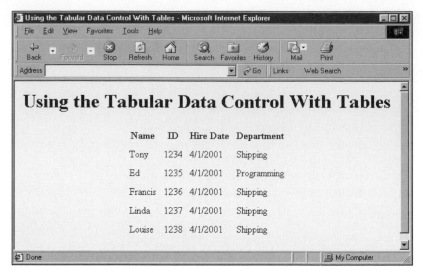

Figure 14.8   Using the TDC control to display a table of data.

Using The XML Data Source Control

"Uh oh," says the novice programmer, "now the big boss wants me to format my database in XML of all things. How can I display it in a browser?" "Well," you say, "one way is to use the XML DSO and data binding." "That will work?" asks the NP hopefully.

As we'll see in Chapters 17 and 18, you can use XML to describe data in a structured way on the Web. XML DSOs have an advantage over other DSOs because you can use XML to structure your data many levels deep. As of Internet Explorer 4, there's an applet that comes with the browser, which lets you create an XML DSO like this:

```
<APPLET
    CODE="com.ms.xml.dso.XMLDSO.class"
    ID="dsoEmployees"
    WIDTH="0"
    HEIGHT="0"
    MAYSCRIPT="true">
    <PARAM NAME="URL" VALUE="employee.xml">
</APPLET>
```

In this case, you pass the XML page that holds the data using the **URL** parameter. The XML data source control supports the usual DSO events:

- **onDataAvailable**—Fires each time a batch of data is downloaded.

- **onDatasetChanged**—Fires when the data set was changed.

- **onDatasetComplete**—Fires when the data is downloaded and ready for use.

- **onReadyStateChange**—Fires when the **ReadyState** property changes.

- **onRowEnter**—Fires when the a new record becomes the current one.

- **onRowExit**—Fires just before exiting the current record.

Internet Explorer 5 goes one step further and integrates XML support directly by using XML *data islands*. You can use XML data islands to embed data in XML format in an HTML page. We'll learn more about data islands in Chapters 17 and 18; as for the XML DSO on the other hand, I'll take a look at it here. In this case, I'll translate the employee database, employee.htm, which we saw in the In Depth section of this chapter, into an XML page, employee.xml. I'll start by giving the XML version:

```
<?xml version="1.0"?>
    .
    .
    .
```

Next, I'll create a new XML tag named **<EMPLOYEES>** (you define your own tags in XML; in more involved applications, you can also specify how those headers are to work, what tags can nest in other tags, and so on):

```
<?xml version="1.0"?>
<EMPLOYEES>
    .
    .
    .
```

I'll give each employee's record a **NAME**, **ID**, **HIRE_DATE**, **DEPARTMENT**, and **TITLE** element like this:

```
<?xml version="1.0"?>
<EMPLOYEES>
    <ITEM>
        <NAME>Tony</NAME>
        <ID>1234</ID>
        <HIRE_DATE>4-1-2001</HIRE_DATE>
        <DEPARTMENT>Shipping</DEPARTMENT>
        <TITLE>Packer</TITLE>
    </ITEM>
```

```
        <ITEM>
            <NAME>Ed</NAME>
            <ID>1235</ID>
            <HIRE_DATE>4-1-2001</HIRE_DATE>
            <DEPARTMENT>Programming</DEPARTMENT>
            <TITLE>Programmer</TITLE>
        </ITEM>
        <ITEM>
            <NAME>Francis</NAME>
            <ID>1236</ID>
            <HIRE_DATE>4-1-2001</HIRE_DATE>
            <DEPARTMENT>Shipping</DEPARTMENT>
            <TITLE>Packer</TITLE>
        </ITEM>
        <ITEM>
            <NAME>Linda</NAME>
            <ID>1237</ID>
            <HIRE_DATE>4-1-2001</HIRE_DATE>
            <DEPARTMENT>Shipping</DEPARTMENT>
        <TITLE>Packer</TITLE>
        </ITEM>
        <ITEM>
            <NAME>Louise</NAME>
            <ID>1238</ID>
            <HIRE_DATE>4-1-2001</HIRE_DATE>
            <DEPARTMENT>Shipping</DEPARTMENT>
            <TITLE>Packer</TITLE>
        </ITEM>
    </EMPLOYEES>
```

That completes employee.xml. It's time to put this XML file to work. In this example, I'll use the XML data source control to bind to the employee.xml file, presenting the user with a set of navigation buttons. I start by adding the XML data source control to a Web page:

```
<HTML>
    <HEAD>
        <TITLE>
            Using the XML Data Source Control
        </TITLE>
    </HEAD>

    <BODY>
        <CENTER>
            <H1>
```

```
              Using the XML Data Source Control
          </H1>

          <APPLET CODE="com.ms.xml.dso.XMLDSO.class"
              ID="dsoEmployees" WIDTH=0 HEIGHT=0 MAYSCRIPT=true>
              <PARAM NAME="URL" VALUE="employee.xml">
          </APPLET>
              .
              .
              .
```

Then I bind this DSO to HTML elements as we've done before in this chapter (see the Immediate Solutions section "Using The MSHTML Data Source Control"):

```
<HTML>
    <HEAD>
        <TITLE>
            Using the XML Data Source Control
        </TITLE>
    </HEAD>

    <BODY>
        <CENTER>
            <H1>
                Using the XML Data Source Control
            </H1>

            <APPLET CODE="com.ms.xml.dso.XMLDSO.class"
                ID="dsoEmployees" WIDTH=0 HEIGHT=0 MAYSCRIPT=true>
                <PARAM NAME="URL" VALUE="employee.xml">
            </APPLET>

        Name: <INPUT TYPE="TEXT" DATASRC="#dsoEmployees"
            DATAFLD="NAME" SIZE=10><P>
        ID: <INPUT TYPE="TEXT" DATASRC="#dsoEmployees"
            DATAFLD="ID" SIZE=5><P>
        Department: <SELECT DATASRC="#dsoEmployees"
            DATAFLD="DEPARTMENT" SIZE=1>
            <OPTION VALUE="Shipping">Shipping
            <OPTION VALUE="Programming">Programming
            <OPTION VALUE="Editing">Editing
            <OPTION VALUE="Writing">Writing
        </SELECT><P>

        Hire date: <SPAN DATASRC="#dsoEmployees"
```

```
                        DATAFLD="HIRE_DATE"></SPAN><P>
            Title: <SPAN DATASRC="#dsoEmployees" DATAFLD="TITLE"></SPAN><P>

            <BUTTON ONCLICK="dsoEmployees.recordset.MoveFirst()" >
                &lt;&lt;
            </BUTTON>
            <BUTTON ONCLICK="if (!dsoEmployees.recordset.BOF)
                dsoEmployees.recordset.MovePrevious()" >
                &lt;
            </BUTTON>
            <BUTTON ONCLICK="if (!dsoEmployees.recordset.EOF)
                dsoEmployees.recordset.MoveNext()" >
                &gt;
            </BUTTON>
            <BUTTON ONCLICK="dsoEmployees.recordset.MoveLast()">
                &gt;&gt;
            </BUTTON>

        </CENTER>

    </BODY>
</HTML>
```

That's all it takes; the results appear in Figure 14.9. As you can see in the figure, the XML data source control can function just like other DSOs. You can also connect the XML DSO to HTML tables—see the next section for the details.

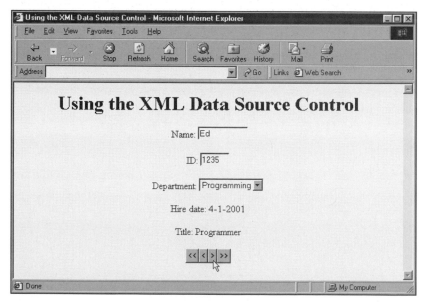

Figure 14.9   Using the XML data source control to navigate through data.

Creating Tables With The XML Data Source Control

In the previous section, we saw that you can use the XML data source control with buttons to navigate through a record set. You can also use the XML data source control with tables, binding it to HTML tables as we've done already in this chapter (see the Immediate Solutions section "Creating Tables With The MSHTML Control"). Here's an example showing how this works:

```
<HTML>
    <HEAD>
        <TITLE>
            Using the XML Data Source Control With Tables
        </TITLE>
    </HEAD>

    <BODY>
        <CENTER>
            <H1>
                Using the XML Data Source Control With Tables
            </H1>

            <APPLET CODE="com.ms.xml.dso.XMLDSO.class"
                ID="dsoEmployees" WIDTH=0 HEIGHT=0 MAYSCRIPT=true>
                <PARAM NAME="URL" VALUE="employee.xml">
            </APPLET>

            <TABLE DATASRC="#dsoEmployees" CELLSPACING=10>
                <THEAD>
                    <TR>
                        <TH>Name</TH>
                        <TH>ID</TH>
                        <TH>Hire Date</TH>
                        <TH>Department</TH>
                    </TR>
                </THEAD>

                <TBODY>
                    <TR>
                        <TD><SPAN DATAFLD="NAME" DATAFORMATAS="HTML">
                            </SPAN></TD>
                        <TD><SPAN DATAFLD="ID" DATAFORMATAS="HTML">
                            </SPAN></TD>
                        <TD><SPAN DATAFLD="HIRE_DATE"
                            DATAFORMATAS="HTML">
```

```
                                </SPAN></TD>
                        <TD><SPAN DATAFLD="DEPARTMENT"
                            DATAFORMATAS="HTML"></SPAN></TD>
                    </TR>
                </TBODY>
            </TABLE>
        </CENTER>
    </BODY>
</HTML>
```

The results of this HTML appear in Figure 14.10. As you can see in the figure, you can use the XML data source control to create and populate HTML tables with data.

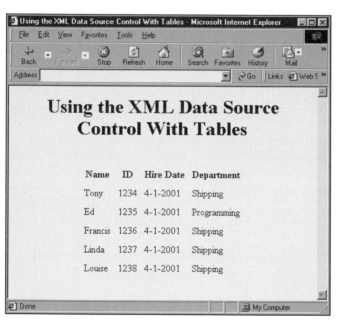

Figure 14.10   Using the XML data source control to display a table of data.

Using The RDS Control

The big boss appears, agitated, and says, "Our competitors are using RDS on their Web site. What is that?" "It's a way of accessing databases on Web sites using Microsoft SQL Server and other database programs." "We need it," the BB says, "add it to our server right away."

You can use the RDS data control to connect to a database application on a Web server, and then bind tags in the Web page to that data control's internal record set. This record set is a special kind of simplified Microsoft ActiveX Data Object (ADO) record set, called an ADO Reduced (ADOR) record set. Here's how you use the RDS data control in a Web page:

```
<OBJECT
    CLASSID="clsid:BD96C556-65A3-11D0-983A-00C04FC29E33"
    ID="dsoRDSControl">
    <PARAM NAME="Connect" VALUE="connection string">
    <PARAM NAME="Server" VALUE="http://server">
    <PARAM NAME="SQL" VALUE="SQL text">
</OBJECT>
```

To use the RDS data control, you need to set only the **SQL**, **Connect**, and **Server** properties using **<PARAM>** elements (which we first saw in Chapter 8), which will automatically create a client-side record set. Usually, you will bind HTML elements to an RDS data control, and then add, edit, and delete records in the client-side record set. After you update the client-side data, you can save the new data to the database by using the control's **SubmitChanges** method.

The RDS control is more complex than the other DSOs we've seen in this chapter. You use the properties of the RDS data control in the following list to configure that control:

- **Connect**—Holds the ADO connection string that you'd use to connect to the database if your application were running on the server.

- **ExecuteOptions**—Indicates whether or not asynchronous execution is enabled. You can set this property to one of these values: **adcExecSync = 1** or **adcExecAsync = 2** (default).

- **FetchOptions**—Indicates the type of asynchronous data fetches and can be one of these values: **adcFetchUpFront = 1**, **adcFetchBackground = 2**, or **adcFetchAsync = 3** (default).

- **FilterColumn**—Specifies the column on which to evaluate the filter criteria. You set this property to a string holding the name of the column on which to filter; you set the actual filtering criterion with the **FilterCriterion** property. To perform the filtering operation, you call the **Reset** method.

- **FilterCriterion**—Specifies the operator to use for a filter; can be **<**, **<=**, **>**, **>=**, **=**, or **<>**.

- **FilterValue**—Sets the data value with which to filter records. You use this property with the **FilterColumn** and **FilterCriterion** properties. To perform the filtering operation, you call the **Reset** method.

- **InternetTimeout**—Holds the number of milliseconds to wait before a request times out.

- **ReadyState**—Holds the progress of the control as it fetches data into its **Recordset** object. Possible values: **adcReadyStateLoaded = 2**, **adcReadyStateInteractive = 3**, **adcReadyStateComplete = 4**. You use the **onReadyStateChange** event method to monitor changes in the **ReadyStateChange** property during an asynchronous query operation.

- **Recordset** and **SourceRecordset**—**Recordset** holds the RDS data control's internal ADOR record set object that it has fetched from the Web. You can set the **SourceRecordset** property to set the record set the control will use. The **Recordset** property is read-only and the **SourceRecordset** property is write-only.

- **Server**—Sets the name of the server you want to use with the RDS data control. The following are some of the ways you can set this property: **<PARAM NAME="Server" VALUE="http://servername">**, **<PARAM NAME="Server" VALUE="http://servername:port">**, or **<PARAM NAME="Server" VALUE="https://servername">**.

- **SortColumn**—Sets the name of the column you want to use for sorting a record set.

- **SortDirection**—Determines if sorts are made in ascending or descending order. The following are the settings for this property: **True** sorts in ascending order, **False** sorts in descending order. To actually perform the sort, you call the **Reset** method.

- **SQL**—Sets the SQL query string used to retrieve the **Recordset** object. This is the actual SQL that the database system on the server will execute.

- **URL**—Refers to the associated URL.

That completes the properties of the RDS data control; it's time to take a look at its methods:

- **Cancel**—Cancels the current asynchronous execution or fetch operation. You use it without any parameters like this: **RDSDataControl.Cancel**.

- **CancelUpdate**—Discards all the pending changes in its **Recordset** object, which means it restores the values since the last **Refresh** method call. This method takes no parameters.

- **CreateRecordset**—Creates a new empty, disconnected **Recordset** object in the RDS data control.

- **MoveFirst**, **MoveLast**, **MoveNext**, and **MovePrevious**—Move to the first, last, next, or previous record in the current record set; they take no parameters.

- **Refresh**—Requeries the data source given by the **Connect** property and updates the **Recordset** object in the RDS data control. This method takes no parameters.

- **Reset**—Executes a sort or filter operator on a record set based on the specified sorting and filtering properties. Here's how you use this method: **RDSDataControl.Reset** *value*. The *value* parameter is **true** (the default) if you want to filter the current "filtered" record set; **false** means that you want to filter the original data.

- **SubmitChanges**—Submits any pending changes of the locally cached updatable **Recordset** object to the data source specified in the **Connect** property. This method takes no parameters.

That completes the RDS data control's methods; I'll take a look at the control's events next:

- **onDataAvailable**—Occurs each time a batch of data is downloaded.

- **onDatasetChanged**—Occurs when the data set was changed.

- **onDatasetComplete**—Occurs when the data is downloaded and ready for use.

- **onError**—Occurs when an error occurs during some operation.

- **onReadyStateChange**—Occurs when the value of the **ReadyState** property changes. You can add code to this event handler when you want to watch the progress of asynchronous operations.

- **onRowEnter**—Occurs when a new record becomes the current one.

- **onRowExit**—Occurs just before exiting the current record.

Here's an example using the RDS data control. In this case, I'll use an RDS data control to connect to the Microsoft SQL Server on a Web server (using the Microsoft Personal Web Server, which I've installed on my machine). I'll use SQL Server to connect to the Nwind.mdb database (which comes with the Microsoft Visual Studio suite as an example database) on the Web server. In this example, I'll use the RDS data control to work with a table named "Employees" in the Nwind.mdb database. Here's how I connect to that table using the RDS control (note that the **Connect** parameter is just the usual ADO connection string you'd use to connect to that database, and the SQL parameter selects the **Employees** table):

```
<HTML>
    <HEAD>
        <TITLE>
            Using The Remote Data Service
```

```
            </TITLE>
        </HEAD>

        <BODY>
            <CENTER>
                <H1>
                    Using The Remote Data Service
                </H1>

                <OBJECT CLASSID="clsid:BD96C556-65A3-11D0-983A-00C04FC29E33"
                    ID="dsoEmployees" HEIGHT=0 WIDTH=0>
                        <PARAM NAME="Server" VALUE="http://default">
                        <PARAM NAME="Connect" VALUE="Provider=SQLOLEDB.1;Persist
                        Security Info=False;User ID=sa;Initial
                        Catalog=Northwind">
                        <PARAM NAME="SQL" VALUE="SELECT * FROM Employees">
                </OBJECT>
                    .
                    .
                    .
```

After you set up the RDS control, you can bind HTML elements to it as we've already done throughout this chapter:

```
<HTML>
    <HEAD>
        <TITLE>
            Using The Remote Data Service
        </TITLE>
    </HEAD>

    <BODY>
        <CENTER>
            <H1>
                Using The Remote Data Service
            </H1>

            <OBJECT CLASSID="clsid:BD96C556-65A3-11D0-983A-00C04FC29E33"
                ID="dsoEmployees" HEIGHT=0 WIDTH=0>
                    <PARAM NAME="Server" VALUE="http://default">
                    <PARAM NAME="Connect" VALUE="Provider=SQLOLEDB.1;Persist
                    Security Info=False;User ID=sa;Initial
                    Catalog=Northwind">
                    <PARAM NAME="SQL" VALUE="SELECT * FROM Employees">
            </OBJECT>
```

```
            First Name:
            <INPUT TYPE="TEXT" DATASRC="#dsoEmployees"
                DATAFLD="FirstName" SIZE=20><P>
            Last Name:
            <INPUT TYPE="TEXT" DATASRC="#dsoEmployees"
                DATAFLD="LastName" SIZE=20><P>

            <BUTTON ONCLICK="dsoEmployees.recordset.MoveFirst()" >
                &lt;&lt;
            </BUTTON>
            <BUTTON ONCLICK="if (!dsoEmployees.recordset.BOF)
                dsoEmployees.recordset.MovePrevious()" >
                &lt;
            </BUTTON>
            <BUTTON ONCLICK="if (!dsoEmployees.recordset.EOF)
                dsoEmployees.recordset.MoveNext()" >
                &gt;
            </BUTTON>
            <BUTTON ONCLICK="dsoEmployees.recordset.MoveLast()">
                &gt;&gt;
            </BUTTON>
        </CENTER>
    </BODY>
</HTML>
```

That's all it takes. The results of this code appear in Figure 14.11. As you can see in the figure, we've been able to open a table from a record set on a Web server. This example is a success.

Similar to the other DSOs in this chapter, you can also bind the RDS data control to tables, and I'll do that as well in the next section.

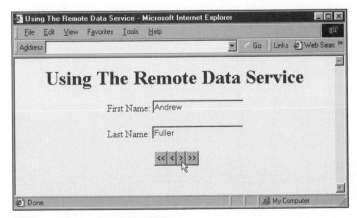

Figure 14.11   Using the RDS.

Creating Tables With The RDS Control

In the previous example, we saw how to use the RDS control in a Web page. This next example uses the RDS data control to populate an HTML table with the first name and last name fields from the **Employees** table of the Nwind database on the Web server. I start by adding an RDS data control to a Web page:

```
<HTML>

    <HEAD>
        <TITLE>
            Using The Remote Data Service With Tables
        </TITLE>
    </HEAD>

    <BODY>
        <CENTER>
            <H1>
                Using The Remote Data Service With Tables
            </H1>

            <OBJECT CLASSID="clsid:BD96C556-65A3-11D0-983A-00C04FC29E33"
            ID="dsoEmployees" HEIGHT=0 WIDTH=0>
                <PARAM NAME="Server" VALUE="http://default">
                <PARAM NAME="Connect" VALUE="Provider=SQLOLEDB.1;Persist
                Security Info=False;User ID=sa;Initial Catalog=Northwind">
                <PARAM NAME="SQL" VALUE="SELECT * FROM Employees">
            </OBJECT>
            .
            .
            .
```

Now you can bind that DSO to a table as we have throughout this chapter, using the **DATASRC** and **DATAFLD** attributes:

```
<HTML>

    <HEAD>
        <TITLE>
```

```
                  Using The Remote Data Service With Tables
            </TITLE>
      </HEAD>

      <BODY>
            <CENTER>
                  <H1>
                        Using The Remote Data Service With Tables
                  </H1>

                  <OBJECT CLASSID="clsid:BD96C556-65A3-11D0-983A-00C04FC29E33"
                  ID="dsoEmployees" HEIGHT=0 WIDTH=0>
                        <PARAM NAME="Server" VALUE="http://default">
                        <PARAM NAME="Connect" VALUE="Provider=SQLOLEDB.1;Persist
                        Security Info=False;User ID=sa;Initial Catalog=Northwind">
                        <PARAM NAME="SQL" VALUE="SELECT * FROM Employees">
                  </OBJECT>

                  <TABLE DATASRC="#dsoEmployees" BORDER = 1>
                        <THEAD>
                              <TR>
                                    <TH>First Name</TH>
                                    <TH>Last Name</TH>
                              </TR>
                        </THEAD>
                        <TBODY>
                              <TR>
                                    <TD><SPAN DATAFLD="FirstName"></SPAN></TD>
                                    <TD><SPAN DATAFLD="LastName"></SPAN></TD>
                              </TR>
                        </TBODY>
                  </TABLE>
            </CENTER>
      </BODY>
</HTML>
```

The results of this HTML appear in Figure 14.12. As you can see in the figure, the RDS data control has connected to the **DataFactory** object on the server and filled the table with data.

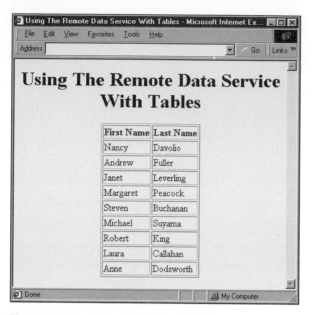

Figure 14.12   Using the RDS with tables.

Behaviors: Attaching To Events

"I keep hearing about Internet Explorer *behaviors*," says the novice programmer, "What do they do for you?" "Well," you say, "you can think of them as you would styles that include scripting." "Can you give me an example?" the NP asks. "Sure," you say, "pull up a chair."

As we saw in the In Depth section of this chapter, the idea behind behaviors is that you can separate code from data by creating HTCs. When you've created a behavior, you can apply it to HTML elements using styles. The example we saw in the beginning of the chapter, glow.htc, made elements glow when the mouse passed over them. To apply this behavior to the text in a **<DIV>** element, I create a style named "glow", which uses the **behavior** keyword, specifying the URL of glow.htc and apply it to the **<DIV>** like this:

```
<HTML>
    <HEAD>
        <TITLE>
            Using Behaviors
        </TITLE>
```

```
        <STYLE>
                .glow {font-size:40pt; font-weight:bold;
                color:white; position:absolute; cursor:default;
                filter:glow(color=yellow, strength=6, enabled=0);
                behavior:url(glow.htc);}
        </STYLE>
    </HEAD>

    <BODY STYLE="background-color: black">
        <CENTER>
            <H1 STYLE="color: white;">
                Using Behaviors
            </H1>
        </CENTER>
        <DIV class="glow" style="top:100; left:40">
            Behaviors are cool!
        </DIV>
    </BODY>
</HTML>
```

I also created glow.htc in the In Depth section of this chapter. In this file, I create the HTC with the **<PUBLIC:COMPONENT>**. Next, I attach functions named **showGlow** and **hideGlow** to the **onmouseover** and **onmouseout** events of the element this behavior will be applied to with the **<ATTACH>** element:

```
<PUBLIC:COMPONENT>

    <ATTACH EVENT="onmouseover" FOR="element" HANDLER="showGlow" />
    <ATTACH EVENT="onmouseout" FOR="element" HANDLER="hideGlow" />

    .
    .
    .
```

All that is left is to implement the **showGlow** and **hideGlow** functions:

```
<PUBLIC:COMPONENT>

    <ATTACH EVENT="onmouseover" FOR="element" HANDLER="showGlow" />
    <ATTACH EVENT="onmouseout" FOR="element" HANDLER="hideGlow" />

    <SCRIPT language="JScript">

    function showGlow()
    {
            element.filters.glow.color = (65536 * 255) + (256 * 255)
            element.filters.glow.enabled = true;
    }
```

```
        function hideGlow()
        {
                element.filters.glow.enabled = false;
        }

    </SCRIPT>
</PUBLIC:COMPONENT>
```

And that's it. You can see the results of this HTML in Figure 14.3 where the words in the **<DIV>** element with the behavior applied to it glow as the mouse passes over them.

However, there's more to behaviors than just attaching them to events—you can create new properties, methods, and events for the elements you apply behaviors to. I'll take a look at how this works in the remaining sections in this chapter.

Behaviors: Creating Properties

The novice programmer appears and says, "I'm hearing all kinds of good things about behaviors. How far can you go with them?" "Pretty far," you say, "you can use **<PUBLIC:PROPERTY>** to create properties for the elements you assign the behavior to, **<PUBLIC:METHOD>** to create methods, **<PUBLIC:EVENT>** to create events, and..." The NP holds up a hand and says, "Sorry I asked."

In this and the next two sections, I'll create a behavior with an HTC, behav.htc, that supports properties, methods, and events. Using this behavior, you can display text in a Web page that changes colors as you watch.

You can see how this behavior works in Figure 14.13 where the color changing text appears at the bottom of the page. To make this example work, you enter the text you want displayed in the top text field, the number of color changes you want to occur in the other text field, and click the Start button to start the color of the text changing. When the text is finished changing colors, the Web page displays the message "Finished!", which you see in Figure 14.14.

Here's what happens behind the scenes: The text is displayed in a **<DIV>** element with the behav.htc behavior applied to it. This behavior has two properties, **text**, which holds the text to display, and **iterations**, which holds the number of color changes you want. When you click the Start button, the JavaScript in the page assigns the two values in the text fields to the two properties, then calls the **go**

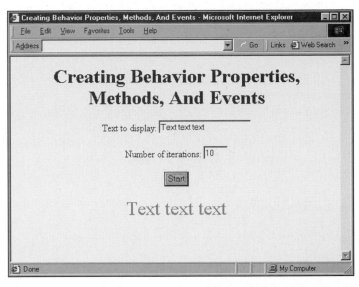

Figure 14.13   Creating a behavior with properties, methods, and events.

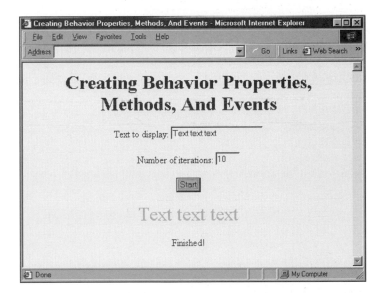

Figure 14.14   Displaying the message "Finished!" after the behavior has completed.

method of the behavior repeatedly to display the color changes (there's one color change for each call to the **go** method). When the number of color changes that you've specified has occurred, a custom event, **oncomplete**, takes place, and the Web page stops calling the **go** method and displays the message "Finished!" in a **<DIV>** element.

For reference, here's the Web page you see in Figures 14.13 and 14.14:

```html
<HTML>
    <HEAD>
        <TITLE>
            Creating Behavior Properties, Methods, And Events
        </TITLE>

        <STYLE>
            .display {font-size:24pt; behavior:url(behav.htc);}
        </STYLE>

        <SCRIPT Language="JavaScript">

            var timer1
            var object1

            function startDisplay()
            {
                object1 = document.all("displayDIV")
                object1.text = document.all("displayText").value
                object1.iterations =
                document.all("displayIterations").value
                timer1 = setInterval("object1.go()", 200)
            }

            function finished()
            {
                clearInterval(timer1)
                document.all("messageDIV").innerText = "Finished!"
            }

        </SCRIPT>

    </HEAD>

    <BODY>
        <CENTER>
            <H1>
                Creating Behavior Properties, Methods, And Events
            </H1>

            Text to display:
            <INPUT TYPE="TEXT" ID="displayText" VALUE="Text text text">
```

```
        <P>
            Number of iterations:
            <INPUT TYPE="TEXT" ID="displayIterations" VALUE="10"
            SIZE=4>

        <P>
            <INPUT TYPE="BUTTON" VALUE="Start"
            ONCLICK="startDisplay()">

        <P>
            <DIV class="display" id="displayDIV"
            oncomplete="finished()">
            </DIV>

        <P>
            <DIV ID="messageDIV">
            </DIV>

    </CENTER>
    </BODY>
</HTML>
```

Here's the HTC, behav.htc, that implements the properties, methods, and events:

```
<PUBLIC:COMPONENT>
<PUBLIC:PROPERTY NAME="text" PUT="setText"/>
<PUBLIC:PROPERTY NAME="iterations" PUT="setIterations"/>
<PUBLIC:METHOD NAME="go"/>
<PUBLIC:EVENT NAME="oncomplete" ID="completeEvent"/>

<SCRIPT LANGUAGE="JavaScript">

    var loopIndex
    var loopMax
    var text

    function setText(data)
    {
        text = data
    }

    function setIterations(data)
    {
        loopIndex = 0
        loopMax = data
```

```
        }

        function go()
        {
            if (loopIndex < loopMax)
            {
                loopIndex++
                element.innerHTML = text
                var newRed = (Math.round(Math.random() * 155) + 100) * 65536
                var newGreen = (Math.round(Math.random() * 155) + 100) * 256
                var newBlue = Math.round(Math.random() * 155) + 100
                var newColor = newRed + newGreen + newBlue

                element.style.color = newColor
            }
            else {
                raiseEvent()
            }
        }

        function raiseEvent()
        {
            var event1 = createEventObject()
            completeEvent.fire(event1)
        }

</SCRIPT>
</PUBLIC:COMPONENT>
```

I'll go through this code in this section and the next two sections. Here, I'll take a look at creating properties for behaviors (the **text** and **iterations** properties), and in the next two sections, I'll create the custom method (the **go** method) and the event (**oncomplete**) we'll need.

When you create a public property for a behavior, you use the **<PUBLIC: PROPERTY>** element. This element has two attributes: **PUT** and **GET**. You use the **PUT** attribute to specify the name of a function that should be called when a new value is assigned to the property and the **GET** attribute to specify the name of a function that should be called when you want to retrieve the value of the property.

The two properties in this example, **text** and **iterations**, store the values for the text to display and the number of times it should change color. I'll just store the values assigned to these properties in internal variables as well as set a loop index to 0, which will keep track of the number of iterations that have already occurred:

```
<PUBLIC:COMPONENT>
<PUBLIC:PROPERTY NAME="text" PUT="setText"/>
<PUBLIC:PROPERTY NAME="iterations" PUT="setIterations"/>

<SCRIPT LANGUAGE="JavaScript">

    var loopIndex
    var loopMax
    var text

    function setText(data)
    {
        text = data
    }

    function setIterations(data)
    {
        loopIndex = 0
        loopMax = data
    }
      .
      .
      .
</SCRIPT>
</PUBLIC:COMPONENT>
```

In the main Web page, the **<DIV>** element that holds the text to display is called **displayDIV**:

```
<DIV class="display" id="displayDIV">
</DIV>
```

This **<DIV>** has the style class **display** applied to it, and this class uses the behavior we're defining:

```
<STYLE>
   .display {font-size:24pt; behavior:url(behav.htc);}
</STYLE>
```

When the user clicks the Start button, the **startDisplay** function is called, and in that function, I create an object from **displayDIV**, and then set the object's **text** and **iterations** properties from the values in the text fields in the page as specified by the user. I also use the **setInterval** function to make JavaScript call the object's **go** method every 200 milliseconds:

```
function startDisplay()
{
    object1 = document.all("displayDIV")
    object1.text = document.all("displayText").value
    object1.iterations = document.all("displayIterations").value
    timer1 = setInterval("object1.go()", 200)
}
```

Every time the **go** method is called, the behavior changes the color of the text. I'll take a look at how to create this method in the next section.

Behaviors: Creating Methods

In this section, I'll add the **go** method to the behavior we developed in the previous section. To add a public method to a behavior, you use the **<PUBLIC: METHOD>** element like this:

```
<PUBLIC:COMPONENT>
<PUBLIC:PROPERTY NAME="text" PUT="setText"/>
<PUBLIC:PROPERTY NAME="iterations" PUT="setIterations"/>
<PUBLIC:METHOD NAME="go"/>
    .
    .
    .
```

This method is responsible for changing the color of the text in the element the behavior is applied to, using a new random color. I can refer to the element the behavior is applied to with the keyword **element**, so I can change its color with the expression **element.style.color**. We also need to keep track of the number of color changes that have occurred to make sure that we don't exceed the number of iterations the user has requested. That number is in the variable **loopMax**, and the current number of iterations that have occurred is in **loopIndex**. Here's what the **go** function looks like:

```
<PUBLIC:COMPONENT>
<PUBLIC:PROPERTY NAME="text" PUT="setText"/>
<PUBLIC:PROPERTY NAME="iterations" PUT="setIterations"/>
<PUBLIC:METHOD NAME="go"/>
    .
    .
    .
    function go()
```

```
{
    if (loopIndex < loopMax)
    {
        loopIndex++
        element.innerHTML = text
        var newRed = (Math.round(Math.random() * 155) + 100) * 65536
        var newGreen = (Math.round(Math.random() * 155) + 100) * 256
        var newBlue = Math.round(Math.random() * 155) + 100
        var newColor = newRed + newGreen + newBlue

        element.style.color = newColor
    }
        .
        .
        .
}
```

What if we've already executed as many iterations as we should? In that case, we can make the custom event, **oncomplete**, occur, which is called *raising* an event. To raise that event, I call a new function, **raiscEvent**:

```
<PUBLIC:COMPONENT>
<PUBLIC:PROPERTY NAME="text" PUT="setText"/>
<PUBLIC:PROPERTY NAME="iterations" PUT="setIterations"/>
<PUBLIC:METHOD NAME="go"/>

<SCRIPT LANGUAGE="JavaScript">

    var loopIndex
    var loopMax
    var text

    function setText(data)
    {
        text = data
    }

    function setIterations(data)
    {
        loopIndex = 0
        loopMax = data
    }

    function go()
    {
```

```
        if (loopIndex < loopMax)
        {
            loopIndex++
            element.innerHTML = text
            var newRed = (Math.round(Math.random() * 155) + 100) * 65536
            var newGreen = (Math.round(Math.random() * 155) + 100) * 256
            var newBlue = Math.round(Math.random() * 155) + 100
            var newColor = newRed + newGreen + newBlue

            element.style.color = newColor
        }
        else {
            raiseEvent()
        }
    }
```

```
</SCRIPT>
</PUBLIC:COMPONENT>
```

In the main page, the **<DIV>** element that displays the color changing text indicates that the function **finished** should be called when the **oncomplete** event occurs:

```
<DIV class="display" id="displayDIV" oncomplete="finished()">
</DIV>
```

In the **finished** function in the main Web page, the code turns off the timer so the color changes stop, and the page displays the word "Finished!":

```
function finished()
{
    timer1 = null
    document.all("messageDIV").innerText = "Finished!"
}
```

I'll implement the **oncomplete** event in the next section by writing the **raiseEvent** function.

Behaviors: Creating Events

In this section, I'll create the **raiseEvent** function that will raise the **oncomplete** event for the behavior we've been developing over the last two sections. To create a public event for a behavior, you use the **<PUBLIC:EVENT>** element. In this case, the name of the event is **oncomplete**, and I'll give it the ID **completeEvent**:

```
<PUBLIC:COMPONENT>
<PUBLIC:PROPERTY NAME="text" PUT="setText"/>
<PUBLIC:PROPERTY NAME="iterations" PUT="setIterations"/>
<PUBLIC:METHOD NAME="go"/>
<PUBLIC:EVENT NAME="oncomplete" ID="completeEvent"/>
    .
    .
    .
```

This event is raised in the function **raiseEvent** (called when all the iterations have been completed). In that function, I create an **event** object with the **createEventObject** method, then pass that event to the **completeEvent** object like this:

```
<PUBLIC:COMPONENT>
<PUBLIC:PROPERTY NAME="text" PUT="setText"/>
<PUBLIC:PROPERTY NAME="iterations" PUT="setIterations"/>
<PUBLIC:METHOD NAME="go"/>
<PUBLIC:EVENT NAME="oncomplete" ID="completeEvent"/>

<SCRIPT LANGUAGE="JavaScript">

    function raiseEvent()
    {
        event1 = createEventObject()
        completeEvent.fire(event1)
    }

</SCRIPT>
</PUBLIC:COMPONENT>
```

As we saw in the previous section, when this event occurs, the code in the main page turns off the timer that's been calling the **go** method repeatedly and displays the word "Finished!" in the page, as you see in Figure 14.14.

This completes the behavior we've been developing in this and the previous two sections—now we've created a behavior with properties, methods, and events. Give it a try. When you enter the text you want to display and the number of color changes you want in the main Web page and click the Start button, you'll see that text appear and change colors as you've directed.

Behaviors: Using Default Behaviors

The following list contains a number of default behaviors that come with Internet Explorer:

- **anchor**—Enables the browser to navigate to a folder view.

- **anim**—Defines an instance of the Microsoft DirectAnimation viewer in an HTML document to render DirectAnimation objects and play DirectAnimation sounds.

- **animation**—Defines a timed animation element in an HTML document.

- **audio**—Defines a timed audio element in an HTML document.

- **clientCaps**—Provides information about features supported by Microsoft Internet Explorer as well as a way for installing browser components on demand.

- **download**—Downloads a file and notifies a specified callback function when the download is complete.

- **event**—Defines a custom event to be fired at a specified time.

- **excl**—Defines a time container that allows only one child element to play at any given time.

- **homePage**—Contains information about a user's home page.

- **httpFolder**—Contains scripting features that enable browser navigation to a folder view.

- **img**—Defines a timed image element in an HTML document.

- **media**—Defines a generic, timed media element in an HTML document.

- **par**—Defines a new timeline container in an HTML document for independently timed elements.

- **saveFavorite**—Enables the object to persist data in a Favorite.

- **saveHistory**—Enables the object to persist data in the browser history.

- **saveSnapshot**—Enables the object to persist data when a Web page is saved.

- **seq**—Defines a new timeline container in an HTML document for sequentially timed elements.

- **time**—Provides an active timeline for an HTML element.

- **time2**—Provides an active timeline for an HTML element or group of elements.

- **userData**—Enables the object to persist data in user data.

- **video**—Defines a timed video element in an HTML document.

To use a default behavior, you specify a URL of the form **#default#*behaviorName*** for the HTC. You also have to know how to use each default behavior before adding it to a Web page. You can find the default behaviors reference at **http:// msdn.microsoft.com/workshop/author/behaviors/reference/reference.asp**.

Here's an example that uses the **USERDATA** default behavior. In this case, I'll use this behavior to save data from a Web page that can be restored at any time, even in a new browser session (such data is called *persisted*). I begin by creating a new style class named **saveable**:

```
<HTML>
    <HEAD>
        <TITLE>
            Using The USERDATA Default Behavior
        </TITLE>

        <STYLE>
            .saveable {behavior:url(#default#USERDATA);}
        </STYLE>
        .
        .
        .
```

I apply this class to a text field that will hold the text to save, connect the function **saveData** to one button, and connect the function **loadData** to another button:

```
<INPUT CLASS="saveable" TYPE="TEXT" ID="text1"
    VALUE="Data Data Data">
<P>
<INPUT TYPE="BUTTON" VALUE="Save Data" ONCLICK="saveData()">
<INPUT TYPE="BUTTON" VALUE="Load Data" ONCLICK="loadData()">
```

In the **saveData** function, I get an object corresponding to the text field, create an attribute I'll name **PersistedValue**, then use the **save** method to invoke the behavior and store the data with the key "SavedData":

```
function saveData()
{
    var object1 = document.all("text1");
    object1.setAttribute("PersistedValue", object1.value);
    object1.save("SavedData");
}
```

14. Dynamic HTML: Drag And Drop, Data Binding, And Behaviors

In the **loadData** function, I want to restore the data to the text field. I do that by getting an object corresponding to the text field, load the data, and restore it to the text field:

```
function loadData()
{
    var object1 = document.all("text1");
    object1.load("SavedData");
    object1.value = object1.getAttribute("PersistedValue")
}
```

Here's what the whole Web page looks like:

```
<HTML>
    <HEAD>
        <TITLE>
            Using The USERDATA Default Behavior
        </TITLE>

        <STYLE>
            .saveable {behavior:url(#default#USERDATA);}
        </STYLE>

        <SCRIPT LANGUAGE="JavaScript">
            function saveData()
            {
                var object1 = document.all("text1");
                object1.setAttribute("PersistedValue", object1.value);
                object1.save("SavedData");
            }

            function loadData()
            {
                var object1 = document.all("text1");
                object1.load("SavedData");
                object1.value = object1.getAttribute("PersistedValue")
            }
        </SCRIPT>
    </HEAD>

    <BODY>
        <CENTER>
            <H1>
                Using The USERDATA Default Behavior
            </H1>
```

```
            <INPUT CLASS="saveable" TYPE="TEXT" ID="text1"
                VALUE="Data Data Data">
            <P>
            <INPUT TYPE="BUTTON" VALUE="Save Data" ONCLICK="saveData()">
            <INPUT TYPE="BUTTON" VALUE="Load Data" ONCLICK="loadData()">
        </CENTER>
    </BODY>
</HTML>
```

You can see the results in Figure 14.15 where the text entered into the text field is stored when the user clicks the Save Data button and restored to the text field when the user clicks the Load Data button. That's it; we've put one default behavior to use. These behaviors can be very useful because they're already built into Internet Explorer.

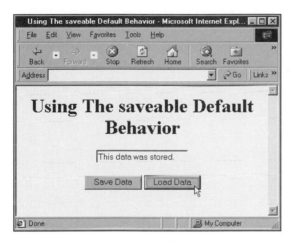

Figure 14.15   Using a default behavior.

14. Dynamic HTML: Drag And Drop, Data Binding, And Behaviors

Chapter 15

Essential Java

In Depth

Even if you haven't programmed in Java, you've probably heard about it—it's that programming language that lets you create *applets*, which you can display in Web pages. Applets are small programs that take over a section of a Web page to display text, images, controls, and they work much like any other program on your computer. For example, you can see a Java applet at work in Figure 15.1. I wrote this applet years ago. It's a word unscrambling game in which users try to unscramble the mixed up word that the applet displays. Users can click one of the checkboxes at the top of the page to make the applet display the unscrambled word, as you see in the figure. They can also click the rotating animated box on the right to get a new mixed up word to work on.

TIP: *If you noticed that all the aspects of this applet can be handled by dynamic HTML today, you'd be right. However, Java runs in nearly all browsers, and dynamic HTML differs radically between browsers, so many developers prefer Java.*

In this chapter, I'm going to work through the mechanics of creating Java programs, including installation issues, writing Java code, making sure your Java program can find what it needs, and displaying simple output. You can use these

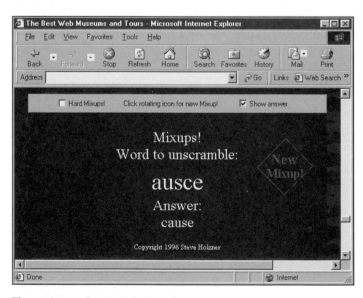

Figure 15.1   An applet at work.

skills when we start writing applets in Chapter 16, where we'll learn how to handle controls like buttons and checkboxes in applets, and work with images, text, and more. In fact, we already have a substantial amount of JavaScript under our belts, so we've got a leg up on Java—JavaScript and Java are not the same, but they're both modeled on C++.

As you might imagine, however, there's way more Java than we can cover here, so if you want to learn more, you might pick up a good book on the subject. There are many, many books available on Java, but without question the best of them is my *Java Black Book* (The Coriolis Group, ©2000), which I recommend without reservation.

Java is a product of Sun Microsystems. The following list of Web sites contains some Java resources that you can use online, most of them at Sun:

- *http://developer.netscape.com/tech/java/*—Netscape's "Java Developer Central."

- *http://java.sun.com*—The main Java site; packed with information.

- *http://java.sun.com/docs/*—The Java documentation is available here.

- *http://java.sun.com/jdk/*—The current Java software development kit is available here.

- *http://java.sun.com/jdk/demos/*—The Sun applet demos.

- *http://java.sun.com/products/jdk/1.2/*—Version 1.2 (the current version as of this writing, officially called Java 2, version 1.2) of the Java software development kit is available here.

- *www.javaworld.com*—Lots of Java resources and discussion.

This next list contains some free online tutorials that you can use to develop your Java skills:

- *http://java.sun.com/docs/books/tutorial/index.html*—Sun's Java tutorial.

- *http://stars.com/Authoring/Java/Intro/*—Tutorial on developing your first applet.

- *www.gamelan.com/javaprogramming/javanotes/*—Gamelan's Java tutorial.

- *www.javacoffeebreak.com*—Online Java tutorial.

- *www-4.ibm.com/software/developer/education/buildapplet/*—IBM's Java tutorial with some cool features.

Note that programming Java is not for everyone, and as you'll see in this chapter and the next chapter, there's really a lot to learn (and these chapters only provide an introduction to Java). Many people prefer to obtain free applets from the Internet instead of writing them from scratch, so here's a starter list of resources for applets you can use in your Web pages (as with other resources, make sure the applets you use are really free of charge before putting them in your own pages):

- *http://freewarejava.com*—This site had no less than 637 free applets last time I checked.

- *http://java.sun.com/applets/index.html*—Sun's collection of free applets.

- *http://java.wiwi.uni-frankfurt.de/*—"The Java Repository," with lots of applets and code.

- *http://javaboutique.internet.com*—A large selection of applets and a nice site.

- *www.ericharshbarger.org/java/*—"The Applet Depot," which had 45 free applets at last count.

- *www.gamelan.com/downloads/freeware/dir.java1.html*—Applets and other free downloads.

- *www.jars.com/jars_resources_java.html*—A large selection of applets.

- *www.javapowered.com/werks.html*—Another large selection of applets.

Writing Java Programs

As you know, your browser already runs Java applets—but how do you create them? That's where Java programming comes in. You write applets as Java code and then compile them with the Java Software Development Kit (the Java SDK; before Java 2, the SDK was called the Java Development Kit [JDK], and some people still call it that). To download the Java SDK (it's free), see the Immediate Solutions section "Getting And Installing The Java SDK" in this chapter. There's a lot to learn to become proficient with the Java SDK, but the results are worth it.

Java programs come in two main types: applications and applets (I'll use the term *program* to refer to both applets and applications). As we've seen, applets are Java programs you can download and run in your Web browser, as in Figure 15.1, and they're what have made Java so popular.

NOTE: *The major Web browsers have sometimes been slow to implement the most recent versions of Java, so Sun has taken charge and created a Java plug-in for Netscape Navigator and Microsoft Internet Explorer. The plug-in implements all the latest features of Java as a Netscape plug-in and an Internet Explorer ActiveX control. We'll discuss this in Chapter 16 in the Immediate Solutions section "Using The Java Browser Plug-In."*

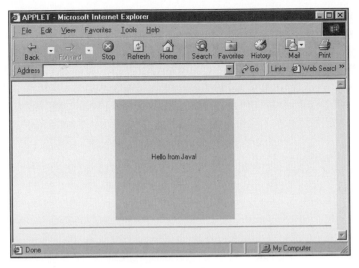

Figure 15.2   Another applet at work.

You can see another applet at work in Figure 15.2 where the applet is running in Microsoft Internet Explorer and is displaying a greeting (I'll create this applet step by step in Chapter 16).

The Java SDK also comes with an applet viewer, which you can use to look at applets. In Figure 15.3, you see the same applet as in Figure 15.2, but this time in Sun's Java Applet Viewer.

Besides downloadable applets, Java also supports *applications* that are designed to be run on the local machine. Java applications work like other computer applications—you can install and run them on your computer. Because they are installed on your computer rather than just downloaded with a Web page, applications have more privileges than applets do by default, such as the capability to read and write files (applets can do that too, but only after you use the Java security tool to grant them higher security access).

Figure 15.3   An applet at work in the Java Applet Viewer.

You need less code for applications than applets, so while we're learning Java in this chapter, I'll create Java applications. The applications I'll use will be the simplest type of Java applications—*console* applications. These are text-based applications you run from the command line (in Windows, this means from the DOS window); they can read and display text. For example, say you have a Java application named **app** that prints out the message "Hello from Java!" as the applet we've just seen does. In this case, the application will display that message in the console. For example, here's how to create an application named **app**, which is stored in a file named app.java (don't look at the details too closely right now because we're going to dissect this example in the Immediate Solutions section "Writing Code: Creating An Application" of this chapter):

```
public class app
{
    public static void main(String[] args)
    {
        System.out.println("Hello from Java!");
    }
}
```

When you use the Java compiler, the file app.java is translated into a *bytecode* file named app.class. The app.class file holds these bytecodes, which is what Java actually reads and interprets to make the program run (bytecode files can be much more compact than the Java code they came from—which means it can be faster to download Java applets than lengthy JavaScript scripts). As we'll see in the Immediate Solutions section "Compiling Code," you use the Java compiler javac to create the bytecode file for app.java:

```
C:\>javac app.java
```

And as we'll see in the Immediate Solutions section "Running Code" of this chapter, it's the file app.class that you use when you run the application, using the tool named **java** (note that you omit the .class part of the app.class filename because Java assumes you'll be running a .class file):

```
C:\>javac app.java
C:\>java app
Hello from Java!
```

You run the application with the **java** command (which runs java.exe, which comes with the Java SDK), passing it the name of the application you want to run. In Unix, the command might look like this, where a percent sign (%) is the command prompt:

```
%java app
Hello from Java!
```

In Windows, it might look like this:

```
C:\>java app
Hello from Java!
```

That's what a Java application looks like. One item that's reassuring—Java code is much like JavaScript code, so the material in Chapters 10 and 11 on JavaScript will help you in this chapter. However, there are some differences; for example, you use the **var** statement in JavaScript to create a variable like this:

```
var counter = 0
```

In Java, variables are *typed*, which means you'll have to specify what type of variable you want to create. Here's how to create an integer variable in Java using the **int** statement (see the Immediate Solutions section "Creating Variables" for all the details):

```
int counter = 0;
```

Another important difference is that Java is much more *object-oriented* than JavaScript is.

Java Is Object-Oriented

Java code is *object-oriented*, and it's important to have some insight into what that means before writing code. Object-oriented programming is really just another technique to let you implement that famous programming dictum: divide and conquer. The idea is that you *encapsulate* data and functions into objects, making each object semiautonomous, enclosing private (that is, purely internal) data and functions in a way that stops them from cluttering the program in general. The object can then interact with the rest of the program through a well-defined interface defined by its public (that is, externally accessible) functions.

Object-oriented programming was first created to handle large programs by separating them into functional units. It actually takes the idea of breaking a program into functions one step farther because objects can have both multiple subroutines and data inside them. The result of encapsulating parts of your program into an object is easily conceptualized and prevents having to deal with all the components that make up the object internally.

Imagine how your kitchen would look filled with pipes, pumps, a compressor, and all kinds of switches that you would need to keep food cold. Every time the temperature of the food got too high, you'd turn on the compressor, open valves, and start cranking the pumps manually. Now wrap all that functionality into an *object*—a refrigerator—in which all those operations are handled internally with the appropriate feedback between the internal parts and handled automatically inside the object.

That's the idea behind encapsulation—taking a complex system that demands a lot of attention, turning it into an object that handles all its own work internally, and it can be easily conceptualized, much like a refrigerator. If the first dictum of object-oriented programming is divide and conquer, the second is surely out of sight, out of mind.

In Java, object-oriented programming revolves around a few key concepts: classes, data members, inheritance, methods, and objects. The following list summarizes the meanings of these terms:

- *Class*—A template from which you can create objects. The definition of the class includes the formal specifications for the class and any data and methods in it.

- *Data members*—The variables that are part of an object; they're how you store the data the object uses.

- *Inheritance*—The process of deriving one class, called the *derived* class, from another, the *base* class, and being able to make use of the base class's methods in the derived class.

- *Method*—A function built into an object. In JavaScript, we called them functions, but in Java, they're methods.

- *Object*—An *instance* of a class. You can think of a class as the *type* of an object, just as **int** is the *type* of the variable named **counter** in this statement: **int counter = 0;**. If a class is a cookie cutter, the cookies are objects.

All these constructs are important to object-oriented programming, and we'll get more details on each of them in the next section.

Classes And Objects

In object-oriented programming, classes provide a sort of template for objects. As mentioned earlier, you can consider a class an object's *type*—just as **int** is the *type* of the variable named **counter** in this statement: **int counter = 0;**.

To create an object, you call a class's *constructor*, which is a method with the same name as the class itself. This constructor creates a new object of the class. When you create a new object, you have to use the Java **new** operator. For example, Java comes with a built-in class named **String** (see the Immediate Solutions section "Creating Strings" in this chapter). You can create a new **String** object named **greeting**, which holds the text "Hello from Java!" by passing that text to the **String** class's constructor like this:

```
public class app
{
    public static void main(String[] args)
    {
        String greeting = new String("Hello from Java!");
                .
                .
                .
    }
}
```

Notice how you specify **String** as the type of this new object, similar to the way you would use **int** as the type of an integer variable:

```
public class app
{
    public static void main(String[] args)
    {
        int counter = 0;
                .
                .
                .
    }
}
```

After creating the new **String** object, you can print out the data in it like this:

```
public class app
{
    public static void main(String[] args)
    {
        String greeting = new String("Hello from Java!");

        System.out.println(greeting);
    }
}
```

Running this application in Windows gives you this:

```
C:\>java app
Hello from Java!
```

So far, it's not very different from treating the **greeting** object as a variable that just holds data. However, objects can also have built-in *methods*. The **String** class has a built-in method named **toUpperCase**, which is a function (in JavaScript, we called them functions; now that they're built into objects, they're called methods) that converts the string's text to uppercase. Here's how I apply this method to the text in the **greeting** object (similar to the way we apply methods to HTML objects):

```
public class app
{
    public static void main(String[] args)
    {
        String greeting = new String("Hello from Java!");
        System.out.println(greeting.toUpperCase());
    }
}
```

And here's the new result:

```
C:\>java app
HELLO FROM JAVA!
```

Besides built-in methods, objects can also hold data in *data members* (also called *fields*). The data members of an object are the variables inside the object. Data members can be accessible outside an object, or you can make them internal to the object for the private use of the methods inside the object. They're much like the properties of the HTML objects we've already seen in this book.

Here's an example showing how you might use an object's data member. Say you have a class named **Data_Class**, and you create an object of this class named **data_object**:

```
Data_Class data_object = new Data_class("Hello from Java!");
      .
      .
      .
```

If **Data_Class** defines a publicly accessible data member named, say, **data**, you can refer to the **data** member of **data_object** using the dot operator (**.**) like this: **data_object.data**. This means you can print out the data in **data_object**, like this:

```
Data_Class data_object = new Data_Class("Hello from Java!");

System.out.println(data_object.data);
```

In this way, you can refer to the data members of an object that the object makes publicly accessible.

There's one more object-oriented concept to master before we get to the code—inheritance.

Inheritance

Inheritance is one of the formally defining aspects of object-oriented programming. Using inheritance, you can *derive* a new class from an old class, and the new class will *inherit* all the methods and member data of the old class. The new class is called the derived class, and the original class is called the *base* class. The idea behind inheritance is that you add what you want to the new class to give it more customized functionality than the base class.

For example, if you had a class named **vehicle**, you might derive a new class named **car** from **vehicle** and add a new method, **horn**, which, when called, prints "beep". In this way, you've created a new class from a base class and augmented that class with an additional method.

Inheritance is an important topic in Java because you can use the huge class libraries available in Java by deriving your own classes from them. We'll learn how to use inheritance in Chapter 16.

And that's all the introduction to Java concepts we'll need before digging into the code—which I'll do now in the Immediate Solutions section.

Immediate Solutions

Getting And Installing The Java SDK

The big boss gives you a call at the last minute—as usual. You have twenty minutes to write a new Web page that will let users get an overview of your company's products. What are you going to do? Knowing how well Java works in cases like this, you select Java as the language of choice to get the task done. Of course, you've got to make sure you have it before you can use it to write applets.

It's time to download and install the Java SDK, so you can create your own applets. You can find it at **http://java.sun.com/jdk/**. After downloading the Java SDK, usually as one executable package that installs itself, follow the installation instructions on the **http://java.sun.com** site.

I'd love to be able to provide the actual installation instructions here, but that's one of the biggest pitfalls that a book discussing Java can fall into. I've been writing about Java ever since it first came out, and it turns out that the actual installation instructions are often very volatile. Because these instructions change frequently, the instructions I had written in various books instantly became obsolete, triggering a landslide of calls and letters. For this reason, the best thing you can do is to see how Sun wants you to install the Java SDK, so please refer to the installation instructions as posted on the Java site. The installation process has been getting easier with every new version and beta of Java, and now typically just involves running the file you've downloaded.

As indicated in the Sun installation instructions, make sure your machine can find the Java tools including the Java compiler. To do this, make sure that the Java bin subdirectory is in your computer's *path*. For example, in Windows, the bin subdirectory is c:\jdk1.2.2\bin for the Java 2 SDK, version 1.2.2. You add a line like the following to autoexec.bat:

```
SET PATH=%PATH%;C:\JDK1.2.2\BIN
```

You must reboot your computer to make these changes take effect. When the bin directory is in the path, you'll be able to use the Java tools directly from the command line instead of having to preface them with a pathname each time you want to use them on the command line.

Writing Code: Creating Code Files

The design team coordinator calls to congratulate you on getting Java installed. You accept the accolades gracefully. "So what programs have you been writing?" the DTC asks. Hm, you think—*programs*?

Java programs are just plain text files made up of Java statements and declarations. We'll start investigating these in the next section. To create a Java program, you should have a text editor or word processor that can save files in plain text format, just as you would HTML pages.

In addition, your programs should be stored in files that have the extension .java. For example, if you are writing an application named **app**, you should store the actual Java program in a file named app.java. You pass this file to the Java compiler to create the actual bytecode file, as we'll see in a few pages.

So far so good—we've got the selection of editor or word processor down. Now how about writing some code?

Writing Code: Creating An Application

The big boss arrives and says, "So now you can write Java? Give me a demonstration!" You turn to your terminal and immediately your mind goes blank. What will you write?

Here's a sample Java application that I'll develop through to the compiling and running stages over the next few sections. Place this code in a file named app.java:

```
public class app
{
    public static void main(String[] args)
    {
        System.out.println("Hello from Java!");
    }
}
```

This application will print out the text "Hello from Java!" when you run it. For example, here's how things would look in a DOS window under Windows:

```
c:\>java app
Hello from Java!
```

Not the most significant of programs, but a good one to get us started. I'll take this program apart line by line now.

public class app

Here's the first line in app.java:

```
public class app
{
    .
    .
    .
}
```

This line indicates that I'm creating a new Java class named **app**. After I translate this class into bytecodes, Java will be able to create objects of this class and run them.

Note the keyword **public** in the previous code. This keyword is an *access specifier*. The **public** access specifier indicates that this class is available anywhere in a program that makes use of it. If you make a class public, Java insists that you name the file after it. That is, you can only have one public class in a .java file. The reason for this is that the Java compiler will translate the .java file into a bytecode file with the extension .class, which means that app.java will be translated into app.class, and if Java needs the app class, it'll know to look in the app.class file. Because Java uses the name of the file to determine what public classes are in the file, you can only have one public class in a file. For this reason, the code for the app class must be in a file named app.java. Note that Java is pretty particular about this and capitalization also counts.

The actual implementation of the class we're defining will go between the curly braces ({ and }):

```
public class app
{
    .
    .
    .
}
```

Java always encloses blocks of code within curly braces. I'll continue building this application by proceeding to the next line of code.

public static void main(String[] args)

The next line of code in our application is as follows:

```
public class app
{
    public static void main(String[] args)
    {
        .
        .
        .
    }
}
```

In this line, I'm creating a method in the **app** class. As we saw in the In Depth section, a method in object-oriented programming is like a function in standard programming—a block of code that you can pass control to, which can return a value. Methods provide handy ways of wrapping code into a single functional unit; when you call a method, the code in the method is executed by Java.

The method, named **main**, is the method that Java will look for when it starts an application (applets do not have a **main** method). When it finds the **main** method, Java passes control to it. We'll place the code we want to execute in this method's code block.

TIP: *You may be wondering about the details of the **main** method. The **main** method must be declared with the **public** access specifier, which means it may be called outside its class. It must be declared **static** as well (technically, this means that **main** is a class method, not an instance method; Java doesn't need to create an object of the **app** class before calling **main**), and it must not return a value when it's finished executing, which is the reason I use the keyword **void** in the previous code (i.e., a return value of type **void** means that there actually is no return value). Finally, note the argument in the parentheses following **main**: **String[] args**. You place an argument list in the parentheses of a method declaration to indicate what values are passed to the method and may be used by the code in the method. In this case, I'm indicating that **main** is passed an array (see the Immediate Solutions section "Creating Arrays" in this chapter) of string values, which I'm calling **args**. These string values hold the values passed from the command line when you start the application; for example, if you typed **java app Hello there**, then "Hello" and "there" would be the two strings in the **args** array. Because I won't use any command-line arguments in this application, I won't use **args** in the code for the **main** method.*

This line of code starts the **main** method. The purpose of this method is to print out the text "Hello from Java!", and I'll do that in the next line of code.

System.out.println("Hello from Java!");

The main method has one line of code in it:

```
public class app
{
    public static void main(String[] args)
    {
        System.out.println("Hello from Java!");
    }
}
```

This is the line of code that actually does all the work. In this case, I'm using some of the code that the programmers at Sun have already created to display the text "Hello from Java!". In particular, I'm using the java.lang package's **System** class here. Libraries of classes are called *packages* in Java, and the **java.lang** package is built into every Java program, which means you don't have to take special steps to make use of it, as you do with other Java packages. The **java.lang** package's **System** class includes a data member named **out**, which is an object itself and has a method named **println** that does the actual displaying of text.

Note also that this line of code ends with a semicolon. This end-of-statement convention is something that Java has inherited from C and C++ (in fact, it has inherited a lot from C and C++). You end nearly all statements in Java with a semicolon. Although JavaScript, as implemented in the major browsers, lets you drop the semicolons at the end of each statement, Java insists that they be there, so we can't skip them here.

That's that. You've created your new application and stored it in a file named app.java. What's the next step? How do you get it to actually *run*? Take a look at the next section.

Compiling Code

The big boss, while chomping on a cigar and standing right behind you as you enter your new Java application into a file says, "Hm," clearly not impressed, "what's next?" "Now," you say, "I have to compile the program and then I can run it." "OK," the big boss says, "amaze me."

To translate a Java program into a bytecode file, you use the Java compiler called javac (on Windows machines, this program is called javac.exe and is located in the bin subdirectory). Here's how you use javac in general:

```
javac [options] [sourcefiles] [@files]
```

Here are the arguments to javac:

• *options*—Command-line options.

• *sourcefiles*—One or more source files to be compiled (such as app.java).

• *@files*—One or more files that list source files.

To compile app.java, I'll use this command (which assumes that app.java is in the C:\ directory—change to the appropriate directory as needed):

```
C:\>javac app.java
```

The Java compiler, javac, takes the file app.java and (assuming there are no errors) compiles it, translating it and creating a new file named app.class. If there are errors, the Java compiler will tell you what they are including what line of code is wrong, as in this case, where I've forgotten the **println** method and tried to use one called **printline**:

```
C:\>javac app.java
app.java:5: Method printline(java.lang.String) not found in class
java.io.Print
Stream.
        System.out.printline("Hello from Java!");
                            ^
1 error
```

When app.java is successfully compiled to bytecodes, the new file app.class contains all Java will need to create objects from the **app** class. So now that we've created app.class—how do you actually run it? See the next section.

Running Code

The big boss is getting impatient. You've written a new application and compiled it without errors the first time (which you can feel proud of), but nothing has really happened that the BB can see. It's time to run the new application.

You run Java applications with the program named "java" (in Windows, for example, this is the java.exe file in the bin subdirectory). The java program, called the java *tool*, is what actually runs the Java environment. For example, to run the application named **app**, located in the file app.class, I can execute this command at the command line (note that you omit the .class part of app.class):

```
C:\>java app
```

The result appears immediately:

```
C:\>java app
Hello from Java!
```

Figure 15.4 shows you how this works in a DOS window in Windows.

That's all it takes—now you've written, compiled, and run your first Java application. Congratulations! (Note that if your application isn't responding, or you want to stop it for some reason, you can type Ctrl+C. If that doesn't work, try the Escape key.)

While we're on the topic of compiling and running code, there is another detail that we should cover—commenting your Java code.

Figure 15.4   Running an application in a DOS window.

Basic Skills: Commenting Your Code

The programming correctness czar comes in and looks at you reprovingly. "What's wrong, PCC?" you ask. "It's your code," the PCC says; "I can't make heads or tails of what's going on in it." "I guess I forgot to comment it," you say. "I guess you did," the PCC says; "Fix it."

Sometimes code can be very cryptic and hard to decipher. For this reason, Java, like JavaScript, lets you place descriptive comments in your code to let you explain to anyone who reads that code how the program works and what it does. As an example, I'll add comments to the application we developed in the previous section.

You can surround a comment of any length with the characters **/*** and ***/** like this:

```
/* This application prints out "Hello from Java!" */

public class app
{
    public static void main(String[] args)
    {
        System.out.println("Hello from Java!");
    }
}
```

The Java compiler will ignore all the text between the **/*** and ***/** markers. You can split comments between **/*** and ***/** across multiple lines like this:

```
/* This application prints out "Hello from Java!"
   Created by: G. Whiz, 1/1/00                  */

public class app
{
    public static void main(String[] args)
    {
        System.out.println("Hello from Java!");
    }
}
```

And like JavaScript, Java also supports a one-line comment, using a double slash (**//**). The Java compiler will ignore everything on a line after the **//** marker, so you can create whole lines that are comments, or just add a comment to an individual line like this:

```
/* This application prints out "Hello from Java!" */

public class app   //Create the app class
{
    //Create main(), the entry point for the application.
    public static void main(String[] args)
    {
        //Print out the message with
        System.out.println("Hello from Java!");
    }
}
```

Commenting your code can be invaluable in team environments where you share your code source files with others, or when someone else is going to take over a project after you.

Basic Skills: Importing Java Packages And Classes

"Hm," says the novice programmer, "I've got a problem. The design team coordinator told me to use the **Date** class to print out the current date in my application, but Java doesn't seem to have ever heard of the **Date** class—I get an error every time I try to use it." "That's because the **Date** class is part of the Java **util** package, and you have to import that package before you can use it." The NP asks, "*Import* it?"

The classes that Sun has created for you to use are stored in class libraries called *packages*. To make a class in a package available to your code, you have to import the package, which means the compiler will search that package for classes. You can also import individual classes that are not part of a package. By default, only the basic Java statements are available to you in an application, that is, the statements in the core **java.lang** Java package. The compiler automatically imports the **java.lang** package for you, but to use the rest of the classes that come with Java, you'll have to do your own importing with the **import** statement. Here's how you use that statement:

```
import [package1[.package2...].](classname|*);
```

Note that you put a dot (.) between package and class names to keep them separate. The standard java packages themselves are stored in a large package called **java**, so the **util** package is really called the **java.util** package (there are other large packages like the **java** package available; for example, the extensive **swing** package is stored in the **javax** package). I can refer to the **Date** class in **java.util** as **java.util.Date**, so here's how I import that class into a program:

```
import java.util.Date;

public class app
{
    .
    .
    .
```

Note that if you're going to use import statements to import classes in a program, the import statements should be at the top of the code. Now I'm free to create an object from the **Date** class using the Java **new** operator (which we saw in the In Depth section of this chapter) like this:

```
import java.util.Date;

public class app
```

```
{
    public static void main(String[] args)
    {
        System.out.println("Today = " + new Date());
    }
}
```

When you run this application, you'll see the current date displayed like this:

```
C:\>java app
Today = Thur Aug 02 12:15:13 EDT 2001
```

As you can see by studying the general form of the import statement in the previous code, there's also a shorthand that will load in all the classes in a package. You can use an asterisk (*) as a wildcard to represent all the classes in a particular package. Here's how that looks if I want to import all the classes in the **java.util** package at once:

```
import java.util.*;

public class app
{
    public static void main(String[] args)
    {
        System.out.println("Today - " + new Date());
    }
}
```

TIP: *Importing packages and classes only indicates to the compiler where to look for code it needs—it does not increase the size of your code. For this reason, the bytecode file app.class will be the same size if you use either the statement **import java.util.Date;** or **import java.util.*;**.*

Importing classes like this is fine if you stick with importing the Sun-provided classes because Java knows where to look for the classes it was installed with. But what if you want to import your own classes or ones provided by a third party?

Here's an example. Say that you have a class named **printer** in a file named printer.java, and that class has one method named **print** like this:

```
public class printer
{
    public void print()
```

```
    {
        System.out.println("Hello from Java!");
    }
}
```

You might want to make use of the **print** method in other classes, as in this case, where I'm creating a new object of the printer class using the **new** operator and using that object's **print** method in an application named **app**:

```
public class app
{
    public static void main(String[] args)
    {
        (new printer()).print();
    }
}
```

To do this, you can import the **printer** class this way:

```
import printer;

public class app
{
    public static void main(String[] args)
    {
        (new printer()).print();
    }
}
```

This works just as it should—congratulations, you've imported a class into a program!

TIP: *This technique works well if printer.class is in the same directory in which you're compiling the application because the Java compiler will search the current directory by default. However, say that you want to store all your classes in a directory named c:\classes. How will the Java compiler find printer.class there? In this case, you have to add the directory c:\classes to the Java variable named **CLASSPATH**—see the Java documentation for more details.*

Creating Variables

"I'm ready to store data in variables," the novice programmer says, "so I should use **var** as I did in JavaScript, right?" "Wrong," you say, "it's a little more involved than that."

As with JavaScript, variables serve as placeholders in memory for data. Unlike JavaScript, however, Java variables come in different *types*. The different types have to do with the format the data is stored in, and how much memory is set aside to hold that data. For example, an integer variable type, the **int** type, is made up of four bytes or 32 bits, and you use it to store integer values. This gives the data in the **int** type a range of possible values between -2,147,483,648 and 2,147,483,647. There are quite a few different variable types built into Java, such as integers, floating point numbers, and individual characters.

Before you use a variable in Java, you must *declare* it, specifying its data type. Here's how you declare variables in Java:

```
type name [= value][, name [= value]...];
```

Here's an example showing how to declare a variable of the **int** type, which means I'll store an integer in it. This variable is named **days**:

```
public class app
{
    public static void main(String[] args)
    {
        int days;
        .
        .
        .
    }
}
```

This code allocates 32 bits of storage in memory and labels the location of that storage, as far as the Java compiler is concerned, as "days", which means you can now refer to that name in code. Here's how I store a numeric value of 365 in **days** using the Java assignment operator (**=**):

```
public class app
{
    public static void main(String[] args)
    {
        int days;

        days = 365;
        .
        .
        .
    }
}
```

To verify that **days** now holds 365, I can print it out on the console this way:

```
public class app
{
    public static void main(String[] args)
    {
        int days;

        days = 365;

        System.out.println("Number of days = " + days);
    }
}
```

Here's the result of this code:

```
C:\>java app
Number of days = 365
```

As you can see, we've created a variable, stored data in it, and retrieved that data to print it on the screen. That's how it works.

As with JavaScript, there's also a convenient shortcut that lets you initialize a variable when you declare it. Here, I'm declaring **days** and initializing it to 365 in one step:

```
public class app
{
    public static void main(String[] args)
    {
        int days = 365;

        System.out.println("Number of days = " + days);
    }
}
```

The **int** type is only one kind of simple variable that you can use. The following list contains more possibilities of types in overview:

- *Boolean*—Holds only two types of values: **true** and **false**.

- *Characters*—Holds representations of characters such as letters and numbers.

- *Floating point numbers*—Refers to **float** and **double** (for double precision), which hold signed floating point numbers.

- *Integers*—Refers to **byte** (one byte), **short** (usually two bytes), **int** (usually four bytes), and **long** (usually eight bytes), which hold signed, whole-value numbers.

Java puts considerable emphasis on its data types. It's a strongly *typed* language; it insists that the simple variables you declare and use must fit into one of the types in the preceding list. Every variable must have a type, and Java is very particular about maintaining the integrity of those types, especially if you try to assign a value of one type to a variable of another type. In fact, Java is more strongly typed than a language like C++. In C++, for example, you can assign a floating point number to an integer and C++ will handle the type conversion for you, but you can't do this in Java—in Java, you have to perform the conversion explicitly.

Creating Arrays

Simple data types of the kind we saw in the previous section are fine for storing single data items, but data is often more complex. Say, for example, that you want to start a new bank, the Java Programming Bank, and need to keep track of the amount of money in every account indexed by an account number. A method of working with compound data is best, and that's what arrays provide.

Using an array, you can group simple data types into a more compound data structure and refer to that new data structure by name. More importantly, you can refer to the individual data items stored in the array by numeric index. This is important because computers excel at performing millions of operations very quickly, so if your data is referenced with a numeric index, you can work through a whole set of data very quickly simply by incrementing the array index and accessing all the items in the array.

Here's an example. In this case, I'll start the Java Programming Bank with 100 new accounts, and each one will have its own entry in an array named **accounts[]**. The square brackets at the end of **accounts[]** indicate that it's an array, and you place the index number of the item in the array you want to access, in the brackets. Here's how I create the **accounts[]** array, making each entry in it the floating point type double for extra precision. First, I declare the array, then I create it with the **new** operator, which is what Java uses to actually allocate memory:

```
public class app
{
    public static void main(String[] args)
    {
        double accounts[];

        accounts = new double[100];
        .
        .
        .
```

Now that I've created an array with 100 items, I can refer to those items numerically, like this, where I'm storing 43.95 in Account 3 and printing out that amount:

```
public class app
{
    public static void main(String[] args)
    {
        double accounts[];

        accounts = new double[100];

        accounts[3] = 43.95;

        System.out.println("Account 3 has $" + accounts[3]);
    }
}
```

Here's the results of this program:

```
C:\>java app
Account 3 has $43.95
```

As you can see, you can now refer to the items in the array using a numeric index, which organizes them in an easy way. In Java, the lower bound of an array you declare this way is 0, so the statement **accounts = new double[100]** creates an array with a first item of **accounts[0]** and a last item of **accounts[99]**.

You can combine the declaration and creation steps into one step like this:

```
public class app
{
    public static void main(String[] args)
    {
        double accounts[] = new double[100];

        accounts[3] = 43.95;

        System.out.println("Account 3 has $" + accounts[3]);
    }
}
```

You can also initialize arrays with values when you declare the array if you enclose the list of values you want to use in curly braces, as we'll see in this chapter (see the Immediate Solutions section "Creating Arrays"). For example, this code creates four accounts and stores 43.95 in **accounts[3]**:

```
public class app
{
    public static void main(String[] args)
    {
        double accounts[] = {0, 0, 0, 43.95};

        System.out.println("Account 3 has $" + accounts[3]);
    }
}
```

Now, let's say that some of the customers in the Java Programming Bank are unhappy; they want a checking account in addition to a savings account. How will you handle that and still keep things indexed by account number?

The **accounts[]** array is a one-dimensional array, which means you can think of it as a single list of numbers that you can index with one number. However, arrays can be multiply dimensioned in Java, meaning that you can have multiple array indexes. In this next example, I'll extend **accounts[]** into a two-dimensional array, **accounts[][]**, to handle both a savings and a checking account. The first index of **accounts[][]** will be 0 for savings accounts and 1 for checking accounts, and the second index will be the account number. Here's how this works in code:

```
public class app
{
    public static void main(String[] args)
    {
        double accounts[][] = new double[2][100];

        accounts[0][3] = 43.95;
        accounts[1][3] = 2385489382.06;

        System.out.println("Savings account 3 has $" + accounts[0][3]);
        System.out.println("Checking account 3 has $" + accounts[1][3]);
    }
}
```

Now that **accounts[][]** is a two-dimensional array, each item in it is referred to using two index values; for example, the savings balance for account 3 is now **accounts[0][3]**, and the checking balance is **accounts[0][3]**. Here are the results when you run this application:

```
C:\>java app
Savings account 3 has $43.95
Checking account 3 has $2.38548938206E9
```

Note that I've given Account 3 a checking balance of $2,385,489,382.06 (wishful thinking) and that Java has printed out 2.38548938206E9. This is Java's shorthand for $2.38548938206 \times 10^9$, not an inconsiderable bank balance by any means.

Creating Strings

Similar to JavaScript, you may have noticed that I've been using the plus (**+**) operator to create the text to print in the examples in this chapter:

```
public class app
{
    public static void main(String[] args)
    {
        double accounts[][] = new double[2][100];

        accounts[0][3] = 43.95;
        accounts[1][3] = 2385489382.06;

        System.out.println("Savings account 3 has $" + accounts[0][3]);
        System.out.println("Checking account 3 has $" + accounts[1][3]);
    }
}
```

That's because text strings are supported by their own class in Java, the **String** class. You can think of the **String** class as defining a new data type. For example, here's how I create a string named **greeting**, which holds the text "Hello from Java!":

```
public class app
{
    public static void main(String[] args)
    {
        String greeting = "Hello from Java!";
        .
        .
        .
```

Now I can treat this string as I would other types of variables, including printing it out like this:

```
public class app
{
```

```
    public static void main(String[] args)
    {
        String greeting = "Hello from Java!";

        System.out.println(greeting);
    }
}
```

Here's the result of this application:

```
C:\>java app
Hello from Java!
```

There are actually two string classes in Java: **String** and **StringBuffer**. You use the **String** class to create text strings that cannot change and **StringBuffer** to create strings that you can modify. As you can see in the previous code, you can use strings as you would any simple data type in Java, even using operators like + and - on them. You'll find all the Java operators in the next section.

Using Operators

"OK," sighs the novice programmer, "I want to multiply two numbers together in Java. In JavaScript, I'd use the multiplication operator, but I suppose it's different in Java?" "Nope," you smile, "same thing."

The most basic way to work with the data in a Java program is with the built-in Java *operators*. For example, say you have stored a value of 46 in one variable and a value of 4 in another. You can multiply those two values with the Java multiplication operator (*) as seen in this code:

```
public class app
{
    public static void main(String[] args)
    {
        int operand1 = 46, operand2 = 4, product;

        product = operand1 * operand2;

        System.out.println(operand1 + " * " + operand2 +
            " = " + product);
    }
}
```

Here are the results of this code:

```
C:\>java app
46 * 4 = 184
```

So what operators are available in Java? Table 15.1 contains all of them—note that nearly all of them are shared by JavaScript as well.

Table 15.1   Java operators.

Operator	Operation Performed	Operator	Operation Performed
++	Increment	--	Decrement
=	Assignment	==	Equal to
+	Addition	+=	Addition assignment
-	Subtraction	-=	Subtraction assignment
*	Multiplication	*=	Multiplication assignment
/	Division	/=	Division assignment
<	Less than	<=	Less than or equal to
<<	Shift left	<<=	Shift left assignment
>	Greater than	>=	Greater than or equal to
>>	Shift right	>>=	Shift right assignment
>>>	Shift right with zero fill	>>>=	Shift right zero fill assignment
^	Logical Xor	^=	Bitwise Xor assignment
|	Logical Or	||	Short-circuit Or
|=	Bitwise Or assignment	~	Bitwise unary Not
!	Logical unary Not	!=	Not equal to
&	Logical And	&&	Short-circuit And
&=	Bitwise And assignment	?:	Ternary if-then-else
%	Modulus	%=	Modulus assignment

Using Conditional Statements: **if, if...else, switch**

The novice programmer appears and says, "How do you create a conditional statement in Java? In JavaScript, I'd use an **if** statement." "With the Java **if** statement," you say. "OK," but what about a **switch** statement?" "With the Java **switch** statement," you say. The NP says, "This is too easy!"

The next step up from using simple operators (see the previous section) is to use *conditional statements*, also called *branching statements*, in your code. You use conditional statements to make decisions based on the value of your data and make the flow of the program go in different directions accordingly. It turns out that Java supports the same kind of conditional statements as JavaScript: **if**, **if...else**, and **switch**.

TIP: *For more details on these statements, see the Immediate Solutions sections "Creating **if** Statements," "Creating **if...else** Statements," and "Creating **switch** Statements" in Chapter 10 on JavaScript.*

For example, say that you wanted to report on the weather, and if it's under 80 degrees Fahrenheit, you want a Java program to print out a message that reads "It's not too hot.". You can do that by checking the current temperature with a Java **if** statement, which compares the value in the variable **temperature** to 80, and if that value is under 80, prints out the message like this:

```
public class app
{
    public static void main(String[] args)
    {
        int temperature = 73;

        if (temperature < 80) {
            System.out.println("It is not too hot.");
        }
    }
}
```

The **if** statement tests whether its condition, the part that appears in parentheses (in this case, **temperature < 80**), is true. Because I've set the value to 73, the **if** statement's condition is true, which means the code in the body of the **if** statement will be executed. Here are the results of this code:

```
C:\>java app
It is not too hot.
```

You can make **if** statements more complex by adding **else** clauses, which must follow an **if** statement and are executed in case the **if** statement's condition turns out to be false. Here's an example:

```
public class app
{
    public static void main(String[] args)
```

```
    {
        int temperature = 73;

        if (temperature < 80) {
            System.out.println("It\'s not too hot.");
        }
        else {
            System.out.println("It\'s too hot!");
        }
    }
}
```

Using Loops: **for, while, do...while**

The novice programmer is back and is still excited about making the move from JavaScript to Java. The NP asks, "Does Java have a **for** loop with the same syntax as the JavaScript **for** loop?" "Yep," you say. "And does it also have a **while** loop?" "Yep," you say. "And a **do...while** loop?" "Yes, yes, yes," you say. "Wow!" says the NP.

Loops are fundamental programming constructs that let you handle tasks by executing specific code repeatedly. Like JavaScript, Java has a **for** loop, a **while** loop, and a **do...while** loop.

TIP: For more details on these statements, see the Immediate Solutions sections "Creating **for** Loop Statements," "Creating **while** Loop Statements," and "Creating **do...while** Loop Statements" in Chapter 10 on JavaScript.

For example, you might want to handle the items in a set of data by working with each item in succession or keep performing a task until a particular condition becomes true. The basic loop statement is the **for** statement, which lets you execute a block of code using a *loop index*. Each time through the loop, the loop index will have a different value, and you can use the loop index to specify a different data item in your data set, as when you use the loop index as an index into an array.

Here's how you use a Java **for** loop in general; note that the statement that makes up the body of the **for** loop can be a compound statement; it can be made up of several single statements enclosed in curly braces:

```
for (initialization_expression; end_conditon; iteration_expression) {
    statement
}
```

You can initialize a loop index in the initialization expression (in fact, you can use multiple loop indexes in a **for** loop), provide a test condition for ending the loop when that test condition becomes false in the end condition, and add some way of changing, usually by incrementing, the loop index in the iteration expression.

Here's an example to make this clear. In this case, I'll use a **for** loop to total the grades of six students in an array and compute the average grade. Here's how this looks in code—note that I am declaring and initializing the loop index to 0 in the initialization expression of the **for** loop, which Java allows you to do, just as you can in JavaScript:

```
public class app
{
    public static void main(String[] args)
    {
        double grades[] = {88, 99, 73, 56, 87, 64};
        double sum, average;

        sum = 0;

        for (int loop_index = 0; loop_index < grades.length;
            loop_index++) {
            sum += grades[loop_index];
        }

        average = sum / grades.length;

        System.out.println("Average grade = " + average);
    }
}
```

This code loops over all items in the **grades** array and adds them, leaving the result in the variable named **sum**, and is then divided by the total number of entries in the array to find the average value. I loop over all elements using a loop index that starts at 0 and is steadily incremented each time through the loop, up to the last item in the array. Here are the results of this code:

```
C:\>java app
Average grade = 77.83333333333333
```

Declaring And Creating Objects

The novice programmer appears, ready to discuss object-oriented programming. "I know all about objects now," the NP says, "only..." "Only what?" you ask. "Only, how do I actually *create* an object?"

You need to declare an object before you can use it. You can declare objects the same way as you declare variables of the simple data types, using the class as the object's type. And you can use the **new** operator to create objects in Java. Let's look at an example using the Java **String** class. To start, I'll declare a new object of the **String** class, **s1**:

```
public class app
{
    public static void main(String[] args)
    {
        String s1;
        .
        .
        .
}
```

Although declaring a simple variable creates that variable, declaring an object doesn't create it. To actually create the object, I can use the **new** operator using this general form, where I'm passing parameters to the class's constructor:

```
object = new class([parameter1 [, parameter2...]]);
```

The **String** class has several constructors, and you can pass quoted strings to one of the **String** class's constructors, so I can create the new object, **s1**, like this:

```
public class app
{
    public static void main(String[] args)
    {
        String s1;
        s1 = new String("Hello from Java!");
        .
        .
        .
}
```

Now the new object, **s1**, exists, and is ready for use. For example, to convert all the characters in **s1** to lowercase, you can use the **String** class's **toLowerCase** method like this: **s1.toLowerCase( );**.

You can also combine the declaration and creation steps into one step, as in this case, where I'm declaring a new **String** object, **s2**, and creating it with the **new** operator all in one line:

```
public class app
{
    public static void main(String[] args)
    {
        String s1;
        s1 = new String("Hello from Java!");

        String s2 = new String("Hello from Java!");
        .
        .
        .
}
```

Classes often have several different constructors, each of which can take a different argument list (that is, different argument types and number of arguments; the Java compiler knows which constructor you want to use by noting the types of the arguments you use and how many arguments there are). In object-oriented terms, these constructors are *overloaded*. For example, the **String** class's constructor is overloaded to take character arrays as well as text strings, so I can create a new object, **s3**, using a character array:

```
public class app
{
    public static void main(String[] args)
    {
        String s1;
        s1 = new String("Hello from Java!");

        String s2 = new String("Hello from Java!");

        char c1[] = {'H', 'i', ' ', 't', 'h', 'e', 'r', 'e'};
        String s3 = new String(c1);
        .
        .
        .
}
```

Sometimes classes will have methods that return objects, which means they'll use the **new** operator internally and you don't have to. Here's an example using a method of the **String** class, **valueOf**, where I convert the number in a **double** variable into text in a **String** object:

```
public class app
{
    public static void main(String[] args)
    {
        String s1;
        s1 = new String("Hello from Java!");

        String s2 = new String("Hello from Java!");

        char c1[] = {'H', 'i', ' ', 't', 'h', 'e', 'r', 'e'};
        String s3 = new String(c1);

        double double1 = 1.23456789;
        String s4 = String.valueOf(double1);
        .
        .
        .
}
```

In addition, you can assign one object to another as I've done here:

```
public class app
{
    public static void main(String[] args)
    {
        String s1;
        s1 = new String("Hello from Java!");

        String s2 = new String("Hello from Java!");

        char c1[] = {'H', 'i', ' ', 't', 'h', 'e', 'r', 'e'};
        String s3 = new String(c1);

        double double1 = 1.23456789;
        String s4 = String.valueOf(double1);

        String s5;
        s5 = s1;

        System.out.println(s1);
        System.out.println(s2);
```

```
        System.out.println(s3);
        System.out.println(s4);
        System.out.println(s5);
    }
}
```

Internally, what's really happening here is that a reference to **s1** is copied to **s5**. What this means in practice is that **s1** and **s5** refer to the *same* object. That's important to know because if you change the instance data in **s1**, it also means you're changing the instance data in **s5**, and vice versa. If two variables refer to the same object, be careful—multiple references to the same object can create bugs that are extremely hard to find, especially when you think you're really dealing with different objects.

At the end of the previous code, I print out all the strings I've created, and here's what appears when you run the program:

```
C:\>java app
Hello from Java!
Hello from Java!
Hi there
1.23456789
Hello from Java!
```

That's how to declare and create objects. It's similar to the way you declare and create simple variables, with the added power of configuring objects by passing data to a class's constructor.

Chapter 16

Creating Java Applets

In Depth

In the previous chapter, we worked through a lot of Java syntax, and in this chapter, it's time to put it to work by creating Java *applets*. We're going to learn how to use the Java Abstract Windowing Toolkit (AWT) to create applets that you can embed in your Web pages.

NOTE: *Java 2 also includes the new Java Swing visual components, but I'll stick to the AWT. Swing takes considerable work to understand the handling of javax packages as well as to understand the various applet panes, just to get started.*

TIP: *There's a lot of depth to Java programming, and of course only some of that depth will fit into this chapter. If you find yourself needing or wanting more details, take a look at my* Java Black Book *(The Coriolis Group, ©2000).*

The Abstract Windowing Toolkit

It's no exaggeration to say that the AWT was the driving force behind Java's popularity. Using the AWT, you can create and display buttons, labels, menus, combo boxes, text fields, and other user-interface controls you expect in windowed programs. The following list contains an overview of the most popular AWT classes:

- **Applet**—Creates an applet.
- **Button**—Creates a button.
- **Canvas**—Creates a canvas you can draw in.
- **Checkbox**—Creates a checkbox.
- **CheckboxGroup**—Creates a radio button.
- **Choice**—Creates a choice control.
- **ComboBox**—Creates a combo box.
- **Dialog**—Creates a dialog box.
- **Frame**—Creates a frame for windowed applications.
- **Label**—Creates a label.
- **List**—Creates a list control.
- **Menu**—Creates a menu.

- **Panel**—Creates a panel that can contain other controls.
- **PopupMenu**—Creates a popup menu.
- **Scrollbar**—Creates a scrollbar.
- **ScrollPane**—Creates a scrollable surface.
- **TextArea**—Creates a two-dimensional text control.
- **TextField**—Creates a one-dimensional text field (called a text box in other languages).
- **Window**—Creates a free-standing window.

The AWT **Applet** class is what you base AWT applets on, and I'll take a look at this class first.

Creating Applets

At last, it's time to build an applet. AWT applets are built on the **Applet** class, which is in the java.applet package, so I'll start by importing that class in a new Java source code file, which I'll call **applet.java**:

```
import java.applet.Applet;
    .
    .
    .
```

The **java.applet.Applet** class is the class that forms the base of standard applets. You *derive* your own applet classes from that class using the **extends** keyword:

```
import java.applet.Applet;

public class applet extends Applet
{
    .
    .
    .
}
```

Deriving a class like this means that our new class is going to *inherit* all the functionality of the **java.applet.Applet** class, including all the built-in functions we'll use (see the discussion of *inheritance* in the In Depth section of Chapter 15 for more information).

So far, so good. Now it's time to add code to this new applet. Applets don't have a **main** method like applications do—in fact, that's the chief code difference between applets and applications. So how can you display text directly in an applet?

16. Creating Java Applets

The actual drawing of an applet is accomplished in its **paint** method, which Java calls when it's time to display the applet. The **java.applet.Applet** class has its own **paint** method, but we can *override* (an object-oriented programming term that means "redefine") that method by defining our own **paint** method:

```
import java.applet.Applet;
import java.awt.*;

public class applet extends Applet
{
    public void paint(Graphics g)
    {
        .
        .
        .
    }
}
```

The **paint** method is actually a part of the Java AWT. Because we'll be using the AWT a great deal in this book, I've imported the AWT classes with the statement **import java.awt.***. Here's how this method works: The **paint** method is passed a Java object of the **Graphics** class, and I'm naming this object **g** in this code. You can use this object's **drawString** method to actually draw the text. In this case, I'll draw the text "Hello from Java!" at location (60, 100) in the applet; coordinates like (60, 100) are measured in pixels from the upper-left corner of the applet, so this position is 60 pixels from the left border of the applet and 100 pixels from the top. Here's what the code looks like:

```
import java.applet.Applet;
import java.awt.*;

public class applet extends Applet
{
    public void paint(Graphics g)
    {
        g.drawString("Hello from Java!", 60, 100);
    }
}
```

That's all it takes. Now, compile applet.java to applet.class using the javac tool as we did in the previous chapter. It looks like this in Windows:

```
C:\>javac applet.java
```

We're almost done. There's just one more step—creating and using a Web page to display the applet in, and I'll take a look at this next.

Running Applets

To display an applet, you can use a Web page with an **<APPLET>** element in it. The **<APPLET>** element has been officially deprecated by the World Wide Web Consortium (W3C) in favor of the **<OBJECT>** element, but no browser, except Internet Explorer, lets you handle applets with the **<OBJECT>** element yet, so I'll stick with the **<APPLET>** element in this chapter.

TIP: *To see how to use **<OBJECT>** in place of **<APPLET>**, see the section "**<APPLET>**—Embedding Applets In Web Pages" in the Immediate Solutions section of this chapter.*

The following Web page, applet.html, will display the applet we've developed (note that I specify the bytecode file for the applet, applet.class, in the **<APPLET>** element):

```
<HTML>
    <HEAD>
        <TITLE>
            Applet Example
        </TITLE>
    </HEAD>

    <BODY>
        <HR>
            <CENTER>
                <APPLET
                    CODE=applet.class
                    WIDTH=200
                    HEIGHT=200 >
                </APPLET>
            </CENTER>
        <HR>
    </BODY>
</HTML>
```

You can open this Web page in a Web browser. Figure 16.1 shows the opened applet in Microsoft Internet Explorer.

There's a handy shortcut you can use with the appletviewer (appletviewer.exe) that comes with the Java Software Development Kit (SDK)—you can embed the **<APPLET>** element right into the Java source code if you put it into a Java comment:

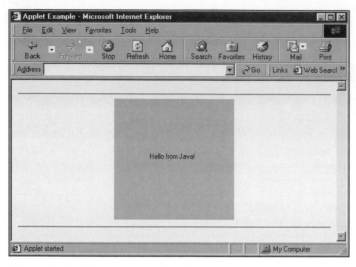

Figure 16.1   Running an applet in Internet Explorer.

```java
import java.applet.Applet;
import java.awt.*;

/*
<APPLET
    CODE=applet.class
    WIDTH=200
    HEIGHT=200 >
</APPLET>
*/

public class applet extends Applet
{
    public void paint(Graphics g)
    {
        g.drawString("Hello from Java!", 60, 100);
    }
}
```

The java compiler, javac, will ignore the **<APPLET>** element, but you can use the appletviewer with this file directly, which means you don't have to create a separate HTML Web page while developing your applet, as here in Windows:

```
C:\>appletviewer applet.java
```

You can see the results in Figure 16.2; I'll use this technique often in this chapter.

Figure 16.2   Running an applet in the Sun appletviewer.

Uploading Applets

You've run the applet you saw in Figures 16.1 and 16.2 on your local computer—but how do you install them on your Web server? You first compile an applet into a bytecode .class file, of course. When you have your .class file, you upload it to your Internet Service Provider (ISP) using a File Transfer Protocol (FTP) program. Some ISPs have Web pages that let you upload files. Contact your ISP's technical staff to determine how to upload files.

You can give the applet the same protection you would give a Web page, making sure anyone can read the applet .class file (for example, in Unix, you might give the applet the permission setting 644, which lets anyone read the file; this is the default protection FTP programs give to uploaded files on Unix systems).

TIP: *Unix file permissions consist of three octal digits corresponding to, in order, the file owner's permission, the permission of others in the same user group, and the permission of all others. In each octal digit, a value of 4 indicates read permission, a value of 2 indicates write permission, and a value of 1 indicates execute permission. You add these values together to set the individual digits in a permission setting—for example, a permission of 600 means that the file's owner, and only the file's owner, can both read and write the file.*

Although you're reading the applet from the Web now, you can still embed the new applet in a Web page with the **<APPLET>** element. You do this by indicating the name of the .class file for the applet as well as telling the Web browser how much space (in pixels) to leave for the applet:

```
<HTML>
    <HEAD>
        <TITLE>
            Applet Example
        </TITLE>
    </HEAD>
```

```
<BODY>

    <CENTER>
        <APPLET
            CODE = "applet.class"
            WIDTH = 300
            HEIGHT = 200

        >
        </APPLET>
    </CENTER>
</BODY>
</HTML>
```

In this case, I've set up a centered 300×200 pixel space in a Web page in which to display the applet, and I've told the Web browser to download the applet.class file and run it.

This example is okay if the applet's .class file is in the same directory as the Web page. On the other hand, if you want to specify a different URL for the applet, you can use the **CODEBASE** attribute of the **<APPLET>** element like this:

```
<HTML>
    <HEAD>
        <TITLE>
            Applet Example
        </TITLE>
    </HEAD>

    <BODY>
        <HR>
        <CENTER>
            <APPLET
                CODE=applet.class
                CODEBASE="http://www.starpowder.com/steve"
                WIDTH=300
                HEIGHT=200 >
            </APPLET>
        </CENTER>
        <HR>
    </BODY>
</HTML>
```

See the section "**<APPLET>**—Embedding Applets In Web Pages" in the Immediate Solutions section for more details about the attributes of the **<APPLET>** element.

Controls In Applets

So far, this applet doesn't actually do anything very useful, like respond to the user. But we can change that. One of the biggest aspects of applets is letting the user interact with the program, and you do that with *events*. When the user performs some action—clicking a button, closing a window, selecting an item in a list, or using the mouse, for example—Java, like JavaScript, considers each of these an event. I'll take a look at how Java event handling works in the Immediate Solutions section "Handling Events."

You use events with controls like text fields, buttons, checkboxes, and so on. Just like HTML, Java supports these controls, and in fact, they work similarly to the way they do in HTML. In the following sections, I'll briefly take a look at the controls we'll see in this chapter.

Text Fields

As in HTML, text fields are the basic text-handling components of the AWT. These components handle a one-dimensional string of text that lets you display text, lets the user enter text, allows you to take passwords by masking typed text, reads the text the user has entered, and more. These components and buttons are the most fundamental AWT components.

Buttons

Buttons provide the user with a quick way to start some action—all you have to do is to click them. Every user is familiar with buttons, and we've already taken a look at buttons in HTML. You can give buttons a caption, such as "Click Me!", and when the user clicks the button, your code is notified if you've registered to handle events from the button.

Checkboxes

Checkboxes are much like buttons except that they are *dual state*, which means they can appear as selected or unselected. When selected, they display a visual indication of some kind, such as a checkmark or an x (the indicator varies by operating system in AWT programming, which is one of the reasons Sun introduced Swing; Swing can display components with the same look across many operating systems).

The user can click a checkbox to select options, such as choosing items in a sandwich, enabling automatic spell checking, or enabling background printing. You use checkboxes to let the user select nonexclusive options; for example, both automatic spell checking and background printing may be enabled at the same time. Radio buttons, however, are a different story.

Radio Buttons

As in HTML, you let the user select one of a set of mutually exclusive options using radio buttons. Only one of a set of option buttons can be selected at one time; for example, using radio buttons, you can let the user select printing color or the day of the week. In the AWT, radio buttons are actually a type of checkbox, and when selected, they display a round dot, a clicked square, or other indicator (again, the visual indicator depends on the operating system). You use radio buttons in groups, and we'll see how this works in the Immediate Solutions section "Creating Radio Buttons."

Graphics In Applets

The final topic I'll take a look at in this chapter is graphics, an important topic in Java. The following list contains some of the AWT graphics methods:

- **draw3DRect**—Draws a 3D rectangle.
- **drawArc**—Draws an arc.
- **drawBytes**—Draws text, given a byte array.
- **drawChars**—Draws text, given a character array.
- **drawImage**—Draws an image.
- **drawLine**—Draws a line.
- **drawOval**—Draws an oval, including circles.
- **drawPolygon**—Draws a polygon.
- **drawPolyline**—Draws a line with multiple segments.
- **drawRect**—Draws a rectangle.
- **drawRoundRect**—Draws a rounded rectangle.
- **drawString**—Draws a string of text.
- **paint**—Called when the applet is to be redrawn.
- **repaint**—Call this method to force the applet to be painted.
- **setBackground**—Sets the background color.
- **setForeground**—Sets the foreground (drawing) color.

Two methods that are particularly worth noting are the **paint** method, in which you paint the applet, and the **repaint** method, which forces the **paint** method to be called and redraws the applet (for instance, when it's been updated).

That's it. Now that we have an overview of applets, it's time to get to the details in the Immediate Solutions section. I'll do that now.

Immediate Solutions

Creating Applets

"Finally!" says the novice programmer; "At last I'm ready to create an applet." "That's right," you say, "now which one would you like to create?" "Hm," says the NP.

You base standard applets on the **java.applet.Applet** class, which is itself subclassed from the **jawa.awt.Container** class:

```
java.lang.Object
|_____java.awt.Component
       |_____java.awt.Container
              |_____ java.awt.Panel
                     |_____java.applet.Applet
```

Let's see an example. Here, I'll create the applet that we saw in the In Depth section of this chapter, which displayed the text "Hello from Java!" in the file applet.java. I start by deriving a new class, **applet**, from the **java.applet.Applet** class like this:

```
import java.applet.Applet;

public class applet extends Applet
{
     .
     .
     .
}
```

To display the message in the applet, I'll use the **paint** method, which the applet inherits from the **Container** class. When an applet is displayed, its **paint** method is called, and you can place the code you want to draw the applet in that method. The **paint** method is passed an object of the **Graphics** class, which is the basis of graphical work in applets. This object supports a method named **drawString**, which I'll use to draw a string of text in the applet. The **Graphics** class is an AWT class, so I'll import the AWT classes when I override the default **Applet paint** method:

```
import java.applet.Applet;
import java.awt.*;

public class applet extends Applet
{
    public void paint(Graphics g)
    {
        .
        .
        .
    }
}
```

Now I customize the overridden **paint** method to draw the text "Hello from Java!" at location (60, 100) in the applet. Applet coordinates are in pixels, so (60, 100) is 60 pixels from the left edge of the applet and 100 pixels below the top of the applet. Here's the code:

```
import java.applet.Applet;
import java.awt.*;

public class applet extends Applet
{
    public void paint(Graphics g)
    {
        g.drawString("Hello from Java!", 60, 100);
    }
}
```

This new **paint** method draws directly on the surface of the applet; note that you also can place controls like buttons and text fields directly on the surface of the applet. We'll see how this works in this chapter in Immediate Solutions sections like "Creating Text Fields" and "Creating Buttons."

You can compile applet.java into applet.class using javac. Now you've created an applet. It's time to get a look at the applet at work—see the next section.

<APPLET>—Embedding Applets In Web Pages

Purpose: Embeds applets in Web pages. Superseded by the **<OBJECT>** element. Deprecated.

Start Tag/End Tag: Required/Required

Supported: [3.2, 4, IE3, IE4, IE5, NS2, NS3, NS4]

Attributes:

- **ACCESSKEY**—Sets the access key for the element. [IE5]

- **ALIGN**—Specifies the alignment of text following or next to the applet; set to: **LEFT**, **RIGHT**, **TOP**, **BOTTOM**, **MIDDLE**, **BASELINE**, **TEXTTOP**, **ABSMIDDLE**, or **ABSBOTTOM**. [3.2, 4, IE3, IE4, IE5, NS2, NS3, NS4]

- **ALT**—Text to be displayed if a browser supports applets but cannot run this one for some reason. Set to alphanumeric characters. [3.2, 4, IE3, IE4, IE5, NS2, NS3, NS4]

- **ARCHIVE**—Used when you've stored the applet in a Java Archive (JAR) or ZIP file to reduce download time. Set to a URL. [4, NS3, NS4]

- **CLASS**—Class of the element (used for rendering). [4, IE4, IE5]

- **CODE**—Indicates a URL pointing to the applet's class. Set to a URL. Required. [3.2, 4, IE3, IE4, IE5, NS2, NS3, NS4]

- **CODEBASE**—Specifies the base URL of the applet if the **CODE** attribute is relative. And if the **CODEBASE** URL is relative, it is treated as such in relation to the current document URL or the **BASE HREF** element. Set to a URL. [3.2, 4, IE3, IE4, IE5, NS2, NS3, NS4]

- **CONTENTEDITABLE**—Set to **TRUE** if the content is editable. [IE5]

- **DATAFLD**—Name of the column of the data source object that supplies the bound data. Set to alphanumeric characters. [IE4, IE5]

- **DATASRC**—Gives the URL or ID of the data source object supplying data bound to this element. W3C says this should be a URL; Internet Explorer says it should be a data source ID. [IE4, IE5]

- **DISABLED**—Indicates if the element is disabled. [IE5]

- **HEIGHT**—Specifies the height of the space reserved for the applet in the Web page. Set to positive pixel measurements. Required. [3.2, 4, IE3, IE4, IE5, NS2, NS3, NS4]

- **HSPACE**—Specifies the padding space allocated to the right and left of the applet. Set to pixel values. [3.2, 4, IE3, IE4, IE5, NS2, NS3, NS4]

- **ID**—Unique alphanumeric identifier for the tag, which you can use to refer to it. [4, IE3, IE4, IE5]

- **LANG**—Base language used for the tag. [IE4, IE5]

- **LANGUAGE**—Scripting language used for the tag. [IE4, IE5]

- **MAYSCRIPT**—Gives the applet access to JavaScript in a page. Stand-alone attribute. [NS3, NS4]

- **NAME**—Name of the applet in the Web browser; applets must be given names if you want other applets or scripts to be able to find and interact with them. Set to alphanumeric characters. [3.2, 4, IE3, IE4, IE5, NS2, NS3, NS4]

- **OBJECT**—Gives the name of the resource that contains a serialized representation of an applet (the applet will be deserialized by the browser). Set to alphanumeric characters. [4]

- **SRC**—Specifies a URL reference to an applet (similar to the **CODE** and **CODEBASE** attributes). Set to a URL value. [IE4, IE5]

- **STYLE**—Inline style indicating how to render the element. [4, IE4, IE5]

- **TABINDEX**—Holds the tab index for the element. [IE4, IE5]

- **TITLE**—Holds additional information (which might be displayed in tool tips) for the element. [3, 4, IE4, IE5]

- **VSPACE**—Specifies the padding space allocated above and below the applet. Set to pixel values. [3.2, 4, IE3, IE4, IE5, NS2, NS3, NS4]

- **WIDTH**—Specifies the width of the space reserved for the applet in the Web page. Set to positive pixel measurements. Required. [3.2, 4, IE3, IE4, IE5, NS2, NS3, NS4]

"OK," says the novice programmer, "I've created an applet and compiled it into a .class file. How do I actually *look* at it?" "You can use the HTML **<APPLET>** element," you say.

When you've created an applet's .class file, you can upload the applet to an ISP (or view it on your own machine) and set its protection (see the In Depth section of this chapter) so it may be read. Next, you can create a Web page using the **<APPLET>** element to display the applet. Technically, the **<APPLET>** element has been replaced by the **<OBJECT>** element (see the end of this section), but in practice, every browser except Internet Explorer has yet to implement this use for **<OBJECT>**, so I'm going to stick with **<APPLET>** in this chapter.

The Web page, applet.html, displays the applet we created in the previous section; note that the only required attributes are the **CODE**, **WIDTH**, and **HEIGHT** attributes:

```
<HTML>
    <HEAD>
        <TITLE>
            Applet Example
        </TITLE>
```

```
        </HEAD>

        <BODY>

            <CENTER>
                <APPLET
                    CODE = "applet.class"
                    WIDTH = 300
                    HEIGHT = 200
                >
                </APPLET>
            </CENTER>
        </BODY>
    </HTML>
```

In this case, I'm not specifying a code base, so I place **applet.class** in the same directory as applet.html. This Web page, opened in Internet Explorer, appears in Figure 16.1. You can also use the Sun appletviewer, which comes with Java, to view applets, opening the Web page in Windows like this:

```
C:\>appletviewer applet.html
```

The results appear in Figure 16.2.

TIP: *The appletviewer that comes in the Java SDK always supports the latest version of Java, so if your Web browser doesn't, and you don't want to install the Java plug-in, you can always use the appletviewer to test your applets.*

In fact, the **<OBJECT>** element is now intended to supersede the **<APPLET>** element. In Internet Explorer, you can now set the **<OBJECT>** element's **CLASSID** attribute like this **<OBJECT CLASSID="java:*filename*.class">**. W3C also suggests providing the appropriate Multipurpose Internet Mail Extension (MIME) type for the applet like this: **<OBJECT CLASSID="java: *filename*.class" CODETYPE="application/octet-stream">**. If your applet is in another location, you can specify that location with the **CODEBASE** attribute like this: **<OBJECT CLASSID="java:*filename*.class" CODETYPE= "application/octet-stream" CODEBASE="*URL*">**.

Handling Non-Java Browsers

"Uh oh," says the novice programmer, "there's a problem. Some users are using a slightly nonstandard Web browser named *SuperWildcat14b*..." "That does sound slightly nonstandard," you say. "And," the NP continues, "it doesn't support Java.

Is there any way to inform those users that they're missing something?" "There sure is"; you say, "pull up a chair and we'll go through it."

If you enclose text inside an **<APPLET>** element, that text will be displayed if the Web browser does not support Java. For example, here's how you might alert users that they're missing your applet:

```
<APPLET code = "applet.class" width = 100 height = 100>
    Sorry, you don't have Java, so you can't see my beautiful applet.
</APPLET>
```

Embedding **<APPLET>** Elements In Code

The novice programmer sighs. "I've been writing applets, and it's always a little bit of a pain." "What is?" you ask. "Writing a Web page with an **<APPLET>** element to test the applet out—isn't there an easier way?" "Sure," you say, "you can embed the **<APPLET>** element directly in the source code file."

The developers at Sun realized that it can be annoying to have to create a Web page to test an applet, so if you use the Sun appletviewer, you can now place an **<APPLET>** element directly into the applet's .java file with a Java comment like this:

```
import java.applet.Applet;
import java.awt.*;

/*
<APPLET
    CODE=applet.class
    WIDTH=200
    HEIGHT=200 >
</APPLET>
*/

public class applet extends Applet
{
    public void paint(Graphics g)
    {
        g.drawString("Hello from Java!", 60, 100);
    }
}
```

After creating the .class file, you can now start the appletviewer with the .java file directly in Windows like this:

```
C:\>appletviewer applet.java
```

Using The **init**, **start**, **stop**, **destroy**, **paint**, And **update** Methods—And Setting Applet Color

The novice programmer is back and says, "My browser has gone all wacky—it draws my applets in gray!" "That's the default for many Web browsers," you say; "But you can change that by adding some initialization code to your applet in the **init** method."

There are a number of important applet methods that your applet will inherit from the **java.applet.Applet** class that you should know about:

- **destroy**—Called when the applet is about to be removed from memory. You can perform cleanup here.
- **init**—Called first; called only once. You initialize the applet here.
- **paint**—Called when the applet is to be redrawn. This method is passed an object of the **Graphics** class, and you can use that object's methods to draw in the applet.
- **start**—Called after **init**. This method is called each time an applet appears again on the screen. That is, if the user moves to another page and then comes back, the **start** method is called again.
- **stop**—Called when the browser moves to another page. You can use this method to stop additional execution threads your applet may have started.
- **update**—Called when a portion of the applet is to be redrawn. The default version fills the applet with the background color before redrawing the applet, which can lead to flickering when you're performing animation, so you often override this method in that case.

You can override (that is, redefine) these methods to customize them as you like. I've already overridden the **paint** method to draw a string of text in the In Depth section of this chapter. Here, I override the **init** method to change the background of the applet to white using the applet **setBackground** method and passing it the **white** property of the Java **Color** class. This applet also provides a skeletal implementation of the other methods listed previously:

```
import java.applet.Applet;
import java.awt.*;

/*
<APPLET
    CODE=applet.class
    WIDTH=200
    HEIGHT=200 >
</APPLET>
*/

public class applet extends Applet
{
    public void init()
    {
        setBackground(Color.white);
    }

    public void start()
    {
    }

    public void paint(Graphics g)
    {
        g.drawString("Hello from Java!", 60, 100);
    }

    public void stop()
    {
    }

    public void destroy()
    {
    }
}
```

The **init** method is a very useful one, and it's commonly overridden because it lets you initialize your applet. In this case, I've changed the background color from the default gray in many browsers to white. Applets excel at graphics, and I'll take a brief look at handling graphics in applets at the end of this chapter; see the section "Drawing Graphics."

TIP: *You can specify colors as **Color.white**, **Color.black**, **Color.cyan**, **Color.magenta**, **Color.pink**, and others. However, you can also create your own colors using color triplets, just as in a Web page. For example, to create a new color, you can specify red, green, and blue values (in the 0 through 255 range) to the **Color** class's constructor like this: **Color c = new Color(red, green, blue);**.*

Using The Java Browser Plug-In

"Hey," says the novice programmer, "there's a problem. I'm using the big two Web browsers, but they don't support the latest Java features; what can I do?" "There's an easy solution," you say; "Use the Java plug-in."

The Java plug-in lets you run the latest Java version applets in Netscape Navigator and Internet Explorer by implementing the Java runtime environment as a plug-in for Netscape and an ActiveX control for Internet Explorer. You can download the plug-in from **http://java.sun.com/products/plugin/**. It's also installed automatically when you install the Java SDK.

To use Web pages with the plug-in, you need to convert their HTML first by using the Sun HTML Converter, which you can also get at **http://java.sun.com/products/plugin/**. The HTML Converter is a Java .class file that you run on HTML pages to convert the **<APPLET>** element to use the plug-in.

To convert a Web page to use the plug-in, you select an HTML file or files in the HTML Converter and click the Convert button. The Converter will change an **<APPLET>** tag like this:

```
<APPLET code=adder.class width=200 height=200></APPLET>
```

into something like this:

```
<!--"CONVERTED_APPLET"-->
<!-- CONVERTER VERSION 1.0 -->
<OBJECT classid="clsid:8AD9C840-044E-11D1-B3E9-00805F499D93"
WIDTH = 200 HEIGHT = 200
codebase="http://java.sun.com/products/plugin/1.2/jinstall-12-
win32.cab#Version=1,2,0,0">
<PARAM NAME = CODE VALUE = adder.class >

<PARAM NAME="type" VALUE="application/x-java-applet;version=1.2">
<COMMENT>
<EMBED type="application/x-java-applet;version=1.2" java_CODE =
adder.class WIDTH = 200 HEIGHT = 200
pluginspage="http://java.sun.com/products/plugin/1.2/plugin-
install.html"><NOEMBED></COMMENT>

</NOEMBED></EMBED>
</OBJECT>

<!--
<APPLET  CODE = adder.class WIDTH = 200 HEIGHT = 200 >
```

16. Creating Java Applets

```
</APPLET>
-->
<!--"END_CONVERTED_APPLET"-->
```

The new HTML file will use the Java plug-in instead of the browser's default.

Reading Parameters In Applets

The big boss appears, chomping on a cigar, and says, "We need to personalize the greeting in our applet by customer." "But there are thousands of customers," you say; "We can't recompile the applet for each one and store each new version on the Web site." "What do you suggest?" the BB asks. What will you say?

You can pass parameters to applets in the **<APPLET>** element, and the applet code can read the value of those parameters, which means that to customize the applet, you only need to supply different parameters in the **<APPLET>** element. To actually get the value of a parameter, you use the **Applet** class's **getParameter** method, passing it the name of the parameter as specified in the **<PARAM>** element (which we first saw in Chapter 8). The **getParameter** method will return the value of the parameter that was set in the **<PARAM>** element.

Here's an example in which I pass a parameter named **string** to an applet; the value of this parameter is the text that the applet should display. Here's how this looks in code:

```
import java.applet.Applet;
import java.awt.*;

/*
<APPLET
    CODE=applet.class
    WIDTH=200
    HEIGHT=200 >
    <PARAM NAME = string VALUE = "Hello from Java!">
</APPLET>
*/


public class applet extends Applet
{
    public void paint(Graphics g)
    {
```

```
        g.drawString(getParameter("string"), 60, 100);
    }
}
```

Using Java Consoles In Browsers

"All this **drawString** stuff is OK," the novice programmer says, "but what about the Java console? What if I use **System.out.println**, which you use for text output in Java applications, in an applet?" "That depends," you say, "on your browser."

Here's an applet that displays a message and uses **System.out.println** to print to the console:

```
import java.applet.Applet;
import java.awt.*;

/*
<APPLET
    CODE=applet.class
    WIDTH=200
    HEIGHT=200 >
</APPLET>
*/

public class applet extends Applet
{
    public void paint(Graphics g)
    {
        g.drawString("Hello from Java!", 60, 100);
        System.out.println("Hello from Java!");
    }
}
```

If you run this applet with the Sun appletviewer, the applet will open in a separate window and you'll see "Hello from Java!" in the console window.

Web browsers often have a Java console as well, although you often have to enable them before using them. The way to enable the Java console differs, unfortunately, not only from browser to browser, but also from version to version. Currently, you enable the Java console in Internet Explorer by selecting Tools|Internet Options, clicking the Advanced tab, and selecting the Java Console Enabled checkbox. The result of the previous applet appears in Figure 16.3 in Internet Explorer's Java console, which pops up when you print to it.

Figure 16.3   Using Internet Explorer's Java console.

In Netscape Navigator, on the other hand, you can open the Java console by selecting Communicator|Tools|Java Console.

Creating Text Fields

"OK," says the novice programmer, "I can draw text in an applet now. But what if I want to let the user *enter* some text?" "For that," you say, "you can use all kinds of text controls, such as text fields."

In Java, text fields are supported with the **TextField** class. Here is the inheritance diagram for the **TextField** class:

```
java.lang.Object
|____java.awt.Component
      |____java.awt.TextComponent
            |____java.awt.TextField
```

Text fields are about the most basic controls you can use in the AWT, so they provide a good starting point. A text field displays and lets the user edit text as displayed on a single line. Here's a text field example. In this case, I'm creating a text field 20 characters wide in an applet's **init** method; note also that I'm importing the AWT classes to be able to use text fields:

```
import java.applet.Applet;
import java.awt.*;

/*
<APPLET
    CODE=applet.class
    WIDTH=200
    HEIGHT=200 >
</APPLET>
*/

public class applet extends Applet
{
    public TextField text1;

    public void init()
    {
        text1 = new TextField(20);
        .
        .
        .
    }
}
```

After creating a new control, you must *add* it to the applet so it's displayed, and that looks like this:

```
    public void init()
    {
        text1 = new TextField(20);
        add(text1);
        .
        .
        .
    }
```

The **add** method adds the control to the current *layout manager*, which decides where the control should be placed. Java comes with a number of layout managers; here, I'll just use the default flow layout manager, which arranges controls like a word processor arranges words, across the first line and then skips to the next line and so on. Now that the text field has been added to the applet, I can place the text "Hello from Java!" in the text field with the **setText** method like this:

```
public void init()
{
    text1 = new TextField(20);
    add(text1);
    text1.setText("Hello from Java!");
}
```

The results of this code appear in Figure 16.4 where you can see the text field with the message we've put into it. The user can also edit that text.

Another basic control is the AWT Button control; I'll use buttons and text fields to discuss event handling, so I'll introduce the Button control in the next section.

Figure 16.4   Adding a text field to an applet.

Creating Buttons

"I'm ready for the next step," the novice programmer reports; "I've added text fields to my applets, what's next?" "Buttons," you say, "pull up a chair and let's talk about it."

Every graphical user interface (GUI) user is familiar with buttons—those elementary controls that you click to signal a program to start some action. For example, you might let the user click a button to change the background color of an application. Buttons are supported in the **java.awt.Button** class, and here is the lineage of that class:

```
java.lang.Object
|____java.awt.Component
     |____java.awt.Button
```

Users can click buttons in your applet to signal that they want to perform some action; for example, you may have a button labeled "Change Color", which, when clicked, changes the background color of the applet using the **setBackground** method. It's easy enough to add a button to an applet; you can do this in much the same way as adding a text field to an applet, as we did earlier in this chapter (see the Immediate Solutions section "Creating Text Fields"). In this case, I'm creating and adding a button with the caption "Click Here!":

```
public class applet extends Applet
{
    TextField text1;
    Button button1;

    public void init()
    {
        text1 = new TextField(20);
        add(text1);
        button1 = new Button("Click Here!");
        add(button1);
          .
          .
          .
    }
```

The real trick is to get something to happen when you click the button, and for that, we'll have to take a look at event handling; see the next section.

Handling Events

"Hey," says the novice programmer, "I've put a button into my applet, but when I click it, nothing happens. What gives?" "What gives," you say, "is that you have to implement event handling."

Event handling—the process of responding to button clicks, mouse movements, and so on—has become a complex topic in Java. Starting with Java 1.1, event handling changed significantly; the current model is called *delegated event handling*. In this model of event handling, you must specifically *register* with Java if you want to handle a particular event, like a button click (the idea is that performance is improved if only the code that handles specific events is informed of those events, and not the rest of your code).

You register for events using an event listener interface. The following list contains the available event listeners and the kinds of events they handle:

- **ActionListener**—Handles action events, such as button clicks.

- **AdjustmentListener**—Handles adjustment events, such as scrollbar movements.

- **AWTEventListener**—Handles AWT events.

- **ComponentListener**—Handles cases where a component is hidden, moved, resized, or shown.

- **ContainerListener**—Handles the cases when a component is added or removed from a container.

- **FocusListener**—Handles the case where a component gains or loses the focus.

- **InputMethodListener**—Handles **input** method events.

- **ItemListener**—Handles the case where the state of an item changes.

- **KeyListener**—Listens for keyboard events.

- **MouseListener**—Listens for the case where the mouse is clicked, enters a component, exits a component, or is pressed.

- **MouseMotionListener**—Listens for the case where the mouse is dragged or moved.

- **TextListener**—Listens for text value changes.

- **WindowListener**—Handles the case when a window is activated, closed, deactivated, deiconified, iconified, opened, or quit.

Each listener is a Java *interface*, and it's up to you to implement the methods of the interface (that is, add those methods to your code, even if you leave them empty). An interface is much like a Java class except that you use the **implements** keyword when inheriting from it instead of from the **extends** keyword. Like classes, interfaces can have methods, and each of those methods is passed a type of event object that corresponds to the kind of event.

- **ActionEvent**—Handles buttons, list controls, double clicks, and menu item clicks.

- **AdjustmentEvent**—Handles scrollbar movements.

- **ComponentEvent**—Handles the case when a component is hidden, moved, resized, or becomes visible.

- **ContainerEvent**—Indicates a change in a container's contents when a component is added or removed. A low-level event.

- **FocusEvent**—Handles the case when a component gains or loses the focus.

- **InputEvent**—Handles checkbox or list item clicks when a choice control selection is made or a checkable menu item is clicked.

- **InputMethodEvent**—Holds information about text that is being composed using an input method.

- **InvocationEvent**—Executes the **run** method when dispatched by the AWT event dispatcher thread.

- **KeyEvent**—Handles input from the keyboard.

- **MouseEvent**—Handles the case when the mouse is dragged, moved, clicked, pressed, released, or the mouse enters or exits a component.

- **PaintEvent**—Occurs when an element is painted.

- **TextEvent**—Occurs when the value of a text field or text area is changed.

- **WindowEvent**—Handles the case where a window is activated, closed, deactivated, deiconified, opened, or quit.

It's time to put some of this knowledge to work. I'll start by adding a new button with the text "Click Here!" to an applet and adding an action listener, which will be notified when the button is clicked. To add an action listener to the button, you use the button's **addActionListener** method, passing it an object that implements the methods of the **ActionListener** interface. This object can be an object of the applet's main class, which means we'll have to implement the methods of the interface in that class.

TIP: You can also unregister an event listener using the **removeListener** method.

Here's how I add an action listener to a button with **addActionListener(this)**; as in JavaScript, the **this** keyword refers to the current object, so here I'm passing the current applet object to **addActionListener**. The result is that Java will send event notifications to the current applet object—note also that I indicate that the **Applet** class now implements the **ActionListener** interface with the **implements** keyword:

```
import java.applet.Applet;
import java.awt.*;
import java.awt.event.*;

/*
<APPLET
    CODE=applet.class
    WIDTH=200
```

```
        HEIGHT=200 >
</APPLET>
*/


public class applet extends Applet implements ActionListener
{
    TextField text1;
    Button button1;

    public void init()
    {
        text1 = new TextField(20);
        add(text1);
        button1 = new Button("Click Here!");
        add(button1);
        button1.addActionListener(this);
    }
}
        .
        .
        .
```

Because action listener events will now be passed to the main **applet** object, I have to implement the methods of the **ActionListener** interface in that object. It turns out that this interface has only one method, **actionPerformed**, which is passed an object of the **ActionEvent** class when the button is clicked:

```
void actionPerformed(ActionEvent e)
```

TIP: *The documentation that comes with Java and the Java Black Book (The Coriolis Group, ©2000) lists every method an interface has, as well as what objects are passed to them, and the methods of those objects.*

ActionEvent objects inherit a method named **getSource** from the **EventObject** class, and this method returns the object that caused the event. This means I can check if this event was caused by the button, **button1**, and if so, place the text "Hello from Java!" into the text field, **text1,** this way in the **actionPerformed** method called when the button is clicked:

```
import java.applet.Applet;
import java.awt.*;
import java.awt.event.*;

/*
```

```
<APPLET
    CODE=applet.class
    WIDTH=200
    HEIGHT=200 >
</APPLET>
*/

public class applet extends Applet implements ActionListener
{
    TextField text1;
    Button button1;

    public void init()
    {
        text1 = new TextField(20);
        add(text1);
        button1 = new Button("Click Here!");
        add(button1);
        button1.addActionListener(this);
    }

    public void actionPerformed(ActionEvent event)
    {
        String msg = new String ("Hello from Java!");
        if(event.getSource() == button1){
            text1.setText(msg);
        }
    }
}
```

This applet appears in Figure 16.5. When you click the button, the text "Hello from Java!" appears in the text field.

Figure 16.5   Supporting button clicks.

Creating Password Fields

"Hey," says the novice programmer, "I want to let users type in a password, but that darn Johnson keeps standing over people's shoulders and watching as they type their passwords." "That's easily fixed," you say; "just set the echo character of the text field to an asterisk or something like that. Problem solved!"

In this case, I'll create a password text field that will display an asterisk (*) each time the user types a character. How can you read the typed password in the text field? You can use the text field's **getText** method, which the text field inherits from the **Component** class. In fact, I'll add a second text field to this program and display the password in that text field when the user presses the Enter key. I'll start by adding two text fields, each 30 characters wide:

```
import java.applet.Applet;
import java.awt.*;
import java.awt.event.*;

/*
<APPLET
    CODE=password.class
    WIDTH=200
    HEIGHT=200 >
</APPLET>
*/

public class password extends Applet implements ActionListener
{
    public TextField text1;
    public TextField text2;

    public void init()
    {
        text1 = new TextField(30);
        add(text1);
        text2 = new TextField(30);
        add(text2);
        .
        .
        .
```

Next, I set the echo character in **text1**, the password text field to '*', and add an action listener to that text field:

```
    public void init()
    {
        text1 = new TextField(30);
        add(text1);
        text2 = new TextField(30);
        add(text2);

        text1.setEchoChar('*');
        text1.addActionListener(this);
    }
```

When the user presses Enter, the **actionPerformed** method is called, so I override that method to set the text in the second text field to the text in the password component:

```
public void actionPerformed(ActionEvent e)
{
    if(e.getSource() == text1){
        text2.setText(text1.getText());
    }
}
```

Here's the entire code for the applet, password.java:

```
import java.applet.Applet;
import java.awt.*;
import java.awt.event.*;

/*
<APPLET
    CODE=password.class
    WIDTH=400
    HEIGHT=200 >
</APPLET>
*/

public class password extends Applet implements ActionListener
{
    public TextField text1;
    public TextField text2;

    public void init()
    {
        text1 = new TextField(30);
        add(text1);
```

```
        text2 = new TextField(30);
        add(text2);

        text1.setEchoChar('*');
        text1.addActionListener(this);
    }

    public void actionPerformed(ActionEvent e)
    {
        if(e.getSource() == text1){
            text2.setText(text1.getText());
        }
    }
}
```

The results of this code appear in Figure 16.6. When the user types a password in the top text field and presses Enter, the password appears in the lower text field (not exactly what you'd call high security).

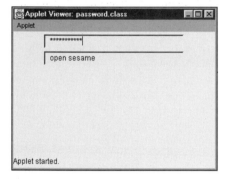

Figure 16.6   Reading passwords in text fields.

Creating Labels

AWT labels are much like AWT text fields except that the user can't edit the text in them. You can use labels to present noneditable text, or, as their name implies, to label other components. Here is the inheritance diagram for the **Label** class:

```
java.lang.Object
|____java.awt.Component
     |____java.awt.Label
```

You can justify the text in a label by passing the fields **Label.LEFT**, **Label. CENTER**, and **Label.RIGHT** to the label's constructor. Here's an example that creates three labels with the various possible text justifications in an example named label.java:

```
import java.applet.Applet;
import java.awt.*;

/*
<APPLET
    CODE=label.class
    WIDTH=200
    HEIGHT=200 >
</APPLET>
*/

public class label extends Applet
{
    Label label1;
    Label label2;
    Label label3;

    public void init()
    {
        label1 = new Label("Hello from Java!", Label.LEFT);
        add(label1);
        label2 = new Label("Hello from Java!", Label.CENTER);
        add(label2);
        label3 = new Label("Hello from Java!", Label.RIGHT);
        add(label3);
    }
}
```

The results of this applet appear in Figure 16.7.

Figure 16.7   Justifying text in a label.

Creating Checkboxes

"Now there's another problem," the novice programmer says; "I want to let users select what they want on a pizza, so I'd like a button, when clicked, to stay clicked so users know what they've already selected." "No problem at all," you say, "don't use buttons." "No?" the NP asks. "No," you say, "use checkboxes."

A checkbox allows the user to select options; when the user clicks a checkbox, a visual indication, such as a checkmark (the indicator varies for each operating system when using the AWT), appears to indicate the option is selected. Clicking the checkbox again deselects the checkbox. In AWT, checkboxes are supported with the **java.awt.Checkbox** class, which has this inheritance diagram:

```
java.lang.Object
|____java.awt.Component
     |____java.awt.Checkbox
```

Note in particular that you can set the state of checkboxes with **setState** and get the state with **getState**.

Here's an example. In this case, I'll add four checkboxes to an applet, and when the user clicks a checkbox, indicate which checkbox was clicked in a text field. Note that checkboxes do not use **ActionListeners** as buttons do; instead, they use **ItemListeners**, which are set up to handle components that can be selected or deselected. The **ItemListener** interface has only one method, **itemStateChanged**, which is passed a parameter of class **ItemEvent**:

```
void itemStateChanged(ItemEvent e)
```

Here's how I add the checkboxes to an applet and add an **ItemListener** to each one in an example named checks.java:

```
import java.applet.Applet;
import java.awt.*;
import java.awt.event.*;

/*
<APPLET
    CODE=checks.class
    WIDTH=200
    HEIGHT=200 >
</APPLET>
*/
```

```
public class checks extends Applet implements ItemListener {

    Checkbox checkbox1, checkbox2, checkbox3, checkbox4;
    TextField text1;

    public void init()
    {
        checkbox1 = new Checkbox("1");
        add(checkbox1);
        checkbox1.addItemListener(this);
        checkbox2 = new Checkbox("2");
        add(checkbox2);
        checkbox2.addItemListener(this);
        checkbox3 = new Checkbox("3");
        add(checkbox3);
        checkbox3.addItemListener(this);
        checkbox4 = new Checkbox("4");
        add(checkbox4);
        checkbox4.addItemListener(this);
        text1 = new TextField(20);
        add(text1);
    }
```

Now I override the **itemStateChanged** method, determining which checkbox was clicked by using the **ItemEvent** object's **getItemSelectable** method:

```
    public void itemStateChanged(ItemEvent e)
    {
        if(e.getItemSelectable() == checkbox1){
            text1.setText("Check box 1 clicked!");
        } else if(e.getItemSelectable() == checkbox2){
            text1.setText("Check box 2 clicked!");
        } else if(e.getItemSelectable() == checkbox3){
            text1.setText("Check box 3 clicked!");
        } else if(e.getItemSelectable() == checkbox4){
            text1.setText("Check box 4 clicked!");
        }
    }
}
```

Note that you can also use the **ItemEvent** object's **getStateChanged** method to determine if the checkbox was selected or deselected; this method returns **Checkbox.SELECTED** or **Checkbox.DESELECTED**. And, of course, you can use the checkbox's **getState** method to make the same determination. You can also set the state of the checkbox with the **setState** method.

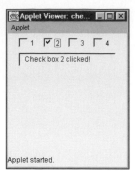

Figure 16.8   Handling checkbox clicks.

The results of this applet appear in Figure 16.8. You can find this applet in checks.java on the CD-ROM accompanying this book.

It's tedious to have so many **if** statements in the if-else ladder in the previous code, so in an example named checks2.java, I can just display the checkbox that was clicked by getting its label directly, like this:

```java
import java.applet.Applet;
import java.awt.*;
import java.awt.event.*;

/*
<APPLET
    CODE=checks2.class
    WIDTH=200
    HEIGHT=200 >
</APPLET>
*/

public class checks2 extends Applet implements ItemListener {

    Checkbox checkbox1, checkbox2, checkbox3, checkbox4;
    TextField text1;

    public void init()
    {
        checkbox1 = new Checkbox("1");
        add(checkbox1);
        checkbox1.addItemListener(this);
        checkbox2 = new Checkbox("2");
        add(checkbox2);
        checkbox2.addItemListener(this);
```

```
        checkbox3 = new Checkbox("3");
        add(checkbox3);
        checkbox3.addItemListener(this);
        checkbox4 = new Checkbox("4");
        add(checkbox4);
        checkbox4.addItemListener(this);
        text1 = new TextField(20);
        add(text1);
    }

    public void itemStateChanged(ItemEvent e)
    {
        text1.setText("Check box " +
            ((Checkbox) e.getItemSelectable()).getLabel() + " clicked!");
    }
}
```

There's another kind of checkbox you can use—radio buttons—and I'll take a look at these in the next section.

Creating Radio Buttons

"Uh oh," says the novice programmer, "there's another problem. I put some checkboxes in my program so the user could select the day of the week, but one user selected Wednesday *and* Friday." "Well," you say, "you should use radio buttons, not checkboxes, to display exclusive options like days of the week."

In AWT programming, radio buttons are a special kind of checkbox; you use radio buttons in groups. Only one radio button in a group may be selected at one time. When the user selects one radio button in a group, the others in the group are automatically deselected.

When you add checkboxes to a checkbox *group*, they become radio buttons automatically. The AWT supports checkbox groups with the **CheckboxGroup** class. Note that because radio buttons are really checkboxes, you can use **Checkbox** methods like **getState** and **setState** with them.

For example, to determine which radio button is selected in a group, use the **CheckboxGroup** class's **getSelectedCheckbox** method, and to set which one is selected, use the **setSelectedCheckbox** method.

Here's an example. In this case, I'll create a checkbox group named **radios** and add four radio buttons to that group. You add a radio button to a checkbox group by adding the group as a parameter in a checkbox's constructor, which turns it into a radio button. Here's what this looks like in an example named radios.java:

```java
import java.applet.Applet;
import java.awt.*;
import java.awt.event.*;

/*
<APPLET
    CODE=radios.class
    WIDTH=200
    HEIGHT=200 >
</APPLET>
*/

public class radios extends Applet implements ItemListener {

    CheckboxGroup radios;
    Checkbox radio1, radio2, radio3, radio4;
    TextField text1;

    public void init()
    {
        radios = new CheckboxGroup();

        radio1 = new Checkbox("1", false, radios);
        add(radio1);
        radio1.addItemListener(this);

        radio2 = new Checkbox("2", false, radios);
        add(radio2);
        radio2.addItemListener(this);

        radio3 = new Checkbox("3", false, radios);
        add(radio3);
        radio3.addItemListener(this);

        radio4 = new Checkbox("4", false, radios);
        add(radio4);
        radio4.addItemListener(this);

        text1 = new TextField(20);
        add(text1);
    }
```

Note that I've added an **ItemListener** to each radio button so I can implement the **ItemListener** interface and the **itemStateChanged** method to indicate which radio button was clicked, like this:

```
public void itemStateChanged(ItemEvent e)
{
    text1.setText("Radio button " +
        ((Checkbox) e.getItemSelectable()).getLabel() + " clicked!");
}
}
```

The results of this code appear in Figure 16.9. You'll find this applet on the CD-ROM as radios.java.

Figure 16.9   Handling radio button clicks.

Using Fonts

"The banner you created for the Company Pride Picnic was good," the big boss says, "but it didn't seem to be bursting with pride." "Why not?" you ask. "Well for one thing," the BB says, "it was only a quarter of an inch tall." "Hm," you say, "guess I better use a bigger font."

TIP: *You can select the type and style of text fonts with the **Font** class. Using this class, you can select a font, like Helvetica, Arial, or Courier, set its size, and specify if it's bold, italic, and so on.*

Let's see an example showing how to use fonts in Java. In this case, I'll let the user type characters, display them in Courier font, and center them in an applet by determining the screen size of the text using the Java **FontMetrics** class's **stringWidth** and **getHeight** methods and the width and height of the applet with the applet's **getSize** method. I'll also let the user specify the size of the text, as

16. Creating Java Applets

well as whether or not it should be italic or bold, and set a **Font** object accordingly. To actually install the font so that when you print text it appears in that font, you use a **Graphics** object's **setFont** method.

Note that I'll also read keystrokes, so I implement the **KeyListener** interface, which has three methods that we have to add to the code: **keyPressed(KeyEvent e)**, **keyReleased(KeyEvent e)**, and **keyTyped(KeyEvent e)**. To get the actual key that was typed in the **keyTyped** method, I use the **KeyEvent** object's **getKeyChar** method. I also use the **repaint** method to force Java to call the **paint** method and repaint the applet (as discussed in the In Depth section of this chapter). Here's what the applet, fonts.java, looks like:

```
import java.awt.*;
import java.awt.event.*;
import java.applet.Applet;

/*
   <APPLET
       CODE=fonts.class
       WIDTH=600
       HEIGHT=200 >
   </APPLET>
*/

public class fonts extends Applet implements ActionListener, KeyListener
{
    String text = "";

    Button boldbutton, italicbutton, largebutton;
    boolean bold = false;
    boolean italic = false;
    boolean large = false;

    public void init()
    {
        boldbutton = new Button("Bold font");
        italicbutton = new Button("Italic font");
        largebutton = new Button("Large font");

        boldbutton.addActionListener(this);
        italicbutton.addActionListener(this);
        largebutton.addActionListener(this);

        add(boldbutton);
        add(italicbutton);
        add(largebutton);
```

```
        addKeyListener(this);
        requestFocus();
    }

    public void actionPerformed(ActionEvent event)
    {
        if(event.getSource() == boldbutton) bold = !bold;
        if(event.getSource() == italicbutton) italic = !italic;
        if(event.getSource() == largebutton) large = !large;
        requestFocus();
        repaint();
    }

    public void paint(Graphics g)
    {
        String fontname = "Courier";
        int type = Font.PLAIN;
        int size = 36;
        Font font;
        FontMetrics fm;

        if(bold) type = type | Font.BOLD;
        if(italic) type = type | Font.ITALIC;
        if(large) size = 72;

        font = new Font(fontname, type, size);
        g.setFont(font);

        fm = getFontMetrics(font);
        int xloc = (getSize().width - fm.stringWidth(text)) / 2;
        int yloc = (getSize().height + fm.getHeight()) / 2;

        g.drawString(text, xloc, yloc);
    }

    public void keyTyped(KeyEvent e)
    {
        text = text + e.getKeyChar();
        repaint();
    }

    public void keyPressed(KeyEvent e) {}
    public void keyReleased(KeyEvent e) {}
}
```

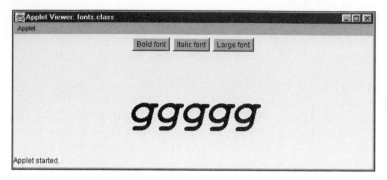

Figure 16.10   Using fonts.

You can see the results in Figure 16.10. When users type text, the text appears centered in the applet, and when they use the Bold font, Italic font, and Large font buttons, the text appears with the corresponding attributes, as you can see in Figure 16.10.

Now it's time to move on to working with images—take a look at the next section.

Handling Images

The big boss says, "About this photo essay you wrote for the company newspaper..." "Yes?" you ask. "Where are the photos?" the BB asks. "Hm," you say, "this looks like a job for the **Image** class."

You can support images in the AWT with the **Image** class, which is derived directly from **java.lang.Object**:

```
java.lang.Object
|____java.awt.Image
```

To load an image into an applet, you can use the **Applet** class's **getImage** method, which has these different forms (Java knows which form you'll be using by the types and number of the arguments you pass):

```
Image getImage(URL url)
Image getImage(URL url, String name)
```

You can specify the URL of the image file you want to read using the **URL** class. You can create a **URL** object using the **URL** class's constructor like this: **URL("http://java.sun.com/products/jdk/1.2/")**. As far as this chapter is concerned, however, I'll use both the **Applet** class's **getCodeBase** and **getDocumentBase** methods to get the URL for the applet itself and use that URL to find the image file.

Here's a short example that just reads in an image, image.jpg, and displays it. To read in the image, I use the **getImage** method, and to draw the image, I use the **Graphics** class's **drawImage** method. For more on the **Graphics** class, see the section "Drawing Graphics," coming up next. Here's the form of **drawImage** that I'll use, which lets me specify the image object to draw and its position in the applet:

```
boolean drawImage(Image img, int x, int y, ImageObserver observer)
```

Note that you have to pass an object that implements the **ImageObserver** interface to **drawImage**. **ImageObserver** objects let you monitor the progress of image loading operations, and there's a default implementation of this interface in the **Applet** class, so you can just use a **this** keyword as the **ImageObserver** object as in this example, image.java:

```
import java.awt.*;
import java.applet.*;

/*
  <APPLET
      CODE-image.class
      WIDTH=500
      HEIGHT=150 >
  </APPLET>
*/

public class image extends Applet
{
    Image image;

    public void init()
    {
        image = getImage(getDocumentBase(), "image.jpg");
    }

    public void paint(Graphics g)
    {
        g.drawImage(image, 10, 10, this);
    }
}
```

Figure 16.11   Displaying an image.

The results appear in Figure 16.11, where you can see the loaded image. This example is a success, and you'll find it in image.java on the CD-ROM.

Drawing Graphics

The big boss appears in a puff of cigar smoke and says, "The design team has come up with a winning program that I want you to write." "What does it do?" you ask. "Lets the user draw lines, rectangles, ovals, or freehand with the mouse," the BB says. "Real cutting edge stuff," you say.

The real core of AWT graphics is the huge AWT **Graphics** class, which is derived directly from **java.lang.Object**. I'm going to put the **Graphics** class to work here by creating the program the big boss wanted—a graphics program that lets the user draw lines, ovals, rectangles, rounded rectangles, and freehand with the mouse, as you see in Figure 16.12.

Here's how this program, draw.class, works: Users click a button indicating what kind of figure they want to draw, which sets a Boolean flag inside the program. When users press the mouse in the drawing area, I store that location as **start**,

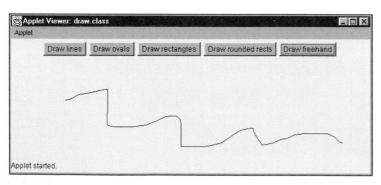

Figure 16.12   Drawing freehand with the mouse.

using a Java **Point** object (which has two data members: **x** and **y**), and when users release the mouse in a new location, I store that location as **end**. Releasing the mouse also repaints the program, and I can select which figure to draw—a line, oval, rectangle, or rounded rectangle—between **start** and **end** based on the Boolean flags set by clicking the buttons.

Drawing freehand with the mouse is a little different, though. In this case, I store up to 1,000 points that the mouse moves over and when it's time to draw the program, I just connect the dots with lines (note that a mouse event is not generated for each pixel the mouse moves over, so I need to draw lines between the mouse locations that Java does report). Here's what draw.java looks like; I'll take a look at the drawing sections in detail in the following pages:

```java
import java.awt.*;
import java.lang.Math;
import java.awt.event.*;
import java.awt.Graphics;
import java.applet.Applet;

/*
  <APPLET
      CODE=draw.class
      WIDTH=600
      HEIGHT=200 >
  </APPLET>
*/

public class draw extends Applet implements ActionListener,
    MouseListener, MouseMotionListener {
    Button bDraw, bLine, bOval, bRect, bRounded;
    Point dot[] = new Point[1000];
    Point start, end;
    int dots = 0;

    boolean mouseUp = false;
    boolean draw = false;
    boolean line = false;
    boolean oval = false;
    boolean rectangle = false;
    boolean rounded = false;

    public void init()
    {
        bLine = new Button("Draw lines");
        bOval = new Button("Draw ovals");
```

```
        bRect = new Button("Draw rectangles");
        bRounded = new Button("Draw rounded rects");
        bDraw = new Button("Draw freehand");

        add(bLine);
        add(bOval);
        add(bRect);
        add(bRounded);
        add(bDraw);

        bLine.addActionListener(this);
        bOval.addActionListener(this);
        bRect.addActionListener(this);
        bRounded.addActionListener(this);
        bDraw.addActionListener(this);

        addMouseListener(this);
        addMouseMotionListener(this);
    }

    public void mousePressed(MouseEvent e)
    {
        mouseUp = false;
        start = new Point(e.getX(), e.getY());
    }

    public void mouseReleased(MouseEvent e)
    {
        if(line){
            end = new Point(e.getX(), e.getY());
        } else {
            end = new Point(Math.max(e.getX(), start.x),
                Math.max(e.getY(), start.y));
            start = new Point(Math.min(e.getX(), start.x),
                Math.min(e.getY(), start.y));
        }
        mouseUp = true;
        repaint();
    }

    public void mouseDragged(MouseEvent e)
    {
        if(draw){
            dot[dots] = new Point(e.getX(), e.getY());
            dots++;
```

```
            repaint();
        }
    }

public void mouseClicked(MouseEvent e){}
public void mouseEntered(MouseEvent e){}
public void mouseExited(MouseEvent e){}
public void mouseMoved(MouseEvent e){}

public void paint (Graphics g)
{
    if (mouseUp) {
        int width = end.x - start.x;
        int height = end.y - start.y;

        if(line){
            g.drawLine(start.x, start.y, end.x, end.y);
        }
        else if(oval){
            g.drawOval(start.x, start.y, width, height);
        }
        else if(rectangle){
            g.drawRect(start.x, start.y, width, height);
        }
        else if(rounded){
            g.drawRoundRect(start.x, start.y, width, height, 10, 10);
        }
        else if(draw){
            for(int loop_index = 0; loop_index < dots - 1;
                loop_index++){
                g.drawLine(dot[loop_index].x, dot[loop_index].y,
                    dot[loop_index + 1].x, dot[loop_index + 1].y);
            }
        }
    }
}

public void actionPerformed(ActionEvent e)
{
    setFlagsFalse();
    if(e.getSource() == bDraw)draw = true;
    if(e.getSource() == bLine)line = true;
    if(e.getSource() == bOval)oval = true;
    if(e.getSource() == bRect)rectangle = true;
    if(e.getSource() == bRounded)rounded = true;
}
```

```
    void setFlagsFalse()
    {
        rounded = false;
        line = false;
        oval = false;
        rectangle = false;
        draw = false;
    }
}
```

That's what draw.java looks like; and in this section, I'll take a look at some of its drawing functions. All of these drawing functions, except freehand drawing, will draw a figure between the locations start and end, which the user indicates by dragging the mouse. Note that to create this program, we'll need to be able to handle the mouse, so I'll start with that.

Using The Mouse

You can work with the mouse using two AWT interfaces—**MouseListener**, which handles mouse clicks, presses, and releases as well as the case where the mouse enters a component and leaves it, and **MouseMotionListener**, which handles mouse movements and drag operations. The following list contains the methods of the **MouseListener** interface, all of which you'll have to implement to use this interface.

- **void mouseClicked(MouseEvent e)**—Called when the mouse has been clicked on a component.

- **void mouseEntered(MouseEvent e)**—Called when the mouse enters a component.

- **void mouseExited(MouseEvent e)**—Called when the mouse exits a component.

- **void mousePressed(MouseEvent e)**—Called when a mouse button has been pressed on a component.

- **void mouseReleased(MouseEvent e)**—Called when a mouse button has been released on a component.

The following are the methods of the **MouseMotionListener** interface, both of which you'll have to implement to use this interface:

- **void mouseDragged(MouseEvent e)**—Called when a mouse button is pressed on a component and then dragged.

- **void mouseMoved(MouseEvent e)**—Called when the mouse button has been moved on a component (with no buttons no down).

Each of the mouse interface methods are passed an object of class **MouseEvent**, and the inheritance diagram for that class looks like this:

```
java.lang.Object
|____java.util.EventObject
    |____java.awt.AWTEvent
        |____java.awt.event.ComponentEvent
            |____java.awt.event.InputEvent
                |____java.awt.event.MouseEvent
```

Let's see a quick example. This applet, mouse.java, will display most of what the mouse can do. To catch particular mouse actions, you just override the corresponding mouse listener method. To get the current location of the mouse from a **MouseEvent** object, you can use the **getX** and **getY** methods. To determine which button was pressed, you can use the **MouseEvent** class's **getModifiers** method, applying **AND** to the result with these fields from the **InputEvent** class's fields: **ALT_GRAPH_MASK**, **ALT_MASK**, **BUTTON1_MASK**, **BUTTON2_MASK**, **BUTTON3_MASK**, **CTRL_MASK**, **META_MASK**, **SHIFT_MASK**. Here's what the mouse.java applet looks like, putting all this to work:

```java
import java.applet.Applet;
import java.awt.*;
import java.awt.event.*;

/*
<APPLET
    CODE=mouse.class
    WIDTH=300
    HEIGHT=200 >
</APPLET>
*/

public class mouse extends Applet implements MouseListener,
    MouseMotionListener
{
    TextField text1;

    public void init(){
        text1 = new TextField(30);
        add(text1);
        addMouseListener(this);
        addMouseMotionListener(this);
    }
```

```java
public void mousePressed(MouseEvent e)
{
    if((e.getModifiers() & InputEvent.BUTTON1_MASK) ==
        InputEvent.BUTTON1_MASK){
        text1.setText("Left mouse button down at " + e.getX() + "," +
            e.getY());
    }
    else{
        text1.setText("Right mouse button down at " + e.getX() + "," +
            e.getY());
    }
}

public void mouseClicked(MouseEvent e)
{
    text1.setText("You clicked the mouse at " + e.getX() + "," +
        e.getY());
}

public void mouseReleased(MouseEvent e)
{
    text1.setText("The mouse button went up.");
}

public void mouseEntered(MouseEvent e)
{
    text1.setText("The mouse entered.");
}

public void mouseExited(MouseEvent e)
{
    text1.setText("The mouse exited.");
}

public void mouseDragged(MouseEvent e)
{
    text1.setText("The mouse was dragged.");
}

public void mouseMoved(MouseEvent e)
{
    text1.setText("The mouse was moved.");
}
}
```

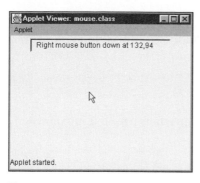

Figure 16.13   Using the mouse.

You can see this applet at work in Figure 16.13. When you move the mouse or use a mouse button, the applet lets you know what's going on.

That gets us up to speed using the mouse in Java—now it's time to turn to the drawing part of draw.java.

Drawing Lines

Using a **Graphics** object, you can draw a line between the points (*x1*, *y1*) and (*x2*, *y2*) with the **drawLine** method:

```
drawLine(int x1, int y1, int x2, int y2);
```

Here's how this looks in draw.java:

```
g.drawLine(start.x, start.y, end.x, end.y);
```

And you can see the results in draw.java in Figure 16.14.

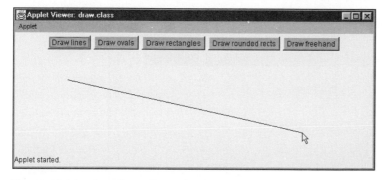

Figure 16.14   Drawing a line with the mouse.

Drawing Ovals

Ellipses, including circles, are called ovals in the AWT, and you can draw them with the **Graphics** class's **drawOval** method:

```
drawOval(int x, int y, int width, int height);
```

Here's how I draw ovals as specified by the user when running draw.java:

```
int width = end.x - start.x;
int height = end.y - start.y;
g.drawOval(start.x, start.y, width, height);
```

And you can see the results in draw.java in Figure 16.15.

Drawing Rectangles

You can draw rectangles using the **Graphics** class's **drawRect** method:

```
drawRect(int x, int y, int width, int height);
```

Here's how I do this in draw.java:

```
int width = end.x - start.x;
int height = end.y - start.y;
g.drawRect(start.x, start.y, width, height);
```

And you can see the results in draw.java in Figure 16.16.

Drawing Rounded Rectangles

You can draw rounded rectangles—rectangles with rounded corners, that is—using the **Graphics** class's **drawRoundRect** method:

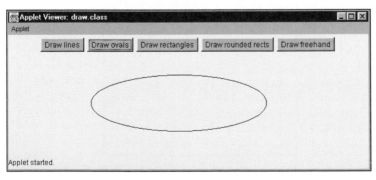

Figure 16.15   Drawing ovals with the mouse.

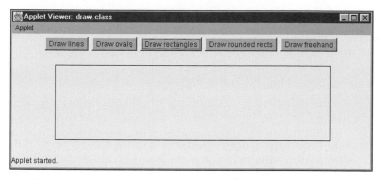

Figure 16.16   Drawing a rectangle with the mouse.

```
drawRoundRect(int x, int y, int width, int height, int arcWidth, int
    arcHeight);
```

You specify the arc width and height in pixels, which specifies the rounding of the corners. Here's how I draw a rounded rectangle in draw.java:

```
int width = end.x - start.x;
int height = end.y - start.y;
g.drawRoundRect(start.x, start.y, width, height, 10, 10);
```

And you can see the results in draw.java in Figure 16.17.

Drawing Freehand

You can let the user draw freehand with the mouse using the AWT **Graphics** class, but you'll have to do it yourself. Here's how I do this in draw.java in the **mouseDragged** method. After determining that the user is drawing freehand by making sure the **draw** flag is true, I save all the mouse locations as the mouse is dragged in an array named **dot[]**:

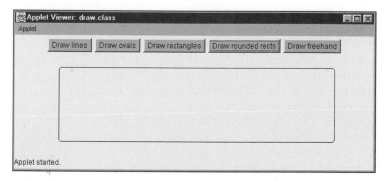

Figure 16.17   Drawing rounded rectangles with the mouse.

16. Creating Java Applets

```
public void mouseDragged(MouseEvent e)
{
    if(draw){
        dot[dots] = new Point(e.getX(), e.getY());
        dots++;
        repaint();
    }
}
```

Then, when it's time to draw the figure, I just connect the dots using lines like this:

```
for(int loop_index = 0; loop_index < dots - 1; loop_index++){
    g.drawLine(dot[loop_index].x, dot[loop_index].y,
        dot[loop_index + 1].x, dot[loop_index + 1].y);
}
```

You can see the results in Figure 16.12.

Drawing Arcs

You can use the **Graphics** class's **drawArc** method to draw arcs (you specify angles in degrees):

```
drawArc(int x, int y, int width, int height, int startAngle, int arcAngle);
```

Drawing Polygons

There are a number of ways to draw polygons and multiple-segment lines with the AWT:

```
drawPolygon(int[] xPoints, int[] yPoints, int nPoints);
```

```
drawPolygon(Polygon p);
```

```
drawPolyline(int[] xPoints, int[] yPoints, int nPoints);
```

Setting Drawing Modes

The AWT also allows you to alternate between two drawing modes, straight painting mode and XOR (exclusive OR) mode, with these methods:

```
setPaintMode();
```

```
setXORMode(Color c1);
```

In paint mode, whatever you paint just covers what's underneath, but in XOR mode, what you draw will be exclusively ORed with a particular color that's already on the screen. This is very useful because when you XOR A with B twice, B is restored, which means that you can draw something on the screen, then draw it using XOR drawing, and whatever was on the screen originally is restored. For example, you may want to let users "stretch" the figures they're drawing in draw.java interactively. To do this, you draw a figure, then when the user moves the mouse, redraw the figure using XOR mode to erase it and redraw it with its new size.

Chapter 17

Essential XML

In Depth

Welcome to Extensible Markup Language (XML). XML is a markup language that you use to describe data, and it allows far more precise structuring of that data than is possible with HTML. In XML, you create your own tags and syntax for those tags, so you can let the document structure follow the data structure. Then you can open the XML document using Internet Explorer. In this chapter and in Chapter 18, I'll take a look at the XML support in Internet Explorer 5 and later (Netscape Navigator doesn't have such support). Using a scripting language like JavaScript, you can reach the various elements of an XML page and make use of your data. I'll start by taking a look at how to create an XML document in this chapter and how to work with it using JavaScript. In the next chapter, I'll take a look at the data binding uses for XML.

The following list contains some resources you can use to learn more about XML:

- *http://msdn.microsoft.com/workshop/xml/index.asp*—Microsoft's discussion of XML.

- *http://msdn.microsoft.com/xml/tutorial/default.asp*—Microsoft's XML tutorial.

- *www.projectcool.com/developer/xmlz/index.html*—Project Cool's in-depth tutorial.

- *www.w3.org/TR/REC-xml*—The latest XML specification. The World Wide Web Consortium (W3C) is in charge of the specification of XML and sets the rules on how to create document type definitions (DTDs) and other elements that we'll see throughout this chapter.

What Does XML Look Like?

I'll create an XML page that holds the purchasing records of several customers, showing how easy it is to create data structures in XML. To start an XML page, you begin with the XML processing instruction **<?xml version = "1.0"?>**, which lets Internet Explorer know that this document is XML, much like the **<HTML>** tag indicates an HTML document.

NOTE: *Internet Explorer is very careful about syntax and insists that everything in the XML processing instruction* **<?xml version = "1.0"?>** *be lowercase.*

Here's the necessary first line of our XML document:

```
<?xml version = "1.0"?>
    .
    .
    .
```

You can name your own tags in XML, and I'll do that here. The body of the XML document should be enclosed in one XML element, which I'll call **<DOCUMENT>**:

```
<?xml version = "1.0"?>
<DOCUMENT>
    .
    .
    .
</DOCUMENT>
```

Now I'll start storing purchasing data by customer. To store this data, I'll create a new element, **<CUSTOMER>**, which goes inside the **<DOCUMENT>** element:

```
<?xml version = "1.0"?>
<DOCUMFNT>
    <CUSTOMER>
    .
    .
    .
    </CUSTOMER>
</DOCUMENT>
```

I can also store the customer's name by creating a new **<NAME>** element, which itself contains two elements—**<LAST_NAME>** and **<FIRST_NAME>**:

```
<?xml version = "1.0"?>
<DOCUMENT>
    <CUSTOMER>
        <NAME>
            <LAST_NAME>Thomson</LAST_NAME>
            <FIRST_NAME>Susan</FIRST_NAME>
        </NAME>
    .
    .
    .
    </CUSTOMER>
</DOCUMENT>
```

Additionally, I store the date of the record as well as the actual customer orders in an **<ORDERS>** element, where I place all the items the customer bought:

```
<?xml version = "1.0"?>
<DOCUMENT>
    <CUSTOMER>
        <NAME>
            <LAST_NAME>Thomson</LAST_NAME>
            <FIRST_NAME>Susan</FIRST_NAME>
        </NAME>
        <DATE>September 1, 2001</DATE>
        <ORDERS>
            <ITEM>
                <PRODUCT>Video tape</PRODUCT>
                <NUMBER>5</NUMBER>
                <PRICE>$1.25</PRICE>
            </ITEM>
            <ITEM>
                <PRODUCT>Shovel</PRODUCT>
                <NUMBER>2</NUMBER>
                <PRICE>$4.98</PRICE>
            </ITEM>
        </ORDERS>
    </CUSTOMER>
        .
        .
        .
</DOCUMENT>
```

I can store the records of as many customers as I want in this XML page. Here's how I add a new customer's record:

```
<?xml version = "1.0"?>
<DOCUMENT>
    <CUSTOMER>
        <NAME>
            <LAST_NAME>Thomson</LAST_NAME>
            <FIRST_NAME>Susan</FIRST_NAME>
        </NAME>
        <DATE>September 1, 2001</DATE>
        <ORDERS>
            <ITEM>
                <PRODUCT>Video tape</PRODUCT>
                <NUMBER>5</NUMBER>
                <PRICE>$1.25</PRICE>
            </ITEM>
```

```
            <ITEM>
                <PRODUCT>Shovel</PRODUCT>
                <NUMBER>2</NUMBER>
                <PRICE>$4.98</PRICE>
            </ITEM>
        </ORDERS>
    </CUSTOMER>
    <CUSTOMER>
        <NAME>
            <LAST_NAME>Smithson</LAST_NAME>
            <FIRST_NAME>Nancy</FIRST_NAME>
        </NAME>
        <DATE>September 2, 2001</DATE>
        <ORDERS>
            <ITEM>
                <PRODUCT>Ribbon</PRODUCT>
                <NUMBER>12</NUMBER>
                <PRICE>$2.95</PRICE>
            </ITEM>
            <ITEM>
                <PRODUCT>Goldfish</PRODUCT>
                <NUMBER>6</NUMBER>
                <PRICE>$1.50</PRICE>
            </ITEM>
        </ORDERS>
    </CUSTOMER>
</DOCUMENT>
```

As you can see, XML provides you with a way of creating and structuring your data in a manner that fits that data. You might wonder how browsers deal with such free-form data. For example, how will a browser know how you want to display **<CUSTOMER>**? This points out a fundamental difference between XML and HTML; XML provides a way of structuring your data, not a method to display it as HTML does (however, you can use Cascading Style Sheets [CSS] or the Extensible Stylesheet Language (XSL) to do just that). Although HTML may indicate what text should be bold and what text italic, XML has no such formatting built-in.

Internet Explorer provides access to the elements in an XML page, as we'll see throughout this chapter, where I'll use JavaScript to access the data in XML pages. It's up to you to interpret the data in the document—Internet Explorer only makes it available to you through an object model with properties and methods.

Internet Explorer actually can display an XML document directly, and you can see the page we've just created in Figure 17.1 (you must give the file the extension .xml to documents you want to view as XML documents).

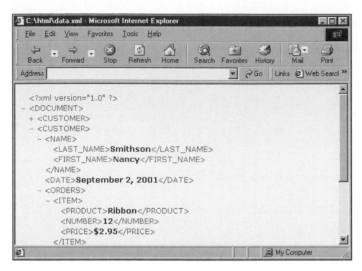

Figure 17.1   An XML document in Internet Explorer.

You can click the plus (+) and minus (-) signs in Figure 17.1 to expand and collapse XML elements. As you see in the figure, I've collapsed the first customer element and expanded the second. In this way, Internet Explorer lets you look at your XML document directly.

In fact, Internet Explorer can even do more—it can check the XML page's syntax. You provide the actual elements in the page and also specify what syntax is legal and what is not. For example, you indicate which elements may contain other elements, exactly what elements an element can contain, as well as how many elements it can contain, and so on. There are two ways of specifying syntax for an XML page—using a *document type definition* (DTD) or an *XML schema*. An XML schema is a Microsoft innovation that serves the same purpose as a DTD, although it's supposed to be easier to create and allows you more control. I'll take a look at both DTDs and schemas in this chapter (see Immediate Solution sections "Creating XML Documents With DTDs" and "Creating XML Documents With Schemas").

The latest technique in Web pages is separating the user interface from data, and in fact, Microsoft calls this the "power and beauty of XML." (The lack of such a separation is the reason W3C didn't adopt Netscape's **<LAYER>** element as official.) On its Microsoft Developer Network (MSDN) Web site, Microsoft says, "XML separates the data from the presentation and the process, enabling you to display and process the data as you wish by applying different style sheets and applications." In practice, what this means is that the real XML processing takes place in code, and you're responsible for writing that code. As the XML tags you use become standardized in your group or corporation, you can exchange XML pages with others. The JavaScript you write can extract the data from the XML page and work with it, even displaying that data to your specification. We'll see quite a few examples of this in this chapter.

From Microsoft's point of view, you can use XML to create:

- An ordinary document.
- A structured record, such as an appointment record or purchase order.
- An object with data and methods, such as the persistent form of a Java object or ActiveX control.
- A data record, such as the result set of a query.
- Metacontent about a Web site, such as Channel Definition Format (CDF) data.
- Graphical presentation, such as an application's user interface.
- XML schemas and types.

We've seen how to create a basic XML document, but there's more to the process. Ideally, XML documents should also be *valid* and *well-formed*, and I'll take a look at what this means before getting into the details of how to work with an XML document's data.

Valid And Well-Formed XML Documents

An XML document is considered *valid* if there is a DTD or XML schema associated with it and if the document complies with the DTD or schema. That's all there is to making a document valid.

TIP: *To check if an XML page is valid, you can open it in Internet Explorer, which will tell you if the document does not comply with the DTD or schema. Also, you might want to check out the Microsoft XML validator page at* **http://msdn.microsoft.com/downloads/samples/internet/xml/xml_validator/default.asp**. *You can download and run the Microsoft validator to test XML documents or enter the URL of an XML document to check it online.*

An XML document is considered *well-formed* if it contains one or more elements, if there is precisely one element (the *root* or *document* element) for which neither the start nor the end tag is inside any other element, and if all other tags nest within each other correctly. In addition, all elements used in the document must either be predefined in XML, DTD, or XML schema.

TIP: *Note in particular the requirement that the entire XML document be enclosed in one element, the root element. This fact will be important when we start working with the contents of XML documents in code because we'll start by getting access to the root element first, and then move to other elements as required. Take a look at the previous XML example where the root element is* **<DOCUMENT>**.

Here's an example. In this case, I'll add a DTD to the XML document we created in the very beginning of the chapter to make it both valid and well-formed (I'll go into how to create DTDs and schemas in a few pages):

```
<?xml version = "1.0" ?>
<!DOCTYPE DOCUMENT [
<!ELEMENT DOCUMENT (CUSTOMER)*>
<!ELEMENT CUSTOMER (NAME,DATE,ORDERS)>
<!ELEMENT NAME (LAST_NAME,FIRST_NAME)>
<!ELEMENT LAST_NAME (#PCDATA)>
<!ELEMENT FIRST_NAME (#PCDATA)>
<!ELEMENT DATE (#PCDATA)>
<!ELEMENT ORDERS (ITEM)*>
<!ELEMENT ITEM (PRODUCT,NUMBER,PRICE)>
<!ELEMENT PRODUCT (#PCDATA)>
<!ELEMENT NUMBER (#PCDATA)>
<!ELEMENT PRICE (#PCDATA)>
]>
<DOCUMENT>
    <CUSTOMER>
        <NAME>
            <LAST_NAME>Thomson</LAST_NAME>
            <FIRST_NAME>Susan</FIRST_NAME>
        </NAME>
        <DATE>September 1, 2001</DATE>
        <ORDERS>
            <ITEM>
                <PRODUCT>Video tape</PRODUCT>
                <NUMBER>5</NUMBER>
                <PRICE>$1.25</PRICE>
            </ITEM>
            <ITEM>
                <PRODUCT>Shovel</PRODUCT>
                <NUMBER>2</NUMBER>
                <PRICE>$4.98</PRICE>
            </ITEM>
        </ORDERS>
    </CUSTOMER>
    <CUSTOMER>
        <NAME>
            <LAST_NAME>Smithson</LAST_NAME>
            <FIRST_NAME>Nancy</FIRST_NAME>
        </NAME>
        <DATE>September 2, 2001</DATE>
        <ORDERS>
            <ITEM>
```

```
            <PRODUCT>Ribbon</PRODUCT>
            <NUMBER>12</NUMBER>
            <PRICE>$2.95</PRICE>
        </ITEM>
        <ITEM>
            <PRODUCT>Goldfish</PRODUCT>
            <NUMBER>6</NUMBER>
            <PRICE>$1.50</PRICE>
        </ITEM>
    </ORDERS>
  </CUSTOMER>
</DOCUMENT>
```

On the other hand, here's a document that is well-formed but not valid (because there is no DTD or schema):

```
<?xml version="1.0"?>
<DOCUMENT>
    <TITLE>
        A Noisy Noise Annoys An Oyster
    </TITLE>
</DOCUMENT>
```

Here is a document that contains a nesting error and no DTD, so it is neither valid nor well-formed:

```
<?xml version="1.0"?>
    <TITLE>
        A Noisy Noise Annoys An Oyster
    <HEADING>
    </TITLE>
        A Study Of Shellfish And Audio Disturbances
    </HEADING>
```

Most XML parsers, like the one in Internet Explorer, require XML documents to be well-formed, but not necessarily valid (most XML parsers do not require a DTD, but if there is one, the parser will use it to check the XML document). The formal specification recommends that your XML documents be both valid and well-formed.

To make an XML document valid, it has to be checked against a DTD or schema. I'll take a look in overview at how to create both of these items and what they look like in the following sections. (Note also that neither a DTD nor a schema is necessary before Internet Explorer will work with an XML document.)

XML Document Type Definitions

We've already seen how easy it is to create XML documents. In fact, if you want to make sure your documents are valid (that is, adhere to the syntax rules you set), you'll need a DTD or a schema. Creating these items is more complex than creating XML documents. I'll take a look at DTDs first. You can use internal or external DTDs with XML documents. Here's an example of an internal DTD—note that you enclose the DTD in a **<!DOCTYPE>** element, providing the name of the root element of the document (which is **THESIS** here) in the **<!DOCTYPE>** element:

```
<?xml version="1.0"?>
<!DOCTYPE THESIS [
    <!ELEMENT THESIS (P*)>
    <!ELEMENT P (#PCDATA)>
]>
<THESIS>
    <P>
        This is my Ph.D. thesis.
    </P>
    <P>
        Do you like it?
    </P>
    <P>
        If so, please give me my Ph.D.
    </P>
</THESIS>
```

The DTD indicates how the syntax of the XML elements you're creating works. For example, what elements can be inside what other elements. This DTD follows the W3C syntax conventions, which means you specify each element with **<!ELEMENT>**. You can also specify that the contents of an element be parsed character data (**#PCDATA**), other elements that you've created, or both. In this example, I'm indicating that the **<THESIS>** element must contain only **<P>** elements, but that it can contain zero or more occurrences of the **<P>** element (which is what the asterisk [*] after **P** in **<!ELEMENT THESIS (P*)>** means). The following list contains the symbols, like asterisk (*), that you can use when defining the syntax of an element:

- *a b*—*a* followed by *b*.
- *a | b*—*a* or *b* but not both.
- *a - b*—The set of strings represented by *a* but not represented by *b*.
- *a?*—*a* or nothing.
- *a+*—One or more occurrences of *a*.

- **a***—Zero or more occurrences of **a**.

- *(expression)*—Surrounding expression with parentheses means it is treated as a unit and may carry the suffix operator **?**, *****, or **+**.

In addition to defining the **<THESIS>** element, I define the **<P>** element so that it can only hold text, that is, parsed character data, with the keyword **#PCDATA**:

```
<?xml version="1.0"?>
<!DOCTYPE THESIS [
    <!ELEMENT THESIS (P*)>
    <!ELEMENT P (#PCDATA)>
]>
<THESIS>
    <P>
        This is my Ph.D. thesis.
    </P>
    <P>
        Do you like it?
    </P>
    <P>
        If so, please give me my Ph.D.
    </P>
</THESIS>
```

In this way, I've specified the syntax of these two elements, **<THESIS>** and **<P>**. We'll learn how to create DTDs and review an extensive example in the section "Creating XML Documents With DTDs" in the Immediate Solutions section.

You can also specify an *external* DTD with the **SYSTEM** attribute in the **<!DOCTYPE>** element like this:

```
<?xml version="1.0"?>
<!DOCTYPE DOCUMENT SYSTEM "dtdthesis.dtd">
<DOCUMENT>
    <P>
        This is my Ph.D. thesis.
    </P>
    <P>
        Do you like it?
    </P>
    <P>
        If so, please give me my Ph.D.
    </P>
</DOCUMENT>
```

17. Essential XML

The file dtdthesis.dtd just contains the **<!ELEMENT>** elements like this:

```
<!ELEMENT THESIS (P*)>
<!ELEMENT P (#PCDATA)>
```

And that's all it takes to create an external DTD. Besides specifying the syntax of XML elements like this, you can also specify which attributes elements can have, as we'll see in "Specifying Attributes In DTDs" in the Immediate Solutions section. In the meantime, I'll take a look at creating XML schemas now.

XML Schemas

XML schemas are Microsoft's alternative to DTDs. If you would like to create valid XML documents for use with Internet Explorer, you can use either a DTD or a schema.

TIP: *Although schemas are supposed to be easier to create than DTDs according to Microsoft, I haven't found them so. In fact, they're usually longer and more complex than the corresponding DTDs.*

NOTE: *The XML Schema implementation that ships with Internet Explorer 5 is based on the XML-Data Note (**www.w3.org/TR/1998/NOTE-XML-data-0105/**) posted by the W3C in January 1998 and the Document Content Description (DCD) Note (**www.w3.org/TR/NOTE-dcd**).*

Here's an example. In this case, I'm creating an XML document with the root element **<TASKFORCE>**. You specify the name of a schema that resides in a separate file with the **XMLS** (XML Schema) attribute in an XML document like this:

```
<?xml version="1.0" ?>
<TASKFORCE XMLS="x-schema:schema1.xml">
    <EMPLOYEE>George Patton</EMPLOYEE>
    <EMPLOYEE>Douglas MacArthur</EMPLOYEE>
    <DESCRIPTION>XML Programming Taskforce</DESCRIPTION>
</TASKFORCE>
```

In this case, I'm indicating that the schema for this XML document is **schema1.xml**. In schema1.xml, you start with the **<SCHEMA>** element like this:

```
<SCHEMA NAME="schema1">
    .
    .
    .
</SCHEMA>
```

To use schemas, you must include the following two lines, which create two XML *namespaces* with the **xmlns** keyword, using the uniform resource names (URNs) for the Microsoft definitions you use in schemas:

```
<SCHEMA NAME="schema1"
    xmlns="urn:schemas-microsoft-com:xml-data"
    xmlns:dt="urn:schemas-microsoft-com:datatypes">
    .
    .
    .
</SCHEMA>
```

The **xmlns** attribute defines an XML namespace. Namespaces were introduced to avoid element and attribute name clashes. For example, the previous code defines a namespace called **dt**, for data type, which includes an attribute named **type**. You may have already defined an attribute named **type**, so to avoid clashes with Microsoft's attribute with the same name, you qualify the Microsoft attributes with the **dt** namespace prefix like this: **dt:type="int"**. You can also qualify element names with namespaces in the same way, such as **<coriolis:document>**, which creates a **<document>** element as defined in the **coriolis** namespace. Namespaces become important when you're importing someone else's XML element and attribute definitions, which you do when creating a Microsoft XML schema. We'll learn how to use namespaces in schemas like this in "Creating XML Documents With Schemas" in the Immediate Solutions section. But we won't need them when creating standard XML documents in this chapter (I'll use DTDs instead of schemas for nearly all examples).

To specify the syntax of an element in a schema, you use the **<ELEMENTTYPE>** element as in this next example. I'm specifying that the **<EMPLOYEE>** and **<DESCRIPTION>** elements can only contain text and that their specifications are *closed*, which means they cannot accept any other content than what is listed (if you leave the specifications open, the element can contain other content than what you list). Note that I'm using the XML shortcut of including a forward slash in front of the closing angle bracket (*/>*), which represents a closing tag:

```
<SCHEMA NAME="schema1"
    xmlns="urn:schemas-microsoft-com:xml-data"
    xmlns:dt="urn:schemas-microsoft-com:datatypes">

    <ELEMENTTYPE name="EMPLOYEE" content="textOnly" model="closed"/>
    <ELEMENTTYPE name="DESCRIPTION" content="textOnly" model="closed"/>
    .
    .
    .
</SCHEMA>
```

Here's how I define the **<TASKFORCE>** element, which can contain both **<EMPLOYEE>** and **<DESCRIPTION>** elements—but can contain *only* elements (not text), which you specify with the **eltOnly** keyword. I'm also specifying that the **<EMPLOYEE>** element must occur at least once, and the **<DESCRIPTION>** element must occur once, but only once in the **<TASKFORCE>** element:

```
<SCHEMA NAME="schema1"
    xmlns="urn:schemas-microsoft-com:xml-data"
    xmlns:dt="urn:schemas-microsoft-com:datatypes">

    <ELEMENTTYPE name="EMPLOYEE" content="textOnly" model="closed"/>
    <ELEMENTTYPE name="DESCRIPTION" content="textOnly" model="closed"/>

    <ELEMENTTYPE name="TASKFORCE" content="eltOnly" model="closed">
        <ELEMENT type="EMPLOYEE" minOccurs="1" maxOccurs="*"/>
        <ELEMENT type="DESCRIPTION" minOccurs="1" maxOccurs="1"/>
    </ELEMENTTYPE>
</SCHEMA>
```

That completes our overview of XML DTDs and schemas; I'll take a look at how to work with XML documents in Internet Explorer 5 next.

XML In Internet Explorer 5

The support for XML in Internet Explorer 5 is fairly substantial. Here's an overview:

- *Direct viewing of XML*—The Microsoft XML implementation lets users view XML directly. You can also view XML using XSL or CSS in Internet Explorer.

- *Extensible Stylesheet Language (XSL) support*—The Microsoft XSL processor, which is based on the latest W3C Working Draft, allows developers to apply style sheets to XML data and display the data in a dynamic and flexible way that can be customized.

- *High-performance, validating XML engine*—The Internet Explorer's XML engine has been enhanced and fully supports W3C XML 1 and XML namespaces, which, as we've seen, let you qualify element names uniquely on the Web and thus avoid conflicts between elements with the same name.

- *XML Document Object Model (DOM)*—The XML DOM is a standard object application programming interface that gives developers control of XML document content, structure, and formats. The Microsoft XML implementation includes support for the W3C XML DOM recommendation and is accessible from Web page script, Visual Basic, C++, and other languages.

- *XML schemas*—Schemas define the rules of an XML document including element names and data types, which elements can appear in combination, and which attributes are available for each element.

At last, it's time to start working with the actual data in an XML document.

Loading XML Documents

To work with an XML document in Internet Explorer 5, you can load it in two ways. To see both ways in action, I'll use the XML document, school.xml, which records a school class on XML including the names of students in the class, like this:

```
<?xml version="1.0"?>
<SCHOOL>
    <CLASS type="seminar">
        <CLASS_TITLE>XML In Theory And Practice</CLASS_TITLE>
        <CLASS_NUMBER>10.306</CLASS_NUMBER>
        <SUBJECT>XML</SUBJECT>
        <START_DATE>1/1/2001</START_DATE>
        <STUDENTS>
            <STUDENT status="attending">
                <FIRST_NAME>Mark</FIRST_NAME>
                <LAST_NAME>Swansburg</LAST_NAME>
            </STUDENT>
            <STUDENT status="withdrawn">
                <FIRST_NAME>Thomas</FIRST_NAME>
                <LAST_NAME>Preston</LAST_NAME>
            </STUDENT>
        </STUDENTS>
    </CLASS>
</SCHOOL>
```

The first way of working with school.xml is to load it in with the **Microsoft. XMLDOM** object, creating a new ActiveX object. To see how this works, I'll read in school.xml and retrieve the name of the second student. After creating a new ActiveX object, I use the **load** method to load in school.xml with JavaScript:

```
<HTML>
    <HEAD>
        <TITLE>
            Finding Element Values in an XML Document
        </TITLE>

        <SCRIPT LANGUAGE="JavaScript">
            function getStudentData()
            {
                var xmldoc;
                xmldoc = new ActiveXObject("Microsoft.XMLDOM");
                xmldoc.load("school.xml");
```

```
                        .
                        .
                        .
                    }
        </HEAD>
</HTML>
```

Now I get the root element of the XML document (which contains all the other elements), using the **documentElement** property of this new object. I'm now free to navigate around the XML document using the **firstChild**, **nextChild**, **previousChild**, and **lastChild** methods, which let you access the child elements of an element, and the **firstSibling**, **nextSibling**, **previousSibling**, and **lastSibling** methods, which let you access elements on the same level. To get the root element of the XML document, you start with the **documentElement** method, then navigate to the second student element and create objects corresponding to the student's first and last names like this:

```
<HTML>
    <HEAD>
        <TITLE>
            Finding Element Values in an XML Document
        </TITLE>

        <SCRIPT LANGUAGE="JavaScript">
            function getStudentData()
            {
                var xmldoc;
                xmldoc = new ActiveXObject("Microsoft.XMLDOM");
                xmldoc.load("school.xml");

                nodeSchool = xmldoc.documentElement;
                nodeClass = nodeSchool.firstChild;
                nodeStudents = nodeClass.lastChild;
                nodeStudent = nodeStudents.lastChild;
                nodeFirstName = nodeStudent.firstChild;
                nodeLastName = nodeFirstName.nextSibling;
                .
                .
                .
    </HEAD>
</HTML>
```

To actually recover the data from the XML document—that is, the content of an element—you use the **nodeValue** property. Here's how I retrieve the name of the second student in school.xml and display it in a **<DIV>** element in the document's body:

```
<HTML>
    <HEAD>
        <TITLE>
            Finding Element Values in an XML Document
        </TITLE>

        <SCRIPT LANGUAGE="JavaScript">
            function getStudentData()
            {
                var xmldoc;
                xmldoc = new ActiveXObject("Microsoft.XMLDOM");
                xmldoc.load("school.xml");

                nodeSchool = xmldoc.documentElement;
                nodeClass = nodeSchool.firstChild;
                nodeStudents = nodeClass.lastChild;
                nodeStudent = nodeStudents.lastChild;
                nodeFirstName = nodeStudent.firstChild;
                nodeLastName = nodeFirstName.nextSibling;

                outputMessage = "Name: " +
                    nodeFirstName.firstChild.nodeValue + ' '
                  + nodeLastName.firstChild.nodeValue;
                message.innerHTML=outputMessage;
            }
        </SCRIPT>
    </HEAD>

    <BODY>
        <CENTER>
            <H1>
                Finding Element Values in an XML Document
            </H1>

            <DIV ID="message"></DIV>
            <P>
            <INPUT TYPE="BUTTON" VALUE="Get Second Student's Name"
                ONCLICK="getStudentData()">
        </CENTER>
    </BODY>
</HTML>
```

Note also that I'm adding a button to the Web page to run the JavaScript that will read the second name. You can see the results in Figure 17.2. When the user clicks the button, the browser reads in school.xml and displays the name of the second student. We've made some progress.

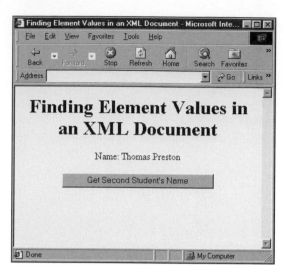

Figure 17.2   Accessing data in an XML document in Internet Explorer.

Using Data Islands

Starting with Internet Explorer version 5, you can also use *data islands* to handle XML. You create a data island with the **<XML>** HTML element, enclosing the XML you want to use in the **<XML>** element like this:

```
<XML ID="XMLID">
    <XMLDATA>
        <DATA>Here's some data!</DATA>
    </XMLDATA>
</XML>
```

The **<XMLDATA>** and **<DATA>** elements are XML elements, so I could have named them anything. Using the **<XML>** element's ID, you can access the XML in the element. You can also use a data island to handle an external XML document by using the **<XML>** element's **SRC** attribute. To get the root element of the XML document, you use the **XMLDocument** property. Here's how I convert the previous example to use a data island instead of the **Microsoft.XMLDOM** object:

```
<HTML>
    <HEAD>
        <TITLE>
            Finding Element Values in an XML Document Using Data Islands
        </TITLE>

        <XML ID="schoolXML" SRC="school.xml"></XML>
```

```
<SCRIPT LANGUAGE="JavaScript">
    function getStudentData()
    {
        xmldoc= document.all("schoolXML").XMLDocument;

        nodeSchool = xmldoc.documentElement;
        nodeClass = nodeSchool.firstChild;
        nodeStudents = nodeClass.lastChild;
        nodeStudent = nodeStudents.lastChild;
        nodeFirstName = nodeStudent.firstChild;
        nodeLastName = nodeFirstName.nextSibling;

        outputMessage = "Name: " +
            nodeFirstName.firstChild.nodeValue + ' '
           + nodeLastName.firstChild.nodeValue;
        message.innerHTML=outputMessage;
    }
    </SCRIPT>
</HEAD>

<BODY>
    <CENTER>
        <H1>
            Finding Element Values in an XML Document Using
            Data Islands
        </H1>

        <DIV ID="message"></DIV>
        <P>
        <INPUT TYPE="BUTTON" VALUE="Get Second Student's Name"
            ONCLICK="getStudentData()">
    </CENTER>
</BODY>
</HTML>
```

This example works as the previous example did, as you see in Figure 17.3. Now we've seen two ways of working with an XML document in Internet Explorer— by loading the document in explicitly and by using a data island. I'll use both approaches in this chapter, but will use data islands mostly because it's the most common technique.

And that's it for the introduction to XML; I'll take a look at the details in the Immediate Solutions section now.

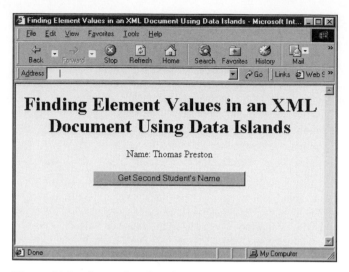

Figure 17.3   Accessing data in an XML document in Internet Explorer with data islands.

Immediate Solutions

Creating XML Documents

"OK," says the novice programmer, "I'm ready to work with XML. Where do I start?" "By creating an XML document," you say. "Lead on," says the NP, "and I'll follow." "It'll be $100 for the first lesson," you say. The NP says, "Uh oh."

We saw in the In Depth section of this chapter that you can create XML elements in a relatively free-form way, defining your own elements. Here's the example I discussed in the In Depth section—note that you must start an XML document with the **<?xml version = "1.0"?>** processing instruction, and that you must have one element that contains all others:

```
<?xml version = "1.0"?>
<DOCUMENT>
    <CUSTOMER>
        <NAME>
            <LAST_NAME>Thomson</LAST_NAME>
            <FIRST_NAME>Susan</FIRST_NAME>
        </NAME>
        <DATE>September 1, 2001</DATE>
        <ORDERS>
            <ITEM>
                <PRODUCT>Video tape</PRODUCT>
                <NUMBER>5</NUMBER>
                <PRICE>$1.25</PRICE>
            </ITEM>
            <ITEM>
                <PRODUCT>Shovel</PRODUCT>
                <NUMBER>2</NUMBER>
                <PRICE>$4.98</PRICE>
            </ITEM>
        </ORDERS>
    </CUSTOMER>
    <CUSTOMER>
        <NAME>
            <LAST_NAME>Smithson</LAST_NAME>
            <FIRST_NAME>Nancy</FIRST_NAME>
        </NAME>
        <DATE>September 2, 2001</DATE>
```

17. Essential XML

```
<ORDERS>
    <ITEM>
        <PRODUCT>Ribbon</PRODUCT>
        <NUMBER>12</NUMBER>
        <PRICE>$2.95</PRICE>
    </ITEM>
    <ITEM>
        <PRODUCT>Goldfish</PRODUCT>
        <NUMBER>6</NUMBER>
        <PRICE>$1.50</PRICE>
    </ITEM>
</ORDERS>
</CUSTOMER>
</DOCUMENT>
```

See the In Depth section of this chapter for the step-by-step construction of this example. You can see this XML document in Internet Explorer in Figure 17.1. Note that although Internet Explorer can deal with XML documents like this, you can also include a DTD or schema to make sure its syntax is acceptable. Take a look at the next few sections for the details on DTDs and schemas.

Creating XML Documents With DTDs

"Hey," says the novice programmer, "there are problems with the data in my XML document!" "Could be a syntax problem," you say, "why not let Internet Explorer check the syntax of your document using a DTD?" "Good idea," says the NP.

You use a DTD to let the browser check your XML document's syntax. DTDs aren't required, but can be a good idea to ensure data integrity. As we saw in the In Depth section of this chapter, you can create internal or external DTDs.

Creating DTDs can be somewhat complex, so I'll work through a second example in this section (there's an example in the beginning of this chapter). Here's the XML document I'll create; the DTD is enclosed in the **<!DOCTYPE>** element:

```
<?xml version="1.0"?>
<!DOCTYPE DOCUMENT [
    <!ELEMENT p (#PCDATA)>
    <!ELEMENT DOCUMENT      (TITLE,SUBTITLE?,PREFACE?,(SECTION | PART)+)>
    <!ELEMENT TITLE         (TITLE2)*>
    <!ELEMENT TITLE2        (#PCDATA)>
    <!ELEMENT SUBTITLE      (p)+>
    <!ELEMENT PREFACE       (HEADING, p+)+>
    <!ELEMENT PART          (HEADING, CHAPTER+)>
```

```
    <!ELEMENT SECTION      (HEADING, p+)>
    <!ELEMENT HEADING      (#PCDATA)>
    <!ELEMENT CHAPTER      (CHAPTERTITLE, p+)>
    <!ELEMENT CHAPTERTITLE (#PCDATA)>
]>
<DOCUMENT>
    <TITLE>
        <TITLE2>
            My Novel
        </TITLE2>
    </TITLE>
    <PART>
        <HEADING>Ice Cream Consumption</HEADING>
        <CHAPTER>
            <CHAPTERTITLE>CHAPTER 1</CHAPTERTITLE>
            <p>I enjoy fishing.</p>
            <p>And I enjoy travel.</p>
            <p>How about you?</p>
        </CHAPTER>
    </PART>
</DOCUMENT>
```

In this code, there are a number of elements: **<DOCUMENT>**, **<TITLE>**, **<PART>**, **<HEADING>**, and so on. I'll start the DTD by declaring the **<p>** element, which I want to hold text only—that is, "parsed character data," as far as XML is concerned—which you specify with the keyword **#PCDATA**:

```
<!ELEMENT p            (#PCDATA)>
       .
       .
       .
```

Next, I declare the root element, **<DOCUMENT>**. I'll set up the **<DOCUMENT>** element to contain a **<TITLE>** tag, possibly a **<SUBTITLE>** tag (by placing a question mark [?] after the **SUBTITLE** declaration) or a **<PREFACE>** tag, and one or more sections or parts declared with the **<SECTION>** and **<PART>** tags. (The pipe [|] means "or", as you can see in the In Depth section of this chapter. To see more about the syntax allowed in a DTD, see the In Depth section of this chapter.)

```
<!ELEMENT p            (#PCDATA)>
<!ELEMENT DOCUMENT     (TITLE,SUBTITLE?,PREFACE?,(SECTION | PART)+)>
       .
       .
       .
```

Next, I declare a **<TITLE>** tag that contains zero or more occurrences of subtitle tags, which I'll call **<TITLE2>**:

```
<!ELEMENT p            (#PCDATA)>
<!ELEMENT DOCUMENT     (TITLE,SUBTITLE?,PREFACE?,(SECTION | PART)+)>
<!ELEMENT TITLE        (TITLE2)*>
        .
        .
        .
```

The **<TITLE2>** element, in turn, can contain character data:

```
<!ELEMENT p            (#PCDATA)>
<!ELEMENT DOCUMENT     (TITLE,SUBTITLE?,PREFACE?,(SECTION | PART)+)>
<!ELEMENT TITLE        (TITLE2)*>
<!ELEMENT TITLE2       (#PCDATA)>
        .
        .
        .
```

Next, I declare the **<SUBTITLE>** element, which must contain one or more paragraphs:

```
<!ELEMENT p            (#PCDATA)>
<!ELEMENT DOCUMENT     (TITLE,SUBTITLE?,PREFACE?,(SECTION | PART)+)>
<!ELEMENT TITLE        (TITLE2)*>
<!ELEMENT TITLE2       (#PCDATA)>
<!ELEMENT SUBTITLE     (p)+>
        .
        .
        .
```

The **<PREFACE>** element must contain one or more **<p>** elements and can contain **<HEADING>** elements, which I specify like this:

```
<!ELEMENT p            (#PCDATA)>
<!ELEMENT DOCUMENT     (TITLE,SUBTITLE?,PREFACE?,(SECTION | PART)+)>
<!ELEMENT TITLE        (TITLE2)*>
<!ELEMENT TITLE2       (#PCDATA)>
<!ELEMENT SUBTITLE     (p)+>
<!ELEMENT PREFACE      (HEADING, p+)+>
        .
        .
        .
```

And I'll specify that the **<PART>** element can be empty, or it can contain **<HEADING>** or **<CHAPTER>** elements:

```
<!ELEMENT p          (#PCDATA)>
<!ELEMENT DOCUMENT   (TITLE,SUBTITLE?,PREFACE?,(SECTION | PART)+)>
<!ELEMENT TITLE      (TITLE2)*>
<!ELEMENT TITLE2     (#PCDATA)>
<!ELEMENT SUBTITLE   (p)+>
<!ELEMENT PREFACE    (HEADING, p+)+>
<!ELEMENT PART       (HEADING, CHAPTER+)>
        .
        .
        .
```

In addition, I'll specify that the **<CHAPTER>** element can be empty, or it can contain **<CHAPTERTITLE>** and **<p>** elements:

```
<!ELEMENT p          (#PCDATA)>
<!ELEMENT DOCUMENT   (TITLE,SUBTITLE?,PREFACE?,(SECTION | PART)+)>
<!ELEMENT TITLE      (TITLE2)*>
<!ELEMENT TITLE2     (#PCDATA)>
<!ELEMENT SUBTITLE   (p)+>
<!ELEMENT PREFACE    (HEADING, p+)+>
<!ELEMENT PART       (HEADING, CHAPTER+)>
<!ELEMENT SECTION    (HEADING, p+)>
<!ELEMENT HEADING    (#PCDATA)>
<!ELEMENT CHAPTER    (CHAPTERTITLE, p+)>
        .
        .
        .
```

Finally, the **<CHAPTERTITLE>** element contains parsed character data like this:

```
<!ELEMENT p            (#PCDATA)>
<!ELEMENT DOCUMENT     (TITLE,SUBTITLE?,PREFACE?,(SECTION | PART)+)>
<!ELEMENT TITLE        (TITLE2)*>
<!ELEMENT TITLE2       (#PCDATA)>
<!ELEMENT SUBTITLE     (p)+>
<!ELEMENT PREFACE      (HEADING, p+)+>
<!ELEMENT PART         (HEADING, CHAPTER+)>
<!ELEMENT SECTION      (HEADING, p+)>
<!ELEMENT HEADING      (#PCDATA)>
<!ELEMENT CHAPTER      (CHAPTERTITLE, p+)>
<!ELEMENT CHAPTERTITLE (#PCDATA)>
```

When you enclose everything in the **<!DOCTYPE>** element, the DTD is complete:

```
<?xml version="1.0"?>
<!DOCTYPE DOCUMENT [
    <!ELEMENT p (#PCDATA)>
    <!ELEMENT DOCUMENT      (TITLE,SUBTITLE?,PREFACE?,(SECTION | PART)+)>
    <!ELEMENT TITLE         (TITLE2)*>
    <!ELEMENT TITLE2        (#PCDATA)>
    <!ELEMENT SUBTITLE      (p)+>
    <!ELEMENT PREFACE       (HEADING, p+)+>
    <!ELEMENT PART          (HEADING, CHAPTER+)>
    <!ELEMENT SECTION       (HEADING, p+)>
    <!ELEMENT HEADING       (#PCDATA)>
    <!ELEMENT CHAPTER       (CHAPTERTITLE, p+)>
    <!ELEMENT CHAPTERTITLE (#PCDATA)>
]>
<DOCUMENT>
    <TITLE>My Novel</TITLE>
    <PART>
        <HEADING>Ice Cream Consumption</HEADING>
        <CHAPTER>
            <CHAPTERTITLE>CHAPTER 1</CHAPTERTITLE>
            <p>I enjoy fishing.</p>
            <p>And I enjoy travel.</p>
            <p>How about you?</p>
        </CHAPTER>
    </PART>
</DOCUMENT>
```

Note that in this case, I defined several elements, but no attributes. To see how to specify attributes as well as elements, see the next section.

Specifying Attributes In DTDs

"Hey," asks the novice programmer, "how do you specify element attributes in a DTD? I know how to specify elements, but not their attributes." "To specify attributes," you say, "you can use the **<!ATTLIST>** element." "How does that work?" the NP wants to know.

You can specify the attributes the elements in a DTD has with the **<!ATTLIST>** element. This element holds a list of the attributes for an element, which you list, one after the other. You can specify default values for attributes as well as whether or not an attribute is required. Here's how you can use the **<!ATTLIST>** element to create attributes for the XML element whose name is ***ELEMENT_NAME***. I'll indicate the three different ways to declare attributes here. In practice, your **<!ATTLIST>** element may have more or fewer lines:

```
<!ATTLIST ELEMENT_NAME
    ATTRIBUTE_NAME TYPE DEFAULT_VALUE
    ATTRIBUTE_NAME TYPE #IMPLIED
    ATTRIBUTE_NAME TYPE #REQUIRED>
]>
```

The first line with ***ATTRIBUTE_NAME*** in it indicates one way to declare an attribute. In this case, I'm specifying an attribute name, its type, and its *default value*. If no value is supplied for the attribute, the default value is used. The usual ***TYPE*** you use for attributes is unparsed character data, **CDATA**. However, you can also used *tokenized types* instead of the **CDATA** type, which are defined by W3C as **ID**, **IDREF**, **IDREFS**, **ENTITY**, **ENTITIES**, **NMTOKEN** (name token), or **NMTOKENS** to indicate the purpose of the attribute if it fits one of these descriptions. You can also set up and use *enumerated* attribute types, which means that the attribute can be set to only those values from an enumeration that you define (such as "Monday", "Tuesday", "Wednesday", "Thursday", or "Friday").

The next line in this example specifies another way to declare an attribute, making it *implied*, which means that it doesn't need to be used in the XML element.

The last line specifies a *required* attribute, which means Internet Explorer will report an error if you omit it.

Here's an example that creates attributes. In this case, I'll create a DTD for the example XML document I created in the In Depth section of this chapter. Here, I'm adding attributes to the **<CUSTOMER>** element—in particular, an attribute named **CITIZENSHIP** that has a default value of "US", an implied **AGE** attribute, and a required **TYPE** attribute. (Again, your **<!ATTLIST>** element may have more or fewer lines depending on how many attributes you want to define for the XML element involved.)

```
<?xml version = "1.0"?>
<!DOCTYPE DOCUMENT [
<!ELEMENT DOCUMENT (CUSTOMER)*>
<!ELEMENT CUSTOMER (NAME,DATE,ORDERS)>
<!ELEMENT NAME (LAST_NAME,FIRST_NAME)>
<!ELEMENT LAST_NAME (#PCDATA)>
<!ELEMENT FIRST_NAME (#PCDATA)>
<!ELEMENT DATE (#PCDATA)>
<!ELEMENT ORDERS (ITEM)*>
<!ELEMENT ITEM (PRODUCT,NUMBER,PRICE)>
```

```
<!ELEMENT PRODUCT (#PCDATA)>
<!ELEMENT NUMBER (#PCDATA)>
<!ELEMENT PRICE (#PCDATA)>
<!ATTLIST CUSTOMER
    CITIZENSHIP CDATA "US"
    AGE CDATA #IMPLIED
    TYPE CDATA #REQUIRED>
]>
<DOCUMENT>
    <CUSTOMER TYPE="Insolvent">
        <NAME>
            <LAST_NAME>Thomson</LAST_NAME>
            <FIRST_NAME>Susan</FIRST_NAME>
        </NAME>
        <DATE>September 1, 2001</DATE>
        <ORDERS>
            <ITEM>
                <PRODUCT>Video tape</PRODUCT>
                <NUMBER>5</NUMBER>
                <PRICE>$1.25</PRICE>
            </ITEM>
            <ITEM>
                <PRODUCT>Shovel</PRODUCT>
                <NUMBER>2</NUMBER>
                <PRICE>$4.98</PRICE>
            </ITEM>
        </ORDERS>
    </CUSTOMER>
    <CUSTOMER TYPE="Solvent">
        <NAME>
            <LAST_NAME>Smithson</LAST_NAME>
            <FIRST_NAME>Nancy</FIRST_NAME>
        </NAME>
        <DATE>September 2, 2001</DATE>
        <ORDERS>
            <ITEM>
                <PRODUCT>Ribbon</PRODUCT>
                <NUMBER>12</NUMBER>
                <PRICE>$2.95</PRICE>
            </ITEM>
            <ITEM>
                <PRODUCT>Goldfish</PRODUCT>
                <NUMBER>6</NUMBER>
                <PRICE>$1.50</PRICE>
            </ITEM>
```

```
         </ORDERS>
      </CUSTOMER>
   </DOCUMENT>
```

Creating XML Documents With Schemas

"Writing DTDs isn't easy," says the novice programmer, "I've heard that you can use Microsoft schemas to do the same thing. How does that work?" "Some people don't find schemas that much easier," you say, "but pull up a chair and let's take a look." The NP rushes off to get coffee.

As we saw in the In Depth section of this chapter, XML schemas are Microsoft's alternative to DTDs. If you want to create valid XML documents for use with Internet Explorer, you can use either a DTD or a schema.

TIP: *For Microsoft XML references and information on how to create schemas, see* ***http://msdn.microsoft.com/ workshop/xml/index.asp***.

Here's the example I presented in the In Depth section of this chapter. This XML document uses a schema named schema1.xml:

```
<?xml version="1.0" ?>
<TASKFORCE XMLS="x-schema:schema1.xml">
    <EMPLOYEE>George Patton</EMPLOYEE>
    <EMPLOYEE>Douglas MacArthur</EMPLOYEE>
    <DESCRIPTION>XML Programming Taskforce</DESCRIPTION>
</TASKFORCE>
```

And here's the schema, schema1.xml, we also developed in the In Depth section:

```
<SCHEMA NAME="schema1"
    xmlns="urn:schemas-microsoft-com:xml-data"
    xmlns:dt="urn:schemas-microsoft-com:datatypes">

    <ELEMENTTYPE name="EMPLOYEE" content="textOnly" model="closed"/>
    <ELEMENTTYPE name="DESCRIPTION" content="textOnly" model="closed"/>

    <ELEMENTTYPE name="TASKFORCE" content="eltOnly" model="closed">
        <ELEMENT type="EMPLOYEE" minOccurs="1" maxOccurs="*"/>
        <ELEMENT type="DESCRIPTION" minOccurs="1" maxOccurs="1"/>
    </ELEMENTTYPE>
</SCHEMA>
```

17. Essential XML

Schemas can get vastly more complex than this, of course. For example, you can specify the data type of elements using the **dt:type** attribute (assuming you create a namespace named **dt** of Microsoft's XML data types, as I have in the immediate preceding code). Here's an example in which I'm specifying that an element can hold integer content:

```
<ElementType name="count" dt:type="int"/>
```

You can also use the **<datatype>** element to do the same thing explicitly:

```
<ElementType name="count">
    <datatype dt:type= "int"/>
</ElementType>
```

The following list contains the possible data types:

- *bin.base64*—Multipurpose Internet Mail Extension- (MIME)-style Base64 encoded binary object.
- *bin.hex*—Hexadecimal digits.
- *boolean*—0 or 1; 0 means false and 1 means true.
- *char*—String; one character long.
- *date*—Date with a subset ISO 8601 format that does not contain time data. For example: 2001-09-02.
- *dateTime*—Date with a subset ISO 8601 format that does contain optional time but not optional zone. Fractional seconds can be as exact as nanoseconds. For example, 2001-04-07T22:00:07.
- *dateTime.tz*—Date with a subset ISO 8601 format does contain both optional time and optional zone. Fractional seconds can be as precise as nanoseconds. For example: 2001-04-07T22:00:07-08:00.
- *fixed.14.4*—Same as "number" except no more than 14 digits to the left of the decimal point and no more than 4 to the right.
- *float*—Real number with no digit limitation; can have leading sign, fractional digits, and optionally, exponent. Values range from 1.7976931348623157E+308 through 2.2250738585072014E-308.
- *int*—Integer with optional sign but without fractions or exponent.
- *i1*—Integer denoted in one byte. A number with optional sign but without fractions or exponent. For example: 7, 119, -123.
- *i2*—Integer denoted in one word. A number with optional sign but without fractions or exponent. For example: 7, 225, -32000.

- *i4*—Integer denoted in four bytes. A number with optional sign but without fractions or exponent. For example: 1, -32000, 278911.

- *number*—Number with no digit limitation; potentially can have leading sign, fractional digits, and optionally, exponent. Precision has a range of 1.7976931348623157E+308 through 2.2250738585072014E-308.

- *r4*—Real number having seven-digit precision; can contain leading sign, fractional digits, and optionally, exponent. Values range from 3.40282347E+38F through 1.17549435E-38F.

- *r8*—Real number having 15-digit precision; potentially can contain leading sign, fractional digits, and optionally, exponent. Values range from 1.7976931348623157E+308 through 2.2250738585072014E-308.

- *time*—Time with a subset ISO 8601 format that does not contain date or time zone. For example: 09:03:54.

- *time.tz*—Time with a subset ISO 8601 format that does not contain date but does contain optional time zone. For example: 09:03:54-07:00.

- *ui1*—Unsigned integer. A number, unsigned, with no fractions or exponent. For example: 231, 6.

- *ui2*—Unsigned integer, two bytes. A number, unsigned, with no fractions or exponent. For example: 18, 211, 56789.

- *ui4*—Unsigned integer, four bytes. A number, unsigned, no with fractions or exponent. For example: 5, 209, 1234500000.

- *uri*—Universal Resource Identifier (URI).

- *uuid*—Hexadecimal digits denoting octets; optional embedded hyphens that are ignored. For example: 195D6A3F-358B4E1D-A439-553A351AAC91.

For more information on schemas, take a look at the Microsoft XML site.

Accessing XML Data By Loading XML Documents

"Hm," says the novice programmer, "now I can create an XML document, and even view it in Internet Explorer. But how can I access the data in it?" You say, "There are two ways—you create an ActiveX object and load an XML page into it, or you can create a data island." "Let's see the first way first," says the NP.

To load an XML document into Internet Explorer, you can create an ActiveX object using the **Microsoft.XMLDOM** object, then use the **load** method to load the XML document. After the document is loaded, you can use the ActiveX object's **documentElement** property to reach the root element of the XML document.

Once you have the root element, you can navigate around the XML document using the **firstChild**, **nextChild**, **previousChild**, and **lastChild** methods, which let you access the child elements of an element, and the **firstSibling**, **nextSibling**, **previousSibling**, and **lastSibling** methods, which let you access elements on the same level.

Let's look at an example from the In Depth section of this chapter, using the XML document, school.xml:

```
<?xml version="1.0"?>
<SCHOOL>
    <CLASS type="seminar">
        <CLASS_TITLE>XML In Theory And Practice</CLASS_TITLE>
        <CLASS_NUMBER>10.306</CLASS_NUMBER>
        <SUBJECT>XML</SUBJECT>
        <START_DATE>1/1/2001</START_DATE>
        <STUDENTS>
            <STUDENT status="attending">
                <FIRST_NAME>Mark</FIRST_NAME>
                <LAST_NAME>Swansburg</LAST_NAME>
            </STUDENT>
            <STUDENT status="withdrawn">
                <FIRST_NAME>Thomas</FIRST_NAME>
                <LAST_NAME>Preston</LAST_NAME>
            </STUDENT>
        </STUDENTS>
    </CLASS>
</SCHOOL>
```

The Web page I developed in the In Depth section of this chapter read in this XML document and by using the navigation methods already discussed, moved to the second student's record. To access the data in that record, I use the **nodeValue** property like this:

```
<HTML>
    <HEAD>
        <TITLE>
            Finding Element Values in an XML Document
        </TITLE>

        <SCRIPT LANGUAGE="JavaScript">
            function getStudentData()
            {
                var xmldoc;
```

```
                    xmldoc = new ActiveXObject("Microsoft.XMLDOM");
                    xmldoc.load("school.xml");

                    nodeSchool = xmldoc.documentElement;
                    nodeClass = nodeSchool.firstChild;
                    nodeStudents = nodeClass.lastChild;
                    nodeStudent = nodeStudents.lastChild;
                    nodeFirstName = nodeStudent.firstChild;
                    nodeLastName = nodeFirstName.nextSibling;

                    outputMessage = "Name: " +
                            nodeFirstName.firstChild.nodeValue + ' '
                        + nodeLastName.firstChild.nodeValue;
                    message.innerHTML=outputMessage;
                }
        </SCRIPT>
    </HEAD>

    <BODY>
        <CENTER>
            <H1>
                Finding Element Values in an XML Document
            </H1>

            <DIV ID="message"></DIV>
            <P>
            <INPUT TYPE="BUTTON" VALUE="Get Second Student's Name"
                ONCLICK="getStudentData()">
        </CENTER>
    </BODY>
</HTML>
```

You can see the results of this HTML and XML in Figure 17.2. Loading an XML document in with the **load** method is one way of accessing it; the other is to use data islands, and you can find the details in the next section.

<XML>—Accessing XML Data With An XML Data Island

Purpose: Creates an XML data island and embeds an XML document in a Web page.

Start Tag/End Tag: Required/Required

Supported: [IE5]

Attributes:

- **CONTENTEDITABLE**—Indicates if the content of the element is editable. [IE5]

- **DISABLED**—Indicates if the element is disabled. [IE5]

- **ID**—Unique alphanumeric identifier for the tag, which you can use to refer to it. [IE5]

- **NS**—Specifies the URL of the XML namespace that the XML content is bound to. Set to a URL. [IE5]

- **PREFIX**—Namespace prefix of the XML contents. Set to an alphanumeric string. [IE5]

- **SRC**—Specifies the source for the XML document. Set to a URL. [IE5]

"Hm," says the novice programmer, "loading in an XML element is OK, but didn't you say something about data islands?" "Yes," you say, "I sure did. You create data islands with the HTML **<XML>** element, and you can mix HTML and XML in this way."

You use Internet Explorer's HTML **<XML>** element to enclose XML data in an HTML Web page, creating a data island, as discussed in the In Depth section of this chapter. Here's an example in which I'm embedding school.xml, the XML document that contains student records that we developed in the In Depth section of this chapter, in a data island:

```
<HTML>
    <HEAD>
        <TITLE>
            Creating An XML Data Island
        </TITLE>

        <XML ID="schoolXML">
            <SCHOOL>
                <CLASS type="seminar">
                    <CLASS_TITLE>XML In Theory And Practice</CLASS_TITLE>
                    <CLASS_NUMBER>10.306</CLASS_NUMBER>
                    <SUBJECT>XML</SUBJECT>
                    <START_DATE>1/1/2001</START_DATE>
                    <STUDENTS>
                        <STUDENT status="attending">
                            <FIRST_NAME>Mark</FIRST_NAME>
                            <LAST_NAME>Swansburg</LAST_NAME>
```

```
                    </STUDENT>
                    <STUDENT status="withdrawn">
                        <FIRST_NAME>Thomas</FIRST_NAME>
                        <LAST_NAME>Preston</LAST_NAME>
                    </STUDENT>
                </STUDENTS>
            </CLASS>
        </SCHOOL>
    </XML>
</HEAD>

<BODY>
    <CENTER>
        <H1>
            Creating An XML Data Island
        </H1>
    </CENTER>
</BODY>
</HTML>
```

You don't need to embed the whole XML document in the data island, however; you can simply use the **SRC** attribute to point to the XML document like this:

```
<HTML>
    <HEAD>
        <TITLE>
            Creating An XML Data Island
        </TITLE>

        <XML ID="schoolXML" SRC="school.xml"></XML>
    </HEAD>

    <BODY>
        <CENTER>
            <H1>
                Creating An XML Data Island
            </H1>
        </CENTER>
    </BODY>
</HTML>
```

Here's the file school.xml:

```
<?xml version="1.0"?>
<SCHOOL>
```

```
<CLASS type="seminar">
    <CLASS_TITLE>XML In Theory And Practice</CLASS_TITLE>
    <CLASS_NUMBER>10.306</CLASS_NUMBER>
    <SUBJECT>XML</SUBJECT>
    <START_DATE>1/1/2001</START_DATE>
    <STUDENTS>
        <STUDENT status="attending">
            <FIRST_NAME>Mark</FIRST_NAME>
            <LAST_NAME>Swansburg</LAST_NAME>
        </STUDENT>
        <STUDENT status="withdrawn">
            <FIRST_NAME>Thomas</FIRST_NAME>
            <LAST_NAME>Preston</LAST_NAME>
        </STUDENT>
    </STUDENTS>
</CLASS>
</SCHOOL>
```

In an example from the In Depth section of this chapter, I demonstrated how to use the navigation methods to get to the second student's record and display that student's name. You navigate around the XML document using the **firstChild**, **nextChild**, **previousChild**, and **lastChild** methods, which let you access the child elements of an element, and the **firstSibling**, **nextSibling**, **previousSibling**, and **lastSibling** methods, which let you access elements on the same level. To get the content of an element, I use the **nodeValue** property. Here's what the JavaScript we developed looked like:

```
<HTML>
    <HEAD>
        <TITLE>
            Finding Element Values in an XML Document Using Data Islands
        </TITLE>

        <XML ID="schoolXML" SRC="school.xml"></XML>

        <SCRIPT LANGUAGE="JavaScript">
            function getStudentData()
            {
                xmldoc= document.all("schoolXML").XMLDocument;

                nodeSchool = xmldoc.documentElement;
                nodeClass = nodeSchool.firstChild;
                nodeStudents = nodeClass.lastChild;
                nodeStudent = nodeStudents.lastChild;
                nodeFirstName = nodeStudent.firstChild;
                nodeLastName = nodeFirstName.nextSibling;
```

```
                outputMessage = "Name: " +
                    nodeFirstName.firstChild.nodeValue + ' '
                  + nodeLastName.firstChild.nodeValue;
                message.innerHTML=outputMessage;
            }
        </SCRIPT>
    </HEAD>

    <BODY>
        <CENTER>
            <H1>
                Finding Element Values in an XML Document Using
                Data Islands
            </H1>

            <DIV ID="message"></DIV>
            <P>
            <INPUT TYPE="BUTTON" VALUE="Get Second Student's Name"
                ONCLICK="getStudentData()">
        </CENTER>
    </BODY>
</HTML>
```

You can see the results in Figure 17.3.

In this case, I used the **XMLDocument** property to get an object corresponding to the HTML document, then used the **documentElement** property of that object to get the root element of the document, but in fact, there's a shortcut for this process. You can simply use the **documentElement** property of the data island directly to get the root element of the XML document like this:

```
<HTML>
    <HEAD>
        <TITLE>
            Finding Element Values in an XML Document
        </TITLE>

        <XML ID="schoolXML" SRC="school.xml"></XML>

        <SCRIPT LANGUAGE="JavaScript">
            function getStudentData()
            {
                var xmldoc;
```

```
            nodeSchool = schoolXML.documentElement;
            nodeClass = nodeSchool.firstChild;
            nodeStudents = nodeClass.lastChild;
            nodeStudent = nodeStudents.lastChild;
            nodeFirstName = nodeStudent.firstChild;
            nodeLastName = nodeFirstName.nextSibling;
            .
            .
            .
```

```
</HTML>
```

Note that these examples simply extract the values of XML elements from an XML document, but not their attributes. To extract attribute values as well, see the next section.

Getting Attribute Values From XML Elements

"One problem," says the novice programmer, "I know I can use the **nodeValue** property to get the content of XML elements, but what about getting the values of *attributes*?" "No problem," you say, "just use the **attributes** property."

Say that you have an XML document named school.xml (as introduced in the In Depth section) where the **<STUDENT>** element has one attribute, **STATUS**:

```
<?xml version="1.0"?>
<SCHOOL>
    <CLASS type="seminar">
        <CLASS_TITLE>XML In Theory And Practice</CLASS_TITLE>
        <CLASS_NUMBER>10.306</CLASS_NUMBER>
        <SUBJECT>XML</SUBJECT>
        <START_DATE>1/1/2001</START_DATE>
        <STUDENTS>
            <STUDENT status="attending">
                <FIRST_NAME>Mark</FIRST_NAME>
                <LAST_NAME>Swansburg</LAST_NAME>
            </STUDENT>
            <STUDENT status="withdrawn">
                <FIRST_NAME>Thomas</FIRST_NAME>
                <LAST_NAME>Preston</LAST_NAME>
            </STUDENT>
        </STUDENTS>
    </CLASS>
</SCHOOL>
```

How can you recover these attribute values? Here's an example showing how it's done. In this case, I'm reading the value of the status attribute of the second student's record. I do that by getting that record's attributes using the **attributes** property, then get the value of the **status** attribute with the **getNamedItem** method like this: **statusStudent = attributes.getNamedItem("status");**. I then get the actual text the attribute was set to this way: **statusStudent.value**. Here's what the JavaScript looks like:

```
<HTML>
    <HEAD>
        <TITLE>
            Finding Attribute Values in an XML Document
        </TITLE>

        <XML ID="schoolXML" SRC="school.xml"></XML>

        <SCRIPT LANGUAGE="JavaScript">
            function getStudentData()
            {
                xmldoc= document.all("schoolXML").XMLDocument;

                nodeSchool = xmldoc.documentElement;
                nodeClass = nodeSchool.firstChild;
                nodeStudents = nodeClass.lastChild;
                nodeStudent = nodeStudents.lastChild;
                nodeFirstName = nodeStudent.firstChild;
                nodeLastName = nodeFirstName.nextSibling;
                attributes = nodeStudent.attributes;
                statusStudent = attributes.getNamedItem("status");
                outputMessage = "Name: " +
                    nodeFirstName.firstChild.nodeValue + ' '
                    + nodeLastName.firstChild.nodeValue + " Status: " +
                    statusStudent.value;
                message.innerHTML=outputMessage;
            }
        </SCRIPT>
    </HEAD>

    <BODY>
        <CENTER>
            <H1>
                Finding Attribute Values in an XML Document
            </H1>
```

```
                    <DIV ID="message"></DIV>
                    <P>
                    <INPUT TYPE="BUTTON" VALUE="Get Second Student's Status"
                            ONCLICK="getStudentData()">
                </CENTER>
            </BODY>
        </HTML>
```

And that's all it takes. You can see the results in Figure 17.4 where you see that the status of the second student is "withdrawn".

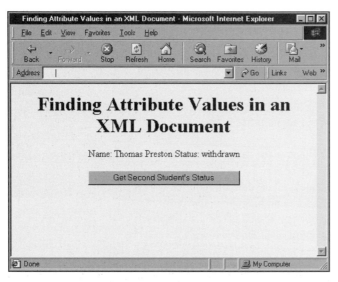

Figure 17.4   Accessing attribute values in an XML document.

Parsing XML Documents In Code

So far in this chapter, I've used the navigation methods like **nextSibling** and **nextChild** to navigate through XML documents. However, I knew just what element I was after and wrote the code accordingly. Usually (that is, when you don't know the exact contents of the files the user is asking you to read), you should parse XML documents, working through the entire document and unpacking the data in it.

One way of parsing an XML document is to use the **childNodes** property, which tells you if an element has any children. In this example, I'll work through the entire XML document, school.xml, displaying all its elements in an HTML Web page:

```
<?xml version="1.0"?>
<SCHOOL>
    <CLASS type="seminar">
        <CLASS_TITLE>XML In Theory And Practice</CLASS_TITLE>
        <CLASS_NUMBER>10.306</CLASS_NUMBER>
        <SUBJECT>XML</SUBJECT>
        <START_DATE>1/1/2001</START_DATE>
        <STUDENTS>
            <STUDENT status="attending">
                <FIRST_NAME>Mark</FIRST_NAME>
                <LAST_NAME>Swansburg</LAST_NAME>
            </STUDENT>
            <STUDENT status="withdrawn">
                <FIRST_NAME>Thomas</FIRST_NAME>
                <LAST_NAME>Preston</LAST_NAME>
            </STUDENT>
        </STUDENTS>
    </CLASS>
</SCHOOL>
```

I'll create a function, **getChildren**, which gets and displays the children of an element (this is a *recursive* function, which means that it can call itself to get the children of an element's children, and so on to many levels in depth). To display the current element's name, I use the **nodeName** property. To start parsing the whole page, then, I just have to call **getChildren** on the root node of the whole document, and I do that in a function named **parseXML**, which I connect to a button in this Web page:

```
<HTML>
    <HEAD>
        <TITLE>
            Parsing an XML Document with Recursion
        </TITLE>

        <XML ID="schoolXML" SRC="school.xml"></XML>

        <SCRIPT LANGUAGE="JavaScript">
            function parseXML()
            {
                documentXML = document.all("schoolXML").XMLDocument;
                divResults.innerHTML = getChildren(documentXML, "");
            }

            function getChildren(nodeXML, indent)
            {
                var text = indent + nodeXML.nodeName + "<BR>";
```

```
                if (nodeXML.childNodes.length > 0) {
                    for (var loopIndex = 0; loopIndex <
                        nodeXML.childNodes.length; loopIndex++) {
                        text += getChildren(nodeXML.childNodes(loopIndex),
                        indent + "    ");
                    }
                }
                return text;
            }
        </SCRIPT>
    </HEAD>

    <BODY>
        <CENTER>
            <H1>
                Parsing an XML Document
            </H1>
        </CENTER>

        <DIV ID="divResults"></DIV>

        <CENTER>
            <INPUT TYPE="BUTTON" VALUE="Parse the XML Document"
                ONCLICK="parseXML()">
        </CENTER>
    </BODY>
</HTML>
```

When you click the button in this page, it will read school.xml and display its structure as you see in Figure 17.5. In this way, you can loop over every element in an XML document. There's one detail to note—Internet Explorer considers more than just elements in the document to be nodes; processing instructions, the text content of elements, the root element, and more are all nodes (see the next section for more information). Usually, you'll just look for specific elements and want to read their data content—the next section discusses the details on how to do this.

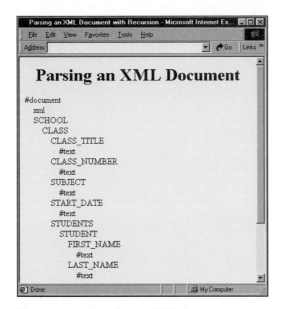

Figure 17.5   Parsing an XML document.

Parsing XML To Get Element Content

In the previous section, we saw how to parse an entire XML document, school.xml, by "walking" through it recursively. However, that example just listed the structure of the XML document. Here, I'll elaborate on that code by also displaying each node's type and content. I do that by checking the **nodeType** property to get the node's type and the **nodeValue** property to get the node's value. Here's the new code—note the different types of items Internet Explorer considers to be nodes in XML documents: processing instructions, the text content of an element, comments, even the document (root) element itself:

```
<HTML>
    <HEAD>
        <TITLE>
            Parsing an XML Document To Get Element Content
        </TITLE>

        <XML ID="schoolXML" SRC="school.xml"></XML>

        <SCRIPT LANGUAGE="JavaScript">
            function parseXML()
            {
                documentXML = document.all("schoolXML").XMLDocument;
```

```
                    divResults.innerHTML = getChildren(documentXML, "");
            }

        function getChildren(nodeXML, indent)
        {
            var typeXML;

            switch (nodeXML.nodeType) {
                case 1:
                    typeXML = "element";
                    break;
                case 2:
                    typeXML = "attribute";
                    break;
                case 3:
                    typeXML = "text";
                    break;
                case 4:
                    typeXML = "CDATA section";
                    break;
                case 5:
                    typeXML = "entity reference";
                    break;
                case 6:
                    typeXML = "entity";
                    break;
                case 7:
                    typeXML = "processing instruction";
                    break;
                case 8:
                    typeXML = "comment";
                    break;
                case 9:
                    typeXML = "document";
                    break;
                case 10:
                    typeXML = "document type";
                    break;
                case 11:
                    typeXML = "document fragment";
                    break;
                case 12:
                    typeXML = "notation";
            }
```

```
            var text = indent + nodeXML.nodeName
            + (nodeXML.nodeValue ?
            "  = " + nodeXML.nodeValue
            + "  (Type: " + typeXML
            + ")<BR>" :
            "  (Type: " + typeXML
            + ")<BR>");

            if (nodeXML.childNodes.length > 0) {
            for (var loopIndex = 0; loopIndex <
                nodeXML.childNodes.length; loopIndex++) {
                text += getChildren(nodeXML.childNodes(loopIndex),
                indent + "    ");
            }
            }
            return text;
        }
    </SCRIPT>
</HEAD>

<BODY>
    <CENTER>
        <H1>
            Parsing an XML Document To Get Element Content
        </H1>
    </CENTER>

    <DIV ID="divResults"></DIV>

    <CENTER>
        <INPUT TYPE="BUTTON" VALUE="Parse the XML Document"
            ONCLICK="parseXML()">
    </CENTER>
</BODY>
</HTML>
```

You can see the results of this HTML and XML in Figure 17.6. As you see in the figure, the code displays not only the type of each node, but also the content if the node is a text node.

On the other hand, some of the elements in school.xml have attributes—so how can we list them too? See the next section for the details.

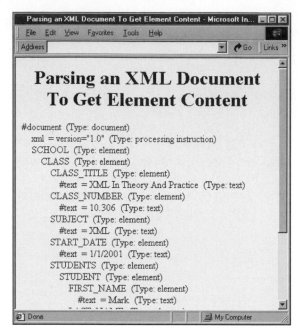

Figure 17.6   Parsing an XML document to get element content.

Parsing XML To Get Attribute Values

In the previous two sections, we developed JavaScript code to display the full structure of an XML document, school.xml, and to display its node types and data. But so far we haven't displayed any attribute values, even though some of the elements in school.xml have attributes:

```
<?xml version="1.0"?>
<SCHOOL>
   <CLASS type="seminar">
       <CLASS_TITLE>XML In Theory And Practice</CLASS_TITLE>
       <CLASS_NUMBER>10.306</CLASS_NUMBER>
       <SUBJECT>XML</SUBJECT>
       <START_DATE>1/1/2001</START_DATE>
       <STUDENTS>
           <STUDENT status="attending">
               <FIRST_NAME>Mark</FIRST_NAME>
               <LAST_NAME>Swansburg</LAST_NAME>
           </STUDENT>
           <STUDENT status="withdrawn">
               <FIRST_NAME>Thomas</FIRST_NAME>
```

```
              <LAST_NAME>Preston</LAST_NAME>
           </STUDENT>
        </STUDENTS>
     </CLASS>
</SCHOOL>
```

To access the attributes of a node, all I have to do is use the **attributes** property
to get access to the **attributes** object. To get the name of the attribute, I can use
the **nodeName** property, and to get the attribute's value, I can use the **nodeValue**
property (Internet Explorer considers attributes to be nodes). All that's left is to
loop over all the attributes an element has, and I can determine the number of
attributes to loop over by checking the **attributes** object's **length** property. Here
is how I list all the attributes of an XML element:

```
<HTML>
    <HEAD>
        <TITLE>
            Parsing an XML Document To Get Element And Attribute Content
        </TITLE>

        <XML ID="schoolXML" SRC="school.xml"></XML>

        <SCRIPT LANGUAGE="JavaScript">

            function parseXML()
            {
                documentXML = document.all("schoolXML").XMLDocument;
                divResults.innerHTML = getChildren(documentXML, "");
            }

            function getChildren(nodeXML, indent)
            {
                var typeXML;

                switch (nodeXML.nodeType) {
                    case 1:
                        typeXML = "element";
                        break;
                    case 2:
                        typeXML = "attribute";
                        break;
                    case 3:
                        typeXML = "text";
                        break;
                    case 4:
```

```
                            typeXML = "CDATA section";
                            break;
                    case 5:
                            typeXML = "entity reference";
                            break;
                    case 6:
                            typeXML = "entity";
                            break;
                    case 7:
                            typeXML = "processing instruction";
                            break;
                    case 8:
                            typeXML = "comment";
                            break;
                    case 9:
                            typeXML = "document";
                            break;
                    case 10:
                            typeXML = "document type";
                            break;
                    case 11:
                            typeXML = "document fragment";
                            break;
                    case 12:
                            typeXML = "notation";
                }

            var text = indent + nodeXML.nodeName
                + (nodeXML.nodeValue ?
                "  = " + nodeXML.nodeValue
                + "  (Type: " + typeXML
                + ")" :
                "  (Type: " + typeXML
                + ")");

            if (nodeXML.attributes != null) {
                if (nodeXML.attributes.length > 0) {
                    for (var loopIndex = 0; loopIndex <
                        nodeXML.attributes.length; loopIndex++) {
                        text += " (Attribute: " +
                            nodeXML.attributes(loopIndex).nodeName +
                            " = " +
                            nodeXML.attributes(loopIndex).nodeValue
                            + ")";
                    }
                }
            }
```

```
            text += "<BR>";

            if (nodeXML.childNodes.length > 0) {
                for (var loopIndex = 0; loopIndex <
                    nodeXML.childNodes.length; loopIndex++) {
                    text += getChildren(nodeXML.childNodes(loopIndex),
                    indent + "    ");
                }
            }
            return text;
        }

    </SCRIPT>
</HEAD>

<BODY>
    <CENTER>
        <H1>
            Parsing an XML Document To Get Element And Attribute Content
        </H1>
    </CENTER>

    <DIV ID="divResults"></DIV>

    <CENTER>
        <INPUT TYPE="BUTTON" VALUE="Parse the XML Document"
            ONCLICK="parseXML()">
    </CENTER>
</BODY>
</HTML>
```

The result of this HTML and XML appears in Figure 17.7 where you can see the names and values of attributes as well as the names and values of the XML elements.

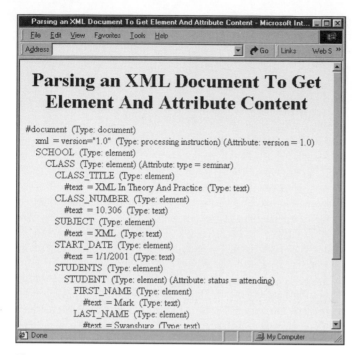

Figure 17.7   Parsing an XML document to get element and attribute content.

Handling Events While Loading XML Documents

"One more question," the novice programmer says, "my XML document is coming in from the Internet and it takes half an hour to load. How can I make sure the document is fully loaded before I use it?" "No idea," you say. The NP says, "Huh?" "Just kidding," you smile and say, "you can use the **ondataavailable** event."

You can use the **onreadystatechange** and **ondataavailable** events to monitor the progress of loading XML documents. You can also check the **readyState** property in the **onreadystatechange** event to determine the status of the document. Here's an example that monitors and displays the progress of loading an XML document:

```
<HTML>
    <HEAD>
        <TITLE>
            Handling XML Loading Events
        </TITLE>

        <SCRIPT LANGUAGE="JavaScript">
```

```
        var xmldoc;

        function loadFile()
        {
            xmldoc = new ActiveXObject("microsoft.XMLDOM");

            xmldoc.onreadystatechange = dataChange;
            xmldoc.ondataavailable = dataAvailable;

            xmldoc.load('school.xml');
        }

        function dataChange()
        {
            switch (xmldoc.readyState)
            {
                case 1:
                    div1.innerHTML += "Data is uninitialized.<BR>";
                    break;
                case 2:
                    div1.innerHTML += "Data is loading.<BR>";
                    break;
                case 3:
                    div1.innerHTML += "Data has been loaded.<BR>";
                    break;
                case 4:
                    div1.innerHTML += "Data loading is complete.<BR>";
                    if (xmldoc.parseError.errorCode != 0) {
                        div1.innerHTML += "An error occurred.<BR>";
                    }
                    else {
                        div1.innerHTML += "File loaded OK.<BR>";
                    }
                    break;
            }
        }

        function dataAvailable()
        {
            div1.innerHTML += 'Data is available.<BR>';
        }
    </SCRIPT>
</HEAD>

<BODY>
    <CENTER>
```

```
            <H1>
                Handling XML Loading Events
            </H1>
        </CENTER>

        <DIV ID="div1"></DIV>

        <CENTER>
            <INPUT TYPE="BUTTON" VALUE="Load the XML file"
                ONCLICK="loadFile()">
        </CENTER>
    </BODY>
</HTML>
```

You can see the results of this HTML and XML in Figure 17.8, which reports each step of the loading process.

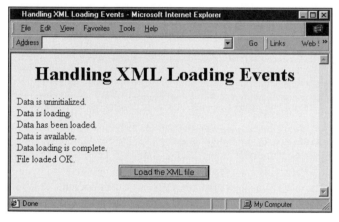

Figure 17.8   Handling XML loading events.

Chapter 18

XML: Data Binding And Record Sets

In Depth

In the previous chapter, we learned how to navigate through Extensible Markup Language (XML) documents by creating an object corresponding to the XML document's root element using methods like **nextSibling**, **lastChild**, and so on. To actually access the data in the elements in the XML document, we used properties like **nodeName**, **nodeValue**, and **nodeType**. However, there's a way of working with data in an XML document that many programmers consider somewhat easier, and that is, letting Internet Explorer treat your XML document as a set of records.

Once Internet Explorer has separated the data in your XML document into records, you have relatively easy access to that data as a record set, which, as the name implies, is a set of the records in your XML document. As we saw in Chapter 14, you can bind the data in a record set to HTML controls and deal with it *en masse* (such as when it's all displayed in a table) or one record at a time (such as when you display the data fields of a record in HTML controls like text fields or select controls). When you move through a record set record by record, you can also access the data in each field of the current record programmatically in script. Many programmers find this easier than using navigation methods, like **nextSibling**, **lastChild**, and so forth. I'll take a look at all of these techniques in this chapter.

NOTE: *This chapter, like the previous one, applies to Internet Explorer only because it has extensive XML capabilities, which other browsers lack.*

Using Data Binding And XML

We discussed data binding in Internet Explorer in Chapter 14. In that chapter, we saw that you can connect HTML files and text files to data source objects (DSOs) in a Web page and bind DSOs to HTML controls like text fields and other HTML elements, such as **<DIV>** elements, in the page. To see which HTML elements you can bind data to and how, see the In Depth section "HTML Bound Tags" in Chapter 14. We also saw in Chapter 14 that Internet Explorer 4 shipped with an XML applet written in Java, which could act as a DSO for XML documents. In this chapter, we'll take full advantage of the XML applet. In addition, you can use data islands in Internet Explorer 5 as DSOs for XML documents, and I'll use them here as well.

Here's an example to start us off. Let's say that I have an XML document named employee.xml, which holds records of several employees—their names, departments, titles, and hire dates:

```
<?xml version="1.0"?>
<EMPLOYEES>
    <ITEM>
        <NAME>Tony</NAME>
        <ID>1234</ID>
        <HIRE_DATE>4-1-2001</HIRE_DATE>
        <DEPARTMENT>Shipping</DEPARTMENT>
        <TITLE>Packer</TITLE>
    </ITEM>
    <ITEM>
        <NAME>Ed</NAME>
        <ID>1235</ID>
        <HIRE_DATE>4-1-2001</HIRE_DATE>
        <DEPARTMENT>Programming</DEPARTMENT>
        <TITLE>Programmer</TITLE>
    </ITEM>
    <ITEM>
        <NAME>Francis</NAME>
        <ID>1236</ID>
        <HIRE_DATE>4-1-2001</HIRE_DATE>
        <DEPARTMENT>Shipping</DEPARTMENT>
        <TITLE>Packer</TITLE>
    </ITEM>
    <ITEM>
        <NAME>Linda</NAME>
        <ID>1237</ID>
        <HIRE_DATE>4-1-2001</HIRE_DATE>
        <DEPARTMENT>Shipping</DEPARTMENT>
        <TITLE>Packer</TITLE>
    </ITEM>
    <ITEM>
        <NAME>Louise</NAME>
        <ID>1238</ID>
        <HIRE_DATE>4-1-2001</HIRE_DATE>
        <DEPARTMENT>Shipping</DEPARTMENT>
        <TITLE>Packer</TITLE>
    </ITEM>
</EMPLOYEES>
```

The main XML document is divided into a number of **<ITEM>** elements, each corresponding to an employee, and each making up one record. So how do you handle employee.xml using data binding? I'll take a look at two ways: One way is by using an HTML table (tabular binding) to display all the data in employee.xml at once, and the other way is single record binding, which displays the data in employee.xml one record at a time.

XML Tabular Data Binding

To bind the data in employee.xml to a table, I'll create a data island for that file, giving the data island the ID **employees**:

```
<HTML>
    <HEAD>
        <TITLE>
            Using XML Data Islands With Tables
        </TITLE>
    </HEAD>

    <BODY>
        <CENTER>
            <H1>
                Using XML Data Islands With Tables
            </H1>

            <XML SRC="employee.xml" ID=employees></XML>
                .
                .
                .
```

Now the records in employee.xml are available to bind to a table, and I do that by setting the **DATASRC** attribute to **employees**:

```
<HTML>
    <HEAD>
        <TITLE>
            Using XML Data Islands With Tables
        </TITLE>
    </HEAD>

    <BODY>
        <CENTER>
            <H1>
                Using XML Data Islands With Tables
            </H1>

            <XML SRC="employee.xml" ID=employees></XML>
```

```
<TABLE DATASRC="#employees" CELLSPACING=10>
        .
        .
        .
```

The fields in each record in employee.xml are **NAME**, **ID**, **HIRE_DATE**, **DEPARTMENT**, and **DATE**, so I bind these fields to cells in a table like this, as we saw in Chapter 14:

```
<HTML>
    <HEAD>
        <TITLE>
            Using XML Data Islands With Tables
        </TITLE>
    </HEAD>

    <BODY>
        <CENTER>
            <H1>
                Using XML Data Islands With Tables
            </H1>

            <XML SRC="employee.xml" ID=employees></XML>

            <TABLE DATASRC="#employees" CELLSPACING=10>
                <THEAD>
                    <TR>
                        <TH>Name</TH>
                        <TH>ID</TH>
                        <TH>Hire Date</TH>
                        <TH>Department</TH>
                    </TR>
                </THEAD>

                <TBODY>
                    <TR>
                        <TD><SPAN DATAFLD="NAME" DATAFORMATAS="HTML">
                            </SPAN></TD>
                        <TD><SPAN DATAFLD="ID" DATAFORMATAS="HTML">
                            </SPAN></TD>
                        <TD><SPAN DATAFLD="HIRE_DATE"
                            DATAFORMATAS="HTML">
                            </SPAN></TD>
                        <TD><SPAN DATAFLD="DEPARTMENT"
                            DATAFORMATAS="HTML"></SPAN></TD>
```

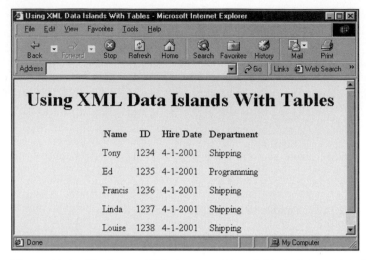

Figure 18.1   Binding an XML document to a table in Internet Explorer.

```
                    </TR>
                </TBODY>
            </TABLE>
        </CENTER>
    </BODY>
</HTML>
```

You can see the results in Figure 18.1 where the data from employee.xml is displayed in a table.

The previous example used Internet Explorer 5 data islands, but you can also use the XML applet, available in Internet Explorer since version 4, as a DSO as well. For example, this code binds employee.xml to a table just as the previous example did:

```
<HTML>
    <HEAD>
        <TITLE>
            Using The XML Applet With Tables
        </TITLE>
    </HEAD>

    <BODY>
        <CENTER>
            <H1>
                Using The XML Applet With Tables
            </H1>
```

```
<APPLET CODE="com.ms.xml.dso.XMLDSO.class"
    ID="employees" WIDTH=0 HEIGHT=0 MAYSCRIPT=true>
    <PARAM NAME="URL" VALUE="employee.xml">
</APPLET>

        <TABLE DATASRC="#employees" CELLSPACING=10>
            <THEAD>
                <TR>
                    <TH>Name</TH>
                    <TH>ID</TH>
                    <TH>Hire Date</TH>
                    <TH>Department</TH>
                </TR>
            </THEAD>

            <TBODY>
                <TR>
                    <TD><SPAN DATAFLD="NAME" DATAFORMATAS="HTML">
                        </SPAN></TD>
                    <TD><SPAN DATAFLD="ID" DATAFORMATAS="HTML">
                        </SPAN></TD>
                    <TD><SPAN DATAFLD="HIRE_DATE"
                        DATAFORMATAS="HTML">
                        </SPAN></TD>
                    <TD><SPAN DATAFLD="DEPARTMENT"
                        DATAFORMATAS="HTML"></SPAN></TD>
                </TR>
            </TBODY>
        </TABLE>
    </CENTER>
</BODY>
</HTML>
```

TIP: *Although I've given the XML applet no space in the Web page in this example (by setting the **WIDTH** and **HEIGHT** attributes to 0), you can let it display its status if you do give it a nonzero area in the Web page. See the Immediate Solutions section "XML Applet Data Access Using Record Sets" in this chapter for more details.*

Besides displaying all the data in employee.xml at once, you can also bind that data to controls and HTML elements, like text fields and **<DIV>** elements, which display the data from only one record at a time.

18. XML: Data Binding And Record Sets

XML Single Record Binding

As we saw in Chapter 14, DSOs consider one record to be the *current* record, and HTML elements that can only display data from one record at a time display data from the current record. You can make other records the current record by using methods we also saw in Chapter 14, such as **moveNext** and **moveLast**.

Here's an example. In this case, I add a data island for employee.xml with the ID **employees** to a new Web page like this:

```
<HTML>
    <HEAD>
        <TITLE>
            Using XML Data Islands With Single Record Binding
        </TITLE>
    </HEAD>

    <XML SRC="employee.xml" ID=employees></XML>
    .
    .
    .
```

Now I bind employees to various HTML elements as discussed in Chapter 14:

```
<HTML>
    <HEAD>
        <TITLE>
            Using XML Data Islands With Single Record Binding
        </TITLE>
    </HEAD>

    <XML SRC="employee.xml" ID=employees></XML>

    <BODY>
        <CENTER>
            <H1>
                Using XML Data Islands With Single Record Binding
            </H1>

            Name: <INPUT TYPE="TEXT" DATASRC="#employees"
                DATAFLD="NAME" SIZE=10><P>
            ID: <INPUT TYPE="TEXT" DATASRC="#employees"
                DATAFLD="ID" SIZE=5><P>
            Department: <SELECT DATASRC="#employees"
                DATAFLD="DEPARTMENT" SIZE=1>
```

```
            <OPTION VALUE="Shipping">Shipping
            <OPTION VALUE="Programming">Programming
            <OPTION VALUE="Editing">Editing
            <OPTION VALUE="Writing">Writing
            </SELECT><P>

            Hire date: <SPAN DATASRC="#employees"
                DATAFLD="HIRE_DATE"></SPAN><P>
            Title: <SPAN DATASRC="#employees" DATAFLD="TITLE"></SPAN><P>
            .
            .
            .
        </CENTER>
    </BODY>
</HTML>
```

So far, this Web page displays the data in the current record, which, when the page first loads, is the first record in employee.xml. However, we need some way to let the user move to other records as well.

Using Record Sets And XML

The kind of record sets that are created in Internet Explorer when you use the XML applet or data islands are subsets of ActiveX Data Object (ADO) record sets called ADOR record sets. These **recordset** objects will present the data from XML documents (but won't let you write changes to the XML document or even perform simple operations on the record set, like sorting the data or filtering it).

To reach the **recordset** object in an XML applet or data island with the ID **employees**, you can refer to **employees.recordset**. The following list contains the properties available in the record sets you create from XML documents:

- **AbsolutePage**—Page where the current record resides.
- **AbsolutePosition**—Position of a **recordset** object's current record.
- **ActiveCommand**—Command object for the **recordset** object.
- **ActiveConnection**—Connection object the **recordset** object belongs to.
- **BOF**—True if the current record position is before the first record.
- **Bookmark**—Unique identifier for the current record in a **recordset** object.
- **CacheSize**—Number of records from a **recordset** object that are cached locally in memory.
- **CursorLocation**—Location of the cursor.

- **CursorType**—Type of cursor used.
- **EditMode**—Indication of editing in progress.
- **EOF**—True if the current position is after the last record.
- **LockType**—Type of database locking used.
- **MaxRecords**—Maximum number of records to return to a record set from a query.
- **PageCount**—Number of pages of data the record set contains.
- **PageSize**—Number of records that make up one page.
- **RecordCount**—Number of records in the record set.
- **State**—State of the object, open or closed.
- **Status**—Status of the current record.
- **StayInSync**—Indication that a hierarchical record set should stay in contact with the data source.

The following are the methods of the **recordset** objects you can create from XML documents:

- **AddNew**—Adds a new record if the record set can be updated.
- **Cancel**—Cancels execution of a pending Execute or Open.
- **CancelBatch**—Cancels a pending batch operation.
- **CancelUpdate**—Cancels a pending update.
- **Clone**—Creates a duplicate record set.
- **Close**—Closes a record set.
- **Delete**—Deletes the current record (or group of records).
- **Find**—Searches the record set.
- **GetRows**—Fetches records to an array.
- **GetString**—Gets the record set as a string.
- **Move**—Moves the position of the current record.
- **MoveFirst**, **MoveLast**, **MoveNext**, and **MovePrevious**—Navigate to various locations in the record set.
- **NextRecordSet**—Clears the current **recordset** object and returns the next record set.
- **Open**—Opens a cursor.
- **Requery**—Re-executes the query that created the record set.
- **Resync**—Refreshes the data in the record set.

- **Save**—Saves the record set in a file.

- **Supports**—Indicates the features the record set supports.

You can also connect scripts to the following events of the XML applet or data islands (see the Immediate Solutions section "Handling Events While Loading XML Documents" in Chapter 17 for an example):

- **onCellChange**—Occurs when the data in a bound control changes and the focus leaves that cell. As of Internet Explorer 5.

- **onDataAvailable**—Occurs each time a batch of data is downloaded.

- **onDatasetChanged**—Occurs when the data set was changed.

- **onDatasetComplete**—Occurs when the data is downloaded and ready for use.

- **onReadyStateChange**—Occurs when the **ReadyState** property changes.

- **onRowEnter**—Occurs when the a new record becomes the current one.

- **onRowExit**—Occurs just before exiting the current record.

- **onRowsDelete**—Occurs when a row is deleted. As of Internet Explorer 5.

- **onRowsInserted**—Occurs when a row is inserted. As of Internet Explorer 5.

To let the user move around the record set based on employee.xml, I can use methods like **employees.recordset.moveNext( )** and so on like this:

```
<HTML>
    <HEAD>
        <TITLE>Using XML Data Islands With Single Record Binding</TITLE>
    </HEAD>

    <XML SRC="employee.xml" ID=employees></XML>

    <BODY>
        <CENTER>
            <H1>
                Using XML Data Islands With Single Record Binding
            </H1>

            Name: <INPUT TYPE="TEXT" DATASRC="#employees"
                DATAFLD="NAME" SIZE=10><P>
            ID: <INPUT TYPE="TEXT" DATASRC="#employees"
                DATAFLD="ID" SIZE=5><P>
            Department: <SELECT DATASRC="#employees"
                DATAFLD="DEPARTMENT" SIZE=1>
```

```
<OPTION VALUE="Shipping">Shipping
<OPTION VALUE="Programming">Programming
<OPTION VALUE="Editing">Editing
<OPTION VALUE="Writing">Writing
</SELECT><P>

Hire date: <SPAN DATASRC="#employees"
    DATAFLD="HIRE_DATE"></SPAN><P>
Title: <SPAN DATASRC="#employees" DATAFLD="TITLE"></SPAN><P>

<BUTTON ONCLICK="employees.recordset.MoveFirst()" >
    &lt;&lt;
</BUTTON>
<BUTTON ONCLICK="if (!employees.recordset.BOF)
    employees.recordset.MovePrevious()" >
    &lt;
</BUTTON>
<BUTTON ONCLICK="if (!employees.recordset.EOF)
    employees.recordset.MoveNext()" >
    &gt;
</BUTTON>
<BUTTON ONCLICK="employees.recordset.MoveLast()">
    &gt;&gt;
</BUTTON>

    </CENTER>
  </BODY>
</HTML>
```

The results appear in Figure 18.2. You can see the fields of a single record displayed in the HTML elements in that Web page. The user can also use the navigation buttons to move around the record set at will.

Having access to the **recordset** object that corresponds to an XML document gives you quite a lot of programmatic control over that data as well. For example, to access the data in the field named **ID** in the current record of a DSO named **employees**, you can use the term **employees.recordset("ID")**. This gives you an easy way to handle the data in an XML document—just divide it into records, access the data in the fields of the current record, and then make the next record the current record with the **moveNext** method and so on, iterating through all the data in the XML document. (Note how much easier this is than using methods like **nextSibling** and **lastChild** or accessing the data in the elements in the XML document using properties like **nodeName**, **nodeValue**, and **nodeType**).

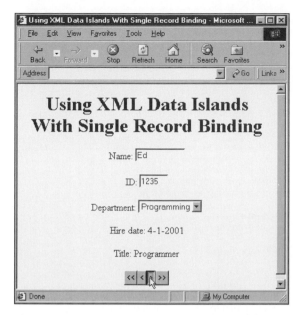

Figure 18.2   Using single record binding with an XML document in Internet Explorer.

Here's an example. In this case, I will loop over all the records in employee.xml, printing out the name and title of each employee (you know when you're at the end of the record set because the record set's **EOF** [end of file] property becomes true) when the user clicks the List Employees button:

```
<HTML>
    <HEAD>
        <TITLE>
            XML Current Record Access
        </TITLE>

        <XML ID="employees" SRC="employee.xml"></XML>

        <SCRIPT LANGUAGE="JavaScript">
            function listEmployees()
            {
                recordSet = employees.recordset

                while (!recordSet.EOF) {
                    div1.innerHTML +=
                    recordSet("NAME") +
                    ", Title: " +
                    recordSet("TITLE") + "<BR>"
                    recordSet.moveNext()
                }
            }
```

```
            </SCRIPT>
        </HEAD>

        <BODY>
            <CENTER>
                <H1>
                    XML Current Record Access
                </H1>
            </CENTER>

            <FORM>
                <INPUT TYPE="BUTTON" VALUE="List Employees"
                    ONCLICK="listEmployees()">
            </FORM>
            <DIV ID="div1"></DIV>
        </BODY>
    </HTML>
```

You can see the results of this HTML in Figure 18.3. As you see in the figure, the data from each record has been printed—and it was relatively easy to reach that data.

And that's it for the overview of this chapter. It's time to start using the XML applet and data islands to bind data to HTML elements and using the **recordset** object to access your XML data directly.

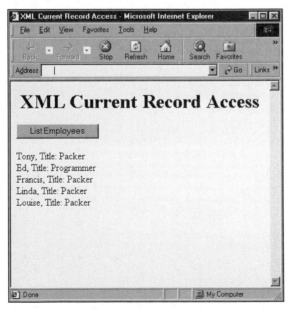

Figure 18.3   Accessing individual records in an XML document in Internet Explorer.

Immediate Solutions

Single Record Data Binding With The XML Applet

"Uh oh," says the novice programmer, "now the big boss wants me to format my database in XML. How can I display it in a browser?" "Well," you say, "one way is to use the XML applet and data binding." "That will work?" asks the NP hopefully.

As discussed in Chapter 14 and the In Depth section of this chapter, since Internet Explorer 4, there's an applet that comes with the browser that lets you create an XML DSO like this (the **MAYSCRIPT** attribute, if set to **true**, indicates that the XML applet may be used with a scripting language like JavaScript):

```
<APPLET
    CODE="com.ms.xml.dso.XMLDSO.class"
    ID="IDNAME"
    WIDTH="0"
    HEIGHT="0"
    MAYSCRIPT="true">
    <PARAM NAME="URL" VALUE="XMLPageURL">
</APPLET>
```

In this example, I'll use the XML document employee.xml presented in the In Depth section of this chapter and bind it to HTML elements using the XML applet. Here's employee.xml:

```
<?xml version="1.0"?>
<EMPLOYEES>
    <ITEM>
        <NAME>Tony</NAME>
        <ID>1234</ID>
        <HIRE_DATE>4-1-2001</HIRE_DATE>
        <DEPARTMENT>Shipping</DEPARTMENT>
        <TITLE>Packer</TITLE>
    </ITEM>
    <ITEM>
        <NAME>Ed</NAME>
        <ID>1235</ID>
        <HIRE_DATE>4-1-2001</HIRE_DATE>
        <DEPARTMENT>Programming</DEPARTMENT>
        <TITLE>Programmer</TITLE>
```

18. XML: Data Binding And Record Sets

```
        </ITEM>
        <ITEM>
            <NAME>Francis</NAME>
            <ID>1236</ID>
            <HIRE_DATE>4-1-2001</HIRE_DATE>
            <DEPARTMENT>Shipping</DEPARTMENT>
            <TITLE>Packer</TITLE>
        </ITEM>
        <ITEM>
            <NAME>Linda</NAME>
            <ID>1237</ID>
            <HIRE_DATE>4-1-2001</HIRE_DATE>
            <DEPARTMENT>Shipping</DEPARTMENT>
            <TITLE>Packer</TITLE>
        </ITEM>
        <ITEM>
            <NAME>Louise</NAME>
            <ID>1238</ID>
            <HIRE_DATE>4-1-2001</HIRE_DATE>
            <DEPARTMENT>Shipping</DEPARTMENT>
            <TITLE>Packer</TITLE>
        </ITEM>
</EMPLOYEES>
```

To bind employee.xml to an HTML table, I start by adding the XML applet to a Web page:

```
<HTML>
    <HEAD>
        <TITLE>
            Using Single Record Binding With The XML Applet
        </TITLE>
    </HEAD>

    <BODY>
        <CENTER>
            <H1>
                Using Single Record Binding With The XML Applet
            </H1>

            <APPLET CODE="com.ms.xml.dso.XMLDSO.class"
                ID="dsoEmployees" WIDTH=0 HEIGHT=0 MAYSCRIPT=true>
                <PARAM NAME="URL" VALUE="employee.xml">
            </APPLET>
            .
            .
            .
```

Then I bind the XML applet to HTML elements as I did in the In Depth section of this chapter, using **moveNext** to move to the next record, **movePrevious** to move to the previous one, and so on:

```
<HTML>
    <HEAD>
        <TITLE>
            Using Single Record Binding With The XML Applet
        </TITLE>
    </HEAD>

    <BODY>
        <CENTER>
            <H1>
                Using Single Record Binding With The XML Applet
            </H1>

            <APPLET CODE="com.ms.xml.dso.XMLDSO.class"
                ID="dsoEmployees" WIDTH=0 HEIGHT=0 MAYSCRIPT=true>
                <PARAM NAME="URL" VALUE="employee.xml">
            </APPLET>

            Name: <INPUT TYPE="TEXT" DATASRC="#dsoEmployees"
                DATAFLD="NAME" SIZE=10><P>
            ID: <INPUT TYPE="TEXT" DATASRC="#dsoEmployees"
                DATAFLD="ID" SIZE=5><P>
            Department: <SELECT DATASRC="#dsoEmployees"
                DATAFLD="DEPARTMENT" SIZE=1>

            <OPTION VALUE="Shipping">Shipping
            <OPTION VALUE="Programming">Programming
            <OPTION VALUE="Editing">Editing
            <OPTION VALUE="Writing">Writing
            </SELECT><P>

            Hire date: <SPAN DATASRC="#dsoEmployees"
                DATAFLD="HIRE_DATE"></SPAN><P>
            Title: <SPAN DATASRC="#dsoEmployees" DATAFLD="TITLE"></SPAN><P>

            <BUTTON ONCLICK="dsoEmployees.recordset.MoveFirst()" >
                &lt;&lt;
            </BUTTON>
            <BUTTON ONCLICK="if (!dsoEmployees.recordset.BOF)
                dsoEmployees.recordset.MovePrevious()" >
                &lt;
```

```
            </BUTTON>
            <BUTTON ONCLICK="if (!dsoEmployees.recordset.EOF)
                dsoEmployees.recordset.MoveNext()" >
                &gt;
            </BUTTON>
            <BUTTON ONCLICK="dsoEmployees.recordset.MoveLast()">
                &gt;&gt;
            </BUTTON>

        </CENTER>

    </BODY>
</HTML>
```

That's all it takes. The results appear in Figure 18.4. As you can see in the figure, the XML applet can function just like data islands when it comes to data binding. You can also connect the XML applet to HTML tables—see the next section for the details.

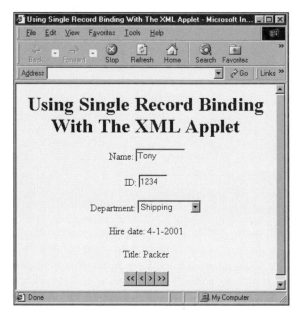

Figure 18.4   Using the XML applet with single record binding.

Tabular Data Binding With The XML Applet

In the previous section, we saw that you can use the XML data source control with buttons to navigate through a record set. You can also use the XML data source control with tables, binding it to HTML tables as we did in the In Depth section of this chapter. Here's an example from the In Depth section showing how this works:

```
<HTML>
    <HEAD>
        <TITLE>
            Using the XML Applet With Tables
        </TITLE>
    </HEAD>

    <BODY>
        <CENTER>
            <H1>
                Using the XML Applet With Tables
            </H1>

            <APPLET CODE="com.ms.xml.dso.XMLDSO.class"
                ID="employees" WIDTH=0 HEIGHT=0 MAYSCRIPT=true>
                <PARAM NAME="URL" VALUE="employee.xml">
            </APPLET>

            <TABLE DATASRC="#employees" CELLSPACING=10>
                <THEAD>
                    <TR>
                        <TH>Name</TH>
                        <TH>ID</TH>
                        <TH>Hire Date</TH>
                        <TH>Department</TH>
                    </TR>
                </THEAD>

                <TBODY>
                    <TR>
                        <TD><SPAN DATAFLD="NAME" DATAFORMATAS="HTML">
                            </SPAN></TD>
                        <TD><SPAN DATAFLD="ID" DATAFORMATAS="HTML">
                            </SPAN></TD>
                        <TD><SPAN DATAFLD="HIRE_DATE"
                            DATAFORMATAS="HTML">
```

```
                                    </SPAN></TD>
                         <TD><SPAN DATAFLD="DEPARTMENT"
                                DATAFORMATAS="HTML"></SPAN></TD>
                      </TR>
                   </TBODY>
                </TABLE>
             </CENTER>
          </BODY>
       </HTML>
```

The results of this HTML appear in Figure 18.5. As you can see in the figure, you can use the XML data source control to create and populate HTML tables with data.

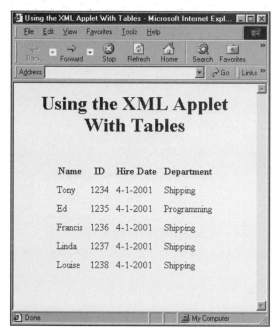

Figure 18.5   Using the XML applet with tables.

Single Record Data Binding With XML Data Islands

The novice programmer says, "What if I want to let the user move through the data in my XML document by just clicking buttons?" "Well," you say, "have you considered using single record data binding with XML data islands?" "How's that?" the NP asks.

Here's an example from the In Depth section of this chapter binding the XML
document employee.xml to various HTML controls by using an Internet Explorer
5 data island to display the fields of a single record from that document:

```
<HTML>
    <HEAD>
        <TITLE>Using XML Data Islands With Single Record Binding</TITLE>
    </HEAD>

    <XML SRC="employee.xml" ID=employees></XML>

    <BODY>
        <CENTER>
            <H1>
                Using XML Data Islands With Single Record Binding
            </H1>

            Name: <INPUT TYPE="TEXT" DATASRC="#employees"
                DATAFLD="NAME" SIZE=10><P>
            ID: <INPUT TYPE="TEXT" DATASRC="#employees"
                DATAFLD="ID" SIZE=5><P>
            Department: <SELECT DATASRC="#employees"
                DATAFLD="DEPARTMENT" SIZE=1>

            <OPTION VALUE="Shipping">Shipping
            <OPTION VALUE="Programming">Programming
            <OPTION VALUE="Editing">Editing
            <OPTION VALUE="Writing">Writing
            </SELECT><P>

            Hire date: <SPAN DATASRC="#employees"
                DATAFLD="HIRE_DATE"></SPAN><P>
            Title: <SPAN DATASRC="#employees" DATAFLD="TITLE"></SPAN><P>

            <BUTTON ONCLICK="employees.recordset.MoveFirst()" >
                &lt;&lt;
            </BUTTON>
            <BUTTON ONCLICK="if (!employees.recordset.BOF)
                employees.recordset.MovePrevious()" >
                &lt;
            </BUTTON>
            <BUTTON ONCLICK="if (!employees.recordset.EOF)
                employees.recordset.MoveNext()" >
                &gt;
            </BUTTON>
```

18. XML: Data Binding And Record Sets

```
                <BUTTON ONCLICK="employees.recordset.MoveLast()">
                    &gt;&gt;
                </BUTTON>
        </CENTER>
    </BODY>
</HTML>
```

That's all it takes. You can see the results of this HTML and XML in Figure 18.2.

Tabular Data Binding With XML Data Islands

"OK," says the novice programmer, "I know I can display the data from single records in XML documents using data islands. But what if I want to see all the data at once?" "In that case," you say judiciously, "you can use tabular data binding."

Tabular data binding binds data to HTML tables. We saw this example, showing how to create tabular data binding to the file employee.xml using a data island, in the In Depth section of this chapter:

```
<HTML>
    <HEAD>
        <TITLE>
            Using XML Data Islands With Tables
        </TITLE>
    </HEAD>

    <BODY>
        <CENTER>
            <H1>
                Using XML Data Islands With Tables
            </H1>

            <XML SRC="employee.xml" ID=employees></XML>

            <TABLE DATASRC="#employees" CELLSPACING=10>
                <THEAD>
                    <TR>
                        <TH>Name</TH>
                        <TH>ID</TH>
                        <TH>Hire Date</TH>
                        <TH>Department</TH>
                    </TR>
```

```
                </THEAD>

            <TBODY>
                <TR>
                    <TD><SPAN DATAFLD="NAME" DATAFORMATAS="HTML">
                        </SPAN></TD>
                    <TD><SPAN DATAFLD="ID" DATAFORMATAS="HTML">
                        </SPAN></TD>
                    <TD><SPAN DATAFLD="HIRE_DATE"
                        DATAFORMATAS="HTML">
                        </SPAN></TD>
                    <TD><SPAN DATAFLD="DEPARTMENT"
                        DATAFORMATAS="HTML"></SPAN></TD>
                </TR>
            </TBODY>
        </TABLE>
    </CENTER>
  </BODY>
</HTML>
```

That's all you need. You can see the results of this HTML and XML in Figure 18.1.

Handling Hierarchical Data

The dedicated database czar appears and says with disdain, "So I hear that Internet Explorer can handle data binding. Well, don't even talk to me about it until it can handle hierarchical record sets." You smile and say, "OK, DDC, shall I teach you all about it? Pull up a chair." The DDC sputters.

One of the biggest assets of XML documents is their ability to store *hierarchical* record sets in which a field in a record can itself hold a whole new record set. In this example, I'll add information about the sales each employee has made to their employee records in employee.xml (introduced in the In Depth section), naming this new file employee2.xml:

```
<?xml version="1.0"?>
<EMPLOYEES>
    <EMPLOYEE>
        <NAME>Tony</NAME>
        <RECORD>
            <ID>1234</ID>
            <HIRE_DATE>4-1-2001</HIRE_DATE>
```

```
                        <DEPARTMENT>Shipping</DEPARTMENT>
                        <TITLE>Packer</TITLE>
                        <SALE>
                            <DATE>4-1-2002</DATE>
                            <AMOUNT>$19000.00</AMOUNT>
                        </SALE>
                        <SALE>
                            <DATE>5-1-2002</DATE>
                            <AMOUNT>$12500.00</AMOUNT>
                        </SALE>
                    </RECORD>
                </EMPLOYEE>
                <EMPLOYEE>
                    <NAME>Ed</NAME>
                    <RECORD>
                        <ID>1235</ID>
                        <HIRE_DATE>4-1-2001</HIRE_DATE>
                        <DEPARTMENT>Programming</DEPARTMENT>
                        <TITLE>Programmer</TITLE>
                        <SALE>
                            <DATE>4-1-2002</DATE>
                            <AMOUNT>$5900.00</AMOUNT>
                        </SALE>
                        <SALE>
                            <DATE>5-1-2002</DATE>
                            <AMOUNT>$23000.00</AMOUNT>
                        </SALE>
                    </RECORD>
                </EMPLOYEE>
                <EMPLOYEE>
                    <NAME>Francis</NAME>
                    <RECORD>
                        <ID>1236</ID>
                        <HIRE_DATE>4-1-2001</HIRE_DATE>
                        <DEPARTMENT>Shipping</DEPARTMENT>
                        <TITLE>Packer</TITLE>
                        <SALE>
                            <DATE>4-1-2002</DATE>
                            <AMOUNT>$1900.00</AMOUNT>
                        </SALE>
                        <SALE>
                            <DATE>5-1-2002</DATE>
                            <AMOUNT>$5300.00</AMOUNT>
                        </SALE>
                    </RECORD>
```

```
        </EMPLOYEE>
        <EMPLOYEE>
            <NAME>Linda</NAME>
            <RECORD>
                <ID>1237</ID>
                <HIRE_DATE>4-1-2001</HIRE_DATE>
                <DEPARTMENT>Shipping</DEPARTMENT>
                <TITLE>Packer</TITLE>
                <SALE>
                    <DATE>4-1-2002</DATE>
                    <AMOUNT>$9000.00</AMOUNT>
                </SALE>
                <SALE>
                    <DATE>5-1-2002</DATE>
                    <AMOUNT>$9500.00</AMOUNT>
                </SALE>
            </RECORD>
        </EMPLOYEE>
        <EMPLOYEE>
            <NAME>Louise</NAME>
            <RECORD>
                <ID>1238</ID>
                <HIRE_DATE>4-1-2001</HIRE_DATE>
                <DEPARTMENT>Shipping</DEPARTMENT>
                <TITLE>Packer</TITLE>
                <SALE>
                    <DATE>4-1-2002</DATE>
                    <AMOUNT>$16000.00</AMOUNT>
                </SALE>
                <SALE>
                    <DATE>5-1-2002</DATE>
                    <AMOUNT>$7600.00</AMOUNT>
                </SALE>
            </RECORD>
        </EMPLOYEE>
</EMPLOYEES>
```

Note that each **<RECORD>** element contains two **<SALE>** elements—and you can consider the two **<SALE>** elements to be a record set in themselves. But how do you make Internet Explorer consider them an actual record set and bind them to HTML elements? All you have to do is refer to this new record set as **RECORD.SALE**, which makes Internet Explorer understand that you mean the record set consisting of **<SALE>** elements in the current record's **<RECORD>** element. Here's an example in code where I'm binding employee2.xml to a table and displaying the **<SALE>** records for each employee as subtables:

```
<HTML>
    <HEAD>
        <TITLE>
            Using XML With Hierarchical Records
        </TITLE>
    </HEAD>

    <BODY>

        <CENTER>
            <H1>
                Using XML With Hierarchical Records
            </H1>

            <XML SRC="employee2.xml" ID=dsoEmployee></XML>

            <TABLE DATASRC="#dsoEmployee" BORDER=1>
                <TR>
                    <TH><DIV DATAFLD="NAME"></DIV></TH>
                    <TD>
                        <TABLE DATASRC="#dsoEmployee"
                        DATAFLD="RECORD">
                            <TR ALIGN = CENTER>
                                <TD>Sales</TD>
                            </TR>
                            <TR>
                                <TD>
                                <TABLE DATASRC="#dsoEmployee"
                                    DATAFLD="RECORD.SALE"
                                    BORDER = 1>
                                    <TR ALIGN = CENTER>
                                        <TH>Date</TH>
                                        <TH>Amount</TH>
                                    </TR>
                                    <TR ALIGN = CENTER>
                                        <TD><DIV DATAFLD="DATE"
                                        dataformatas="TEXT">
                                        </DIV></TD>
                                        <TD><DIV
                                        DATAFLD="AMOUNT"
                                        dataformatas="TEXT">
                                        </DIV></TD>
                                    </TR>
                                </TABLE>
                                </TD>
```

```
                    </TR>
                 </TABLE>
              </TD>
           </TR>
        </TABLE>
     </CENTER>
  </BODY>
</HTML>
```

You can see the results of this HTML and XML in Figure 18.6. Each sales record set is displayed as a subrecord set of the associated employee's record. This example is a success—now we're handling hierarchical record sets as XML data.

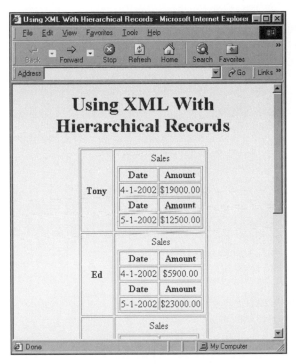

Figure 18.6   Displaying hierarchical XML data.

Handling Variable Size Hierarchical Data

In the previous section, we saw how to handle hierarchical record sets, but in those cases, each **<RECORD>** element had the same number of **<SALE>** elements. What if each **<RECORD>** element had a different number of **<SALE>** elements? To explain this situation, I'll create a new XML document, employee3.xml, where the employees have varying numbers of sales:

```
<?xml version="1.0"?>
<EMPLOYEES>
    <EMPLOYEE>
        <NAME>Tony</NAME>
        <RECORD>
            <ID>1234</ID>
            <HIRE_DATE>4-1-2001</HIRE_DATE>
            <DEPARTMENT>Shipping</DEPARTMENT>
            <TITLE>Packer</TITLE>
            <SALE>
                <DATE>4-1-2002</DATE>
                <AMOUNT>$19000.00</AMOUNT>
            </SALE>
            <SALE>
                <DATE>5-1-2002</DATE>
                <AMOUNT>$12500.00</AMOUNT>
            </SALE>
            <SALE>
                <DATE>5-5-2002</DATE>
                <AMOUNT>$12500.00</AMOUNT>
            </SALE>
        </RECORD>
    </EMPLOYEE>
    <EMPLOYEE>
        <NAME>Ed</NAME>
        <RECORD>
            <ID>1235</ID>
            <HIRE_DATE>4-1-2001</HIRE_DATE>
            <DEPARTMENT>Programming</DEPARTMENT>
            <TITLE>Programmer</TITLE>
            <SALE>
                <DATE>4-1-2002</DATE>
                <AMOUNT>$5900.00</AMOUNT>
            </SALE>
        </RECORD>
    </EMPLOYEE>
    <EMPLOYEE>
        <NAME>Francis</NAME>
        <RECORD>
            <ID>1236</ID>
            <HIRE_DATE>4-1-2001</HIRE_DATE>
            <DEPARTMENT>Shipping</DEPARTMENT>
            <TITLE>Packer</TITLE>
            <SALE>
                <DATE>4-1-2002</DATE>
```

```
                    <AMOUNT>$1900.00</AMOUNT>
                </SALE>
                <SALE>
                    <DATE>5-1-2002</DATE>
                    <AMOUNT>$5300.00</AMOUNT>
                </SALE>
            </RECORD>
    </EMPLOYEE>
    <EMPLOYEE>
        <NAME>Linda</NAME>
        <RECORD>
            <ID>1237</ID>
            <HIRE_DATE>4-1-2001</HIRE_DATE>
            <DEPARTMENT>Shipping</DEPARTMENT>
            <TITLE>Packer</TITLE>
            <SALE>
                <DATE>4-1-2002</DATE>
                <AMOUNT>$9000.00</AMOUNT>
            </SALE>
            <SALE>
                <DATE>5-1-2002</DATE>
                <AMOUNT>$9500.00</AMOUNT>
            </SALE>
        </RECORD>
    </EMPLOYEE>
    <EMPLOYEE>
        <NAME>Louise</NAME>
        <RECORD>
            <ID>1238</ID>
            <HIRE_DATE>4-1-2001</HIRE_DATE>
            <DEPARTMENT>Shipping</DEPARTMENT>
            <TITLE>Packer</TITLE>
            <SALE>
                <DATE>4-1-2002</DATE>
                <AMOUNT>$16000.00</AMOUNT>
            </SALE>
            <SALE>
                <DATE>5-1-2002</DATE>
                <AMOUNT>$7600.00</AMOUNT>
            </SALE>
            <SALE>
                <DATE>5-3-2002</DATE>
                <AMOUNT>$7200.00</AMOUNT>
            </SALE>
        </RECORD>
```

```
            </EMPLOYEE>
    </EMPLOYEES>
```

I'll use the following HTML page, as I did in the previous section, to display this page, however, this one uses employee3.xml:

```
<HTML>
    <HEAD>
        <TITLE>
            Using XML With Different Size Hierarchical Records
        </TITLE>
    </HEAD>

    <BODY>

        <CENTER>
            <H1>
                Using XML With Different Size Hierarchical Records
            </H1>

            <XML SRC="employee3.xml" ID=employees></XML>

            <TABLE DATASRC="#employees" BORDER=1>
                <TR>
                    <TH><DIV DATAFLD="NAME"></DIV></TH>
                    <TD>
                        <TABLE DATASRC="#employees"
                        DATAFLD="RECORD">
                            <TR ALIGN = CENTER>
                                <TD>Sales</TD>
                            </TR>
                            <TR>
                                <TD>
                                <TABLE DATASRC="#employees"
                                    DATAFLD="RECORD.SALE"
                                    BORDER = 1>
                                    <TR ALIGN = CENTER>
                                        <TH>Date</TH>
                                        <TH>Amount</TH>
                                    </TR>
                                    <TR ALIGN = CENTER>
                                        <TD><DIV DATAFLD="DATE"
                                        dataformatas="TEXT">
                                        </DIV></TD>
                                        <TD><DIV
```

```
                              DATAFLD="AMOUNT"
                              dataformatas="TEXT">
                              </DIV></TD>
                          </TR>
                      </TABLE>
                      </TD>
                  </TR>
              </TABLE>
          </TD>
      </TR>
  </TABLE>
  </CENTER>
  </BODY>
</HTML>
```

And in fact, this works. You can see the results in Figure 18.7. Each **<SALE>** record set is correctly displayed, even though they have a different number of records.

You can also create the same page using the XML applet instead of data islands:

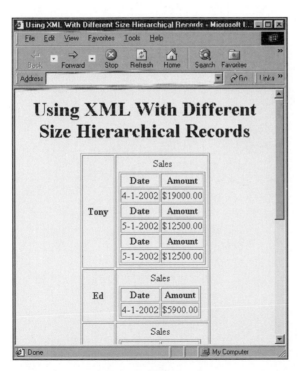

Figure 18.7   Displaying different sizes of hierarchical XML data.

```
<HTML>
    <HEAD>
        <TITLE>
            Using XML With Different Size Hierarchical Records
        </TITLE>
    </HEAD>

    <BODY>
        <CENTER>
            <H1>
                Using XML With Different Size Hierarchical Records
            </H1>

            <APPLET CODE="com.ms.xml.dso.XMLDSO.class"
                ID="employees" WIDTH=0 HEIGHT=0 MAYSCRIPT=true>
                <PARAM NAME="URL" VALUE="employee3.xml">
            </APPLET>

            <TABLE DATASRC="#employees" BORDER=1>
                <TR>
                    <TH><DIV DATAFLD="NAME"></DIV></TH>
                    <TD>
                        <TABLE DATASRC="#employees"
                        DATAFLD="RECORD">
                            <TR ALIGN = CENTER>
                                <TD>Sales</TD>
                            </TR>
                            <TR>
                                <TD>
                                <TABLE DATASRC="#employees"
                                    DATAFLD="RECORD.SALE"
                                    BORDER = 1>
                                    <TR ALIGN = CENTER>
                                        <TH>Date</TH>
                                        <TH>Amount</TH>
                                    </TR>
                                    <TR ALIGN = CENTER>
                                        <TD><DIV DATAFLD="DATE"
                                        dataformatas="TEXT">
                                        </DIV></TD>
                                        <TD><DIV
                                        DATAFLD="AMOUNT"
                                        dataformatas="TEXT">
                                        </DIV></TD>
                                    </TR>
```

```
                              </TABLE>
                             </TD>
                         </TR>
                     </TABLE>
                 </TD>
             </TR>
         </TABLE>
     </CENTER>
  </BODY>
</HTML>
```

XML Applet Data Access Using Record Sets

The novice programmer appears and says, "How do I get my data out of an XML document again? I'm getting lost with this **nextSibling** and **previousChild** stuff." "Why not think of your XML document as a record set?" you ask, "That way, you can move through your data and access it easily." "Wow," says the NP, "how does that work?"

As we saw in the In Depth section of this chapter, you can access the record set exposed by the XML applet or data island with the **recordset** property. You can reach the fields of the current record using **employees.recordset("NAME")**, which refers to the value in the **NAME** field in the current record. You can loop over all the data in the record set, printing out the name and title of each employee like this:

```
<HTML>
    <HEAD>
        <TITLE>
            XML Current Record Access
        </TITLE>

        <SCRIPT LANGUAGE="JavaScript">
            function listEmployees()
            {
                recordSet = employees.recordset

                while (!recordSet.EOF) {
                    div1.innerHTML +=
                    recordSet("NAME") +
                    ", Title: " +
                    recordSet("TITLE") + "<BR>"
```

```
                        recordSet.moveNext()
                }
            }
        </SCRIPT>
    </HEAD>

    <BODY>
        <CENTER>
            <H1>
                XML Current Record Access
            </H1>
        </CENTER>

        <APPLET CODE="com.ms.xml.dso.XMLDSO.class"
            ID="employees" WIDTH=400 HEIGHT=50 MAYSCRIPT=true>
            <PARAM NAME="URL" VALUE="employee.xml">
        </APPLET><P>

        <FORM>
            <INPUT TYPE="BUTTON" VALUE="List Employees"
                ONCLICK="listEmployees()">
        </FORM>
        <DIV ID="div1"></DIV>
    </BODY>
</HTML>
```

And that's all it takes. The result of this Web page, which uses the XML applet, appears in Figure 18.8. As you can also see in the figure, the XML applet will display its current status if you set the **WIDTH** and **HEIGHT** parameters in the **<APPLET>** element to nonzero values. The background of the applet's display is green if the current operation was a success, and red otherwise.

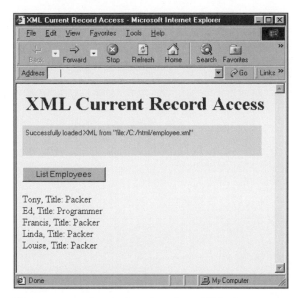

Figure 18.8   Accessing data in an XML document using a record set.

XML Data Island Access Using Record Sets

In the previous topic, we saw how to access data in an XML document using the XML applet. You can also access data in an XML document using XML data islands. Here's an example from the In Depth section of this chapter displaying the name and title of each employee:

```
<HTML>
    <HEAD>
        <TITLE>
            XML Current Record Access
        </TITLE>

        <XML ID="employees" SRC="employee.xml"></XML>

        <SCRIPT LANGUAGE="JavaScript">
            function listEmployees()
            {
                recordSet = employees.recordset

                while (!recordSet.EOF) {
                    div1.innerHTML +=
                    recordSet("NAME") +
                    ", Title: " +
```

```
                        recordSet("TITLE") + "<BR>"
                        recordSet.moveNext()
                }
            }
        </SCRIPT>
    </HEAD>

    <BODY>
        <CENTER>
            <H1>
                XML Current Record Access
            </H1>
        </CENTER>

        <FORM>
            <INPUT TYPE="BUTTON" VALUE="List Employees"
                ONCLICK="listEmployees()">
        </FORM>
        <DIV ID="div1"></DIV>
    </BODY>
</HTML>
```

You can see the results of this HTML and XML in Figure 18.3.

Searching XML Data Using The XML Applet

Because you can access the data in each field of the records of an XML document, you can manipulate that data easily. In this case, I'll create an example that works by searching the data in an XML document for a specific entry.

In particular, I'll use the employee.xml example we've used throughout the chapter and let the user search for employees by name. I'll also add a second employee with the name Louise to employee.xml to make sure we catch multiple matches:

```
<?xml version="1.0"?>
<EMPLOYEE>
    <ITEM>
        <NAME>Tony</NAME>
        <ID>1234</ID>
        <HIRE_DATE>4-1-2001</HIRE_DATE>
        <DEPARTMENT>Shipping</DEPARTMENT>
        <TITLE>Packer</TITLE>
```

```
        </ITEM>
        <ITEM>
            <NAME>Ed</NAME>
            <ID>1235</ID>
            <HIRE_DATE>4-1-2001</HIRE_DATE>
            <DEPARTMENT>Programming</DEPARTMENT>
            <TITLE>Programmer</TITLE>
        </ITEM>
        <ITEM>
            <NAME>Francis</NAME>
            <ID>1236</ID>
            <HIRE_DATE>4-1-2001</HIRE_DATE>
            <DEPARTMENT>Shipping</DEPARTMENT>
            <TITLE>Packer</TITLE>
        </ITEM>
        <ITEM>
            <NAME>Linda</NAME>
            <ID>1237</ID>
            <HIRE_DATE>4-1-2001</HIRE_DATE>
            <DEPARTMENT>Shipping</DEPARTMENT>
            <TITLE>Packer</TITLE>
        </ITEM>
        <ITEM>
            <NAME>Louise</NAME>
            <ID>1238</ID>
            <HIRE_DATE>4-1-2001</HIRE_DATE>
            <DEPARTMENT>Shipping</DEPARTMENT>
            <TITLE>Packer</TITLE>
        </ITEM>
        <ITEM>
            <NAME>Louise</NAME>
            <ID>1240</ID>
            <HIRE_DATE>4-1-2001</HIRE_DATE>
            <DEPARTMENT>Programming</DEPARTMENT>
            <TITLE>Programmer</TITLE>
        </ITEM>
    </EMPLOYEE>
```

To let users search for an employee by name, I'll add a text field to a Web page and let them enter the name they want to search for. When they click the Search Database button, a function named **findEmployees** will search employee.xml for matches to the name entered.

To search for a match in a case-insensitive way, I'll convert both the name to search for and the names in employee.xml to uppercase in code, and then display the names and titles of any employees whose name matches:

```
<HTML>
    <HEAD>
        <TITLE>
            XML Data Searching With The XML Applet
        </TITLE>

        <SCRIPT LANGUAGE="JavaScript">
            function findEmployees()
            {
                toFind = form1.text1.value.toUpperCase()
                recordSet = employees.recordset;

                while (!recordSet.EOF) {
                    var currentName = ""
                    currentName += recordSet("NAME")
                    currentName = currentName.toUpperCase()
                    if (currentName.indexOf(toFind) >= 0) {
                        div1.innerHTML +=
                        recordSet("NAME") +
                        ", Title: " +
                        recordSet("TITLE") + "<BR>"
                    }
                    recordSet.moveNext()
                }
            }
        </SCRIPT>
    </HEAD>

    <BODY>
        <CENTER>
            <H1>
                XML Data Searching With The XML Applet
            </H1>

            <APPLET CODE="com.ms.xml.dso.XMLDSO.class"
                ID="employees" WIDTH=400 HEIGHT=50 MAYSCRIPT=true>
                <PARAM NAME="URL" VALUE="employee.xml">
            </APPLET><P>

            <FORM ID="form1">
                Employee(s) to find: <INPUT TYPE="TEXT" NAME="text1">
                <BR>
                <BR>
```

Figure 18.9   Searching an XML document with the XML applet.

```
                <INPUT TYPE="BUTTON" VALUE="Search Database"
                    ONCLICK="findEmployees()">
            </FORM>
        </CENTER>
        <DIV ID="div1"></DIV>
    </BODY>
</HTML>
```

You can see the results in Figure 18.9. I searched for employees with the name Louise, and as you can see in the figure, there are two matches. That's all there is to it—now we're searching XML documents for data.

Searching XML Data Using XML Data Islands

In the previous section, we saw how to search through a file, employee.xml, for specific employees by name. Here's what employee.xml looks like now (I've added two employees with the name Louise to make sure we can find multiple matches):

```
<?xml version="1.0"?>
<EMPLOYEE>
    <ITEM>
```

```
            <NAME>Tony</NAME>
            <ID>1234</ID>
            <HIRE_DATE>4-1-2001</HIRE_DATE>
            <DEPARTMENT>Shipping</DEPARTMENT>
            <TITLE>Packer</TITLE>
        </ITEM>
        <ITEM>
            <NAME>Ed</NAME>
            <ID>1235</ID>
            <HIRE_DATE>4-1-2001</HIRE_DATE>
            <DEPARTMENT>Programming</DEPARTMENT>
            <TITLE>Programmer</TITLE>
        </ITEM>
        <ITEM>
            <NAME>Francis</NAME>
            <ID>1236</ID>
            <HIRE_DATE>4-1-2001</HIRE_DATE>
            <DEPARTMENT>Shipping</DEPARTMENT>
            <TITLE>Packer</TITLE>
        </ITEM>
        <ITEM>
            <NAME>Linda</NAME>
            <ID>1237</ID>
            <HIRE_DATE>4-1-2001</HIRE_DATE>
            <DEPARTMENT>Shipping</DEPARTMENT>
            <TITLE>Packer</TITLE>
        </ITEM>
        <ITEM>
            <NAME>Louise</NAME>
            <ID>1238</ID>
            <HIRE_DATE>4-1-2001</HIRE_DATE>
            <DEPARTMENT>Shipping</DEPARTMENT>
            <TITLE>Packer</TITLE>
        </ITEM>
        <ITEM>
            <NAME>Louise</NAME>
            <ID>1240</ID>
            <HIRE_DATE>4-1-2001</HIRE_DATE>
            <DEPARTMENT>Programming</DEPARTMENT>
            <TITLE>Programmer</TITLE>
        </ITEM>
    </ITEM>
</EMPLOYEE>
```

Although I used the XML applet in the previous section, I'll use an XML data island here to allow the user to search the XML document:

```
<HTML>
    <HEAD>
        <TITLE>
            XML Data Searching Using Data Islands
        </TITLE>

        <XML ID="employees" SRC="employee.xml"></XML>

        <SCRIPT LANGUAGE="JavaScript">
            function findEmployees()
            {
                toFind = form1.text1.value.toUpperCase()
                recordSet = employees.recordset;

                while (!recordSet.EOF) {
                    var currentName = ""
                    currentName += recordSet("NAME")
                    currentName = currentName.toUpperCase()
                    if (currentName.indexOf(toFind) >= 0) {
                        div1.innerHTML +=
                        recordSet("NAME") +
                        ", Title: " +
                        recordSet("TITLE") + "<BR>"
                    }
                    recordSet.moveNext()
                }
            }
        </SCRIPT>
    </HEAD>

    <BODY>
        <CENTER>
            <H1>
                XML Data Searching Using Data Islands
            </H1>

            <FORM ID="form1">
                Employee(s) to find: <INPUT TYPE="TEXT" NAME="text1">
                <BR>
                <BR>
                <INPUT TYPE="BUTTON" VALUE="Search Database"
                    ONCLICK="findEmployees()">
            </FORM>
        </CENTER>
        <DIV ID="div1"></DIV>
    </BODY>
</HTML>
```

And that's all there is to it. You can see the results in Figure 18.10, which is much like Figure 18.9 in the previous section.

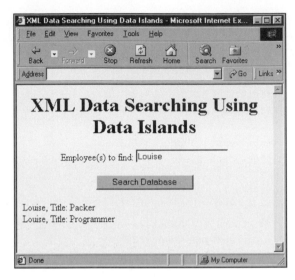

Figure 18.10   Searching an XML document with a data island.

Chapter 19

Essential Perl

(continued)

In Depth

In this chapter, I'll discuss creating Common Gateway Interface (CGI) scripts on Web servers, which will let you create Web pages on the server. This is a great method to use for interacting with the user, including letting the user click checkboxes and radio buttons, entering text for guest books, participating in multiuser chat, and using Web hit counters—and sending data back to a script on the server. CGI also supports server push, cookies, server-based databases, games, shopping carts, site searches, redirecting browsers to new Web sites, uploading files, and much more. To create CGI scripts that run on the Web server and send HTML pages to browsers, I'll use the most popular CGI scripting language, Perl (Practical Extraction and Reporting Language).

There's a great deal more to Perl than we can cover in one or two chapters, so for more details you might want to check out a good book on Perl. There are many books on Perl, but without a doubt, the best of them is my *Perl Black Book* (The Coriolis Group, ©1999), which examines all the topics mentioned in the previous paragraph and much more—it's the most complete Perl book available.

In this chapter, I'll work through the basics of Perl programming, and in Chapter 20, put them to work creating a Web page that can interpret buttons, radio buttons, checkboxes, scrolling lists, password fields, text fields, and more. The user can enter data using these controls, click the Submit button, and the CGI script on the server will summarize the data entered by the user and display it in a new Web page in the browser.

TIP: *Because this is only an introduction to Perl, keep in mind that the Perl coverage in this chapter unavoidably skips a great of Perl programming, including such topics as writing and reading data to and from files (for example, when you want to store user comments in a guest book on your Web server). If you become frustrated trying to understand a topic, please refer to the* Perl Black Book *(The Coriolis Group, ©1999) for all the details.*

Here's a sample Perl script that you can install on your server and, when opened in a Web browser, will display an HTML text area with the text "Welcome To Perl!" in it:

```
#!/usr/local/bin/perl

use CGI;
```

```
$co = new CGI;

print $co->header,

$co->start_html(-title=>'CGI Example'),

$co->center($co->h1('Welcome To Perl!')),

$co->start_form(),

$co->textarea
(
    -name=>'textarea',
    -default=>'Welcome To Perl!',
    -rows=>10,
    -columns=>60
),

$co->end_form(),

$co->end_html;
```

You can see the results of this CGI script in Figure 19.1. We'll learn how to create scripts like this in Chapter 20. In this chapter, we'll build the foundation of Perl programming that we'll need.

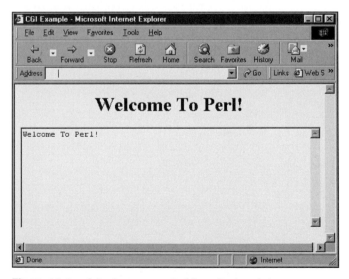

Figure 19.1   A text area created by a Perl script.

There are many, many Web pages available on Perl for additional study (a random Web search turns up a mere 1,527,903 pages mentioning Perl). The following is a list of some good ones:

- *Comprehensive Perl Archive Network (CPAN) (**www.cpan.org**)*—You can get Perl, Perl modules, Perl extensions, and tons of other Perl items here. This is the most comprehensive source for information about Perl. If you browse through CPAN, you're sure to see lots of valuable code ranging from Perl language extensions to image handling and from Internet modules to database interfaces.

- *Online Perl documentation (**www.cpan.org/doc/manual/html/pod/ perl.html**)*—This site has the official Perl documentation.

- *Perl home page (**www.perl.com**)*—You can find source code and Perl ports for various operating systems, documentation, modules, bug reports, and a Perl frequently asked questions (FAQ) list. The FAQ is at **www.perl.com/ perl/faq**.

- *Perl language page (**www.perl.com**)*—This site includes Perl overviews, news, resource lists, and software as well as a list of Perl mailing lists.

- *Perl Mongers (**www.pm.org**)*—This nonprofit organization works to establish Perl user groups. There are countless numbers of groups—visit the site for lists.

Many other sites having to do with special Perl interests, such as security, CGI programming, and more, are available—just search the Web if you want to be overwhelmed.

The following list contains a number of Usenet groups for Perl programmers:

- *comp.lang.perl.announce*—A low-traffic group.

- *comp.lang.perl.misc*—A high-traffic site that also posts a Perl FAQ.

- *comp.lang.perl.modules*—A group about creating modules and reusing your own or someone else's code.

- *comp.lang.perl.tk*—A group about the connection between Perl and the Tcl language's Tk toolkit. The Tk toolkit supports many visual controls, like buttons, menus, and so on, that you can use with Perl, and it's become pretty popular.

If you're interested in CGI programming, take a look at comp.infosystems. www.authoring.cgi—it doesn't have Perl in the name, but it's a good place to talk with others about Perl CGI programming.

In the next section, we'll begin to create Perl programs. Fortunately, we have some knowledge of creating Perl programs because, like JavaScript and Java, Perl is based on C++. We are familiar with many constructs used in Perl, such as **if** and **while** statements.

Creating Perl Programs

Like JavaScript, and unlike Java, Perl is parsed and executed at runtime instead of being compiled into binary form and then run. This means that Perl programs are actually scripts, and they're run by the Perl interpreter named perl (note the lowercase "p"). The Perl interpreter is probably already installed on your Web server, and we'll learn how to use it on Web servers in the next chapter. For development purposes, however, you might want Perl on your local machine. You can download the latest version, a very good one for Windows is the ActiveState Perl implementation, from **www.perl.com/pub/language/info/software.html**.

TIP: *When creating your own Perl programs, a good asset to have is the Perl documentation, which comes with Perl. You can also view it online at* **www.cpan.org/doc/manual/html/pod/perl.html**.

Creating Perl scripts can be very easy. All you have to do is save a plain text file with the Perl code you want in it. In the Immediate Solutions section "Writing Code: Creating Code Files" of this chapter, I'll run scripts locally and give such files the extension .pl. In Chapter 20, we'll create CGI scripts and use the extension .cgi. For example, say you have a file named hello.pl with the following Perl statement in it, which is designed to print out the message "Hello from Perl!":

```
print "Hello from Perl!\n";
```

Note that the **\n** character represents a newline character, which makes the output skip to the next line. Like Java, Perl insists that each statement ends with a semicolon (**;**). If you have Perl installed on your computer, you can run this script in an MS-DOS session in Windows:

```
C:\>perl hello.pl
```

When you do, the message "Hello from Perl!" is displayed at once:

```
C:\>perl hello.pl

Hello from Perl!
```

This gives us our start with Perl scripts—I'll press on to explain how to work with data.

Handling Data In Perl

In this chapter, I'll discuss how Perl handles two types of data: *scalar variables* and *lists*. Scalar variables hold a single data item, and lists hold multiple data items. From the outset, it's important to understand the difference between scalar variables and lists. Although scalar variables are actual data types—that is, you can allocate storage for them—there is no list data type in Perl. The difference between scalar variables and lists is one of *context*, not data types—Perl knows if you're working in what it calls *scalar context* or *list context*. Many Perl functions and operators are sensitive to context, so if your code uses such a function or operator in list context—for example, you might assign its return value to a list—that's a signal to Perl that you expect a list of data items. If the function is used in scalar context, Perl knows you expect a scalar.

Scalar Variables

Scalar variables are what many programming languages refer to as simple variables (and in Perl, they're also often just called scalars), and they hold a single data item, such as a number or a string. Scalars are called scalars to differentiate them from constructs that can hold more than one item, like arrays. (In scientific terms, a scalar is a simple numeric value, whereas vectors can have multiple values, and in fact, one-dimensional arrays are often called vectors in programming.)

You preface a scalar variable's name with a dollar sign (**$**). In Perl terms, **$** is the *prefix dereferencer* for scalars. Using it for scalars means that Perl will know how to treat your scalar—and that none of your scalar variable names will conflict with reserved words in Perl (i.e., the words built into the Perl language). You don't need to declare variables in Perl before using them as you do in Java (there is no **var**, **int**, or **float** statement in Perl).

TIP: *There is a different type of prefix dereferencer for each data format in Perl: **$** for scalars, **@** for arrays, and **%** for hashes.*

There are two main types of scalars: numbers and strings. You assign values to a scalar variable with the assignment operator (**=**) like this:

```
$scalar1 = 5;
$scalar2 = "Hello there!";
```

You can also use Perl operators and functions with scalars. The operators and functions you use usually depend on whether the data in the scalar is a number or a string. Keep in mind that scalar variables represent actual memory locations that store a single item of data—a string or a number. They're the fundamental unit of data storage in Perl.

Lists

As you can gather from their name, lists are just that: lists of data elements. As mentioned earlier, unlike scalars, there is no specific list data type, but the concept of lists in Perl is very important. A list is a construct that associates data elements, and you can specify a list by enclosing those elements in parentheses and separating them with commas. In the following code, I'm printing out the elements in the list ("H", "e", "l", "l", "o") with the **print** function, which is designed to take a list argument:

```
print ("H", "e", "l", "l", "o");
```

Hello

Note that in this case, I did not assign the list ("H", "e", "l", "l", "o") to a variable before printing it because there is no explicit list variable type in Perl.

You can also omit the parentheses when working with lists if you don't need them to indicate that you want to work in list context and if there's no possibility of confusion, as in this case, where I pass "H", "e", "l", "l", "o" to the **print** function:

```
print "H", "e", "l", "l", "o";
```

Hello

The functions built into Perl are divided into two groups: those that expect scalar arguments and those that expect lists (although many functions are written to take either).

Scalar And List Context

How does Perl know when to treat data as a scalar and when to treat data as a list? It makes its decision based on the context. There are two main contexts: scalar context and list context (these in turn are broken down as well: for example, numeric context and text string context are both scalar contexts).

That is to say, if Perl is expecting a list (for instance, when you use a function that only takes a list), it treats your data as a list. If it's expecting a scalar, it treats your data as a scalar. In other words, the way the data is treated is *implicit* in Perl programming, based on the context in which you use that data, and not explicitly set in code. If you're working with functions that take or return list arguments, for example, those arguments are automatically treated as lists.

After scalars and lists, the next step in data organization is to use an array.

Arrays

Arrays let you organize a list of items by numeric index, and let you refer to those items using that index. Being able to access data items by index is often invaluable in code because you can increment or decrement that index and work through the entire array under programmatic control.

You can create an array by assigning a list to an array variable, which starts with a **@** in Perl (**@** is the array prefix dereferencer):

```
@array = (1, 2, 3);
```

You refer to the individual elements of a simple array by indicating the index of the element inside brackets (**[** and **]**) and by substituting **$** for **@**—note that array indices are 0-based in Perl:

```
print $array[0];
```

1

TIP: *It's often confusing to novice Perl programmers that you use **$** as the prefix dereferencer when referring to individual array elements instead of **@**. But when you consider that Perl uses the prefix dereferencer to determine the type of a variable, it makes sense, because an individual element in a simple array is a scalar, whose prefix dereferencer is **$**.*

There's another type of array that Perl supports besides standard arrays—associative arrays, also called *hashes*.

Hashes

Novice programmers often start using Perl with no idea of what a hash is, but a little programming experience makes them an expert on the topic because they're ubiquitous in Perl. As mentioned previously, hashes are also called associative arrays, and they work very much like arrays except that you use text string keys—not numeric indices—to organize data in a hash. This is useful for data that you want to reference with a name, such as "title" instead of by number as you would with a standard array. (In this way, working with hashes may be considered one step closer to true database programming than working with standard arrays.)

When you create a hash, you associate a value, such as **apple** used here, with a key, **fruit** in this case:

```
$hash{'fruit'} = 'apple';
```

Note the similarity to working with standard arrays. The main difference is that you use curly braces ({ and }) with hashes when referring to a specific item, not straight brackets ([and]) as with standard arrays, and that you index values with a text string key—such as **fruit** used here—not a numeric index. Note also that, as with arrays, when you refer to single values in a hash, you use the **$** prefix dereferencer.

You can refer to the new value in the hash to print it out like this:

```
$hash{'fruit'} = 'apple';
print "$hash{'fruit'}\n";
```

apple

The prefix dereferencer for hashes is %, and, as with arrays, you can create hashes with list assignments. When you do so, you can associate the values stored in the hash with text keys using key/value pairs like this:

```
%hash = (
    'fruit'    , 'apple',
    'sandwich' , 'hamburger',
    'drink'    , 'bubbly',
);
```

Now you can refer to the values in the hash by key like this:

```
%hash = (
    'fruit'    , 'apple',
    'sandwich' , 'hamburger',
    'drink'    , 'bubbly',
);
```

```
print "$hash{'fruit'}\n";
```

apple

Organizing your data into hashes is often more intuitive than using arrays because you can use text keys to retrieve your data from a hash, which is beneficial for setting up data records. For example, note how much clearer this is:

```
print $employees{'name'};
```

than using a numerically indexed array:

```
print $employees[13];
```

Like JavaScript and Java, Perl has operators based on C++ (although with a number of additions). I'll take a look at them in overview next.

Operators

Using operators, you can manipulate your data, even if it's just a simple addition function, by using the addition operator (**+**) in this way:

```
print 2 + 2;
```

4

The Perl operators, in descending order of precedence (i.e., the first line has highest precedence and so is evaluated first), appear in Table 19.1. The column labeled Associativity indicates which direction the operator looks for its arguments, to the right or left.

Table 19.1   Operator precedence.

Operator(s)	Associativity
terms and leftward list operators	left
->	left
++ --	n/a
**	right
! ~ \ and unary + and -	right
=~ !~	left
* / % x	left
+ - .	left
<< >>	left
named unary operators file text operators	n/a
< > <= >= lt gt le ge	n/a
== != <=> eq ne cmp	n/a
&	left
	^	left
&&	left
||	left
.. ...	n/a
?:	right

(continued)

19. Essential Perl

Table 19.1   Operator precedence **(continued).**

Operator(s)	Associativity
= += -= *= etc.	right
, =>	left
rightward list operators	n/a
not	right
and	left
or xor	left

Conditional Statements

As in JavaScript and Java, conditional statements let you direct code execution depending on logical tests that you make. In other words, conditional statements let you make decisions in code and act on them.

You use conditionals to perform tests on data and take the appropriate actions. For example, I might want to test the value in **$variable** to see if it's equal to 5. I can use an **if** statement to do that. If the value is 5, the code will display the string, "Yes, it's five.\n"; otherwise, the code displays the string, "No, it's not five.\n":

```
$variable = 5;

if ($variable == 5) {
    print "Yes, it's five.\n";
} else {
    print "No, it's not five.\n";
}
```

Yes, it's five.

The **if** statement is a compound statement, which means you use curly braces to delimit the code block(s) in it. Note that because Perl skips white space, including newlines, you can write the previous code like this:

```
$variable = 5;

if ($variable == 5) {
    print "Yes, it's five.\n";
}
else {
    print "No, it's not five.\n";
}
```

However, you *cannot* use the JavaScript-style **if** statement syntax, which makes the curly braces optional if a code block only includes one line. Note that I'm creating a Perl comment here by prefacing the comment text with a sharp character (**#**):

```
$variable = 5;

if ($variable == 5)                    #wrong!
    print "Yes, it's five.\n";
else
    print "No, it's not five.\n";
```

Besides the conditional statements we've seen in JavaScript and Java, Perl also adds others, such as **unless**, which we'll see throughout this chapter. Perl also includes loop statements.

Loop Statements

Loop statements are also a powerful part of programming because they let you perform iterative operations on sets of data, and that's something computers excel at—quick, repetitive calculations. Loop statements continue executing the code in the loop body until a conditional test, which you specify, is met.

Here's an example **for** loop, which calculates a factorial value. The loop index is a variable called **$loop_index.** Note how much this looks like the corresponding JavaScript or Java **for** loop:

```
$factorial = 1;

for ($loop_index = 1; $loop_index <= 6; $loop_index++) {
    $factorial *= $loop_index;
}
print "6! = $factorial\n";

6! = 720
```

Using a loop index, you can index the values in a data set, working through that data value by value as in this case, where I iterate through an array. Perl fills the expression **$#*arrayname*** with the index value of the last element in the array named **@*arrayname***:

```
@array = ("one", "two", "three");
for ($loop_index = 0; $loop_index <= $#array; $loop_index++)
{
```

```
    print $array[$loop_index] . " ";
}
```

one two three

That's it. Conditional statements let you make decisions in code, and loop statements let you handle repetitive operations on your data. There are two more skills we'll need to discuss before we can start writing CGI scripts in Chapter 20: using Perl modules and creating objects in Perl.

Using Perl Modules

Java comes with many classes already created for you as well as packages of classes, and you can add them to your programs with the **import** statement. Similarly, there are hundreds of Perl *modules* available, some of which come with Perl, and some of which you can obtain from the CPAN site. In the next chapter, we'll use the CGI module to create CGI scripts. To add a module to your script, you can add a **use** statement to your code. Here's an example in which I'm using the Perl **integer** module, which adds support for integer math:

```
use integer;
print 5/3;
```

Integer math discards the remainders of division operations, so the result of this division is 1:

```
use integer;
print 5/3;
```

1

Modules also can contain *submodules*. For example, the **Time** module has a submodule named **Local**, which includes the function **timeLocal**, which lets you determine the number of seconds since the Perl epoch began (dated to 1/1/1970) to 1/1/2000 like this (note the **::**, which is how you separate module and submodule names):

```
use Time::Local;
print timelocal(0, 0, 0, 1, 1, 2000);
```

949381200

We'll need one more skill for the next chapter—creating objects.

Creating Objects

In Chapter 20, we'll use the CGI module to create CGI scripts. Like much of modern Perl, the CGI module is object oriented (for more on object-oriented programming, see the discussion in the In Depth section of Chapter 15). To create a Web page to send back to a Web browser, I include the CGI module and use the **new** operator to create an object named **$co** of the CGI class:

```
use CGI;
$co = new CGI;
```

The variable **$co** really contains a *reference* to a new CGI object (for more Perl references, see the *Perl Black Book*, The Coriolis Group, ©1999), and you can access its data members and methods using the arrow operator (**->**) like this, where I'm calling the new CGI object's **header** method:

```
use CGI;
$co = new CGI;
print $co->header;
```

The **header** method returns the header text of a Web page (such as **Content-Type: text/html** text, which tells the browser what kind of document is being sent to it), and when the script runs as a CGI script, the **print** function will send that header back to the browser as we'll see in the next chapter.

And that brings us up to speed—it's time to turn to the details of Perl programming in the Immediate Solutions section.

Immediate Solutions

Writing Code: Creating Code Files

The design team coordinator calls to congratulate you on getting Perl installed. You accept the accolades gracefully. "So what scripts have you been writing?" he asks. "Hm," you say, "Scripts?"

Perl scripts are just plain text files made up of Perl statements as needed. To create a Perl script, you should have a text editor or word processor that can save files in plain text format.

As you already know if you edit your own HTML pages, saving text in plain text format is a simple achievement that's beyond many fancy word processors. You might have trouble accomplishing this feat with some word processors. However, in Microsoft Word, you can save plain text files using the File|Save As dialog box. The general rule is, if you can type the file out at the command line (for example, in DOS on both DOS- and Windows-based computers) and not see any odd, nonalphanumeric characters, it's a plain text file. The real test, of course, is if Perl can read and interpret your script.

NOTE: *One big difference between text files in Unix and MS-DOS/Windows is that Unix files use a single character at the end of each line, and MS-DOS/Windows files use two characters (i.e., a carriage return and a line feed). This can be a problem when you move scripts from one operating system to another, because Perl, on the target system, may have problems with scripts written on the source system. (Note that many FTP programs now automatically convert line endings to the correct version for the target system.)*

You can name your Perl code files just about any way you want to—no special extension is necessary. However, the very popular Windows port—Win32 ActiveState Perl—associates the extension .pl with Perl scripts, so you can run them just by double-clicking them. In fact, file extensions can be useful when you come back to long lists of files three years from now and wonder what kind they are. For these reasons, I'll use the extension .pl for scripts in this chapter. Just bear in mind that you don't have to use this extension or any other (including the other popular Perl script extension, .p).

So far so good—we've finished our discussion on the selection of an editor or a word processor. Now how about writing some code.

Writing Code: Statements And Declarations

The big boss is looking over your shoulder. You've got your editor open and are about to start impressing the BB with your Perl expertise. The BB is waiting— what will you type?

Perl statements come in two forms: simple and compound. A simple statement is an expression that performs some specific action. In code, a simple statement ends with a semicolon (;) as you can see in the following code line. We'll use the print function to display the string "Hello!", followed by a newline character, **\n** (see "Basic Skills: Text Formatting" in the Immediate Solutions section later in this chapter for more on characters like **\n**), which skips to the next line:

```
print "Hello!\n";
```

Compound statements are composed of expressions and blocks. Blocks are delimited with curly braces in Perl ({ and }) and can hold multiple simple statements. You do not place a semicolon after the curly braces. Here's an example in which I use a block to create a compound **for** loop statement, which is the most basic of the Perl loops:

```
for ($loop_index = 1; $loop_index <=5; $loop_index++) {
    print "Hello ";
    print "there!\n";
}
```

If you enter either of the previous scripts into a file, such as hello.pl, you've created a Perl script. The next step is making sure you can connect that script and the Perl interpreter to get the script to run.

Writing Code: Finding The Perl Interpreter

The big boss is still looking over your shoulder as you type at your workstation. You've created your first lines of Perl script. The BB is mighty impressed. But how do you make sure that script can find the Perl interpreter? The BB says, "I'm waiting...."

There are two principal ways to make sure a Perl script can find the Perl interpreter: explicitly and implicitly. I'll look at them both in the following sections.

Finding Perl Explicitly

You can find Perl by passing your script to perl, the Perl interpreter, explicitly from the command line like this:

```
C:\>perl hello.pl
```

This assumes, of course, that Perl has been installed correctly on your machine, which means it's in your command path. If it isn't, you'll find yourself having to use the fully qualified path to the Perl executable like this in MS-DOS:

```
D:\>c:\perl\bin\perl hello.pl
```

I don't recommend using the fully qualified path and instead suggest you add Perl to your path if it's not already there (as mentioned earlier, it should be in your command path if Perl was installed properly).

Finding Perl Implicitly

Besides passing your script to Perl explicitly, you can also make sure your script can find Perl by itself. This means you can run your scripts more like a stand-alone command, like this in Unix (where the % is the command prompt):

```
%hello.pl
```

Or, if you have named the Perl script's file without an extension like this:

```
%hello
```

This looks more like a system command, which is the idea. Making sure your script can find Perl by itself differs by operating system, and I'll take a look at the major possibilities in the following sections.

Unix

You can let Unix know that your file is Perl script by making the following line the first line of your script (bear in mind that you don't need this line if you invoke the Perl interpreter explicitly as discussed previously):

```
#!/usr/local/bin/perl
```

If you use the special **#!** syntax, it must be the very first line in your script. This line refers to the standard location of Perl on most Unix systems. Note that Perl might be at a different location on your machine, such as /usr/bin/perl (on many machines, the paths /usr/bin/perl and /usr/local/bin/perl are aliased to be the same).

To specify that you want to use Perl 5, you might have to use a line like this on many systems:

```
#!/usr/local/bin/perl5
```

MS-DOS

In MS-DOS, you can make sure your script knows where to find Perl by converting that script into a .bat batch file with the pl2bat.bat utility. This utility comes with ActiveState's port of Perl. For example, let's say you had this Perl script, hello.pl:

```
print "Hello!\n";
```

You could use pl2bat.bat to convert it into a .bat file, hello.bat, which you can run directly from the command line. Here's how you'd convert hello.pl to hello.bat:

```
C:\>pl2bat hello.pl
```

Here's the resulting batch file, hello.bat:

```
@rem = '--*-Perl-*--
@echo off
if "%OS%" == "Windows_NT" goto WinNT
perl -x -S "%0" %1 %2 %3 %4 %5 %6 %7 %8 %9
goto endofperl
:WinNT
perl -x -S "%0" %*
if NOT "%COMSPEC%" == "%SystemRoot%\system32\cmd.exe" goto endofperl
if %errorlevel%==9009 echo You do not have Perl in your PATH.
goto endofperl
@rem ';
#!perl
#line 14
print "Hello!\n";

__END__
:endofperl
```

Rather than going through this step, you may find it more to your liking to pass your script to Perl explicitly in MS-DOS, especially during development (or even to create a .bat file with the following command in it):

```
C:\>perl hello.pl
```

Windows 95/98 And Windows NT

The ActiveState port of Perl for Windows 95/98 and Windows NT is very handy because it modifies the Windows Registry to connect the .pl extension with the Perl interpreter automatically.

All you need to do is double-click the Perl script to run it. However, when you do, the script opens an MS-DOS window, runs, then immediately closes the MS-DOS window. To solve this problem, see "Basic Skills: Avoiding Immediate Script Closings In Windows" in the Immediate Solutions section of this chapter.

Macintosh

Macintosh Perl scripts automatically have the appropriate Creator and Type, so that double-clicking them will invoke MacPerl, if it's been installed correctly.

Now it's time to actually run your script; see the next section.

Running Perl Code

You've finished writing your Perl script, and the big boss is watching over your shoulder. The company's future hinges on your new script. "OK," says the BB, "it's the big moment. How do you get all this to run?"

Assume you have a short file named hello.pl containing this Perl script:

```
#!/usr/local/bin/perl

print "hello\n";
```

Getting scripts like this to run is a basic Perl step. There are many variations, and I'll take a look at them in some detail in the following sections.

If Your Script Can Find Perl

If your script can find Perl, you can run the script easily. In Unix, this means that you've included a line like **#!/usr/local/bin/perl** as the first line in your script (which we'll do in CGI scripts in the next chapter). In Unix, you make the script an executable file with **chmod** like this: **chmod +x hello.pl**. Also, make sure the script is in your path (e.g., check your .login file and look for **set path** commands). Then you just run the script at the command line like this:

```
%hello.pl
```

In Windows and on the Macintosh, just double-click the script file to run it (make sure you've given the script file the extension .pl in Windows, which is the extension that the ActiveState software connects to the Perl interpreter).

In MS-DOS, after you've used the pl2bat.bat batch file to convert your script into a .bat file, just run the .bat file at the DOS prompt like this:

```
C:\>hello
```

You can also invoke Perl from the command line explicitly, and I'll take a look at these possibilities next.

If You Want To Use Perl From The Command Line

To run a script explicitly with the Perl interpreter, make sure perl is in your path and use the **perl** command. You can place your script in a file and pass that file's name to the Perl interpreter. For example, if the following code line is the contents of the file hello.pl (note that I'm omitting the **#!** line, which isn't needed because I'm running the Perl interpreter explicitly):

```
print "Hello!\n";
```

then you could run that script this way, specifying that file name:

```
C:\>perl hello.pl

Hello!
```

TIP: *To end a Perl script while it's running—for example, while it's waiting for input from you, but you want to quit— you can press Ctrl+C.*

Basic Skills: Text Input And Output

Perl treats input and output as *channels*, and you work with these channels using *file handles*. A file handle is just a value that represents a file to Perl. You get a file handle for a file when you open that file.

There are three predefined file handles that you can use with text: **STDIN**, **STDOUT**, and **STDERR**. **STDIN** is the normal input channel for your script, **STDOUT** the normal output channel, and **STDERR** the normal output channel for errors. By default, **STDIN** corresponds to the keyboard and **STDOUT** and **STDERR** to the screen. I'll use predefined file handles throughout this chapter, for instance, see the next section, where I use **STDOUT** to display text.

Basic Skills: Using The **print** Function

The programming team coordinator is mighty pleased with your new script, which handles no end of data and does no end of data crunching. The script finally ends and you turn triumphantly to the PTC. "But," the PTC asks, "where's the output?" You think: *output*? "Try the **print** function," the PTC says.

To print text to a file, including to **STDOUT**, you use the **print** function. It may be the most commonly used function in Perl. We've already seen the print function in this chapter, but I'll take a more systematic look at it in this section. The **print** function has these forms:

```
print FILEHANDLE LIST
print LIST
print
```

If you don't specify a file handle, **STDOUT** is used. If you don't specify a list of items to print (note that such a list may be made up of only one item), the **print** function prints whatever is in the special Perl variable **$_** to the output channel. The variable **$_** is the default variable that holds input from the input channel (see "Basic Skills: Using The Default Variable **$_**" in the Immediate Solutions section for more information).

Here's an example where I just print "Hello!" and a newline character to the output channel:

```
print "Hello!\n";
```

Hello!

The **print** function is really a list function that takes a list of items. This means that you can pass a list of items to print, separating the list items with commas like this:

```
print "Hello ", "there!\n";
```

Hello there!

If you want to print a string a number of times, you use the Perl **x** repetition operator like this:

```
print "Hello!\n" x 10;
```

Hello!
Hello!
Hello!
Hello!
Hello!
Hello!
Hello!
Hello!
Hello!
Hello!

Or like this if you want to draw a horizontal line made up of hyphens:

```
print "-" x 30
```

```
- - - - - - - - - - - - - - - - - - - - - - - - - - - - - -
```

Basic Skills: Text Formatting

You've gotten your script to print out some data at last, and the programming team coordinator is very pleased. But the PTC wants the data to appear in table form, so you've got to print out tab characters. Hm, you think—how do you print tabs?

You can perform some basic text formatting using *escape characters*. An escape character is a special character that you preface with a backslash (\). It indicates to functions like print, which handles text strings, that the escape character is a special character that should be specifically interpreted. Some of the escape characters and what they represent appear in Table 19.2.

Table 19.2 Escape characters.

Escape Character	Means
\"	double quote
\033	octal char
\a	alarm (bell)

(continued)

Table 19.2   Escape characters (continued).

Escape Character	Means
\b	backspace
\c[	control char
\e	escape
\f	form feed
\n	newline
\r	return
\t	tab
\x1b	hex char

For example, here's how you can display double quotes in a printed string:

```
print "\"Hello!\"\n";
```

"Hello!"

And here's how to use tabs:

```
print "Hello\tfrom\tPerl.\n";
```

Hello   from   Perl.

Here's how to create multiline output using the \n newline character:

```
print "Hello\nfrom\nPerl.\n";
```

Hello
from
Perl.

Keep in mind that this is just basic text formatting and that more complex formatting is possible.

Basic Skills: Commenting Your Code

Your new script is so popular that the home office has distributed it to all the field offices. But now you're getting calls and emails from all over asking what line 14 does, if you really meant to do that in line 28, if line 42 is really legal code, and what about line 56—surely that's an error? As you hang up the phone wearily, you wonder if there is a better way to let other programmers know just how your programs work. There is—you can comment your code.

When you create complicated scripts, you may want to add comments—that is, a reminder or explanatory text ignored by Perl—to make the structure and workings of these scripts easier to understand. In Perl, you preface comments with a **#** because Perl will ignore all the text on a line after the **#** symbol. Here's an example:

```perl
#!/usr/bin/perl -w       # Use Perl with warnings
my $count = 0;           # $count used to match {}, (), etc.
my $statement = "";      # $statement holds multi-line statements
local $SIG{__WARN__} = sub {}; # Supress error reporting

while (<>) {             # Accept input from the keyboard

    chomp;               # Clean up input
    while (/{|\(|\[/g) {$count++};     # Watch for {, (, etc.
    while (/}|\)|\]/g) {$count--};     # Pair with }, ), etc.

    $statement .= $_ . " ";    # Append input to current statement

    if (!$count) {       # Only evaluate if {, ( matches }, ) etc.

        eval $statement; # Evaluate the Perl statement
        if($@) {print "Syntax error.\n"};  # Notify of error
        $statement = ""; # Clear the current statement
        $count = 0       # Clear the multi-line {, ( etc. count

    }
}
```

Comments can help programmers reading your code at a later date to understand what's going on. Keep in mind that the programmer you help may be yourself.

Basic Skills: Reading Typed Input

Well, your new Perl calculator is a terrific success—it adds 7 + 7 and prints out 14 every time. The big boss is very happy with it. "Let me try it," the BB says, "How do you enter the numbers to add?" You say, "Enter them? You can't do that—the calculator only adds 7 + 7 and that's it." "No good," says the BB, "you've got to let users type in their own numbers to add." So how do you do that?

As we've seen earlier, you can use the **print** function to display output—but how do you accept input? You can read input from the **STDIN** file handle, simply by using angle brackets (**<** and **>**). For example, here's how to use a **while** loop (just like the JavaScript or Java **while** loop) to read each line the user types, storing those lines in a variable named **$temp,** and printing out each line:

```
while ($temp = <STDIN>) {
    print $temp;
}
```

When you run this script and type, for example, "Hello!", the script echoes what you've typed:

```
while ($temp = <STDIN>) {
    print $temp;
}

Hello!
```

In fact, as is often the case in Perl, there's a short way to do this—take a look at the next section.

Basic Skills: Using The Default Variable $_

When you use the construct **<STDIN>** without assigning its return value to a variable, Perl automatically assigns that return value to a special variable named **$_**. This variable, called the default variable, is a special variable that many Perl functions use as a default if you don't specify another. This means you can use the **print** function without specifying a variable at all to print the contents of **$_**. (There are plenty of other special variables too, like **$!**, which hold the current error if there is one.)

In fact, you can omit the **STDIN** altogether if you just use the angle brackets < and > alone without specifying any file handle—**STDIN** is used by default. (Perl is full of defaults like this, which can make things easier for experts but opaque for novices. That may explain why the experts like it.) Here's how the code from the previous section looks after making use of these shortcuts:

```
while(<>) {
    print;
}
```

This is really a short version of this code, which does the same thing:

```
while($_ = <STDIN>) {
    print $_;
}
```

Some stylists have objected to the overuse of **$_** because its implicit, behind-the-scenes nature can be very hard to keep track of over many pages of code. That is, if you have five pages of code to look over, you might miss some operation that implicitly sets **$_** on page three and think that the **$_** used on page five holds the same value as in the code on page one. However, Perl scripts are typically rather short, and even if they're not, the operations that use **$_** are typically localized and not spread over many pages.

Note that there's no way to provide a set of simple rules to make it clear when you can use **$_** and when you can't, because some of the Perl functions use **$_** and some don't. This means that you have to make this determination on a function-by-function basis.

When you're used to working with **$_**, it usually makes programming much easier, even if it's more confusing to the uninitiated. Here's an example where every statement uses **$_** implicitly:

```
while (<>) {
    for (split) {
        s/m/y/g;
        print;
    }
}
```

What does this script do? It breaks the line you type into words, loops over those words, converts all m characters to y characters, and prints the result. Here, I've typed in "them" and get back "they":

```
%perl mtoy.pl

them
they
```

So how does this code look if you put the **$_** default variable back in explicitly? It looks like this—note how much cleaner the previous code is without the explicit **$_** symbol:

```
while ($_ = <>) {
    for $_ (split / /, $_) {
```

```
            $_ =~ s/m/y/g;
            print $_;
        }
    }
```

Using **$_** is a learned skill in Perl. You can use it with some loops, functions, and constructs, but not with others. It's one of the things that can make the learning curve steeper. But when you know what you're doing, you'll use **$_** implicitly all the time—it becomes second nature. We'll see which loops, functions, and constructs use **$_** in this and the next chapter.

Basic Skills: Cleaning Up Typed Input

Program quality control is on the phone with a complaint about the code you wrote, which was supposed to take simple "yes" or "no" responses from the user. But the actual strings that are showing up when the program is run, all have a newline character appended to them: "yes\n" and "no\n". What's going on?

Input read from **STDIN** includes everything the user has typed, including the newline character at the end. To get rid of that newline, you can use the **chop** or **chomp** functions. Here's how you use **chop**:

```
chop VARIABLE
chop LIST
chop
```

This function chops off the last character of a string and returns the character chopped. If *VARIABLE* is omitted, **chop** chops the default variable **$_**. For example, look at this script:

```
while (<>) {
    print;
}
```

When the script prints out each line of input, you'll see that each line is followed by a newline (to end a script like this, press Ctrl+C). However, if you chop the input, there will be no newline when the scripts prints out each line:

```
while (<>) {
    chop;
    print;
}
```

Besides using **chop**, you can also use **chomp**:

```
chomp VARIABLE
chomp LIST
chomp
```

The **chomp** function is a safer version of **chop**. It removes any line ending that corresponds to the current value of **$/**, which is the special Perl variable holding the input record separator (and defaults to a newline). This function returns the total number of characters removed. It's usually used to remove the newline from the end of an input record. If **VARIABLE** is omitted, it chomps **$_**.

Basic Skills: Avoiding Immediate Script Closings In Windows

Program quality control is on the phone again—there's a problem with your script when it runs in Windows. The user is very patiently double-clicking your script to run it and watches as something flickers on the screen—that's all that happens. Can you fix it?

Here's what's happening if you're using Perl for Windows—when you double-click a file with the extension .pl, an MS-DOS window appears, the script executes, and then the MS-DOS window closes immediately without giving you the chance to see the script's output.

You can fix this if you make the script wait for keyboard input after executing. Just add these two lines to the end of your script:

```
print "Hello!\n";

print "Press <Enter> to continue...";
<STDIN>
```

The result appears in Figure 19.2. The script executes and then waits until you press the Enter key.

You can make the previous two lines of code even shorter because **<>** is the same as **<STDIN>**:

```
print "Hello!\n";

print "Press <Enter> to continue...";
<>
```

Figure 19.2   Holding a Perl script open in an MS-DOS window.

Creating Scalar Variables

The novice programmer says, "OK, I can get a Perl script to print something out, but what about handling data?" "Good question," you say, "let's start with scalar variables."

As we saw in the In Depth section of this chapter, scalar variables can hold simple data items, such as numbers and strings. Here's an example—note that to add strings together, you use the dot operator (.) (see "Using Strings In Scalar Variables" in the Immediate Solutions section of this chapter for more details):

```
$count = 1;
print "The current count is " . $count;
```

```
The current count is 1
```

The name you use for a scalar variable may contain letters, numbers, and underscores. Such a name must start with **$**, which stops it from conflicting with reserved words in Perl. A scalar variable's name can be long—although the length is platform dependent, a variable's name can be at least 255 characters long.

TIP: *In fact, scalar variable names can also contain single quotes, although that practice is now deprecated.*

Because scalar variable names begin with a **$** and don't conflict with Perl reserved words, you can write them in lowercase, which most programmers do.

(Almost all Perl reserved words are lowercase except for file handles like **STDIN** or implicitly called functions like the **BEGIN** block in a package.)

Note in particular that scalar variable names are case sensitive—**$variable1** is not the same as **$Variable1**—which is something to bear in mind if your operating system is not otherwise case sensitive, like MS-DOS.

After the initial **$**, you can start a variable name with any letter or an underscore. In fact, you can even use a number as the first character after the **$**, but if you start a variable name with a number, it must be made up of all numbers. You can even use nonalphanumeric and nonunderscore characters in variable names, but if you do, that variable name can be made up of only two characters, the **$** and one character after the **$** (just like the built-in Perl special variables, such as **$_**).

The **$** symbol that starts all scalar variables is called a "funny character" in Perl. As mentioned in the In Depth section of this chapter, it's called a prefix dereferencer. The following are the data prefix dereferencers in Perl and what they're used for:

- **$**—Scalar variables
- **%**—Hash variables (i.e., associative arrays as detailed in Chapter 20)
- **@**—Arrays

Unlike many other programming languages, you don't need to declare scalar variables in Perl to use them. The first time you use a scalar, Perl will create it if it doesn't already exist.

NOTE: *Note the possibility of spelling errors—you might inadvertently misspell a variable and consequently create a new, uninitialized one. Perl does not consider this an error, and it's very hard to find when you're trying to debug your code.*

However, the scalars you create this way are available to code throughout the current package, which means, if you don't divide your code into packages, it's available anywhere in the script. Such scalars are called global and have global *scope*. The scope of a variable consists of all the code in which you can access it.

TIP: *It's often desirable to limit the scope of variables, however, and it will become a consideration if you start dividing code into blocks when creating subroutines. There are two ways to declare variables with restricted scope—you use the **my** or **local** keywords. See the Perl Black Book (The Coriolis Group, ©1999) for more information.*

Using Assignment Operators On Scalars

The programming team coordinator is carefully going through your code. "All these new scalars are fine," the PTC says, "but you never seem to assign any data to them." "Well," you say, "how do you do that?" "Use scalar assignment," the PTC says.

How do you place data in a scalar variable? You use the assignment operator as in the following example where I place the value 5 in a variable named **$variable1**:

```
$variable1 = 5;
```

String assignments work much the same way:

```
$variable1 = "Hello there!";
```

Besides single assignments, you can perform multiple assignments in the same statement like this:

```
$x = $y = $z = 1;
```

In this case, each scalar is set to the same value, 1, as you see by printing them out (I'll use the **join** list function later in "Joining A List Into A String" in the Immediate Solutions section):

```
$x = $y = $z = 1;
print join (", ", $x, $y, $z);
```

1, 1, 1

There are a great many operators that you can use besides assignments on scalars, of course—you can perform addition, subtraction, multiplication, and so on like this:

```
$x = $x + 2;
$x = $x - 2;
$x = $x * 5;
```

Using Numbers In Scalar Variables

So what kinds of numbers can you work with in Perl? Perl supports a variety of numeric formats, which are listed in Table 19.3.

Note in particular the underlined numeric format, which lets you format digits in a number in groups of three for easy recognition of numbers, like 1,234,567 (Perl will generate an error if the underscores bind groups of anything but three digits):

```
$variable1 = 1_234_567;
```

TIP: *There's one more sticky point here: numeric precision. Because Perl is a cross-platform language, and because the precision of stored numeric values differs by machine (unfortunately—for this reason, there's no way to list the kind of numeric precision you can expect), there's the possibility that you might have different results using the same code on different machines. It's something to watch out for.*

Table 19.3   Perl numeric data types.

Type	Example
Floating	1.23
Hex	0x123
Integer	123
Octal	0123
Scientific	1.23E4
Underlines	1_234_567

Handling Truth Values In Perl

You've explained to the novice programmer that scalars can hold numbers and strings in Perl. The novice programmer nods, impressed, and asks, "What about the values **true** and **false**, how does Perl store those?" "Pull up a chair," you say, "and I'll go over it."

There are two ways to store **true** and **false** values using scalars, corresponding to the two scalar contexts, the numeric and string contexts. Here's the rule to remember: In numeric context, 0 is **false** and *any* other value is **true**, and in string context, the empty string, "", is **false** and *any* other value is **true**.

The fact that any nonzero value represents **true** is especially useful in constructs like loops. For example, it keeps this **while** loop going because **<>** always returns something, even if the user enters a blank line (in which case, **<>** returns a newline character because it always appends a newline character to what the user enters):

```
while(<>) {
    print;
}
```

Programmers often rely on the fact that any nonzero or nonempty string is **true**. You'll find it frequently in Perl code like this, where I'm checking the value of the divisor to avoid dividing by zero (note that this is not the greatest programming practice—for clarity I should check **$bottom** against 0 explicitly, but this example is to give you an indication of a common programming practice):

```
if ($bottom) {
    $result = $top / $bottom;
}
else {
    $ result = 0;
}
```

Using Strings In Scalar Variables

You're writing your new Perl text editor and have to decide how to save that text. If you were writing your program in C, you'd be working with awkward character arrays. Can Perl do any better? It sure can. Besides numbers, scalar variables can also hold strings like this:

```
$variable1 = "Hello!";
```

Perl allocates space to match the length of your strings; so theoretically, they can grow very large. As far as Perl is concerned, the difference between strings and numbers is one of context—if you use a scalar in numerical context (which you can force by adding 0 to a scalar), Perl treats the scalar's value as a number. If you treat the scalar as a string, Perl does too. For example, there are two sets of comparison operators in Perl, one for use on scalars when you're treating them as strings, and one for use when you're treating them as numbers.

You can also use the escape characters in Table 19.2 in strings. For example, to place a double quote in your text, you can use the \" escape character this way:

```
print "I said, \"Hello\".";
```

I said, "Hello".

And note that you use the dot operator (.) to add two strings together:

```
$count = 1;
print "The current count is " . $count;
```

The current count is 1

Currently, Perl stores the characters in a string in ASCII format, which is to say, as one character per byte (note that this means, among other things, that string sorts are done based on ASCII values). However, now that Perl is becoming more locale sensitive, this will probably change in the future as it starts incorporating two-byte character sets to handle Japanese and other character sets, so don't count on one byte per character in your code.

Using Variable Interpolation

The programming team coordinator is looking over your code again. "What are all these dots in code like **print "The value at" . $index . "is" . $value**?" "Just the Perl string concatenation operator," you say, "which adds two strings together." "Use string interpolation," the PTC says, "because the code will be cleaner."

When you enclose a string that includes variable names in double quotes, Perl automatically substitutes the value stored in that variable into the string. For example, if you have a variable named **$text** that holds the word "Hello":

```
$text = "Hello";
```

then you can use that variable by name in double quotes, and Perl will substitute the contents of that variable—the string **Hello**—for the variable:

```
$text = "Hello";
print "Perl says: $text!\n";
```

Perl says: Hello!

This process is called *interpolation*. In particular, Perl has interpolated the value in the variable **$text** into the string enclosed in double quotes.

However, if you use single quotes, not double quotes, Perl will not perform interpolation:

```
$text = "Hello";
print 'Perl says: $text!\n';
```

Perl says: $text!\n

This means that you use single quotes when you don't want Perl to try to evaluate the expressions you place in single quotes.

What if you want to interpolate a variable as part of another word and not a word by itself? For example, what if **$text** held the prefix "un", which you wanted to prepend to the word "happy"? Clearly, you can't use an expression like **$texthappy**, which would cause Perl to search for a variable named **$texthappy**, not interpolate **$text** to create the word "unhappy". Instead, you use **{** and **}** to set off the name of the variable you want to interpolate as part of a word this way:

```
$text = "un";
print "Don't be ${text}happy.";
```

Don't be unhappy.

You can also use backticks—the backwards leaning single quote (`)—to cause Perl to pass a command to the underlying operating system. For example, in Unix, you can execute the **uptime** command (which shows how long the host computer has been up) this way:

```
$uptime = `uptime`;
print $uptime;
```

4:29pm up 18 days, 21:22, 13 users, load average: 0.30, 0.39, 0.42

It works the same way in MS-DOS; there's no MS-DOS **uptime** command, but I can execute a command like **dir** this way:

```
$dirlist = `dir`;
print $dirlist;
```

Directory of C:\perlbook\temp

```
.              <DIR>        10-07-99  4:02p .
..             <DIR>        10-07-99  4:02p ..
TEMP     PL          3,535  10-07-99  4:06p T.PL
```

Programmers often use interpolation to concatenate strings, as I do here in this example:

```
$a = "Hello";
$b = "there";
$c = "$a $b\n";
print $c;
```

```
Hello there
```

Defining A List

Now that you're a Perl professional, technical support has sent over some code for you to check. Everything is going well until you get to the line **($name, $id, $unit) = ("Sam", 1332, "Sales");**. What the heck is going on here? You call technical support to report an error in the code. "That's not an error," the technical support specialist says, "that's a list assignment."

As discussed in the In Depth section of this chapter, Perl allows you to assemble scalar variables (and other types, like hashes and arrays) into *lists*. A list represents a number of items that you can work with as a whole. Lists are very important in Perl, and in fact, the built-in functions in Perl are divided into two groups: those that can handle scalars and those that can handle lists (although some functions can handle both).

There is no specific list data type in Perl because using lists is really a coding technique, and it doesn't represent a data storage format. However, there is a list operator, which is a pair of parentheses, and you can create a list by using commas to separate elements inside a pair of parentheses. For example, the expression **(1, 2, 3)** returns a list with three elements: 1, 2, and 3.

The **print** function is a list function, and if you pass it a list, it will concatenate (i.e., join) the elements in the list into one string. For example, if you pass it the list **(1, 2, 3)**:

```
print (1, 2, 3);
```

then **print** will display 123:

```
print (1, 2, 3);
```

123

In fact, you can even omit the parentheses:

```
print 1, 2, 3;
```

123

You can also add a comma after the last list element if you like, which makes it easy to add future elements (you'll often see this in Perl code, and I mention it here so you won't have to wonder what's going on when you see it):

```
print (1, 2, 3,);
```

123

Assigning Lists To Other Lists

You can assign one list to another using the assignment operator (**=**). For example, here's how you assign the elements in the list (**$c, $d**) to the respective elements in the list (**$a, $b**):

```
($a, $b) = ($c, $d);
```

In this way, you can treat lists as assignable entities. The two lists can even contain some or all of the same variables, as in this case, where I swap the contents of two variables, **$a** and **$b**, using list assignments without using a temporary variable:

```
($a, $b) = ($b, $a);
```

The lists you assign to each other can even be of different sizes, as in this example, where **$a** and **$b** receive the first two elements, respectively, of the longer list:

```
($a, $b) = (1, 2, 3);
print $a;
```

1

```
print $b;
```

2

On the other hand, if you assign a list to a scalar, you'll just get the last element of the list:

```
$a = (2, 4, 6);
print $a;
```

6

When you work with a list in your code, you're working in list context. As we'll see when handling arrays (see the Immediate Solutions section "Creating Arrays" later in this chapter), you can create an array, which has the prefix dereferencer @, by passing it a list of data because the array knows about list context:

```
@a = (2, 4, 6);
print @a;
```

246

In fact, the array knows so much about list context that when you assign it to a scalar, you actually get the number of elements in the array (and not, as you might expect of a straight list, the last element in the array):

```
@a = (2, 4, 6);
$a = @a;
print $a;
```

3

Also, take a look at the reverse process where we try to assign a scalar to a list like this:

```
($a, $b, $c) = 1;
```

In this case, only **$a** gets a value (**$a** will equal 1) and the other two variables will not be assigned any value.

Joining A List Into A String

You're getting kind of tired of the print function concatenating all the items in the list you pass it. For example, **print ("Now", "is", "the", "time")** displays "Nowisthetime", which looks a little less than professional when it comes up on the client's screen. Is there any way to format a list into a string that makes sense?

There is. To concatenate—that is, join—the elements of a list into a string, you can use the Perl **join** function, which works like this in general:

```
join EXPR, LIST
```

This function surrounds the strings in *LIST* with the value in *EXPR* and joins them into a single string, returning that resulting string. For example, here's how to handle the list ("Now", "is", "the", "time") a little better by separating the elements with spaces:

```
print join(" ", ("Now", "is", "the", "time"));
```

```
Now is the time
```

EXPR can be more than one character. For example, you can also use commas and spaces together—which is great for printing out a list:

```
print join(", ", ("Nancy", "Claire", "Linda", "Sara"));
```

```
Nancy, Claire, Linda, Sara
```

Here's another example showing how you can join the elements in the list ("12", "00", "00") with a colon between fields to create the string 12:00:00:

```
print join (":", "12", "00", "00");
```

```
12:00:00
```

Of course, you don't need to specify any characters to use when joining list elements, as in this case, where I pass the empty string, """, to join H, e, l, l, o, which results in output just as **print** would have displayed it:

```
print join ("", H, e, l, l, o);
```

```
Hello
```

Creating Arrays

The programming correctness czar wants to know why you're using 40,000 separate variables in the company's payroll program to hold the names of employees. "Well," you say, "we have 40,000 employees, and..." The PCC says, "Use an array and index it by employee ID." So how do you create arrays?

Array variables start with an **@**; otherwise, the same naming convention that scalars use applies. In Perl, a standard array is one-dimensional and it holds its elements, one after the other, in a single row like this: [1, 2, 3]. The power of arrays is that you can refer to each element in the array by index—the first element is element 0, the next element is element 1, and so on. Using array indices, you can iterate over all the data in the array using a loop.

You can create an array by assigning a list to an array variable this way:

```
@array = (1, 2, 3);
```

To see the data in the new array, you can print it like this (note that **print** treats the array as a list and concatenates the elements as "123"):

```
@array = (1, 2, 3);
print @array;
```

123

As with scalars, Perl creates arrays when you first refer to them, and the arrays created have global scope—that is, they are universally accessible. You can refer to individual array elements by index using **[** and **]** and the **$** prefix dereferencer; you use **$** because the individual element of a standard array is a scalar:

```
@array = (1, 2, 3);
print $array[0];
```

1

Besides numbers, of course, you can store other types of scalars, like strings, in an array:

```
@array = ("one", "two", "three");
print @array;
```

onetwothree

Note that because Perl skips over white space (including newlines) when handling lists, you can set up your array assignment this way as well (as usual with lists, the final comma in the list is optional):

```
@array = (
    "one",  "two",  "three",
    "four", "five", "six",
);

print @array;
```

onetwothreefourfivesix

You can use the **x** repetition operator as in this case, where I create an array of 100 zeroes:

```
@array = (0) x 100;
```

You can use the **..** notation (called the range operator) as well. This example fills **@array** with the numbers 1 through 10:

```
@array = (1 .. 10);
```

When you refer to an array element that doesn't exist yet, Perl creates it automatically:

```
@array = (1, 2, 3);
$array[5] = "Here is a new element!";
print "$array[5]\n";
```

Here is a new element!

Programmers who use other languages often wonder if you can allocate resources for arrays before using them in Perl. In fact, you can extend arrays to an arbitrary length after you've created them using the previous technique—just refer to an element that doesn't exist yet. If you "grow" an array to the size you want to use this way, you do in fact, save some time over constructing an array element by element.

Using Arrays

You've been able to create a new array and add elements, impressing the programming correctness czar. In fact, you've been able to store the names of all 40,000 employees in a single array. "OK," the PCC says, "Now how are you going to access the data in that array?" You think—*access* it?

After creating an array, you can refer to the individual elements of an array as scalars by prefacing the array name with **$** and using a numeric index in square brackets:

```
@array = ("one", "two", "three");
print $array[1];
```

two

In other words, you can treat a standard array as an indexed collection of scalars simply by enclosing that index in square brackets. You can also work with the elements in an array en masse, as here, where I copy one array to another:

```
@a1 = ("one", "two", "three");
@a2 = @a1;

print $a2[1];
```

two

Because you use an index to access array elements, arrays can function as lookup tables, as in this example, where I translate a decimal value the user types in (0 through 15) into a hexadecimal digit:

```
while(<>) {
    @array = ('0' .. '9', 'a' .. 'f');
    $hex = $array[$_];
    print "$hex\n";
}
```

Creating Hashes

The novice programmer is in trouble again. "I just can't get used to thinking of everything in terms of numbers," the NP says, "I've stored all my data in an array, but I always get mixed up: Is the index of the day of the week 491 or 419?" "Well, NP," you say, "you should use a hash. With a hash, you can index your data with text string keys like 'weekday'. Problem solved."

Hashes are also called associative arrays, which might be a more descriptive name. Instead of using a numeric index to retrieve a value, you use a *key* (i.e., a text string), which is associated with that value.

Because you refer to the values in a hash with keys, not numbers, it's often more intuitive to store your data in a hash rather than an array. However, it can be more difficult to set up loops over the data in a hash, precisely because you can't directly index data in a hash with a numeric loop index.

You preface a hash variable's name with % like this where I set up an empty hash:

```
%hash = ();
```

As with arrays, you use the **$** prefix dereferencer when working with individual hash elements. For example, here's how I place a few items in our new hash (**fruit** is the first key in the hash, and it corresponds to the value **apple**; **sandwich** is the second key and corresponds to the value **hamburger**, and so on):

```
%hash = ();

$hash{fruit} = apple;
$hash{sandwich} = hamburger;
$hash{drink} = bubbly;
```

Note that you use curly braces—**{** and **}**—to dereference a hash element, not square brackets—**[** and **]**—as you do with arrays.

At this point, you can refer to individual elements in the hash by key value like this:

```
%hash = ();

$hash{fruit} = apple;
$hash{sandwich} = hamburger;
$hash{drink} = bubbly;

print $hash{sandwich};
```

hamburger

In this way, we've created a hash with keys and values associated with those keys.

You do not need to create an empty hash in order to start filling it. If you start working with a hash that does not yet exist, Perl creates it automatically. This means that this code works just as well as the previous code:

```
$hash{fruit} = apple;
$hash{sandwich} = hamburger;
$hash{drink} = bubbly;
```

```
print $hash{sandwich};
```

hamburger

You may recall that Perl ignores white space when reading a new array's elements, making constructs like this convenient if you have lots of array elements:

```
@array = (
    "one",  "two",  "three",
    "four", "five", "six",
);
```

In the same way, you can create a hash like this, specifying the key/value pairs you want to fill the hash with:

```
%hash = (
    'fruit'    ,  'apple',
    'sandwich' ,  'hamburger',
    'drink'    ,  'bubbly',
);

print "$hash{'fruit'}\n";
```

apple

In fact, there's a synonym for a comma (=>). Using this operator makes the relationship between keys and values clearer, so programmers often write hash creation statements like this:

```
%hash = (
    fruit    => apple,
    sandwich => hamburger,
    drink    => bubbly,
);
print "$hash{fruit}\n";
```

apple

Note that the **=>** operator is not doing anything special—it really is just the same as a comma operator except for one thing: It forces any word to the left of it to be interpreted as a string. For example, this statement:

```
print "x"=>"y"=>"z";
```

xyz

is the same as this one:

```
print "x", "y", "z";
```

xyz

You can use keys with spaces in them, as in this case, where I'm creating a hash element with the key **ice cream**:

```
$hash2{cake} = chocolate;
$hash2{pie} = blueberry;
$hash2{'ice cream'} = pecan;
```

You can reference this item in the way you'd expect:

```
$hash2{cake} = chocolate;
$hash2{pie} = blueberry;
$hash2{'ice cream'} = pecan;

print "$hash{'ice cream'}\n";
```

pecan

You can also use double-quote interpolation to create hash keys, or of course, use variables directly:

```
$value = $hash{$key};
```

Hashes provide a powerful technique for storing your data, but keep in mind that you can't reference the values in a hash directly with a numeric index.

Using Hashes

"OK," says the novice programmer, "I've created my new hash and loaded it up with data. I'm all set to go. There's only one problem: How do I get that data out of the hash again?" "No problem," you say, "just use the keys you've set up."

After you've created a hash, you can use it by addressing the values in the hash by key like this:

```
$value = $hash{$key};
```

In addition, you can place elements in the hash simply by using the assignment operator, as in this example from the previous topic:

```perl
$hash{fruit} = apple;
$hash{sandwich} = hamburger;
$hash{drink} = bubbly;

print $hash{sandwich};
```

hamburger

If you use a hash in a list context, it interpolates all the key/value pairs into the list:

```perl
$hash{fruit} = apple;
$hash{sandwich} = hamburger;
$hash{drink} = bubbly;

print join(" ", %hash);
```

drink bubbly sandwich hamburger fruit apple

This example illustrates an important point: The items in a hash are *not* stored in the order in which you inserted them. Perl stores them in its own order for efficiency because it assumes you'll be retrieving those items using a key and not relying on the order in which they're stored.

If you use a hash in a scalar context, it returns a value of **true** if there are any key/value pairs in the hash.

Hashes are not quite as convenient to use in loops as arrays are because you don't use an easily incremented numeric index with a hash. However, Perl supplies various ways of improving this situation. One such way is the **each** function, which returns successive key/value pairs:

```perl
$hash{fruit} = apple;
$hash{sandwich} = hamburger;
$hash{drink} = bubbly;

while(($key, $value) = each(%hash)) {
    print "$key => $value\n";
}
```

drink => bubbly
sandwich => hamburger
fruit => apple

Another way to work with hashes in loops is the **keys** function, which returns a list of the keys in a hash, making those keys almost as easy to handle as a numeric index:

```
$hash{fruit} = apple;
$hash{sandwich} = hamburger;
$hash{drink} = bubbly;

foreach $key (keys %hash) {
    print $hash{$key} . "\n";
}
```

bubbly
hamburger
apple

Using Perl Operators

The operators in Perl are much the same as in JavaScript or Java, with a few additions. You can find the Perl operators listed in Table 19.1. The Perl operators are mostly like the ones we've seen in JavaScript or Java, but the relational and equality operators are worth a closer look; see the next two sections.

Using Relational (Comparison) Operators

"Look," says the novice programmer, "I'm alphabetizing a list of strings with this comparison code: **if ($a < $b)**...." "Hold on right there," you say, "there's a problem. You're using the wrong comparison operator."

Perl relational operators are binary operators that perform comparisons, returning 1 for **true** and **false** otherwise. The relational operators, like greater than or equal to, less than or equal to, and so on appear in Table 19.4.

Note in particular that you use one set of operators for numeric comparisons and another for string comparisons (the string comparisons are done using ASCII values), which are listed in Table 19.4. Also note that the greater than or equal to operator is **>=**, not **=>**, which is the comma synonym operator.

Table 19.4   Relational operators.

Operator	Data Type	Returns
<	numeric	**true** if left operand is less than right operand
<=	numeric	**true** if left operand is less than or equal to right operand
>	numeric	**true** if left operand is greater than right operand
>=	numeric	**true** if left operand is greater than or equal to right operand
ge	string	**true** if left operand is greater than or equal to right operand
gt	string	**true** if left operand is greater than right operand
le	string	**true** if left operand is less than or equal to right operand
lt	string	**true** if left operand is less than right operand

Here's an example where I check the user's input numerically, displaying an error message if that input is greater than 100:

```
while (<>) {
    if ($_ > 100) {
        print "Too big!\n";
    }
}
```

You can also use the logical operators, like **&&** and ||, or their low precedence cousins, the **and** operator and the **or** operator, to connect logical clauses together, as in this example, where I require user input to be a letter between **k** and **m**:

```
print "Please enter letters from k to m\n";
while (<>) {
    chop;
    if ($_ lt 'k' or $_ gt 'm') {
        print "Please enter letters from k to m\n";
    } else {
        print "Thank you - let's have another!\n";
    }
}
```

Using Equality Operators

Perl supports the equality operators listed in Table 19.5. Note that, like the relational operators, there are separate sets of operators to use on numbers and on strings. Also note the very useful **!=** operator, which tests for inequality.

Here's an example where I ask users to type the character "y" and keep displaying an error message until they do:

```
print "Please type the letter y\n";
while (<>) {
    chop;
    if ($_ ne 'y') {
        print "Please type the letter y\n";
    } else {
        print "Do you always do what you're told?\n";
        exit;
    }
}
```

Here's the output the user might get from this code:

```
Please type the letter y
a
Please type the letter y
b
Please type the letter y
c
Please type the letter y
y
Do you always do what you're told?
```

Table 19.5   Equality operators.

Operator	Type	Returns This
!=	numeric	**true** if left operand is not equal to right operand
<=>	numeric	-1, 0, or 1 depending on whether left operand is numerically less than, equal to, or greater than right operand
==	numeric	**true** if left operand is equal to right operand
cmp	string	-1, 0, or 1 depending on whether left operand is less than, equal to, or greater than right operand
eq	string	**true** if left operand is equal to right operand
ne	string	**true** if left operand is not equal to right operand

Using The **if** Statement

"I've got a decision to make," the novice programmer says. "What is it?" you ask. The NP says, "The question is, is the value of **$budget** greater than or less than 0?" You ask, "What's the difference?" The NP says, "If **$budget** is less than 0, I'm fired." "OK," you say, "better check it with an **if** statement."

As in JavaScript and Java, the **if** statement is the core conditional statement in Perl. This statement checks a condition specified in parentheses and, if that condition evaluates to **true** (i.e., nonzero or not an empty string), the statement executes the code in the associated block.

You can also use an **else** clause to hold code that is executed if the statement's condition is **false**, and you can use **elsif** (note: not **else if** or **elseif** as in other languages) clauses to perform additional tests on other conditions. Here's how you use the **if** statement in general:

```
if (EXPR) BLOCK
if (EXPR) BLOCK else BLOCK
if (EXPR) BLOCK elsif (EXPR) BLOCK ... else BLOCK
```

Note the expression **EXPR**. That is the expression that determines the program flow in this statement; if **EXPR** evaluates to **true**, the code in the succeeding block is executed. If **EXPR** evaluates to **false**, the code in the succeeding block is not executed—instead, the code in the following **else** block, if there is one, is executed.

If there is no **else** statement, Perl looks for an **elsif** statement, which is an **else** statement combined with a new **if** statement, so it includes a new condition to be tested. If the condition in an **elsif** statement evaluates to **true**, the code in its block is executed; if it evaluates to **false**, Perl looks for a following **elsif** statement, and the test begins again.

Note that you can only have one **else** statement following an **if**, but you can have many **elsif** statements, each with their own conditions. And the **else** statement must follow any **elsif** statements.

That's how **if** statements work. Let's look at an example. In this case, I'm using the equality operator (**==**) to check if a variable equals 5, and if so, indicate that result to the user with a message:

```
$variable = 5;

if ($variable == 5) {
    print "Yes, it's five.\n";
}
```

Yes, it's five.

Note the expression in the parentheses. That expression is a logical expression, which evaluates to **true** or **false** (and because any nonzero or nonempty string is regarded as **true**, you can get pretty creative with the **if** statement's condition); if **true**, the code in the block following the **if** statement is executed.

You can use multiple logic clauses in the **if** statement's condition by tying them together with operators like **&&** and **||** (or the **and** operator and the **or** operator) like this:

```perl
use integer;

$variable = 5;

if ($variable < 6 && $variable > 4) {
    print "Yes, it's five.\n";
}
```

Yes, it's five.

You can also include code in an **else** clause, which is executed if the preceding **if** statement's condition evaluates to **false**:

```perl
$variable = 6;

if ($variable == 5) {
    print "Yes, it's five.\n";
} else {
    print "No, it's not five.\n";
}
```

No, it's not five.

You can also add **elsif** clauses to perform an arbitrary number of tests. In this case, if the first condition is **false**, the second is tested; if the second condition is **false**, the next is tested, and so on. If none of the conditions are **true**, the code in the **else** clause is executed:

```perl
$variable = 2;

if ($variable == 1) {
    print "Yes, it's one.\n";
} elsif ($variable == 2) {
    print "Yes, it's two.\n";
} elsif ($variable == 3) {
```

```
    print "Yes, it's three.\n";
} elsif ($variable == 4) {
    print "Yes, it's four.\n";
} elsif ($variable == 5) {
    print "Yes, it's five.\n";
} else {
    print "Sorry, can't match it!\n";
}
```

Yes, it's two.

That's it for the formal **if** statement. Before finishing this topic, we might note that you can use **if** as a modifier with simple statements like this:

```
while (<>) {
    print "Too big!\n" if $_ > 100;
}
```

It's good to know Perl can do this, but this is not the same as using the **if** statement—this is the **if** *modifier*. For the details on this and other statement modifiers, see "Modifying Statements With **if**, **unless**, **until**, **while**, And **foreach**" in the Immediate Solutions section later in this chapter.

The Reverse **if** Statement: **unless**

The programming correctness czar, an expert in C++, takes a look at your code doubtfully. "What's this statement?" the PCC asks, "It starts with **unless**." "Sure," you say, "that's the **unless** statement." "What's that?" the PCC asks. "Sort of a reverse **if**," you say, "and it's perfectly legal."

The **unless** statement is indeed much like a reverse **if** statement. It works the same way as **if** except that it executes code in the associated block if the specified condition is **false**, not **true**. Here's how you use **unless**—note that there's a parallel form using **unless** for every form of the **if** statement:

```
unless (EXPR) BLOCK
unless (EXPR) BLOCK else BLOCK
unless (EXPR) BLOCK elsif (EXPR) BLOCK ... else BLOCK
```

Note the expression **EXPR**. That is the expression that determines the program flow in this statement; if **EXPR** evaluates to **false**, the code in the succeeding block is executed. If **EXPR** evaluates to **true**, the code in the succeeding block is not executed—instead, the code in the following **else** block, if there is one, is executed.

If there is no **else** statement, Perl looks for an **elsif** statement, which is an **else** statement combined with a new **if** statement, so it includes a new condition to be tested. If the condition in an **elsif** statement evaluates to **true**, the code in its block is executed; if it evaluates to **false**, Perl looks for a subsequent **elsif** statement, and the test begins again.

Note that you can only have one **else** statement following an **unless**, but you can have many **elsif** statements, each with their own conditions.

That's how the **unless** statement works. Here's an example that shows how **unless** acts as a reverse **if** statement:

```
$variable = 6;

unless ($variable == 5) {
    print "No, it's not five.\n";
}
```

No, it's not five.

Here's an example that uses an **else** clause:

```
$variable = 6;

unless ($variable == 5) {
    print "No, it's not five.\n";
} else {
    print "Yes, it's five.\n";
}
```

No, it's not five.

Here's an example using **elsif** clauses (note that there is no **elsunless** statement):

```
$variable = 2;

unless ($variable != 1) {
    print "Yes, it's one.\n";
} elsif ($variable == 2) {
    print "Yes, it's two.\n";
} elsif ($variable == 3) {
    print "Yes, it's three.\n";
} elsif ($variable == 4) {
    print "Yes, it's four.\n";
} elsif ($variable == 5) {
    print "Yes, it's five.\n";
} else {
```

```
    print "Sorry, can't match it!\n";
}
```

Yes, it's two.

That's it for the formal **unless** statement. Before finishing this topic, we might note that you can use **unless** as a modifier with simple statements like this:

```
while (<>) {
    print "Too small!\n" unless $_ > 100;
}
```

As with the **if** modifier, it's good to know Perl can do this, but this code is not the same as using the **unless** loop—this is the **unless** modifier. For the details on this and other statement modifiers, see "Modifying Statements With **if**, **unless**, **until**, **while**, And **foreach**" in the Immediate Solutions section later in this chapter.

That's it for the built-in conditional statements, **if** and **unless**. Now it's time to take a good look at loops, starting with the **for** loop.

Looping With The **for** Loop

"I'm fed up with this," the novice programmer declares. "With what?" you ask. "Adding all these values one by one," the NP says, "I must have two dozen addition statements in my code." "Get rid of them," you say, "and use a **for** loop."

As in JavaScript and Java, you use the **for** loop to iterate over the statement(s) in the loop body, usually using a loop index. Here's how you use the **for** loop in general:

```
LABEL for (EXPR1; EXPR2; EXPR3) BLOCK
```

The first expression, ***EXPR1***, is executed before the body (i.e., ***BLOCK***) of the loop is executed, and that's where you do any initialization, such as setting the initial value of a loop index, which counts how many times the loop has executed.

The second expression, ***EXPR2***, is tested before each loop iteration (i.e., each time before the body of the loop is executed) and, if **false**, terminates the loop (note that the body of the loop may not even be executed once if the condition turns out to be **false** when the loop starts). This is how you specify when the loop is to end. For example, you might check the value of the loop index, if you're using one, and terminate the loop if the loop index has reached a certain value.

The third expression, ***EXPR3***, is executed after each loop iteration. You can use this expression to get ready for the next iteration of the loop by, for example, incrementing a loop index if you're using one.

The actual code executed each time through the loop, that is, the body of the loop, is in ***BLOCK***.

There are a number of ways to use this loop; the classic way is with a simple loop index like this, where I use a loop variable named **$loop_index** to print "Hello!" 10 times:

```
for ($loop_index = 1; $loop_index <= 10; $loop_index++) {
    print "Hello!\n";
}

Hello!
Hello!
Hello!
Hello!
Hello!
Hello!
Hello!
Hello!
Hello!
Hello!
```

Note how this works: The first expression in the **for** loop initializes the loop index, the next expression is the test that must evaluate to **true** for the loop to continue looping, and the third expression, executed after each loop iteration, increments the loop index. Using a loop index like this is one way of making sure the **for** loop only executes a certain number of times.

Looping With The **foreach** Loop

Technical support is on the phone asking for your help. "The code loops over a list with a **while** loop, and..." "Stop right there," you say, "I see the problem. When you're looping over a list, you should use a **foreach** loop if you can. Problem solved."

Although it's actually the same loop as **for** (see the previous section), programmers often use **foreach** when using a variable to iterate through a list (i.e., you can read the loop as "for each element in..."). Here's how you (usually) use **foreach**:

```
LABEL foreach VAR (LIST) BLOCK
```

This loop iterates over a list, setting the variable *VAR* to be each successive element of the list, and executes the code in *BLOCK*. You can refer to *VAR* in the code in *BLOCK* so your code can work on each successive element in the list.

The **foreach** loop is specifically designed to let you work with a list of elements without needing to use an index to iterate over the elements in the list. Instead of iterating a loop index, a loop variable is automatically filled with a new element from the list after every iteration. You don't have to worry about ending the loop when you reach the end of the list because it's done automatically.

Here's an example using **foreach** on a list. In this case, I sum the values in an array without using an array index:

```
@array = (1, 2, 3);
$running_sum = 0;

foreach $element (@array) {
    $running_sum += $element;
}

print "Total = $running_sum";

Total = 6
```

If you don't supply a loop variable name, **foreach** uses **$_** as the loop variable, which can be convenient if you're using functions that use **$_** by default, like **print**. Here's an example where I print out the elements of an array while relying on the default variable **$_**:

```
@array = ("Hello ", "there.\n");

foreach (@array) {print;}

Hello there.
```

Looping With The **while** Loop

The novice programmer is in trouble again. "My code," the NP says, "reads in lines from a file using a **for** loop, but I don't know when to terminate the loop." "Well," you say, "how many lines are there in the file?" "That's just it," the novice programmer says, "I have no idea." "The solution is clear," you say, "use a **while** loop."

The **while** loop is a significant one in Perl because you can use it to execute code over and over while a condition that you specify remains **true**. Here's how you use it:

```
LABEL while (EXPR) BLOCK
LABEL while (EXPR) BLOCK continue BLOCK
```

This loop executes the code in **BLOCK** as long as **EXPR** is **true**. The code in a **while** loop's **continue** block, if there is one, is executed every time the loop executes fully, or if you use a loop command that explicitly goes to the next iteration of the loop.

The **while** loop is an easy one to use. Here's an example in which I keep adding the users' savings until they've made a million dollars:

```
$savings = 0;
while ($savings < 1_000_000) {
    print "Enter the amount you earned today: ";
    $savings += <>;
}

print "Congratulations, millionaire!\n";
```

Using The Reverse **while** Loop: **until**

You've got a variable named **$error** and want to keep looping while **$error** remains **false**. You can set up a while loop like this: **while (!$error)**, which will work, but looks a little clumsy. There is a better way to do this in Perl—use the **until** loop like this: **until ($error)**.

The **until** loop is the same as the **while** loop except that it tests its condition in the reverse logical sense. Here's how you use this loop:

```
LABEL until (EXPR) BLOCK
LABEL until (EXPR) BLOCK continue BLOCK
```

This loop executes the code in **BLOCK** as long as **EXPR** is **false**, not **true** (as a **while** loop would). The code in an **until** loop's **continue** block, if there is one, is executed every time the loop executes fully, or if you use a loop command that explicitly goes to the next iteration of the loop.

This loop is just like a reverse-logic **while** loop. Here's an example that keeps looping and echoing what the user types *until* the user types "q":

```
until (($line = <>) eq "q\n") {
    print $line;
}
```

Now
Now
is
is
the
the
time
time
q

Here's another example in which I use a loop index to print the string "Hello!" 10 times using an **until** loop:

```
$loop_index = 1;
until ($loop_index > 10) {
    print "Hello!\n";
    $loop_index++;
}
```

Hello!
Hello!
Hello!
Hello!
Hello!
Hello!
Hello!
Hello!
Hello!
Hello!

Modifying Statements With **if, unless, until, while,** And **foreach**

"I've heard," the programming correctness czar says, adjusting an imperious monocle, "that you can use **if** at either the beginning or the end of a statement in Perl. How odd." "Not only that," you say enthusiastically, "the same goes for **unless**, **while**, and **until**." The monocle drops as the PCC's eyebrows shoot skyward. "What," the PCC asks, "will they think of next?"

It's true—besides the formal conditional and loop statements in Perl, you can also use statement modifiers like these at the end of a standard statement:

```
if EXPR
unless EXPR
until EXPR
while EXPR
foreach EXPR
```

The statement modifiers work much the same way as the formal conditional and loop statements, but they're often easier to read. For example, suppose the big boss asks you to create a Christmas program that would echo any character but "L" (you ask the BB: why doesn't it echo "L"? "No 'L'," the big boss says, "get it? *Christmas*." "Oh," you say.). You could write that code using an **unless** statement like this:

```
while (chomp($input = <>)) {

    unless ($input eq 'L') {print "You typed: $input\n"};

}
```

This works, but it reads a little backwards—"L" is the exception, not the rule, so if you were describing what the code does, you'd probably say something like "echo the typed character unless that character is an L," not "unless the typed character is an L, echo the typed character."

Using statement modifiers, you have a way of making the code read a little easier. You can use **unless** as a modifier, so I can rewrite this code this way, which reads more like what you'd actually say if you were describing what the code does:

```
while (chomp($input = <>)) {

    print "You typed: $input\n" unless $input eq 'L';

}
```

In other words, modifiers are largely a convenience mechanism—they don't change how the code works as much as how it reads.

TIP: *This being Perl, the previous statement isn't quite true—there is one difference between using loop statements and the corresponding loop statement modifiers: The loop statement modifiers do not support **continue** blocks.*

Here's another example in which I use the **if** modifier to print the message "Too big!\n" if the user enters a value above 100:

```
while (<>) {
    print "Too big!\n" if $_ > 100;
}
```

And here's another example where I use the **until** modifier to keep prompting users for more input until they type "q":

```
print "Please enter more text (q to quit).\n" until (<> eq "q\n");
```

This example points out an important aspect of statement modifiers—they're evaluated before the rest of the statement, just as you'd expect if they were at the beginning of the statement (the idea is that using statement modifiers just modifies how the code reads, not how it works). Note how the code accepts input from the user (who starts by typing "Hello?") *before* printing anything out:

```
print "Please enter more text (q to quit).\n" until (<> eq "q\n");
```

```
Hello?
Please enter more text (q to quit).
Why should I?
Please enter more text (q to quit).
q
```

Using **while** as a modifier, you can create a **while** loop where you print out what the user types in like this:

```
print while (<>);
```

Note how the value returned from **<>** in this case is automatically tested (to see if it's defined) and assigned to **$_** as it would be in a straightforward **while** loop.

And here's an example where I use **foreach** as a statement modifier:

```
print "Current number: $_.\n" foreach (1 .. 10);
```

```
Current number: 1.
Current number: 2.
Current number: 3.
Current number: 4.
Current number: 5.
Current number: 6.
Current number: 7.
Current number: 8.
Current number: 9.
Current number: 10.
```

Using The **die** Statement

What if there's a problem and you want to display an error message when you end the program? You can use the **die** function, which works like this in general:

```
die LIST
```

This function prints the value of **LIST** to **STDERR** and stops the program. Here's an example where I try to open a nonexistent file (you'll invariably see a **die** statement tacked onto the end of an **open** statement this way in Perl):

```
$filename = "nonexist.pl";
open FileHandle, $filename or die "Cannot open $filename\n";
```

This script ends with this error message:

```
Cannot open nonexist.pl
```

Creating Objects

In Chapter 20, we'll use the CGI module to create CGI scripts. The CGI module is object oriented (for more on object-oriented programming; see the discussion in the In Depth section of Chapter 15). To create a Web page to send back to a Web browser, I include the CGI module and use the **new** operator to create an object named **$co** of the CGI class:

```
use CGI;
$co = new CGI;
```

The variable **$co** really contains a *reference* to a new CGI object (for more references, see the *Perl Black Book*, The Coriolis Group, ©1999), and you can access its data members and methods using the arrow operator **->** like this, where I'm calling the new CGI object's **header** method:

```
use CGI;
$co = new CGI;
print $co->header;
```

The **header** method returns the header text of a Web page. When the script runs as a CGI script, the **print** function will send that header back to the browser as we'll see in the next chapter.

Chapter 20

CGI Scripting With Perl

In Depth

In this chapter we'll learn about Web programming using Common Gateway Interface (CGI) scripts. For many programmers, this is the most exciting chapter of this book.

CGI programming is all about creating and using CGI scripts. In Perl programming, a CGI script is just a Perl program in a file that (typically) has the extension .cgi. You place CGI scripts on your Internet Service Provider (ISP) Web server, and the scripts will create Web pages dynamically using Perl code, responding to user actions. From now on, we'll be sending output to Web browsers, not to the console.

Creating Web pages on the fly can make your Web pages come alive by using buttons, scrolling lists, popup menus, and much more. Using CGI, users can interact with your Web pages, access databases, run programs, play games, even make purchases on the Web. Perl is the power behind interactive Web pages for tens of thousands of programmers.

The beauty of CGI programming in Perl is that you use code to create the Web page you want, responding dynamically to the user. Perl CGI programming is the same kind of programming used in Chapter 19 except that your code runs on a Web server. Also, **STDIN**, **STDOUT**, and **STDERR** are not tied to the console. Other than that, it's just Perl, so the skills you've already developed are applicable in this chapter. The only change is the input/output (I/O), and it really isn't terribly different.

When you run a Perl CGI script, the standard I/O filehandles are different from programs you write to work with the console. The following list describes how **STDIN**, **STDOUT**, and **STDERR** are set up for CGI scripts:

- **STDIN**—Provides the input to your script from HTML controls, like buttons, text fields, and scrolling lists. This information is encoded, and to parse this information, you use a Perl module like CGI.pm to fill variables with the data from a Web page.

- **STDOUT**—Goes back to the user's Web browser. To create a new Web page, you just print that Web page's HTML to **STDOUT** directly or use the methods of modules like CGI.pm to create the HTML you want, and then send that to **STDOUT**. (It's often easier to write the HTML using those methods than to write the HTML yourself, that is, in terms of making sure angle brackets match, the right tags enclose other ones, and so on).

- **STDERR**—Goes to the Web server's error log. This is not very useful for the majority of CGI programmers because they don't have easy access to their ISP's server log. However, you can redirect **STDERR** to **STDOUT** if you want to; see "Debugging CGI Scripts" in the Immediate Solutions section of this chapter for more information.

CGI Programming With CGI.pm

In this chapter, we're going to master the essentials of CGI script programming using CGI.pm, the CGI module that comes with Perl. I'll create two CGI scripts—the first is cgi1.cgi, which creates a Web page full of HTML *controls* (buttons, scrolling lists, radio buttons, popup menus, and so on). When the user clicks the Submit button in that Web page, the Web browser will send the data in those controls to a second CGI script, cgi2.cgi. In that script, I'll read and report that data back to the user. Using this approach, you'll learn how to use all the common HTML controls in CGI scripts.

Before we begin, I'll make the assumption that you have an ISP, a Web site, and can upload your Web pages to that site (which is usually a simple matter of using an FTP program or using an ISP Web page that can upload files). I'll also assume that your ISP runs Unix, which is the usual operating system for Web servers that can run Perl.

You'll also need to be able to run CGI scripts on your ISP; some ISPs do not allow this, usually for security reasons. Some ISPs restrict your CGI scripts to a directory in your account named cgi-bin or just cgi, and that directory must have special permission before you can execute any scripts. There can be other restrictions as well; for example, some Web servers will not allow your CGI script to execute system commands using the backticks operator (`` ` ``) because it's a big source of security leaks.

Assuming you can run CGI scripts, you must not forget to set any pertinent permission levels for those files (without compromising your security or your system's security). Unix file permissions consist of three octal digits corresponding to, in order, the file owner's permission, the permission of others in the same user group, and the permission of all others. In each octal digit, a value of 4 indicates read permission, a value of 2 indicates write permission, and a value of 1 indicates execute permission. You add these values together to set the individual digits in a permission setting. For example, a permission of 600 means that the files owner, and only the file's owner, can both read and write the file.

On a Unix machine, you can use the **chmod** command to set permissions like this: **chmod 755 script.cgi**. The number 755 is a common permission setting for CGI scripts because it gives the file's owner read, write, and execute permission, and gives everyone else read and execute permission, which they'll need to use your CGI script.

Increasingly, ISPs are not allowing users shell access to the Web areas of the ISP for security reasons. However, many modern FTP programs will allow you to set file permissions as well as upload files, and this is becoming the most common way of setting CGI script permissions instead of using the **chmod** command directly in a shell. If your FTP program doesn't let you set file permissions using octal values like 755, give your CGI script read and execute permissions for all three levels of users, and give the owner level write permission as well.

NOTE: *For more information on the uploading process for your ISP, check with your technical support specialists—if they're accessible.*

So how do you create a CGI script? Theoretically, it's very easy: Your CGI program just executes normal Perl code like any Perl program when it's called by a Web browser (i.e., when a Web browser navigates to your CGI file's URL). Anything you print to the standard output channel is sent to the Web browser.

You must use a line like **#!/usr/local/bin/perl** as the first line of your CGI script because you can't invoke Perl on these scripts directly (e.g., by typing their name at the command prompt like **C:\>perl script.cgi**), which means that they have to find Perl by themselves. See the Immediate Solutions section "Writing Code: Finding The Perl Interpreter" in Chapter 19 for more details.

If your CGI script executes a command—for example, **print "Hello!"**—that text is sent back to the browser and "Hello!" appears in the Web page. But that's a very rudimentary use of a CGI script. What if you want to read input from controls in a Web page? What if you want to create those controls using a script? To perform these functions and more, I'll use the CGI.pm package that comes with Perl.

CGI.pm comes with Perl, so if you have Perl installed on your system, you should have CGI.pm. Since the release of Perl 5, CGI.pm has been object oriented, although a simpler, function-oriented interface still exists. I'll use object-oriented CGI programming in this chapter, but will also take a look at the function-based interface, so you can choose that way of coding if you like. See "Non-Object-Oriented CGI Programming" in the Immediate Solutions section later in this chapter.

When a user calls your CGI script, either directly by its URL or through a Web page, and clicks the Submit button, data from that page (such as the data in HTML controls) is encoded and sent to your script; that data is appended as text to the end of the URL of your script. To read that data, most programmers use a module like CGI.pm to decode the data and store it in variables.

To start using CGI.pm, you use its **new** method to get a CGI object, then call its various methods. There's a method corresponding to every major HTML tag, and calling a method generates the tag using the attributes you pass. You can also get the data sent to your CGI script from a Web page using the **param** method. I'll take a look at programming with CGI.pm in more detail now.

CGI.pm methods can take *named parameters*, which means you can pass the name of the HTML attribute you're setting as well as the value you're setting it to as a key/value pair. Here's an example in which I use a CGI object to create a Web page, using that object's methods to create HTML tags. In this case, I am passing named parameters to the CGI.pm **textarea** method to create an HTML **textarea** control (a **textarea** is like a two-dimensional text box), giving it a name ('textarea'), and a size (10 rows and 60 columns). Note that the hyphen before the attribute name in a named parameter is optional, so you could write **-name=>'textarea'** as **name=>'textarea'** if you prefer:

```perl
#!/usr/local/bin/perl

use CGI;

$co - new CGI;

print $co->header,

$co->start_html(-title=>'CGI Example'),

$co->center($co->h1('Welcome to CGI!')),

$co->start_form(),

$co->textarea
(
    -name=>'textarea',
    -rows=>10,
    -columns=>60
),

$co->end_form(),

$co->end_html;
```

The CGI.pm methods like **textarea** only return HTML. To get that HTML into a Web page, you use the **print** function to send it to **STDOUT**. In fact, scripts that use CGI.pm can simply be one long **print** statement, as in the previous code. This code creates a complete Web page with an HTML **textarea** control in it:

```
<!DOCTYPE HTML PUBLIC "-//IETF//DTD HTML//EN">
<HTML>
<HEAD>
<TITLE>CGI Example</TITLE>
</HEAD>

<BODY>
<CENTER>
<H1>Welcome to CGI!</H1>
</CENTER>
<FORM METHOD="POST"  ENCTYPE="application/x-www-form-urlencoded">

<TEXTAREA NAME="textarea" ROWS=10 COLS=60>
</TEXTAREA>

</FORM>
</BODY>
</HTML>
```

I only used the attributes of the **<TEXTAREA>** element to set up that element as you see here: **<TEXTAREA NAME="textarea" ROWS=10 COLS=60>**. But what if I wanted to enclose HTML content between the opening and closing tag? For example, what if I wanted to enclose the text "Welcome to CGI!" between **<P>** and **</P>** tags like this: **<P>Welcome to CGI!</P>**?

In this case, the text "Welcome to CGI!" is the content of the element, not an attribute. If you're going to pass the content of an element as well as attributes to CGI.pm, you enclose the attributes in a hash to let CGI.pm know they're attributes, and then pass the actual content as the argument(s) following that hash, like this (yes, I know it's confusing, but that's the way official CGI programming in Perl works):

```
#!/usr/local/bin/perl

use CGI;

$co = new CGI;

print $co->header,
```

```
$co->start_html(-title=>'CGI Example'),

$co->center($co->h1('Welcome to CGI!')),

$co->start_form(),

$co->textarea
(
    -name=>'textarea',
    -rows=>10,
    -columns=>60
),

$co->end_form(),

$co->p({-align=>center}, 'Welcome to CGI!'),

$co->end_html;
```

This code produces this Web page:

```
<!DOCTYPE HTML PUBLIC "-//IETF//DTD HTML//EN">
<HTML>
<HEAD>
<TITLE>CGI Example</TITLE>
</HEAD>

<BODY>
<CENTER>
<H1>Welcome to CGI!</H1>
</CENTER>

<FORM METHOD="POST"  ENCTYPE="application/x-www-form-urlencoded">

<TEXTAREA NAME="textarea" ROWS=10 COLS=60>
</TEXTAREA>

</FORM>

<P ALIGN="center">
Welcome to CGI!
</P>
</BODY>
</HTML>
```

The curly braces create a hash and let CGI.pm distinguish between HTML tag attributes and the tag contents; the attributes go in the hash.

Methods that create HTML tags in CGI.pm are called HTML *shortcuts*. You'll find the available HTML shortcut methods in Table 20.1; note that they have the same name as the HTML tags they create. These methods are called shortcuts because they let you create HTML easily. (Note that if you prefer, you can simply print HTML directly to **STDOUT** without using CGI.pm HTML shortcuts—and sometimes it's easier than using shortcuts.)

If you want to specify the attributes of an HTML element you create using one of these HTML shortcut methods, you need to pass those attributes in a hash, even if you're not giving the element any content. You also have to provide a key/value pair for each attribute. If the attribute does not have a value, pass an empty string (""). On the other hand, if you're just passing text you want to use as the tag's content and not any attributes, you can pass the text directly as an argument to the HTML shortcut. Here are some CGI HTML shortcut examples and the HTML they create:

```
p();                              ----> <P>
p('Hello there');                 ----> <P>Hello there</P>
p('Hello', 'there');              ----> <P>Hello there</P>
p({-align=>right});               ----> <P ALIGN="RIGHT">
p({-align=>right}, 'text');       ----> <P ALIGN="RIGHT">text</P>
p({-align=>right}, 'text');       ----> <P ALIGN="RIGHT">text</P>
p({-align=>right}, ['text1', 'text2']); ----> <P ALIGN="RIGHT">text1</P>
                                              <P ALIGN="RIGHT">text2</P>
```

Table 20.1   CGI.pm HTML shortcuts.

a	address	applet	b	base
basefont	big	blink	body	br
caption	center	cite	code	dd
dfn	div	dl	dt	em
font	form	frame	frameset	h1
h2	h3	h4	h5	h6
head	html	hr	i	img
input	kbd	li	ol	p
pre	samp	Select	small	strong
sup	table	td	th	title
Tr	tt	ul	var	

Notice in particular, the last example; I'm passing a hash of attributes and an *array* of element contents. When you pass an array of content arguments, an element with the given attributes is created for *each* item in the array.

You may be surprised to find that the names of HTML controls, like the **textarea** control, do not appear among the list of HTML shortcut methods because the default text in a **textarea** control is actually placed in the content of the **<TEXTAREA>** tag like this, where the default text in this text area is "Hello!":

```
<!DOCTYPE HTML PUBLIC "-//IETF//DTD HTML//EN">
<HTML>
<HEAD>
<TITLE>CGI Example</TITLE>
</HEAD>

<BODY>
<CENTER>
<H1>Welcome to CGI!</H1>
</CENTER>

<FORM METHOD="POST"  ENCTYPE="application/x-www-form-urlencoded">

<TEXTAREA NAME="textarea" ROWS=10 COLS=60>
Hello!
</TEXTAREA>

</FORM>
<P ALIGN="center">
Welcome to CGI!
</P>
</BODY>
</HTML>
```

However, CGI.pm does treat controls with HTML shortcuts. You use attributes to set up controls, not HTML content. In this case, you use the **-value** attribute to set the default text in the text area like this:

```
#!/usr/local/bin/perl

use CGI;

$co = new CGI;

print $co->header,
```

```
$co->start_html(-title=>'CGI Example'),

$co->center($co->h1('Welcome to CGI!')),

$co->start_form(),

$co->textarea
(
    -name=>'textarea',
    -value=>'Hello!',
    -rows=>10,
    -columns=>60
),

$co->end_form(),

$co->p({-align=>center}, 'Welcome to CGI!'),

$co->end_html;
```

This code produces the preceding HTML, where the **<TEXTAREA>** element has both content text and attributes.

Note that I pass the attributes to the **textarea** method in a simple list, not in a hash. Until version 2.38 of CGI.pm, you always passed attributes in a list to control-creation methods like **textarea**. But in more recent versions, you can pass them in a hash if you prefer, which is more consistent with the way you pass attributes to HTML shortcuts.

Another item worth noting: If you call control-creation methods, like **textarea,** with just one argument (like **$co->textarea('text1')**), not one or more pairs of arguments (like **$co->(-name =>'textarea', -value=>'Hello!')**), then that single argument is taken to be the control's name.

CGI.pm also supports a simple function-oriented programming interface if you don't need its object-oriented features. I'll take a look at a function-oriented CGI.pm example at the end of this chapter in the Immediate Solutions section "Non-Object-Oriented CGI Programming."

Creating HTML Controls In cgi1.cgi

To see how CGI.pm works, and to create some code you can use in your own CGI scripts, I'll write two scripts in this chapter: one that creates a Web page full of controls, like text fields, checkboxes, and radio buttons—including a Submit button—and another script that reads the data the user has entered into that Web page. Both CGI scripts consist of little more than one long print statement, which I use to create a Web page by sending text to **STDOUT** (i.e., to the Web browser).

The first CGI script is cgi1.cgi. For the sake of reference, it appears in Listing 20.1. How do you run this script? You just navigate to it using a Web browser. When the user opens this CGI script in their Web browser by navigating to its URL (such as **www.yourstarpowder.com/user/cgi/cgi1.cgi**), the script returns a Web page containing HTML controls and text, displaying a sample Web page survey that the user can fill out. This survey appears in Netscape Navigator in Figures 20.1, 20.2, and 20.3.

As you see in Figure 20.1, the Web page welcomes the users with an image and suggests that if they don't want to fill out the survey, they can jump to the CPAN site with a hyperlink.

Scrolling down the page (see Figure 20.2), the survey asks for users' names with a text field and their opinions with an HTML text area.

Scrolling farther down the page (see Figure 20.3), you see even more controls in the survey page: checkboxes, scrolling lists, radio buttons, a password control, popup menus, and Submit and Reset buttons. These controls are there to accept more survey data from users. We'll learn how to create these controls from a CGI script throughout this chapter.

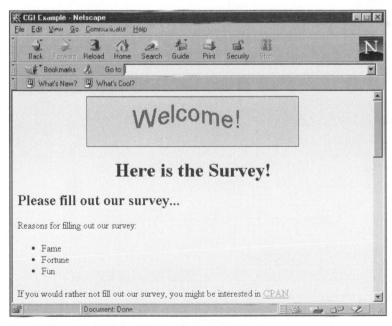

Figure 20.1   Text, a bulleted list, and a hyperlink.

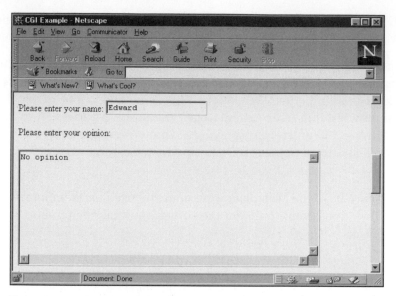

Figure 20.2   A text field and text area.

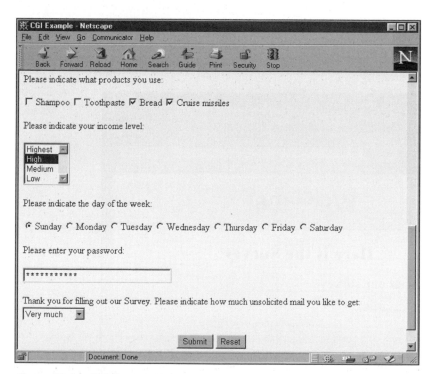

Figure 20.3   HTML controls.

When users click the Submit button at the bottom of the survey, the Web browser collects all the data from the controls in the Web page and sends that data to another CGI script, cgi2.cgi.

The cgi2.cgi script reads the data sent to it and produces a summary of that data in a new Web page. For reference, cgi2.cgi appears in Listing 20.2, and the results of that script appear in Figure 20.4, where you can see the summary of the data a user entered in the survey Web page. The HTML created by cgi1.cgi appears in Listing 20.3 and the HTML created by cgi2.cgi appears in Listing 20.4.

Note that in this chapter, I'm creating a survey page full of HTML controls using a script, cgi1.cgi. I'm doing this to demonstrate how to create Web pages that contain controls using the CGI.pm shortcut methods. However, as we saw in Chapter 12, you can create a Web page with an HTML form full of controls directly in HTML. In other words, it's not necessary to create the survey page using a CGI script at all, you can use HTML to do it instead. In fact, you can use the HTML Web page that cgi1.cgi creates, which you see in Listing 20.3. That Web page can be displayed in a browser directly, and when the Submit button is clicked, the browser will send all the necessary data to cgi2.cgi. For more on creating Web pages with forms and controls in HTML, see Chapter 12. Also see "Calling A CGI Script From An HTML Web Page" in the Immediate Solutions section of this chapter for an example.

20. CGI Scripting With Perl

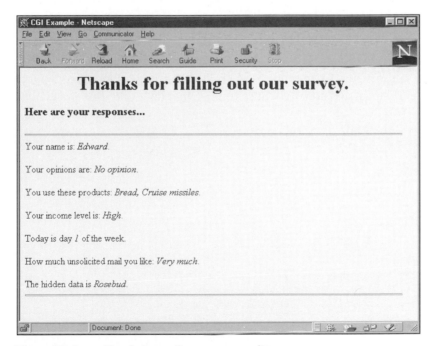

Figure 20.4   cgi2.cgi shows the survey results.

How does the survey Web page know where to send the survey data? All the controls in that page are in the same HTML form. As we saw in Chapter 12, a form is not a visible Web page entity; it's simply an HTML construct that contains a collection of controls. The form's **ACTION** attribute holds the URL of cgi2.cgi. When the user clicks the Submit button, the Web browser sends the data from the controls in the form to that URL. In cgi2.cgi, the code reads the data the user has entered and displays it.

You can use the HTML **<FORM>** element to create an HTML form. In the following example, I place a text field in a form along with Submit and Reset buttons and indicate that the text in the text field is to be sent to **http://www. starpowder.com/username/cgi/cgi2.cgi** when the user clicks the Submit button:

```
<FORM METHOD="POST" ACTION=
    "http://www.starpowder.com/username/cgi/cgi2.cgi"
    ENCTYPE="application/x-www-form-urlencoded">
    <INPUT TYPE="text" NAME="text" VALUE="">
    <INPUT TYPE="submit" NAME="Submit" VALUE="Submit">
    <INPUT TYPE="reset">
</FORM>
```

To see more on how to use HTML to create forms that let you call CGI scripts from Web pages, see Chapter 12 and "Calling A CGI Script From An HTML Web Page" in the Immediate Solutions section of this chapter.

It's also possible to use a CGI script to create a Web page that has an HTML form in it. You use the **start_form** method to create a form in a Web page, which you write in a CGI script and specify where to post that data, like this in cgi1.cgi:

```
#!/usr/local/bin/perl

use CGI;

$co = new CGI;

print $co->start_form
(
    -method=>'POST',
    -action=>"http://www.yourserver.com/user/cgi/cgi2.cgi"
);
```

If you call **start_form** without any arguments, the Submit button will post (i.e., send) the form's data back to the same CGI script that created the Web page; see

"Creating Image Maps" in the Immediate Solutions section for an example. This means that you can send data from a form back to the same script that generated that form. For example, the first time you call the script, it can generate one Web page; when you call it again with data from a form in that page, it can read and use the data to create a new page. Again, see "Creating Image Maps" in the Immediate Solutions section to see how this works.

After creating a form, you can add HTML controls to that form, such as a text area this way:

```perl
#!/usr/local/bin/perl

use CGI;

$co = new CGI;

print $co->start_form
(
    -method=>'POST',
    -action=>"http://www.yourserver.com/user/cgi/cgi2.cgi"
),

$co->textarea
(
    -name=>'textarea',
    -value=>'Hello!',
    -rows=>10,
    -columns=>60
);
```

You can add a Submit button to the form with the **submit** method, a Reset button with the **reset** method, and end the form with the **end_form** method:

```perl
#!/usr/local/bin/perl

use CGI;

$co = new CGI;

print $co->start_form
(
    -method=>'POST',
    -action=>"http://www.yourserver.com/user/cgi/cgi2.cgi"
),
```

```
$co->textarea
(
    -name=>'textarea',
    -value=>'Hello!',
    -rows=>10,
    -columns=>60
),

$co->submit('Submit'),

$co->reset,

$co->end_form;
```

Now when the user clicks the Submit button, the data from the controls in the form is sent to cgi2.cgi. The next step is to actually read that data.

Reading Data From HTML Controls In cgi2.cgi

When the user clicks the Submit button in an HTML form, the data from the controls in the form is posted to your CGI script. And when the data arrives, you can use the CGI.pm module's **param** method to read it.

You call the **param** method with the name you've given to a control (you give a name to a control with the **-name** attribute), and the return value is the data that is in the control. To see if any data is available, you can call the **param** method with no arguments; if it returns a value of **true**, there is some data from an HTML form waiting for you.

Here's an example from cgi2.cgi. In this case, I'm reading the data the user typed into a text field named "text" and a text area named "textarea" and printing them in a new Web page:

```
#!/usr/local/bin/perl

use CGI;

$co = new CGI;

if ($co->param()) {
    print
        "Your name is: ",$co->em($co->param('text')), ".",
        $co->p,

        "Your opinions are: ",$co->em($co->param('textarea')), ".",
```

```
        $co->p,
              .
              .
              .
}
```

We'll learn more about how to read the data from HTML controls throughout this chapter. That's it. We've discussed how to create HTML pages that call CGI scripts and how to read the data they send. Now it's time to start writing some actual code.

Listing 20.1   CGI script for cgi1.cgi

```perl
#!/usr/local/bin/perl

use CGI;

$co = new CGI;

$labels{'1'} = 'Sunday';
$labels{'2'} = 'Monday';
$labels{'3'} = 'Tuesday';
$labels{'4'} = 'Wednesday';
$labels{'5'} = 'Thursday';
$labels{'6'} = 'Friday';
$labels{'7'} = 'Saturday';

print $co->header,

$co->start_html
(
    -title=>'CGI Example',
    -author=>'Steve',
    -meta=>{'keywords'=>'CGI Perl'},
    -BGCOLOR=>'white',
    -LINK=>'red'
),

$co->center($co->img({-src=>'welcome.gif'})),

$co->center($co->h1('Here is the Survey!')),

$co->h2('Please fill out our survey...'),

"Reasons for filling out our survey:",
$co->p,
```

```
$co->ul
(
    $co->li('Fame'),
    $co->li('Fortune'),
    $co->li('Fun'),
),

"If you would rather not fill out our survey, ",

"you might be interested in ",

$co->a({href=>"http://www.cpan.org/"},"CPAN"), ".",

$co->hr,

$co->start_form
(
    -method=>'POST',
    -action=>"http://www.yourserver.com/username/cgi2.cgi"
),

"Please enter your name: ",

$co->textfield('text'), $co->p,

"Please enter your opinion: ",

$co->p,

$co->textarea
(
    -name=>'textarea',
    -default=>'No opinion',
    -rows=>10,
    -columns=>60
),

$co->p,

"Please indicate what products you use: ", $co->p,

$co->checkbox_group
(
    -name=>'checkboxes',
```

```perl
    -values=>['Shampoo','Toothpaste','Bread','Cruise missiles'],
    -defaults=>['Bread','Cruise missiles']
),

$co->p,

"Please indicate your income level: ",

$co->p,

$co->scrolling_list
(
    'list',
    ['Highest','High','Medium','Low'],
    'High',
),

$co->p,

"Please indicate the day of the week: ",

$co->p,

$co->radio_group
(
    -name=>'radios',
    -values=>['1','2','3', '4', '5', '6', '7'],
    -default=>'1',
    -labels=>\%labels
),

$co->p,

"Please enter your password: ", $co->p,

$co->password_field
(
    -name=>'password',
    -default=>'open sesame',
    -size=>30,
),

$co->p,

"Thank you for filling out our Survey. Please indicate how
much unsolicited mail you like to get: ",
```

```perl
$co->popup_menu
(
    -name=>'popupmenu',
    -values=>['Very much','A lot','Not so much','None']
),

$co->p,

$co->hidden
(
    -name=>'hiddendata',
    -default=>'Rosebud'
),

$co->center
(
    $co->submit('Submit'),
    $co->reset,
),

$co->hr,

$co->end_form,

$co->end_html;
```

Listing 20.2   CGI sript for cgi2.cgi

```perl
#!/usr/local/bin/perl

use CGI;

$co = new CGI;

print $co->header,

$co->start_html
(
    -title=>'CGI Example',
    -author=>'Steve',
    -meta=>{'keywords'=>'CGI Perl'},
    -BGCOLOR=>'white',
    -LINK=>'red'
),

$co->center
```

```
(
    $co->h1('Thanks for filling out our survey.')
),

$co->h3
(
    'Here are your responses...'
),

$co->hr;

if ($co->param()) {
    print
        "Your name is: ",$co->em($co->param('text')),
        ".",
        $co->p,

        "Your opinions are: ",$co->em($co->param('textarea')),
        ".",
        $co->p,

        "You use these products: ",$co->em(join(", ",
        $co->param('checkboxes'))), ".",
        $co->p,

        "Your income level is: ",$co->em($co->param('list')),
        ".",
        $co->p,

        "Today is day ", $co->em($co->param('radios')),
        " of the week.",
        $co->p,

        "Your password is: ",$co->em($co->param('password')),
        ".",
        $co->p,

        "How much unsolicited mail you like: ",
        $co->em($co->param('popupmenu')),
        ".",
        $co->p,

        "The hidden data is ",$co->em(join(", ",
        $co->param('hiddendata'))),
```

```
                ".";
      }

      print $co->hr;

      print $co->end_html;
```

Listing 20.3   HTML page generated by cgi1.cgi

```
<!DOCTYPE HTML PUBLIC "-//IETF//DTD HTML//EN">
<HTML>
<HEAD>
<TITLE>CGI Example</TITLE>
<LINK REV=MADE HREF="mailto:Steve">
<META NAME="keywords" CONTENT="CGI Perl">
</HEAD>

<BODY BGCOLOR="white" LINK="red">
<CENTER>
<IMG SRC="welcome.gif">
</CENTER>
<CENTER>
<H1>Here is the Survey!</H1>
</CENTER>
<H2>Please fill out our survey...</H2>
Reasons for filling out our survey:
<P>
<UL>
<LI>Fame</LI>
<LI>Fortune</LI>
<LI>Fun</LI>
</UL>
If you would rather not fill out our survey, you might be interested in
<A HREF="http://www.cpan.org/">CPAN</A>.
<HR>
<FORM METHOD="POST"
ACTION="http://www.yourserver.com/username/cgi/cgi2.cgi"
ENCTYPE="application/x-www-form-urlencoded">
Please enter your name:
<INPUT TYPE="text" NAME="text" VALUE="">
<P>
Please enter your opinion:
<P>
<TEXTAREA NAME="textarea" ROWS=10 COLS=60>
No opinion
</TEXTAREA>
<P>
```

```
Please indicate what products you use:
<P>
<INPUT TYPE="checkbox" NAME="checkboxes" VALUE="Shampoo">Shampoo
<INPUT TYPE="checkbox" NAME="checkboxes" VALUE="Toothpaste">Toothpaste
<INPUT TYPE="checkbox" NAME="checkboxes" VALUE="Bread" CHECKED>Bread
<INPUT TYPE="checkbox" NAME="checkboxes" VALUE="Cruise missiles" CHECKED>
Cruise missiles
<P>
Please indicate your income level:
<P>
<SELECT NAME="list" SIZE=4>
<OPTION  VALUE="Highest">
Highest
<OPTION SELECTED VALUE="High">
High
<OPTION  VALUE="Medium">
Medium
<OPTION  VALUE="Low">
Low
</SELECT>
<P>Please indicate the day of the week:
<P>
<INPUT TYPE="radio" NAME="radios" VALUE="1" CHECKED>Sunday
<INPUT TYPE="radio" NAME="radios" VALUE="2">Monday
<INPUT TYPE="radio" NAME="radios" VALUE="3">Tuesday
<INPUT TYPE="radio" NAME="radios" VALUE="4">Wednesday
<INPUT TYPE="radio" NAME="radios" VALUE="5">Thursday
<INPUT TYPE="radio" NAME="radios" VALUE="6">Friday
<INPUT TYPE="radio" NAME="radios" VALUE="7">Saturday
<P>
Please enter your password:
<P>
<INPUT TYPE="password" NAME="password" VALUE="open sesame" SIZE=30>
<P>
Thank you for filling out our Survey. Please indicate how
much unsolicited mail you like to get:
<SELECT NAME="popupmenu">
<OPTION  VALUE="Very much">Very much
<OPTION  VALUE="A lot">A lot
<OPTION  VALUE="Not so much">Not so much
<OPTION  VALUE="None">None
</SELECT>
<P>
<INPUT TYPE="hidden" NAME="hiddendata" VALUE="Rosebud">
<CENTER>
```

```
<INPUT TYPE="submit" NAME="Submit" VALUE="Submit">
<INPUT TYPE="reset">
</CENTER>
<HR>
<INPUT TYPE="hidden" NAME=".cgifields" VALUE="radios">
<INPUT TYPE="hidden" NAME=".cgifields" VALUE="list">
<INPUT TYPE="hidden" NAME=".cgifields" VALUE="checkboxes">
</FORM>
</BODY>
</HTML>
```

Listing 20.4   HTML page generated by cgi2.cgi

```
<!DOCTYPE HTML PUBLIC "-//IETF//DTD HTML//EN">
<HTML>
<HEAD>
<TITLE>CGI Example</TITLE>
<LINK REV=MADE HREF="mailto:Steve">
<META NAME="keywords" CONTENT="CGI Perl">
</HEAD>
<BODY BGCOLOR="white" LINK="red">
<CENTER>
<H1>Thanks for filling out our survey.</H1>
</CENTER>
<H3>Here are your responses...</H3>
<HR>
Your name is: <EM>Edward</EM>.
<P>
Your opinions are: <EM>No opinion</EM>.
<P>
You use these products: <EM>Bread, Cruise missiles</EM>.
<P>
Your income level is: <EM>High</EM>.
<P>
Today is day <EM>1</EM> of the week.
<P>
Your password is: <EM>open sesame</EM>.
<P>
How much unsolicited mail you like: <EM>Very much</EM>.
<P>
The hidden data is <EM>Rosebud</EM>.
<HR>
</BODY>
</HTML>
```

Immediate Solutions

Using PerlScript

I'll start the programming topics off in this chapter in a way you might not expect—with *PerlScript*. PerlScript is an interpreted language that works with some Web browsers (you should make sure your users have it before you work with it). Although PerlScript is beyond the scope of this book, it's worth knowing that it exists because instead of writing a full-scale CGI program, you may be able to do what you want to do just by embedding some PerlScript in a Web page. Here's an example where I use PerlScript to say "Hello!" in a Web page:

```
<HTML>
<HEAD>
<TITLE>PerlScript Example</TITLE>
</HEAD>

<BODY>
<H1>PerlScript Example</H1>

<SCRIPT LANGUAGE="PerlScript">
$window->document->write("Hello!");
</SCRIPT>

</BODY>
</HTML>
```

This Web page appears in Internet Explorer in Figure 20.5.

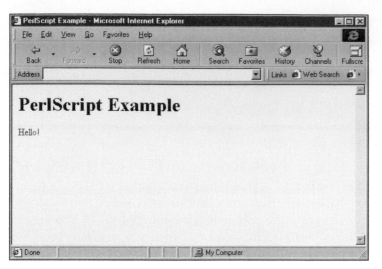

Figure 20.5   A PerlScript example.

Starting An HTML Document

"OK," says the novice programmer; "I'm ready to start creating CGI scripts with CGI.pm. Where do I start?" "You start," you say, "by creating an HTTP header."

To start an HTML document, you create a CGI object by creating an HTTP header with that object's **header** method (I'll create a simple header here, although you can create more complex ones with cookies and other attributes) and start the HTML document with the **start_html** method. The **header** method just prints out "Content-Type: text/html", which tells the browser what type of document is being sent.

The **start_html** method creates a **<HEAD>** section for the Web page and allows you to specify various attributes for the **<BODY>** part, such as the background and link color. Here's how I start the survey Web page example in cgi1.cgi—note that to get the output from the header and **start_html** into the Web page, you use the Perl **print** function:

```
#!/usr/local/bin/perl
use CGI;

$co = new CGI;

print $co->header,
```

```
$co->start_html
(
     -title=>'CGI Example',
     -author=>'Steve',
     -meta=>{'keywords'=>'CGI Perl'},
     -BGCOLOR=>'white',
     -LINK=>'red'
)
```

Displaying Images

The novice programmer appears and says, "So how do I display an image in a Web page that I'm creating from a CGI script?" "No problem at all," you say, "use the **img** method."

The CGI.pm **img** method creates **<IMG>** elements you use to display images. Here's an example from cgi1.cgi:

```
$co->center
(
     $co->img
         (
              {-src=>'welcome.gif'}
         )
)
```

In this case, I'm displaying the image welcome.gif in the survey Web page. You can see the results in Figure 20.1. Here is the HTML created:

```
<IMG SRC="welcome.gif">
```

The attributes you can set in the **img** method are **-align**, **-alt**, **-border**, **-height**, **-width**, **-hspace**, **-ismap**, **-src**, **-lowsrc**, **-vspace**, and **-usemap**.

Creating HTML Heads

"Great," says the novice programmer, "I've put a welcome banner into my dynamically generated Web page. Now—what about creating headings like **<H1>** and **<H2>**?" "No problem at all," you say, "just use methods like **h1** and **h2**."

You can use CGI.pm methods, like **h1**, **h2**, **h3**, and so on, to create HTML headings corresponding to the **<H1>**, **<H2>**, and **<H3>** elements.

For example, here's how I create two headings, an **<H1>** heading and an **<H2>** heading, at the top of the survey Web page created by cgi1.cgi, welcoming the user to the survey:

```
#!/usr/local/bin/perl
use CGI;

$co = new CGI;

print
        .
        .
        .
$co->h1('Here is the Survey!'),

$co->h2('Please fill out our survey...')
```

And you can see the results in Figure 20.1. Here is the HTML created:

```
<H1>Here is the Survey!</H1>
<H2>Please fill out our survey...</H2>
```

The possible attributes you can set are **-align** and **-class**.

Centering HTML Elements

"Hm," says the novice programmer, "I've put an **<H1>** heading into my Web page, but it's aligned to the left of the Web page. How do I center HTML elements?" You say, "You can often use the **-align** attribute in a tag, or, if you want to center a number of elements, use the **center** method."

You can center text by printing **<CENTER>** elements with the CGI method **center**. Here's an example in which I center the **<H1>** element created in the last section:

```
#!/usr/local/bin/perl
use CGI;

$co = new CGI;
```

```
print
        .
        .
        .

    $co->center($co->h1('Here is the Survey!')),

    $co->h2('Please fill out our survey...')
```

You can see the results of this code in Figure 20.1.

Creating A Bulleted List

"I want to introduce my dynamically created Web page with a bulleted list of items," the novice programmer says, "How do I do that?" "That's no problem," you say, "you can use methods like **ul** and **li**."

You can create unordered bulleted lists with the **ul** and **li** CGI methods, which create **<UL>** and **<LI>** elements.

For example, here's how I display a bulleted list to the user in the survey Web page in cgi1.cgi, indicating some good reasons to fill out the survey:

```
#!/usr/local/bin/perl
use CGI;

$co = new CGI;

print
        .
        .
        .

"Reasons for filling out our survey:",

$co->p,

$co->ul
(
    $co->li('Fame'),
    $co->li('Fortune'),
    $co->li('Fun'),
)
```

The results of this code appear in Figure 20.1. Here's the actual HTML created:

```
<UL>
<LI>Fame</LI>
<LI>Fortune</LI>
<LI>Fun</LI>
</UL>
```

You can use the **-compact** and **-type** attributes with **ul** and the **-type** and **-value** attributes with **li**.

Creating A Hyperlink

"OK," says the novice programmer, "I have another question—how do I create hyperlinks using CGI.pm?" "No trouble," you say, "just use the **a** method."

You can create a hyperlink with the **a** CGI method as in this case, where I offer users another URL to jump to if they're not interested in filling out the cgi1.cgi survey:

```
#!/usr/local/bin/perl
use CGI;

$co = new CGI;

print
        .
        .
        .
"If you would rather not fill out our survey, ",

"you might be interested in ",

$co->a({href=>"http://www.cpan.org/"},"CPAN"), "."
```

The results of this code appear in Figure 20.1. Here's the actual HTML created:

```
If you would rather not fill out our survey, you might be interested in
<A HREF="http://www.cpan.org/">CPAN</A>.
```

You can use these attributes with the **a** method: **-href**, **-name**, **-onClick**, **-onMouseOver**, and **-target**.

Creating Horizontal Rules

"Hm," says the novice programmer, "I want to separate the content of my HTML page using horizontal rules. Is there an **hr** method?" "There sure is," you say, "and it creates **<HR>** elements for you."

To create horizontal rules using the **<HR>** element, you just use the CGI **hr** method:

```
#!/usr/local/bin/perl
use CGI;

$co = new CGI;

print
    .
    .
    .
$co->hr
```

That's all you need to create a horizontal rule. The attributes you can use with **hr** are **-align**, **-noshade**, **-size**, and **-width**.

Creating An HTML Form

"OK," says the novice programmer, "I'm ready to start putting controls in my Web page. I want to use buttons, and text fields, and..." "Whoa," you say, "before you start, you have to set up an HTML form to hold those controls."

To use HTML controls in a Web page, you must enclose them in an HTML form. I used the CGI **start_form** method in the survey example cgi1.cgi to create a form, so that when the user clicks the Submit button (which I'll add soon), the data from the controls in this form is sent to the script that will produce the data summary, cgi2.cgi. I target cgi2.cgi by placing its URL in the form's **ACTION** attribute:

```
#!/usr/local/bin/perl
use CGI;

$co = new CGI;

print
    .
    .
    .
```

```
$co->start_form
(
    -method=>'POST',
    -action=>"http://www.yourserver.com/user/cgi/cgi2.cgi"
)
```

Note that all the following controls, up to the Immediate Solutions section "Ending An HTML Form," are enclosed in the form because executing **start_form** inserts a **<FORM>** tag into the Web page. Here is the actual HTML created by the previous code:

```
<FORM METHOD="POST"
ACTION="http://www.yourserver.com/username/cgi/cgi2.cgi"
ENCTYPE="application/x-www-form-urlencoded">
```

And these are the attributes you can use with **start_form**: **-action**, **-enctype**, **-method**, **-name**, **-onSubmit**, and **-target**.

If you call **start_form** without any arguments, the Submit button will post (i.e., send) the form's data back to the same CGI script that created the Web page. See "Creating Image Maps" in the Immediate Solutions section for an example. Also see "Calling A CGI Script From An HTML Web Page" in the Immediate Solutions section to see how to create HTML forms using HTML directly, so you can call CGI scripts from Web pages that you write manually.

Working With Text Fields

"This is great," says the novice programmer, "now I've created a form to put HTML controls in. The first control I want to use is a text field. How do I create one?" "That's easy," you say, "you use the **textfield** method."

To create an HTML text field, which allows the user to enter text, you use the CGI method **textfield**. Here's how I create and name a text field that will hold the user's name in cgi1.cgi:

```
#!/usr/local/bin/perl
use CGI;

$co = new CGI;
```

```
print
        .
        .
        .
"Please enter your name: ",

$co->textfield('text')
```

You can see the resulting text field at the top of Figure 20.2. Here's the actual HTML created:

```
Please enter your name:
<INPUT TYPE="text" NAME="text" VALUE="">
```

These are the attributes you can use with **textfield**: **-maxLength**, **-name**, **-onChange**, **-onFocus**, **-onBlur**, **-onSelect**, **-override**, **-force**, **-size**, **-value**, and **-default**.

How do you read the data in a text field once the user clicks the Submit button to send the form to you? See the next section.

Reading Data From HTML Controls

"Hm," says the novice programmer, "now that I've added a text field to my Web page, how can I read the data in that text field when the user clicks the Submit button and sends that data to my CGI script?" "You can use the CGI.pm **param** method," you say, "pull up a chair, and we'll take a look."

When the user clicks the Submit button in the survey example, the Web browser posts the data in the form to cgi2.cgi, and in that script, I use the CGI method **param** to read the data in the text field.

To use **param**, I pass it the name I've given to the text field, "text" (see the previous section), and display the data the user entered in the text field this way (the **em** method creates an **<EM>** tag, which translates to italics in most browsers):

```
#!/usr/local/bin/perl
use CGI;

$co = new CGI;
```

```
print "Your name is: ",
    $co->em($co->param('text')),
    ".";
```

You can see the results in Figure 20.4. That's how to read the data in a control—just pass the name of the control to the **param** method. Note that if you call **param** without any arguments, it'll return **true** if there is any data waiting, and **false** otherwise.

Working With Text Areas

"I can't fit all the text I need into a text field," the novice programmer says, "Is there anything bigger?" You say, "Sure—text areas."

As we saw in Chapter 12, unlike a text field, an HTML text area can hold several rows of text. Here's how I create a text area in cgi1.cgi to hold any opinions the user wants to enter, giving the text area 10 rows, 60 columns, some default text, and a name, "textarea":

```
#!/usr/local/bin/perl
use CGI;

$co = new CGI;

print
    .
    .
    .
"Please enter your opinion: ",

$co->p,

$co->textarea
(
    -name=>'textarea',
    -default=>'No opinion',
    -rows=>10,
    -columns=>60
)
```

You can see the results in Figure 20.2. Here's the actual HTML created:

```
Please enter your opinion:
<P>
<TEXTAREA NAME="textarea" ROWS=10 COLS=60>
No opinion
</TEXTAREA>
```

These are the attributes you can use with the **textarea** method: **-cols** (also **-columns**), **-name**, **-onChange**, **-onFocus**, **-onBlur**, **-onSelect**, **-rows**, **-override**, **-force**, **-value**, **-default**, and **-wrap**.

And here's how I use the CGI **param** method to read the text from the text area in cgi2.cgi, the CGI script that reports the survey data, which is shown in Figure 20.4:

```
print  "Your opinions are: ",
    $co->em($co->param('textarea'))
    , ".";
```

Working With Checkboxes

"This one's a little tougher," says the novice programmer, "how do I set up a group and HTML checkbox controls and give them each a caption?" "Get some coffee," you say, "and we'll go over it."

You can create checkboxes in a group (you group checkboxes together so the names of all the boxes that are checked are reported in the same list).

In the following example, I use the CGI method **checkbox_group** to create a group of checkboxes in cgi1.cgi, which will let users indicate what commercial products they use. In this case, I name the checkbox group, pass an array of labels for the checkboxes, and list the default checkboxes I want to appear clicked when the Web page first appears in another array like this:

```
#!/usr/local/bin/perl
use CGI;

$co = new CGI;

print

    .

    .

    .

"Please indicate what products you use: ",
```

```
$co->p,

$co->checkbox_group
(
    -name=>'checkboxes',
    -values=>['Shampoo','Toothpaste','Bread','Cruise missiles'],
    -defaults=>['Bread','Cruise missiles']
)
```

You can see the results in Figure 20.3. Here's the actual HTML created:

```
Please indicate what products you use:
<P>
<INPUT TYPE="checkbox" NAME="checkboxes" VALUE="Shampoo">Shampoo
<INPUT TYPE="checkbox" NAME="checkboxes" VALUE="Toothpaste">Toothpaste
<INPUT TYPE="checkbox" NAME="checkboxes" VALUE="Bread" CHECKED>Bread
<INPUT TYPE="checkbox" NAME="checkboxes" VALUE="Cruise missiles" CHECKED>
Cruise missiles
```

I read and report the checkboxes that were checked using this code in cgi2.cgi, which is shown in Figure 20.4. Note that **param** returns a list of checkbox names, and I use **join** to create a string from that list:

```
print "You use these products: ",
    $co->em(join(", ",
    $co->param('checkboxes'))),
    ".";
```

Working With Scrolling Lists

"How about HTML scrolling lists?" the novice programmer asks, "Can I create them too?" "Yes," you say, "if you use the **scrolling_list** method."

A scrolling list displays a list of items that can scroll if all the items cannot be displayed at once. You create a scrolling list with the CGI.pm **scrolling_list** method.

Here's how I create a scrolling list in cgi1.cgi to let users select their income level. I name it "list", place the items **Highest**, **High**, **Medium**, and **Low** in it, and select **High** by default:

```
#!/usr/local/bin/perl
use CGI;
```

```
$co = new CGI;

print
      .
      .
      .
"Please indicate your income level: ",

$co->p,

$co->scrolling_list
(
    'list',
    ['Highest','High','Medium','Low'],
    'High',
)
```

You can see the results in Figure 20.3. Here's the actual HTML created:

```
Please indicate your income level:
<P>
<SELECT NAME="list" SIZE=4>
<OPTION  VALUE="Highest">
Highest
<OPTION SELECTED VALUE="High">
High
<OPTION  VALUE="Medium">
Medium
<OPTION  VALUE="Low">
Low
</SELECT>
```

These are the attributes you can set with the **scrolling_list** method: **-default**, **-defaults**, **-labels**, **-multiple**, **-name**, **-onBlur**, **-onChange**, **-onFocus**, **-override**, **-force**, **-size**, **-value**, and **-values**.

Here's how I read the selected item in cgi2.cgi, which is shown in Figure 20.4:

```
print "Your income level is: ",
    $co->em($co->param('list')),
    ".";
```

Working With Radio Buttons

"Now I can work with checkbox controls," says the novice programmer, "but the options I want to present are exclusive—in fact, I want to let the user choose the day of the week—so I need to use an HTML control where only one of a set can be selected at one time." "That," you say, "is the radio button control."

As we saw in Chapter 12, you can use HTML radio buttons to let the user select one of a number of exclusive options. For example, in cgi1.cgi, I use seven radio buttons to let the user indicate the day of the week.

In this case, I create a set of radio buttons that operate in a group (i.e., the user can only select one radio button from the group) named "radios", give those radio buttons the values 1 through 7, and use a hash named **%labels** to hold the label of each radio button with the **radio_group** method:

```
#!/usr/local/bin/perl
use CGI;

$co = new CGI;

$labels{'1'} = 'Sunday';
$labels{'2'} = 'Monday';
$labels{'3'} = 'Tuesday';
$labels{'4'} = 'Wednesday';
$labels{'5'} = 'Thursday';
$labels{'6'} = 'Friday';
$labels{'7'} = 'Saturday';

print
    .
    .
    .
"Please indicate the day of the week: ",$co->p,

$co->radio_group
(
    -name=>'radios',
    -values=>['1','2','3', '4', '5', '6', '7'],
    -default=>'1',
    -labels=>\%labels
)
```

You can see the results in Figure 20.3. Here's the actual HTML created:

```
<P>Please indicate the day of the week:
<P>
<INPUT TYPE="radio" NAME="radios" VALUE="1" CHECKED>Sunday
<INPUT TYPE="radio" NAME="radios" VALUE="2">Monday
<INPUT TYPE="radio" NAME="radios" VALUE="3">Tuesday
<INPUT TYPE="radio" NAME="radios" VALUE="4">Wednesday
<INPUT TYPE="radio" NAME="radios" VALUE="5">Thursday
<INPUT TYPE="radio" NAME="radios" VALUE="6">Friday
<INPUT TYPE="radio" NAME="radios" VALUE="7">Saturday
```

Now we've created radio buttons in a Web page from a CGI script. These are the attributes you can use with **radio_group**: **-cols** (or **-columns**), **-colheaders**, **-default**, **-labels**, **-linebreak**, **-name**, **-nolabels**, **-onClick**, **-override**, **-force**, **-rows**, **-rowheaders**, **-value**, and **-values**.

And here's how I read and report which radio button was selected in cgi2.cgi, which is shown in Figure 20.4:

```
print "Today is day ",
    $co->em($co->param('radios')), "
    of the week.";
```

Working With Password Fields

"Uh oh," says the novice programmer, "that darn Johnson was looking over my shoulder when I was typing my password into the page created by my CGI script." "Uh oh," you say, "you better use a password field control." The NP asks, "You can do that?"

You use a password field to let the user enter a password. A password field is just like a text field except that it appears as an asterisk, so no one can read what you're typing. In fact, Web browsers protect password fields by not allowing you to copy the data in it and paste it elsewhere.

You create a password with the **password_field** method as in this code from cgi1.cgi:

```
"Please enter your password: ",

$co->p,

$co->password_field
(
```

```
        -name=>'password',
        -default=>'open sesame',
        -size=>30,
    )
```

You can see the results in Figure 20.3. Here's the actual HTML created:

```
Please enter your password:
<P>
<INPUT TYPE="password" NAME="password" VALUE="open sesame" SIZE=30>
```

These are the attributes you can use with **password_field**: **-maxLength**, **-name**, **-onChange**, **-onFocus**, **-onBlur**, **-onSelect**, **-override**, **-force**, **-size**, **-value**, and **-default**.

Here's how I read and report what the user typed into the password control in cgi2.cgi, which is shown in Figure 20.4:

```
print
    "Your password is: ",$co->em($co->param('password')),
    ".";
```

Working With Popup Menus

"Hm," says the novice programmer, "I've got a lot of choices to present to the user in the page my CGI script generates. How can I do that?" "Easy," you say, "just use a popup menu."

An HTML popup menu—familiar to Windows users as a drop-down list box and discussed in Chapter 12 as a **<SELECT>** HTML control—presents a list of items that the users can open by clicking a button that usually displays a down arrow. The users can select an item in that menu, and you can determine which item they choose.

Here's how I ask the users how much unsolicited mail they want from the survey by placing items in a **<SELECT>** control using the CGI **popup_menu** method:

```
#!/usr/local/bin/perl
use CGI;

$co = new CGI;

print
```

```
"Thank you for filling out our Survey. Please indicate how
much unsolicited mail you like to get: ",
```

```
$co->popup_menu
(
    -name=>'popupmenu',
    -values=>['Very much','A lot','Not so much','None']
)
```

You can see the results in Figure 20.3. Here's the actual HTML created:

```
Thank you for filling out our Survey. Please indicate how
much unsolicited mail you like to get:
<SELECT NAME="popupmenu">
<OPTION  VALUE="Very much">Very much
<OPTION  VALUE="A lot">A lot
<OPTION  VALUE="Not so much">Not so much
<OPTION  VALUE="None">None
</SELECT>
```

These are the attributes you can set with the **popup_menu** method: **-default**, **-labels**, **-name**, **-onBlur**, **-onChange**, **-onFocus**, **-override**, **-force**, **-value**, and **-values**.

And here's how I read and display the user's selection in cgi2.cgi, which is shown in Figure 20.4:

```
print "How much unsolicited mail you like: ",
    $co->em($co->param('popupmenu')),
    ".";
```

Working With Hidden Data Fields

The novice programmer says, "Hm, I'm writing a game and want to hide the secret word in a Web page so I can read it in a CGI script. But when I store that word in a password field, it looks pretty amateurish." "I'll bet," you say, "you should use a hidden field instead."

You can store data in a hidden field in a Web page, which is invisible to the user. This technique is useful if you want to store data pertinent to a Web page that will be posted back to a script. To create a hidden field, you use the **hidden** method.

Here's how I store hidden data in the survey Web page created by cgi1.cgi:

```
#!/usr/local/bin/perl
use CGI;

$co = new CGI;

print
    .
    .
    .
$co->hidden(-name=>'hiddendata', -default=>'Rosebud');
```

Here's the actual HTML that's generated:

```
<INPUT TYPE="hidden" NAME="hiddendata" VALUE="Rosebud">
```

These are the attributes you can use with **hidden**: **-name**, **-override**, **-force**, **-value**, **-values**, and **-default.**

And here's how I display the data in the hidden field in cgi2.cgi, which is shown in Figure 20.4:

```
print "The hidden data is ",$co->em(join(", ",
    $co->param('hiddendata'))),
    ".";
```

Creating Submit And Reset Buttons To Upload Data From An HTML Form

"OK," says the novice programmer, "I've added the controls to my HTML form—now how can the user actually send the data in those controls to my CGI script?" "Easy," you say, "you use a Submit button in a form. When the user clicks that button, the data from the controls in your form is sent to the CGI script you designated when you created the form."

To upload the data in a form, the user must click a Submit button. You create a Submit button with the CGI.pm **submit** method. You can also create a Reset button using the **reset** method, which clears the data in the form.

Here's how I add Submit and Reset buttons to the survey Web page created by cgi1.cgi:

```
#!/usr/local/bin/perl
use CGI;

$co = new CGI;

print
    .
    .
    .
$co->center
(
    $co->submit,
    $co->reset,
)
```

Note that this creates two buttons, one with the caption Submit and one with the caption Reset, which is shown in Figure 20.3. Here's the actual HTML created:

```
<CENTER>
<INPUT TYPE="submit" NAME="Submit" VALUE="Submit">
<INPUT TYPE="reset">
</CENTER>
```

You can set the caption used in this button with the **-value** attribute. When the user clicks the Submit button, the data in the form in cgi1.cgi is posted to cgi2.cgi for decoding and use. The attributes you can set with the **submit** method are **-name**, **-onClick**, **-value**, and **-label**.

Ending An HTML Form

"OK," says the novice programmer, "I've added my controls to my Web page—I'm ready to go!" "Not so fast," you say, "don't forget to end the form using the **end_form** method."

All the controls we created in the previous topics of this chapter's Immediate Solutions section are part of the same form in the survey page we created in cgi1.cgi. I created that form with the **start_form** method and to end the form, I use the **end_form** method:

```
#!/usr/local/bin/perl
use CGI;
```

```
$co = new CGI;

print

    .

    .

    .

$co->end_form
```

This method just returns **</FORM>**, which I print to the Web page to end the HTML form.

Ending An HTML Document

"OK," says the novice programmer, "I've written my Web page and put a form in it—*now* I'm ready to go!" "Not so fast," you say, "don't forget to end the Web page with the **end_html** method."

To end an HTML document, use the CGI **end_html** method, which returns the **</BODY></HTML>** tags that should end a Web page (even though most browsers do not require these closing tags, it's still a good idea to put them in).

Here's how I end the survey Web page in cgi1.cgi:

```
#!/usr/local/bin/perl
use CGI;

$co = new CGI;

print

    .

    .

    .

$co->end_html;
```

That completes cgi1.cgi. When you navigate to this CGI script, you see the Web survey page that appears in Figures 20.1, 20.2, and 20.3. When the user enters data into that page and clicks the Submit button, the data in that page is sent to cgi2.cgi, which displays a summary of that data shown in Figure 20.4.

Note that by dissecting this example, you can see in detail how to create and read the data in most HTML controls.

Calling A CGI Script From An HTML Web Page

To call a CGI script from an HTML Web page, you can create an HTML form using HTML, as in this case, where I'm adding a text field to a form:

```
<FORM METHOD="POST"
ACTION="http://www.yourserver.com/username/cgi/cgi2.cgi"
ENCTYPE="application/x-www-form-urlencoded">
Please enter your name:
    <INPUT TYPE="text" NAME="text" VALUE="">
    <INPUT TYPE="submit" NAME="Submit" VALUE="Submit">
    <INPUT TYPE="reset">
</FORM>
```

When the user clicks the Submit button, the data in the text field is sent to cgi2.cgi. If the user clicks the Reset button, the text in the text field is cleared.

Here's a complete Web page in HTML that displays the survey you see in Figures 20.1, 20.2, and 20.3. When you click the Submit button, it sends its data to cgi2.cgi:

```
<HTML>

<HEAD>

<TITLE>CGI Example</TITLE>
</HEAD>

<BODY BGCOLOR="white" LINK="red">

<CENTER>
<IMG SRC="http://www.yourserver.com/username/cgi/welcome.gif">
</CENTER>
<CENTER>
<H1>Here is the Survey!</H1>
</CENTER>

<HR>

<FORM METHOD="POST"
ACTION="http://www.yourserver.com/username/cgi/cgi2.cgi"
ENCTYPE="application/x-www-form-urlencoded">

Please enter your name:
<INPUT TYPE="text" NAME="text" VALUE="">
<P>
```

```
Please enter your opinion:
<P>
<TEXTAREA NAME="textarea" ROWS=10 COLS=60>
No opinion
</TEXTAREA>
<P>
Please indicate what products you use:
<P>
<INPUT TYPE="checkbox" NAME="checkboxes" VALUE="Shampoo">Shampoo
<INPUT TYPE="checkbox" NAME="checkboxes" VALUE="Toothpaste">Toothpaste
<INPUT TYPE="checkbox" NAME="checkboxes" VALUE="Bread" CHECKED>Bread
<INPUT TYPE="checkbox" NAME="checkboxes" VALUE="Cruise missiles" CHECKED>
Cruise missiles
<P>
Please indicate your income level:
<P>
<SELECT NAME="list" SIZE=4>
<OPTION  VALUE="Highest">
Highest
<OPTION SELECTED VALUE="High">
High
<OPTION  VALUE="Medium">
Medium
<OPTION  VALUE="Low">
Low
</SELECT>
<P>Please indicate the day of the week:
<P>
<INPUT TYPE="radio" NAME="radios" VALUE="1" CHECKED>Sunday
<INPUT TYPE="radio" NAME="radios" VALUE="2">Monday
<INPUT TYPE="radio" NAME="radios" VALUE="3">Tuesday
<INPUT TYPE="radio" NAME="radios" VALUE="4">Wednesday
<INPUT TYPE="radio" NAME="radios" VALUE="5">Thursday
<INPUT TYPE="radio" NAME="radios" VALUE="6">Friday
<INPUT TYPE="radio" NAME="radios" VALUE="7">Saturday
<P>
Please enter your password:
<P>
<INPUT TYPE="password" NAME="password" VALUE="open sesame" SIZE=30>
<P>
Thank you for filling out our Survey. Please indicate how
much unsolicited mail you like to get:
<SELECT NAME="popupmenu">
<OPTION  VALUE="Very much">Very much
<OPTION  VALUE="A lot">A lot
```

```
<OPTION  VALUE="Not so much">Not so much
<OPTION  VALUE="None">None
</SELECT>
<P>
<INPUT TYPE="hidden" NAME="hiddendata" VALUE="Rosebud">
<CENTER>
<INPUT TYPE="submit" NAME="Submit" VALUE="Submit">
<INPUT TYPE="reset">
</CENTER>
<HR>
<INPUT TYPE="hidden" NAME=".cgifields" VALUE="radios">
<INPUT TYPE="hidden" NAME=".cgifields" VALUE="list">
<INPUT TYPE="hidden" NAME=".cgifields" VALUE="checkboxes">

</FORM>

</BODY>

</HTML>
```

Creating Image Maps

"Hmm," says the novice programmer, "I'd like to create a clickable image in my Web page—an image map. Can I do that?" "Sure," you say, "you just use the **image_button** method."

To create an image map that the user can click, use the **image_button** method. When the user clicks that image map, the coordinates of the mouse are sent to your script. If you've named the image map control "map", the coordinates returned to your script will be in **map.x** and **map.y**.

Here's an example. In this case, I create an image map named "map" using an image from the file map.gif this way:

```
#!/usr/local/bin/perl

use CGI;

$co = new CGI;

print $co->header,

$co->start_html('Image Map Example'),
```

```
$co->h1('Image Map Example'),

$co->start_form,

$co->image_button
(
    -name => 'map',
    -src=>'map.gif'
),

$co->p,

$co->end_form,

$co->hr;
    .
    .
    .
```

Because I haven't passed any arguments to the **start_form** method, the data in
the form will be sent back to the same CGI script when the user clicks the image
map. I can read and display the location of the mouse click if that data is sent to
the script, which I check by determining if the **param** method indicates there's
data waiting like this:

```
#!/usr/local/bin/perl

use CGI;

$co = new CGI;

print $co->header,

$co->start_html('Image Map Example'),

$co->h1('Image Map Example'),

$co->start_form,

$co->image_button
(
    -name => 'map',
    -src=>'map.gif'
),
```

```
$co->p,

$co->end_form,

$co->hr;

if ($co->param())
{
    $x = $co->param('map.x');
    $y = $co->param('map.y');
    print "You clicked the map at ($x, $y)";
}

print $co->end_html;
```

The results appear in Figure 20.6. As you can see in the figure, the user can click the image map to send data to the script, and that script creates a new Web page indicating where the image map was clicked using pixel coordinate measurements. This example is a success.

TIP: *Another resource to check out is the CGI::Imagemap module from CPAN.*

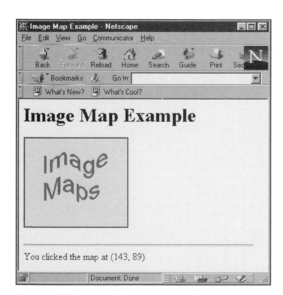

Figure 20.6   Creating and using image maps.

Creating Frames

"How about creating frames?" the novice programmer asks, "Can I do that with CGI.pm?" "Sure you can," you say, "by using an HTML shortcut. But, don't forget, you can also just print the HTML you want to a Web page." "I haven't forgotten," the NP says, "I just want to use CGI.pm to do it."

You can create frames using the CGI.pm HTML shortcuts **frameset** and **frame**. Here's an example where I create a Web page with two frames in it:

```perl
#!/usr/local/bin/perl

use CGI;
$co = new CGI;

print $co->header,

$co->frameset(
    {-rows=>'40%,60%'},

    $co->frame
    ({
        -name=>'top',
        -src=>'http://www.yourserver.com/username/cgi/a.htm'
    }),

    $co->frame
    ({
        -name=>'bottom',
        -src=>'http://www.yourserver.com/username/cgi/b.htm'
    })
);
```

The results appear in Figure 20.7. As you can see, you can use CGI.pm to create frames. The attributes you can use with **frameset** are **-rows** and **-cols**. Use the following attributes with **frame**: **-marginwidth**, **-name**, **-noresize**, **-scrolling**, and **-src**.

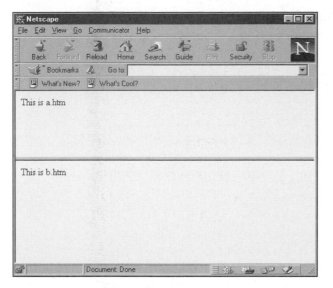

Figure 20.7   Creating frames.

Non-Object-Oriented CGI Programming

"I'm being sent to the western affiliate again," says the novice programmer, "and they don't like object-oriented programming—how can I use CGI.pm?" "Well," you say, "you can use the CGI.pm module's function-oriented interface instead."

We've used the object-oriented methods of the CGI package in this chapter, but the CGI package also has a function-based interface. (Note that not all the object-oriented CGI methods are supported in the function-based interface.)

Here's an example that uses the function-based CGI interface. This code displays a text field with a prompt to users to enter their names. When they do and click the Submit button, the data in the text field is posted back to the same CGI script, which uses the **param** function to display the name a user entered at the bottom of the returned Web page:

```perl
#!/usr/local/bin/perl

use CGI qw/:standard/;
```

```
print header,

    start_html('CGI Functions Example'),

    h1('CGI Functions Example'),

    start_form,

    "Please enter your name: ",

    textfield('text'),

    p,

    submit, reset,

    end_form,

    hr;

if (param()) {

    print "Your name is: ", em(param('text')), hr;

}

print end_html;
```

You can see the results of this script in Figure 20.8.

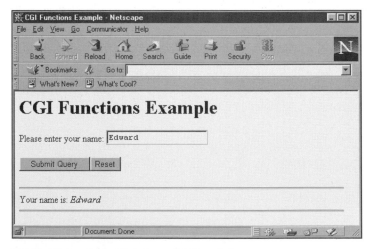

Figure 20.8   A function-based CGI script.

Debugging CGI Scripts

The novice programmer is running in circles and screaming "Error 500: Internal Server Error! Error 500: Internal Server Error! Error 500: Internal Server Error!" You smile and say, "I know just what's wrong—you're trying to debug a CGI script and all you ever see from the server is a Web page that says 'Error 500: Internal Server Error', and it's impossible to find out what's really going wrong, isn't that so?" The NP screams, "Error 500: Internal Server Error!"

When there's a problem with a CGI script, the Web server will often return a Web page that says something like "Error 500: Internal Server Error", and that inscrutable message has paralyzed more than one CGI programmer with frustration. To find out what's going wrong, you need to take a look at the script itself. The following may help you to debug your CGI script.

Is It Executable?

This is the equivalent of the line in hardware manuals that asks: Did you plug it in? Sometimes, you might forget to give a CGI script the proper permission to let it run, such as 555 or 755. The important point here is to make sure the script is executable, because if it's not, you'll get Error 500 when you call it.

If there's a problem with access permission—for example, you may not have permission to read the script, or the script may try to work with a resource that it has no permission for—you'll usually get a "Permission Denied" message.

Is Its Syntax Okay?

The biggest source of Error 500 problems is syntax errors. Fortunately, there's an easy way to check a script's syntax locally without having to run it on a Web server. To check the script's syntax, run it under Perl at the console using the **-w** switch to see warnings and use the **-c** switch so Perl will only parse—and not run—the script to inform you of any syntax problems:

```
C:\>perl -w -c script.cgi

script.cgi syntax OK
```

This should take care of most errors. However, if the script's syntax is okay, but you're still getting Error 500, it's time to try running the script locally.

Running A Script Locally

CGI.pm lets you run CGI scripts locally without having to run them on a Web server. For example, say you had the following CGI script that you wanted to test. All I'm doing here is displaying the data from a text field named "text" sent to this script:

```
#!/usr/local/bin/perl

use CGI;

$co = new CGI;

print $co->header,

$co->start_html
(
    -title=>'CGI Example',
    -author=>'Steve',
    -meta=>{'keywords'=>'CGI Perl'},
    -BGCOLOR=>'white',
    -LINK=>'red'
),

"Your name is: ",

$co->em($co->param('text')), ".",

$co->end_html;
```

You can run this script at the command line. But what about the data for the control named "text" that this script expects? You can pass that like this on the command line:

```
% perl script.cgi text=George
```

When you do, CGI.pm prints out on the console what it would send to the Web server like this:

```
% perl script.cgi text=George

Content-Type: text/html

<!DOCTYPE HTML PUBLIC "-//IETF//DTD HTML//EN">
<HTML>

<HEAD>
<TITLE>CGI Example</TITLE>
<LINK REV=MADE HREF="mailto:Steve">
<META NAME="keywords" CONTENT="CGI Perl">
</HEAD>
```

```
<BODY BGCOLOR="white" LINK="red">
Your name is: <EM>George</EM>.
</BODY>

</HTML>
```

If you have more than one parameter to fill, you can also pass them on the command line like this:

```
% perl script.cgi text1=George text2=Georgette text3=Georgie
```

In fact, you can redirect a whole file full of such data to a script like this:

```
% perl script.cgi < input.txt
```

Besides setting the values of parameters passed to your script this way, in addition you can set environment variables that your script might read, like **CONTENT_LENGTH**, **HTTP_USER_AGENT**, **QUERY_STRING**, **REQUEST_METHOD**, or others. You can set those environment variables locally; however, the actual command varies by operating system. In the Unix csh shell, you can use a command like this:

```
setenv REQUEST_METHOD "POST"
```

In the Unix bash shell, it looks like this:

```
export REQUEST_METHOD "POST"
```

And in Windows/MS-DOS, you do this:

```
set REQUEST_METHOD = "POST"
```

If you can't find the problem locally, you'll have to try to find it when the script runs on the Web server. That can be difficult because messages written to **STDERR** actually go to a server's error log. Most programmers don't have access to a server's error log—and even if you do, it can be very hard to find the actual message that corresponds to the error that occurred when your script ran. On the other hand, you can redirect **STDERR** to your Web browser.

Redirecting **STDERR** To Your Browser Or A File

To redirect **STDERR** to the Web page created by a CGI script, you redirect it to **STDOUT** like this:

```
open (STDERR, ">&STDOUT");
```

Sometimes it's better to keep a log of errors, and you can do that yourself like this:

```
open (STDERR, ">error.log");
```

Another option is to use CGI::Carp.

Using CGI::Carp

In the previous chapter, I used the Perl function **die** to handle errors, and you can use it in CGI programming too. However, it's standard practice to replace **die** with the corresponding function in the CGI::Carp module because this module produces messages that are more useful for CGI scripts.

Here's how you can use CGI::Carp:

```
use CGI::Carp;

die "A serious error occurred, so quitting.";
```

You can also redirect error messages from **die** to a file instead of **STDERR** by passing a filehandle to the **carpout** function:

```
use CGI::Carp qw(carpout);

open(FILEHANDLE, ">error.log");

carpout(\*FILEHANDLE);
```

And you can even require that fatal error messages get sent to the browser with the **fatalsToBrowser** method like this:

```
use CGI::Carp qw(fatalsToBrowser);

die "A serious error occurred, so quitting.";
```

TIP: *You might also want to take a look at the CGI::LogCarp module from CPAN.*

Index

T

U

Index of HTML Tags

</>

What's On The CD-ROM

The *HTML Black Book* companion CD-ROM contains elements specifically selected to enhance the usefulness of this book, including code for the book's projects as well as the following and much more:

Underline: PC Software:

- *Applet FX Freeware Edition*—A package of 20 high-quality Java effects.
- *AutoEye*—(Demo version.) AutoEye offers professional designers a new way to make their photographs look their best by reclaiming lost color an detail.
- *Coffee Cup HTML Editor++*—A full-featured HTML editor.
- *Edit Revolution*—Freeware HTML, Javascript, CSS, Perl, and text editor for Windows 95 and above.
- *Net Toob*—Easy to use and integrate software that works with multiple browsers. It plays *all* the digital video standards, as well as real-time MPEG-1 audio and video.
- *Page Submit*—Freeware software that guides you through the process of submitting your Web page to search engines.
- *Photo/Graphic Edges*—(Demo version.) Gives you incredible control over the edge effect to create unique feathered deckles, custom edges, and creative matte backgrounds.
- *Ulead Gif Animator Lite*—(Demo version.) The industry standard for GIF Animation.

Underline: Mac Software:

- *AutoEye*—(Demo version.) AutoEye offers professional designers a new way to make their photographs look their best by reclaiming lost color and detail.
- *HTML Gorm*—A powerful application for creating HTML forms.
- *HTML.edit*—An HTML editor for the Mac.
- *Net Toob*—Easy to use and integrate software that works with multiple browsers. It plays *all* the digital video standards, as well as real-time MPEG-1 audio and video.
- *Photo/Graphic Edges*—(Demo version.) Gives you incredible control over the edge effect to create unique feathered deckles, custom edges, and creative matte backgrounds.
- *Table Tool*—An application that makes the process of creating HTML tables easy.

System Requirements

Software

- Window 95/98/NT or Macintosh System 8 or higher
- Table Tool application for Macintosh requires HyperCard Player 2.1 or later

Hardware

- Intel (or equivalent) Pentium 100MHz processor is the minimum platform required; an Intel (or equivalent) Pentium 133MHz processor is recommended
- RAM: Windows 32MB required; Macintosh 32MB required
- CD-ROM drive